CHANGING WORLDS

A silent struggle was taking place between entrenched conservatism and the fragile new thinking.
"Hanoi Life under the Subsidy Economy, 1975–1986," Museum of Ethnology, Hanoi, 2006–7.

Changing Worlds

VIETNAM'S TRANSITION FROM COLD WAR
TO GLOBALIZATION

David W. P. Elliott

OXFORD
UNIVERSITY PRESS

Oxford University Press is a department of the University of Oxford.
It furthers the University's objective of excellence in research,
scholarship, and education by publishing worldwide.

Oxford   New York
Auckland   Cape Town   Dar es Salaam   Hong Kong   Karachi
Kuala Lumpur   Madrid   Melbourne   Mexico City   Nairobi
New Delhi   Shanghai   Taipei   Toronto

With offices in
Argentina   Austria   Brazil   Chile   Czech Republic   France   Greece
Guatemala   Hungary   Italy   Japan   Poland   Portugal   Singapore
South Korea   Switzerland   Thailand   Turkey   Ukraine   Vietnam

Oxford is a registered trade mark of Oxford University Press
in the UK and certain other countries.

Published in the United States of America by
Oxford University Press
198 Madison Avenue, New York, NY 10016

Library of Congress Cataloging-in-Publication Data
Elliott, David W. P.
Changing worlds : Vietnam's transition from the Cold War to globalization / David W.P. Elliott.
    p.   cm.
Includes bibliographical references and index.
ISBN 978-0-19-538334-8 (cloth); 978-0-19-937758-9 (pbk)
1. Vietnam—Politics and government—1975– 2. Vietnam—Foreign relations. 3. Vietnam—Economic policy—1975–
4. National security—Vietnam. I. Title.
DS559.912.E45   2012
959.704′4—dc23   2011052938

9 8 7 6 5 4 3 2 1

Printed in the United States of America
on acid-free paper

To Mai
Who Shared the Journey
With Love

Contents

Preface to the Paperback Edition

THE HISTORICAL CHAPTER examined in this book ended in 2007, and the research was essentially concluded in that year. It is always tempting to see how the passage of time has affected the analysis done right at the close of the period analyzed in this book, which assesses Vietnam's efforts to come to terms with the dramatic changes of the post–Cold War period and the era of globalization. It is also tempting to assess the extent to which the course of events after 2007 has confirmed or altered the trajectory of Vietnam's policies and engagement with the world as presented in the first edition of the book.

Nevertheless, in the concluding section of the first edition of *Changing Worlds* I observed that "This is not a book of prognostication" and offered only a few qualified thoughts about Vietnam's future, and this caveat still stands. The reason is that the main focus of this study is on a completed historical chapter—the period from 1975 when Vietnam confidently envisaged a future within the orthodox parameters of socialist development and the socialist world in an international system divided into antagonistic blocs, and 2007 when its entry into the World Trade Organization capped a contested evolution from the two-worlds framework of the Cold War to the complexities of deep integration into a single globalized world system.

The decision to acknowledge the unity of the new global system and to opt for deep integration with it does, of course, have profound implications for Vietnam's future, though the way Vietnam's next historical chapter will unfold is still difficult to predict, even with the benefit of observing what has happened in the years since "taking the plunge" into the turbulent waters of the globalized world. One might have thought that the 2008 global financial crisis would give even the most ardent Vietnamese reformers pause about the uncertainties that come with global integration, but the evidence so far is that the plunge was irreversible (though curiously the exact point at which this happened is still not clearly understood[1]) and, as happened after the earlier 1997 Asian financial crisis, Vietnam's integrationist course was not derailed despite the ammunition that the unpredictable turbulence of this darker side of globalization offered to opponents of reform and integration in Vietnam.

But, if the story moving forward has not significantly changed since the first edition of *Changing Worlds*, what about the perspective looking backward on the period it covered? Here, there has been a significant development; the publication of the remarkable book by the Vietnamese journalist Huy Duc called *The Winning Side* (*Ben Thang Cuoc*, published in two volumes—which I will cite as *BTC I* and *II*) first disseminated on the internet and then published in Vietnamese in the United States in 2012. The author explains his ironic title in the following way: "My book begins its chronicles with April 30, 1975, the day when many believed North Vietnam liberated South Vietnam. Taking a cautious look back at the last three decades, many are stupefied by the impression that 'the liberated' turned out to be the North."[2]

Without necessarily endorsing this provocative observation (although *Changing Worlds* does have a section titled "The South Shall Rise Again" which explores this theme[3]), I certainly agree with many highly qualified observers that this is a remarkable book, offering many unique and rare insights into the inner world of Vietnamese elite politics.[4] The *New York Times* characterized this book as "perhaps the first critical, comprehensive history of Vietnam since 1975 by someone inside the country."[5] In the end, I think that this insider account reinforces most of the analysis of *Changing Worlds*, which was based on Vietnamese sources but still subject to the limitations of being written by an outside observer.

Still, there are innumerable examples of insights and revelations that I wish had been available to me when I wrote the first edition, which confirm or enlarge upon key points of analysis and interpretation dealing not only with the details of political struggles within Vietnam's leadership over the ways to respond to globalization, but even more importantly for this book, the impact of mind-sets and ideas and the role that they played in the outcome of these struggles. It would be pointless to try to incorporate the multiple revelations from this massive two volume work, but I would like to mention a few examples, and hope that this may induce the interested reader to read Huy Duc's magnum opus in conjunction with this book. *The Winning Side* was written with a different purpose and focus from *Changing Worlds*, but the portrait it paints of the events and key characters in this story is a very useful complement to what I have tried to present.

The first example is his portrayal of the disastrous attempt to impose socialism on the South right after the Communist victory of 1975 and the unification of the country the following year. This episode had a significant impact on subsequent events in several ways. First, it was an economic and political disaster, and provided a powerful negative example of the rigid version of socialism that then Party leader Le Duan and others represented. This failure subsequently led to a search for a better way, and to the reform process which officially started in 1986.

The search for a way out of South Vietnam's economic crisis set in motion a chain of events which ultimately transformed the policies and institutions in North Vietnam that the leadership had rashly attempted to impose on the South, and spilled over into the security and diplomatic spheres. The improvised responses to the economic crisis in the South led to the resurfacing of some economists who had served under the pre-1975 Saigon government who were an important source of reform ideas. A young professor of economics recalled that "his generation began to encounter the idea of a market economy from a series of articles written in the newspaper *Tuoi Tre* and, after that in *Lao Dong Chu Nhat* ... The articles written prior to 1975 [in South Vietnam] by Professors Nguyen Van Ngon, Pho Ba Long ... began to be put to use." The circulation of these ideas eventually led to a demand by Vietnamese students to drop Marxist economics as a required part of the Ho Chi Minh City University of Economics.[6] In February 1990, Nguyen Van Hao, an advisor to the World Bank and a former Deputy Premier of Saigon, who had left Vietnam in 1981 but had remained in touch with Vo Van Kiet, was asked by Kiet to return to Vietnam for consultations. Nguyen Xuan Oanh, a former International Monetary Fund economist and also a Republic of Vietnam Vice Premier (whose photo appears in the first edition of *Changing Worlds*) was also consulted by Vietnam's top leaders.

The significance of this is that the resurfacing of market economy ideas from the old Saigon government era expanded the repertoire of alternatives to the command economy orthodoxy. As Jeffrey Legro has argued "Not only must political actors undermine the old orthodoxy, they need to replace it with a new orthodoxy. Consolidation is shaped in part by two types of factors: (1) the number of prominent ideas in a society that might serve as a replacement for the dominant orthodoxy, and (2) the perceived initial results of such new ideas."[7] The intrusion of market ideas which had been the object of a ruthless political suppression campaign (the "socialist transformation campaign") in South Vietnam in the mid-1970s into the policy debate in the 1980s was an important contributing factor to the growth and ultimate ascendency of reform ideas.

Involvement in the debacle of the "socialist transformation campaign" in the South weakened the position of the opponents of reform in the period following 1986. Some anti-reformers tried to minimize their ties to "socialist transformation" in the South, and pin the entire responsibility on the then Party leader Le Duan. Others, however, attempted to exonerate Le Duan from blame for Vietnam's earlier economic blunders. Following the collapse of the Soviet Union, Le Duan's closest aide said during a review of the early decision to impose socialism on the South, "It is really hard to sit here now, following the collapse of the Soviet Union, and talk about this old story." Another aide to Le Duan, who had at one time been the head of the Faculty of Marxist-Leninist economics at the Ho Chi Minh Higher Party School, recalled that "Although Brother Three (Le Duan) was very uneasy faced with the realities of development in the South, at that time one would have to have been terribly creative to have escaped the dogmatism of the entire Communist camp. This creativity would have had to be based on a mature theoretical foundation, which we were lacking. Our theoreticians had all studied in China and other socialist countries, and our Party school originated from Chinese teachers." Another assistant of Le Duan, Professor Tran Phuong, who an informed observer called a 'liberal economist' [*mot nha kinh te tu do*] also had to admit that "Prior to the collapse of the Soviet Union, our heads were still imprisoned in the dogmatism of Marxism."[8]

The fact that Vietnam's mistakes were now blamed on ideological conformism with the socialist bloc concepts and policies which were inappropriate for Vietnam, was a considerable departure for their earlier pride in being part of such an enlightened and powerful bloc and the desire to emulate more advanced socialist countries. But, as the examples just cited on the revival of discussion of market economics in the 1980s shows, the inability to challenge command economy orthodoxy was not entirely due to lack of alternative ideas in circulation, although these ideas were considered outside the sphere of acceptability and politically dangerous at the time. This, in turn, underlines the exceptional courage of the early reformers who accepted the risks of challenging the conventional wisdom. It also showed that the reformers would have to be protected and promoted at the very top of the leadership in order to have an impact.

Even if the old thinking was generally shared by the leadership, including some who later became converts to reform ideas, the death of Le Duan prior to the 1986 "reform" Sixth Party Congress eliminated a significant obstacle to what became known as "new thinking" (*tu duy moi*). His transitional successor, Truong Chinh, played a decisive role in moving Vietnam toward economic reform. As *Changing Worlds* pointed out, this was especially ironic in that Truong Chinh had been previously identified as a rigid and hard line ideological purist, who took the blame for the disastrous overzealous land reform of the 1950s in North Vietnam.[9] In the 1980s he turned out to be a pragmatic realist (a label which some had earlier ascribed to Le Duan's wartime leadership, in contrast with Truong Chinh's insistence on maintaining socialist orthodoxy and opposition to Le Duan's "whatever works" approach.[10]). Truong Chinh's investigations of the economic problems of the South are described in *Changing Worlds*, largely based on the account of Hanoi economic historian Dang Phong and a retrospective newspaper series on this period in the liberal newspaper *Tuoi Tre*, for which Huy Duc once worked.[11] To this account *BTC* adds a crucial insight into how this learning experience in the South was carried back to the North by Truong Chinh: ". . . in November 1985 he travelled back to Haiphong and, according to the economist Tran Nham, 'the vivid reality of the South had left a deep imprint on the reform thinking of Truong Chinh.'"[12]

It was not only the rigidity of the old thinking which led to the disastrous campaigns against the middle class and petty traders in the South after 1975, and the disruptive persecution of the overseas Chinese residents who were the core of the vestigial market economy in the South, but also a growing concern that economic ties with the outside world were a Trojan Horse, that would serve as a conduit for subversion.[13] Economic ties were potential avenues for penetration and control of Vietnam by external forces. It is well known that the 1978 persecution of Vietnam's Chinese ethnic minority stemmed from this concern, but Huy Duc's account underlines this with specificity.

The China factor is a recurrent issue in this story. *Changing Worlds* shows that there was a significant overlap between the opponents of internal reform, external integration with the globalizing economy and cooperation with the capitalist powers who were integral elements of it, and the advocates of closer ties between Vietnam and China as an alternative to the seductive but (to conservatives) threatening ties with former adversaries and their purported schemes of "peaceful evolution" aimed at subverting the last remnant communist systems.

Huy Duc's book reinforces the account of the China factor in *Changing Worlds* over relations with the PRC and with revealing detail about the extent to which the Vietnamese leadership was divided and how this affected the outcome of the debate over the pace and scope of Vietnam's global integration. Some specific revelations are: 1. the role of Chinese instructors in setting up the Party training institute where Marxist-Leninist economics was taught—important because blinkered adherence to this orthodoxy was cited by many Vietnamese leaders as a reason for their tardy adjustment to reality during Vietnam's decade-long economic crisis following 1975, and delay in responding to the challenges of globalization. 2. Paradoxically, the adversarial relationship between Vietnam and China that developed after 1975 also prevented Vietnam's reformers from citing China during Deng Xiaoping's reforms as a model of how a socialist system could adopt market mechanisms. Despite Gorbachev's perestroika, the Soviet advisors who were called in the late 1980s to help Vietnam formulate a response to its economic woes were themselves still stuck in the old orthodoxies and were themselves, as Huy Duc shows through interviews with leading Vietnamese economists of the period, part of the problem rather than part of the solution. 3. During the 1990s, after Vietnam's reluctant rapprochement with China as the Soviet Union went into free fall, Vietnamese opponents of reform advocated closer political ties with China as an alternative to reconciling with former adversaries in the capitalist world. *Changing Worlds* records the fact that this "China card" eventually foundered as China became an increasing security concern to Vietnam[14] but, again, Huy Duc provides important confirming detail. It was the eclipse of the China option that finally cleared the way for deep integration in the globalizing system of international relations and economic ties.

The collapse of the Soviet Union was the main factor that forced Vietnam to reconcile with China, and also the final blow to the old model of a socialist command economy. The Leninist political structures of Vietnam largely persisted (with some minor exceptions such as the increasing role of the National Assembly and a modest attempt to establish limits and accountability to Party rule), even while the Marxist economic model was challenged and some of the key Marxist ideological constructs, most importantly the centrality of class struggle in political life, were downplayed and largely ignored. The international implication of this was that it helped pave the way for a more relaxed view about the inevitable tensions involved in Vietnam's relations with countries with different social systems, which was an essential precondition to pursuing a path of deep integration with the globalizing world.

A key turning point in the collapse of the Soviet model in Vietnam was the series of events in the communist bloc during the turbulent year of 1989—the "Year of Living Dangerously" is the chapter title for this period. *The Winning Side* contributes a number of revelations which enlarge our understanding of this pivotal year both in the communist countries and within Vietnam itself. I will illustrate these with several examples. The first is the *BTC* account of extent and gravity of the economic crisis in Vietnam that dramatically escalated in 1988, which made the external crisis of 1989 all the more unsettling. This is noted in *Changing Worlds* but the impact it had on Vietnam's leadership was not sufficiently stressed. The Soviet Union had, in its terminal stage, revived the pragmatic market thinking of Lenin in the New Economic Policy period of the Soviet Union, which filtered back to Vietnam both through the large numbers of Soviet economic advisors brought in by Vietnam (who had earlier merely reinforced the old command economy model) and Vietnamese students trained in the Soviet Union during the Gorbachev era.

But it was a development much more important than "new thinking" that shut the door on a return to the old ways. Professor Dao Xuan Sam observed that "Fortunately for Vietnam, the Soviet Union itself refused to grant the sum of money they had said would be necessary to halt inflation – if not, it was quite possible that Vietnam would have gone back to the old subsidy regime."[15] It became increasingly clear to Vietnam's leaders that the alternative to the constraints of the interdependence (or "mutual dependency" as it was often called at the time) was greater dependency on the Soviet Union. Integration into the globalizing economy, on the other hand, offered a path to a more independent economy.

Changing Worlds covers the economic and political crisis in the South in the decade following 1975, but not the subsequent crisis in North Vietnam in the period just before and during the momentous year of 1989. Huy Duc writes that "At the beginning of 1988 a famine broke out in twenty one provinces and towns in the North, with 9.3 million people lacking food, among which 3.6 million have to skip meals and are seriously famished." A National Assembly report revealed that "In some places, people died of hunger." A reporter wrote that "Almost the whole country was short of food, and in a few provinces it seemed like the famine of 1945 [in which up to two million people died in North Vietnam, creating a societal crisis that paved the way for the successful communist seizure of power in that year]. Beggars flooded Hanoi in unusual numbers, not as isolated individuals as before, but in entire families. In some places there was nothing to eat at all." *BTC* concludes that this shocking immiseration "changed the thinking of a number of leaders and forced the Party to change some of its policies" including a return to quasi private farming (the individual contract system) used in an earlier crisis.[16] The famine had been reported at the time, based on official Vietnamese requests for aid[17], but Huy Duc's vivid account casts new light on the extent of the internal crisis in Vietnam as it headed into the "Year of Living Dangerously" and is an important explanation for the changing views of many in the leadership about the need for systemic reform. In addition, it shows why the reforms initiated in the South to cope with crises in that region were eventually extended to the North, the original model of socialist economics.

Another significant *BTC* revelation concerns the lengthy stay of Vietnam's leader at the time in East Germany, at a time when Vietnam was engulfed in a sea of troubles both domestically and externally. *Changing Worlds* speculates on the reasons for this extended stay, but there was no conclusive information available prior to Huy Duc's reporting on what actually transpired during this critical visit. *Changing Worlds* devoted several paragraphs to the October 1989 three week stay of Party leader Nguyen Van Linh in East Germany, and noted that he and other Vietnamese leaders had always viewed East Germany as a success story, and proof that old style socialism was economically successful and as proof that a rigid authoritarian regime was still viable even in a world of vertiginous change. The unusual length of Linh's stay in Berlin at a time of great crisis at home and abroad for Vietnam was mentioned, as was the rumor that he had a heart attack while there, which could explain the prolonged stay. Huy Duc's account, drawing largely on interviews with the prominent reform economist Le Dang Doanh who accompanied Linh on that trip (and who plays a key role in the events discussed in *Changing Worlds*) discloses graphic details of Linh's health condition, and the profound impact that this close up encounter with the unraveling communist world had on Linh. A major reason for the length of Linh's stay in East Germany was a desperate attempt to persuade Gorbachev and other communist leaders to rally in defense of the unraveling socialist world and to continue high levels of aid to Vietnam.

Prior to his departure in October 1989 for East Berlin, Linh had discussed with the Vietnamese politburo the idea of persuading Gorbachev to convene a meeting of communist states to rally against the disintegration of the socialist bloc. Unfortunately for Linh, his remark in a meeting (presumably with East Germans) that "Gorbachev is the biggest opportunist on the planet" reached Gorbachev's ears, and Gorbachev sarcastically referred to it in a grudgingly granted and demeaning meeting with an ailing Linh. "The biggest opportunist on the planet greets comrade Nguyen Van Linh," said Gorbachev. Nevertheless Gorbachev politely listened to Linh's pleas to save the socialist bloc and also to continue to subsidize Vietnam's forthcoming economic development plan. "That's really tough, that's really tough," said Gorbachev, "the Vietnamese comrades will simply have to take care of it themselves."[18]

In addition, the East Germans, once firm friends and supporters of Vietnam, largely ignored Linh, and his appeals to other communist leaders to rally together fell on deaf ears as they worried about their own futures. Now that we know these details of the Linh-Gorbachev meeting, it is even harder to understand why the Vietnamese leadership clung to the illusion that the socialist world as they knew it would somehow weather the storm. The great shock registered in Hanoi when the Soviet Union finally dissolved is evidence of the denial of reality by a leadership generation so encased in a belief system that what was obvious even to the casual observer in 1989—that the socialist world would never be the same—did not sink in to many in the politburo until the actual demise of the Soviet Union in late 1991. This, in turn, helps us to appreciate the formidable challenge faced by the Vietnamese reformers who insisted that fundamental changes were needed, and why the decade of the 1990s was a decade of policy stalemate between reformers and conservatives.

In 1988, Truong Chinh passed away after slipping and falling down a flight of stairs. His replacement was Nguyen Van Linh, who was initially hailed as a "new thinker" and reformer. As *Changing Worlds* describes, Linh retreated back into the old orthodoxies in the face of the collapse of Communism in Eastern Europe and Vietnam's own economic troubles. *BTC* relates the concern of Linh and his entourage that they get out of East Berlin before a possible collapse would leave them vulnerable and trapped in a hostile situation in the middle of the capitalist world "without a dollar in their pockets," so they found a doctor to get the ailing Nguyen Van Linh in shape to travel, and hurriedly grabbed the next flight out of Berlin as the German Democratic Republic dissolved before their eyes.[19]

This led to an alliance between Linh and the ideological conservatives, which was implied in *Changing Worlds*, but made explicit in *BTC*. Even so, some reformers managed to insert the words "market economy" into the main text for the crucial 1991 Seventh Party Congress, sugar coating with what they considered empty verbiage (market economy "under the control of the state") in order to placate the conservatives. The conservatives were not fooled, however, and vigorously protested. At this critical juncture, another unlikely figure salvaged the reform agenda or at least kept it alive: Do Muoi, the stodgy manager of Vietnam's command economy in an earlier period joined forces with the reformer Vo Van Kiet. *BTC* asserts that "If the two persons, Do Muoi and Vo Van Kiet had not resolutely defended it, in 1991 the concept of a market economy might not have been put on the agenda of the Communist Party of Vietnam." This was not, says Huy Duc, a mere question of words; the struggle between the reformers and their opponents shows that "the 'struggle between the two paths' in the Party really began at that time."[20]

The pivotal year in the 1990s decade, characterized in *Changing Worlds* as a period of "wary reconciliation" and "uncertain transition," was 1995, when a confluence of domestic and external events created the conditions for an eventual breakthrough in Vietnam's stalled progress toward reform and global integration. This was the year that Vietnam joined, ASEAN, and normalized relations with the United States and the European Union. It was also the year of preparing for the Eighth Party Congress, at which a major generational turnover of the top leadership was expected. This did not happen, for reasons discussed in *Changing Worlds*, but the nature and intensity of the conflict between reformers and their opponents is underlined further by the details concerning the leadership struggles provided by Huy Duc.

The focal point of this struggle was a letter to the politburo sent by reformist Premier Vo Van Kiet, a blistering critique of the opponents of reform and integration which stirred a virulent counter-attack from conservatives. The contents of this letter have been well known, and it is discussed in *Changing Worlds*. It is the reaction to the letter, how-ever, which was less well documented. And, it was at this point that a new development occurred in Vietnamese elite politics, the political intrusion of the military—and omi-nously the military intelligence branch—into the affairs of the Party leadership at the highest level. This part of the story was known only by unverifiable documents circu-lating on the internet, and *Changing Worlds* discussed this development with great cau-tion and many caveats, owing to the difficulties of documentation.

We discover from Huy Duc that there was considerable substance to the allegations in these internet documents of sinister activities and power plays by the steadily expanding military intelligence organization known as General Directorate II (GD II). Ironically it was Vo Van Kiet who, to his later regret, signed the 1997 order that expanded the powers of this body, and politicized it by taking it from a position subordinate to the Army Gen-eral Staff and placing it under the "direct and absolute control of the Party." This on the surface would seem to insure that the military intelligence organization would not have an independent role. Mao Zedong had famously stated that "power grows out of the barrel of a gun" but, less famously, added that "Our principle is that the Party commands the gun, and the gun must never be allowed to command the Party." But following Kiet's order, things did not exactly work out that way. The conservative ideologists consistently warned of a Western plot to "de-politicize the armed forces" and the consequence was to turn part of the military into a partisan combatant in Vietnam's internal political strug-gles. GD II was employed by anti-reform Party leaders to use its technical expertise for political surveillance and even manufacturing of false charges of conspiracy—against General Giap, among others.[21] *Changing Worlds* mentioned some of these reported inci-dents, but underlined the difficulty of verifying them.[22] *BTC* unveils a quite detailed and plausible picture of the sinister side of the GD II, which I could only dimly grasp from unverifiable bits and pieces of information on the internet.

Even so, *Changing Worlds* observed that "it is an irony that among the rare instances in which there is public evidence of a potentially destabilizing power struggle in Vietnam, it has involved the military—or, more specifically, an element of the military intelligence branch . . ."—referring to GD II.[23] In addition to the KGB-like intrusion into matters of "internal security," GD II aligned itself with the opponents of deep integration to sabo-tage major policies like the U.S.-Vietnam Bilateral Trade Agreement. GD II sent slanted reports of the progress of the negotiations to selected individual politburo members in an effort to derail the process. According to the Vietnamese trade negotiator, "Looking back at the reports of GD II, one sees that most of them had the purpose of influencing the ranks of Vietnam's leadership, by creating an unfavorable mind set in external activities, tending to push toward confrontation with America. I don't understand why, after reading these kinds of reports, the politburo didn't demand that they be corrected."[24]

I stress the importance of understanding the impact of GD II on the story told in this book, because the overreach of the seemingly formidable alliance between the conserva-tive ideological theoreticians (who tried to brand reform and integration as a political "deviation"—a dangerous label which could lead to extreme retribution), and this rogue element of the military, which provided some real muscle to that anti-reform group, undermined their apparent success in stalling the reform process in the 1990s in what proved to be a pyrrhic victory. One of the important propositions of a theoretical model drawn on by this book, from the writings of Jeffrey Legro is that in order to change a deeply entrenched mind set, it is necessary not only to show a better alternative, but to discredit the old orthodoxy.[25]

The better alternative was provided by the reformers. Discrediting the old orthodoxy was unwittingly assisted by the anti-reform unholy alliance. *Changing Worlds* observed that "The apparent success of partial reform in the mid-1990s which had seemed to validate the conservative line on going slow and minimizing change was called into question by the end of the decade, as Vietnam's economy had reaped the easy gains of reform, and stalled as the unresolved issues of reform blocked further progress. This, in turn, strengthened the position of the reformers, who had been arguing for bolder action, and brought to the surface again the central issue of whether or not the main danger for Vietnam was falling behind in the race for economic development or risking destabilization by opening up. The conservatives had been somewhat discredited on the national-security front by the failed China card of Le Kha Phieu, criticism of the territorial treaties with China for giving away too much, meddling in political intrigues, and by their own involvement in the widespread networks of corruption, made easier by the partially reformed system, which created artificial monopolies and rewarded political influence which could be translated into cash—the worst of both worlds."[26]

It should be noted that one of the problems of relying on Huy Duc's account is that we have to take his word for the authenticity of the sources he cites. Another problem is that his reportorial style is anecdotal, not analytical. He sometimes cites sources who say contradictory things, and does not pause to analyze or evaluate the relative merits of the assertions. Even so, I think we can have confidence in the accuracy of his accounts based on personal interviews, and a reasonable degree of confidence in documents he draws upon and second hand hearsay that he reports. It is mostly consistent with what outside scholars and observers have reported, and contains much more elaborating and informative detail.

So it is with Huy Duc's account of the reaction to Vo Van Kiet's 1995 letter to the politburo. *Changing Worlds* cites the comment of journalist and author Robert Templer that this letter "touched off an intense political struggle, and ultimately diminished the influence of the conservatives."[27] Kiet dismissed the conservatives scare talk about "peaceful evolution" and imperialist plots, and declared that "In today's world there is no antagonistic contradiction between imperialism and socialism . . ." He remarked on the diversity and inclusiveness in the new globalized system and dismissed the idea of retreating into a cloistered international sub-system of the rump remnants of the once formidable communist bloc (in other contexts Kiet reminded the conservatives of Vietnam's security tensions with China, and the fact that North Korea had opposed Vietnam's invasion and occupation of Cambodia, undercutting the security rationale for "socialist solidarity"). *Changing Worlds* observed that "this letter seems to be a watershed in the evolution of Vietnam's new thinking about international relations, in that it represents a leader at the top of Vietnam's political system explicitly closing the chapter of the 'two worlds' mentality and spelling out the logical consequences of abandoning this 'us and them' mentality."[28] Kiet argued that it would be a "disaster for the country" if the 1996 Eighth Party Congress "timidly passed up the opportunity" to take advantage of globalization and "make the people wealthy, the country strong, create an egalitarian and civilized society."[29]

The conservative backlash to Kiet and his letter led to the installation of what turned out to be an interim Party leader, the political general Le Kha Phieu, who was essentially a front man for conservative Party ideologists and the economic and political interests of those in the military and other sectors who benefitted from political monopolies on commercial ventures and rent or profits from the sale of politically procured valuable land. The self-interested element of this anti-reform coalition ultimately helped undermine the claim of the conservative Party ideologists, who were the most visible opponents of reform, that they were standing up for lofty ideals and sacred principles. A politburo member (later dismissed for political intriguing) called Kiet's letter "100% deviationism." Kiet pointed out that the "deviationism" that the conservatives accused the reformers of was actually a charge better leveled at the corrupt use of political power for profit (Kiet himself was accused by conservatives of nepotism and his wife of large scale corruption).[30]

The final contribution of *BTC* to our understanding of the issues raised in *Changing Worlds* does, in fact, point the way toward the future; the question of the significance of generational turnover in the leadership. But here, *BTC* is somewhat disappointing. It observes that the leadership elected at the Tenth Party Congress of 2006, the point at which our story ends, "still had some people who had grown up in wartime," but notes that by and large this was a group that belonged to the generation of "becoming cadres" and no longer a "generation of revolutionaries."[31] This is another way of stating Max Weber's "routinization of charisma" proposition about the drop-off in political appeal and authority following the passing of movement founders and succession by followers who have fewer claims to rule by virtue of heroic deeds. But beyond that observation, there is little discussion of the character and future impact of this generation, and its implications for the evolution of Vietnam's political system. Thus there is little to add to the discussion of this topic in the first edition of *Changing Worlds*.

To simplify a more extended discussion of this subject in *Changing Worlds*, I advanced the view that we would see far less of the personalized political conflicts that characterized the story of Vietnam's reforms and integration in the future. It is more likely that the system itself will submerge the individuals who run it and the conflicts will be struggles over turf and benefits rather than great matters of state. This means that it is unlikely that we will see transformational leaders like Truong Chinh and Vo Van Kiet in the future.

But it also means that domineering "just say no" figures like Le Duan and Le Duc Tho will not find it easy to halt a gradually evolutionary process. It may even mean that discordant elements of the political system, like the rogue military intelligence branch or the group of conservative ideologues, in the future (though the jousting over polemical terminology continues[32]) will be hammered down like the proverbial nail that sticks out. Whether this process leads to a more open and participatory system is open to question, however. It is equally possible that the challenges of globalization to the powers of the state to control its political and economic environment, and the entrenchment of localism and familism described in *Changing Worlds* will lead to a weaker, but not necessarily more liberal state. What may eventuate is a system that is self-perpetuating, but also self-evolving—perhaps in ways that neither the current leadership nor outside observers could anticipate. So, in the end, both *Changing Worlds* and *The Winning Side* will be more helpful in understanding the past than as guides to the future. Vietnam's modern history suggests that it is impossible to understand the present, let alone the future, without reference to shaping forces that produced it. Hopefully this book will be a small contribution to that understanding.

Preface

ALTHOUGH I WROTE my graduate-school dissertation on the political system of the Democratic Republic of Vietnam (North Vietnam), which focused largely on the decade between 1954 and 1964—that is from the division of Vietnam at the end of the First Indochina War to the escalation into direct US military action in the Second Indochina War—I would be the first to admit the limits of my understanding of the subject, even after extensive documentary research and interviews with a number of people who had lived in North Vietnam during this period. So what led to the foolhardy decision to proceed with a second attempt to understand the notoriously secretive political system of communist Vietnam?

In part, it was due to a gradual opening up of Vietnam to the outside world and the fascination of watching what amounted to a Vietnamese version of glasnost, as more and more veils of secrecy fell to the ground. In addition, as the process unfolded, the expanded range of public issues, life choices, and diversity of opinion at all levels of society made the study of Vietnam infinitely more interesting. Between my first visit to unified Vietnam in 1982, and my last substantial research trip, from December 2006 to January 2007, extraordinary change occurred.

My 1982 visit was to a country still paranoid about foreigners and external threats, and was marked by several tense encounters with the public security branch and police, despite my status as an official guest of the Ministry of Foreign Affairs. On the street, I was routinely addressed as *dong chi* (comrade) because it was inconceivable to most Vietnamese at the time that a foreign visitor would not be from a fraternal socialist country. Even those who suspected that I was something different were at a loss as to the appropriate form of address for someone outside the familiar and restricted categories of visitors, so "comrade" was a safe bet.

Normal social and personal contacts between Americans and citizens of Vietnam were out of the question in 1982. A Hanoi meeting with my sister-in-law, who had joined the Viet Minh and persevered in the jungles during the anti-French Resistance, was a stiff and awkward affair, not least because the American connection put them under suspicion in that politically tense era—despite the fact that the meeting was authorized at a very high level. I feared it would not be possible to have a normal relationship with any citizen of socialist Vietnam in my lifetime.

By 2007, after a number of intervening visits to Vietnam, mostly accompanied by my wife, who had been raised in presocialist Hanoi, contacts with relatives were warm, familial, and unconstrained—even in the case of a first meeting with several families on the maternal side of my wife's clan, which included several who worked in the party ideological sector, and who had kept a discreet distance during earlier visits. By this time I had developed close and cordial relations with a number of academics and government researchers whom I had met over the years. Far from being an illustration of the regime's fears of a drift toward "peaceful evolution" and slackening loyalties, the deep patriotism and commitment to making the regime better, rather than undermining it, was a prominent feature of the many Vietnamese who interacted easily and spontaneously with foreigners—a far cry from the tense and wary encounters of 1982. It was an ease based on a self-confidence that was not easy to sustain in the prereform period, and the product of a major shift in the collective mindset of the Vietnamese elite during this period.

Looking back from the perspective of the relaxed and generally open Vietnam of 2007, the stifling and oppressive political atmosphere of 1982 seems very remote. Small wonder that it is difficult for a younger generation of foreign scholars, and even younger Vietnamese, to fully appreciate how far Vietnam has come in terms of liberalizing its political system and adopting a posture of openness. Even though the coercive arm of the regime is still active in suppressing dissidents and some religious and ethnic groups, and direct inquiry into many sensitive political areas by foreign scholars is still not possible, the extraordinary contrast between these two points in time underlines the profound and extensive transformation that has taken place in Vietnam over the course of several decades.

The 1982 trip was an outgrowth of an encounter with the Vietnamese delegation to an international conference on Cambodia at Chulalongkorn University in Bangkok in June 1980, led by the head of the Philosophy Institute, Pham Nhu Cuong. He was hardly an armchair, ivory-tower philosopher. In Vietnam, "philosophy" was the study of Marxist-Leninist dialectics, and Professor Cuong was the designated polemical heavy hitter who would slug it out with the Chinese delegation to the conference at a time of very high tensions (less than two years after the invasion and occupation of Cambodia by Vietnamese forces, Hanoi's troops had just made an alleged incursion into Thai territory). Professor Cuong's message was clear: Vietnam's security had been intolerably threatened by

China and its cat's paw, Pol Pot. This was the face Vietnam presented to the outside world at the time: fiercely combative, persuaded that any sign of conciliation would completely unravel Vietnam's position, and convinced that it was the world against Vietnam—a stark life or death struggle between "us" and "them."

I had edited a book which attempted to unravel Vietnam's reasons for invading and occupying Cambodia. Complex though these reasons were, from Hanoi's perspective they fit comfortably into a familiar paradigm; Vietnamese territory under threat from a more powerful foreign enemy who, in collusion with local proxies, wanted to impose its will on Vietnam's policies and politics. Later, as the Cold War reached its terminal stage, Vietnam concluded that this occupation was a strategic error of major proportions and that its security would have to be achieved by other means, and based on fundamentally different assumptions. That is the starting point of this book.

It was in Bangkok that I met for the first time Luu Doan Huynh, a long-time senior analyst at the Ministry of Foreign Affairs' Institute of International Relations, then serving in the Vietnamese embassy in Thailand. Over the course of many subsequent trips to Vietnam, Mr. Huynh provided keen insight and sage counsel. A key figure in the McNamara seminars on the Vietnam War held in Hanoi in the mid-1990s, the exceptional qualities of Mr. Huynh were very visible.[1] He had also been involved in my June 1982 trip to Vietnam. My very presence in Vietnam at that time evidently had been the subject of political debate between some officials, who wanted to diversify Vietnam's foreign contacts and begin to open up to the larger world beyond their socialist and Third World friends, and other conservative officials who felt that this trip was a gratuitous concession to someone who had once been in the enemy camp, was a "complicated element" who did not fit clearly into the framework of "friend or enemy," and who could provide an opening for subversion through undesirable contacts with Vietnamese citizens. My contacts were carefully limited to meetings with members of various state social-science institutes and government officials, who were impressive and articulate, but very restricted in the parameters of permissible topics and ideas, especially in conversation with an American visitor.

What I encountered in 1982 was a closed society, beleaguered and aggrieved in its dealings with much of the outside world, in a high state of political tension and, though I did not fully understand it at the time, sharply divided about how to resolve the many domestic and external problems it faced. Still, that impressive group of specialists I encountered in the institutes and elsewhere showed that Vietnam had a rich endowment of human resources, if only they could be allowed to realize their potential by removing the political, ideological, and organizational obstacles that limited their contributions to Vietnam's development in the era before the *doi moi* reforms.

In retrospect, one of the most interesting meetings during this trip was with the then minister of culture, Tran Do, who was a former deputy political commissar of the guerrilla forces in the South during the war. Do became the highest-ranking political dissident in Vietnam prior to his death in 2002. In 1982, however, General Do appeared bemused to be sitting in his office at the Ministry of Culture talking with a former member of US military intelligence and employee of the Rand Corporation in Vietnam about Do's intransigent tract on the dangers of cultural subversion (in which foreigners played a prominent part), which had recently been published, and his role in the Tet Offensive. Among the people I met on that trip, he was the last person that I could imagine becoming a fervent democracy advocate. Although there are many distinctive reasons for Tran Do's political and ideological transformation, and though he went much farther than most in his advocacy of political reform, it does parallel some of the broader but less extreme changes that took place in the Vietnamese elite in the period from the early 1980s into the new century.

My 1982 visit was jointly sponsored by the Ministry of Foreign Affairs (MOFA) and the State Commission for the Social Sciences (SCSS, as it was known then, before it became the National Center for the Social Sciences and Humanities and then the Vietnam Academy of Social Sciences). My liaison with MOFA was a veteran of Dien Bien Phu, the resourceful Le Trung Nghia, whose imposing demeanor and revolutionary credentials helped overcome the initial resistance of some who were either opposed to the idea of my visit, or reluctant to take the risk of being implicated with it, in the event political tides shifted once again. I met with Nguyen Khanh Toan, the director of SCSS; Dao Van Tap of the SCSS; Huu Tho, deputy editor of *Nhan Dan*; Duong Hong Hien, a prominent agricultural specialist (and, unbeknown to him, a cousin of my wife), who was in the South to do surveys and studies related to the ill-fated attempt to collectivize agriculture there; Le Cong Binh; Nguyen Khac Vien, the editor of *Vietnamese Studies* and interpreter of Vietnam to the outside world; Hoang Nguyen; and Tran Do, minister of culture. Historian Phan Gia Ben was helpful during my stay in Ho Chi Minh City, as was historian Luu Phuong Thanh. The topic of most of my interviews was revolutionary history, and I did not pursue the issues of reform and international relations that are the subject of the present book.

The first major academic conference in the social sciences involving both Western academics and Vietnamese officials, academics, and analysts was organized and funded by the US Social Science Research Council in June 1990, after some delay and after a crucial round of vigorous debate about economic reform had somewhat subsided.[2] Over the course of this conference I was introduced to many of the key figures in Vietnam's reform process. I was fortunate to be in Vietnam and Cambodia in 1991 with former senator Dick Clark, who met with a number of top leaders in both countries at this critical phase of terminating Vietnam's occupation of Cambodia.

I also had the good fortune to participate in the larger US–Vietnam dialogue project organized by Senator Clark and sponsored by the Aspen Institute. In visits to Vietnam and various conferences involving American and Vietnamese officials in other locales, I met political figures, notables, and academics who would play a remarkable role in the story of Vietnam's opening to the outside and in its internal reform process, called *doi moi* or "renovation." Two of the most intrepid and admirable were the mathematician

Phan Dinh Dieu and the reform economist Le Dang Doanh, pioneering advocates of ideas that were far ahead of their time, both politically and intellectually. These two models of integrity are true "profiles in courage." Even if they did not carry the day in the lonely and politically exposed early years of reform, the example of their ultimate impact on Vietnam's adaptation to a new world, even when their bold advocacy threatened their personal interests, reinforced my views about the importance of ideas in political behavior.

I should also mention encounters with two remarkable figures in Vietnamese diplomacy in the context of various trips and conferences organized by Senator Clark; Foreign Minister Nguyen Co Thach, a shrewd and skillful statesman, whose brilliant and controversial tenure in this office ran aground on the shoals of Vietnam's complex politics, and his apparent successor, Deputy Foreign Minister Le Mai, whose untimely death cut short a very promising career. I first met Foreign Minister Thach in a brief but memorable encounter on the flight from Bangkok to Hanoi on my 1982 trip. It was clear that he was very supportive of my visit and the opening up it portended. I subsequently learned that there were other officials who had a quite different view. In 1991, I sat in on a meeting between Senator Clark and Thach, during which Thach underlined his commitment to reform and outreach by presenting Clark with a published Vietnamese translation of Paul Samuelson's classic introductory textbook on economics, which Thach had commissioned.

John McAuliff, founder of the Indochina Reconciliation Project, played a notable role in trying to maintain open lines of communication between Vietnam and the outside world. I joined a tour group that he led, visiting Cambodia and Laos, which resulted in several important contacts in those countries. Mary McDonnell, Vietnam program director of the Social Science Research Council, arranged support for many academic exchanges, which was also helpful in this regard, including the 1990 social sciences conference mentioned above.

In 1994, on a brief visit to Hanoi, I had unusual feedback on what I thought was the esoteric topic of Vietnam's "strategic culture," in a curious meeting requested by a very high-ranking official of Vietnam's Ministry of Public Security. He was under the impression that "strategic culture" meant "strategy of culture" (which is the only way it could be translated into Vietnamese), and that the paper was a cryptic blueprint for an American-sponsored plot of cultural subversion of Vietnam. This accelerated my interest in the subject of "peaceful evolution," which was emerging as a primary concern to many Vietnamese leaders just at that time—though it had been prefigured by Tran Do's writings on "decadent culture" in the early 1980s.

My education in the economic dimension of Vietnam's external policies was furthered by a research trip to Vietnam in the summer of 1995, funded by the Haynes Foundation. I was accompanied by my Pomona colleague Stephen Marks, a specialist in American policies on trade and development, who subsequently focused his Southeast Asian research on Indonesia. In this respect, I must also express gratitude for the pioneering work of Adam Fforde on Vietnam's economic reforms, and Dang Phong's work on economic history of the reform period. This trip provided valuable insight on Vietnam's efforts to integrate into the global and regional economy.

The International Conference on Vietnamese Studies met in Hanoi in July 1998. Up to that date, it was the largest international gathering of academic researchers on Vietnam. The National University of Hanoi and the National Center for Social Sciences and the Humanities in Vietnam cosponsored the conference. The venerable revolutionary icon General Vo Nguyen Giap put his stamp of approval on this venture by his prominent keynote appearance. The conference was organized by Professor Phan Huy Le and his remarkable Center for Cooperation, which facilitated various academic exchanges—a pioneering venture in the opening up of academic ties between Vietnam and the United States, Europe, and Japan. Professor Le is a truly extraordinary person, who has helped to create an entire academic field in Vietnam (he was one of the "four pillars" of the Vietnamese history faculty which was founded after 1954), and led the way in the opening up of Vietnam to scholarly exchange. I was astounded by his vast knowledge and extraordinary range of contacts throughout the entire Vietnamese political elite, which did so much to facilitate my research in the most sensitive area of Vietnamese life, its security and diplomatic policies, even though this subject was not in the mainstream of academic exchanges, and the sensitivity of this project had a considerable potential downside for whoever sponsored it—even for someone of the unique eminence and prestige of Professor Le. His extensive networks of personal connections with leading figures in every sphere of Vietnamese life gave me a sense of the distinctive intimacy of intra-elite connections because of the relatively small size of the political and cultural elite, and its concentration in Hanoi, Hue, and Ho Chi Minh City. Thanks to these contacts, I was able to talk with a number of people outside the normal orbit of an international-relations specialist, such as Dr. Chu Hao, vice minister of the Ministry of Science, Technology and Environment, and a number of distinguished historians.

Prof. Le's pathbreaking 1998 conference on Vietnamese Studies and the Enhancement of International Cooperation certainly marked a turning point in the growing evolution of an "epistemic community," linking Vietnam and foreign scholars. It was a privilege to cochair a panel at this conference with General Nguyen Dinh Uoc, director of Vietnam's Institute of Military History. At this conference I also met Dr. Nguyen Huu Nguyen, a prominent military historian, and a former combatant in My Tho province in the Mekong Delta, where I had lived for four years during the war. He introduced me to some important memoirs and to the historiography of the war in that area, which provided valuable insights for my research on the subject. Dr. Nguyen, attached to the Ho Chi Minh City Social Sciences and Humanities Center, accompanied me on a tour of that province in 2006. Encounters like this would have been hard to imagine in earlier times, as he pointed out in an article he wrote after the 1998 conference about the novelty of the unscripted "corridor meeting" between two scholars who had served in the military forces of the opposing sides of the Vietnam War.

Research trips in 1999 and 2000 were made possible by a generous grant from the Smith Richardson Foundation, which supported extensive travel throughout most of Northeast and Southeast Asia, to meet with academic and government specialists knowledgeable about Vietnam, and to do further interviews in Vietnam. These interviews made it clear that Vietnam had taken further substantial steps in moving toward regional integration, including the security and political spheres, though it was also apparent that Vietnam's partners and interlocutors still perceived that the SRV leadership was hesitant to take the final plunge into deep global integration. This research provided the basis of chapters 5 and 6 of this book ("Wary Reconciliation" and "Uncertain Transition"), which focus on the critical period of the mid- and late 1990s, when Vietnam was struggling with the question of whether or not to opt decisively for deep integration into a globalizing world.

My 2006–7 visit was part of an academic exchange between Pomona College, where I teach, and Vietnam National University in Hanoi, funded by the Luce Foundation and facilitated by the American Council of Learned Societies. My host, professor and dean of the Faculty of International Relations, Pham Quang Minh, was a gracious and dynamic scholar heading up Vietnam's Faculty of International Relations. His students were exceptionally bright and well informed, and they indicate that Vietnam's future leaders will have an even more sophisticated grasp of the global environment in which they are situated than those who went before. Professor Minh spent a semester in 2006 at Pomona College. He facilitated my 2006–7 visit to Vietnam, sponsored in part by the same ACLS grant that had brought Professor Minh to Pomona College, and introduced me to a wide range of academics and government officials. I had the honor of being invited to give a lecture to the students in the Faculty of International Relations at the University of Hanoi during this stay. In 1982, this faculty did not exist, and it would have be inconceivable for an American professor to have such access to Vietnam's premier university, which had long been insulated from the outside world out of a concern that it might become the conduit for unwanted ideas infiltrating Vietnam. It was through Dean Minh that I had the opportunity to meet and interview his predecessor, Vu Duong Ninh, who was in many ways the founder of the academic program of study of international relations in Vietnam.

Academic contacts in many of my visits were made through the National Center for Social Sciences and Humanities. In this regard, I must especially thank Nguyen Duy Quy, director of the National Center for Social Sciences and Humanities, and Nguyen Duy Thong, director of the International Cooperation Department of that organization, and, of course Nguyen Khanh Toan, the director of the precursor State Commission on the Social Sciences in 1982, during my first visit to postwar Vietnam.

MOFA cosponsored my 1982 trip, and was a frequent point of contact for interviews and insights in succeeding years. I would like to acknowledge my thanks to foreign ministers (the late) Nguyen Co Thach, Nguyen Manh Cam, Nguyen Dy Nien, and (the late) deputy foreign minister Le Mai, as well as leading ministry officials Nguyen Manh Hung, Pham Cao Phong, Tran Minh Tuan, and Nguyen Van Tho.

The specialists at Vietnam's Institute of International Relations (IIR), the think tank and training center of the Ministry of Foreign Affairs, were generous with their time and ideas over the course of a number of visits: the perceptive senior analysts Luu Doan Huynh and Phan Doan Nam, and IIR directors Vu Duong Huan, deputy directors Dao Huy Ngoc, Bui Thanh Son, and Nguyen Ngoc Dien; Ha Hong Hai, deputy editor of *International Studies Review*; Pham Cao Phong, in his capacity as coordinator of the International Peace and Security Studies Program. I am also indebted to the insights of IIR analysts Hoang Anh Tuan, Le Linh Lan, Nguyen Thai Yen Huong, Luan Thuy Duong, and Nguyen Duc Duong, as well as Nguyen Vu Tung, who accompanied Luu Doan Huynh for my final interview with him.

In the sphere of economic issues, I was greatly assisted by Dang Phong who, in addition to his own research on which I relied, introduced me to Phan Van Tiem, deputy director of the State Finance and Currency Council, and Tran Phuong, a leading economic policy-maker of the prereform era. On a 1995 visit to focus on economic issues, Vo Dai Luoc and Le Van Sang of the International Economy Institute, Le Nhat Thuc of the Foreign Trade Institute, and Luu Bich Ho of the State Planning Commission were informative.

Among other key research institutes and their members who shared their expertise were Dr. Pham Duc Thanh, Chu Viet Cuong, and Pham Nguyen Long at the Institute of Southeast Asian Studies, Do Duc Dinh and the Institute of African Studies, Dao Tri Uc and the Institute of Law and Government, and officials of the umbrella state organization that coordinated them, known throughout much of this period as the State Committee on Social Science Research. I was also able to meet with members of the External Relations of the National Assembly thanks to Nghiem Vu Khai, Tran Van Phac, and Nguyen Thi Ngoc Phuong.

Although it was difficult to arrange meetings in the army and security sectors of Vietnam, I am indebted to the following for agreeing to meet with me: Security Ministry: Senior Colonel Nguyen Quang Binh (director general of the International Relations Department), Cuc truong, Cuc Quan he Quoc te, Ministry of Defense: Senior Colonel Le The My (head of international studies, Department of the Institute for Military Strategy), Senior Colonel Dr. Nguyen Vinh Tu (senior researcher, Institute for Military Strategy). *People's Army Newspaper*: editorial writer and international-relations commentator Ho Quang Loi. Meetings with members of the Party Central Committee's External Relations section, Bui The Giang, Le Vinh Thu and Nguyen Xuan Son were interesting, as were conversations with members of the Ho Chi Minh National Political Academy to discuss the role of ideology.

In documenting the analysis in this study, I have relied primarily on written sources, but the interviews with those mentioned above were crucial in getting a better understanding of underlying issues and personalities involved in the fascinating collective dialogue about Vietnam's appropriate response to the disappearance of the familiar Cold War world, and its venture into uncharted waters. I have also relied on some crucial documents circulated on the internet, whose provenance and authenticity cannot be confirmed with absolute certainty. Given the long tradition of politically inspired fabrication in Vietnam, it would be foolhardy to insist that the reader can place absolute confidence in these sources, although I been able to verify the authenticity of most of them with reasonable certainty. The exceptional and unprecedented access these documents provide into the once-impenetrable inner world of Vietnamese politics means that neglecting these sources would deprive us of key insights.

The trail leading toward a deeper understanding of Vietnamese politics and society has been blazed by a number of distinguished scholars, to whom I owe a deep intellectual and personal debt for their inspiration and generosity. David Marr introduced me to the academic study of Vietnam, and is a pioneer in the study of Vietnamese history who has left an indelible mark on the field. Carlyle Thayer is perhaps the best-informed student of contemporary Vietnamese politics and a leading authority on foreign policy and the Vietnamese military. I have relied heavily on the provocative and elegantly argued work of Adam Fforde on the Vietnamese economy, among others. Bill Turley, Brantly Womack, Ben Kerkvliet, Gareth Porter, Jayne Werner, Hy Van Luong, Mark Sidel, Lew Stern, and Nguyen Manh Hung are scholars with whom I have had long-standing and gratifying personal associations, and whose work has influenced my own—along with other scholars who I have not had close personal ties with, such as Heonik Kwan, whose brilliant studies of Vietnamese society heavily influenced the final chapter of this book.

Murray Hiebert was one of the best-informed journalists during this period. As the reader will discover, I greatly profited from a number of perceptive journalists who reported on some of the most sensitive political issues of the times, which foreign academics were rarely able to penetrate. Along with Hiebert's *Chasing The Tigers*, Robert Templer's *Shadow and Wind*, Bill Hayton's *Rising Dragon*, and David Lamb's *Vietnam Now* are penetrating studies of changing Vietnam. Nayan Chanda's *Brother Enemy* remains a classic.

In addition to the many interviews done in Vietnam, I traveled extensively in Asia to talk with specialists on Vietnam and the region to get their informed and close-up views of Vietnam's post–Cold War transformation, thanks to the generous grant from the Smith Richardson Foundation. They are listed below, generally (though not in every case) after the country in which the interviews took place, even when the person interviewed was not a citizen of that country.

Australia: Alan Behm, Greg Polson, Peter Calver, Rosemary Greaves. Paul Dibb, Miles Kupa, Bill O'Malley, David Glass, Ben Kerkvliet, David Marr, Frank Frost.

Cambodia: Lao Mong Hay, Kao Kim Hourn, Khieu Kannarith, Uch Kiman, Chan Prasith.

China: Beijing: Dao Shulin, Gu Yuanyang, Han Feng, Jai DuQiang, Lin Zhonghan, Pan Wei, Yu Xiang, Zhao Baoxu, Zhang Xizhen. Shanghai: Ma Ying, Tian Zhongqin, Wu Xinbo, Yang Jiemian. Quangxi: Gu Xiaosong, Nong Lifu, Wei Hui.

xxx

Preface

Indonesia: Kusnanto Anggoro, H.D. Assegaff, Bantaro Bandoro, Hashim Djalal, Clara Joewono, Hadi Soesastro, Rizal Sukma, Jusuf Wanandi.

Japan: Yasuo Endo, Motoo Furuta, Isao Kishi, Hirohide Kurihara, Hisashi Nakatomi, Kurt Radke, Masaya Shiraishi, Yoshihide Soeya, Seichiro Takagi, Okabe Tatsumi, Susuma Yamagagi.

Laos: Soubanh Srithirath.

Malaysia: Zakaria Ahmad, Chandran Jeshurun, J.N. Mak, K.S. Nathan, Lee Po Ping.

Republic of Korea: Bae Geung Chan, Yong Kyun Cho, Dong-Ju Choi, Dong-Hwi Lee, Lee Yong-joon, Insun Yu, Suk Ryul Yu.

Singapore: Amitav Acharya, Khong Yuen Foong, Melina Nathan, David Koh, Ang Cheng Guan, Kwa Chong Guan, Russell Heng, Kishore Mahbubani, Tin Maung Maung Than.

Taiwan: Chen Hurng Yu, Robert Hsieu, Lin Yu-fang.

Thailand: Boonsrang Niumpradit, Kavi Chongkittavorn, Khien Theeravit, Kusuma Snitwongse, Piti Kumpoopong, Pranee Thiparat, Sihasak Phuangketkeow, Suchit Bunbongkarn, M.R. Sukumbhand Paribatra, Vutti Vuttisant, Withaya Sucharithanarugse.

United States: US Department of State: Dorothy Avery, Desaix Anderson, Jim Bruno, Ray Burghardt, Michael Eiland, Denis Harter, Pete Peterson, Karen Stewart. US Department of Defense: John Bose, Pete Bostwick, John Cole, Frank Miller, Phuong Pierson, Tom Racquer, Howie Tran, Tim Wright.

Finally, I would like to thank the people at Oxford University Press who made this book possible. Foremost among these is Dave McBride, executive editor for law and politics, whose interest in the manuscript was crucial, and whose extremely perceptive and patient editorial guidance made it a much better book. I owe him a profound debt of gratitude for his support and encouragement. Caelyn Cobb, assistant editor for law and politics at OUP managed the very complex production process with efficiency and great skill. Venkat Raghavan Srinivasa Raghavan at TNQ, was instrumental in coordinating the final phase of copyediting, which was done by Michael Durnin with exceptional sensitivity and meticulous attention to the many pitfalls of a manuscript replete with many references in the Vietnamese language.

CHANGING WORLDS

I

Introduction

IN THE AFTERMATH of the fall of Saigon in 1975 and the unification of Vietnam under Hanoi's communist rule, its leaders' world view was decisively shaped by the external context of the Cold War. The origins of that conflict were already evident at the time Vietnam's August 1945 revolution launched the three-decade struggle that would lead to independence and a commitment to building a communist regime. As the newly unified Vietnam embarked in 1976 on an ambitious program of socialist construction in the North and socialist transformation in the South, top party officials had a clear view of its objectives and strategy, the nature of international relations, and Vietnam's place in the world.

Although the Sino-Soviet split had already shaken the ideological foundations of the high Cold War period, and deteriorating relations with China and conflict with Cambodia had injected an element of geostrategic complexity into the world of ideological orthodoxy that had guided Vietnam's revolutionary leaders, it was not until the collapse of the Soviet Union and the end of the Cold War that a profound and comprehensive rethinking of all elements of Vietnam's foreign and strategic policies, along with critical aspects of its political, social, and economic life, was forced on them.

Economic stagnation in the early 1980s had already stimulated a substantial reevaluation of the Vietnamese Communist Party's policy orthodoxy, culminating in a sweeping program of economic reform, initiated in 1986. These reforms, however, had still been legitimized by parallel efforts in the Soviet Union and China, and did not in themselves fundamentally challenge the world view of Vietnam's communist leaders.

The beginning of a fundamental shift in the system of international relations was evident by the mid-1980s and provided another reason to question the hitherto accepted world view of the Vietnamese party leaders. Gareth Porter's seminal analysis of this period notes that the then party leader, Le Duan, generally regarded as a pillar of orthodoxy on the subject of the irreconcilable divide between the communist and capitalist worlds, had conceded by mid-1984 that "Vietnam was building socialism in a 'new world situation'"[1] But Porter also notes that despite these early harbingers of "new thinking" in the mid- and late 1980s Vietnamese party leaders "did not completely abandon their view of the world as a struggle between two systems, and there were signs of lingering ambivalence among Hanoi's leaders about how much emphasis should be placed on the overriding importance of the global economy and the orthodox theme of struggle" with the capitalist world.[2] This book will trace the gradual displacement of the old world-view of the party elite by the new thinking which now dominates the scene, despite pockets of resistance on the part of an "old guard"—now reduced in numbers and influence.

Nearly two decades after the collapse of the Soviet Union and the dissolution of the communist bloc, Vietnam's party theoreticians insist that the great changes in domestic and foreign policy that followed 1989 are still consistent with the tenets of Marxism-Leninism. Is this only a front devised by Vietnam's rulers to downplay or to hide from its citizens the collapse of a vanished world and discredited ideology, or does it still affect the beliefs and actions of Vietnam's leadership?

Are today's party leaders schizophrenics who simultaneously inhabit parallel universes? Have they built a new system on the shaky foundations of the old, without consideration for the possible instability that this architectural and conceptual contradiction might entail? Or does pragmatism rule the day, leaving the reformers a free hand as long as they pay lip service to the old formulas?

On the occasion of the thirtieth anniversary of the end of the Vietnam War, *Los Angeles Times* journalist David Lamb wrote an article titled "War Is History for Vibrant Vietnam," which opened by stating that "Thirty years after the fall of Saigon, the firmly communist nation has a flourishing economy, social freedom and deep ties with the U.S. Half the nearly 83 million people in Vietnam were born after Saigon fell." Lamb apparently is using "it's history" in a distinctly American sense; if it is "history," it is no longer relevant to today's concerns and has been largely forgotten. His article posed the question, "So what have the decades since brought to a country that Air Force Gen. Curtis LeMay once suggested the United States should bomb "back to the Stone Age"?" His answer was, "Ironically, if you took away the still-ruling Communist Party and discounted the perilous decade after the war, the Vietnam of today is not much different from the country U.S. policymakers wanted to create in the 1960s." Lamb characterized the Vietnam of 2005 as a "peaceful, stable presence in the Pacific Basin," noting the substantial reduction in the size of its army and a strong market-driven economy with a flourishing private sector and growing middle class. "The United States is a major trading partner, and Americans are welcomed with a warmth that belies the two countries' history."[3]

Could it be that the ideological passions and intense political commitments of revolutionary Vietnam have vanished with hardly a trace? Has Vietnam become merely another

Asian soft-authoritarian regime, with its state economic sector largely reduced to a form of crony capitalism? Is Vietnam today more or less what it would have become if the Saigon side had won—except with a different leadership group in control? Was the struggle only about who ruled, not how they ruled?

The reader should be cautioned that this book in no way is intended as a triumphalist tract proving that the Vietnamese revolutionaries have seen the error of their previous ways and are in the process of becoming "us." It does not accept or support the "end of history" view that there is only one destination for Vietnam and all other countries in the world to reach. On the contrary, the era of globalization is characterized by its unleashing of forces of diversity along with its homogenizing tendencies. As a result of globalization, Vietnam has a widely expanded repertoire of models and examples to choose from in responding to the challenges and opportunities of globalization. In addition, the societal changes set in motion in Vietnam in the past several decades by internal factors have in many ways led to a return to distinctive cultural practices and ideas that had gone underground during the Cold War and Vietnam's prolonged revolutionary struggle, as the final chapter of this book will discuss.

In 1976, no informed observer in Vietnam would have anticipated a world without an "order" that expressed the main ideological division of the time, between communism and capitalism, imperialism and "progressive humanity." The driving forces of global change had been laid out by Marx and supplemented by Lenin. Friends and enemies were sharply defined and the conflict between them was an essential feature of the dynamics of international relations. A Vietnamese foreign policy based on the undiscriminating idea of being friends with all who would be friends with it would have jarred the confrontational instincts and attitudes of a triumphant leadership, still savoring the heady experience of defeating the formidable leader of the imperialist world. The idea of Vietnam (and China, along with a shrunken non-Marxist Russia) participating in an interdependent global market economy and joining the World Trade Organization, founded on capitalist principles, would have seemed fantastic. Membership in the Association of Southeast Asian Nations (ASEAN) would likewise have been unthinkable. As for the United States, what was sought was not access to the huge American market (and even a low-key security relationship, with visits by the US Navy and the Secretary of Defense) but reparations for war-inflicted damage.

Since this book takes the year 1975 as the starting point of the study of Vietnam's transformation over the next three decades, it is helpful to remind ourselves of the mindset of Vietnam's leaders in the heady period following the military victory in Vietnam. Adam Fforde and Stefan de Vylder write: "After national reunification in 1975, the Vietnamese national leadership was composed of individuals whose political education had occurred during the 1930s. People talk about the time just after reunification as being intoxicating, a time when people could seriously imagine that Vietnam could become an industrialized country by the year 2000, 'after four to five Five Year Plans.'"[4] This would not, however, take place in a placid or benign international environment. Continued antagonism between the socialist and capitalist worlds was assumed, despite the end of the armed conflict involving Vietnam. Growing tensions between China and Vietnam complicated this world view, but they only intensified Hanoi's view that its development would happen despite the international environment, not because of it.

Many years ago, Professor Arnold Wolfers posited the difference between two conceptions of international relations and national security. The first was a traditional view of the centrality of "possession goals"—the defense (or conquest) of territory and the protection (or undermining) of national sovereignty and independence. "Milieu goals" are more abstract, and involve attempts to create a regional or international environment that advances national interests and, unlike the possession paradigm, can be win–win rather than zero sum. In today's terms, the best example would be China's (and Vietnam's) conclusion that stable regional and global environments are essential for the international economic prosperity that has become the lynchpin of their economic development strategy.

As I have argued elsewhere, Vietnam has traditionally viewed its national security in very conventional terms, of protection of territory from encroaching powers (China, France, the U.S.) or seizing territory to expand the realm to the south (the Nam Tien, or Southward March). Vietnam's rulers have traditionally viewed international relations in starkly realist terms; a world of power and contestation, in which the "strong did what they will and the weak did what they must."[5]

It might be said that periodic decisions at various historical periods to acquiesce in a Chinese-dominated "system" or regional environment was in some ways similar to the current decision to join the U.S.-dominated system of international relations. But Vietnam's strategic thinking until quite recently has been almost exclusively focused on how to defuse the threat from a larger power and how to manipulate power balances to best advantage in order to defend its own territory, sovereignty, and independence—the emotional slogan that galvanized Vietnam's political class in 1945 and continues to resonate even in today's interdependent world.

Charles Tilly memorably said that war shaped the modern state: "the state made war and war made the state." Creating military power tended "to promote territorial consolidation, centralization, differentiation of the instruments of government, and monopolization of the instruments of coercion, all the fundamental state making processes."[6] Although Tilly's focus was primarily the formation of the modern European state, it can apply to the modern Vietnamese state, which was created from revolution and consolidated in war against external intervention. A political system designed to assert independence may find it difficult to adjust to the constraints of interdependence which characterize the current international system. The shift from a total focus on political and military security to economic growth requires different processes and institutions than the garrison state.

And yet, the picture of a dramatic shift from assertive sovereignty to constraining interdependence is somewhat misleading in the case of Vietnam. Precisely because of the fact that the Vietnamese state emerged in a period of intense conflict, internal and international, the leaders of the revolutionary movement were compelled to accept a level of dependency which belied the inspirational rhetoric of sovereignty and independence. This was evidenced at several key junctures of modern Vietnamese history, most notably in the 1950s, when Vietnam bowed to Chinese and Soviet pressure to agree to a compromise settlement of the First Indochina War in 1954. And it was constrained from pursuing its goal of national unification in the late 1950s by Soviet pressure and Chinese indifference.

More importantly, Vietnam adopted an economic model that resulted in a high degree of dependence on outside economic assistance, mainly from the Soviet Union and China. Fforde and de Vylder note that the "trend toward import dependency was increased by the onset of U.S. bombing, after which high levels of foreign aid helped maintain output and consumption. . . . [T]his helped create a particular type of dependency, in which the 'modern' sector could almost detach itself from the rest of the economy and float upon levels of commodity aid . . . This syndrome was reinforced in the late 1980s by the increased Soviet aid program at that time . . . [which came to an end with the collapse of the Soviet Union in 1991]."[7]

Vietnam was forced to confront the extent of its dependency on external support as aid from its erstwhile allies evaporated. Another important consequence of this economic reality check in the 1980s was that the party leadership was also forced to abandon its illusions of a Soviet-style forced march to modernity (an advanced socialist economy by the year 2000) and absorb the fact that the advanced sector of Vietnam's economy that could be considered under some degree of state control was a negligible percentage of the whole, perhaps five percent. Prior to the reforms, the relative insignificance of the state sector of the economy "created the contradictory picture of an ambitiously expansionary and aid-financed state unable to control an economy still largely based on subsistence farming and small-scale local trade. Instead it relied ever more heavily upon external assistance to maintain its levels of activity."[8]

Ironically, given Vietnam's fierce adherence to the ideal of sovereignty and independence, entrance into an interdependent global economy created the conditions for a more modern and self-reliant economy than was the case during the Cold War period. Because of deeply ingrained suspicions of capitalism, many of Vietnam's leaders were reluctant to acknowledge this challenge to their belief system, and remained deeply suspicious of the perils of extensive engagement with the world economy, fearing it was a trap ("peaceful evolution"), which would undermine Vietnam's political regime.

Perhaps the biggest mental adjustment for Vietnam's leaders since 1975 was acknowledging that the country had been relegated to the wings of the world stage, after being in the limelight for several decades. Even a decade after the end of the Second Indochina War, a history of Vietnam's foreign relations proudly noted that "In the last 40 years Vietnam and Indochina was the only place in the world that had continuous conflict. . . . and also the only place that in 40 years had three international conferences with the participation of all the major countries, members of the UN Security Council. . . . [T]he anti-American Resistance . . . of Vietnam was viewed as a historic confrontation, and Vietnam was regarded as the place where the contradictions of the era were concentrated."[9]

Coming as it did only one year before the bold decision to embark on a program of sweeping economic reform, this 1985 reaffirmation of the hard-line views of the previous decades raises the question of the relationship of Vietnam's internal crisis to the transformation of the world views of most of its leaders. Was the catalyst of change, the shift in the political alignments of Vietnamese leadership in 1986, mainly due to the policy failures of party leader Le Duan and his close associates and their inability to solve the internal economic crisis that had grown steadily worse since 1975? Or was it 1989 and the end of the Cold War—which suggests a more abrupt and far-reaching system shock that went far beyond questions of a state-controlled economy and was largely triggered by changes in Vietnam's external environment?

We will explore each of these factors in detail, but here it is important to examine the underlying analytic issue: was the transformation in Vietnam between 1975 and 2005 (or even 1995, by which time the most sweeping reorientations were already well underway) a gradual process, one in which change took place only in certain sectors and remained contested by important segments of the leadership; or was the main change abrupt, comprehensive, and definitive? To what extent did the dynamics of change in the economic sphere spill over into the military and security sphere of Vietnamese politics? Vietnam's transition from 1975 to 2005 was gradual, but punctuated with sharp discontinuities; first the conflict with China and Cambodia in the late 1970s, the economic reforms of 1986, the end of the Cold War in 1989, and the rapprochement with China in 1991. But the big turning points in ideological shifts have been fairly distinct.

One way of approaching these issues is to start by examining the second hypothesis; that it was a single abrupt shock, the collapse of the socialist bloc and disintegration of the Soviet Union, which prompted a thoroughgoing reassessment of Vietnam's relation to the world and which, in turn, affected its internal policies and politics. In this case, the 1986 turn in economic policy was a tactical expedient, limited to one sector of the regime. As one might expect, the explanation seems to validate elements of both positions. Having already engaged in what became known as "fence breaking," the later more sweeping change of thinking was made easier. It was a combination of spillover from the economic renovation into other areas of Vietnamese politics, the disappearance of Soviet aid, the fear of becoming weaker by failing to keep pace with economically dynamic neighbors, and the need for a stable and peaceful external environment in which to pursue economic development which led to major shifts in foreign and security policies.

But even though the new thinking in economic reforms was a facilitating condition—or even a necessary condition—for the subsequent new thinking about diplomacy and strategy, it could not by itself determine the outcome of the post-1989 decision about the nature of the international system and Vietnam's place in it. The decision to embark on a path of economic reform was an essential ingredient of Vietnam's paradigm shift, but not the primary cause of the fundamental change in the way the leadership viewed the world after the end of the Cold War. If true, this suggests that the shift was primarily due to changing external factors rather than an outgrowth of the internal transformation started in the early 1980s, and points to 1989 as a pivotal year, even though the subsequent adjustment to this shock took nearly a decade to evolve and take root in Vietnam. Still, by the turn of the new century it became apparent to many in the Vietnamese elite that after a decade of stalled reform their national interests required a bolder engagement with the global economy and acceptance of deep integration with it.

Since this book is primarily about Vietnam's foreign and security policies, 1989 is a logical starting point to examine the process of change. But even if it is confirmed that much of the new thinking in the area of international relations was forced on Vietnam by this dramatic global transformation, there are a number of subsidiary questions that remain, concerning not only the main topic of how and when this change in thinking happened (that is, the extent to which it was evolutionary and improvisatory), but also what practical impact it had on policies (did new policies flow from new thinking, or was the new thinking simply retrofitted onto pragmatic adjustments that had been imposed on Vietnam by force of circumstance?), how comprehensive was the reassessment (to use the jargon of the "realist" school of international relations was it merely adaptive or tactical change, or did it involve "complex learning," based on the acceptance of new paradigms and different fundamental assumptions?) and, finally, to what extent the new ideas have become entrenched at the leadership level (are there important issues that are still contested that challenge the fundamental conclusions of the new thinking?). Even if the external factors are found to be decisive, this does not exclude the possibility that internal factors were crucial to Vietnam's reorientation or that the economic reforms of 1986 were an indispensable condition for the later, more comprehensive reevaluations of the old orthodoxies.

Jack Levy's important article on learning and foreign policy behavior notes that "Kenneth Waltz and other neorealists allow for two forms of learning in international politics. One is the process of socialization in which states assimilate the norms of the system (i.e., learning). Systemic structure also acts as a selector by rewarding some behaviors and punishing others: states that fail to learn the causal laws or the norms of the international system cannot compete and so drop out of the system. This second process is better described as the selection of a system of rational adapters rather than learning. . . . Hence, neorealist theory and learning models provide different explanations for foreign policy change, and we should not confuse the two."[10]

From the neorealist vantage point, Vietnam's eventual extensive integration into the international system and downplaying of much of its revolutionary ideological heritage can be simply explained in Darwinian terms. It was a case of adjusting to the requirements of the dominant system or facing international isolation and marginalization, or state failure. Levy sketches out the alternative view of why states change their foreign policies (and therefore their behavior). "Neorealists emphasize the rational and efficient adjustment to changing structural incentives, whereas learning theorists emphasize significant variations in individual responses to structural changes deriving from variations in cognitive structures, beliefs, and processes." [11] In other words, the neorealists assert that there is a universal rationality at work that explains the behavior of elites. The only variation between cases is due to different circumstances and therefore different incentives. The alternative view is that different societies respond differently because of distinctive historical and cultural legacies that shape the outlook of decision-making elites.

One of the themes of this book is that the elements in the Vietnamese leadership who became concerned that an attempt to preserve the old system intact would result in losing everything eventually prevailed over those who wanted to cling to the status quo to retain their power and positions. Although the underlying story is extremely complex, the main thesis of this book can be simply stated. The debate about adapting to the post–Cold War era that took place among Vietnam's political elite was essentially between those who rejected jettisoning some of the most fundamental ideological assumptions about how the world worked and, along with them, the contention that the party's legitimacy rested on the claim that it was right in every instance and always had been, and those in favor of a substantial rethinking of assumptions and a switch to what has come to be known as "performance-based legitimacy."

Supporters of the idea that the party would have to justify its rule by results included some fairly conservative and hard-line pragmatists who supported performance-based legitimacy and who justified limited reforms on nationalist and national-interest grounds. But one might argue that it was a subset of this group, who have been controversially labeled "reformers" and who advocated fundamental changes in both ideas and policies, who were the "learners" and who not only adjusted to new realities but changed their minds about fundamental issues because of the new realities.

With a few exceptions on the margins of the Vietnamese political system, both "conservatives" and "reformers" wanted to preserve the socialist regime, but disagreed on how best to accomplish this. A closely related point is that the advocates of performance-based legitimacy also favored elevating economic development to the top national priority and downgrading military force as an instrument of policy, as well as relaxing the paralyzing and even paranoid obsession with security that had inhibited opening up to the new world of globalization.

Fear of "falling behind" in economic development and being unable to survive in a competitive world where power was increasingly based on economic success were important factors in both Vietnam's domestic reforms and changes in its international relations. This could easily fit a rational-choice or neorealist structural-adjustment paradigm. This study does not, therefore reject these explanations, but regards them as incomplete. There were more fundamental changes taking place in the minds of the elite of Vietnam than mere grudging recalibration of the minimum requirements for survival in the new international context and some profound changes in the deep social and cultural structures of the country that provided the context for the new thinking.

Compared to Russia and China, Vietnam was a somewhat special case because the obstacles to both adjustment and learning were very imposing, given the close identification of the old thinking with the existing leadership and its claims to legitimacy.[12]

Among his many important insights on idea change ("learning") and foreign policy, Levy discusses the related questions of whose learning is most relevant to understanding foreign policy change and the importance of timing in applying the lessons learned.

> We have seen that learning is neither necessary nor sufficient for policy change. Individual learning has little impact unless those who learn are in a position to implement their preferred policies or to influence others to do so. Different people learn different things and at different rates, and which ideas have the greatest impact is as much a political as an intellectual question. . . . As Nye argues, "Shifts in social structure and political power determine whose learning matters." Although some debate the relative explanatory power of learning and political power, the key question is how intellectual and political processes interact to shape policy.
>
> Shifts in political power determine when conditions are ripe for political leaders to put their ideas and policy preferences on the political agenda and effect a change in policy.[13]

Finally, Levy observes that "Not all learning is from the top down, and political and technical specialists in certain policy communities attempt to sell their ideas to political leaders. Their success depends on the power of their ideas, their degree of consensus on those ideas, their access to people in leadership positions, their political skill in creating and exploiting that access, and particularly on the match between the ideas of the specialists and the interests of the leadership and the extent to which specialists are empowered by leaders."[14] This point is especially important for this study, because much of the idea change that led to major policy shifts in Vietnam came from specialists and technocrats who were authorized by top political leaders to range beyond previous limits on acceptable ideas.

In thinking about these issues, I have greatly benefitted from the superb analysis of Jeffrey Legro in his book *Rethinking the World*.[15] Legro's book was written with a somewhat different focus (great-power strategies and international order) than the present study of Vietnam's adaptation to the post–Cold War era, but there are many important insights that are quite relevant to some of the central analytic issues mentioned above. The first of these is Legro's insistence on the importance of the world of collective ideas. Specialists in the study of international relations will immediately prepare themselves for another rehashing of the contemporary "great debate" in the academic field of international relations between realists, neoliberals, and "constructivists." This was not Legro's primary intention in *Rethinking the World*, nor is it mine in this work.

Still, it is not accidental that the blurb for *Rethinking* proclaims the book "as yet another nail in the coffin of realist theory as it shows that power relationships, unfiltered by prior collectively held ideas about cause and effect in international relations, tell us little about major power behavior." Leaving aside the issue of whether explanations of great-power behavior can also be applied to smaller powers, the focus on the role of ideas is certainly central to my own study, as it was to Legro.

"If there is a default explanation for discontinuous shifts in social ideas," writes Legro, "it is 'external shock'—typically such big events as war, revolution, or economic crisis. . . . Embedded mindsets endure for relatively long periods of time, but then they change under the pressure of dramatic events, giving way to ideas that last until the next crisis."[16] But, he notes, there is a problem with this simple formula: "Similar shocks seem to have different effects: some leading to change and some not."[17] Since it is not my purpose to present Vietnam's "rethinking of the world" in comparative perspective, this analysis does not bear the same heavy burden of proof in demonstrating why the case under review does or does not conform to a general pattern.

But, once again, Legro's analysis is relevant for the examination of the particular case of Vietnam, especially his contention that the range of ideas in play regarding foreign policy determines the parameters and likely direction of policy change.[18] Legro is careful to point out that ideas do not of themselves cause change in foreign policy, but interact with other factors.[19] So we must explore how the specific events that led to change were understood and interpreted in the light of the prevailing orthodoxy at the time of these events. That is the main task of this book.

In order to address some general conclusions relevant to the issues raised by Legro, let us preview some points made in the conclusion of this book. Was it the post–Cold War transformation of the global power structure that led Vietnam down the path it subsequently took? Or the positive and negative incentives of the global economy? Was the significant shift in collective ideas among the Vietnamese political elite a cause or a consequence of these objective factors?

Among these idea changes, three stand out as fundamental and transformational. The first was the rejection of the Marxist central-planning model in the 1980s, and the related undermining of the idea that the party (and its leadership) was always right, far-seeing, and wise. The second was the shift from confrontation to accommodation marked by Resolution 13 (1988; see below, chapter 3) and the decision to withdraw from Cambodia, along with the related upgrading of economics as Vietnam's top priority, and the downgrading of military force as the ultimate guarantor of Vietnam's national interests. The third was the 1991 adoption of a policy of "becoming friends" with all countries who would agree to normal relations with Vietnam—which implicitly rejected the zero-sum "us against the enemy" (*dich-ta*) foundation of previous Vietnamese strategic thinking.

These three developments took place in a context of crisis, but the hammer-blow shock did not come until the final collapse of the Soviet Union in 1991. This definitively undermined any possibility of avoiding real change. It marked the beginning of the end for the conservative resistance to reform and opened the way for the subsequent decisions to reconcile with former adversaries, to join ASEAN, and to embark on a path of deep integration with the global economy. It was not, therefore, a single "external shock" that led to the changes, but a shock following an extended crisis which had weakened resistance to change that was the *coup de grâce* for the old ways. The changes did not take place immediately following the collapse of the Soviet Union, but unfolded in fits and starts over the next decade until the internal debate surrounding them was resolved.

We must also ask not only why the change in Vietnam's thinking about international relations took place when it did, but why it took the form that it did—why did the Vietnamese leadership formulate the alternative to the previous orthodoxy in the way it did? Legro demonstrates that it is not enough merely to discredit the old thinking, the new thinking has to be legitimized and consolidated. "Not only must political actors undermine the old orthodoxy, they need to replace it with a new orthodoxy. Consolidation is shaped in part by two types of factors: (1) the number of prominent ideas in a society that might serve as a replacement for the dominant orthodoxy, and (2) the perceived initial results of such new ideas."[20]

This book tells a story which has a beginning (the post-1975 economic crisis in Vietnam), a middle (the early post–Cold War struggle between reformers and conservatives), and an end (the subsequent eclipse of the "old thinking" and the plunge into deep integration with the global economy). The irony is that the end may mark the beginning of yet another chapter in the transformation of modern Vietnam, as the world that it decided to enter after much hesitation itself encountered a crisis of ideas and confidence in 2007–2008. But that is another story.

The American reaction to the global economic crisis does, however, offer an illustration of Legro's point about the impact of sudden shock on ideas, and the related issue of how the policy action of elites depends on the presence or absence of replacement concepts and alternatives—also a critical point in the Vietnam story. The dominant free-market orthodoxy and faith in the "rational market" collapsed almost overnight, as evidenced in the former chairman of the Federal Reserve Alan Greenspan's startling admission that his guiding ideology of forty years had been wrong. "The whole intellectual edifice collapsed in the summer of last year," he said in 2008. Prior to this, doubt had already emerged about the validity of the "rational market" ideology, even as early as the 1970s. "By the end of the century they had knocked most of its underpinnings. Yet there was no convincing replacement, so the rational market continued to inform public debate, government decision making and private investment policy well into the first decade of the twenty-first century—right up to the market collapse of 2008."[21] Of course, the importance of ideas and rational discourse is more obvious in a democratic society but, as this book will attempt to demonstrate, ideas are also consequential in authoritarian systems.

There are obvious, if ironic, parallels between the crisis of confidence in the global economy in 2007–2008 and the post-1989 crisis in the Soviet bloc. Some scholars have argued that idea change was a fundamental element of the transformation in Soviet behavior that led to the end of the Cold War—and ultimately to the collapse of the

Soviet Union. Larson and Shevchenko write that "Between 1985 and 1991, the foundation of Soviet foreign policy changed from a Marxist-Leninist view of inevitable conflict between capitalism and socialism to an idealist vision of cooperation between
states in solving global problems. Mikhail S. Gorbachev fundamentally altered Soviet
foreign policy theory and practice by adopting the ideals of the new thinking, including
global interdependence, universal human values, the balance of interests, and freedom
of choice. Nor was this just rhetoric; he accepted the dismantling of Soviet medium-
range missiles in Europe and asymmetric reductions in Soviet conventional forces,
withdrew support from communist movements, and helped mediate an end to regional
conflicts in the developing world. He applied the principle of freedom of choice to
Eastern Europe, culminating in his decision to tolerate the fall of communism and to
acquiesce to Germany's unification. The change in Soviet foreign policy was a fundamental shift in identity, in how the Soviet Union viewed itself in relation to the rest of
the world."[22]

Despite the vast differences between the situation of the Soviet Union in its final phase,
and Vietnam, the Larson–Shevchenko analysis raises an issue that is central to this study:
did the new thinking in Vietnam, concerning the nature of the international system and
Vietnam's place in the world, have an impact on actual policy and behavior beyond an
inevitable readjustment to new power realities and the compulsions of national interest?
Larson–Shevchenko write that neither idea-based nor power adaptation explanations
adequately explain why Gorbachev went as far and as fast as he did in abandoning old
approaches. They supplement these explanations with an interpretation that stresses the
importance of identity politics and the need to find a new and fitting international role
for Russia. "We argue that Gorbachev and his like-minded associates chose the idealistic
new thinking over competing foreign policy programs because it offered a new global
mission that would enhance Soviet international status while preserving a distinctive
national identity."[23]

In the case of Vietnam, we have to explain why the "new thinking" about Vietnam
and the world emerged; how, why, and when it eclipsed the "old thinking," as well as
what, beyond the compulsion of unavoidable adjustment to circumstances beyond
Vietnam's control, impelled the translation of new thinking into concrete actions and
policies, and why these took the form they did. Did Vietnam's early response to the end
of the Cold War also involve "a fundamental shift in identity," in how Vietnam "viewed
itself in relation to the rest of the world" as was the case in the Russia? We would expect
that, to the extent that policies and actions were more than simple adjustment to forces
beyond the nation's control, as in the case of the Soviet Union, it might have something
to do with finding a new role in the international system that was not only compatible
with Vietnam's interests but also with the national self-image ("preserving a distinctive
national identity").

This study argues that the idea shift in Vietnam was essentially from socialist orthodoxy, sustained by conservative fear of change and obsession with regime maintenance

(defined narrowly as preserving as much as could be salvaged of the existing ideological framework in order to resist demands for more extensive change that might threaten the current power holders), to a broader, more traditional view of national interest as preserving and enhancing the status of Vietnam in the world and improving the welfare of its people. This resulted in a sharper distinction between the current power holders and the enduring national interests of the Vietnamese state, which had been blurred during the long revolutionary struggle by the constructed mythology of preternaturally wise and resolute party leaders who had presided over an epic drama of national salvation. It is understandable that the view that top party leaders are only custodians of the national interest, and not in themselves the embodiment of the national interest, raised further questions about selection of leaders, political accountability, and other fundamental political issues.

One of the most important explanations for the shift in the Vietnamese leadership's view of the world from confrontation to integration was a reformulation of the analytic foundations of its Marxist views on development and their implications for Vietnam's future. Porter notes the qualified acceptance as early as 1984 of the idea of a division of labor within the socialist economic system and the emergence of a single world market. Previously Vietnam, recalling its history as a colony exploited by the capitalist West for its natural resources, had rejected the idea of being a "hewer of wood and a drawer of water" in the socialist division of labor, consigned to an inferior economic niche as a supplier of raw materials to the advanced socialist economies. Vietnam's self-image was of a "'sovereign economic unit developed to a high level . . .', meaning that each member of the [socialist] bloc would have a heavy industry sector that would make it independent of more developed states for most basic manufactured goods."[24]

In terms of "ideological hegemony," the transition in new thinking was from socialist orthodoxy to the quest of the early nationalist modernizers for "wealth and power."[25] That, of course, was also the avowed goal of the conservatives who opposed much of the new thinking—but their recipe for attaining "wealth and power" was gradually discredited, and they reverted to a tenacious defense of the status quo that entrenched them in power, fearing the risks of deeper integration into the globalizing postwar international community, and passing up what the reformers saw as vital windows of opportunities to catch up with the rest of the world.

As noted earlier, Fforde and de Vylder have documented the pervasive dependency which was the actual result of Vietnam's quest for economic autonomy through socialist industrialization. Porter writes that "After reunification in 1975, Hanoi still did not envision Vietnam participating in an international division of labour" but, by the mid-1980s (and even before the pivotal 1986 "reform" party congress), "the Vietnamese leadership now accepted the need for Vietnam to participate actively in the global capitalist-dominated division of labour as well as the division of labour within COMECON [the Soviet-led economic bloc]."[26] This recognition that continuing down the same orthodox path would only entrench Vietnam's economic dependency was reinforced by the model of successful East Asian export-led growth during the 1980s. These changing views of the nature of the global economic system planted seeds of contradiction between traditional Vietnamese nationalism and Vietnam's historical attachment to the ideal of autonomy and independence—which had so often been compromised—and are important factors in explaining the intellectual transition to an acceptance of deep integration in a single world system.

The Marxist and nationalist components of the Vietnamese revolution had always coexisted, and still do, but nationalism became increasingly prominent as the socialist component of Vietnam's identity served mainly to isolate it from most of the rest of the world, and led to greater dependence on the last remaining ideological soul mate, Vietnam's traditional problem, China. Furthermore, when Vietnamese looked at the major trends (*xu the*) of the current era, they saw mainly a scientific–technological revolution coupled with an explosively expanding global market economy. One of the leading reform voices of the 1980s, Foreign Minister Nguyen Co Thach, said that the world economy "is entering a period of the most profound changes since the industrial revolution some 200 years ago," and that the economies of the world were now "linked with one another in an integrated whole, which is the world economy." In Porter's estimate, "Thach was thus moving away from the traditional Vietnamese view of the world as a struggle between the two camps for dominance to one in which states with different systems faced similar challenges in a single overarching economic system."[27] Some Vietnamese leaders still clung to the dreams of a socialist world, but that was clearly a hope for the distant future. Ironically, it was this resurgence of nationalist concern for Vietnam's place in the world that led to the expanded internationalism of its deep integration into the world economy and international institutions like ASEAN and the World Trade Organization (WTO).

A major theme of the reformers, which paved the way for acceptance of the new thinking, and a central topic of this book, is the growing consensus among Vietnam's leaders that the primary danger to Vietnam came not from hostile forces in the capitalist world bent on destroying communism in Vietnam, but from "falling behind" (*tut hau*). In addition to the popular dissatisfaction with the regime's economic mismanagement and the hardships of life, which severely undermined the prestige that the revolutionary leadership had gained from its wartime exploits, Vietnamese nationalist sentiment was deeply pained by the position of the country as an impoverished and marginalized actor in a world that was passing them by.

Of course at the time of the emergence of perestroika, the Vietnamese leadership was aghast at Gorbachev's reforms (which had also been motivated by fear of falling behind in the era of globalization) and the new thinking associated with them as they unfolded, and Gorbachev continues to be reviled as an apostate whose blunders and miscalculations crippled the socialist movement. Apart from the political and ideological gulf separating Gorbachev and the Vietnamese leadership of that time (and its successors), Vietnam's position as a peripheral actor on the international stage meant that its situation and role in the world was so different from that of the Soviet Union that even had it wanted to follow in Gorbachev's footsteps, his new thinking would not have been a particularly helpful guide. Still, the content of Gorbachev's new thinking in foreign policy was well known to the Vietnamese, and inevitably must have expanded their conceptual repertoire when it came to thinking about the nature of international relations in a changing world.

A good illustration of the extent to which change in views about socialism and the Cold War ideals of the Vietnamese party and state has penetrated into Vietnamese society, at least at the level of the political elite, is the popular reaction in Hanoi to the extraordinary 2006 exhibition held, appropriately enough, at the Vietnam Museum of Ethnology. This event, an exhibition called *Hanoi Life under the Subsidy Economy 1975–1986*, was termed by one Western journalistic account "the surprise hit of the summer."[28]

Vietnam's economic transformation in recent years has been so rapid that the items on display seem like antiquities from a bygone age—even though most are only about 20 years old. The exhibit, which opened in June and runs through December, features recreation of general stores filled with dreary state-made goods—complete with ration coupons and mannequins standing in line. For most of those who lived through the hard times, the exhibit is a reminder of how far they've come. For their children, raised during the "doi moi" [renewal] economic reforms, it's a window into a world they've only heard about. With the economy growing at an average 7 per cent each year and more than half of Vietnam too young to remember the hardships of the post-war economy, the ethnology museum set out to bridge the generation gap with its exhibit, according to curator Nguyen Van Huy.[29]

"The younger generation who did not live in the subsidy economy can hardly understand how their parents lived," said Huy, "So our approach is to look at that time through the eyes of ordinary people." As his next comment made clear, however, these visitors, residents of the national capital, were hardly "ordinary people." "Response has been overwhelming. On weekends, about 2,000 visitors—about five times the usual attendance—pack into the museum. The parking lot overflows with motorcycles and even private cars, which are so new in Vietnam that the museum had to create a special parking place for them. 'Those are the rich people who bring their children to tell them about their life in the past,' Huy said."[30] In other words, these are the children of the elite, and the next generation of leaders in Vietnam.

Despite these striking evidences of change in outlook, and though few would want to return to the spartan days of Cold War and revolution, there are not many voices calling for radical change of regime, although there has been pressure for expanded political participation and accountability within the existing party and state institutions. Vietnam is a somewhat special case with regard to the "number of prominent ideas in a society that might serve as a replacement for the dominant orthodoxy," as Legro puts it. First of all, as a tightly controlled authoritarian society, with an explicit and highly specified ruling ideology, there has not been much room for the gestation of ideas which would challenge the dominant ideology. Moreover, the adjustment to the shock of the collapse of the communist world was presided over by the same people who had jealously preserved the prior orthodoxy, and radical change would be an implicit repudiation of their past leadership.

Yet Vietnam also has two conditions that counteract what would appear to be insuperable obstacles to new ideas. The first is that during the long civil war, alternative ideas of social, economic, and political organization were widely circulated by the former Saigon regime and its patron, the United States. (Hanoi's leadership insists that it was a war against imperialism and its proxies, and not a "civil war," but it is clear that Saigon's decades of rule left a profound imprint on the South which, as we will see, ultimately filtered up to the North.) Finally, there are many highly educated and articulate individuals and groups in the Vietnamese diaspora who have sharply challenged not only the old orthodoxy, but Hanoi's response to the changed international environment.

Some Vietnamese revolutionaries even argue that there were ample precedents for a more liberal and flexible approach to making revolution and building socialism, which had been derailed by prolonged leftist phases. In this view, the reform decisions were a matter of getting back on the right track after a prolonged period of deviation. Hoang Tung, the longtime editor of the party newspaper from the 1950s to the 1980s, writes,

> A swing to the left led to the economic and social crisis of 1975–1985, forcing us to renovate our development path. Our Doi Moi (Renovation) started in 1986, but in reality it was only returning to an old path laid out in 1929, 1941, and 1945, encouraging the development of a national commercial sector, and the expansion of economic contacts with other countries, broadening the market economy, and bringing about self management control in the commercial production of each form of the economic system. The State would only manage administratively, and guide the macro economic level, putting forth a development strategy for the country.[31]

There are, of course, many variables in examining the role of ideas and new thinking in Vietnam's adjustment to the post–Cold War world. The formative experiences of the political leadership, its cohesion and political style, generational differences, and the extent to which popular attitudes are relevant or influential in decision-making are some of the factors that need to be considered. The fact that these elements are reflections of a broader pattern of change, and that the study of Vietnam's leadership and its decisions is always aimed at a moving target, makes the task even more complex.

The residual impact of decades of warfare is clear. Le Dang Doanh, perhaps the most eminent of Vietnam's reform economists, observes that,

> There is something specific to Vietnam, it is the war mentality. The country was more or less one of the fiercest battlefields of the last century. The heritage, besides

the cost, is that a lot of people still believe that there are a lot of enemies around. Many don't understand that the world has changed, that there are nowadays co-operation and competition, and that competition is not war. Indeed, Vietnam is engaged in a lot of co-operation and it is done within a permanent competition. For some of the people, it is still difficult to understand the difference. They look at any issue as if they are in a fight. In their mind, there are only win-lose situations as during the war, but no win-win solutions.[32]

Yet there are significant differences in attitudes between this war-hardened leadership and the populace at large, Doanh asserts, as well as between the older and younger generations.

The society at large is not really affected by this perception. The people are friendly and do not see the competition as a matter of life and death. I would say it is rather at the elite level of the country that such perception is, in some quarters, still very much alive. Look at the way Vietnam enters into trade agreements. It is very clear, on closer analysis, that the State is always hesitating as to how and with whom to sign a trade agreement. There is still a lot of argument about the way we should conduct the diversification of our trade or relationship with one country or another. The latest example is the argument arising about the United Nations University. Are we going to accept one to be here or are we going to turn it down? The argument is not about education needs, but rather about the influence of the backers of the University and the role such influence can play.[33]

"Why so much paranoia about the influence of ideas?" asked the interviewer. Doanh replied

Maybe we should look at history. A very striking phenomena [sic] is that, when Ho Chi Minh took power in 1946, traveling on a French warship on his way home from Fontainebleau, he could invite a lot of Vietnamese intellectuals trained in France to come back with him, to organize the resistance against the French Today, if Vietnam wants to catch up with a knowledge-based economy, it must attract again a lot of the overseas Vietnamese, living in France, or in the US and elsewhere to come back to Vietnam to help our society to understand what marketing is, what economic management is, so on and so forth. But it didn't happen and one wonders why what Ho Chi Minh did, the leadership can't do today.

The problem, in this view, seems to be that Vietnam is caught between a single-minded authoritarian system that thinks it can impose change at will, and a democratic system that has political procedures to work out differences. Vietnam has an authoritarian collective leadership which, however, is divided into different interest groups and networks, and is paralyzed by the lack of mechanisms to resolve its conflicts. Reaching consensus is possible, but it is always fragile and transitory. Politics in this collective-leadership system is perpetual renegotiation, which makes it difficult to achieve policy consistency on long-term objectives. Perhaps what is needed is a strong leader to facilitate the importation of ideas, asked the interviewer. "People need to focus on one man," responded Doanh. "To take your example, we do not have a Deng Xiaoping to focus the energy and make the decision, but we actually need one."

"If a collective leadership, to a point, brings different views coming from various segments together, how can it build a strong consensus on contentious issues such as the switch to a market economy?" asked the interviewer. "What can be said because it is obvious is that the consensus must be reached daily, in other words, every day, for every new decision, a new consensus must be reached," Doanh answered. "Its is undoubtedly a matter of generation. I like to compare that situation with that of physics before and after the quantum theory. Physicists of the classic physics did not understand quantum physics, and to support their views, even remarkable physicists went astray, while the new generation immediately accepted the quantum theory of Max Planck. In Vietnam, in a manner of speaking, we are in a similar situation. The new generation will come with new conceptions and a new understanding of the world and the new paradigm will be accepted readily, probably because of the internet and new technology developments everyone can witness."

Interviewer: "Can then Vietnam afford to wait for an old generation to go and a new one to take the lever, because it seems to me that it is a rather long process?"

Doanh: "I really do hope that we could shorten that natural process, to move forward as fast as possible. The problem is to catch the train of the XXIst century as soon as possible."[34]

This study will examine in detail the emergence of divergent views on key policy issues, primarily in the security and foreign-policy domain, in an attempt to determine how much of the actual policy change that eventuated can be plausibly traced to ideas and new thinking, as opposed to purely reactive concessions to reality, rudderless pragmatism, compromises between competing interest coalitions, or even the perennial of Cold War Vietnam-watchers, power struggles within the leadership. With respect to this latter point, during the Cold War period, many outside observers thought that there might be different policy coalitions in the leadership during the Vietnam. There were even some who claimed to be able to identify hardened "factions" (e.g., "organized opinion groups," which blended struggle over policy with struggle over power)—a term which aroused great controversy among observers of communist politics during the Cold War. Following the Cold War, a parade of dissidents and quasi-dissidents in Vietnam have asserted this view even more forcefully, often with compelling, if unverifiable, documentation.

In addition, there is ample room for changes in the sphere of foreign policy which would not threaten the hold of the leadership—except for those identified with failed policies, which can be dealt with by offering a "sacrificial lamb," as happened in the case of Foreign Minister Nguyen Co Thach, who was removed from power both to appease China, and as a precondition of normalization, and because his politburo colleagues claimed he had not been sufficiently consultative in managing the high-risk confrontation with China. Indeed, it has been the leadership that has taken the lead in policy revision in this area.

But these changes have also been influenced by external and internal pressures, and prompted by two fears. The first is that if Vietnam did not find a way to tap into global growth, its economy would be left behind not only the Asian "tigers," but any state that is able to take advantage of the opportunities of the global market. A stagnant economy will be unable to fund an adequate security force, and the kind of technological infrastructure required by modern armies will be difficult to build. In this case, in addition to Vietnam falling behind its neighbors, if its leadership cannot satisfy its people's craving for a better life in a region of dynamic growth where others prosper, there would eventually be domestic political repercussions.

Nevertheless, the main arbiters of the permitted boundaries of new thinking are the current leaders in Vietnam. We will deal more specifically with the theoretical implications of this study in a later chapter, but it is appropriate to state here that the focus on collective idea change at the level of political elites raises the issue of what agents are involved in this change.

If this is a study of collective idea change within Vietnam's political elite, how can we define the group we are talking about? The most obvious answer is that, when talking about the elite, "we know it when we see it." These are the people who matter most in the political life of Vietnam. To paraphrase an old American commercial, "when they speak, people listen." They are the ones who write in the government press and are written about. The members of the political elite most relevant to this study are, of course, those who can make a difference in policy areas dealing with external relations. There is no single standard for inclusion in this category, but some rules of thumb may provide an operational definition.

In the first place, the Vietnamese Communist Party controls political life in Vietnam, and it has a very clear standard of inclusion in its own inner ruling group; membership in the party's Central Committee (160 elected members in the 2006 Tenth Congress Central Committee). This might be expanded to include all delegates to the periodic party congresses which elect the Central Committee, although this larger group is clearly less relevant to policy- and decision-making in the external affairs and security field. There were 1,176 delegates at the 2006 Tenth Party Congress. The political elite would include all members of the state bureaucracy who are in policy-making positions, perhaps down to the third echelon of the ministries, or leading cadres and analysts in various state commissions and institutes that have functions related to policy development, implementation, interpretation, or evaluation. These include the "think tanks" of the Vietnamese Academy of Social Sciences, the Vietnamese Academy of Science and Technology, and similar organizations, as well as the major universities and institutions of higher education. It has been reported that Vietnam has 100,000 people with advanced degrees. An ongoing biographical dictionary project aimed at establishing a record of Ph.D. degree holders has produced three volumes with 3,000 entries, though this is not yet a complete or comprehensive list of all Vietnamese Ph.D. holders. Although most of these are in technocratic or minor bureaucratic positions, and often their training does not meet international standards expected of this academic degree, it does suggest a deep reservoir of educated people, many of whom are influential enough to belong to the political elite. To this must now be added a growing managerial and technocratic class working in the private or semiprivate sector, along with literary, creative, and performing artists who play a central role in Vietnam's intellectual life.

Over the three decades of reform, the size and composition of the political elite changed. In part, this was simply a byproduct of Vietnam's population growth; from a population (North and South) of around 30 million in 1960, the combined population grew to around 47 million in 1975 and 84 million in 2007. Although it cannot be assumed that the size of the political elite grew proportionately, it certainly grew significantly—especially after 1975 and reunification of the country. Another important factor in the growth of the elite is the expansion of higher education. The pool of qualified potential members of the elite has grown along with the expansion of higher education. In a globalizing world in which information and knowledge are increasingly the key to success, education is a necessary qualification for most leadership positions.

In addition to intensifying existing regional diversity at the elite level, the growth in the size of the elite has also led to increased diversity of interests, background, and opinions within the elite, as the prominence of southerners in the reform process attests. A possible exception to this may be a decline in the prominence of revolutionary elites coming from the hardscrabble provinces of upper central Vietnam, in particular Nghe An and Ha Tinh, through a combination of being "northernernized" over many years of living in Hanoi, and often having a skill set (revolutionary zeal and loyalty would be a prominent part of this) that is decreasingly relevant to the party's needs in an era of development and globalization.[35]

Some Vietnamese from other regions have felt that this regional group was over-represented because of its close ties with the early party leaders of the revolution (Ho Chi Minh himself was from this region). But like many topics worthy of study, this issue can be only mentioned here, and the observation is based on impressionistic evidence. The way regionalism in general affects elite politics is a critically important topic, but one which would require a major research effort to sort out.

The move to a market economy and the increasing salience of private interests and of important leaders in the private or public–public sectors have also added to the complexity of discourse within the elite. We will discuss the debate about the extent to which party members can engage in private business, but one of the key elements of the debate is the question of how the party can represent the emerging entrepreneurial sector of society if it does not include them among its members.

In addition to changes in the size and composition of the political elite, there have been important changes in the ways ideas circulate among them. The most significant is the relaxation of tight ideological and political control over the expression of ideas. Democratic centralism was supposed to be a device for encouraging intraparty debate up to the point of decision, after which everyone would fall in line and support whatever had been decided at the top. As many party members themselves have stated, until recent years, this never produced real debate in the party. In addition, the felt need to maintain an image of party infallibility (with some exceptions, such as admission of error in land reform, and the more recent reassessments of the failures of central planning or its strategic mistake in invading Cambodia) limited how candid party discussion could be about policy alternatives, even in its own ranks.

This study will examine the emergence of new thinking among a small vanguard of the elite, and the conditions under which the once unthinkable eventually became mainstream. It will also note changes in the dynamics of the political system that made the spread of new thinking possible, though this book is not primarily focused on a study of the Vietnamese political system per se. Finally it will consider in a concluding chapter the broader societal transformation that paralleled the evolution in thinking at the elite level and which was both a cause and a consequence of idea change at the top levels of society. But fundamentally this is a book about how a political elite, shaped in an environment of conflict and revolutionary struggle, adjusted to a new global environment and to challenges for which their life experience and intellectual formation had not prepared them. For this reason it might be best to start the tortuous process of tracing the changes in thinking about the transformation of the international system and its implications for Vietnam by examining how this leadership itself, and its predecessors in the prior two decades, have analyzed the process of adopting "new ideas" to meet a new situation.

2

On the Eve of *Doi Moi* Reform (1975–1986)

MAJOR SHIFTS IN the collective mindset of a political elite have frequently resulted from an external crisis which jolts the conventional wisdom about the nature of the world they live in and their country's place in that world, and opens the way for new understandings and different ideas about international engagement. Such crises are typically caused by war, internal upheaval, or economic distress. As Jeffrey Legro observes, "Embedded mind sets endure for relatively long periods of time, but then they change under the pressure of dramatic events, giving way to ideas that last until the next crisis." Of course, crisis can only be a partial explanation for collective idea-change, because the same event, or same type of event, may not have a uniform impact across societies. Some upheavals lead to significant change in some places, but not in others.[1] Moreover, major shifts in collective ideas can take place in increments and be affected by more than one crisis as the "embedded mindset" crumbles. Finally, splits within an existing elite consensus, which open the way for new ideas, can be the paradoxical result of backlash against attempts by members of the leadership to enforce an unquestioning adherence to old ways and old ideas that have proven to be ineffectual or even disastrous in the face of crisis.

Although Vietnam was certainly not a major player on the international scene a decade after the termination of the Second Indochina Conflict, it was buffeted by the same shock that the great powers had to confront at the end of the Cold War.[2] In addition, Vietnam was undergoing wrenching internal change at precisely this time. There had been considerable "new thinking" about economics during the 1980s (and even earlier), but it was not until 1989 that new thinking expanded to the larger sphere of diplomacy, security, and strategy, the changing nature of the international system, and its implications for

Vietnam. It is not coincidental that the temporarily stalled economic reforms were rein-vigorated in 1989, and that the new thinking on internal reform and the new thinking about international relations became interlinked.

Although Vietnam's reforms were officially (if tentatively) launched in 1986, their origins were back in the late 1970s. The year 1989 marked a major turning point in the reform process—though both what happened in Vietnam's economy and why it happened are still subjects of vigorous debate among economists. As we shall see, some economists insist that Vietnam's leaders had opted for "shock therapy" and a "big bang" approach toward shifting from a command economy to a market economy, while others reject the idea that state policy had a major impact on economic behavior. Since this book is more about the impact that factors like economic crisis had on the thinking of Vietnam's leaders about Vietnam and the international system, their perceptions, intentions, conclusions, and beliefs are as important as the objective reality. This chapter will explore the ways in which the new thinking about economics paved the way for a more fundamental reassessment of the Vietnam's place in the world.

ADAPTATION OR LEARNING? RETHINKING ECONOMICS PREPARES THE GROUND FOR RETHINKING SECURITY

As noted in the introduction, this study does not attempt to engage in comparative analysis, but the main subject of this chapter also happens to be a central area of debate among those who study the Gorbachev era in the Soviet Union. Many scholars assert that Gorbachev's dramatic break with conventional thinking in Soviet foreign policy was driven by the failure of the Soviet economy. Domestic priorities, it is argued, "required a shift in resources away from military spending and external commitments, which in turn required a reevaluation of the cold war paradigm, Soviet state interests, and strategies to achieve them."[3]

A related question, posed by the dramatic changes in elite conceptions of the place of Russia in the world in the final phase of the Cold War, is: how much of this was a tactical retreat forced by circumstances (which took on a momentum beyond the control of the reformers and went in directions they did not anticipate), and how much reflected a fundamental rethinking of the basic assumptions of generations of Soviet leaders? To put it in theoretical terms, how much was "adaptation" and how much was "learning"? James Moltz argues that there were competing economic models (Gorbachev's and Boris Yeltsin's, for example) and that these models themselves derived from the differing political interests of their respective advocates. Celeste Wallander argues more generally that internal economic crises often played a critical role in Soviet foreign-policy change. These arguments have led several Sovietologists to contend that Soviet foreign-policy change under Gorbachev derived more from political change than from learning.[4] Because the new thinking in Vietnam first emerged in the economic area, prior to the great geostrategic shocks of 1989–91, similar questions could be asked about the connection between the economic and the foreign policy and security dimensions of Vietnam's ideational and policy shifts in the late 1980s and after.

Fforde and de Vylder succinctly describe the beginnings of the conceptual transition of Vietnam's views of socialism and the nature of the state in the mid-1980s. The Sixth Party Congress of 1986 launched what they term a "soft reform" socialism, which resulted in internal liberalization and the "opening up of the economy to the private sector and the outside capitalist world." By 1989, the economic reforms were accelerated by the introduction of a market economy without, however, the creation of effective capital markets and appropriate state institutions. This, in turn, led to inflation and instability in a system suspended between the old and the new, setting the stage for the deepening of economic reform in the 1990s, "which was initiated by the 1992 interest reforms, the rising inflow of foreign direct investment, the growth of the private sector and strong de facto privatization and the resumption of multilateral lending in late 1993." Fforde and de Vylder then point out the implications of this for our subject of collective idea-change within the Vietnamese political elite. "How could Vietnamese Marxist-Leninists grapple with, and then explain, such a reality? The simple answer is this: through debate."[5] As we shall see, the debate was protracted, and eventually led to direct political confrontations among the top leadership precisely because the issue was the basic identity of the regime and its relation to the outside world.

It also raised the question of the possible dangers of attempting partial or half-way reform, and building a new edifice on the foundation of an incompatible base—a point which recurs repeatedly in this study. The danger of partial reform is ending up between two worlds, with the negatives of each, but not the positives.

At the pivotal 1986 Sixth Party Congress which sanctioned the launching of *doi moi* or economic renovation, the external context was very much in the foreground. Vietnam still lived in a world divided into friends and enemies—in effect, in two worlds. Interior Minister Pham Hung's speech at the congress made this clear. "In the first stage of the period of transition to socialism in our country, the struggle to defeat the multifaceted war of sabotage waged by the hegemonists [China] in collusion with imperialism is closely linked to the struggle to determine 'who will triumph over whom' in the context of the socialist and capitalist systems. Therefore, the tense, decisive, complex, and long-range characteristics of that struggle will increase constantly. The struggle to determine 'who will triumph over whom' in the context of the two systems will take place throughout the period of transition to socialism in our country, especially in its first stage."[6] The fact that China (the "hegemonists") was lumped into the enemy camp was a complication and adaptation of the earlier and simpler view of capitalist versus socialist worlds, but the fundamental idea of antagonistic and irreconcilable "camps" persisted at the Sixth Party Congress even as the logical coherence of the concept began to disintegrate.

Along with the internal economic shocks of the post-1975 period, Vietnam had to cope with a sudden transformation of the international landscape. First was the rapid

collapse of its relations with China, and the related issue of Vietnam's invasion and occupation of Cambodia. Then came the rise of Gorbachev and perestroika and, finally, the
fall of the Berlin Wall. Although dissolution of the Soviet Union took another few years,
the fall of the Berlin Wall and the implosion of the Eastern European communist regimes
made it abundantly clear that the winds were not blowing in a direction favorable to
socialism or the remnants of the Soviet "camp."

Vietnam's invasion of Cambodia in 1978 and overthrow of the Chinese-supported Pol
Pot regime was not a "proxy war," as China and the United States termed it, in which
Vietnam was merely serving as an instrument of Soviet pressure on China, but the invasion and occupation were enabled by the backing of a superpower. Without continued
backing from the Soviet Union, and in the face of serious economic distress, Vietnam had
little choice but to bow to reality and accept China's dominance in the region and, eventually, to normalize relations with the United States and ASEAN. The language of "who
will triumph over whom," still central to party rhetoric in the "reform party congress" of
1986, ultimately disappeared, though it was briefly revived in its most extreme rhetorical
form during the turbulent changes of 1989. But the further question is, did Vietnam's
leaders make a virtue of necessity by embracing the idea of "changing worlds" even beyond
what stark necessity demanded?

This chapter lays the groundwork for exploring the relationship between the economic
shock and the strategic shock, and the relative impact that each had on the leadership's
new thinking about the way Vietnam would relate to the world in the aftermath of the
big changes of 1989. The primary analytic task is to examine how the foundations for the
subsequent response to the great shock of the collapse of socialism in the Soviet Union
and Eastern Europe were laid. Legro emphasizes the importance of external shock in
inducing "discontinuous shifts in social ideas." But let us also recall that Legro points out
the importance of what precedes the shock. "Foreign policy idea change (and continuity)
depends on preexisting ideas. Collective ideas fundamentally shape their own continuity
or transformation (1) by setting the terms and conditions of when change is appropriate
and (2) constituting the most likely option(s) for the new orthodoxy."[7]

We will explore the origins and early evolution of the economic reform process up to
the shocks of 1989–91. With respect to the economic reforms, a persuasive school of
thought maintains that it was not the leadership or any "policy" shifts that instigated the
reform, but that the hard economic facts on the ground drove the reform from the
bottom up. In addition, some maintain that the reforms were a gradual evolutionary
process and reject the idea that there was either a landmark turn in the road at the 1986
Sixth Party Congress, which gave the signal to abandon the attempts to enforce a comprehensive command economy, or a "big bang" in 1989, when the reforms were first
formulated in concrete and comprehensive terms.

This may be true, and we shall examine its implications in this chapter, recognizing
that in terms of the purely economic dimensions of the reform, the nonexpert must defer
to the economists. But even if the leadership was following and not leading in economic

reform, it is still highly relevant to the question of the extent to which being compelled to abandon orthodoxy in one central area of the regime's belief system made the leadership more receptive to new ideas in the area of foreign policy and national security.

The leadership and its policies are, after all, the main object of this study. And, in the area of diplomacy and strategy, even though the leadership may be compelled by force of circumstances to do things it does not want to do, the diplomatic and strategic dimensions of politics are the exclusive domain of the state, unlike the economy, and it is unlikely that significant change would take place unless intentionally directed by the regime. To the extent that new thinking about diplomacy and strategy is forced on a reluctant party leadership by external factors beyond their control, it would be similar to the "bottom up" forces that compelled the economic changes in Vietnam after 1975. But in this case it would be "top down," in the sense that pressures from above the level of the national government (the international system) are driving the change, as well as "bottom up," since the internal economic crisis compounded the external threat.

One way of measuring the extent to which change has been embraced by the party leadership because they see the world in a new light and view the changes as a means of seizing opportunities, rather than grudgingly engaging in damage control with tactical adjustments, is to explore the "roads not taken." If there were, in fact, no alternatives but to "integrate" (*hoi nhap*) into the international system (dominated largely by Western, capitalist, and democratic countries), then it would be difficult to say whether any new thinking involved really made a difference. Again, to use the language of the realists, this could simply be a temporary tactical adjustment to power realities.

EARLY CHALLENGES TO ORTHODOXY

Chapter 3 will deal with the geostrategic changes of 1989. This chapter will provide an overview of the economic reforms and a survey of the interpretive debates over the causes and consequences of the reforms. From the perspective of contemporary Vietnam, the conventional story of the reform is one of heroes and villains. The negative figures in the morality play of reform are the party secretary general Le Duan (party leader from 1960 to 1986) and his most important supporter, Le Duc Tho, who controlled the organizational machinery of the party. Another major figure in this story was Do Muoi, later secretary general of the party, often identified as opposing reform during his tenure in the 1990s, and the person in direct charge of "socialist transformation" in the late 1970s. Do Muoi was also the leader who made the penitential trip to China in 1991 to apologize for past transgressions and restore relations.

Le Duan conveniently died just before the Sixth Party Congress (regularly referred to as the "historic Sixth Party Congress") of December 1986, which opened the way for experimentation by providing protection for reformers, who had up until this time been under constant threat of punishment as "revisionists" and antiparty elements. With the threatening presence of Le Duan (and Le Duc Tho) removed, open debate and discussion about the causes of Vietnam's economic crisis became permissible. That there was no clear reform agenda at this time does not diminish the importance of making possible rational policy debate and "facing the facts."

Some participants in this debate later attempted to downplay the role of Le Duan as an obstacle to policy innovation and idea change in the late 1970s and early 1980s (see the discussion of Vo Van Kiet and the comments of General Le Duc Anh below), but the general consensus is that he was unyielding and dogmatic in clinging to orthodoxy. An even clearer example of the opponents of change, and a recognizable face attached to the label of "conservative," was the head of the Party Organization Department and Henry Kissinger's former diplomatic adversary, Le Duc Tho.

One of the early postwar confrontations between advocates of change and doctrinaire conservatives took place in 1982, when Le Duc Tho attempted to depose Tran Do, his one-time comrade-in-arms in revolutionary struggle (they shared a common prison experience and were in the top echelon of command in South Vietnam during the latter phase of the conflict), from his position as minister of culture. Tran Do would seem to be an unlikely "reformer," given his hard-line views about the threat of cultural subversion—the progenitor of "peaceful evolution"—but apparently he was viewed as sympathetic to the desires of artists and writers to be granted more freedom of expression. Le Duc Tho viewed Tran Do's receptivity to these pleas for more openness as subversive and threatening to the existing power structure, which he was committed to preserve intact and unchallenged.

In Tho's view, ideas inevitably had political consequences. Even Tran Do's predilection for long hair and bell-bottom trousers was a form of "lax" behavior that would inevitably lead to "lax" ideas and a loss of political control. Do describes how his supporters tried to contain the damage of Le Duc Tho's attack by focusing on questions of style and behavior (he was "too nice" and lenient with subordinates and sloppy in dress and appearance). Tho insisted that this was simply another manifestation of Do's more serious failing, the politically fatal charge of holding "erroneous viewpoints" (*sai lam ve quan diem*). Prior to the 1982 Fifth Party Congress, Tho unexpectedly convened a meeting of ministry of culture officials to confront Tran Do, and inform him that he was being removed from his ministerial post and would not be selected to the Central Committee in the upcoming party congress.

One of the collaborators of Le Duc Tho, who played a role in the scripted meeting of accusation against Tran Do (which was probably the key factor in his later conversion to democracy advocate and dissident and his expulsion from the party), read the following charges (as Do remembered them several decades later): "Comrade Tran Do often reveals a viewpoint that is extremely erroneous; that the situation is completely new so that the approach to leadership has to be changed [*phai thay doi cach lanh dao*]. If you hold that it is completely new, that means rejecting everything that has been done up to now. It is also because of this erroneous viewpoint that comrade Tran Do does not accept things as they are [*khong chap nhan nhung cai da co*], and wants to seek out things that are completely new, which he calls 'new thinking' [*tu duy moi*] and 'new style of leadership' [*phong cach moi*] in the leadership of culture and literature."[8]

This is one of the earliest uses of the term "new thinking" that I have come across. Tran Do may be applying this term retroactively, but it is clear that he did, in fact, represent the vanguard of high-level party members who felt that Vietnam's situation had fundamentally changed since the old doctrines had been formulated, and that an assessment of the implications of the "new realities" was imperative.[9] At the time Tran Do was, if not in a minority, at least on the political defensive, and nearly alone in expressing his views openly. Part of the story of collective idea-change in an authoritarian system is that the vanguard active agents of change are always in a small minority because the risks of baldly stating that the "emperor has no clothes" are very high. Many others may feel, intuitively or based on observation and analysis, that the imposed orthodoxy is wrong or self-defeating, but will not say so until a different political climate reduces the risks of being in a dissident minority. How this political climate evolved, permitting both the open expression of "new ideas" and spreading the acceptance of these new ideas, is the story of this and subsequent chapters.

There are a number of testimonials by informed participants in the Vietnamese political process to the perils and frustrations of being an early innovator, coming up with the right idea at the wrong time. We will consider some of these later, in this and succeeding chapters. For the moment, let us simply illustrate the point by the following statement by General Le Duc Anh (who led Vietnamese forces in Cambodia, became head of state, and later came under a dark cloud of political controversy over unresolved issues about his revolutionary past, which his alleged sponsor for party membership, Le Duan, is said to have covered up). In an attempt to claim that Le Duan and others were early proponents of reform, Anh presented some evidence of earlier flexibility on economic management, and argued that the seeds of reform had been planted well before the Sixth Party Congress, but that conditions were not right until 1986. "It was Le Duan himself that was the first person to discover 'the peasant question.' Forty-five percent of agricultural production came from the 5 percent of land allotted to families, and the other 95 percent only produced about 50 percent of the total. Thus the peasants didn't have a motivation to farm, and it was necessary to create one for them. Because of this, comrade Kim Ngoc, the party secretary of Vinh Phuc province, put forth the policy of contracting to the family, and he was supported by very few people at first. Too bad that at the time this matter was too novel and it ran counter to the ways of thinking and doing things that had been in place for a long time, so that this thinking [*tu duy*] by Kim Ngoc and the support of brother Le Duan did not receive majority support. In exchanges with people, brother Le Duan was often heard to repeat a firmly and enthusiastically held view: 'the truth is concrete [*chan ly la cu the*], revolution is creativity; so that often the revolutionary path has to cross through a lot of trials before creativity can find the truth.'"

After offering some unconvincing illustrations of Le Duan's foresight in economic matters—such as setting up a joint venture with the Soviet Union to exploit Vietnam's oil, even though Vietnam knew the Soviet Union did not have the best qualifications for the job—Anh portrays Le Duan as a visionary of reform who was stymied only because he was ahead of his time and conditions were not ripe. In Anh's view, Le Duan's great wisdom was in holding back some exploration blocks and not giving everything to the Soviet venture. "For this reason I think that though we usually say that the Sixth Party Congress was the critical juncture of the nation's *doi moi*, and that is correct, that doesn't mean that it was only at the Sixth Party Congress that we had reform. This thought had been nascent from the time of the Fourth Party Congress, and was even more apparent in the Fifth Party Congress, and on the threshold of the Sixth Party Congress, the situation and conditions in all respects (ideological understanding, socioeconomic . . .) were ripe for our party to decide to publicly announce the policy of comprehensive *doi moi* of the country's economy."[10]

Whatever Le Duan's role in suppressing or tolerating "premature reformists," his enforcer of party discipline, Le Duc Tho, was powerful and implacable enough to be able to impose heavy costs on anyone questioning orthodoxy. Despite Tho's machinations, however, Tran Do was re-elected to the party Central Committee at the Fifth Party Congress in 1982, based on his high standing among his fellow revolutionaries and impressive record of wartime accomplishment. But Tho used his powerful position as head of the Party Organization Department to remove Do from his position as minister of culture and saw to it that he did not obtain any other position.

Prior to the Sixth Party Congress, which was presided over by Nguyen Van Linh as the newly elected party secretary general, and which opened the way for new thinking and reform, Tran Do had a conversation with Linh, who asked him why he had not initially been on the list of those slated for election to the Fifth Central Committee. Tran Do explained in detail the maneuvering of Le Duc Tho and the charges leveled against him. "Brother Linh attentively listened and looked pensive. Finally, when it came time to leave, he exclaimed—neither happy nor sad—'Well, the two of us have been criticized for being liberal [*tu do*, literally "freedom-ists"]. You were liberal in the field of literature and I was liberal in economics.' Both of us laughed. At that time Linh and I were both members of the Fifth Central Committee, but Linh still held the important post of party secretary of Ho Chi Minh City, and I didn't have any particular job. Before parting to go back, I said to Brother Linh, 'Back then out in the jungles, how beautiful our life was. In life or death we had each other, and loved each other as family. And now only five years after peace look at all these things that are happening.' Linh laughed and said 'In the end, everything will turn out fine.'"[11]

NARRATIVES AND COUNTERNARRATIVES OF REFORM

Not surprisingly, the principal villain in this now conventional story is Le Duc Tho, who viewed resolute resistance to change as the only way to keep himself, his favored faction, and his patron Le Duan in power. Like Tran Do, Le Duc Tho also had occasion to reflect on the lost world of revolutionary solidarity and idealism. Tho was eased out of the politburo in 1986 and died in 1990, having witnessed the great crisis of socialism, but not yet the final collapse of the Soviet Union. Near the end of his life, Tho wrote a poem reflecting his sadness about the course of events. A foreign reporter observed that,

> Judging by a poem he wrote, published two weeks before his death from cancer, he died an unhappy man. His victory over Henry Kissinger, it would seem, was not his but America's—15 years after unification the values of free-wheeling Saigon had triumphed.

> In the past we had strong emotion
> Sharing life and death, sharing a bowl of rice and a shirt
> But now people take money
> And individuality as a measure for emotion and feelings
> The sense of camaraderie has faded.[12]

Considering the number of hardened guerrilla revolutionaries who had become embittered targets of Tho's political vendettas, it is not hard to see why the "camaraderie had faded." As noted at the beginning of this chapter, attempts to enforce unquestioning adherence to old ways and old ideas that prove to be ineffectual or even disastrous in the face of crisis can end up shattering the existing consensus. In this sense, by destroying the solidarity of the revolutionary elite and breaking up a once-monolithic consensus among them, Le Duc Tho was an unwitting facilitator of the new thinking about reform.

The heroes in this conventional wisdom story are the party leaders who had ruled the South after 1975. Nguyen Van Linh and Vo Van Kiet were the most prominent of these. Truong Chinh, once known as an unbending ideologue and defender of orthodoxy, also played a key role by going to the South, observing the desperation measures employed to keep factories running and the urban population fed, and signing off on them, even though they were in clear violation of party policy. Nguyen Van Linh replaced Truong Chinh as party general secretary at the Sixth Congress and gained a reputation as a resolute reformer, and the leader who had put Vietnam back on a sustainable track.

There is considerable truth in these portrayals, but also some problems. First, a number of scholars have challenged the idea that reform is a story of personalities, or even of formal decision-making, as we shall see in a later chapter. Martin Gainsborough, who did extensive research on the economy of Ho Chi Minh City in the late 1990s, noted that, "A tendency to personalize the reform process—and hence to see change as a product of actions by individual leaders—is also widespread in the Vietnam literature."[13] As an example, he cites the case of leaders like Nguyen Van Linh and Vo Van Kiet as the personification of "reform." The fact that a succession of reform leaders had risen to the top after being in charge of affairs in South Vietnam (Vo Van Kiet after Linh, and Phan

Van Khai after him) led many to conclude that reform was associated with experience in South Vietnam. "By the 1990s, the 'Southerner, therefore reformer' thesis was firmly established."[14]

This is an important caution to accepting too quickly the conventional narratives of reform. For one thing, some unlikely Northerners (like Truong Chinh) played a key role in launching the reforms. For another, some prominent Southern figures such as Pham Hung (like Vo Van Kiet, a native of Vinh Long province in the Mekong Delta) were opposed to many of the fence breaking measures taken in the South. Vo Van Kiet recounts the heated arguments he had with Pham Hung, who was then a deputy prime minister, but ascribes the differences to Hung's national responsibilities and mission to keep the "big picture" in mind, while Kiet was trying to cope with urgent problems in the South.[15] But if it is true that not all Southerners were reformers (so that the formula "Southerner, therefore reformer" is misleading) it is also true that many were much more inclined to challenge orthodoxy than in other areas of Vietnam. Vo Van Kiet recalls that when he was the party secretary of Ho Chi Minh City in the early post-1975 period, it was not so much a question of pursuing a reform policy agenda as dealing with crises. Still, this was viewed by many leaders in the North as unprincipled cutting of corners that was undermining socialism. "We ran ourselves ragged groping for any way of unraveling the difficulties. Comrade Pham Van Dong called me the 'Chairman of rice' [*chu tich gao*] and 'Chairman of pigs' [*chu tich heo*]. There were some comrades who pinned on me the label "fence-breaking general" [*tuong vuot rao*]. Several times a year I would go to Hanoi to report on things. In these conferences not a few comrades were unsympathetic to the measures which the city had taken."[16] Pham Van Dong's "Chairman of pigs" was, says Kiet, good-natured humor.[17] Still, it is not the kind of label usually associated with a heroic builder of socialism.

Despite the clear North–South differences in risk-taking and willingness to challenge orthodoxy, it is misleading to conclude that all "reformers" had the same agenda, or that all reformers were also political "liberals." Still, as the introduction to this book tries to argue, there is one fundamental axis along which it is possible to use labels of "reformers" and "conservatives"—that is the spectrum between those whose main concern was that Vietnam would fall hopelessly behind in the global race for economic development and those whose main concern was regime preservation and salvaging the status quo. In this sense, the relevant labels would be "primarily nationalist" and "primarily regime preservation" oriented. A fuller discussion of this issue is in chapter 7, "Taking the Plunge."

The most obvious alternative to the focus on individuals or elites in looking at the vast changes that took place in Vietnam in the three decades following 1975 is to consider it either part of a self-generated process, driven by impersonal forces rather than considered policy, or a societal transformation taking place at the grassroots level, independent of any formal governmental design—or both. We will return to this issue in subsequent chapters. In this context, I simply register agreement with the caution about overpersonalizing the "reform story" but, at the same time, contend that it cannot be ignored. It is, after all, a story largely told by the Vietnamese themselves. Even though it has clearly been manipulated by political elites to make themselves and the regime look good, the broad outlines of the "conventional wisdom" reform narrative appear to be widely accepted in Vietnam. Since this book is a study of ideas, it could not ignore this story because it might be exaggerated or manipulated, or even untrue (and I am reasonably convinced that the general outlines of the story provide an important, if incomplete, description and explanation of the reforms).

More importantly, while economic processes are an important part of the post-1975 transformation of Vietnam, this study concentrates on how collective idea-change was either a cause or a consequence (or both) of that transformation. It is ultimately about perceptions concerning Vietnam's place in the world and the changing nature of its external environment. Given this topic, it is inevitable that this study will focus not only on ideas, but on ideas at the level of the political elite. We should try to understand how close these ideas come to reflecting the realities of Vietnam—indeed that is title of the concluding chapter of this book ("Rhetoric and Reality"), but the first task is to attempt to understand the Vietnamese elite perception of that reality.

In addition to the conceptual issue of understanding change in terms of process or individuals, there are problems even with the inner logic or consistency of the personalized conventional narrative of reform. For example, some reports from that period claim that Truong Chinh was actually aligned with Le Duc Tho in opposition to Nguyen Van Linh's elevation to party secretary general.[18] In addition, in running Saigon Nguyen Van Linh had, by virtue of his position, been the overseer of the disastrous economic policies that turned an enfeebled but still viable postwar economy into a shambles. However much he may have disagreed with the policies, he carried them out. His main virtue was in turning a blind eye to some of the desperation measures taken by a few bold factory managers to keep their enterprises producing, and in ignoring the blatant violations of policy necessary to procure enough rice for Saigon to avoid starvation. Linh had been put in charge of the socialist transformation of the South right after the takeover of Saigon, but progressively distanced himself from that role with a shifting series of jobs, and eventually withdrew, or was removed, from his post in the politburo.[19]

Some retroactive accounts claim that the problem was a temporary deviation from the good intentions of reformers like Nguyen Van Linh because of (usually unspecified) leaders issuing inappropriate policy directives from the North. The point of this view is the at least *someone* in the party had the right answers, even if they could not be implemented for a time. The alternative is to admit that the entire party was disastrously wrong about its basic orientation for an extended period of time—which would lead to a credibility gap which even the harshest critics of Le Duan would rather avoid. But since this is a study of significant shifts in ideas and world view in Vietnam's leadership, we need to examine critically this conventional wisdom story, of a few strategically placed bad apples deflecting the party from its own clear vision and better instincts. As we shall see in the next chapter, Nguyen Van Linh, widely viewed as a bold reformer, reacted to the changes of 1989 with rhetoric about proletarian dictatorship and imperialist perfidy that was at least as harsh as anything the purported "conservatives" had ever said.

The "conservatives"—with the exception of Le Duan and Le Duc Tho, for whom "conservatism" meant keeping themselves in a position of unchallenged power—are also hard to categorize. Mai Chi Tho (pseudonym of the younger brother of Le Duc Tho), later in charge of the coercive arm of the party, would hardly seem likely to be a critic of the imposition of hard-line political and economic policies on the South immediately following the takeover in 1975, but his account of this period offers a vivid illustration of the gap between the new rulers in the South and the ordinary people and their lifestyle, as well as an unvarnished admission of the desperate poverty that stemmed from the regime's policies.

Even those who are unlikely paladins of reform (or their supporters) have tried to recast their role as the consensus grew that the prereform management of the economy was a disaster and those in office at the time scrambled to distance themselves from responsibility for it. Apart from apologias from close associates of Le Duan,[20] some reformers like Vo Van Kiet tried to soften the hard edges of Le Duan's leadership in the post-1975 period, as we shall see. The hard-nosed Mai Chi Tho, brother of the even more intransigent Le Duc Tho, and a lifetime official in the public-security branch, tried to reinvent himself and recast his role during the hard years after 1975. Not only was he a reluctant cop, he told the redactor of his biography, but he was sympathetic to the plight of all those unfortunate victims of the reeducation camps[21] and socialist transformation campaign.[22]

Mai Chi Tho's image-polishing biography states that, "It could be said that the time Nam Xuan [his nickname] was Chairman of the People's Committee [of Ho Chi Minh City] (1978–1984) was the most difficult time of the period before reform." In order to link Tho to the reformers, the biography says, "When speaking of the collective leadership of that time, people mentioned comrades Nguyen Van Linh, Vo Van Kiet, and Mai Chi Tho as outstanding leaders along with the cadres and people of the city who were looking for strong remedies for development, at the time called 'fence breaking.' The struggle for *doi moi* in the city was very rich in many dimensions." In this version, Mai Chi Tho was the target of the sarcastic and menacing criticisms from high-level visitors from Hanoi, such as "odor of Yugoslavia," "fattening up the Chinks [*nuoi beo Ba Tau*], enriching the capitalists." By 1982 when the politburo came down to check on things, there was whispering about "coming in to put down the rebellion." "This is one of the darkest periods in our history," he reportedly said. "If we don't do *doi moi* we're dead."[23] Unlikely as it sounds, there is some evidence from other sources that Mai Chi Tho was something of a "reformer," although even after sifting through rival hagiographies it is hard to say.[24]

In a 2006 interview, Mai Chi Tho recalled that, "After the victory of April 30, 1975, with the policy of 'Advancing quickly and strongly toward socialism,' right after the Liberation the [party] center gave Ho Chi Minh City the responsibility of immediately carrying out two plans known by the secret designators X1 and X2, on the subject of 'Reforming the capitalist economy,' which is usually called 'hitting the compradore bourgeoisie.'"[25] In Mai Chi Tho's view, "the X1 campaign was somewhat acceptable [*tam duoc*] because we carried out the reform of the bourgeoisie who had ties to the imperialists, even though among them were a considerable number who were purely focused on 'doing business' [*chi thuan tuy lam kinh te*]. But when it came to carrying out campaign X2, the errors were clearly exposed. Because the 'quotas' [*chi tieu*] assigned were higher, for an extended period of time tens of thousands of workers, youth, and older and students and pupils hit the streets with slogans and banners, as well as loudspeakers in hand, shouting resounding slogans like 'down with the compradore bourgeoisie,' which scared the 'rich' [*lop nguoi giau*] out of their wits. But a preliminary check of over 2,000 'X2 targets' [*doi tuong*] came up with . . . only three targets! This arbitrary [*duy y chi*] policy had led to a horrific decline, which changed the face and the substance of the city, completely wiping out the strong points and existing material base of the 'Pearl of the Orient.'"[26] The property confiscated was misappropriated, or spoiled in storage, leaving a huge pile of damaged and useless confiscated goods. From "a consumer city and one of the biggest commercial centers in the aftermath of Campaigns X1 and X2 'the entire industrial production of the city was paralyzed and totally depleted.'"[27]

The severity of the burden on the ordinary people can be gauged by the immiseration of even the leading cadres and their families. For five years the son of the one-time figurehead leader of the National Liberation Front, Nguyen Huu Tho, a mid-level youth leader in the city, had to line up along with thirteen- and fourteen-year-olds at 3 A.M. to buy bread to supplement his family's meager diet. The (2006) party leader of Ho Chi Minh City, Nguyen Minh Triet, had to raise pigs to increase his income. In the North, life was also hard.

Mai Chi Tho recalls being assigned to a lavish French-style villa (he calls it a "chateau") with a swimming pool and tennis court. The swimming pool was used to raise African carp, until it became impossible to get anything to feed them, so the swimming pool turned into a stagnant breeding ground for frogs. The tennis court went unused because it symbolized an "aristocratic sport" and was planted with sweet potatoes.[28] This provides a good baseline for measuring the shift in attitudes as Vietnam "changed worlds." Thirty-five years later, the once reviled "colonialist" and "aristocratic" sports of golf and tennis were, as we shall see, enthusiastically embraced both the by the leadership—impelled to join the ASEAN fraternity of golf-crazy leaders on the links—and the emerging Vietnamese "yuppie" class.[29]

A 2005–6 series of newspaper accounts detailed the severity and pervasiveness of the economic crisis, along with the various ruses employed to survive in an environment in which adherence to official edicts meant unemployment, factory closures, and starvation. The vividness and concrete detail of these accounts show that this period has not been forgotten, and many writers bemoan the loss of time for Vietnam's development.

A leading analyst of international relations and one-time assistant to the foreign minister recalled his own shock at the poverty he found on a return from an overseas posting. His first visit was to his sister's house, but she was not home. Growing hungry, he went all over Hanoi looking for something to eat. There was money in his pocket, but nothing to buy. Returning to his sister's home, he saw some squash hanging on a trellis and knocked a couple down, took them in the house, cooked and ate them. This left a lasting impressing about the failings of the "subsidy regime" (prereform) period, and explained why he and others became receptive to the need for fundamental economic reform. Speaking of the exhibition of life during the "subsidy" period that was then (2006) creating a stir in Hanoi, he commented that his own personal experience and feeling typified that of many others like him living under conditions which had been tolerable in war, but not what people had expected after peace had arrived.[30]

Clearly someone or some group of people was responsible for this disaster. It is now convenient to lay the full blame on the deceased Le Duan, since the alternative would be to blame the more recent leadership (almost all reformers, but almost all with deep involvement in the debacle of "socialist transformation" of the South), or to blame the entire party, whose reputation for infallibility is central to its claims to legitimacy.

UNLIKELY REFORMERS

Even the Northern leadership of the early postwar period has been the subject of revisionist attempts to explain away the failures of "socialist transformation" and exonerate the party. A recent (2005) party province leader in the South, who had been studying in Hanoi in the mid-1970s (and claims to regret not being on hand in the South to "gain merit" in the socialist transformation campaign), claims that Premier Pham Van Dong told an assembled group of Southern cadres in Hanoi, in September 1975, "You comrades are here in order to visit places, look and learn in a discriminating manner. Don't imitate the North—if you force them into the mold of cooperatives [like those in the North] there will be a great outcry."[31] Pham Van Dong also has been identified as the person responsible for bringing a Soviet delegation of specialists on Lenin's New Economic Policy to lecture to middle- and high-ranking cadres in Hanoi.[32]

Another example of the attempt to exonerate the Northern leadership is the polishing of Truong Chinh's image as a strong reformer from the outset. As already noted, he has been portrayed as the interim party leader who engineered the transition from the heavy-handed Le Duan to the reformer Nguyen Van Linh. In fact, Hanoi insiders claimed that Truong Chinh aligned himself with Le Duc Tho to oppose Linh's elevation to the position of party secretary general.[33] The author of a flattering 2005 biography of Truong Chinh, portraying him as a leader of the new thinking, claims that by 1982, Truong Chinh had become convinced that the economic crisis could not be allowed to drag on. He convened a group of North Vietnamese economists "comprised of people with a new-thinking [a term that had not yet been used in Vietnam] mentality in order to research a number of theoretical and practical issues as a basis for determining a path and steps to take in the immediate future."[34]

Vo Van Kiet also tried to improve the posthumous image of Le Duan. Following Le Duan's death and Truong Chinh's appointment to succeed him, his reputation as a hard-liner actually, in Kiet's view, made it easier for him to clear the way for the "reform" Sixth Party Congress.[35] "I must say that at that time it was only comrade Truong Chinh who had the deep theoretical understanding, had the image of a comrade who went all out to adhere to principle, and had some elements of an orthodox hard-liner [*co phan cung theo kieu chinh thong*], who could have organized the Sixth Party Congress—the Congress of Reform. The thing that I find amusing is that the 'author' [*tac gia*]—or more accurately the 'editor-in-chief' [*chu bien*] of *doi moi* was a person like Truong Chinh who was regarded as an all-out 'hard-liner' [*het suc cung*]." The quality that made Truong Chinh receptive to change, Kiet argues, was that even though he fought hard for his beliefs, he had a willingness to listen to people who had ideas (*co tu duy*) that were "serious and well grounded" (*dung dan, du co so*) and dared to tell the truth.[36] Kiet added that "Comrade Truong Chinh usually listened very attentively, his questions and his facial expressions told me that this comrade was able to grasp [*y thuc duoc*] many new things that came up in the course of real-world experience [*thuc tien*], even though this ran counter to the things that had always been regarded as correct or orthodox. With respect to the policy of industrial and commercial transformation in the South, comrade Truong Chinh did not manifest a fiercely determined attitude like a number of other cadres."[37]

Truong Chinh had fiercely cracked down on "fence breakers" during the war, to the dismay of more pragmatic leaders, including Le Duan, who had been willing to sacrifice socialist rectitude for anything that would get more production for the wartime emergency. The most famous case was the party leader of Vinh Phu province, who was sacked for tolerating fence breaking in agricultural production. During the economic crisis of the early 1980s, Truong Chinh admitted to a close associate he had been wrong and ascribed the error in part to faulty information. At this juncture (early 1980s) Truong Chinh subtly reversed his long-standing view that the "relations of production" were more important than the "forces of production," that is, that the right economic organization would produce the best results and that the way to increase production was to have tight central planning and agricultural cooperativization.

In an intriguing example of twisting old dogmatic formulas to justify new thinking, he told his newly appointed assistant, economics professor Tran Nham, that now the "relations of production" were the key to solving the problem of unleashing the productive forces in the economy—an ambiguous formulation which might be construed to mean that the constraints of orthodox socialist planning and collectivization might have to be loosened in order to revive the economy. This is an excellent example of a tactic often used by more radical advocates of reform, disguising new ideas in familiar terminology. The central issue in this arcane Marxist play of terminology was whether a state-controlled economy (socialist relations of production) should guide Vietnam's development, or whether the market should decide. At its most fundamental level, it was the age-old debate among Marxists and reformers about material incentives and human nature itself.

The group convened by Truong Chinh was supplemented by another collection of brains trusters for the party leaders in Ho Chi Minh City, called the Saturday Group, this one drawn largely from prominent economists who had served the former South Vietnamese regime. The Hanoi economic historian Dang Phong terms this Saturday Group of non-Marxist economists "a rather special phenomenon, not only for Vietnam, but for other socialist countries" at that time. Relying on Dang Phong's research of this period, the journalists who, several decades later, recorded the views and events of the "Eve of reform" (*dem truoc doi moi*), list the various measures recommended by these economists, setting up special rice-growing zones in the upper Mekong Delta that would encourage high production (presumably by freeing producers from restraints and offering incentives), setting up test sites for shareholder-owned banks, establishing zones for assembling goods for exports and, finally, making fundamental wage and monetary reforms. The result was that "this was breakthrough thinking [*dot pha tu duy*] that contradicted most of the main ideas of the time."[38]

THE SOUTH SHALL RISE AGAIN?

The question of which group of brains trusters was most influential in shaping the longer-term trajectory of reform is difficult to answer, but the question is in itself important. Of course, the direct impact of a small group of former Saigon economists was minimal, but they symbolically represented the survival of an alternative vision of economics and society to the one which was officially designated as the end state of "socialist transformation." One way of looking at the reforms is that they set in motion a progressive triumph of the advocates of an alternative to socialism. Taking this line of argument a step further, it might be viewed as the "revenge of the South," since the spectacular failure of the rash attempt to impose a Northern model of socialism on the South not only backfired, but rebounded on the North by a form of "blowback," which ended up eroding the basis of the Northern orthodox model and taking the North along the path blazed by the South during the early postwar economic crisis.

An intriguing parallel is what Kevin Phillips, the innovator of the Republican Party's Southern strategy, portrays in a recent book as the revenge of the South for the humiliation of defeat in the Civil War. In a chapter titled, tongue partly in cheek, "The United States in a Dixie Cup," Phillips elaborates on the Southernization of American politics. "Back in 1860, who could have guessed? Very few southerners that year ever got a chance to vote for or against Abraham Lincoln and the Republican party. . . . This makes the turnabout of the last century and a half especially stark. The Republican presidential nominee took all eleven ex-Confederate states in both 2000 and 2004." Phillips observes that among Western countries this magnitude of reversal of regional dominance is unique to America. He attributes it to "the transfer, over five decades, of deep seated fealty to southern folkways and sectionalism from the Democrats to the Republicans. So what psychology reversed and why?"[39] The additional factor at play in the Vietnamese case of the "Southernization" of national politics was the fundamental challenge to the ideological and institutional structure of the state, which had been built in the North after 1954.

As mentioned above, Martin Gainsborough, who did extensive research on state enterprises in Ho Chi Minh City in the 1990s, has challenged the view that the city was a hotbed of reform, in the sense of a state- or even local-government-directed policy, but he also acknowledges the magnitude of the change and that, "Ho Chi Minh City's political economy is now far removed from any pre-reform state-socialist blueprint."[40] Most accounts of the past three decades of change in Vietnam assign an important role to the dynamism of the Southern economy in driving transformation in other areas of Vietnam. And it is certainly worth noting that Southerners have played an exceptionally prominent role in Vietnam's national leadership.

I am not arguing that there is a direct parallel between the Southernization of American politics and the Southernization of Vietnam, and certainly not that sectional differences in Vietnam will inevitably produce political pluralism and a competitive party system. But though it took a different form, there has been a notable Southernization of Vietnamese politics that could not have been anticipated in 1975. In 1994, the *New York Times*'s Steven Erlanger observed that "in most important respects, it is really the south that finally won the war. . . . For the young, increasingly in the north as well as in the untamable, pleasure-seeking south, the only ideology is 'song voi' or 'living quickly'"[41]

There are several reasons for this. The most obvious is that as Vietnam was forced to abandon its command economy, subsidized largely by the Soviet Union, and integrate into the global economy, this naturally gave the comparative advantage to the dynamic economy of the South, a residual legacy of the old capitalism as well as a consequence of the greater resources of the South. The remembered experience of having lived in a market economy not only made it easier for the South to adopt many of the features of this kind of an economy. "Vietnam's situation (especially in the South) was somewhat different from the other Socialist countries in that the private economy and the market system had never been systematically eliminated."[42] Dang Phong compared this to a camel's hump, which is capable of storing nourishment for long trips across the desert.[43]

The existence of an alternative to the Northern model of socialism is significant because, as Legro argues, "Not only must political actors undermine the old orthodoxy, they need to replace it with a new orthodoxy. Consolidation is shaped in part by two types of factors: (1) the number of prominent ideas in a society that might serve as a replacement for the dominant orthodoxy, and (2) the perceived initial results of such new ideas."[44] Remembrance of the old system in the South constituted a possible alternative (point one), and the clear record of effective results from the fence breaking in the South constituted the confirming initial results (point two).

A crucially important element of the South's advantages in surviving the catastrophe of "socialist transformation" was its links to the outside world, in the form of overseas Vietnamese remittances and "care packages" of consumer goods. Even more important, in terms of the later "opening up" of the economy and integration into the global market, was the long-standing and strong ties of Chinese residents in South Vietnam with family and commercial networks throughout Asia. The extent to which these connections made this group a target during the "socialist transformation" campaign and even more when the charge of treasonous relations to China were added to the economic crimes of capitalist ties, and the persecution and expulsion of large numbers of ethnic Chinese from both North and South Vietnam, has now been glossed over. As Dang Phong notes, "It was only private individuals who had the capacity to provide investment capital, purchase goods and to make contacts abroad with foreign businessmen to exchange goods. In reality the only private individuals who could do this were the Hoa [ethnic Chinese in Vietnam]. They not only had capital, but also had relations with prime producers inside Vietnam as well as close relations with overseas Chinese in Hong Kong and Singapore."[45]

Dang Phong's history of the reform process makes it clear how vital these external contacts were to the party leadership in the South. "At the end of 1979, Ho Chi Minh City's exports from abroad were nearly completely cut off. Vo Van Kiet, the city party secretary, and Mai Chi Tho, head of the Ho Chi Minh City People's Committee struggled to find ways to import some raw materials and other critical goods, in order to sustain production in the city units. This along with the running around to procure rice of the Foodstuff Corporation, required them to find a form of fence breaking that would not cause the whistle to be blown on them."[46]

On an inspection tour in the South, bodyguards accompanying Deputy Prime Minister Do Muoi (Do the Tenth—i.e., tenth child in the family) procured ten kilos of rice to bring back with them for their own use—or possibly to sell on the black market. At a checkpoint in My Tho this illegal (because untaxed and out of channels) cargo was discovered. The bodyguards were forced to admit that this was the deputy prime minister's vehicle, in the hope of being waved on. To their surprise they were harangued; "We don't give a damn whether it's Do the Tenth or Do the Eleventh," and the rice was confiscated—a revealing display of local contempt for central authority, as well as the hypocrisy of the central authorities themselves.

Another illustration of the defiance of stifling central-government attempts to control local commerce and force even sales of desperately needed food supplies into state-controlled channels is Mai Chi Tho's revelation that, at that time, even his own public-security police, in charge of enforcing these unpopular controls, illegally purchased rice on the black market, put on civilian clothes, and requisitioned Jeeps, stashing the contraband rice in the trunk.[47] The need to resort to disguise and subterfuge for actions which violated state policies, and the hypocrisy involved, led to the questioning even by the most zealous agents of state control of the wisdom and efficacy of these ideologically driven and counterproductive edicts. This internal crisis of belief became an important source of new thinking.

These desperation measures in the struggle for economic survival in the South are part of an inconvenient chapter of Vietnamese history, which the current authorities would rather set aside. But some ethnic Chinese in the South were surreptitiously allowed by local party authorities to reactivate their commercial ties in the Southeast Asia region in some key industries like textiles.[48] According to Dang Phong, the tiny private economy of that period comprised enterprises exporting to socialist countries and the occasional influx of hard currency from the few visitors, like crew members of commercial ships, but these sources were only one-tenth of what the overseas Vietnamese contributed (itself a paltry 2 million dollars) to the private economy.[49] In addition, the recent nonsocialist experience of the South made it nearly impossible for the Northern command economy to work there—leading to the crisis which set the economic reform process in motion.[50]

But perhaps the most important immediate cause of the resurgence of the South was that the party leaders there were far from the orthodoxy of Hanoi, confronted with a desperate economic situation that could not be resolved by orthodox measures or coercion and, most importantly, were politically insulated from charges of deviationism or treason by their wartime accomplishments. It is an apparent irony that the hardest and toughest of the wartime guerrilla leaders were also the most pragmatic and flexible in peace. This group not only spearheaded the reforms but some of them even became advocates of a more open political system in Vietnam.

The highly charged political atmosphere in the South of the period between 1975 and the Sixth Party Congress in 1986 made it risky to challenge the orthodoxy proclaimed from Hanoi, which was primarily aimed at asserting political control rather than economic efficiency. This went through several phases. First came the X1–X2 socialist transformation, which was aimed mainly at South Vietnam's urban middle class, which had not, on the whole, supported the revolution. Then as relations with China deteriorated in the late 1970s, the Hoa, with their vital overseas contacts, were targeted.

"I SMELL THE ODOR OF YUGOSLAVIA!"

In the early 1980s, the furtive violations of Hanoi edicts on collectivization and the command economy were interpreted by some party leaders as treasonous political opposition. "Crushing the rebellion" (*dep loan*) was the title of one of the installments in the mid-2006 *Tuoi Tre* series on "fence breaking" (*xe rao*), the term that was used to describe the "breaking out" (*dot pha*) from the restraints of official policy. A cabinet minister from Hanoi visiting Ho Chi Minh City in mid-1982, having just stepped off the plane, exclaimed, "I smell the odor of Yugoslavia!" As the account of this incident noted, "the meaning was that the 'odor' was capitalism."[51] Most of the politically aware people in

Vietnam at that time had a vivid memory of the Cold War–era polemics by first the Soviet Union, and then China, against Yugoslavia's attempt to forge an independent political model, and its pathbreaking economic reforms. Vietnam's party leadership had duly fallen in line and issued its own harsh denunciations of Yugoslavia.

This was more than "revisionism"—a political slap at the Soviet Union during Vietnam's tilt toward China in the 1963–4 period. "Revisionism," was only an ideological error, and a polemical term mainly related to the Sino-Soviet dispute—a quarrel that still remained within the "socialist camp." "Yugoslavia," however, was code for "deviationism" from the party line, advocating abandoning socialism, and even treason. (Ironically, China had not only abandoned its censure of Yugoslavia by 1978, but adopted it as a fruitful source of lessons about economic reform.)[52]

It is not surprising, therefore, that the reformers proceeded cautiously, and did not try to attack the main policies of the command economy head on. "The breakouts in Vietnam were special because they didn't directly 'declare war' on the politics and programs, but usually went about it with delicacy and indirection. If the policies were like ancient walls of a fortress, the breakout assaults did not use heavy artillery but only cuts with a knife, and were done like the trowel of a mason removing the mortar between bricks on a wall. At some point, the knife cuts and the trowel could bring down an entire wall without breaking things or shaking the earth. It was even possible to salvage many of the materials to use for new projects."[53]

The economic historian Dang Phong describes the mindset and atmosphere of this period.

> We had chosen a circuitous and rather long and wasteful road, which we originally thought was a straight road, and the shortest, easiest, and fastest one. The conventional broad highway of history has often been mistaken for a twisting road full of danger and hardships, which should be avoided, so road signs were placed there warning of "danger." For anyone to pull up and remove those warning signs was itself dangerous. It is a pleasant irony [*thu vi*] that almost all of the people who took the lead in "breaking out" [*dot pha*] were revolutionary warriors who had defended the nation and the party—Vo Van Kiet, Nguyen Van Chinh, Nguyen Van Hon . . . had waded through blood during the anti-American Resistance. It would be hard for anyone to be suspicious of their conviction [*lap truong*] or character [*pham chat*]. Or, to be more precise, it would be hard to "pin the crime" [*bat toi*] of opposing socialism on them. Because of this they were able to survive and had the necessary prerequisites to persuade and mobilize. . . . The course of revolution and resistance had these "knights in shining armor" to break out even in the case of difficulties encountered in peacetime.[54]

Another retrospective article on the reforms also emphasizes that it was the patriotic credentials of the former revolutionary leaders in the South that allowed them to provide

political protection for defying Hanoi's dictates, and create a climate in which the improvisation that led to the new thinking about economic policy could survive. "Almost all
the fence-breaking organizations, who ran counter to the established policies, were
people who had taken the lead on the battlefield. In the economic sphere they continued
to fight because of the common cause. In the struggle within the ranks of the comrades,
their selfless sacrifices had to be acknowledged [*Cuoc chien dau trong hang ngu dong chi
phai chap nhan nhung hi sinh khong mo chi*]."[55]

For reformers in Saigon (including the pragmatists who simply wanted to feed the
population and get the factories going again), these political warnings from the Northern
leadership and its inspection teams came at a very bad time, just as Saigon and the Southern economy had begun to emerge from the worst of the postwar crisis. The Fifth Party
Congress in March 1982 made it clear that party leader Le Duan would not tolerate
departures from orthodoxy, and the message was aimed at the improvisations in the
South. At the party congress, Le Duan said, "Some party members [had] failed to 'uphold
revolutionary quality.'" He continued, "'In order to keep the party ranks clean, following
this congress we must resolutely expel from the party as soon as possible all opportunists,
all those whose revolutionary spirit has been paralyzed, exploiters, smugglers, specula-
tors, persons involved in corruption and bribery and oppressors of the masses.'"[56]

In the summer of 1982 Hanoi was sending "dozens" of inspection and oversight groups
to Ho Chi Minh City to "crush the rebellion" (*dep loan*).[57] "Even today (2006) none of
the top cadres of Ho Chi Minh City will ever forget the meetings of the politburo
between August 10 and August 18, 1982." Mai Chi Tho, the chairman of the Ho Chi
Minh City People's Committee at the time, was brusquely ordered from his hospital bed
to attend the meetings. "If you can't do it, then quit!" the Northern emissary said. The
upshot of the meetings was a reaffirmation of the strict controls of the command
economy, which the Southern leaders were ordered to pass on to the "fence breaking"
enterprises. The warning was reinforced with a continuing stream of inspection teams
from the North.[58]

Pham Hung, a former head of COSVN, the party headquarters for the revolution in
South Vietnam, was the minister of the interior at the time, and was dispatched at the
end of August 1982 to send the message to the South that challenging the command-
economy dictates from Hanoi was a security problem, and therefore treasonous.[59] As a
later journalistic account noted, "As is known, at the end of 1982 and the beginning of
1983, a heavy political atmosphere enveloped Ho Chi Minh City."[60]

During the summer of 1983, during Le Duan's absence on a trip to Moscow, Truong
Chinh, Premier Pham Van Dong, and Vo Chi Cong (a politburo member with extensive
revolutionary experience in the South prior to 1975) traveled to the South to assess the
critical economic situation. Nguyen Van Linh, who had voluntarily withdrawn from the
politburo because of personality and policy clashes with Le Duan and Le Duc Tho, and
was the party head of Ho Chi Minh City, requested that the factory managers who had
to deal with the realities of the economy be allowed to directly brief this politburo

delegation. Attempting to calm their nerves as these low-level cadres prepared to brief the top leaders, Linh told them, "don't worry comrades … you have done very well and done the right thing. The Central Committee couldn't possibly know the details of everything you have done, so it is up to us to make a direct report. This is a matter of saving ourselves and not waiting for Heaven to save us." These meetings became known as the "Dalat affair" since they were held in that town. Following this series of meetings the politburo members asked to take a hands-on tour of the factories and enterprises to see for themselves. Having done this, Truong Chinh is reported to have said, "It turns out that everything that we have been told in Hanoi is completely wrong."[61]

OASES IN THE DESERT

This tour of the South by several of Vietnam's top leaders (minus Le Duan) relieved the political pressure on the reformers. "The 'Dalat affair' and the on-the-spot fact-finding trip of Truong Chinh in Ho Chi Minh City not only was a cool and fresh breath of air soothing the stifling atmosphere, and relieving the pessimism of the units that had been engaged in fence breaking, it also created important conditions for the people's *doi moi*, which was formalized in the resolutions of the Sixth Party Congress." Truong Chinh said to one factory manager, "So there are oases in the desert." Premier Pham Van Dong had to reassure the flustered and frightened cadre that this was meant as a compliment.[62]

It is revealing that desert metaphors came quickly to mind in describing this period. A desert (which does not exist in Vietnam) is the exact opposite of the traditional image of prosperity—lush green and well-irrigated rice fields. Truong Chinh's "oases in the desert" comment could mean only that the environment of orthodox state socialism surrounding these "oases" of incipient reform were as barren as the Sahara—which Dang Phong alluded to (see above) when he analogized surviving remnants of the premarket economy in the South to "the camel's hump, which is capable of storing nourishment for long trips across the desert." Truong Chinh's remark is all the more important because it was contemporaneous with the crisis of the early 1980s. Even without a direct challenge to existing orthodoxy, the subversive impact of this kind of spontaneous image reveals a significant loss of faith in the old certitudes.

The alleged receptivity of some top leaders to the clear evidence that their policies were not working is a good illustration of the retroactive heroic narrative of reform, which elevates the role of some of the top leaders while placing the blame on Le Duan. Nguyen Van Linh, for example, was alleged to be a consistent reformer from the moment the war ended in 1975.[63] One of the notable quotes attributed to him was his reported statement that, "We want to reach socialism, but we want to go by airplane, not by bicycle."[64] One of the series of retrospective articles on reform appearing in the press in 2005–6 called Nguyen Van Linh and Vo Van Kiet "the great meritorious statesmen of reform [*dai cong than*]." *Cong than* used to be a term of opprobrium in the party lexicon, indicating someone who was motivated only by seeking the status of high office (*cong than dia vi*) and its reinstatement as a label of honor is a measure of how much the new thinking has affected the old political rhetoric.[65]

Vo Van Kiet later tried to absolve Le Duan of blame for the errors of the postwar period, by noting that everyone to some extent subscribed to the conventional wisdom principles of the command-economy model of socialism. Kiet also asserts that Le Duan was willing to countenance the reining in of some of the excesses of the socialist transformation campaign, such as forbidding impoverished itinerant peddlers to sell their wares. He even claims, in a memorial essay (which would naturally accentuate the positive), that Le Duan discussed policies that prefigured the *doi moi* reforms, and maintained that it was necessary to retain the "multisectoral" economy of the pre-1975 Saigon (e.g., allow the continuation of private commerce) and warned against the kind of rural collectivization that had been done in the North. Of course these cautions were soon overtaken by the disastrous socialist transformation campaign, but even in this case, Kiet implies that Le Duan was not the leading proponent of this policy, and observed, "I didn't see him really pushing" the policy.[66]

Kiet provides a telling account of the governing mindset of the post-1975 period, which impeded the development of new thinking about economic policy. "I understand that Brother Three [Le Duan] realized that what was taking place did not meet the requirements of the situation and needed to be changed. However, he was unable to transcend the framework of the economic model that enveloped the entire socialist camp. Although there were many questions raised by the social and economic difficulties, I never saw him formally set them out in front of the politburo or assign a group to research the fundamental essence of the problem, which was that the centralized system of subsidies had been 'revered' [*ton vinh*] as one of the [basic] principles for many years. Thinking back over that period, any thoughts that were different from 'approved official thinking' [*tu duy chinh thong*] were subject to serious accusations. In the COMECON (SEV) bloc Poland and Hungary were fiercely attacked and criticized." Noting the comment about the "odor of Yugoslavia," Kiet wrote, "Now there are times when I ask myself, 'isn't it a shame that at the time we didn't have an agency or [social] scientist who specialized in economics to organize research that would have dug deeply into the ideas of Brother Three?' And even worse, there wasn't anyone who raised a voice in criticism of the irrationalities of the old system and proposed a new system. I only wish that the Fourth Party Congress (1976) had even a little bit of the Sixth Party Congress—how different our country would be now." Still, said Kiet, he understood that it would have been difficult given the framework of assumptions at that time to break out of the old thinking. At most, there could be only incremental and improvised change. "We ourselves at the city leadership level, had just stepped from a situation where we 'only knew about fighting' to become administrators of the society and economy, and had no idea about how to distinguish among systems [*co che*] but simply operated by inertia [*quan tinh*]. Because of this, although we also wrestled with this [*tran tro*] and groped our way along, and had a number of innovative ideas which were termed 'fence breaking' [*vuot rao*], overall we tied ourselves up in the general regime of that time."[67]

LOOKING BACK ON THE CONCEPTUAL LIMITS OF THE PREREFORM PERIOD

Kiet's account presents a vivid picture of the political pressures that reinforced conformity. It also validates Legro's point that some acceptable alternative to the status quo must emerge for collective idea-change to happen. At this time, fundamental reform was not possible within the ideological horizons and permitted political boundaries of the time. The conceptual gulf that separates the thinking of this period "on the eve of reform" from the Vietnam of the twenty-first century is illustrated by an anecdote related by the economic historian Dang Phong. After the liberal newspaper *Tuoi Tre* ran a series of articles in 2005–6 on the problems of reform, "on the eve," including several by Dang Phong, he received a phone call from a young friend who demanded to know why the fence breaking was such a big deal. Ho Chi Minh City "didn't have enough rice, the people of the Mekong Delta had rice to sell, so going down and buying it was the commonsense thing to do. What is there to merit praising the leaders of the city for courageously breaking out, for daring to think for themselves, carry it into action, and face the consequences?" The next day Phong's students all had the same reaction. He concluded, "It turns out that the young generation can't picture how rigid the structural and conceptual [*tu duy*] obstacles of that time were."[68]

It clearly required a crisis, if not a shock, to enable the new thinking to flourish. "In reality, it has to be admitted that it was only then, a time when the economic and social situation of the country had hit bottom and was on the brink of the abyss of chaos and danger, that the concepts of revolutionary pragmatism were accepted [*chap nhan*]—it wasn't easy."[69]

The reality check of Truong Chinh's visit to the South in 1983 had an impact. "It was precisely this direct and comprehensive set of meetings that caused Brother Five, Truong Chinh, to have some new thoughts [*suy nghi moi*]. One could view this as an important development of that period."[70] On the death of Le Duan in July 1986, Truong Chinh became interim party leader and paved the way for Nguyen Van Linh's election as party leader in December 1986, at the Sixth Party Congress, which put reform and new thinking on the agenda, even though it was not until 1989 that significant changes were introduced.

Some important steps had been taken in 1985 that marked a significant break with party orthodoxy and had a major impact on the lives of the Vietnamese. Sophie Quinn-Judge notes that, "It was not until 1985–1986 that changes in economic policies began to look secure and the party's punitive attitude toward capitalist success changed." In part this was due to the changes in the Soviet Union under Gorbachev, as well as the reforms of Deng Xiaoping—though the adversarial relationship between Vietnam and China made it difficult to openly acknowledge the Chinese reforms. "It was in 1985 that Vietnam attacked the 'subsidy system,' which was a way of life in the communist world.

In June the party announced the end of subsidies in foodstuffs for government workers and the introduction of cash salaries indexed to the cost of living."[71]

But if the economic reforms in China and the Soviet Union helped to legitimize "fence breaking" within an accepted political and conceptual framework, much of the impetus for change came from noncommunist sources. As an important study of the Vietnamese economic reforms observes, "through the 1980s the source of inspiration was increasingly not the Soviet Union, but the spectacular economic development experienced in the newly industrialized countries of Southeast Asia."[72] The fact that an alternative model of development existed, which was not American or European capitalism (looked on with suspicion in Vietnam because of the association with imperialism), and which had been proven successful in other Asian countries, made the example of the "tiger economies" attractive to Vietnamese reformers.

One of the most significant features of the mindset on the reform-minded party leaders on the eve of the 1986 Sixth Congress was that they felt Vietnam's economic problems could be compartmentalized and resolved from within and by pragmatic adjustments that would not fundamentally challenge the basic ideological foundations and assumptions of the party. Most importantly, security issues arising from the changing international situation were viewed as entirely separate from the economic issues. Resolving Vietnam's challenges in 1986 could be done by a two-track approach— one for internal problems and another for external challenges.

Looking back from the vantage of 2006, Vo Van Kiet said, "The situation now is not like it was at the time of the Sixth Congress, when there were big changes in the international situation. When the situation is at an impasse, you had to change at the top, and change thinking, as at the Sixth Congress." In contrast, Kiet felt that in 2006 the situation was less urgent and more favorable, and Vietnam could be incremental and discriminating in responding to the challenges of the time. But today's leaders, said Kiet, are much more aware of the linkage between the international context and Vietnam's internal problems. "I would put it this way: the comrades who are in charge today have a knowledge, understanding, and ability to engage with the outside that is many times greater than it was fifteen or twenty years ago—to say nothing of the wartime period. Compared with the time I worked here [Ho Chi Minh City], the leading comrades have access to international information and contacts to research what is going on outside which are entirely superior, and their understanding is quite broad."[73]

BREAKING DOWN THE BARRIERS TO NEW THINKING: THE SIXTH PARTY CONGRESS OF 1986

The major impact of the Sixth Party Congress was in breaking down the barriers to open discussion of Vietnam's mounting problems and not reverting to the default bromides of more indoctrination and more effort. This dramatically expanded the range of policy debate and political discussion, and allowed the new thinking to come out in the open. Without this green light to open discussion, it would have been impossible to attempt a systematic program of reform, and the "fence breakers" and "new thinkers" would have furtively gone their own way, ignoring party directives and protecting the desperate improvisations as best they could. This was recognized by Nguyen Van Linh who, even in opposition, focused on convincing the top leaders, because he knew that clandestine and partial responses to Vietnam's problems would not solve them.[74]

Clearly the command economy was not only contributing to the economic distress, but measures like the compulsory sale of rice to the state and irrational price controls were creating hostility toward the party and government. The head of the Institute of Economics declared to a select audience at the Ho Chi Minh party school, the ideological training center for high-level cadres, "the current (rice) purchase and sale regime is 'buying like robbers and selling like dogs'"; that is, the peasants had to sell their rice to the government at confiscatory prices (one-tenth the market price), which made it unprofitable to grow, and buyers of rice had to scramble to purchase the declining supply of rice.[75]

Le Duan's death in July 1986, and his replacement by Truong Chinh, cleared the path for putting basic issues on the table at the Sixth Party Congress, scheduled for December 1986. As the congress approached, it became clear that there were sharp divisions within the party leadership on fundamental economic and political questions. One participant in the discussions leading up to the congress described a preliminary "steering meeting" that afterward was termed the "the conference of three points of view" (*hoi nghi ba quan diem*). "The debates and discussions showed that though the draft documents had been carefully prepared, they had not yet touched on the fundamental causes of the crisis (*khung hoang*) and because of this could not show the way out of this in the face of the real-life demands that were producing a boiling atmosphere of reform. These fierce debates focused on three concepts that needed to be changed." The first of these was Vietnam's continuing adherence to the conventional Soviet doctrine of giving priority to heavy industry in economic development. The second concerned the "big bang" approach to rapid and total "socialist transformation" of the South, and the third had to do with Vietnam's controlled prices and subsidy system which tried to circumvent market economics.[76]

Truong Chinh added several voices of reform to the generally conservative group that was drawing up the policy documents for the congress, sent them off to the resort town of Do Son, and told the group to revise the documents. Three "new thinkers" were added, but they found the "old guard" of defenders of ideological purity (Hoang Tung, editor of the party newspaper, and Dao Duy Tung, the party's ideological chief) had taken charge and reinstated all the "old thinking" into the drafts, while Truong Chinh and the politburo were preoccupied with personnel issues. Finally, one of the reformers challenged the retreat to orthodoxy. The matter was brought to Truong Chinh, who endorsed putting reformist ideas back on the agenda. Even so, the documents avoided terms like "market economy" and referred vaguely to "socialist commercial accounting" (*hach toan kinh doanh Xa Hoi Chu Nghia*).[77]

The Sixth Congress concluded with a direct admission of failure of the command economy. "In the past ten years (1975–1985) we have made a lot of mistakes in determining our objectives and approach to building the material and technological foundations for socialist reform and economic management. The concrete targets for determining and administering prices, currency exchange and the steps taken in revising wages and prices have been established without careful preparation and were not suitable for the real situation. Errors in the leadership and administration of the economy over the last five years (1980–1985) in distributing and transporting food were very serious."[78]

Outside observers of the Sixth Party Congress sensed a party in disarray. It appeared to be riven with factionalism, the army was disgruntled, and the South was proving difficult to manage. Some Hanoi officials saw the South as "the source of corruption, political deviation, and 'many-faceted sabotage.'" Thai Quang Trung, a very well-informed historian of the party, based in Paris, asserted that, "South Vietnam is in a state of moral secession."[79]

Despite these problems, the *New York Times* report noted several signs of political relaxation in the congress; a more open attitude toward outsiders, a decline in the amount of ideological rhetoric that is usually a staple of big party gatherings, and the prominence given to the example of reform in the South. In contrast to the negative and alarmist views of the situation in the South held by many Northern party leaders, the official press began to present more upbeat picture. Hanoi Radio described Ho Chi Minh City as "a dynamic example of economic development for provinces throughout the country."[80]

DELAYED REACTION TO THE SIXTH PARTY CONGRESS

No detailed or long-range reform program came out of the Sixth Congress, and there was considerable passive resistance by conservative elements in the party. "There was agreement on the need to change thinking about economics," said one account, "but there were still foot dragging [*tri keo*] and regrets."[81] A former Third Force activist from the Saigon era, Ly Chanh Trung, boldly told the National Assembly, "It is certain that the resolution of the Sixth Congress cannot possibly be implemented because the state machinery is still mandarinal, capricious, arbitrary, divorced from the people, and, because of all that, entirely impotent, even though they have concentrated all power in their hands. Certainly the resolution of the Sixth Congress can only be implemented by a state machinery renovated by democratization."[82] This kind of talk in a very public setting was highly unusual, and the call for democratization was not a mainstream position of the reformers. But it did suggest that a very different political atmosphere had emerged.

Between the Sixth Party Congress of 1986 and the first systematic reforms in 1989, there was no real program of reform. It is symptomatic of this limited and improvised approach that the main "flag carrier" of reform, party secretary general Nguyen Van Linh, tried to maintain the impetus of the Sixth Congress by publishing a series of newspaper articles under the heading "Things That Have to Be Done Right Away." Opening up the political system, however, was not one of these things, as we shall see in the next chapter. Still, Linh was concerned not only about radical voices like Ly Chanh Trung, but also about the undercurrent of resistance to the Sixth Congress decisions that simmered under the surface, manifested mainly by what Linh termed "a terrifying silence [*im lang dang so*]."[83]

If Ly Chanh Trung was the exception in boldly calling for democracy, there were clear signs that the "fence breaking" and "new thinking" in the economic sphere were spilling over into other areas. Quinn-Judge observes that, "Significantly, in these early days of reform Linh's program of change included the removal of certain intellectual controls. This period became known as the time of *coi troi* (loosening the bonds or untying), the closest thing that Vietnam would have to the policy of glasnost or openness in the Soviet Union." It was during this period that two notable novelists appeared on the scene, with highly critical accounts of aspects of life in Vietnam that had long been out of bounds. Duong Thu Huong's *Paradise of the Blind* and Bao Ninh's searing account of the tragic face of war (*Sorrows of War*) were sensational departures from the previous timidity of Vietnamese writers. Nguyen Van Linh reflected a more tolerant approach to previously repressed groups such as Catholics and the overseas Chinese community, and ordered an end to discrimination against intellectuals who had served under the former Saigon regime. Most of the military officers of the Saigon army still in "reeducation camps" were released in 1988.[84]

Other voices outside the party contributed to the widening of conceptual horizons. Among these, certainly one of the most interesting was the mathematician Phan Dinh Dieu, who boldly challenged the leadership and the conventional wisdom, and ultimately produced a striking analysis of the implications of the dramatic changes in the world for Vietnam. This analysis used concepts and terminology familiar to Vietnamese Marxists (Dieu was not a party member) but creatively recast them into new model, composed of familiar elements, but pointing in a very different direction.

Appropriately enough, for a figure who played a prominent role in stretching the boundaries of elite discourse, Dieu was a pioneer in developing Vietnam's information technology strategy.[85] As a nonparty member, Dieu was included in institutions such as the Fatherland Front, a powerless organization of eminent people outside the party, which supposedly symbolized their inclusion in the political process. He was also one of the few figures in the National Assembly who was not a member of the Communist Party. In 1981, he petitioned the external relations committee of the National Assembly to pursue a less confrontational policy toward the rest of the world to relieve Vietnam's isolation. During this period, Dieu created a sensation within the elite by stating at a public meeting that party secretary general Le Duan had performed meritoriously for Vietnam during the war, but the best thing he could under current circumstances was resign.[86] Dieu's nonconfrontational, scholarly, and often distracted manner may have softened the reaction to this bombshell, but it certainly set a new standard for bold public expression.

The fact that Phan Dinh Dieu was not jailed for this challenge to the party leader contributed to the impression that he was a tolerated, or even designated or "licensed," dissident.[87] If such a category exists, it is a rare species, as Dieu is a unique figure in Vietnamese life. Even as a tolerated dissident, there were limits. In the early 1980s Premier Pham Van Dong asked Dieu to write up in memo form those things that he could not say publicly. Dieu pointed to the then current concept of the "three interests" (*ba loi ich*) which was a formula stressing the convergence of the interests of the individual, state, and society, and urged giving primacy to using personal interest (*loi ich ca nhan*) to aid development. This was an example of building on familiar ideas and terminology and taking them in new directions. In a play on words, Dieu changed the slogan, "each person for every person" to "each person for themselves" (*khong phai moi nguoi vi moi nguoi nhung moi nguoi vi chinh minh*) and argued that this would make the best contribution to society. Dong subsequently used this line in a speech.[88] This concept was developed further in a major 1988 article, written by Dieu.

Based on a report that he delivered to a subcommittee of the State Commission on the Social Sciences in early 1988, Dieu wrote a speech which was published later in 1988 in the last issue of *To Quoc*. *To Quoc* (The Fatherland), was the organ of the Vietnamese Socialist Party (Dang Xa Hoi Viet Nam), a United Front group that had been formed at the time of the founding of the Vietnamese state as a symbolic gesture to noncommunist intellectuals before this party was disbanded in 1988.[89] Dieu published this prophetic analysis of the implications for Vietnam of the current global changes taking place in the final issue of *To Quoc* before it was ordered by the party to suspend publication because the Socialist Party it represented had been dissolved—just at the time the need to cultivate better relations with Vietnam's intellectuals outside the party in a time of rapid and uncertain transformation was becoming obvious.

Dieu's article, titled "Some Observations About Today's Era and Our Path," was notable for several conceptual innovations that later were adopted explicitly or implicitly, in whole or in part, by the party (without, of course, any acknowledgment of Dieu's pioneering analysis). The first major innovation was in reconceptualizing the fundamental Marxist periodization of history (primitive society, slave society, feudalism, capitalism, communism). Instead, Dieu portrayed humanity as going through three stages; from agricultural production, to production of machines, and then to the stage of "informaticizing" (*giai doan tin hoc hoa*) the world. The implications of this (spelled out in greater detail in Dieu's subsequent writings) are that Vietnam must depend on an educated elite of scientific technocratic people (exactly the constituency of the soon-to-be-defunct Socialist Party), whose brainpower cannot be harnessed by central planning and top-down authority. This in turn led to an intensification of his activities as an advocate of democracy.

This formulation also points away from an inevitable clash between capitalism and communism, with the inevitable triumph of the latter. Dieu implied a kind of convergence between social systems in speaking of a *chinh the*, which is rendered in some dictionaries as "a perfect whole" or a "totality." This is the foundation of a conception of a "one world" international system, and a variety of related ideas such as interdependence, which was just entering Vietnamese elite discourse, and globalization, which would become a central concept in the 1990s. Most importantly, it is based on the assumption that all countries in the world are driven by the same dynamics and headed in the same direction. There is a strong emphasis on economic forces driving historical change, which is in the Marxist tradition, but with technological innovation rather than class struggle the underlying engine of transformation.

Dieu wrote that the world was being transformed by the scientific–technological revolution from a resource-based to a "brainpower-based" (*tri tue*) economy. "In that transformation the world increasingly has many linkages which create a totalistic system [*he thong chinh the*]. At the same time, within that totality there are many differences; while there is an advanced segment of the world which has crossed the threshold into a new stage, the third stage [informaticization] of the civilization of human kind [*van minh nhan loai*], the largest segment has not yet passed beyond the threshold of the first stage of this civilization of human kind. The important thing is that it is a **totality** but not a **homogenous** [*thuan nhat*] [world]; and also it is **differentiated** [*khac biet*] but not **compartmentalized** [*biet lap*]."[90] He adds that, "When the character of a world system, and of a totalistic world, is reinforced, then relations among countries, especially the relations of interdependence [*phu thuoc lan nhau*] and the survival and development of every nation will have an integral connection to the survival and development of the entire world system." In turn, the unifying trends he sees will gradually reduce conflicts between different social systems and interdependence will reduce the role of war in settling differences.[91]

The extent to which this idea of a common civilization and humanity had been incorporated into mainstream official thinking within two decades is illustrated by the complaints about the concept made by diehard conservatives whose displeasure showed that they had lost the ideological battle (see chapter 9, "Rhetoric and Reality"). In 2006 Nguyen Duc Binh, who had dominated Vietnam's ideological discourse for several decades (but was now retired), wrote; "After the catastrophe of the collapse of the Soviet Union and Eastern Europe, *should we continue along the socialist path or not?* Or: should we stop talking about socialism, stop talking about Marxism-Leninism, and just do what it takes to have a 'prosperous people, strong country, just society, democracy, and civilization' and consider that enough?"[92]

The "prosperous people, strong country" language was the key political language of the Ninth's Party Congress's main resolution in 2001. The depth of the rift between hardcore conservatives like Nguyen Duc Binh and the twenty-first-century mainstream of the party is evident in his dismissal of this aspiration as unworthy and inadequate ("and consider that enough?"). The reason for his concern is evident; if there is comprehensive global civilization, it will naturally reflect the values of its dominant segment, that is, common civilization leads to capitalist ascendancy. The fact that these ideas still raised hackles in 2006 is an indication of the extent to which Dieu was ahead of his time in 1988.

Perhaps anticipating this kind of response, Phan Dinh Dieu's 1988 answer to Nguyen Duc Binh's question was, "Our goal is socialism. But the concept of socialism is being renovated [*doi moi*] and we must change our awareness on this subject. And could it be that for us, a poor underdeveloped country, socialism is a goal toward which we are headed, not an immediate objective? The transitional road to it is long, and comprises many stages. We have to determine our goal for the immediate stage," which, he said, is getting out of poverty. "We are part of the world and have to find our role in the world within a general equilibrium of the system. What position is the most beneficial to us? That depends on our capabilities." In the short term this will mean becoming a "hired hand" in the world economy. To get beyond that will depend on brainpower capable of engaging with the cutting-edge issues in a world that is increasingly becoming an information economy—the third stage of human development.

The diplomatic and strategic corollary of this was self-evident to Dieu. "If we are poor and underdeveloped, our goal in the coming decades must give priority to developing production and escaping from poverty and backwardness. *By every means*, increasing production and making many products for society is the most needed thing at present. To meet this 'benign' [*hien lanh*] objective, the confrontational [*gay gat*] slogans such as 'who will defeat whom' [*ai thang ai*] and pointless tense relations are not appropriate."[93]

Nguyen Duc Binh posed his bitter quasirhetorical questions (do you accept socialism as defined by me or not?) in 2006 and asked, "After the dissolution of the Soviet Union and Eastern Europe, the capitalists seized the majority of the world, the political map was fundamentally transformed. Was this the 'end of history' in that capitalism was the pinnacle of the civilization of humanity?"[94] At the same time, in the same pages of the party theoretical journal, other writers were routinely referring to a world of unified values and aspirations. "Through dialogue people will tie together all civilizations and accomplishments of civilization to create a common legacy for humanity."[95]

In the late 1980s, however, the idea of a unified global civilization based on core shared values, even as an aspiration, was definitely far outside the mainstream of Vietnamese thinking, which was still largely based on the assumption of coexistence of incompatible ideological blocs. New thinking was also both hindered and stimulated by the stalling of reform in 1988 and the emergence of severe food shortages and land disputes in the South. At the beginning of the year, Nguyen Van Linh complained about bureaucratic and political resistance to the economic reforms. "'If you have a new policy, but the people think and act according to very old style,' Linh told foreign journalists recently, in a tone of exasperation, 'the resolutions—no matter how good they may be—are still kept in the drawer.'"[96]

By the summer of 1988, the foot dragging had been compounded by real economic crisis as a concern for the leadership. Kenneth Richburg of the *Washington Post* reported that Vietnam's leaders seemed "paralyzed in a political gridlock, unable to resolve differences over how to loosen economic restraints without giving up some political control." He found the Vietnamese public disillusioned after their earlier high hopes for reforms and rapid improvement in living conditions were not realized. "Such sentiments mark a dramatic reversal from one year ago, when the mood was upbeat, signs of the new liberalization were palpable, and government officials and analysts proudly proclaimed that 'the winds of change are blowing.'"[97]

Some analysts portrayed the slowing of reform and the inability to resolve pressing issues as the consequence of a combination of discord at the top level and generational gaps between the most enthusiastic reformers and the older leadership. Le Duc Tho, though officially retired since the 1986 Sixth Party Congress was thought by some to be still effectively operating behind the scenes and a factor in the resistance to reform.[98]

In addition to the persisting problem of disagreements at the top, Vietnam was undergoing a general transition in leadership, which was to take another decade to complete. The selection of Do Muoi as prime minister in June 1988 was viewed by many as a transition to a younger generation of leaders, but the failure to promote rising figures like Vo Van Kiet to the top position appeared to be both cause and symptom of the stalemate between reform and reaction that continued to characterize Vietnam in the aftermath of the Sixth Party Congress. The continuing hold of the older generation also served to prevent the emergence of new thinking and thus was a continuing obstacle to fundamental collective idea change. "Muoi's election by the National Assembly last June underscored the fact that Vietnam faces a leadership transition crisis. . . . Vietnam's rigid brand of communism, its underfunded education system and its Confucian-style pattern of promotion based on age and seniority are being blamed for stifling creativity and discouraging new young talent from emerging." The director of international cooperation in the Ministry of Higher Education asserted that, "It is very difficult to identify rising stars. . . . The structure of society does not give rise to new faces. We know that for a long time we did not pay enough attention to creative thinking."[99]

The fact that there had been an electoral competition, albeit a very constrained choice, and that the results were publicly announced, was a change, but the results of this guided democracy were probably not what the more vocal reformers had in mind in calling for political reform. Vo Van Kiet had been touted as a rising star of reform, but only received 30 percent of the National Assembly vote. It was also observed that the new prime minister, Do Muoi, had been the major figure in the ill-fated "socialist transformation" in the South and was presumptively a conservative antireformer (though his later record showed more flexibility than his earlier record seemed to indicate).[100] Still, the cautious introduction of electoral changes within the party did signal a recognition of the need to find a mechanism to rejuvenate the leadership. In June 1988, the Central Committee agreed to a new system in which every time an election is held for the top leadership, one-third of the Central Committee must also be replaced.[101]

At the same time Vietnam was undergoing a protracted leadership transition in the late 1980s, the slow progress of the reforms was complicated by the dramatic changes in the international context, leading Vietnam to reassess its position on Cambodia, which it had invaded and occupied in 1979, and which had isolated it in the region and in the world. Even before the fall of the Berlin Wall, Hanoi's leaders had decided to withdraw from Cambodia, and the seeds for a major shift in foreign policy had been planted. In many ways the new thinking stimulated by the economic crisis had cleared the way for the even more dramatic shifts in Vietnam's thinking about how to relate to the external environment even though economic reform seemed stalemated as Vietnam entered the crisis year of 1989.

3

The Year of Living Dangerously (1989)

VIETNAM'S INTERNAL ECONOMIC crisis in the 1980s was paralleled by a concurrent intensification of external problems. The immediate issue was Vietnam's occupation of Cambodia, but this was tied to larger questions such as relations with China, the United States, and members of ASEAN. And, as relations with those countries remained tense, Vietnam's most important international supporter, the Soviet Union, was deeply enmeshed in its own problems. The direct connection between the economic and diplomatic issues was the embargo imposed on Vietnam by the United States after 1975, and internationalized after Vietnam's invasion of Cambodia, which significantly contributed to Vietnam's economic stagnation.

The year 1989 was a year of rapid transition. A series of successive external developments constituted sequential "minishocks," which cumulatively added up to a major shock to the assumptions on which the world view of Vietnam's leaders had been based. It is not surprising that there was inconsistency and a mixture of "old" and "new" in the reactions to fast-moving events. On the one hand, the fears raised by the prospect of dissolution of the "socialist camp" and of the Soviet Union itself, led Nguyen Van Linh, the party leader and a "reformer," to warn of a threat to Vietnam's own political system. On the other hand, Vietnam's leaders also realized that major changes were needed to avoid being isolated and left behind its neighbors, who were experiencing rapid economic growth. Although Linh had been forced to confront serious internal problems in late 1988, and other leaders had publicly revealed Vietnam's difficulties at that time, Linh appeared confident at the beginning of 1989 that the pace of change was manageable.

However, other voices in Vietnam expressed doubt and uncertainty about both the international situation and Vietnam's ability to adjust.

Even the confident Linh became alarmed by the summer of 1989 and retreated to Cold War paranoia. Inevitably the open atmosphere of debate and "new thinking" was dampened considerably by threats against those who wanted to push the envelope of reform. In October, Premier Do Muoi emphasized how important it was to maintain strong economic ties with the Soviet Union and Eastern Europe and to treat them as the anchor of Vietnam's foreign economic relations. By the end of the year, Linh had revised his hard line somewhat and sketched the outlines of a new conception of national security, though the accompanying diplomatic strategy was a hybrid of the old and the new. Still, even Linh emphasized that the domestic *doi moi* reforms must continue because they were essential to keep Vietnam from encountering the same problems as the Soviet and Eastern European countries.

BREACHING THE WALLS OF THE FORTRESS: NEW REALITIES LEAD TO A REASSESSMENT OF OLD POLICIES AND DOCTRINES

The turmoil in the communist world prompted many long-time revolutionaries to reassess their understanding of the ideology that they had embraced as a tool to achieve national liberation and social justice in Vietnam. The veteran Southern party leader Tran Bach Dang observed, "The reality of Vietnam after the revolution is different from what I imagined when I joined the party. . . . Life has shown us that it is much more complicated. The thing is, we received Marxism in a theoretical sense, not in a full sense, and the information was not very precise. Marxism came to Vietnam through the interpretation of Stalin and Mao Zedong. It was simplified to a great extent. And now we read the classic works of Marx and other founders, and we find that things were not so simple. Though the social conditions under which Marx wrote his works are not the same as now, the principles are the same. Yet those principles were not interpreted precisely correctly."[1]

As noted in the previous chapter, the political debate in the 1980s was conducted largely by indirection. Even Nguyen Van Linh did not directly confront those who disagreed with him. A retrospective view claims that radical reform views were held by a small minority and that "[b]ecause of this, party secretary general Nguyen Van Linh didn't engage in face-to-face struggles with these people."[2] (Of course it could also have been true that this was an influential minority, and that Linh was wary of moving on them too hard or too fast—or even that he agreed with much of what they had to say, at least at the beginning.) As Dang Phong put it, the advocates of change pursued an incremental strategy, likened to breaching the walls of a fortress by chipping away at the mortar between the bricks, piece by piece: "the trowel could bring down an entire wall without breaking things or shaking the earth. It was even possible to salvage many of the materials to use for new projects."[3]

The nationalist halo still protected the party, but the leadership was increasingly forced to draw on this past legacy of accumulated credit, rather than renew their prestige with positive current accomplishments. A report from the *Washington Post*'s Kenneth Richburg in October 1989 nicely captures this attitude.

Richburg reported that there was a feeling in some informed quarters that the old guard who had risen to power during forty years of conflict were still respected for their wartime contributions, but were not equipped to deal with the problems of peace, and that they did not fully understand the problems confronting Vietnam. "Our leaders are patriotic and they belong to a class that would be respected by any nation in the world," said one intellectual, "But their way of thinking and their age has betrayed their patriotism."[4]

During 1989, the two most important bases of legitimacy for the rule of the Vietnamese Communist Party were brought into question. The first was the nationalist legacy from the lengthy struggle for Vietnamese independence. In the name of this struggle, the party had demanded unquestioning obedience in carrying out its policies. The second was the idea that Vietnam was a valued member of a socialist community that was growing in power and influence as its members marched toward communism. The party's policies were validated because they drew on the same doctrinal basis as did the policies of the more powerful and economically advanced socialist countries. This source of external legitimation was threatened by the admission of error by the Soviet Union, and by the ideological and political confusion in the countries of Eastern Europe—to say nothing of China and its unsettled spring of 1989.

With regard to Vietnam's own situation, even more than the earlier errors of the land-reform movement, which caused the party to apologize to its victims and initiate a "rectification of errors campaign" in the 1950s, the damage to Vietnam's standard of living inflicted by doctrinaire post-1975 economic blunders eroded some of the prestige and confidence that the party had gained by 1975. By mid-1989, the admission of the extent of the damage caused by these policies was unequivocal.

As abandonment of communism in Eastern Europe picked up speed in late 1989 and 1990, and the Soviet Union stood by while its ideological sphere disintegrated, Vietnam's leaders were taken aback. "There is no question that the Soviet party's decision to abandon its absolute political dominance, at least in principle, has come as a shock to Vietnam's leaders, Eastern European diplomats and some Vietnamese officials say. 'They didn't expect it,' an Eastern European diplomat said of the Vietnamese. 'In fact, I think they thought it was impossible.'"[5]

CHANGING WORLD VIEW

As Carlyle Thayer has written, the changes in the Soviet Union had a major impact on Vietnam's reassessment of its foreign policy. "Vietnam's ideologically derived world-view began to change in tandem with a re-thinking of Soviet foreign policy. It was not until

May 1988, however, that Vietnam's new foreign policy orientation was codified." The new view was distilled in politburo Resolution 13 which called for a "multidirectional foreign-policy orientation," and was a seminal moment in Vietnam's response to the changes in the international system. As Thayer points out, there was an economic aspect of this decision in that Vietnam now defined its main task as taking advantage of favorable world conditions in order to lay the foundation for economic development and stabilize its domestic situation. The policy laid out in Resolution 13 "thus set in motion changes in Vietnamese national and foreign policies which contributed to a diplomatic settlement of the Cambodian conflict in October 1991."[6]

The precursor of Resolution 13, the landmark document that previewed Vietnam's post–Cold War foreign policy and embodied Vietnam's final decision to withdraw from Cambodia, was a politburo Resolution 32 of July 1986, which initiated the process of new thinking about Vietnam and the world. Because there was not a sufficient consensus within the party, and because conditions were not yet right (including Vietnam's reluctance to make the necessary concessions to get a Cambodian settlement at this time), the full impact of this decision was not felt until two years later. But it was a watershed moment in reordering priorities, most notably by giving priority to economic development over military security and redefining the main mission of diplomacy.

As I will argue in subsequent chapters, the main axis of opinion along which "reformers" and "conservatives" can be identified is one that places the concern of falling further behind in economic development at one end, and maintaining as much as possible of the political control system and its supporting ideology of "socialism" at the other. This 1986 identification of economic development as Vietnam's top priority, and the portrayal of military expenditures as a drag on Vietnam's economy was the most visible point at which the balance between military and economic priorities began to shift, with momentous consequences for Vietnam's view of its relationship to the external world. This was the necessary condition for the far-reaching decisions about integrating into the region and the world that unfolded over the next fifteen years.

Looking back twenty years later, one of Vietnam's premier diplomatic analysts explained the importance of Resolution 32.

After liberating the South and unification of the country, although meeting many difficulties created by thirty years of war, Vietnam had established a position of very high prestige on the world stage. However, because of subjective mistakes, voluntarism, impatience, we had stumbled into a socioeconomic crisis and were diplomatically isolated. Recognizing this situation, opposition forces exploited these Vietnamese difficulties to and colluded with each other to oppose us. We had very few friends remaining. A number of countries which had previously supported Vietnam during the anti-American Resistance distanced themselves from us. The relations between our country and the countries of ASEAN and the big powers (except for the Soviet Union and India) encountered many hang-ups [*vuong mac*] that couldn't be untangled, causing our national security to become unstable at a time when we had to confront tensions on borders at both ends of the country. At that time, the economic difficulties continued to pile up because we had very large military and national defense expenditures.[7]

Phan Doan Nam stresses the importance of Vietnam adopting a view of proactively (*chu dong*) shaping the external environment. This is in contrast to its previous concern with a reactive diplomatic judo, deflecting aggressive encroachments into its security sphere, and stress on finding ways of exploiting contradictions and weaknesses on the part of its opponents. As discussed elsewhere, this reactive approach is most suitable for the pursuit of "possession goals" with the relatively simple objective of defending and securing territory, as opposed to a more complex "milieu goal" of proactively and cooperatively constructing a favorable external (global or regional) environment.[8] "To escape from this difficult situation, in July 1986, the politburo met and issued Resolution 32 which clearly set out guidelines [*chu truong*] and revised diplomatic policies, and moved toward a solution in Cambodia. The resolution clearly stated: the external mission of Vietnam is to . . . proactively [*chu dong*] create a condition of stability for economic construction." This would require pursuing a policy of peaceful coexistence with China, ASEAN, and the United States, and building Southeast Asia into a "region of peace, stability, and cooperation."[9]

While the major shift from a default view of national security that put military concerns as the top priority, to top priority for economic development, was a momentous turn in the road in terms of new thinking about Vietnam and the external environment, it was still controversial within the party and not backed up by a realistic appraisal of the painful concessions that Vietnam would have to make to extricate itself from Cambodia and focus on economic development. "Only after the Sixth Party Congress [December 1986] when our party set forth a comprehensive statement of policy direction, first of all about economic renovation, and the politburo put out Resolution 13 on May 20, 1988 on the external mission and policy in the new situation, did our diplomacy undergo an important transformation. With the heading 'steadfastly maintain peace to serve economic development,' Resolution 13 emphasized that the diplomatic mission was to serve political stabilization, and that first priority would be given to economic development."[10]

VIETNAM'S WITHDRAWAL FROM CAMBODIA AND NEW CONCEPTIONS OF SECURITY

Vietnam's withdrawal from Cambodia was decided in 1988, and implemented in 1989. There were many reasons for this decision, but the changing policy of the Soviet Union was perhaps the most significant. Changing Soviet foreign policy and the decision to reduce aid to allies created tensions that were evident in the 1988 remarks of the Soviet ambassador to Vietnam that, "'I can say that important progress has been achieved in Soviet–Vietnamese relations. Looking at the immediate future, we may see numerous great difficulties."[11] There was a direct and immediate link between the Soviet decision to pull out of Afghanistan and the Vietnamese decision to withdraw from Cambodia.[12]

Karen Sutter writes that, "The Soviet Union also played an important diplomatic role in facilitating the Cambodia settlement. Following the initiation of the Soviet withdrawal from Afghanistan in January 1988, Vietnam withdrew 25,000 soldiers from Laos in the spring of 1988. After talks between [Vietnam's Foreign Minister Nguyen Co] Thach and Soviet leaders on May 18, 1988, Vietnam announced on May 26 that it would withdraw half of its troops from Cambodia by the end of 1988 and all of its troops by 1990." Soviet–Chinese diplomacy was also crucial for the end game in Cambodia. "During a meeting in Harbin in September 1990, just prior to the Jakarta talks, China and the Soviet Union both agreed to suspend military support for Cambodia."[13]

Premier Do Muoi went somewhat farther in elaborating on the new concept of security that was emerging in Vietnam at the end of the "year of living dangerously." In a major speech in December 1989, on the anniversary of the establishment of the armed forces of Vietnam, Muoi said that in the new conditions, economic development would be more tightly integrated with security than before, and that the armed forces would need to sustained at a level "just enough" (*vua du*) to assure Vietnam's defense. In the age of globalization and interdependence, the economic factor in international relations had become the key to national security. "Weakness in the economy and defense and political instability are great dangers to the independence and security of the country."[14]

Muoi's speech laid out the broad outlines of new security concepts, which would be further refined and developed during the next decade. The key elements were a redefinition of security that placed greater emphasis on economic development, which military security narrowly defined would have to support, and which required a recognition of a single global economic system, broadening the range of Vietnam's international partners and "adding friends while reducing enemies."

This emerging new security conception was the product of lessons learned during the collapse of communism in Eastern Europe in 1989, and the great changes taking place in both the Soviet Union and China. Although elements of this new conception can be traced back through the year 1989 and even earlier, it was only at the end of that year that they were combined and elaborated in the speech of Do Muoi—ironically a leader with a reputation as a conservative—in terms much clearer than the purported reform leader Nguyen Van Linh. Even then, this emerging view of what would come to be known as "comprehensive security" was not uncontested. The year 1989 was replete with political jolts, as Linh and other leaders tried to apply the brakes to the reform process, for fear that it would spin out of control and Vietnam would go the way of the Eastern European communist regimes.

LEADERSHIP UNCERTAINTY IN THE FACE OF CRISIS

Even before the unsettling events of the "year of living dangerously," the Vietnamese leadership showed signs of confusion about how to respond to rapid change as the Cold War wound down, as Vietnam's own internal policies were undergoing significant revision, and as signs of political unrest emerged, especially in the South. Vice Premier Vo Van Kiet's lengthy report to the National Assembly in December 1988 reflected the confusion and uncertainty among the party's top leaders in the face of the internal crisis of that time. "In the past, the party used to make decisions on everything. Now, it is the party's policy to merely set the guidelines. The rest is left to the National Assembly. If the National Assembly does not make the appropriate decisions, then, we, members of the Council of Ministers, will meet with deep bewilderment when it comes to implementation. . . . I really feel very bewildered and do not know what to do. I really feel very bewildered. May I tell you, comrades, that only the National Assembly can resolve this issue. There is no way for the Council of Ministers to resolve it. The party only sets forth the guidelines. The rest is left to the National Assembly. The decisions rest with the National Assembly."[15] Kiet was pleading to the National Assembly to take care of the details of policy implementation and allow the party to address itself only to broad policy issues, which was not, in itself, a new development. Even so, this remarkable expression of uncertainty by a top party leader was an indication of the ideological and political confusion of the period, which provided an opening for new thinking to spread.

A year later, the perceptive journalist Steven Erlanger revisited Vietnam and reported that the leadership was still uncertain about how to proceed as the momentum of change in the Soviet Union approached its decisive and terminal stage. "'This is the biggest crisis in the socialist camp since 1917,' a party member said. 'Right now the leadership just doesn't know what to do.'"[16]

The uncertainty about how the Vietnamese party should respond to the unprecedented changes in the communist world was reflected in a party official's response to a question about political change in Vietnam, such as adoption of a multiparty system. "When pressed . . . Nguyen Van Dang, deputy editor of the *Communist Review*, the party's theoretical journal, finally said: 'It's very difficult to give an answer. The party leaders are meeting now.'" Even this desperate hope that the party, in its collective wisdom, would come up with some answers on how to deal with the baffling change didn't offer much solace. A younger editor, taking notes in the interview just cited, at one point asked to say something. "Don't be surprised if we change our policy," he said passionately, "The only people who continue with the same policy forever are either stupid or dead." As this report also noted, however, there was no evidence of widespread popular pressure for political change, which was viewed as destabilizing and a threat to economic progress.[17]

The year 1989 opened on an uncertain note. In December 1988, party leader Nguyen Van Linh found it necessary to go to the South to resolve a series of land disputes that were threatening to spin out of control. Xinhua, the official Chinese news agency, reported that the Vietnamese Communist Party had set up a committee to deal with the ideological fallout from the conflicts over land in southern Vietnam. Nguyen Van Linh was put in charge of this effort. Despite his reputation as a reformer, the party group headed by Linh ascribed the turmoil involving land disputes in the South as the result of trends of "'adoring capitalism,' 'suspecting socialism,' and 'denying the revolutionary fruits.'" Although Linh called for more party democracy, openness, and candidness in acknowledging problems in order to assuage the tensions in the South, he also called for a reinforcement of ideological orthodoxy, appealed to local leaders to "beat back the viewpoints attempting to lower the prestige of socialism and refute Marxism and Leninism," and sternly warned that "democracy must be accompanied by discipline and obedience to law."[18]

While Linh was putting out fires in the South, Vice Premier Vo Van Kiet made public the leadership's broader concerns about Vietnam's direction. Xinhua reported that, "A high Vietnamese official said today Vietnam is worried about 'serious trials and big difficulties' in its domestic situation." Premier Vo Van Kiet told the National Assembly that "big problems have occurred" and as a result "the people are facing hardship."[19]

Linh's trip to the South to nip potentially destabilizing domestic political unrest in the bud illustrated that the party had (for the moment) adopted the view that it was political rigidity and failure to address the needs of the people that were a major factor in the troubles of the Eastern European socialist regimes. While Xinhua was hardly a disinterested observer during this period of continuing tensions between China and Vietnam and serious unrest in China itself, the gist of these reports is confirmed by the Vietnamese press and other reporting.

The substance of the "land disputes" seems to have involved an unwise party decision to reintervene in the agricultural sector to avert a severe rice shortage in 1988. The *Christian Science Monitor* reported that there were instances of famine and malnourishment in the north with an estimated three to seven million people hungry. This "brush with famine has reaped a harvest full of changes in Vietnam," the *Monitor* reported. "The resulting embarrassment to the ruling Communist Party, and the possibility of another famine in 1989, has put the country's leadership on a virtual war footing and brought about manifold political tremors. One is a breakout of civil unrest in the South.... This dramatic back step from old-style Marxism unleashed bureaucratic chaos. It also uncorked resentments rooted in the confiscation of southern farmland from 1977 to '83."[20]

At the time, informed observers felt that this crisis strengthened the hands of the reformers and pragmatists, rather than the conservatives. "'The food crisis has pushed Vietnam into a high degree of pragmatism about its future,' says a Hanoi-based Western diplomat. 'The party's progressives have had to confront the conservatives in order for the party to show the people that it can do something.' The famine caused heads to roll."[21]

This article also reveals how complex the political labels of "conservative" and "reformer" were, and how opaque Vietnamese politics was to outsiders. Having confidently stated that the crisis had benefited the reformers, the unidentified foreign observer then asserted that it was actually the conservatives who had come out ahead politically.

"The biggest political casualty was Vo Van Kiet, the acting prime minister, who lost his job in June to a conservative, Do Muoi. In a mea culpa, Mr. Kiet took responsibility for not convincing the politburo of the depth of the crisis at a key February meeting."[22] There is probably no way to resolve these complexities, but they do illustrate the crisis and confusion in Vietnam as 1989 commenced.

Another fallout of the food crisis in late 1988 was that Vietnam's leaders became acutely aware of the limitations of self-sufficiency and the necessity of improving economic links with the outside world. "Hanoi also learned that few nations will come to its aid. The response to pleas for food was weak, Vietnamese officials say. They blame themselves in part for hesitating to announce the crisis."[23]

PRESSURES FOR CHANGE

There was talk of "democracy" in Vietnam during this period, but it was intended to underline the importance of greater responsiveness and accountability to economic and social problems, not to undermine the control of the party. A typical article in the party press during this period stressed that the root of the turmoil in Eastern Europe was that they had not paid adequate attention to the standard of living of their people. "Violating the principle of material interests, no matter what the circumstances and whatever the reason, will always lead to negative reactions from people, will erode their ties to society, and will reduce or even completely rapidly annihilate their good will and enthusiasm for their work."[24] This was a long way from the party wartime exhortations to the populace not to think of themselves, but only of the party and the struggle.

Now the party explained the upheavals in Eastern Europe with a bluntly materialist analysis of living conditions—the kind of "economism" for which Lenin castigated his socialist opponents, fearing that it would lead away from revolution to a mere humanitarian concern with raising living standards. In the 1950s and 1960s, orthodox communists (and the Chinese) had scornfully denounced Hungary's "goulash communism" and other Eastern European attempts to turn away from Spartan central planning to attempts to raise standards of living. The Hanoi hard-liners' criticism of economic policy in the South in the early 1980s (see chapter 2) as having the "odor of Yugoslavia" was an echo of this orthodoxy, but by the late 1980s it was under serious challenge.

The *Washington Post* reported in October 1989 that Vietnam's leaders also had to contend with growing frustration at the slow pace of change—a problem sharpened by heightened popular expectations that the leadership itself had unleashed. Much of the criticism was directed against Nguyen Van Linh, despite his reputation as a reformer. "'The man who pushes the plow is too old, said another intellectual here. 'He has spoiled everything.' 'I don't think the reform process is going as I wished,' said Tran Ngoc Chau, executive editor of *Tuoi Tre*, the Communist Party youth newspaper, which has been a champion of liberalization. 'In the beginning we did not imagine all of the problems that we faced.'" In the face of unrest, and even small demonstrations protesting living conditions, local authorities were forced to respond. Most of these expressions of discontent "were quickly addressed by local Communist authorities, who generally seem willing to defuse tensions by listening to popular grievances."[25]

Although the major economic reforms were not instituted until 1989, the government had some accomplishments to its credit. Inflation had been reduced from around 400 percent in the 1986–8 period to about 30 percent in 1989. In 1989, Vietnam became a net exporter of rice for the first time since the end of the Vietnam War. Some Western observers began to see Vietnam as a candidate to follow the footsteps of the Asian "tiger" economies. World Bank appraisals were positive, comparing Vietnam to South Korea on the eve of its economic takeoff in 1965.[26] The picture from the perspective of Vietnam's leaders and ordinary Vietnamese was not as rosy, however.

A FORK IN THE ROAD

Even before the tumultuous events of 1989—Tian An Men Square and the fall of the Berlin Wall, Vietnam had reached a fork in the road, and made a decision that meant going forward into an unknown future, with no turning back. Steven Erlanger, the *New York Times* Southeast Asia correspondent, noted in April 1989 that "for some Vietnamese, the long occupation of Cambodia is a metaphor for Vietnam's recent and ongoing 'renovation': a more realistic policy at last emerging after a tremendous sacrifice by the peasant class in pursuit of a miscalculated and dogmatic adventure by an unchanging and relatively unsophisticated elite. 'In the end,' one Vietnamese official said, 'this is our version of Afghanistan.' Vietnam would be forced by its own declining economy to change. It needed jobs and Western investment that had been blocked by its Cambodian occupation. '[W]e stayed too long. We can no longer afford to be isolated in the world when our neighbors in Southeast Asia are developing with such speed.'"[27]

As this and other contemporaneous reports pointed out, the decision to change direction in Cambodia was due to the combination of internal economic problems and the changing external environment. It is also clear from these reports that there was a broad consensus on the withdrawal, even though some more conservative leaders had their doubts about the wisdom of this move. Erlanger's report gives a good indication of the spectrum of views, from intellectuals who wholeheartedly embraced the change, to the army leadership, who grudgingly accepted the inevitability of the move. A Vietnamese writer observed that Vietnam had shown a talent for fighting. "But as you know, over time we made many mistakes, and one was to be so big-mouthed and proud about our victory over the United States. We were so proud over our victory for so long a time, and we thought we could have a victory in everything else."[28]

The military endorsement of this policy shift was more qualified but reflected an understanding that this was a matter of necessity, not choice. One example of this is especially revealing. Major General Tran Cong Man, editor of *Quan Doi Nhan Dan* (Army People's Daily), provided two further reasons—"error and pride." He still felt the invasion of Cambodia was a justified response to Khmer Rouge provocations, but admitted that Vietnam had made mistakes during its occupation of Cambodia, including not preparing their Cambodian allies to take over their own affairs. From this, he learned that "the revolution of each country and the independence of each country must be managed by each nation themselves. And the support of others can only be secondary."[29]

The Vietnamese political leadership had been forced to confront both the economic consequences of a draining and costly war, and the political impact of accountability for a foreign and security policy that was a failure, compounding the failures of economic policy since 1975. The impact of Cambodia penetrated deeply into the society. "Nearly every family here has a relative or friend who served in Cambodia, and they have been told, as they were again on the day the pullout was announced, that Vietnamese soldiers have 'gloriously fulfilled their duty to help the Cambodian people wholeheartedly and unselfishly.'"[30]

At the same time, there was a perception that Vietnam had not derived clear security benefits from the occupation of Cambodia, and that the burden had not been equitably shared—unlike the previous conflicts against the French and the Americans. General Man acknowledged difficulties in reintegrating soldiers returning from Cambodia. "'They fight very well,' he said of the veterans, 'but when they come back home, some cause trouble. First they feel they have showed devotion and sacrifice on the battlefield, and when they come back, they are not treated in proportion to what they have given. They feel treated inequitably.'" Other people in Vietnam also encountered difficulty. Erlanger observed that "every family also struggles to make ends meet in a country where the average wage is about $6 a month and a surgeon is paid less for an operation than the cost of fixing a punctured bicycle tire." Nevertheless, the returning soldiers felt that they deserved more consideration for their sacrifices.[31]

The economic costs of the Cambodian occupation were heavy. "Intellectuals say most people believe the price was too high." About 20,000 Vietnamese died and more than 47,000 were wounded in the border fighting between 1977 and 1978, according to General Man. Approximately 15,000 more died among the further 50,000 casualties in the following decade. The financial costs were estimated at 2 million dollars a day throughout most of the 1980s, mostly covered by Soviet aid.[32]

In addition, the idea that Vietnam was fulfilling its "internationalist duty" by protecting and nurturing a fellow socialist regime in order to consolidate a growing community of communist countries had lost its allure as the very concept of a world of fraternal communist countries dissipated. "Let the Cambodians build any 'ism' they want to," said a novelist and screenwriter with revolutionary credentials. "It's up to them. Perhaps the kingdom [of Cambodia] will come back. But let them build a regime suitable to themselves."[33] Six months later, as the last of the Vietnamese troops withdrew from Cambodia, General Man said, "If we withdraw, the Khmer armed forces will grow up and make their own effort. If we stay there we don't know how long we would have to remain."[34]

The *New York Times*'s Steven Erlanger's remarkable reportage in 1989 provides a valuable glimpse into a moment in time that marked a crucial turning point for Vietnam, as it embarked on an uncharted path without a clear idea of the ultimate destination. Both those who wanted to cling to the familiar path and those who had concluded that this was a dead end had a clear sense that this was a rare moment of transition, in which the future hung in the balance and the risks of miscalculation were very high. "'There is a struggle going on for the soul of Vietnamese socialism,' said a prominent editor. 'It is between the bureaucratic conservative mechanism and the new mechanism of the market, between the theorists and the pragmatists, and it is a struggle inside each one of us.... I think this period is the hardest time, because it is the transition between the old and the new. But in the last few years we've forced a little light from the coals, and the stagnant ice is melting. All over the world and in other socialist countries, hundreds of millions of people recognize that they must live as life is and work as life demands, and not as the ice demands.'"[35] Some officials openly spoke of the aged and transitional nature of the leadership and some privately hoped that a new generation would emerge less affected by personal experience in building "an outdated and borrowed form of socialism."[36]

POLITICAL RETRENCHMENT AND ACCELERATED ECONOMIC REFORM IN THE FACE OF RAPID CHANGE

The top party leaders became concerned that the ice was melting too quickly, and decided to issue some clear political and ideological guidance that would keep the advocates of fundamental change on the socialist reservation. Party leader Nguyen Van Linh issued a statement at a party Central Committee meeting in late March 1989 that reaffirmed the party's "leading role," rejected a move toward pluralist democracy, and stated that the state would "legislate limitations to private businesses . . . to preserve the communist character of the nation."[37]

The party also realized that it could no longer compartmentalize its economic development from its foreign-policy strategy, pursuing geostrategic goals without regard to the impact they had on Vietnam's development—the economic embargo resulting from the invasion of Cambodia was the main example of this. The Sixth Plenum of the Sixth Party Congress (March 1989) put forth a resolution which "clearly pointed out the need to strongly shift the focus in foreign policy from political relations to political–economic relations," said a later review of foreign policy during this period.[38]

One bellwether of Vietnam's changing view of the international system was its policy shift on relations with Yugoslavia. As mentioned earlier, Yugoslavia had become the symbol of an alternative to a tightly controlled two-bloc (or two-world) system, as well as a challenge to the orthodox command-economy model of the Soviet Union. At various times Yugoslavia was castigated by the USSR and China for being "revisionist" and daring to promote a heterodox version of socialism. It was this that Vietnam's party conservatives had in mind when, in the early 1980s, they detected an "odor of Yugoslavia" in the South. Where economic pluralism existed, they reasoned, political defiance could not be far behind.

On top of this, Yugoslavia had condemned Vietnam for the invasion of Cambodia which, given Belgrade's influence in the nonaligned movement, was a major diplomatic setback for Vietnam, not easily forgotten. But Gorbachev had made restoration of good relations with Yugoslavia a major priority, and succeeded in normalizing relations between the two countries in 1988. (And, as noted above, China quickly abandoned its censure of Yugoslavia when Deng Xiaoping consolidated his position nearly a decade earlier following the death of Mao.) The key paragraph of the joint statement, which Vietnam undoubtedly noted with great interest, was, "Consistent respect for the autonomy and independence of parties and socialist countries in defining their own paths of development made it possible to eliminate the factors that led to the conflict between the Communist Party of Yugoslavia and the All-Union Communist Party (Bolsheviks) and the Cominform in 1948. This is of great significance not only for mutual relations between the CPSU [Communist Party of the Soviet Union] and the LCY [League of Communists of Yugoslavia], but also for the development and establishment of socialism as a world process."[39]

This was, in effect, a proclamation of the end of the sharp bipolarity in the international system that had, in any case, long ago ceased to be a reality, with the nonaligned movement, the Sino–Soviet split, and the Third Indochina Conflict between contending communist parties. But Vietnam found it difficult to forgive Yugoslavia for its condemnation of the Vietnamese occupation of Cambodia, and it was not until the Vietnamese troop withdrawal was nearly complete that Hanoi turned to normalizing relations, with a high-level visit to Belgrade carrying the "fraternal greetings" of Vietnam's top leaders.[40]

By September 1989, the leadership's concern about external events had intensified as events in the Soviet Union and Eastern Europe, as well as the Tian An Men Square incident showed how easily change could spin out of control. Erlanger reported that Nguyen Van Linh delivered two hard-line speeches calling for a ideological crackdown on intellectuals and warning against the dangers of Western subversion in harsh Cold War language, to the dismay of his supporters among Vietnam's intellectual and journalistic elite.[41]

By this time it had become apparent that Vietnam's gamble in leaving Cambodia would not lead to an immediate payoff, as the United States made it clear that it would not lift the economic embargo unless a list of additional conditions was fulfilled. Vietnam was in danger of being caught between a disintegrating socialist world and a capitalist world that would not accept it as a member. The withdrawal from Cambodia was "now believed unlikely to lead to the United States' lifting its embargo on Vietnam. . . . At the same time, radical changes elsewhere in the Communist world—in China, the Soviet Union, Poland and Hungary in particular—seem to have shocked the party leadership here and increased a sense of threat and isolation."[42] The difference between Poland's Solidarity and Yugoslavia's workers councils was, in Hanoi's view, that Solidarity was a counterrevolutionary movement supported by imperialist intervention aimed at overthrowing socialism in Poland.[43]

Internally, the situation in Vietnam appeared to have stabilized. A series of articles in Nhan Dan in the summer of 1989 surveyed the major state-owned enterprises (SOE) with a series of interviews with the key SOE managers. The interview of the manager of a state-owned mine bore the subhead, "The shock is past, though many difficulties remain, the first steps to take measures appropriate to the market have been taken."[44] The term *cu xoc* came into common currency at this time. It was a borrowing from the French *coup choc*, and its increasing application to unexpected events that threw Vietnam off balance may have been an alternative to Vietnamese terms such as *khung hoang*, which would indicate extreme crisis and unmanageable turmoil. "Shock" seemed to imply that an external upheaval had seriously impacted Vietnam, but that with appropriate measures, the adverse consequences could be minimized.

Some economists refer to the major economic reforms undertaken in 1989 to reenergize the flagging *doi moi* reform process as "the big bang." There is considerable debate about whether this is the appropriate way to describe and understand what happened in the Vietnamese economy during 1989, and the actual impact of the reforms. Fforde and de Vylder's outstanding study of the economic transition in Vietnam argues that in studies of the reforms, too much attention has been paid to policy makers and their political decisions about the reforms, and that much of the actual change was driven by economic forces beyond the control of the decision makers. "Top-down assumptions about the nature of change seem to go well with interpretations of events in terms of rapid and rather discontinuous change: big bang reforms are seen to have taken place in Vietnam [in 1989]." Fforde argues that much of the economic change in 1989 was the culmination of processes set in motion earlier, and the result of the state simply getting out of the way. "Micro level adaptation and the reduction of plan distortion had by 1989 prepared the Vietnamese economy for a shift to generalized market-based exchange without too much upheaval."[45] "Too be even more critical," they conclude, "we believe that big-bang metaphors are meaningless when applied to Vietnam." If this is the case, finding direct and immediate causal linkages between Vietnam's domestic economic policy and the changing external situation may be problematic, especially in the case of the fast moving events of 1989.

NGUYEN VAN LINH REVERTS TO "OLD THINKING" ABOUT THE TWO-WORLDS INTERNATIONAL SYSTEM

If big-bang metaphors are meaningless when applied to Vietnam's economic reforms, perhaps the same could be said for big-bang metaphors in the area of Vietnam's external relations. Despite the major upheavals of 1989, the Vietnamese response was really a process of adjustment over an extended period of time. Indeed it would be hard to locate a key turning point in Vietnam's journey from a "two worlds" framework, to an acceptance of membership in a of a diverse international system, dominated largely by democratic powers and centered around an integrated global market economy. During 1989—especially toward the end of that year—the outlines of a new approach to Vietnam's external relations became dimly visible, but it took a number of years for this to evolve into a coherent conception. In addition, though 1989 was a year of progress toward new thinking about security and the global system, it was also punctuated by reversals and reversions to the old thinking.

Nevertheless, the fatal blow to the "two worlds" concept had been struck by Mikhail Gorbachev in December 1988 in his momentous speech to the United Nations. The idea of a common civilization and common humanity was central to Gorbachev's stunning speech, which, in effect, declared an end to the two-worlds conception of international politics. "Today we have entered an era when progress will be based on the interests of all mankind. Consciousness of this requires that world policy, too, should be determined by the priority of the values of all mankind. The history of the past centuries and millennia has been a history of almost ubiquitous wars, and sometimes desperate battles, leading to mutual destruction. . . . However, parallel with the process of wars, hostility, and alienation of peoples and countries, another process, just as objectively conditioned, was in motion and gaining force: The process of the emergence of a mutually connected and integral world. Further world progress is now possible only through the search for a consensus of all mankind, in movement toward a new world order. . . . The formula of development 'at another's expense' is becoming outdated. In light of present realities, genuine progress by infringing upon the rights and liberties of man and peoples, or at the expense of nature, is impossible."[46]

The world focused on Gorbachev's dramatic offer to withdraw Soviet troops from Eastern Europe and along the Chinese border, even though the larger global vision of Gorbachev was equally important. China immediately responded positively to the Soviet Union, meeting one of its conditions for normal relations. Vietnam did not respond for two weeks. At the time, some diplomatic observers were puzzled by this reaction. "[D]iplomatic observers in [H]anoi are surprised at [V]ietnam's delayed reaction to this major diplomatic initiative by its main ally. They said [H]anoi's support seems to be reluctant and hard to explain."[47] In retrospect, it is easy to understand Vietnam's shock and displeasure. Gorbachev had just destroyed the foundation of their world view, though it took some time for Vietnam to officially adjust to this new reality.

As change in other socialist countries accelerated in mid-1989, Nguyen Van Linh reverted to the Cold War language of antagonistic world systems. Just as he had endorsed the view in the 1986 "reform" party congress that the main political question in the world was "who will defeat whom," Linh accused the United States of trying to undermine Communist countries. "He spoke of the 'escalating' battle between the Communist camp and a fundamentally unchanged capitalist world 'with its very insidious schemes and tricks.'"[48] Linh's hard-line speech to the party Central Committee at the end of August

1989 is worth examining in detail because it was the most militant and explicit statement of the "two worlds" theory after a period of more moderate rhetoric. Although the party has never abandoned the general concept of "two worlds" and the inevitable triumph of socialism, the anti-Western hostility and general paranoia of this speech gradually dissipated over time. But Linh's vehement reiteration of the old formulas was probably a rebuke to Gorbachev, or an attempt to bring him back to his senses.

"Now more than ever before, the imperialists are especially concentrating the spearhead of their offensive against the socialist countries with frenzied acts and insidious tricks. They are rejoicing at what US President Bush has been waiting for day and night. We are now living in the final period of an idea, at the final chapter of the communist experiment," Linh told the assembled party leaders. Linh noted that the purpose of this August meeting of the party Central Committee had been to assess the impact of international developments, which were affecting Vietnam. In addition to the "insidious schemes of the imperialists," he warned of negative ideological influences from "other" socialist countries. "We have initially analyzed the process of reform which is being carried out in a number of socialist countries. Besides the achievements scored by these countries, we sympathize with them over newly arising difficulties and express our profound concern over the danger threatening socialism in some fraternal socialist countries. The plenum noted that the above-said international situation, with different degrees of seriousness, is affecting Vietnam. In view of the schemes of imperialism, in view of the negative influences of the wrong ideological tendencies in a number of socialist countries, and in view of our party's renovation policy, the majority of our cadres and party members have still clearly shown a correct and firm ideological stance. This reflects the steadfast revolutionary tradition of our party, a genuine Marxist-Leninist party built, educated, and trained by Uncle Ho. On the other hand, we also noted that, in view of the abovementioned situation, there have appeared some deviant ideological viewpoints among a handful of cadres and party members. We cannot disregard these manifestations because they can spread. Moreover, there still exists in our society a breeding ground for these poisons. There has also been the impact of wrong ideological currents coming from outside. It is precisely for this reason that the seventh plenum of the party Central Committee, with a serious and frank attitude, has discussed these problems and has arrived at important conclusions. These conclusions are the basis for carrying out ideological work and organizing political activities at all levels and in all sectors to create unanimity of views within the party and among the people and to step up production and work so as to achieve the objective of stabilizing the socioeconomic situation."[49] The surprising conclusion, then, is that in the face of all these threats, the appropriate response is to make sure that the reforms succeed in stabilizing "the socioeconomic situation." In other times a threat of this magnitude would have called for political repression and purges.

Still, Linh's description of the international system is a classic statement of the "two worlds" concept. "For a long time in the past, when analyzing the world situation, we unanimously noted that in the world there are two camps, the socialist camp and capitalist camp, and four fundamental contradictions. . . . However, for a long time after that we did not talk about it any more. Is it true that these theses have become old-fashioned? No, absolutely not. In my opinion, this is our serious shortcoming, especially in ideological work. This, more or less, has led certain persons to mistakenly believe that the nature of imperialism has changed." Linh emphasized that "as long as imperialism exists and as long as the socialist revolution has not yet achieved victory on a world scale, the value of these Leninist theses remains intact."

Linh asserted that as imperialism reaches its inevitable end things become more complicated and its demise will not be readily apparent, but gradual and subtle. "We should not assume that imperialism will die a simple, superficial death. It is the death of a social and economic structure that could go on for centuries and may happen partially, step by step. . . . Imperialism continues to alter its forms, methods, and tactics to suit the situation, while maintaining its true nature. The imperialists are frantically attempting to defend themselves in order to prolong their death. "This means that even more vigilance would be required as imperialists devise more subtle tactics to stave off their demise."[50] To assert that "imperialism" was in its death throes at the very moment of terminal decline in the socialist world was certainly the mark of a leadership in deep denial.

Linh gave another speech in late September 1989 to the army newspaper *Quan Doi Nhan Dan* in which he highlighted the dangers of "peaceful evolution" (*dien bien hoa binh*), which was to become an obsession with party conservatives for the next decade. "Peaceful evolution" will be analyzed in greater detail in chapter 4, but its proximate origins can be traced to this period in 1989, when the party leaders concluded that "imperialist and reactionary forces" were attempting to use a variety of political, economic, social, and cultural means to destroy the remaining communist countries from within. Addressing a military audience, Linh said, "In the past we had to fight the enemy with actual weapons, and defeating them was not easy. Today, under conditions of peace, we have to struggle with the enemy's 'peaceful evolution' on every front, and defeating them will be even more difficult, fierce, and complicated."[51]

In an address to the party's ideological training institute at the end of September 1989, Nguyen Van Linh laid out an uncompromising view of Marxism as a total ideology and capitalism as a dead end. Noting that "some people" were alleging that Marxism was out of date, an antiquated remnant of a nineteenth-century thinker analyzing nineteenth-century problems, Linh forcefully asserted that it would continue to be Vietnam's guide into the post–Cold War era. "There has never been a scientific and revolutionary theory like Marxism-Leninism. It is a 'comprehensive and logically tight [*chat che*] theory which gives people a total world view' and a theory that not only aims at 'understanding the world, but also changing it.'" Linh confidently concluded that, "Capitalism will certainly be replaced by socialism, because that is the law of human history, which no one can deny." Linh warned against using the cover of *doi moi* to engage in a rejection of fundamental principles of Marxism-Leninism. "That is revisionism, pure and simple," he said, using the dreaded term that had destroyed the careers of party members and even sent them to jail.[52] This was hardly an auspicious atmosphere for new thinking—especially in the field of external relations.

However, this attempt to mandate ideological orthodoxy by fiat and threat proved inadequate to stem the tide of doubt or restore the old certainties. Even seasoned revolutionaries like Tran Bach Dang had begun to entertain doubts about the totalism and analytic power of traditional Marxism-Leninism. In early 1990, one of Hanoi's leading ideologists wrote about the "ideological task" with a new tone of flexibility and introspection. Vu Huu Ngoan wrote that it was time to emphasize persuasion rather than compulsion in ideological work. "To put it another way," he wrote, "we cannot forbid people to think [*tu duy*], but can only guide their way of thinking." Even more interesting was Ngoan's statement that, "If in the past our ideological task aimed at sharpening the contradictions between the enemy and ourselves, and struggling to resolve the contradictions in a way that would bring victory to the people, today the ideological task has to deal with a new situation: resolving contradictions among the people, internal to socialist society." This more defensive view of propaganda can also imply that the major problems for communist societies were internal, not external.[53]

Reform-minded intellectuals and journalists found themselves in a difficult position during this period of political instability and transition. One official noted that, "The problem now is that there is no clear ideological line," but added that, paradoxically, "It is very easy to cross it." One senior journalist called Linh's speech "clumsy." "It was the language of 45 years ago, and it depressed many people."[54] Some party leaders tried to reassure concerned foreign observers that this language was for domestic consumption only. One of Linh's top aides assured Western diplomats that Linh's hard line was intended mainly to appease hard-liners in the leadership, and did not signify a retreat from economic reform.[55]

Although the arena of policy discussion had expanded, especially in the economic sphere, the party was determined to keep control over the discussion agenda. In late 1989, a new press law was promulgated with great fanfare. As Bui Tin recalled, a number of journalists from Southeast Asia requested visas to cover the story. After listening to a long-winded briefing, a reporter from *The Nation* in Bangkok cabled his editors that the main points could be briefly stated: the party will maintain tight control over the press, and will prohibit private newspapers. In other words, nothing had changed. Bui Tin said that even as a deputy editor of the party newspaper *Nhan Dan*, he felt that he was an object of political scrutiny by the organizational branch of the party.[56]

In the autumn of 1989, as the changes in Eastern Europe were accelerating, Nguyen Van Linh traveled to East Germany to get a first-hand look. Bui Tin describes the Vietnamese view of East Germany as a hard-line old-guard regime, which had rejected Gorbachev-style reforms. Despite its relatively advanced technology (compared to most other socialist countries), "this country had stood aside from *doi moi* and *ngay thang* ["straightforwardness"]' (perestroika and glasnost), because they thought that they had accomplished these things a long time ago, and stood in the ranks of the ten most highly industrialized economies in the world." Despite this economic development, East Germany's major assistance to Vietnam had been in the form of advice and technical assistance in the security and counterespionage fields.[57]

Whether it was for advice on how to keep things in Vietnam under control or simply to take a closer look at the changes in Eastern Europe, Nguyen Van Linh led a delegation to attend the fortieth anniversary of the founding the German Democratic Republic.[58] *Nhan Dan* pictured Linh with Erich Honecker, the hard-line GDR leader and noted the "cordial" (*than mat*, which could also be rendered as "intimate") talks between the two leaders. Linh's discussions with Gorbachev were also described as "cordial." Honecker's speech to the assembled dignitaries was titled, "We will continue to advance along the path to socialism."[59] After the anniversary celebrations, *Nhan Dan* announced that Linh was going to "rest for a period in Eastern Germany."[60] He spent a week "resting," during this period of rapid and turbulent change swirling around him, and returned to Hanoi, met at the airport by the key politburo members.[61] There were rumors in the international press that Linh had suffered a stroke, and was receiving medical care in East Germany, suggesting that no political significance should be read into this prolonged stay abroad during a crucial moment of transition.[62] The fact that Linh was quite active following his return to Vietnam suggests that either his health condition was not as serious as reported, or that it was a diplomatic cover for his extended stay in the GDR.

At this time, it appears as though East Germany was a kind of talisman of the socialist future, at a time when the Vietnamese leadership was increasingly unsure of where Gorbachev was taking the Soviet Union. East Germany represented both a model of retaining strict political control during a period of change and a model of socialist economic transformation. In addition, the Vietnamese press portrayed the GDR as proof positive that the socialist development model was superior, and that history was still moving in a favorable direction. "Today, along with America, the Federal Republic of Germany, and Japan, the countries that export innovation, the GDR and the Soviet Union are the countries that comprise most of the advanced industry in the world." The GDR was held up as a proof of the superiority of socialism, "which is being demonstrated in an even more effective manner." Its superiority over advanced capitalist countries, and West Germany, was that the capitalists left most of the scientific and technical sector in private hands—an argument that reflected the essentially theological belief that socialism was not only politically and morally superior, but more effective as well.[63]

This was the last gasp of the doctrinaire view that the existing (as opposed to theoretical and future) socialist model was superior to the capitalist model. Very soon the GDR economy would be revealed as a hollow shell, as it was submerged by the powerful economic force of West Germany. At this juncture, the collapse of the USSR and GDR models left the Vietnamese party ideologists in somewhat of a quandary, since relations with China had not yet reached the point that China's reforms could be cited as worthy of emulation.

Soon the capitalist "tiger economies" of Asia would become examples for Vietnam to consider, because conditions in these Asian countries were more similar to Vietnam's, and because they had seemed to accomplish economic miracles while maintaining tight political control. A decade later, the party ideologists reaffirmed the ultimate superiority of socialism as a development model, but had to admit that there was no clear example or blueprint to show what it would look like. The erosion of the belief in the clear path toward the future had a profound impact in opening the way for new thinking.

DIFFICULT FOREIGN POLICY CHOICES IN A PERIOD OF IDEOLOGICAL TRANSITION

An example of Vietnam's ambivalence in fully embracing new thinking is the statements about Vietnam's economic ties toward the end of 1989. At this point, Vietnamese leaders still expressed a commitment to the primacy of their relations with the Soviet Union and Eastern Europe, and the centrality of their COMECON (Council for Mutual Economic Assistance—the Soviet-led economic bloc of Eastern European countries which Vietnam had joined in 1978) membership to Vietnam' s economic future, just as that organization was on the verge of collapse (which happened in 1991). Pham Van Dong published a prominent article in *Nhan Dan* in November 1989, urging strengthening solidarity with the Soviet Union. "As comrades and sincere fraternal brothers of the Soviet people, the Vietnamese people are carefully following the process of profound renovation [*doi moi*] in the Soviet Union in the sincere hope that the communists [*nhung nguoi Cong San*] and the people of the Soviet Union [this was a very unusual case of differentiating between a specified group of "communist people" within the larger entity termed the "people"] will overcome every obstacle to successfully achieve their mission of reorganization [*cai to*—the Vietnamese translation of "perestroika"—i.e., not *doi moi*] and bring a new strength to the country so that it will move forward, and elevate its position as the first and most powerful socialist state in the world today."[64]

In Pham Van Dong's view, the advantage of economic ties to the Soviet Union was that the Soviet Union was helping to build the base of the Vietnamese economy by giving aid to construct factories and productive enterprises, and was training scientists and technicians, while trade with the capitalist countries only brought in luxury consumer goods. This was a legacy of the physiocratic and Confucianist contempt for mere commerce that was imprinted in the minds of many of the older generation of Vietnamese leaders. In the same month, Premier Do Muoi admitted that Vietnam had a serious trade imbalance, and was running up external debt in consequence. For a variety of reasons, including the economic embargo by the United States, foreign investment was not sufficient to have an impact on economic development. The bottom line, according to Do Muoi, was that, "with respect to partners in cooperation and expanding external economic relations, we will continue to give first place to cooperation with the Soviet Union, Laos, and Cambodia, and other socialist countries, strive to cooperate with Third World countries, and developed capitalist countries along with the various international economic organizations. We place importance on cooperation with countries in the region both for reasons of economic interest and the interest in preserving peace and stability in the region."[65]

There was a clear tension between the priority assigned to the politicized economic relations with COMECON, Laos, and Cambodia, and economic ties with market economies—certainly as far as "efficiency" (the title of Muoi's article) was concerned. It is revealing that at the end of 1989 Vietnam's leaders still urged priority to ties with other communist countries, even while cautiously seeking out other partners. Dong scolded some economic officials for wanting to slight their obligations to COMECON in favor of more profitable trade elsewhere. He concluded with an acknowledgment of the Soviet Union's problems, but said, "As in any new undertaking, the cooperation between Vietnam and the Soviet Union is going through a process of experimentation and is overcoming obstacles step by step in order to develop and increase efficiency. These initial difficulties are inevitable, due to the difference in the level of development between the two countries, and differences in the form and level of reforms [*doi moi*] in planning and in utilizing the relationship between commodities and money." Nevertheless, he asserted, these problems can be resolved and Vietnamese–Soviet cooperation expanded still further.[66]

Despite his earlier warnings about ideological orthodoxy and "revisionism," by the end of 1989 Linh was calling for new thinking in the sphere of national security. It is important to note that his starting point was the familiar concept of a close "special relationship" with client regimes on Vietnam's flanks in Laos and Cambodia (where Vietnam hoped to maintain the relationship even though their combat troops were gone), and diplomatic and economic support from the Soviet Union on the global stage. Vietnam also was tentatively moving toward an accommodation with China, but made the painful concessions required only after the withdrawal of Soviet support, and the impending collapse of the Soviet Union itself had become more obvious, and only at the cost of serious discord among the top Vietnamese leaders. The formal restoration of diplomatic relations (the subject of the next chapter) did not occur until November 1991.

In an article written for the military journal *Quan Doi Nhan Dan* and republished in the party newspaper in mid-December 1989, Nguyen Van Linh reiterated the reasons Vietnam had intervened in Cambodia a decade earlier: it saw itself under attack from both the north and the southwest. Linh reminded his readers that China's 1979 invasion of Vietnam in response to the Vietnamese invasion of Cambodia was not the only evidence of Chinese hostility, and cited China's previous assault and occupation of Vietnamese-controlled islands in the Spratly chain. He also reminded his readers of the dangers of "peaceful evolution" and US strategies of low-intensity warfare and military deterrence (which, he implied, were aimed at Vietnam) and, while stressing that preserving the peace was now a paramount concern, it should not lead to a loss of vigilance.[67]

In the face of all these concerns, Linh argued, new thinking about the role of military force was needed. The past experience from the "liberation struggle" was "precious" but not relevant to the current circumstances. This article formulated an early version of a concept that would later be termed "comprehensive security." "You cannot protect the Fatherland without a strong military. But political, economic, and diplomatic [*doi ngoai*] factors also play a key role in the mission of defending the country. We must organize and mobilize each facet: struggle and construction, politics and economics, creating a comprehensive strength [*suc manh tong hop*] to defend the Fatherland, just as we knew how to develop comprehensive strength to defeat the enemy during war." [68]

To protect Vietnamese security interests, Linh wrote, defining the right political goals was paramount. Internally this involved continuing to adhere to socialism under party leadership, while externally the aim was to "unite and closely cooperate with the Soviet Union and the socialist countries, while resolutely and patiently removing the obstacles for a friendly relationship with China, and broadening all aspects of relations with all nations in the world, including those with different political systems in order to increase the number of friends and decrease the number of enemies, while actively engaging in the life of the international system [*tich cuc tham gia doi song quoc te*]." The political objectives, Linh emphasized, were the key to an effective national defense and security approach. [69]

This important formulation of Vietnam's approach to "defending the Fatherland" at the end of the "year of living dangerously" contains many of the seeds of Vietnam's emerging post–Cold War conceptions of security. Of these, four are especially important: the idea of comprehensive security, the importance of diversification of external ties, "engaging in the life of the international system," and the primacy of economic development over military spending. All of these pointed away from a traditional approach to security. First, "comprehensive security" marked a shift from "possession goals" toward "milieu goals" in Vietnamese thinking about security, and reflected a relative downgrading of the military component of security. Second, the idea of diversifying relationships regardless of political system implicitly rejected a "two worlds" view of the international system. And, third, "engaging in the life of the international system" combined both of these elements, in that it accepted the idea of a pluralistic constellation of actors in the international system, and mandated an active engagement with the system within its own parameters and rules—again a difference from the Cold War attempt to operate only within the confines of an "antisystem" of socialist countries who tried to pose an alternative to the capitalist and Western dominated system of the post–Second World War period.

The fourth element of the emerging Vietnamese conception of security in the post–Cold War era was that economic strength was the most indispensable element of comprehensive strength, and that Vietnam's relations with the outside world had to be harnessed to the goal of economic development. "*Building the economy* is the central task of national construction. Economic construction is an urgent requirement of the life of the people, a requirement for national development and catching up with the developed countries of the world, and also a *requirement of national defense and security*. [emphasis in original] Economic difficulties, the backwardness of the country, the constraints on the people who are in a state of backwardness and poverty, weaken the political and military potential . . . [ellipsis in original] of national defense, and puts the country in danger of becoming insecure. Economic crisis can lead to social and political crisis, and lead to an internal collapse (naturally in the circumstances of the current class struggle in the world it is hard to exclude the impact coming from the outside)."[70]

The fear of falling behind and becoming an economic cripple in a competitive world was precisely the nationalist "wealth and power" concern that had worried the Club of Former Resistants and other revolutionaries. This argument was also aimed at softening the blow of severe budgetary cuts for the military, and the article discussed how the military could revise its posture in a people's war direction, which would place more reliance on militias and less on conventional forces to fulfill its defensive obligations to national security.

The diplomatic strategy that would support this new security concept was a mixture of old and new. On the one hand, it would emphasize solidarity with the socialist countries, and improved relations with China, while on the other hand Vietnam would try to improve relations with India and Third World countries, as well as ASEAN and the United States. The tensions between these objectives is evident in Linh's conclusion that Vietnam needed to maintain "Vigilance and resolve to smash the aggressive hostile plots, while at the same time firmly seeking ways to resolve disputes between nations through negotiations."[71] The language and the objectives are a combination of Cold War alignments and rhetoric, and a transition to post–Cold War diplomacy.

The following year, 1990, would invalidate many of the Cold War aspects of this formulation, and accelerate the new directions. The pace at which this transformation from old to new should occur was the subject of heated controversies in the party leadership, ultimately leading to the expulsion of one politburo member and the termination of the political career of another, Foreign Minister Nguyen Co Thach, who had been the most highly visible face of Vietnamese diplomacy for a decade.

Finding the right balance between competing objectives was also divisive. Some leaders concluded that the old world of international relations was gone for good, and that Vietnam would have to explore ways of accommodating to the new post–Cold War system. Other leaders urged vigilance against "peaceful evolution," which implied that the dominant forces in the world were still hostile to Vietnam's fundamental interests (or at least the interests of the Communist Party in Vietnam). These conservative elements wanted a balance tipped in the direction of vigilance, while the reformers were willing to accept higher risks in the pursuit of economic development.

HOW MUCH FUNDAMENTAL IDEA-CHANGE TOOK PLACE DURING THE "YEAR OF LIVING DANGEROUSLY"?

Many years after the 1989 crisis, Linh is viewed by the party leadership as the savior of Vietnamese communism, who remained steadfast in a time of crisis and kept reform within bounds, revitalizing the regime rather than destroying it. A 2005 retrospective on how Linh dealt with the advocates of moving beyond socialism describes the situation as a time when socialist countries of Eastern Europe and the Soviet Union were collapsing, "causing a big ideological and psychological shock in our people's feelings." At the same time, "imperialism tightly enveloped us with an embargo and ceaselessly put out rumors and ideological attacks in order to shake our ideological convictions."[72] Moreover, there was an internal economic crisis in Vietnam, with production shortfalls and scarcity of goods and food, and unemployment. Vietnam's factories were outmoded and inefficient and there was no "outlet" (*dau ra*) for Vietnam's goods, because the export markets of the Soviet Union and Eastern Europe had been cut off. "In this situation there emerged a rightist opportunist ideology that tried to find a way out for the economy. They said that whether something was 'socialist' or 'capitalist' didn't make any difference for commerce—whatever you wanted to call it, it was all right as long as production increased and the livelihood of the people was improved."

"Whatever you want to call it" was an echo of Deng Xiaoping's famous statement that "it doesn't matter whether a cat is black or white, as long as it catches mice." "It is not hard to see that this ideology emerged from the economic difficulties and pressures. . . . However, at that time the number of people with this outlook was only a minority and it didn't forcefully express itself, and its impact was not great."[73]

For this reason, Linh, it was asserted, did not attack his critics head-on but got his points across by face-to-face conversations or by raising issues in conferences and setting the agenda. He would indicate that it was necessary to solicit investment from capitalists and to help Vietnam get rich. You could even accept the rise and prosperity of Vietnam's entrepreneurs, the "socialist" bourgeoisie, because they were held in check by Vietnam's socialist framework. To reassure cadres about the expansion of private wealth, Linh revealingly noted, "They can become rich and have a lot of money, but at best they can only eat one chicken. Their spare money will be invested in production in goods for society, which will create more jobs and can be exported to get foreign currency."[74] Linh appears to have been confident that the heavy hand of socialism would keep these budding capitalists in check, and restrict them to "eating one chicken a day."

One of the important influences on the new thinking in Vietnam was the example of the Soviet Union, which had traditionally been viewed by the party as the Vatican of doctrinal authority—even when Vietnam went its own way with respect to specific policies. The Sino–Soviet dispute had taken its toll on the idea of doctrinal infallibility, but Vietnam's close relations with the Soviet Union in the post-1975 period had reaffirmed Moscow's salience in Vietnam's own discussions of theory and doctrine.

The central doctrinal concept of international relations shared by Vietnam and the Soviet Union had been the division of the world into two irreconcilable "camps," and the question of "who would defeat whom." There is still debate over when Vietnam abandoned these ideas, and cleared the path for "changing worlds." As noted in the previous chapter, the Vietnamese premier Pham Hung repeated the phrase "who will triumph over whom" in the National Assembly meeting of January 1987, which was held to discuss the "reform" Sixth Party Congress.

It is important to recall that Vietnam soon after decided on a very significant revision of its foreign policy in the seminal Resolution 13 in 1988, which introduced the concepts of "diversification" and "multilaterilization" of Vietnam's foreign policy. The seeds of the idea of interdependence and moving away from a polarized view of two hostile and irreconcilable "camps" were planted in Resolution 13.

One careful study of Vietnamese political rhetoric during the 1980s and early 1990s provides a useful inventory of both the broad doctrinal shifts (and the various rhetorical and polemical strategies reflected in the ideological debates of this period), and the new terminology that was introduced—much of it originating from the Soviet Union. An early Vietnamese response to the pivotal 27th Congress of the Soviet Communist Party was made by Hoang Tung, who had been editor-in-chief of the party newspaper *Nhan Dan* from 1954 to 1982. Eero Palmujoki characterizes Tung's assessment of the 27th Congress as drawing the conclusion that, "with respect to international relations the basic assumptions remained intact." However, the author asserts that, "Obviously the Soviet's own emerging lack of confidence in the formal doctrine's ability to deal with the complex questions of the future in international relations made him remove the *ai thang ai* ["who will triumph over whom"] and the three revolutionary currents from his vocabulary."[75]

As we have seen, the "who will triumph over whom" language remained prominent even after the December 1986 Sixth Congress in Vietnam (and is still used two decades later) but the significance and meaning of this belligerent term did begin to shift in 1986. The basic issue at stake was whether the international system was sharply divided into two worlds, one of which was destined by the laws of history to obliterate the other.

As Palmujoki's study of rhetoric persuasively demonstrates, there was a significant shift in Vietnam during the several years following 1986 to a more pluralistic view of the international system. Over time, the fact that Vietnam was, in fact, "changing worlds" was somewhat obscured by the adoption of the concept of a diverse and nonpolarized international system, and related concepts which attempted to situate a still coherent "socialist camp" in a more pluralistic and interdependent international system. One of these concepts was the idea of an "international order," whose rules and characteristics were not a function of ideological alignments or differences in political and economic systems. Another was the concept of international relations as a subject of study and analysis that had no explicit political or ideological framework of assumptions. (It was not until 1995 that the National University of Vietnam established an autonomous program of international relations separate from the courses in Marxism-Leninism.)

Perhaps the most important polemical device to obscure the erosion of the "two worlds" and "who will triumph over whom" was the reemphasis on a standard Marxist concept of a "transition to socialism." From 1986 on, this concept played a key role in explaining the continued adherence to the idea of an ultimate socialist triumph, in the face of disarray and the dissolution of the communist world. The idea that these are only

temporary difficulties inherent in a complex process of "transition" allows the theoreticians to avoid the awkward questions about the present and near future by an assertion
that it will all turn out right in the end, and that after the long dark night of socialist
disintegration, there will be a bright dawn of communism. We will return to this concept
in a later examination of how Vietnam's party leaders have portrayed Vietnam's place in
the world and its destiny in the twenty-first century.[76]

If Hoang Tung downplayed the implications of the 27th Soviet Party Congress in his
March 1986 article in the party's theoretical journal, an article in the next month's issue
was more explicit in moving toward new thinking in international relations. This article
was written by a prominent member of the Ministry of Foreign Affairs, Luu Van Loi.[77]
The most distinctive feature of this analysis, in the view of one specialist, was that Loi's
arguments "departed radically from the old revolutionary pragmatism, where the goals
determined the way reality was conceived. Loi's point of view was that the existing
reality should be defined before the goals are explicated."[78] This was the equivalent of
the observation cited earlier, that a time of rapid and uncertain transition, when the
"stagnant ice is melting," Vietnam must learn to "work as life demands, and not as the ice
demands."

This view reflects an advocacy of a deideologized or realist approach to international
relations and, by implication, a rejection of Marxism-Leninism as a guide to foreign
policy.[79] Palmujoki cautions that Loi's views were an "exception in cadre discourse" at the
time, but concludes that, along with the similar views expressed by Hoang Tung, they
illustrate "the extent of the doctrinal disintegration in Vietnam shortly after the Soviet
27th Party Congress."[80]

With respect to reform, the Vietnamese were insistent on using the term *doi moi*, or
renovation, rather than a more direct translation of the Soviet term *perestroika*, which is
more accurately translated as "restructuring" and, in the eyes of the Vietnamese, had the
implication of a more thoroughgoing reform, involving not only the economic system,
but the political system as well, which the Vietnamese leadership emphatically rejected.[81]

Still, the acceptance of the Soviet concept of "dependency" (as in mutual dependency—
not to be confused with "dependency theory," a staple of the Third World left) had important implications for the "two camps" doctrine and the zero-sum, "who will triumph over
whom" mentality. "Dependency" (*su tuy thuoc*) was a precursor to the concept of "interdependence" (*su tuy thuoc lan nhau*) and, ultimately, globalization.[82] As noted above, Do
Muoi's important speech on armed-forces day, December 1989, used the term *su rang buoc*
("constraining ties") as another way of characterizing interdependence and spoke of
"interdependence" as a matter of converging interests (*tuy thuoc lan nhau ve loi ich*).[83]

As Palmujoki argues, "the concept of dependency which referred to the new structure
of international relations, gave a justification for the setting of concrete aims, which were
often economically motivated. Both patterns were based on the acceptance of the fact
that dependency meant that possibilities for independent action were limited. The old
starting point, whereby the two opposing camps were independent themselves without

mutual interaction, was no longer valid. Accordingly, the new contradictions of the world have united it into a single entity."[84]

Some Vietnamese commentators resisted the implications of this, insisting that there was still an unbridgeable gap between the two sides in the Cold War, and denounced the "illusion of fishing from both sides."[85] Other international relations specialists, however, expanded on a concept borrowed from discussions of wartime strategy, using the language of "scenarios" and a power politics analysis which reflected the world as it was, without ideological contextualization. As the nature of international relations moved more toward globalization-related issues in the 1990s, this realist form of geopolitical analysis gradually disappeared, but it was another form of deideologizing international relations during the critical period of new thinking in the late 1980s and early 1990s.

The boldest example of new thinking in the diplomatic and security areas came from Foreign Minister Nguyen Co Thach. It is not surprising that Thach, who leaned toward the "scenario" format of analyzing foreign-policy and strategic issues, also adopted a realist view of what the international changes of the late 1980s meant for Vietnam, and advocated adjusting Vietnam's foreign policy on the basis of a realpolitik strategy of using regionalism to counterbalance China, which he viewed in quite traditional power-politics terms as the most dangerous threat to Vietnam. The "China threat" required an improvement of relations with ASEAN—across the divide of the "two camps."[86] This idea of regionalism was related to the concept of interdependence and the idea of joining an interdependent community across ideological lines for both security and economic reasons—a preview of Vietnam's foreign-policy evolution in the 1990s. Still, Thach's resolute opposition to normalization of relations with China ultimately contributed to his removal from office, as we shall see in the next chapter, and made "playing the ASEAN card," to balance China, less attractive to some other Vietnamese leaders.

4

Changing Partners in a Changing World (1990–1991)

ALTHOUGH THE COLLAPSE of the Soviet Union was a protracted process, it still caught the Vietnamese leaders off guard and they found it difficult to acknowledge the full implications of this pivotal event until the final demise of the communist regime. Vietnam had been heavily reliant on the USSR for both economic assistance and diplomatic support. When these evaporated in 1990–91, the party leaders had to scramble to mitigate the negative consequences.

To some extent, preparations had been made to insure against Vietnam becoming isolated, and to alleviate the negative consequences of the obvious shift in Soviet policies even before it was clear that the USSR was breaking up and the old system was doomed. Vietnam's decision in 1988 to withdraw from Cambodia was a recognition that in the shifting international environment, its existing security and diplomatic strategy would have to be significantly adjusted. Initial attempts to improve relations with China and some members of ASEAN, as well as the United States, were part of this prudent policy shift. Yet Hanoi clung to the possibility that it could still count on Moscow for some support until the finality of the collapse of the Soviet Union dashed this hope.

With its preferred patron in shambles, Vietnam's leaders turned to China as a replacement. Both the ancient past and recent history made this a difficult choice, but the alternatives seemed even worse—being set adrift in a turbulent and changing international system without a safe haven or an anchor. The US refusal to proceed toward normalization even after the Vietnamese troops had been withdrawn from Cambodia seemed to foreclose the remaining option of integrating into a US-dominated system. So Vietnam's leaders decided that their only recourse in the immediate post–Cold War period was to change partners in a changing world.

The move to restore a close relationship with China underscored what might be termed Vietnam's security dilemma in the post–Cold War period. On the one hand, without the Soviet Union as a counterbalancing superpower patron Vietnam could not afford to persist in its open defiance of its giant neighbor, China. In addition, the fact that China was the most important remaining communist country made it vital for Vietnam to preserve some elements of the old "fraternal friendship" among socialist countries in order to validate its own continued adherence to Marxism-Leninism as the central organizing principle of its political regime. But the dilemma lay in the fact that China was also the main security threat to Vietnam's both because of unresolved territorial disputes and simply because of its proximity and overwhelming size.

This security dilemma made it difficult for Vietnam to maintain a stable and long-lasting strategic relationship with China that served Vietnam's core national interests. When Vietnam had the chance to diversify its options in the mid-1990s by joining ASEAN and establishing diplomatic relations with the United States, it did so. And despite attempts in the late 1990s to revitalize strategic and ideological ties with China and shelter under the protective umbrella of the most powerful remaining communist country, a combination of Chinese reluctance and nationalist backlash in Vietnam undercut this approach. By the year 2000, Vietnam decided to "take the plunge" into deep global integration, and diversified its strategic and diplomatic options—the subject of later chapters. But initially the shock of the Soviet collapse at the end of the Cold War accelerated Vietnam's decision to normalize relations with China and had the immediate impact of temporarily postponing the decision to "change worlds" by deep integration into the rapidly globalizing post–Cold War international system.

DOWNSIZING THE "COMMUNIST WORLD" CONCEPT

It took nearly two years following the withdrawal of Vietnamese troops from Cambodia to achieve a fundamental breakthrough in the normalization of relations with China. Even then, normalization came at the expense of painful concessions for the Vietnamese, and a reluctant acknowledgment that Vietnam would have to reconcile itself to Chinese domination in the region. The compensation for this strategic setback was that Vietnam could point to China's continuing adherence to socialism as evidence that the communist world, though shrunken in size and numbers, remained a significant element of the international system. China, however, refused to play the role of the ideological centerpiece of the diminished communist world, as Vietnam urged it to do and, while maintaining close party ties, firmly kept its diplomatic and strategic relationship with Vietnam largely on a state-to-state basis even after normalization.

The setback to the once-grand visions of a communist world emerging in triumph over the capitalists was a jolt to the believers in Vietnam. It didn't help that some in the capitalist world rubbed salt into the wound by referring to the remaining remnants of the communist world (China, Vietnam, North Korea, and Cuba) as "the lonely hearts club." In October 1991, a disconcerted Vietnamese delegation attended the last congress of the Cambodian Communist Party, during which it renounced communism and switched its name to the Cambodian People's Party. Vietnam's chief ideologist, politburo member Nguyen Duc Binh, who had in past years visited Cambodia to set up a counterpart to the Vietnamese Higher Party Training Institute,[1] tried to put the best face he could on the explanation from Chea Sim, the head of the former Cambodian Communist Party and now the head of the new People's Party, which had renounced communism. Binh "expressed the firm support of the Vietnamese Communist Party for the Cambodian people's platform," as he witnessed the evaporation of the fruits of his labors when the Party Training School was rededicated as the Institute of Sociology.[2] In the visitors' section at the congress, the Vietnamese ambassador sat at the end of an empty row of seats in conspicuous isolation, until the solicitous Cuban ambassador moved next to him in a gesture of solidarity.[3] (Cuba was eventually itself forced to adjust to the new realities of the post–Cold War era, but it was not until 1995 that Fidel Castro made his first visit to China, which he had dutifully attacked for years on behalf of the by then defunct Soviet Union.)[4]

The Vietnamese leadership tried to downplay the significance of this further erosion of an already diminished socialist camp. Discussing the Cambodian reforms with a Western reporter, a "source close to the Vietnamese leadership" dismissed them as "tactical changes" in a continuing struggle within the Cambodian leadership over the extent of its commitment to socialism. Nonetheless, the fact remained that the Marxist People's Revolutionary Party of Kampuchea had changed its name to the Cambodian People's Party, while dropping all references to socialism and Marxism-Leninism and endorsing multiparty democracy as well as the market economy. Trying to put the best face on this ideological defection, the Vietnamese source said that, "Cambodia is not ready for socialism right now. To have socialism, you need to have a developed economy."[5]

With the "lonely hearts club" now reduced to four countries, party leader Do Muoi spoke out in defense of the idea of a surviving, if diminished, socialist world in October 1991. In a speech to party cadres he noted the demise of communism in the Soviet Union and Eastern Europe and admitted that, "Faced with this situation . . . some people have worried if our country could hold fast and continue to develop on the socialist path."[6] Do Muoi said that "'hostile forces are intensifying their offensive in order to suppress the remaining socialist countries'—China, Vietnam, Cuba and North Korea. 'Our people are determined to defend the revolutionary gains and will let no force destroy them,' said Muoi."[7]

Some years later, Prime Minister Vo Van Kiet pronounced a more definitive epitaph on the communist world, emphasizing that foreign and security policies would now be derived from the domestic needs and national interests of each country rather than any sense of solidarity or identity of interests based on regime type. But he also asserted that the remaining socialist countries would be targets because of their anomalous political and social systems. In a 1996 newspaper interview, Kiet said "The face of the world showed great changes after the collapse of the Soviet Union. Naturally in the case of the countries that are still led by communist parties as well as in the national capitalist countries [*nhung nuoc tu ban dan toc chu nghia*], the forces of imperialism will not leave them alone."[8]

The phrase "national capitalist countries" was an attempt to readjust traditional Marxist terminology to changing circumstances. The term "tu ban dan toc" originally referred to the class of "national bourgeoisie" in a colonial or semicolonial country whose resentment at their political subjugation to the colonial power and patriotism put them at odds with the ruling structure. Kiet was applying this term to small and medium-sized capitalist states, rather than a native capitalist class within a colonial state. The term apparently was intended to draw a distinction between large predatory capitalist states (imperialists), and non-predatory smaller capitalist states, a subtle way of indicating that it was not capitalism itself that was the threat, but imperialism—downplaying the Leninist view that imperialism was the logical outgrowth and ultimate expression of capitalism. As we will see in chapter 5, in the context of the mid-1990s this was a necessary ideological formulation in view of Vietnam's entry into ASEAN, dominated by "national capitalist" states. It also served to move away from the idea that the security strategies and foreign policies of states are derived from their political and economic systems. The further implication is that external policies no longer derive from membership in an ideologically constructed bloc, but rather the national interests of each country.

In the general environment of change following the collapse of the Soviet Union, the relations of each of the remaining socialist country would be determined by its own situation. "In these conditions," Kiet said, "bilateral and multilateral relations have a diverse character, and in the case of countries with different political regimes, all external relations are primarily dependent on the internal and external policies of each country. Precisely for this reason, although there were still four remaining socialist countries, Vietnam, China, Cuba, and the Democratic People's Republic of Korea, it is not as though these countries had similar external policies. Apart from the goal of socialism, each of these countries has different national characteristics, and even the path to socialism of each country is not completely similar."[9] At the time of the Soviet collapse, however, some Vietnamese leaders still hoped to save what they could of their ties with the remaining socialist countries, and hoped that China might constitute the core of a sort of rump socialist camp.

VIETNAM'S FAILED ATTEMPT TO SALVAGE THE REMNANTS OF SOCIALIST SOLIDARITY

Vietnam's early hopes that China would play the role of the steadfast center of a down-sized communist world were dampened when China de-emphasized the aspect of ideological solidarity at the time of formal normalization of relations between the two countries a few weeks later, in November 1991. "'For the moment, the Chinese don't want to appear too communist,' said a source close to the Vietnamese leadership. 'They don't want to give the impression that this is an ideological alliance.'"[10]

Perhaps China had also been discouraged about the prospects of leading such a reduced fragment of the once-imposing communist bloc not only by the small numbers and relative international insignificance of the fellow members of the "lonely hearts club" but also by the reluctance of some members to accept a subordinate role in such an axis. Cuba's self-importance and long-standing ties to the Soviet Union made it an unlikely camp follower. And in September, in connection with the impending visit to China of North Korea's Kim Il Song the following month, a North Korean spokesperson stated that "'We cannot apply Marxism to our country, and Marxism cannot give comprehensive scientific answers to the rapidly changed situation.'"[11]

There was another reason for China's reluctance to embrace Vietnam as an ideological soul mate; the old nationalist frictions between the two countries. In addition to the complex historical legacy, which made the Chinese reluctant to deal with Vietnam as an equal partner, the emotions of the 1979 border war were still fresh (even though it was China that had invaded Vietnam). When General Vo Nguyen Giap was sent to visit China in September 1990, as a "specially invited guest," to attend the Asian Games (a Vietnamese diplomat claims that the Chinese put out the word that it was Giap who requested the invitation as a supplicant), the famed Vietnamese general requested to meet some of his military counterparts, including General Yang Dezhi who had led the incursion into Vietnam in February 1979. "There's no way I would ever meet him," fumed Yang, "the grass on our soldiers' graves is still green."[12]

As the process of normalization progressed, it became clear that the relationship between China and Vietnam would not be primarily based on ideological solidarity, as some of Vietnam's leaders hoped, but on a partial convergence of national interests, a shared desire to avoid instability in their region in order to pursue economic development, and the stark geographical facts of sharing a border. Although Vietnam's formal normalization of relations with China in November 1991 following the collapse of communism in the Soviet Union earlier that year marked a "change of partners," China could not, and did not want to, step into the role of the ideological center of the "socialist camp" that the Soviet Union had abdicated.

This chapter will examine the Vietnamese reaction to the decline and fall of the Soviet Union in 1990 and 1991, and its efforts to achieve diplomatic normalization with China during the same period. This was accompanied by a search for an alternative to the vanished world of the once-imposing "communist bloc" by taking steps to normalize relations with some members of ASEAN and the United States, and to diversify its diplomatic and strategic options in an increasingly unipolar world, which will be the subject of the next chapter.

RECOVERING FROM THE 1989 SHOCKS: VIETNAMESE OPTIMISM TEMPERED
WITH APPREHENSION AT THE START OF THE YEAR OF THE HORSE (1990)

January 27, 1990, ushered in the Year of the Horse. A festive Tet edition of the party news-paper featured pictures of Vietnamese dancers in colorful fake traditional costumes, sharing the front page with a picture of a smiling Uncle Ho receiving a presentation of Tet flowers from an adoring, rosy cheeked, young girl. One of the few articles of substance in this otherwise feature-heavy Tet issue was by the paper's deputy editor, Bui Tin, writing under his pen name, Thanh Tin, titled "Spring colors of the current [of history]." To the outside observer, there was nothing remarkable about this article, labeled as a "reportage on current affairs by Thanh Tin." It excoriated the imperialists for their predatory behavior in the Third World, and asserted the capitalists were doomed to collapse of their own antagonistic internal contradictions.[13]

In view of the anxiety of Vietnam's "year of living dangerously" (1989), Bui Tin's article, reviewing the past year and looking forward to the new year, was exceptionally optimistic. After reciting the dangers of the imperialist threat, and the woes of the communist countries of Europe, he concluded "But on this day of spring we shouldn't be flustered and discouraged. The arrival of spring is a law of nature [*qui luat*]. Going with the flow of the people's wishes and with the laws of history, socialism will be victorious. That means genuine socialism, socialism that has not been transformed into something else [*bien dang*], socialism that is imbued with a deep sense of humanism and humanitarianism [*nhan van va nhan dao*] and socialism that has a full component of democracy. That is the profound current of human history resplendent in spring colors like the earth under-going the inevitable renewal [*doi moi*] to spring on this day."[14]

Not everyone read Bui Tin's article as an orthodox and upbeat message, however. In his memoirs, Tin writes "At the beginning of 1990, the resolution of the Eighth [Central Committee] plenum, determined that the collapse of the socialist countries in Eastern Europe was due to plots to overthrow them by imperialism and the reactionary gangs inside and outside those countries, of the CIA and the Vatican. . . . When this was published in *Nhan Dan* everyone took note of it in silence [was this the "terrifying silence" that Nguyen Van Linh had earlier noted?] . . . But when I met with them alone, most of them said that this was a subjective and nonsensical determination, that it was the people themselves in each country who had risen up to overturn the mandarinal, undemocratic, and arbitrary regimes that had gone counter to the wishes of the people. In the light of this, I wrote an article in the Tet 1990 issue of *Nhan Dan* with the title "Spring colors of the current [of history]," which observed that, 'What had to happen has happened. The people of Eastern Europe have rejected their regimes, which are lacking in democracy and social equality. They couldn't bear the injustices and poverty forever. The actual socialism of today is far from scientific socialism. . . . This article was regarded as running counter to the party central committee's resolution. Many friends among the young journalists enthusiastically approved of my observation. They shook my hand and praised me for writing the article. But when it was raised in official meetings, when people in the organization attacked me, they sat in silence and didn't approve of it or join the discussion."[15]

Bui Tin did not, of course, use such direct language in his article. But looking back on this essay in retrospect, the blunt message is certainly there. It is instructive to examine the language used at the time to make such a message politically palatable. In the guise of the orthodox political terminology of the time, a bold message was being communicated. Here is the way Bui Tin formulated his daring views: A basic requirement for the socialist countries of Eastern Europe to salvage socialism is "that each communist party has to adequately and seriously reflect on itself, and build a party with a real sense of responsibility, that is closely linked to the people, that elevates its level of intelligence to the standard of the age, strongly and resolutely reject the old bad habits and ailments [such as] being divorced from reality, the bad trait of mandarinism and lack of democracy, estranged from the people, conservative, stagnant; [they must] *lose* the bad, broken, and deformed . . . and *achieve* a genuine socialism, *achieve* a high level of democracy, *achieve* social justice, and *achieve* development." (emphasis in original)[16]

What Bui Tin was attempting to do was to employ the approved party political terminology in a new way—a kind of postmodernist deconstruction of the old ideological edifice, using the same terms but in a context that gave them a quite different meeting. None of the criticism of the Eastern European regimes used words that were not staples of party self-criticism. Even the idea of a fuller democracy was a recurrent theme of the reform period, though it meant more efficient "democratic centralism" rather than Western-style democracy. Bui Tin had introduced a somewhat different element to the debate about democracy. Rather than advocating multiparty democracy or pluralism or any of the formal trappings of "bourgeois democracy," which would have amounted to a call for the liquidation of the current regime, Tin stressed the element of accountability to the people—which had been a core element in party dogma (the party as the servant of the people) but had clearly not been the reality—as the language about "divorced from reality" and "estranged from the people" illustrates. The repetition of what the communist parties must *achieve* to save themselves was a clear assertion that in Eastern Europe (and by implication in Vietnam) self-congratulatory claims of success by the party leadership are not enough.

Perhaps even bolder was the implication in Bui Tin's article that each party was on its own, to sink or swim with its own actions and achievements. As noted earlier, by mid-decade this had become a mainstream conclusion, as the comment of Vo Van Kiet in 1996 that "in that general environment of change, the relations of each of the remaining socialist country are determined by their own policies" illustrates. In 1990, this was not a politically acceptable position, however.

Despite the Tet festiveness and Bui Tin's optimism, the great changes in the Soviet Union were deeply unsettling. Even in early 1990, the implications for a doctrinal stance based on basking in the glow of the Soviet Union were clear. Vietnam, like Eastern Europe, was on its own. This was a remarkable stance for the deputy editor of the party newspaper to assume. The editor of *Nhan Dan*, however, was too much of an organizational loyalist to back up this position. Not only was Bui Tin rebuked by his party organization (presumably *Nhan Dan*'s party committee) but Ha Dang shortly thereafter published (without clearing it at higher levels) a blistering attack written by a conservative general against Solidarity, which had just taken power in Poland through a democratic election. The result was international ridicule at Vietnam's retrograde posture and a protest from the Polish embassy. The following year, the alliance of ideological and military conservatives made another attempt to roll back the clock by publically praising the "loyal comrades in the Soviet Union" who conducted the ill-fated coup against Gorbachev and represented the last gasp of communism in Russia.[17]

SOCIALISM IS DEAD; LONG LIVE SOCIALISM! VIETNAM ATTEMPTS TO DEFINE A SOCIALIST FUTURE IN THE FACE OF WORLD WIDE SOCIALIST COLLAPSE

The party's position, reflected in mid-January 1990 by a draft of the Central Committee on "Building Socialism in the Transition Period," was also optimistic, but for more conventional ideological reasons. It was true, the draft said, that the capitalist world was looking good, and the socialist world was in disarray, but appearances are deceiving. Even though communism has collapsed in some countries, others will draw appropriate lessons from this and get socialism back on track. As for the capitalist countries, after taking a setback with the loss of colonies, they recovered as a result of taking advantage of the scientific–technological revolution. But this is only a temporary reprieve, argued the draft statement. Eventually the contradictions between the increasingly socialized forces of production and private ownership will fundamentally weaken the capitalist world.[18]

The generational gap in responding to the collapse of Eastern Europe and the Soviet Union was especially notable, considering that Vietnam was undergoing its own generational transformation in the leadership which, however, took nearly a decade more to accomplish. The historical sketch of the formation of the post–Second World War system of international relations in this document illustrates why, for the older generation of revolutionaries, it was very difficult to accept the idea that a formerly colonized country like Vietnam could have constructive relations with capitalist countries, given their history of colonial exploitation; colonialism was inextricably tied to the idea of capitalism in the minds of these revolutionaries.

One of the biggest mental leaps in the new thinking about international relations was the realization that the emerging new system of international relations might require a deep interdependence with former exploiters and adversaries—especially since this generation had been raised on the belief that the defeat of colonialism would also sound the death knell for capitalism, and the socialist world would emerge triumphant. Still the seeds of interdependence or even integration into a global market economy were already planted.

At the same time this document laid out the main political interpretation of the implications of communism's demise in Europe (in a period of transition such setbacks are inevitable, but a scientific understanding of the forces of history shows that the transition, by definition, will end up with a communist world), the party leaders saw some opportunities presented by the global market economy. "Peace, the international economy, technology transfers, cultural and information exchanges will become a general trend, and provide favorable conditions for developing countries."[19]

IN A TIME OF GREAT CHANGE WHAT IS THE MAIN THREAT?

Still reeling from the tumultuous events of 1989, the Vietnamese leadership was forced to reevaluate fundamental questions about Vietnam's approach to the outside world. Deputy Foreign Minister Tran Quang Co's extraordinary account of the debates over Vietnam's external policies in the late 1980s and early 1990s contains an invaluable synopsis of the key issues of controversy. Probably the most fundamental of these was the question of where the main threat to Vietnam lay. "There was a dispute [about whether] the danger of peaceful evolution [was] greater than the danger of falling behind economically. From this came the idea that for a nation the strength of national defense and security was the key, not the social and economic strength of each country." The relative priority of ideological orthodoxy and regime preservation versus national strengthening and economic development was the central issue, and all other questions of diplomatic strategy and security conceptions would be largely influenced by the way this question was answered.

Although conservatives demanded that regime preservation be given priority over economic development, if the main threat to Vietnam was falling behind in the race for development, then the urgent necessity was to do whatever it would take to accelerate the growth of Vietnam's economy. This was the obvious conclusion, whether the starting point was realpolitik calculations (Vietnam could not afford to let the national capabilities gap between it and its neighbors grow), neoliberal calculations (the name of the game was now economic growth and prosperity, and success in this area would be the measure of success for any leadership), or even a constructivist vantage (internally, Vietnamese nationalism would demand that Vietnam take its proper place in the world and not be considered an international "loser," and externally, successful Vietnamese diplomacy would require more cooperation and integration with the region and the world, which would best be achieved by a common commitment to a stable environment conducive to economic growth and the adoption of a "win-win" approach to relations with other countries).

The countervailing rationale was mostly based on a concern for holding steadfastly to Marxism-Leninism and the idea of an inherent antagonism between "two worlds" that was an integral part of this view. At bottom, this was a regime preservation strategy.

The Communist Party was the glue that held the regime together, and many party conservatives felt that its legitimacy would be threatened by adopting a more pragmatic, "whatever it takes" approach that would elevate economic growth to the position of the decisive factor in determining both internal and external policies.

EMERGENCE OF THE CONCEPT OF COMPREHENSIVE SECURITY AND IMPLICATIONS FOR THE ROLE OF MILITARY FORCE

The gradual acceptance of the concept of "comprehensive security"—which included every aspect of national strength, from economic, to political, to cultural, as well as the traditional military component—was forced on the leadership as the world became more complex and Vietnam's security concerns expanded from preservation of territory and sovereignty ("possession" goals) to adjusting to a globalized international system in which global and regional stability was the key to economic growth and prosperity ("milieu" goals).

For different reasons, the concept was useful to both conservatives and reformers. "Comprehensive security" could be interpreted by conservatives concerned about "peaceful evolution" as a concept that underlined the importance of political and ideological factors, as well as purely military threats. But in the lead-up to the Seventh Party Congress, some military leaders were uneasy about the possibility that the regular armed forces would be downsized to economize and divert resources to economic development. Thus there was a divergence of interest between some political conservatives, who wanted more of a "people's army," and military professionals who wanted a more elite, better trained and equipped force. "It is necessary to come up with a plan for building a regular, elite, and seasoned people's armed forces capable of simultaneously developing the quintessence of the country's traditional military art and adjusting itself to the country's existing conditions. Some comrades discussed this matter in a relatively profound fashion [and argued that] . . . decisive strength lies in the troops' ever-improving quality."[20]

What was the role of military force in the post–Cold War world for a country like Vietnam? The draft political resolution of the Seventh Congress seemed to suggest that military force was an extension of diplomacy, or a backup for unexpected contingencies, and not an end in itself. Thus the size of the armed forces would depend largely on the external threat perception, rather than being mainly a function of Vietnamese internal politics. As noted in chapter 3, Do Muoi had called in December 1989 for a military strength that was "just sufficient."[21] In addition, if the assessment of the external environment depended primarily on milieu factors that required a diplomatic or economic assessment, the traditional defense establishment might have less to say about the level of threat than if the issue was defense of Vietnamese territory. Even if regime preservation were the main goal, the best means of assuring it would not necessarily be through a large or well-equipped military establishment, since the problem would be mainly political.

A discussion of the draft statement of the Seventh Party Congress political report said, "The first question is as follows: 'Should national defence, security and foreign policy be included in the same chapter?' There are two different views here. Comrade Ngo Minh Man, deputy director of the Dong Nai Military School, and some other cadres suggested that the issue of national defense and security should be included in a separate chapter."[22] A military officer supporting the single chapter organization argued that "the inclusion of national defense, security, and foreign policy into one chapter is proof of the party's flexibility in handling national affairs in the new situation. National defense, security, and foreign policy all belong to a political system designed to fulfil a common objective, namely building and defending the Fatherland."[23]

There was a large overlap between the groups which, for purposes of simplicity, we will also call the "conservatives" and the "reformers," but at the outer edges of the policy preferences and beliefs of each group there were significant, even fundamental differences, which became clearer as the debate continued throughout most of the 1990s. In essence, the conservatives placed defense of the party and existing power structure above the strengthening the country through economic growth and "increasing friends and decreasing enemies." The title of one of Le Duan's polemical tracts of the 1970s was "This nation and socialism are one," and this conservative assertion of the identity of unchallenged party supremacy with Vietnam's supreme national interest in the post-1989 internal debates continued to reflect this view.[24] But the opposition to this "conservative" position came from a surprising quarter.

FEAR OF "FALLING BEHIND" STIMULATES A NATIONALIST CRITIQUE OF THE POLICY OF REGIME MAINTENANCE AT ALL COSTS

Both the realpolitik and the nationalist reasons for not allowing Vietnam to fall further behind converged in one important group—the former guerrilla leaders in South Vietnam who called themselves the "Club of Former Resistants." The choice of the term "club" to describe the group was meant to take advantage of the fact that while the constitution would not permit the spontaneous formation of political parties, other types of ostensibly nonpolitical associations were permitted. It also reflected their common identity as former guerrilla leaders in the South. But the term "club" was politically provocative. The Hungarian revolt of 1956 had been ignited by groups of intellectuals like the Petofi Club, as Mao pointed out on the eve of the Cultural Revolution in explaining why all heterodox opinion had to be stamped out. The lesson was that "clubs" inevitably lead to political opposition to the party.

The first issue of a clandestinely circulated paper published by this group contained a speech to the group by its director, Nguyen Ho, on December 18, 1988, at the Worker's House of Culture. Ho, who was later to become a prominent dissident and democracy advocate, said, "Previously the American imperialists thought that with half a million US troops, a million puppet troops, millions of tons of bombs and ammunition, hundreds of billions of dollars, thought they could force Vietnam to give in and the people of Vietnam to move away from the Communist Party. But the reality was that in the end the Vietnamese people defeated the Americans and won the praise of all humankind."[25]

However, argued Nguyen Ho, this was not a tale with a happy ending. "But in the last thirteen years the Americans haven't spent a dollar or a single soldier and their postwar plan for Vietnam has been realized in the following way: Vietnam hasn't advanced to socialism (rich and powerful, prosperous and happy). Vietnam is the poorest and most backward country in the world at the present." It was clear that, in the beginning at least, this was not an attack on the party but, rather, an admonition to the party to get its act together and get rid of corrupt members who were undermining its prestige and impeding Vietnam's development. "The influence and prestige of the party and socialism has seriously declined among the people and in the world. That is a great disaster for the party and the people of Vietnam. The reason for this situation is that there have been people in the leading and administrative organs of the state who have monopolized many areas of activities—especially in the economic field—and have regularly gone counter to the resolutions of the party."[26]

These veteran guerrilla leaders were distressed that, rather than becoming more respected and powerful as a result of its epic military victory, Vietnam had become more isolated and had fallen far behind its neighbors in terms of the traditional measure of national achievement set down by Asia's nineteenth- and early twentieth-century nationalist reformers—"wealth and power." Ho added that, "Defeating aggressors hundreds of times more powerful than us shows that the Vietnamese are a heroic, intelligent, creative, hard working and resilient people. Because of this there is nothing, no matter how difficult, that our people cannot do. But why in the past thirteen years [after Liberation] haven't we seen the building of a happy life for ourselves although the 'four dragons' have emerged in Southeast Asia—four 'tigers' who are strong, wealthy, and happy including Thailand, South Korea, Taiwan, and Singapore? The reason is that the leadership has committed serious errors, and these very errors have led to the pinning down of the country so it can't develop. For this reason we former resistants, the majority of whom are retired, with many years of life left, must actively contribute to the struggle for renovation and carrying out the resolution of the Sixth Congress and the Central Committee resolutions of the party. Because the mission we have pursued has not yet been completed and is only half done—we have independence but not happiness, freedom or socialism. We struggle so that deeds can match words, so that the resolutions of the party can become a vibrant reality bringing clothes and food and happiness for the people, and restoring the confidence of the people in the party and in socialism."[27]

It is noteworthy that at the time this speech was given (December 1988) the aim of these critics was to "restore the confidence of the people in the party, and in socialism." Over the next decade, some of the "former resistants" went into open opposition to the party and advocated multiparty democracy; Nguyen Ho went into open opposition to the party at the time of the pivotal Central Committee meetings of March 1990, which led to the ouster of politburo member and reformer Tran Xuan Bach. Ho was arrested later that year.

INTEGRATION OR ASSIMILATION INTO THE WORLD SYSTEM?

In addition to these disgruntled Southern guerrilla leaders, who saw the fruits of their sacrifices being squandered, many reformers saw that Vietnam would have to integrate with the post–Cold War global system in order to avoid isolation and backwardness. One obvious implication was that Vietnam would have to be more closely tied to the evolving post–Cold War international system. Initially, the advocates of closer integration in the global system used the term *hoa nhap*—"to assimilate." Eventually this was officially rejected as an acceptable term because it implied that Vietnam would be absorbed into a capitalist dominated system, and become transformed into the image of the dominant forces in the world, capitalist and democratic countries. Instead, the party ultimately decided that the appropriate term would be *hoi nhap*—"to integrate" into or join the global system but not be swallowed up and transformed by it.

Some analysts continued to use the term *hoa nhap* to refer to assimilation into an abstract historical process, like globalization which transcended human agency and is a compelling force for all governments—that is, it was not a question of submitting to the dictates of international organizations or powerful capitalist nations. An illustration of the way the two terms are employed is an article by a Vietnamese economist on Vietnam's integration (*hoi nhap*) into ASEAN. "The market economy creates a force of attraction [*suc cuon hut*] for every government. Development in isolation according to a closed door [*khep kin*] and stand-alone [*biet lap*] policy will not be able to prevail against superior technological forces [*uu the ky thuat*] and global interconnectedness [*lien ket co tinh quoc te*]. Each nation's market is merging [*hoa nhap* = being assimilated] into the regional and global markets. This is a favorable opportunity for every country to rapidly attain the preconditions for assimilation [*hoa nhap*] into the current of the global economy but, at the same time it is also a stern challenge for slow developing countries, if they don't know how to take advantage and respond flexibly and creatively to the opportunity." The cautions about *hoa nhap* are that it should mean, "Assimilation without losing control [*tu chu*], and not being passive or waiting for things to happen [*cho y lai*]. Respecting the assistance of friends but at the same time holding firm to the principles of cooperation in a spirit of self-reliance and self-strengthening, and preserving sovereignty in all aspects."[28]

In some ways the tacit alliance between the nationalist Southern guerrilla leaders, appalled at the prospect of falling behind their neighbors, and the reformers who wanted a more productive and efficient economy, reflected a convergence on a fundamental point: national interest was more important than ideology. This was the basic fault line of the post–Cold War debate on Vietnam's foreign and security policies. As Tran Quang Co summarized it, the controversy about "assembling forces" and strategic alliances centered on this issue. There was "a common view on diversifying relations. But there was still controversy over gathering forces on the basis of ideological outlook or on the basis of national interest, or while saying diversification, at the same time emphasizing ideological outlook [*y thuc he*] and the necessity of seeking strategic allies."[29] Subsequent analyses of the reasons for the collapse of the Soviet Communist Party identified "de-ideologization" as one of the key demands of the political reforms that ultimately undermined the party's authority.[30] The implication is that ideology is a necessity for maintaining party rule, whether or not it leads to effective policy—presumably because it reinforces the need for an authoritative party center, which keeps everyone on the same page.

FRIENDS, ENEMIES, AND STRATEGIC ALLIES IN THE POST–COLD WAR WORLD

The question of "strategic allies" revolved around a fundamental determination of who was a "friend" and who was an "enemy." The answer to this question depended on whether the analysis rested on a realpolitik foundation, or was premised on ideological assumptions. The realpolitik answer took a more negative view of China and more positive view of the United States and noncommunist countries, while the ideological view led to the reverse conclusion.

As Vietnam's overall foreign policy was undergoing a sweeping reevaluation in the spring of 1990, some Vietnamese asked, "Why were the other countries in the region worried about China, while Vietnam placed its hopes on China (as a strategic ally)?"; "Was the expansionist hegemonistic face of China the main one, or was it socialism?"; "What was the real nature of 'socialism with Chinese characteristics'?" The "big question" underlying these issues was whether the main threat to Vietnam was falling behind economically or peaceful evolution, and, consequently, how Vietnam should define its relations with China—was it a "strategic" or a "special relationship"?[31] These questions, in turn, led to an equally fundamental issue: "Is concentrating on economic development the only way or the most effective way to reinforce stability and escape from the social and economic crisis in the country and raise the international status of our country, and cope with 'peaceful evolution'? Have we given a high enough priority to economic development?"[32]

For both those with primarily strategic concerns and those advocating giving priority to economic development, expanding relations with China was a priority. By mid-1991, it was clear that the drying up of aid and markets in the Soviet Union and Eastern Europe would necessitate a reorientation of Vietnam's foreign economic policy. Even reformers and advocates of diversifying Vietnam's external relations saw expanding economic relations with China as a vital part of compensating for what had been lost. In August 1991,

Vo Van Kiet responded to a question about Vietnam's economic ties with China by stating that, "In the past few years the volume of merchandise exchanged between China and Vietnam has been rather large. The three provinces of China that share a border with us have a total of 200 million people. This is a big market, and has the potential for beneficial mutual exchange that will be critical for both sides. This market can compensate for the recent shrinking of the Soviet and Eastern European markets."[33]

Despite the convergence between economic reformers and conservatives advocating closer ideological and strategic ties with China on the issue of expanding trade relations, there were important differences about the overall nature of the relationship between Vietnam and China. Some conservatives wanted to focus external economic ties to China insofar as possible for fear of being assimilated into the capitalist orbit through economic dependency, and the forces it would unleash within Vietnam for the kind of sweeping reform that the conservatives feared. The danger, of course, was exchanging one risk of dependency for another.

POLITICAL REFORM ALONG WITH ECONOMIC REFORM?

The balance of political power among the advocates of these differing positions began to tilt in early 1990. Tran Xuan Bach was elected to the politburo at the Sixth Party Congress in 1986 and, the following year, assigned by the politburo to read foreign news and digest it for them—serving as a kind of filter through which what was going on in the world outside Vietnam would be screened.[34] Although he was initially a protégé of Nguyen Van Linh (and some observers felt he was being groomed as Linh's successor) Bach became known to foreign journalists as "Vietnam's Boris Yeltsin"[35]—which turned out not to be a career-enhancing label, as the Vietnamese leadership became alarmed about the course of Soviet politics in late 1989 and early 1990.

Bach started the year 1990 by participating in what Radio Vietnam termed a "frank and open-minded debate" about reform issues with leading party members in Hanoi and the Hanoi party committee.[36] The main issue was the relationship between political and economic reform.[37] This must have appeared to his politburo colleagues as an attempt to build up an independent political base of support right in the national capital. The implicit call for political liberalization to support the economic reforms put Bach far apart from most of his fellow politburo members. It probably did not come as a surprise to party insiders that Bach was thrown out of the politburo and stripped of his party positions at the next Central Committee meeting in March 1990, "for having seriously violated the party's organizational principles and discipline, leading to many bad consequences."[38]

According to the official party spokesperson, the central policy issue in question at this very contentious meeting was whether economic or political reform was the main priority. But Bach's main political transgression seems to have been his public maneuvering and self-promotion and open calls for democratization. A Western news account of this meeting recapitulates this meeting: "At the end of an unusually lengthy 2½-week Central Committee meeting—called in part to formulate a Vietnamese response to the changes underway throughout the socialist world—Hanoi's Communist rulers seemed to reject recent calls for accelerated political reform while reaffirming their commitment to continue a three-year-old policy of economic liberalization. . . . as for political reform, the communiqué said, 'political stability is the most important thing.'"[39]

The *Washington Post*'s Kenneth Richburg reported that Major General Tran Cong Man described the Central Committee meetings as "extremely vigorous, suggesting sharp differences over such questions as, Should we give priority to economic renovation or political renovation?" while other sources indicated that Bach was purged as much for egotistic grandstanding as for his policy positions The harsh retribution against Bach was considered by some Vietnamese insiders as a temporary overreaction to the events in Eastern Europe, which "could soften once the initial shock wears off."[40] Explaining why Bach was removed, Tran Bach Dang, a former Southern guerrilla leader and adviser to Nguyen Van Linh, who had himself incurred the party's displeasure more than once in his own career, said, "His way of reform would have led to demonstrations and strikes, but without giving the people enough to eat."[41]

LESS THAN TWO WORLDS BUT MORE THAN ONE WORLD: IS THERE A FUTURE FOR COMMUNIST STATES IN A SINGLE, PLURALISTIC WORLD SYSTEM?

At a Vietnamese–Soviet symposium in February 1990 on the role of the Communist Party, the leading Soviet ideologist R. G. Yanovsky asserted that there were fundamental similarities between the challenges faced by the Soviet Union and Vietnam, despite their different levels of development and different circumstances, implying that Vietnam should follow the Soviet path of reform. Of course, he noted, there were distinctive aspects of reform in both countries, but the key was to recognize the diversity and pluralism of the socialist world. Each country would have to find its own form of communism. Moreover, said Yanovsky, successful reform in the Soviet Union would not only benefit its own people but "create new possibilities for strengthening the contributions of socialism to the development of the world, with a reciprocal impact among all countries and peoples [*tac dong lan nhau giua tat ca cac nha nuoc va dan toc*]."[42]

This formulation implied that there was more than simply a loss of cohesion in a "pluralistic" socialist camp. Yanovsky's further implication, that there is a single pluralistic world system to which the communist countries can "contribute," rather than a clear communist alternative which will eventually emerge victorious over the "other world," seems to have irritated Vietnam's chief ideologist Nguyen Duc Binh (who played a prominent role at the symposium and was singled out by Yanovsky for presenting a forceful argument that Vietnam's *doi moi* the correct path of reform and was bound to succeed).[43]

Nguyen Duc Binh responded in the party newspaper, arguing that *doi moi* is absolutely essential, but it is equally important to keep it from leading to demands for bourgeois democracy. He explicitly acknowledged the party's mistakes in the economic domain, and endorsed the people's right to engage in "fence breaking" and defying party policy, because it threatened their livelihood. But, in an implied rebuke to the Soviet approach, it was crucial to maintain absolute party control when it came to political matters, stating that "we cannot fail to be dictatorial with regard to the enemies of the people. Even in a number of fraternal socialist countries, when carrying out democracy and glasnost [*cong khai*, a specific reference to the Soviet Union], we can clearly see that out there in society there are elements who are estranged from the regime [*xa la voi che do*], to say nothing of political opportunists who are scheming to use democracy and glasnost to attack the party in order to carry out devious plans that are contrary to the interests of the people. If you are not dictatorial with these enemies of the people, the very democracy of the people cannot be guaranteed."[44]

Nguyen Duc Binh defiantly attempted to invoke the immutability of a world divided into irreconcilable blocs just at the time it was dissolving. According to one account of this speech, Binh "made strong arguments to support his view that the world is now divided into two confronting camps." He was quoted as saying that "In my opinion, the key conflict in the world today is between the bellicose policy of empirical [*sic*] hegemony from the US, and other forces committed to fighting against world domination to preserve national sovereignty, independence, democracy, peace, equality, and human dignity." Binh would continue to pursue the idea of two hostile worlds into the next century, and he was certainly not alone among the old guard conservatives in this.[45]

THE END OF THE SOVIET UNION

One of the last official statements of solidarity with the Soviet Union and confidence in its future came a few weeks before the internal shakeup resulting in Tran Xuan Bach's ouster. The fifteenth meeting of the Vietnam–Soviet Interministerial Council on Science and Technology convened in Ho Chi Minh City on March 6, 1990, with Foreign Minister Thach, now also a vice-premier, heading the delegation. News reports said the Soviet representative expressed his country's continuing strong support for Vietnam, but the Soviet cutbacks in their foreign aid programs was also mentioned, and the theme of conference seems to have been making Soviet aid "more efficient," which suggests the problem was better management of a declining amount of aid.

A *Nhan Dan* communiqué said that Premier Do Muoi and Soviet Vice-Premier Gusev "affirmed the determination of the two countries to develop and elevate even higher the cooperation in every field, consistent with the *doi moi* policy line of the Vietnamese

Communist Party and the renovation [*cai to*, the term used to translate "perestroika"] policy of the Communist Party of the Soviet Union, aimed at bringing new strength to socialism in all [socialist] countries [*dem lai suc manh moi cho chu nghia xa hoi o moi nuoc*], contributing to the strengthening of peace, security, and cooperation in Asia-Pacific and the world."[46] This appears to have been the last such meeting until 1994, after Russia agreed (in 1993) to assume the commitments made to Vietnam by the former Soviet Union (but it presumably was cautious in extending new commitments).

Nguyen Van Linh granted a press interview to Mainichi Shimbun in April 1990, the first granted by Vietnam's top leader to a noncommunist foreign journalist since the events of 1989. Responding to a question about the big changes going on in the Soviet Union, the major source of economic aid for Vietnam, Linh replied: "Every country has to solve its own problems in its own way. By doing this, it will be able to get past the tensions and challenges, and will certainly be able to gain final victory." The Mainichi report (reprinted on the front page of *Nhan Dan*) said "This [comment] shows us that he [Linh] stressed the role of 'national self determination' in resolving the dangers." With respect to Soviet support, Linh said "The Soviet Union is still oriented toward the goal of building socialism and carrying out perestroika [*cai to*] under the leadership of the Communist Party." In a lukewarm endorsement of the ties with the Soviet Union, Linh said, "We have no reason not to have good relations with the Soviet Union—on the contrary we must strengthen this friendly relationship." On the question of the reduction in Soviet aid, Linh commented, "This will certainly have an impact. But we have great understanding toward the Soviet Union, which is encountering economic difficulties. We will encounter more difficulties, and will have to become more self sufficient in order to get through this."[47]

But by June 1990, the uncertainty and paranoia in Vietnam had intensified. Western journalists reported that "Worry about domestic economic turmoil and the global crisis of communism is causing authorities to get even tougher with dissidents and people they don't trust," including the suppression of the Club of Former Resistance Fighters and detention or expulsion of a small number of foreigners. These reports maintained that conservatives had gained the upper hand, and that the political concern over events in the communist world was having a negative impact on Vietnam's economic reforms, "'There is a tremendous sense of insecurity' in top party ranks, said a source with access to many officials. 'There is a tightening up, and everybody is more cautious and afraid to say anything. They don't acknowledge it, but you can see it in their faces.'"[48]

Bui Tin tells us that in July 1990, a few months after the contentious party plenum in March, the Vietnamese leaders became alarmed at the critical reevaluation of Stalin in the Soviet Union, and issued an order forbidding the Vietnamese media to make any reference to Stalin. The fact that Stalin suddenly became a nonsubject while the topic was vigorously debated in the Soviet Union underlined the parting of the ways between Vietnam and the Russian link to historical communism, including the more positive chapters, such as the fight against fascism. Older Vietnamese revolutionaries had been trained to view Stalin with reverence, and even children in the DRV were taught that it was Stalin who had put food on their table and brought smiles to their faces. Vietnam's official poet laureate, politburo member To Huu, was famous (or infamous) for his embarrassingly overdone paeans to Stalin.[49] Tran Xuan Bach, the expelled politburo member who had evidently undergone a fundamental ideological conversion, had raised the hackles of his politburo colleagues in early 1990 by lumping Stalin together with Mao and Pol Pot.

With the historical roots of the party's ties to the Soviet Union now a delicate subject, and the increasing uneasiness of the Vietnamese leaders with Gorbachev, Marxism-Leninism in Vietnam was faced with the challenge of having to redefine itself. Since the Soviet Union itself was headed for what Marx once termed "the dustbin of history," it clearly could not serve as a model of the march toward communism and a concrete illustration of what the Vietnamese theoreticians had always called the "absolute superiority" (*tinh hon han*) of socialism. The solution for this problem, still in process long after the collapse of the Soviet Union, is to universalize the analysis and message, and point to the imagined wonderful future offered by Marxism-Leninism, while noting that it is not surprising that such a vision is difficult to achieve, and that there have been stumbles and reverses along the way. We shall return to this point in the final chapter.

REMOVING THE PRIMARY OBSTACLE TO NORMALIZATION WITH CHINA AND ESCAPING VIETNAM'S DIPLOMATIC ISOLATION: THE CAMBODIAN END GAME

We have examined the internal reforms which the 1986 Sixth Party Congress set in motion, but we should also recall the foreign-policy aspect of this pivotal political event—especially with respect to Vietnam's relations with the Soviet Union. Tran Quang Co, who was appointed deputy foreign minister with special responsibility for resolving the Cambodian question right after the Sixth Party Congress, made the observation about the Sixth Party Congress that there was a close connection between new thinking in domestic reforms and new thinking in external relations. However, the analysis of the implications for Vietnam's occupation of Cambodia stressed adapting to external geopolitical shifts more than extending the logic of Vietnam's internal reforms to the foreign policy sphere. Co wrote that, "The Sixth Congress unfolded in the context of a tendency toward consolidating peace in the developing world, and the big countries going deeply into an accommodating [*hoa hoan*] relationship of each pair, the US–USSR, the US and China, and the USSR and China. The most direct and powerful influence on the Cambodian question and Vietnam was the accommodation between the Soviet Union and China."[50]

"It wasn't accidental," wrote Co, " that Resolution 32/BCT21 of July 9, 1986, which declared that it was necessary to have a political solution for the Cambodian question and move toward normalization of relations with China . . . came into being right before

Gorbachev's Vladivostok speech (July 28 1986)."[51] In this speech, Gorbachev announced the removal of the "three obstacles" to better relations with China; withdrawing from Afghanistan, terminating clashes along the Sino-Russian border, and resolving the Cambodian question.

At the time, it was felt that Vietnam could extricate itself from Cambodia but maintain a friendly regime in power and predominant influence in its backyard with "special relationships" with Cambodia and Laos ("a solution for the Cambodian question must hold fast to the accomplishments of the Cambodian revolution, hold fast to the unity of the three countries of Indochina"). This "special relationship" policy of trying to maintain influence in Cambodia indirectly through a client regime came into being right before Gorbachev's Vladivostok speech. In that speech, Gorbachev announced that "The Cambodian question cannot be settled in far-off capitals, including the United Nations, but must be settled between Vietnam and China, the two neighboring socialist countries."[52] The withdrawal of Soviet support from Vietnam's claim to predominant influence in Indochina and disengagement from the diplomacy of the Cambodian settlement doomed the idea of a painless withdrawal from Cambodia by placing China in a decisive diplomatic role.

Vietnam was thus put on notice that the Soviet Union would no longer play the role of superpower patron, and that Vietnam should think about making its own accommodation with China. It was also an implied Soviet recognition that Vietnam fell within China's sphere of influence. But Gorbachev also noted that there were ideological as well as realpolitik factors at work in this situation; China and Vietnam were "neighboring socialist countries."

Following the December 1989 Malta summit between Gorbachev and George H. W. Bush that essentially amounted to a declaration that the Cold War was over, the Soviet Union sent an emissary to explain the situation to Vietnam's leaders. Vietnamese reports of this summer reveal that Vietnam was a distant and powerless observer to this pivotal development, which would eventually radically change its calculations about the nature of the global system. "Comrade Do Muoi thanked the Soviet leadership for keeping him informed of this important political event," said an official Vietnamese commentary, Do Muoi repeated the Soviet position that this was a great step toward world peace, but the commentary was silent on the larger implications of this event.[53] This was among the last occasions on which Vietnam would dutifully endorse the latest twist of Soviet global policy, for it was now clear that the Cold War came was coming to a close and Vietnam was losing a patron—and possibly a partner as well.

Presumably the Vietnamese had their own sources of information and had picked up on the panic and confusion at the top levels of the Soviet leadership that had led them to make a deal on the key issues of the Cold War in Europe—German unification and independence in Eastern Europe. An authoritative account of the Malta summit relates that a

Soviet official said, "Gorbachev and [foreign minister] Shevardnadze 'had a very keen feeling that we had to accomplish a huge maneuver without losing time. We felt the Soviet Union was in freefall, that our superpower status would go up in smoke unless it was reaffirmed by the Americans.'"[54] Gorbachev told Bush "we don't consider you an enemy anymore."[55]

As a result of the Soviet change of policy, Vietnam had to face reality. "Also in the period from 1986 to 1988 the economic and social crisis in our country reached a high plateau. In the face of the urgent requirements of the international and domestic situations, our party decided that in the area of external affairs we would shift to a new phase of new struggle and peaceful coexistence with China, ASEAN, and the US, in order to rapidly rebuild our economy and develop in peace. The period of struggle aimed at a total victory of the Cambodian revolution, under the illusion that the 'situation is irreversible,' had come to an end, and we had to acknowledge the reality of a step-by-step struggle to achieve a political solution for the Cambodian question."[56]

In Tran Quang Co's realpolitik view, the Cambodian situation would be decided by the great powers, not the regional actors (Vietnam and ASEAN) or the contending parties within Cambodia. The Soviet retreat from its own backyard of Eastern Europe did not suggest that the Soviets would give Vietnam much support in Cambodia, and the Soviets had been pressuring Vietnam to withdraw since Gorbachev's Vladivostok speech of 1986. In Co's analysis, "on the surface it looked like the factions in Cambodia and the neighboring countries would play the key role in deciding the Cambodian question because they were the parties whose interests were most closely involved [*co loi ich sat suon*]. But if you examine it carefully, then you will see that the big powers will play the decisive role. In researching a solution, we naturally had to concentrate on the factors that directly affected the third tier [the contending factions in Cambodia], but we couldn't possibly overlook tremors of change [*dong thai*] among the countries in the first tier, the strategies of the big countries, the US, the Soviet Union and, especially China. In our view, China, unlike the Soviet Union and America, constantly changed its strategy"[57] Considering Gorbachev's post-Vladivostok turnabout in policy toward China and Asia, this is a remarkable statement.

REALISM, NATIONAL INTEREST, AND IDEOLOGY IN VIETNAM'S ADJUSTMENT TO THE NEW STRATEGIC SITUATION

Along with Foreign Minister Thach, Tran Quang Co saw the necessity of using a national-interest model in analyzing the impending problems for Vietnam's diplomacy and national security. This was entirely consonant with the nationalist traditions of Vietnam, but ran counter to the political interests of some of Vietnam's top party leaders, who were mainly concerned about the ideological aspects of diplomatic alignments and the implications for maintaining an image of solidarity among communist countries and infallibility of the party leadership. This group essentially wanted to shift to an alignment with China if the Soviet connection were threatened, because this would at least preserve the ideological construct of two antagonistic worlds, and preserve the viability of Vietnam's communist regime.

The idea of pursuing a kind of Bismarckian diplomacy of maneuver was raised by Thach after the Sixth Party Congress and the recognition that the Soviet Union would not longer be a guarantor of Vietnam's international interests. Tran Quang Co states that at a "heated" politburo meeting on April 14, 1987, Thach rejected the view that the Cambodian issue could be resolved only by making a bilateral deal with China, and recommended instead a policy of diplomatic maneuver involving the United States and the Soviet Union along with China. "[I]f we only lock horns along one path with China, that is not correct," said Thach.[58]

Tran Quang Co recalled that, "I personally deeply reflected on that idea. For a long time I often felt that we were in a somewhat dependent position with the big brother Soviet Union and the second son China both in thought and in action, so that we had self imposed restrictions on our foreign policy actions in the world and in Southeast Asia." But, though noting this dependency which constrained Vietnam's freedom of maneuver on Cambodia, Co evidently did not see a way out of the impasse as long as Vietnam's diplomacy was confined to its relations with the great communist powers. If Vietnam remained isolated from the noncommunist world and "if we only looked at China, and if China saw that we were weak and isolated, they would take a hard line with us. Precisely for this reason, China had forced us to make one concession after another." The Soviet Union could not be of much help. "On the other side, Gorbachev, because of his big-power interest, whether intentionally or not, had pushed Vietnam into the box of 'having to resolve the Cambodian question with China.'"[59] The implication of this analysis was that Vietnam would have to diversify its relations with the noncommunist world in order to extricate itself from the "box" of asymmetrical dependency on China, so aptly depicted by Brantly Womack.[60] Although Co's analysis pinpointed the problem, it would take another half a decade to devise a strategy based on the implications of the need to diversify external relations and carry it out.

When the events of 1989 occurred, there was spirited debate within the Central Committee and the politburo about what the implications were for Vietnam's relations with the Soviet Union and China. After the Tian An Men Square incident in June 1989, a favorite line among some top Vietnamese leaders was "however expansionist China may be, it is still a socialist country." In other words, the ideological support to help sustain communism in Vietnam was more important than the conflicts of national interest, an indication of how deeply unsettling the possibility of the unraveling of communism spreading to China was to the Vietnamese party leaders, who undoubtedly knew that if communism collapsed in China, it would be very difficult for it to survive in Vietnam.

THE "RED SOLUTION": RESTORING IDEOLOGICAL
SOLIDARITY WITH CHINA?

Tran Quang Co and his Foreign Ministry colleagues debated at length over whether the key aspect of China was its "expansionist hegemonism" or the fact that it was evidently holding firm to its identity as a communist regime. Prior to 1989 the Vietnamese leadership seemed to have a consensus on the conclusion that China did not share common interests with Vietnam or any other socialist country in defending socialism against imperialism. "China proclaims that it is protecting socialism, but it never proclaims that is defending socialism in [the socialist] countries of the world. This means that China is only protecting the socialism and hegemonism of China."[61]

This consensus shattered in the turmoil of 1989. According to Tran Quang Co, in the 1989 crisis of socialism "in a number of branches of party central and even in the politburo there arose different views about how to evaluate Tian An Men as well as the situations in the Soviet Union and Eastern Europe. At this time the favored line was 'however expansionist it may be, China is still a socialist country.'"[62]

Tran Quang Co and the Foreign Ministry challenged the prevalent view that China's determination to remain a communist country should be the determining element in Vietnam's relations with it, on the grounds that China itself based its policies on transient calculations of national interest, and not on ideological or political solidarity. "In our view: China at present has two faces, a socialist face and a hegemonistic expansionist face. Its socialist nature is most clearly demonstrated in its internal policies and economic structures. But the foreign-policy line of China still retained its traditional expansionist hegemonist nature. The unchanging aspect of China is its hegemonism. But what China uses as a tool to achieve this policy is the 'ten thousand changes' [e.g., tactical flexibility in pursuing an unchanging objective in periods of change and transition—a reference to the Chinese maxim, borrowed by Ho Chi Minh as the doctrinal cornerstone of Vietnamese diplomacy 'from an unchanging stance, respond to ten thousand changes' (*di bat bien, ung van bien*)]. Depending on their own interests at any given time, a given country might become China's friend or its enemy."[63]

The term used to suggest slippery and unprincipled deceit on China's part is, when applied by the Vietnamese to themselves, always viewed in a positive light. The venerable phrase "respond to ten thousand changes" had always been the justification for tactical flexibility in Vietnamese revolutionary strategy—but always in the context of unrelenting adherence to long-term strategic objectives—and was a useful concept, sanctioned both by tradition and famously used by Ho Chi Minh, to provide cover for specific policy shifts. But it could also serve as a rationale for changing the entire conceptual basis of thinking about foreign policy. The term could suggest a realist, nonideological approach to international relations. A top theoretician of the party ideological journal traced the concept back to key turning points in modern Vietnamese history, like the August 1945 revolution, and asserted that "The concept 'from an unchanging stance, respond to ten thousand changes' is the foundation of the new style methodology of creative thinking."[64]

Needless to say, the main focus in applying this concept has been on clever tactical moves to divide and confuse an enemy, but it has also served to pave the way for a less ideological approach toward foreign policy. The same author wrote, in another context, "When moving into a new stage, as Lenin warned, the strong points of yesterday cannot possibly persist into the present." Thus, "On the basis of 'from an unchanging stance, respond to ten thousand changes,' the party must find its own path, consistent with the reality of the country. This path manifests faithfulness to the past, but isn't bound by the past."[65]

At the time of the collapse of the Soviet Union, this break with the immediate past was not easy, however. The animosities stirred up by Vietnam's post-1975 conflict with China were a serious obstacle to rapprochement, as were the inevitably humiliating terms that China imposed as the cost of restoring normal relations. Emphasizing the communist ideology that the two leaderships shared would help disguise the painful power disparities which were the real basis of the rapprochement, possibly provide some deterrent to China's leadership in pushing Vietnam around (a violation of socialist "solidarity"), and have the significant benefit of validating Vietnam's beleaguered communist regime by the survival of a major communist state.

The issue of building a relationship with China on the basis of ideological solidarity or maintaining a more cautious and distant stance based on the conflicting national interests split the Vietnamese leadership at the highest level, as Tran Quang Co's account attests. Nguyen Van Linh and others wanted to sound out China on the possibility of a "red solution" in Cambodia, based on a coalition of the rival communist groups, which would cut out Prince Sihanouk and the noncommunist groups. This would be an appeal to China to acknowledge that the ideological interests it shared with Vietnam should override the conflicts in national interest.

On June 5, 1990, Vietnam's party leader, Nguyen Van Linh, invited the Chinese ambassador in Hanoi to the state guest house to "have an intimate talk to show a respectful attitude." Linh made an acknowledgement of past mistakes in Vietnam's relations with China, evidently to satisfy Deng Xiaoping's criticisms of what he viewed as Vietnamese ingratitude and insolence. Anticipating the arrival of a Chinese envoy to discuss improving bilateral relations, Linh stressed that his agenda was to "discuss matters relating to socialism" because "the imperialists are plotting to exterminate socialism . . . they are plotting peaceful evolution." Although Linh labeled the Soviet Union "the bulwark of socialism" it was "encountering a lot of issues." Linh expressed his willingness to go to China to meet with its leaders, "to restore friendly relations. You comrades have only to say the word and I will come . . . China needs to raise the flag of socialism high and resolutely defend Marxism-Leninism." With regard to Cambodia, "brother Linh put forward the idea of the 'red solution' to settle it. 'There is no reason why communists can't talk with each other,' they meet with Sihanouk, to say nothing of meeting with each other."[66]

As noted earlier, China was not enthusiastic about relating to Vietnam on an ideological plane. In the case of Cambodia, it would involve accepting Vietnam's client, the Hun Sen regime (which renounced its communist identity the following year), as well as treating Vietnam with a greater degree of parity as an ideological soul mate. China was more interested in achieving its diplomatic objectives (and saw a leading role for the distinctly non-communist but anti-Vietnam and pro-China Prince Sihanouk, who the Vietnamese were trying to exclude from power) than in assisting Vietnam in bolstering its internal and external political position on such nebulous grounds as "defending socialism." Because of its size and influence, China was confident that its regime would survive under any circumstances, while Vietnam's party leaders felt much more vulnerable.

Deputy Foreign Minister Tran Quang Co conducted the negotiations with the Chinese deputy foreign minister. His account of this period reveals the deep splits within the Vietnamese leadership on how to deal with China. Co was strongly opposed to the "red solution" in Cambodia because it would legitimize Pol Pot and the Khmer Rouge. The problem was that party leader Nguyen Van Linh had already raised this possibility with the Chinese and showed his hand. General Le Duc Anh subsequently called Co to tell him not to raise the issue of the "red solution" unless the Chinese did, on the grounds that it was premature to envision the reconciliation of the two rival Cambodian sides and that if the Vietnamese concession on including the Khmer Rouge in a solution leaked it would be damaging to Vietnam.

Foreign Minister Thach discovered from Co's debriefing on the first round of talks that he had followed the military's instructions. Thach emphatically opposed the "red solution" but was furious that Co had taken instructions from the military. "Whose ideas are you going to listen to?" asked Thach, "The minister of defense or the minister of foreign affairs?" Co replied that as a cadre of the Foreign Ministry, he would follow the minister of foreign affairs, but with the additional understanding that Thach was speaking as a member of the politburo. At this juncture, Co realized that there were serious divisions among the top Vietnamese leadership. "At the time I was truly stunned by the reaction of brother Thach but, at the same time, I could also sense that the signs of division in the politburo were quite deep."[67]

Co recounts that the Chinese negotiator took full advantage of the serious splits among the Vietnamese leadership, and constantly reminded him of Nguyen Van Linh's views, with a not so subtle reminder that the Chinese were sure that the Vietnamese negotiators would not go against the wishes of their leader.[68] (Henry Kissinger would no doubt be pleased that Le Duc Tho's tactic in the Paris negotiations on Vietnam of reading newspaper accounts of political divisions over the war in America, which Kissinger found aggravating, was now being used against the Vietnamese.)

After the first round of negotiations with the Chinese, Tran Quang Co made his report to the politburo. "As the person directly negotiating with China, I presented the Foreign Ministry's report to the politburo, which included an evaluation of the devious aims [*y do*] that China wanted to achieve in this negotiation. The devious aim [*y do*] of China with respect to relations with Vietnam concerning the Cambodian issue has been clearly revealed over the course of these meetings. China's strategy is to place highest priority on the struggle to win over the US and the Europeans and ASEAN to serve their goal of the 'four modernizations.' Their policy toward Vietnam, and also toward the Soviet Union and other countries has to serve this highest interest, and not cause the slightest negative influence on China's relations with the US, the Europeans, and ASEAN. Precisely for this reason, China is not responding to the proposals of General Secretary Nguyen Van Linh and Le Duc Anh to the Chinese ambassador prior to the negotiations."[69]

Co's analysis of the reasons for China's diffidence in responding to Vietnam's attempt to move the relationship onto a political footing, by stressing the shared interest in salvaging what was left of communism, is a masterpiece of realism. He noted that China didn't respond to the Vietnamese proposals made by Linh because they had concluded that Vietnam had been weakened by the situation in the Soviet Union and Eastern Europe, as well as by Vietnam's own overblown (in China's estimation) fear of peaceful evolution. "Because of this they used our strong desire [*khat khao*] to cooperate with China to pressure us in the negotiations." In addition, China "unceasingly passed on information about its activities in the Paracel and Spratly islands with the intent of both pressuring us and reassuring the US and ASEAN that there is nothing to worry about in the relations between China and Vietnam, and that this relationship is of no more concern than China's relations with other Southeast Asian countries."[70] Of course, the Chinese were not mistaken when they saw Vietnam's concerns about the collapse of communism as an exploitable vulnerability.

Vietnam's diplomats noted that as far as their interests were concerned the world was changing. The old ideological divide was being erased by a confluence of interests among the major powers, including the United States, along with the Soviet Union and China. This was evidenced by the tendency to resolve matters relating to Cambodia within the framework of the permanent members of the UN Security Council. On top of this, US secretary of state James Baker indicated in August that he would be willing to discuss a Cambodian solution with Vietnam's representative to the UN.

These developments raised fundamental questions for Vietnam in understanding the nature of the international system in which its diplomacy was conducted. And, at the same time Vietnam had the rug pulled out from its diplomacy by a changing Soviet Union, it was also forced to recognize that its own interests were increasingly diverging from those of its (still) communist protégés in Phnom Penh.

THE END OF ILLUSIONS: VIETNAM SETTLES FOR ACCOMMODATION WITH CHINA RATHER THAN PARTNERSHIP OR POLITICAL SOLIDARITY

During the summer of 1990, the changes set in motion by the events of the previous year began to alter the dynamics of international diplomacy. Tran Quang Co's account of the crucial phase in the normalization of Vietnam–China relations amply illustrates this transformation. As the politburo continued to debate whether to try to cut a deal with China based on common ideology (the "red solution") or engage in the more unpredictable diplomacy of the United Nations, which would also involve the United States and ASEAN. Co consulted the venerable Pham Van Dong, now an "adviser" to the top leadership. Dong told Co in early August 1990, "We must dare to play the game with the UN and the Security Council, with the US and the Europeans. We need to utilize the American factor in the new situation. . . . The plan is very good in theory, but the key is how to implement it. . . . We shouldn't put forth demands that are too great [such as] 'holding firm to the results of the (Cambodian) revolution.' If our friends could get 50% in a general election, that would be ideal."[71]

Not long after this conversation, China issued a surprise urgent invitation to Premier Do Muoi (soon to replace Nguyen Van Linh as party general secretary) and Pham Van Dong to meet in remote Chengdu (the Chinese said this was necessary to preserve secrecy) to engage in an effort to resolve the Cambodian problem and achieve a breakthrough in normalizing relations between China and Vietnam. This came as a surprise, because China up until then had adamantly insisted that the Cambodian question would have to be resolved to its satisfaction before it would negotiate the normalization.

Tran Quang Co's analysis was that China now had to change its position because its top priority, economic development, had been impeded by the sanctions imposed after Tian An Men. Accelerated diplomacy by other parties (including the United States, Japan, and ASEAN) and the elimination of the major factor that had unified the position of China and ASEAN (the Vietnamese occupation of Cambodia), along with growing ASEAN concerns about China's intentions in the region, was threatening China's ability to control the outcome of the Cambodian settlement—hence the incentive to quickly cut a deal with Vietnam.

Nguyen Van Linh and Pham Van Dong led a Vietnamese delegation to meet with the Chinese in Chengdu in early September 1990, which, significantly, did not include Foreign Minister Nguyen Co Thach, whom Beijing considered excessively anti-Chinese. In politburo meetings Thach had expressed his opposition to both the "red solution" in Cambodia and betting all Hanoi's diplomatic cards on a presumed shared interest between Vietnam and China in joining forces to "save socialism," as Nguyen Van Linh and some other politburo leaders advocated. Thach's position had been weakened by his failure to demonstrate any results by playing the "American card." In the end, the party leadership decided to throw the stridently anti-Chinese Thach overboard to appease Beijing.

Despite vague Chinese indications that Deng Xiaoping would attend the Chengdu meetings (which persuaded Pham Van Dong to attend and add his seniority and prestige to the occasion), Deng was nowhere in evidence, and Jiang Zemin, along with Li Peng, did the talking for China. Vo Van Kiet later concluded this was a deliberate insult to Vietnam, and that the delegation "had fallen into a trap" by sending a senior leader without reciprocation by China. As the Vietnamese delegation quickly discovered, China was not interested in the "red solution" or an ideological alliance of any kind with Vietnam.

"If, in the current international situation, the two communist parties join hands, it won't be advantage for either of us," the Vietnamese were told. This reluctance to invoke ideological solidarity by cultivating party-to-party relations between the rival communist factions in Cambodia didn't stop China from circumventing the anti-PRC Vietnamese Foreign Ministry and delivering diplomatic communications through the Vietnamese Party Central Committee's External Department, even though China's insistence on keeping its relations with Vietnam primarily on a nonideological state-to-state basis would suggest that diplomacy should be carried on through normal government to government contacts, rather than party-to-party channels. This in turn suggests that China would invoke party-to-party solidarity only when it suited its own interests, and it continued to resist Vietnam's appeals to replace the Soviet Union as the "bulwark of socialism" in a changing world.

Labeling the Chengdu meeting as a diplomatic defeat for Vietnam, Tran Quang Co said that the main explanation was that Vietnam had deceived itself by clinging to the belief that China was interested in an ideological alliance to defend against the imperialists' "peaceful evolution" plot to finish off the remaining communist countries. The debacle of the failed attempt at a "red solution" was an important step in the ultimate fading of the power of the specter of "peaceful evolution" cited by Vietnam's conservatives as a reason for resisting coming to terms with the integrative forces of a globalizing post–Cold War system.

Adding insult to injury, the Chinese gleefully revealed tapes of their discussions with Vietnam's leaders agreeing to a preponderance of anti–Hun Sen forces in a coalition government—in effect selling out Vietnam's own main client in Cambodia, which was the dominant force in Cambodia at the time—to Hun Sen himself, as well as a variety of other parties. One of the aims of this revelation of supposedly secret negotiations was to establish an image of Vietnam to its ally as duplicitous and unreliable, and to sow discord within the Vietnamese leadership. In this they succeeded: in a politburo meeting in mid-May 1991, Pham Van Dong expressed his regret at being railroaded into endorsing an unwise policy. Premier Do Muoi also regretted the outcome, on the grounds that it would make Vietnam an unreliable friend in the eyes of its partners. Nguyen Co Thach also told party leader Linh that he had made a serious mistake.[72]

On the SRV's national day, September 2, 1990, the day preceding the opening of secret negotiations between Vietnam and China in Chengdu, Premier Do Muoi's major address for the occasion acknowledged Li Peng's call for the "two neighbors" (not "two comrades") to restore normal relations and find a political solution for the Cambodian problem. Muoi recalled the assistance of the Soviet Union and China to Vietnam during its armed struggles, and said that "Today, during our task of renewing [doi moi] the country, the assistance of international friends will have a great significance."

One reading of this is that Vietnam was signaling that it was turning from geopolitical moves on the global chessboard to economic development—in which normalizing relations with China would be helpful, but not as essential as it would be in the strategic realm. Earlier in the speech, Do Muoi had said, "The international situation is evolving in a very complex manner. The crisis in the Eastern European socialist countries is extremely serious, and will have a not insignificant impact on building socialism in our country. The enemy forces are carrying out many activities to sabotage the development and protection of the Fatherland of our people."[73]

As a further indication that the Vietnamese leadership was shifting its view of the nature of international relations, Do Muoi sketched the broad outlines of what would become known as "globalization" (*toan cau hoa*). "The scientific and technological revolution and the trajectory [*xu the*] of economic globalization [*quoc te hoa nen kinh te the gioi*] is offering the people's of the world many great possibilities to develop." Acknowledging that "many mistakes had been made" in economic policy "over many years," Muoi stated that "At present, we are facing the reality that the living standard and level of development of our people is too low. That is a tense situation and a big challenge for our people."[74]

The impetus for the Chengdu concessions in the interest of normalizing relations with China was both realpolitik (compensating for the loss of Soviet support and bowing to the realities of China's improved strategic position) and ideological (preserving and strengthening the diminished core of communist countries). Do Muoi's September 1990 speech, a further elaboration of his speech of December 1989 (discussed in chapter 3), also indicates that Vietnam was attempting to think through the implications of this new era of international relations, in which neither realpolitik nor ideological factors would be decisive in solving Vietnam's most pressing problem, its economic backwardness. For the moment, however, divesting itself of the Cambodian albatross and finding an accommodation with China that would allow Vietnam to focus on its economic development was essential.

Although the Vietnamese delegation to Chengdu had made the major concession of agreeing to a Chinese proposal which could tilt the proposed governing mechanism in Cambodia in the favor of Hun Sen's opponents, Nguyen Van Linh and military leader Le Duc Anh flew to Phnom Penh and tried to persuade their Cambodian client Hun Sen to agree to collude with the Pol Pot forces, because the big picture was the imperialists trying to destroy socialism, and the Cambodians could do their part to save it by achieving a reconciliation between the Hun Sen communists and the Khmer Rouge. Nguyen Van Linh told the Cambodian leaders, "'We must see that there are also contradictions between China and the imperialists on the question of Cambodia. We must have a strategy to exploit these contradictions. Don't struggle with China to the point that it pushes them to close ranks with the imperialists.' Le Duc Anh elaborated on this argument: 'The Americans and the West want to have a pretext to eliminate communism. They are eliminating it in Eastern Europe. They have announced that they will eliminate communism throughout the entire world. Clearly they are the direct and dangerous enemy. We have to look for an ally. That ally is China.'"[75] The red solution was still in play in the minds of these Vietnamese party and military leaders, but without China's support it was doomed to fail.

The red solution also alienated Vietnam's Cambodian ally. The Vietnamese ambassador reported that after this meeting, the attitude of Hun Sen toward the Vietnamese changed—which ultimately led to the scene described above of the "lonely" Vietnamese ambassador Ngo Dien being forced to witness the dissolution of the Cambodian Communist Party.

The upshot was a Vietnam with no communist patron and no communist client. Tran Quang Co was probably not alone in concluding that the Chengdu meetings were a "stain on Vietnam's diplomacy." Not only had Vietnam revealed a desire to pursue an anachronistic policy of ideological solidarity with China, but China's sly revelation of Vietnam's failure to achieve a "red solution" and its betrayal of an ally undermined Vietnam's attempt to diversify its foreign policy and gain more room for maneuver. China's stance had made this the only feasible diplomatic alternative to Vietnam's total dependence on China.

Even the remarkably candid account by Tran Quang Co of the Chengdu meetings between Vietnamese and Chinese leaders does not mention a reported Chinese proposal, which went far beyond the issue of Cambodia. A British newspaper reported that Western intelligence sources claimed that China had offered to replace commodities that the Soviet Union could no longer supply, give back a substantial portion of the Spratly Islands (a region with potential oil deposits). "In return for its assistance, China demanded that Hanoi 'co-ordinate'—in other words subordinate—its foreign policy to that of Peking. 'It came very close,' said an intelligence source in Bangkok. 'And that is what really amazes me, rather than their eventual refusal. The carrots to Hanoi were very big, and they had to think long and hard before rejecting the whole package. It just shows how desperate the Vietnamese are.'"[76] In fact, Vietnam's deteriorating strategic situation would soon lead it to grudgingly accept the subordinate role which China demanded—even without the carrots.

THE SEVENTH PARTY CONGRESS: A HOLDING OPERATION

In contrast to the optimism that marked the beginning of 1990, reflected in the *Nhan Dan* Tet article of Bui Tin and the January 1990 draft of the Central Committee on "Building Socialism in the Transition Period," the following year opened on a much more pessimistic note. "This year Tet, which fell on February 15, was somber, with little spent on imported explosives, and for good reason," wrote the *New York Times*'s Steven Erlanger. "'Dear comrades, 1991 is the year we will face unprecedented challenges,' Prime Minister Do Muoi, recently told the National Assembly. A Western banker here puts it more bluntly: '1991 looks like a disaster for Vietnam.' Many of the economic gains so evident last year have been undermined by political indecision, infighting and corruption." The collapse of the Soviet Union and Eastern Europe and the trauma of Tian An Men Square "have frightened Vietnam's aging leaders. The Politburo has stalled economic reforms begun in late 1987. Vietnam still seeks foreign investment, but foreigners now see increased risks." Moscow's decision to cut its aid in Vietnam in half and Vietnam's continued isolation and the American led economic embargo added to Vietnam's woes.[77]

The accumulating difficulties led to further strains within the leadership and arguments in the politburo. Beyond the question of diplomatic tactics and strategy was a growing divide on the fundamental assessment of the international situation, which came into the open at a the same pivotal politburo meeting in April 1991 in which Pham Van Dong had expressed his regrets for not being more alert to the down side of the Chengdu decisions. At this meeting, Nguyen Co Thach presented his analysis of the international situation, and General Le Duc Anh introduced the officer who headed military intelligence to give the military view, giving a mere colonel the same platform and prominence as a politburo member and minister. (Years later there was a flurry of internet documents alleged to be from Southern revolutionary veterans which charged Anh with falsifying his revolutionary credentials, sponsoring a military intelligence organization that committed a variety of abuses of power—including, according to some charges, an attempted coup against party secretary general Le Kha Phieu.) This military intrusion into party decision-making at the highest levels was unprecedented, and contributed to the polarization and fragmentation which produced paralysis of decision making and implementation that plagued Vietnam over the next decade.

The viewpoints on fundamental perceptions of the external environment were so divergent that an irritated Pham Van Dong suggested that the different bureaucracies meet and work out a common understanding. This indicates that, as of this point, there was no formal mechanism (such as an equivalent of the US National Security Council to reconcile diplomatic and military strategy—far less to include the key component of internal security and regime stability) to coordinate the various elements of external policy, except within the politburo. Thus "comprehensive security" was an emerging concept, but there was no bureaucratic mechanism to achieve the coordination between various elements of the State that the concept implied.

Monitoring implementation of party policies was the ostensible function of the party secretariat, but studies of communist ruling systems generally conclude that because the secretariat is usually an instrument of the party secretary general and an extension of his power, it does not function well in times of collective leadership, when the locus of power over both policy and implementation shifts to the politburo.[78] Using the politburo both as a debating forum over basic policy and as a mechanism for resolving bureaucratic disputes would overload the political circuits, and compound the policy differences by making them questions of power and turf among Vietnam's top leaders. This situation did, however, make it clear that in a more complicated world, a better coordinating mechanism for Vietnam's external relations was needed, and that diplomatic, military, security, and economic interests sometimes would clash.

Following the discordant politburo meeting in April 1991, a meeting was convened in early May with representatives of the diplomatic, military, and security bureaucracies to work out their differences. According to Tran Quang Co, this meeting did not have a satisfactory outcome, and the politburo held a three-day series of meetings in mid-May to address the conflicting viewpoints. From his vantage as an observer at these meetings, Co witnessed a replay of the arguments on both fundamental questions (friends and enemies, China, peaceful evolution) and specific issues (Cambodia, ASEAN) that had been raging for a year, with no conclusive resolution prior to the June 1991 Seventh Party Congress.

A foreign-policy specialist affiliated with the Central Committee said that the shock of the events of summer 1991 was even more unsettling to the party leadership than the turbulent events of 1989, and that there were heated debates about the proper course of action. The issues in contention centered on how much Vietnam would have to open up to compensate for the collapse of the socialist world, with an emerging consensus that Vietnam would have to open up to some degree "for the sake of the country, for the system itself."[79]

He recalls that there was also growing agreement that it was a mistake to align with a military bloc. Since 1986 most party leaders felt that it was not appropriate to follow a single model. Vietnam should voluntarily learn from others and pick out the best features for its own model. Because there were many similarities between Vietnam and China, he said, China could be "a source of information, a reference," but he and some others did not foresee the relationship developing much deeper. Vietnam had made its pitch, and China did not respond positively. "China watches us closely and we watch them closely."[80] Clearly some others in the party hoped for more from China, but China's price—Vietnamese acknowledgment of Chinese regional hegemony—was still considered too high.

The ideological and political turmoil was not confined to the top level of the political system in Vietnam at this time. Consternation and uncertainty pervaded the political elite. Phan Dinh Dieu recalls that "Contradictions were converging in 1991. There were strong clashes [of viewpoints]." The arts took the lead in challenging the conventional wisdom followed by the sciences. There was a reaction from those holding to the "old thinking" because of the collapse of Soviet Union and Tian An Men Square. In a conference of academics and institute leaders convened in preparation for the Seventh Party Congress, Dieu reiterated what he had been saying for nearly a decade. The head of the Social Sciences Institute commented that "we all agree with what Dieu said, but only he dared say it."[81]

The Seventh Party Congress was essentially a holding operation, reaffirming the leadership's commitment to the communist system, and replacing Nguyen Van Linh with the equally senior Do Muoi, whose reformist credentials were rather mixed, considering his earlier career as a central planner and his role in leading the socialist transformation of the South after 1975. Bui Tin noted that Muoi's notable career accomplishments were overseeing the heavy-handed post-1975 "socialist transformation" campaign in the South, and single-mindedly pushing through the construction of Vietnam's most controversial construction projects, the Ho Chi Mausoleum and the two "construction projects of the century," the Thang Long bridge across the Red River (which had been destroyed by American bombing) and the Hoa Binh hydroelectric dam, which became a monument to the deficiencies of Soviet engineering. "Both these projects represented the defect of subjective voluntarism [*duy y chi*, the idea that you only have to will something to be done and it will happen], and brushing aside the ideas of the scientific–technological establishment, which once in motion could not be stopped and could not be fixed, and were a colossal waste of time and money. . . . Many Hanoi intellectuals often said 'lack of understanding plus zeal equals making a mess of things.'"[82] Still, the record shows that the most prominent high-level statements reflecting new thinking about the evolving international system and its implications for Vietnam were the two speeches by Do Muoi, in December 1989 and September 1990, discussed above.

This represented a power transition (Muoi took the opportunity to purge some supporters of Le Duc Tho, such as Foreign Minister Nguyen Co Thach, following Tho's death the previous year) but not a generational transition. (This also shows the complexity of labeling; most people would place Thach on the "reformer" side of the spectrum—witness his enthusiastic embrace of Paul Samuelson's economic text—and Tho a resolute opponent of all change.) It is a testament to the complete bankruptcy of the prereform approach to economics and governance that Do Muoi continued the main line of the economic reforms, and a validation of Jeffrey Legro's important point about the discrediting of alternatives being a key to consolidating policy and ideational change. But it is also not surprising that his leadership was marked by caution and conservatism and a long delay in giving power to a younger generation of leaders. He led Vietnam from the 1991 Seventh Party Congress to the end of 1997, thus putting his stamp on Vietnam's policies throughout most of the decade of the 1990s.

Vo Van Kiet, a southerner with a more established record as a reformer, became premier. In a later retrospective account of the main features of the Seventh Congress, the following points were noted. The Seventh Party Congress met in June 1991 at a time that it was clear that the Soviet Union had been radically transformed and might be on the brink of dissolution. Retrospective official party accounts of this turbulent period admit that, "Some of our cadres, party members, and people showed signs of demoralization—to say nothing of those who wanted to 'take a different road.' All the enemy forces were moving in with a fierce counter attack on the remaining socialist countries, among them Vietnam." As an attempt to steady the ship, the Party Congress affirmed Vietnam's commitment to follow the road to socialism but, recognizing that there was no longer an orthodox model to provide guidance, the congress "identified six special characteristics of Vietnamese socialism and seven basic directions to guide the process of building socialism during the transition to socialism."[83] The "six special characteristics" were probably intended to illustrate that Vietnam had its own distinctive model of socialism that would not succumb to the fate of the Eastern European countries and the Soviet Union.

DECIDING ON THE ROAD TO TAKE: BUT THE MAP REMAINS SKETCHY

The major theme of the Seventh Congress was the "transition to socialism." This reaffirmed that Vietnam would maintain its political and ideological system even as communism collapsed in Europe and the Soviet Union. The fact that reform and experimentation were permitted—indeed demanded—by the uncertainties of a transition helped justify Vietnam's departure from formerly orthodox communist policies. And the uncertainty of the transition was compensated for by the assertion that, by whatever the route, the final destination would be the communism that Marx had foreseen. This was perhaps another application of Ho Chi Minh's adage "from an unchanging stance, respond to ten thousand changes" (*di bat bien, ung van bien*), which counseled strategic clarity and firmness of purpose along with tactical flexibility. Or, it might have been merely making the best out of an intractable reality.

At the time of the Seventh Party Congress in mid-1991, even the reformers appear to have accepted the position that Vietnam's period of groping and confusion was over. Vo Van Kiet told a Vietnamese journalist shortly after the Congress that, "We have the advantage of the fact that the Seventh Party Congress had laid down a policy line for *doi moi*, and we don't have to learn on the job [*vua lam, vua tim toi*, seeking the way while going ahead with the work], as after the Sixth Party Congress. That means the road to take is clear even though it might not be the road to bliss [*hoan lo*], but we have enough confidence in it to move straight down this road."[84] Vietnam's improvisation was not yet at an end, however. Deng Xiaoping advised that even China would have to "grope its way across the stream, feeling for stepping stones." A well-regarded economic specialist said that Do Muoi had picked up this phrase and applied it to Vietnam in 1993,[85] so clearly the Seventh Party Congress decision to set the course toward socialism still left open important questions about specific policies. It should also be noted that the absence of a specific blueprint for *doi moi* meant that it was more difficult for the reformers to act in concert to highlight and promote specific alternatives to existing policy but, at the same time, it gave them more freedom to improvise and presented less of a target for conservative critics. *Doi moi* was more a mindset than a specific program.

The fact that the Soviet and Eastern European models of communism had failed was now held to be irrelevant to Vietnam. Marx had specified three different scenarios regarding the transition to communism. The first, transformation of an advanced capitalist society to communism, had never happened. The second was the path of the Soviet Union and Eastern Europe. Economist Tran Nham wrote in the party newspaper, that in the third case, of, "Making the transition from moderately or low developed capitalism to socialism . . . there have been some models of this transition pattern, but to date none has been successful and they have been harshly criticized."[86]

Fortunately for Vietnam, said Professor Nham, the failure of the second model (the Soviet Union and Eastern Europe) does not affect Vietnam, because its transition to socialism will take a third path. "Making the transition from a precapitalist colonial society to socialism, bypassing the capitalist socioeconomic form. It was only a century ago that Marxism-Leninism predicted this pattern of transition and there has been scant guidance on its implementation. Practical experience in this field has also been negligible. Generally speaking, we are still in the process of searching and discovering, and success has been marginal while difficulties and mistakes have been numerous. The transition to socialism in our country follows the third pattern. For this reason, in principle the models and theories of the first two patterns are inapplicable; nor can the experience derived from these transition patterns be used as the basis for examining the transition period in Vietnam."[87] Making a virtue of necessity, consigning the Soviet Union and European models of socialism to irrelevancy, deprived Vietnam of the confidence that there was a proven path to communism, but it was also a consolation in that it could be used to show that Vietnam's communist aspirations were not doomed to failure.

FOREIGN POLICY IMPLICATIONS OF THE COLLAPSE OF THE SOVIET UNION

A central problem of the Seventh Congress was to redefine Vietnam's foreign policy to take into account the collapse of communism in Eastern Europe and the changes in the Soviet Union. The economic necessity of replacing lost Soviet assistance was clear, but so was the political price that too eager a pursuit of assistance from the capitalist world would entail among the regime's core of supporters. Requesting aid from China was a tempting alternative but, as noted earlier, the political price was very high. The withdrawal of Soviet subsidies forced Vietnam to purchase indispensable imports with scarce hard currency at greatly inflated prices. Most Soviet imports, including vital commodities such as oil and fertilizer, were seven times more expensive in 1991 than the previous year.[88]

This was not merely an economic issue. "How to cope with such economic strains, and how much they may require further economic changes or relations with the West, are fundamentally political and ideological questions," a party member told a *New York Times* reporter. "The leadership knows it must deal with the West," the party member said, but "if you go too far, you lose the respect of your people, whom you pushed to fight Western imperialism and the rule of the dollar," The party member concluded "you can't accept all the premises of either socialism or capitalism . . . And the situation just gets worse."[89]

The political report of the Seventh Party Congress declared: "With this unfavorable international condition unfolding, in June 1991, our party convened the Seventh Party Congress which set forth the external policy line of independence, sovereignty, openness [*rong mo*], diversification [*da dang hoa*], and multilateralization [*da phuong hoa*] of international relations." This approach was summarized by the slogan "Vietnam wants to become the friend of all countries in the world community, and struggle for peace, independence, and development." The congress also confirmed that "the mission of our external relations was to 'preserve peace, expand friendly and cooperative relations and create favorable conditions for building socialism and protecting the Fatherland, while at the same time actively contributing to the common struggle of the peoples of the world for peace, national independence, democracy, and social progress.'"[90]

A foreign journalist noted the increased interest among Vietnam's leaders in alternatives to the past reliance on economic ties with socialist countries. "Vietnam's new leaders, pursuing capitalism to cure the country's ailing economy while remaining strongly committed to a socialist political system, are looking for new friends to help them out." In one of his last pronouncements prior to retirement, Communist Party leader Nguyen Van Linh told delegates to the Seventh Party Congress "We want to cooperate equally on the basis of mutual benefit with all countries without discriminating between different sociopolitical systems."[91]

Although the main story of 1990–91 for Vietnam in overall strategic terms was changing partners from the Soviet Union to China, the declarations of the Seventh Congress clearly recognized that normalizing relations with China was an essential but not sufficient step in responding to the changing external environment. The focus on expanding cooperative relations with a broad and diverse range of countries and the use of the terms "diversification" and "multilateralizion" clearly indicated that the old stratagem of premising external relations on the assumption of a world sharply divided into antagonistic blocs, and cultivating an alliance with a major power in the "socialist camp," was no longer an adequate response to the complexities of the post–Cold War era.

THE SHOCK OF THE ABORTIVE COUP AGAINST GORBACHEV AND THE FINAL DISSOLUTION OF THE SOVIET COMMUNIST PARTY

Vietnam did not give up on the old world-view easily. When an abortive coup against Gorbachev to restore the old system was launched, the Vietnamese leadership was fleetingly hopeful that something could be salvaged from the wreckage of 1989. Having given its tacit support to this attempt to turn back the clock in Russia, the Vietnamese leadership was taken aback when the coup failed. "The Soviet events appeared to shock Hanoi, and Vietnamese leaders reacted slowly."[92] William Branigan of the *Washington Post* reported that two top Communist Party leaders in Vietnam confirmed that the collapse of the abortive attempt to restore the old communist system in Russia was a shock to the Vietnamese leaders, and accelerated their rapprochement with China. "Still, officials here vowed that the Vietnamese party would stick to its ideology and would not be overthrown. 'There is no other way than socialism for defending our independence and development,' said Tran Cong Man, a retired lieutenant general. Thai Ninh, the vice chairman of the party's ideology and culture committee, predicted major difficulties for the Vietnamese military, which is heavily dependent on Soviet equipment. 'But this doesn't mean that we will collapse also,' he said. . . . Vietnam would not abandon its path even if it becomes the last Communist state on Earth."[93]

Gorbachev's response to the coup was to dissolve the Soviet Communist Party. Prior to this, Vietnam had stoutly defended the Soviet Union against all detractors, and charged that all "bad mouthing [*noi xau*] and slander [*boi nho*] of the Soviet Union were aimed at diminishing the prestige and influence of the Soviet Union," with the purpose of "enticing this or that country to follow them, threaten them, and creating pressure on those countries, encouraging them to follow their own path which, in reality, is a plot to detach them from the bloc of socialist countries, creating dissension between them and the Soviet Union, destroying the bloc solidarity of the socialist community."[94]

Following the August 1991 coup and dissolution of the Soviet Communist Party, Vietnamese ideologists had to retreat from defending the Soviet Union as the core of the communist world, to an abstract and theoretical explanation of why communism had a future, even though it had died in its own birthplace. By the end of 1991, the party's theoretical journal admitted that "it is hard to see what the Soviet Union will become, because the situation is evolving in a very complicated way, and often surpasses one's ability to predict. But one thing is for certain; whatever the direction that the Soviet Union evolves, you absolutely cannot say that socialism, as a theory and a political system, has collapsed." The reasons given were basically that, whatever the setback in its place of origin, communism remained valid as a theory, and although one model of communism had collapsed, there still remained others to keep the flame alive.[95] Clearly the coup and its aftermath marked the end of Vietnam's hopes that communism would survive in the Soviet Union, making rapprochement with China even more urgent.

THE END GAME OF NORMALIZATION WITH CHINA

On October 23, 1991, the diplomatic settlement of the Cambodian conflict was concluded in Paris. The following month, Do Muoi and Premier Vo Van Kiet traveled to Beijing to formalize the normalization of relations between Vietnam and China, on November 5, 1991. Tran Quang Co bitterly titled the section in his memoirs on the final step of the normalization process "the end of a stage in the journey, but not the turning of a page in history," to underline his view that the results of Vietnam's normalization of relations with China did not lead to everyone "living happily ever after." Even at the time, the joint declaration suggested a relationship that would be cautious and distant, certainly not based on the close ideological solidarity that some of Vietnam's leaders had sought. The joint declaration said: "Vietnam–China relations will abide by the principles of respect for each other's sovereignty and territorial integrity, and mutual nonaggression and noninterference in each other's internal affairs. . . . Relations between Vietnam and China are not an alliance relationship, and will not return to the relationship of the 1950s and 1960s."[96]

As the last echoes of the Cold War faded away, Vietnam had been forced to change partners in a changing world, but China did not turn out to be the substitute for the previously supportive Soviet Union that some in Hanoi had hoped it would be. In fact, relations became even more strained in the next few years over a variety of territorial issues which took another decade to resolve. Primary reliance on China was clearly not going to be a viable strategy for Vietnam in the post–Cold War era. It took a year after normalization for China to offer Vietnam a paltry $14 million dollars in loans.[97] The alternative for Vietnam was to diversify its diplomatic options, and this required establishing better relations with the noncommunist world, especially its Southeast Asian neighbors and the United States.

5

Wary Reconciliation (1992–1995)

CHANGING PARTNERS DID not solve Vietnam's problem of devising a new strategy for dealing with the post–Cold War world. It was a move on the global chessboard, but not only were the rules of the game changing, so was the nature of the game. The global chessboard was of decreasing relevance to an emerging system of globalization in which economics was supplanting realpolitik issues and ideological conflicts as the central concern.

Still, for Vietnam there were some unresolved geostrategic issues that needed to be addressed. The "normalized" relationship with China remained fraught with difficulties (there would be territorial clashes over the next decade), and China had made it clear that this was a very limited partnership, and not an ideological alliance to reconstitute a diminished socialist world. The most important consequence of normalization of relations with China was to end a dangerously adversarial relationship with Vietnam's powerful neighbor, now that Vietnam no longer had a superpower patron to back it up. It did not in itself resolve the problem of Vietnam's isolation in the post–Cold War world.

For this reason, Vietnam also initiated a process of improving relations with the noncommunist world, especially its former enemies, Vietnam's ASEAN neighbors, and the United States. The new approach of enlarging the range of Vietnam's international contacts was marked by a series of visits in Asia and that significantly expanded the range of personal contacts of Vietnam's top party leaders. These visits were more important as symbolic gestures than for any tangible immediate diplomatic results, but they indicated a trajectory that led, over time, to Vietnam's diplomatic integration into the region and the global system, symbolized by its joining ASEAN in 1995 and campaigning to become a nonpermanent member of the UN Security Council in 2008–9. They were also vitally important in helping the isolated Vietnamese leadership learn about how the noncommunist world worked through direct observation.

VIETNAM'S LEADERS EXPLORE THE OUTSIDE WORLD

While the attention of the region and the world was focused on Vietnam's entrance into ASEAN, establishment of diplomatic relations with the United States, and ties with the European Union, Vietnam was undergoing a major internal change in the way it viewed the outside world and interacted with it. Vietnam's party leader Do Muoi, who had traveled within Southeast Asia as part of Vietnam's normalization diplomacy with ASEAN, made the first trip taken by the top Vietnamese Communist Party leader to Japan and South Korea, in April 1995. A press account of this unprecedented venture by Vietnam's party leader to "Asia's bastions of capitalism" and his audience with Japan's imperial couple noted that it "would have been unimaginable just five years ago when Vietnam was almost completely isolated from the world."[1]

Later in 1995, Do Muoi visited Australia and New Zealand, which some reporters characterized as the first visit of a Vietnamese party leader to "Western" countries—Australia and New Zealand—since Ho Chi Minh's visit to France in 1946.[2] The visit to Australia was marked by protests from the Vietnamese community in Australia and a diplomatic snub by the opposition leader, underlining the more exposed and risky nature of this kind of visit.[3]

Vietnam's previous party leader, Nguyen Van Linh, had visited India, a traditionally supportive quasi-ally, in 1982, and had gone to Singapore in 1992 after he had left office. After becoming party leader, Do Muoi had also traveled to India, in 1992, Singapore and Thailand in 1993, and Malaysia in 1994. But these trips were the exceptions and not the norm, and involved a supportive country (India), a tightly controlled authoritarian state (Singapore), a tightly controlled and somewhat supportive state (Malaysia), and a close neighbor (Thailand). That the top party leader emerged from the inner sanctum of the traditionally secretive and insulated corridors of power to venture onto unfamiliar terrain is an indicator of the extent of internal transformation required of Vietnam in its commitment to reconcile with former adversaries and integrate into the international system.

For years it had been considered too dangerous to risk the security and dignity of the top party leader outside a friendly and controlled environment. The party secretary general had traditionally been concealed from public view by layers of secrecy and, even in the post-1954 period, rarely traveled outside Vietnam even to friendly socialist countries. Surrounded by enemies, the top leader was protected like a queen bee. Now, instead of hunkering down to repel assaults on Vietnam's territory and letting the diplomats do the front-line contacts with a hostile world, Do Muoi saw the necessity of sallying out to explore the world outside despite the risk entailed, as a step toward proactive interaction with an environment which had been viewed as hostile and threatening.

The experiences, beliefs, and perceptions of the top party leaders in Vietnam are a pivotal element of the story of Vietnam's "changing worlds," for they themselves had lived largely in a world of their own—a world within a world. A Chinese writer of the Mao period coined the phrase "the world of the party" to describe the inner core of the Maoist-dominated belief system and its ability to contain the thoughts and assumptions of writers and set the agenda for them.[4] Although the issue here is somewhat different, the phrase "world of the party" usefully describes the conviction of the top leaders that they could shape reality outside their "world" to conform to the visions and desires of those who lived inside the charmed circle of party leaders. The more the top party leaders were directly exposed to these external realities, the more difficult it would be to cling to their imagined visions of the world beyond the corridors of power. The outreach of top leaders that was part of the reconciliation process also helped to defuse some of their more extreme paranoid convictions, which had long been reinforced by isolation and secrecy.

Some foreign observers felt that this intensification of interest in the outside world reflected a more relaxed and self confident Vietnam, now clearly committed to reform and opening up to its neighbors and others. A Swedish aid official and academic who had been a close observer of Vietnam since the 1970s reported that, "During a conversation I had with (the new) Prime Minister Vo Van Kiet in January 1992, he spoke with self-confidence, in virtually a new language, about the results of the reform program. He sounded like a person who had jumped into an unknown ocean of reform without knowing if he would ever reach the shore, and who now, finally, felt certain that he would make it." In hindsight (as the present work argues), this conclusion was premature. There was a backlash to this reform enthusiasm of leaders like Kiet, and "taking the plunge" did not happen until 2000. It did, however, have an immediate effect on opening up Vietnam's foreign relations, as Vietnam now sought to learn from the experiences of other countries.[5] The opening up would also affect relations with countries that had previously had adversarial relations with Vietnam.

This was a wary reconciliation, however. It took Vietnam nearly a year after normalizing relations with China to digest the changes in the international situation and take the next steps toward reestablishing ties with its former adversaries, in a flurry of diplomacy at the end of 1992 and the beginning of 1993. By 1995, Vietnam had joined ASEAN, established full diplomatic relations with the United States, and forged closer economic and diplomatic ties with Europe, both bilaterally and through ASEAN.

IMPACT OF RECONCILIATION DIPLOMACY ON VIETNAM'S INTERNATIONAL SELF-IMAGE

On his trip to Japan, Muoi sounded a faint echo of the "beauty queen" theme, touting Vietnam's attractiveness to foreign investors and imagining that its resources and growth potential would make it irresistible to infatuated capitalists. While pleading for more aid to alleviate Vietnam's spiraling debt to Japan, Muoi also appealed for more "daring" investment from Japanese companies, and brushed aside the suggestion that prudent investors should wait for Vietnam to get its own act together with respect to risk and cumbersome procedures.[6] Clearly the Vietnamese leader, perhaps influenced by the "cowboy investors" from Taiwan and South Korea who had plunged in despite the risk, felt that the rapacious capitalists couldn't keep their hands off the Vietnam prize, and he was not especially concerned about doing what it took to create a more stable investment climate in Vietnam.

Some Vietnamese analysts used a variation of this theme, in which the "beauty queen" was no longer specifically Vietnam but the entire Southeast Asian region, which was so favorably situated economically and geopolitically that the great powers couldn't resist "paying constant attention" (*thuong xuyen quan tam*) to it. "It's not accidental that the history of the nations in this region is, for the most part, one of struggling to resist foreign aggression," said a Vietnamese economist.[7]

This view of Vietnam's irresistibility to investors and intrinsic importance in international affairs was challenged by the new realities of the global system. One of the many consequences of the end of the Cold War was that Vietnam had been relegated farther from its once central position on the international stage. To some extent, this was a neglect that benefited Vietnam, considering the price it had paid for being on the front pages of the world press during the Vietnam War, but it was also galling to its self-image of a nation that counted in the world (or had at one time). By joining ASEAN, Vietnam had increased its international importance and therefore its desirability as a partner or, at the other extreme, an object to be exploited. Now, getting the best of both worlds, it had strengthened its capacity to fend off excessive or unwanted attentions by gaining the backing of ASEAN. But in joining ASEAN, Vietnam became one player among a number, and found that it had to serve an apprenticeship to establish the bona fides necessary to be a trusted and influential partner in the organization.

"NEW THINKING" ABOUT THE INTERNATIONAL SYSTEM: 1992–1995

The period 1992–1995, spanning an interval from the collapse of the Soviet Union and normalization of relations with China through full membership in ASEAN and diplomatic recognition by the United States, was also a time of significant change in elite views of the nature of the international system, and its implications for Vietnam. Although the old guard remained in control of the political system, generational change at the top was limited, and the few outspoken reformers at high levels had been purged or sidelined, a fundamental shift nevertheless took place in the realm of "new thinking" about international relations and their implications for Vietnamese diplomacy and security. This raises the important question of how much of the new thinking came from the top, and how much filtered up from the surrounding infrastructure of analysts, think tanks, diplomats, economists, intellectuals, and economic managers.

Let us recall Jeffrey Legro's analysis of how and why collective ideas about international relations change. "If there is a default explanation for discontinuous shifts in social ideas," writes Legro, "it is 'external shock'—typically such big events as war, revolution, or economic crisis. . . . Embedded mind-sets endure for relatively long periods of time, but then they change under the pressure of dramatic events, giving way to ideas that last until the next crisis."[8] The abrupt end of the Cold War and the collapse of Vietnam's main supporter certainly qualifies as a major "external shock," and it had been preceded by the economic shock of the 1980s which, by undermining the old ways of conceiving socialism, had cleared the way for new thinking in the external sphere.

Legro also demonstrates that it is not enough merely to discredit the old thinking, the new thinking has to be legitimized and consolidated. Consolidation of new ideas is influenced by the number of existing ideas that could potentially replace the old orthodoxy and the "perceived initial results of such new ideas."[9] This would suggest that new thinking cannot be entirely a top-down process, since the consolidation of new ideas also depends on formulation of a coherent alternative, which is the province of specialists, and dependent on effective implementation by the bureaucracy.

Applying this to the case of Vietnam, we may posit that the acceptance of new thinking about the changed world and Vietnam's place in it required more than a recognition by the political elites that the Cold War was over and that Cold War thinking was now obsolete. As Legro argues, new thinking must also draw on alternative ideas that make sense to the elites who have abandoned the old thinking. The more these new ideas could build on the old, or alternative conceptions that had survived despite party orthodoxy, the more likely they would be to succeed. Finally, they must be validated by visible results.

The "wary reconciliation" was set in a context of new ideas about the nature of the international system and their implications for Vietnam's diplomacy and security. Before we trace the evolution of Vietnam's response to the end of the Cold War, we will summarize the culmination of these ideas in the various versions of new thinking that had been distilled by key actors in Vietnam's external relations by mid-decade—the endpoint of this chapter—after the milestone rapprochements with ASEAN, the United States, and other former members of the rival Cold War bloc.

A good overview of both the rationale for new thinking and the outlines of the content of this new thinking is the special issue of the Foreign Ministry's house journal, *Nghien Cuu Quoc Te* (International Studies) of September 1995. The occasion was a commemoration of fifty years of Vietnamese diplomacy, but the subtext was a summation of the new thinking since the end of the Cold War, on the occasion of Vietnam's new status as a more "normal" country—now a member of ASEAN and recognized by the United States. As Foreign Minister Nguyen Manh Cam observed in his introduction, the conference on which this special issue was based was both a retrospective of three generations of Vietnamese diplomacy and an assessment of the current challenges that diplomacy must address.[10]

Cam observed that "one of the shortcomings frequently mentioned [in the confer-ence] was that there were many times when we didn't change our thinking in a timely fashion, and did not grasp the changes in the face of international relations at various historical turning points in a timely manner, and had shortcomings in researching and forecasting strategy, which persists in managing the richly diversified external activities in the new era."[11] This was an acknowledgment that Vietnam had stuck too long with its Cold War assumptions and mentality.

Cam left it for others to present and justify the new thinking. But the common thread in all of these analyses of the transformation of international politics was a conviction, long held and fostered by the Vietnamese Communist Party, that the party's leaders had a special insight into the inner workings of history, which made their guidance in matters of politics, domestic and international, indispensable. The fact that the key to unlocking the secret code of international transformation was not explicitly classical Marxism was less important than the party leadership's continuing role as a group of illuminati, whose wisdom about the esoteric inner secrets of history legitimated their power.

Vietnam's deputy foreign minister, Dinh Nho Liem, admitted in a 1995 article that the party had not foreseen the collapse of communism, but argued that its continuing role as a prescient analyzer and forecaster of trends and events was still the foundation of Vietnam's external policy. "The only thing we failed to anticipate was the situation in the (former) Soviet Union and Eastern Europe (just as the entire world did not anticipate it). The [party] resolutions concerning external affairs are among the intellectual products con-cerning external matters that have both a real impact and provide the foundation for our current external policy as well."[12] This continuity between the old doctrinaire Marxist-Leninist, ideologically derived analysis, and the newer more cosmopolitan and universalis-tic structural analysis was reinforced by the ease with which technological–economic determinism was substituted for class struggle and politico-economic determinism.

The key difference between the dynamics of the old world and the post–Cold War era was that even the frictions and competitive aspects of international relations in an era dom-inated by the quest for economic development would not lead to armed conflict or open struggle between countries, despite their different political and socioeconomic makeups. Deputy Foreign Minister Liem observed that, "The scientific and technological revolution and the developments of the forces of production have given rise to new issues for every country; the nations have reduced their military commitments [*su cam ket quan su*] and are focusing on internal consolidation and the *hectic competition in the economic and scientific-technological areas* [italics in original]. The trajectory of struggle and cooperation within peaceful coexistence among countries with different regimes is expanding daily."[13] But, of course, tensions and potential conflicts would continue to exist.

Phan Doan Nam, a senior analyst in the Foreign Ministry's think tank with a reputa-tion for incisive conceptual thinking, downplayed the role of the end of the Cold War in producing many of the changes in international relations that had become the subject of Vietnam's reexamination of its position in the world. He noted that many conflicts of the

Cold War era persisted into the post–Cold War period because the underlying dynamics were not a product of the now-vanished superpower competition. In particular, Nam observed that the forces that undermined the division of the world into rival economic blocs were already evident in the 1970s and 1980s, and thus a unified global economy was more a cause than a consequence of the end of the Cold War. "The division of the world into two adversarial economies and two adversarial markets ran counter to the trajectory [*xu the*] of development even in the 1970s and 1980s. This explains why when the Soviet Union and the countries of Eastern Europe collapsed, the socialist countries of Asia remained stable and continued to develop as at present." However, he cautioned, "In reality, if the Asian socialist countries hadn't launched their reforms and renovated their thinking, especially their economic thinking, they would have found it difficult to avoid the fate of the Soviet Union and Eastern Europe."[14] Significantly North Korea, the exception to the reforming changes of "Asian socialist countries," was rarely mentioned in Vietnamese discussions about the changing world. North Korea was a clear example of the alternative to integration—anachronistic pursuit of an extreme version of the command economy, total societal control, and insulation from outside influences. Even Vietnam's hardest-line conservatives were not interested in this model and most Vietnamese analysts, like Phan Doan Nam, passed over North Korea in silence.

Another factor in Vietnam's strategic calculations that had not changed with the end of the Cold War was its geographical location. In his 1995 overview of Vietnamese external relations, Nguyen Manh Cam noted that there was a traditional view in Vietnam that "one can choose friends, but no one can choose their neighbors; our security and [national] interest are always linked to our neighbors and the countries in the region."[15] No one in his audience of diplomats had to be reminded that this was a reference to the rationale for normalizing relations with China and joining ASEAN.

It is significant that Foreign Minister Cam gave priority to the regional dimension of diplomacy before analyzing the role of the great powers. During the Cold War, Vietnamese diplomacy and security strategy were set in the larger global context. The problem was a distant superpower adversary, and the main ally was another distant superpower. Vietnam felt that it could afford to confront its neighbors, China and ASEAN. In the new global context, Vietnam would have to deal with its own immediate surroundings first and foremost.

In many ways the study of Vietnam's normalization with ASEAN tells us more about the evolution and consolidation of Vietnam's post–Cold War new thinking about the world than its more or less simultaneous normalization of relations with the United States, which is why we address the issue of joining ASEAN prior to examining Vietnam's post–Cold War relations with the United States. The reason that the ASEAN case is especially instructive about the new thinking is that it required a reconceptualization of the nature of the international system, the nature of political power and influence in the world, the connection between regional and global issues, and Vietnam's approach toward strategy and diplomacy. It also marked a fundamental break with the zero-sum view of international relations of the Cold War "two camps" period, and with the view that all foreign policy and external strategy was derived from the ideological complexion (*y thuc he*) and political system of the various states in the international system. I will argue in chapter 6 that Vietnam's normalization with the United States demanded far less conceptual adjustment, and would have happened even if the Cold War had not ended (the hold-up in establishing full diplomatic relations was mainly on the US side).

Foreign Minister Cam summarized the nature of the global changes set in motion by the end of the Cold War. "The world is passing through a period of regime transition from the old international order which has broken up, to the new international order which is in the process of formation."[16] It was the former foreign minister, Nguyen Co Thach—who had been sacked in 1991 to propitiate China—who was left with the task of analyzing the nature of this process of transition.

Thach drew upon some analytic tropes that were familiar and accepted in Vietnam. The first was an extended realpolitik analysis of evolution of the international system since 1945, and the new power realities and their implications for Vietnam. The focus was on military strategic issues and the relations between the big powers. The early phase of the Cold War was, in Thach's view, an attempt by the United States to become the world hegemon, using anticommunism to legitimate its power. The Cold War led to an arms race among the big powers. The nuclear standoff led to the big powers opting for peaceful coexistence. America became bogged down and weakened by its intervention in Vietnam. China tried to sabotage détente between the United States and the Soviet Union. The Soviet Union agreed to arms reductions and opted for perestroika. After the collapse of the Soviet Union, the United States became the sole superpower.

But, in Thach's view, the apparent victory of the United States in the Cold War was not all bad news from the point of view of Vietnam. First of all, rather than producing a unipolar world, Russia still had enough power to act as a counterweight to the United States, and "the bipolar and tripolar world has become a multipolar world."[17]

Secondly, the new multipolar world is driven by economic competition and not by the quest for military or political dominance (though other Vietnamese analysts questioned this conclusion, pointing to the famous 1992 Defense Department draft strategy paper advocating suppression of potential challengers to American power). And, even though the capitalist model of a market economy had now fully eclipsed the Marxist model, the "third industrial revolution" offered less-developed countries the chance to catch up with the advanced countries "without necessarily being compelled to follow the path of the advanced capitalist countries."[18] Nevertheless, Thach had concluded as early as 1990 that the capitalist road had to be carefully studied, and even commissioned the translation of the classic American introductory economics text of MIT professor Paul Samuelson and ordered his staff to read it.[19]

Although Thach's analysis of the rise and fall of the Cold War owed much to the traditional realist view ("The notable point of international relations in the past fifty years is that national interest increasingly became the dominant factor"[20]), there was also a quasi-Marxist analysis of why the world had changed, substituting technological determinism for economic determinism, while also emphasizing the dominance of economic forces in the new international system. For the class struggle as the main agent of historical change, Thach substituted the "third industrial revolution" as the force driving change in the global economy, and he argued that economic forces have become the determining agents of change in global politics, surpassing ideological conflicts and military power balances.[21]

"The elimination of the world that was divided into two opposing social systems has created new and very favorable possibilities for the forces of production to reach their full potential," wrote Thach, using the familiar Marxist vocabulary. Then, applying it to a new phenomenon, he went on to say that, "The globalization of the world economy is creating conditions for a new international division of labor on the scale of the entire globe. At the same time, mutual dependence [*tuy thuoc lan nhau*] between big and small countries also has expanded to a larger scale."[22]

A SINGLE WORLD SYSTEM AND THE PRIMACY OF ECONOMIC POWER

The abandonment of the concept of a world sharply divided between antagonistic systems, the prelude to the victory of the communist world over the capitalist world, was a fundamental conceptual shift that paved the way for viewing international relations in "win-win" rather than zero-sum terms. Soviet premier Nikita Khrushchev was famous for his 1956 boast to the capitalist world that "we will bury you."[23] By the mid-1990s, it was clear that the few remaining communist states would live in a world that did not reflect their dreams and aspirations for a very long time—at the very least. The remaining party theoreticians dutifully catalogued the flaws and contradictions of capitalism, but the traditional Marxist-Leninist vision could not provide a credible alternative, let alone aspire to be the shaping force of the international system.

Deputy Foreign Minister Vu Khoan had also employed a quasi-Marxist analysis of the forces of global change and underlined the devaluation of military power in the post–Cold War era. Khoan also noted the changing nature of the concept of national security. "Previously, in speaking of the means of defending sovereignty, national security, and territorial integrity, to say nothing of even international standing and influence, often people stress military strength and violent methods. Today [1993], military strength still has an important significance, but it no longer holds a 'monopoly' [*doc ton*]. In the face of the changes on the world stage, it is not accidental that the main tendency of nations is to adjust their defense strategy in the direction of 'sufficiency' [*du manh* = sufficient strength, an alternative to preponderant military strength]." The lesson of the past half-century was that military losers like Japan and Germany had become economic winners, while the Soviet Union, a nuclear power of the first rank, "had disintegrated, and its territorial integrity is no more." The lesson is that military power by itself is no longer enough, Khoan concluded.[24]

The underlying structural dynamic of international change, Khoan argued, is the "tra-jectory" (*xu the*) of the scientific, technological, and industrial revolution which had led to dramatically accelerated economic growth, uneven development, and increasingly dense interdependence (*tinh rang buoc lan nhau ngay cang dam*). This creates the paradox of offering an unprecedented opportunity for less-developed countries to catch up, but at the same makes the threat of falling further behind even more serious. Moreover, there was the additional paradox of proliferating economic "opponents," even at a time when the threat of military opponents had declined. "Some people have the view that in war, there is only one enemy, while in economic competition everyone is an opponent [*doi thu*], and because of this there is a struggle that is no less tense and complex [than war]."[25]

Vu Khoan nevertheless urged Vietnam to realistically consider its options. In the light of the changed world, what were these options? "There are only two choices," he argued, "either shut yourself in completely [*khep kin*] or act in a way appropriate to the trajectory of the times [he used the term *xu the*, which might be translated as "tendency," "trajec-tory," or "direction of change"] and objective reality."[26]

Khoan concluded that world history had demonstrated that attempts to seal off a country from the international system had led those countries only to fall further behind. And in today's world, "total closure" is not even an option. As a consequence, "the best choice is to adequately recognize the main tendency [*xu the*] and objective reality, and find an appropriate way of dealing with it." Going with the main flow of global change will not only let a country better pursue its national interests, it will educate it to avoid being taken advantage of by other countries who know how to make these changes work for them.[27]

FRAMING THE ALTERNATIVES: ISOLATION OR INTEGRATION

This analysis by one of Vietnam's deputy foreign ministers contains one of the most complete outlines of the transitioning new thinking about international relations in this early post–Cold War period. It marked an important development in the consolidation of the new thinking, in that it framed the options in a stark and simplified either–or manner. If a closed-door policy was no longer possible in the globalized world, this vali-dated whatever the alternative was defined to be—in this case integration into the global market economy, which required normalization with the United States, regional inte-gration (which required membership in ASEAN), and transformation to a market economy. The reformers advocating integration could support their contention with the argument that it was the only realistic option.

The focus on the failure of a closed-door approach was a surrogate argument for admit-ting the failure of not only the command-economy model, the core of conventional Marxist-Leninist state organization (whose deficiencies had been acknowledged since the beginning of *doi moi*), but also on many of its underlying political and theoretical assumptions. The Marxist economic vision had not even survived within the "socialist camp," let alone proved capable of winning over those outside the socialist world. But castigating the closed-door approach did have the advantage of not directly repudiating the entire socialist project, which would have meant the delegitimation of Vietnam's regime and ruling elite. As we shall see, the advocates of limited reform, while agreeing that Vietnam must open up, also stressed the importance of salvaging the state-owned enterprises as a symbol of continuity with the past and a commitment to remaining a socialist regime.

Even though the reformers used indirection and allusion, which avoided attacking these fundamental Marxist assumptions directly, and concentrated mainly on the stubborn realities Vietnam now faced, conservatives continued to express reservations about the desirable extent of this integration and the potential pitfalls, such as "peaceful evolution." But they could not defend the old command-economy system, with its curious combination of autarky and isolation from the economic networks of the most dynamic regional growth center in the world economy and its dependency on Soviet and Chinese aid. As noted earlier, there were no Vietnamese advocates of the North Korean approach. If the command economy and the "closed door" were the only alternative to Vietnam's past policies, and one which had already failed, the conservatives were placed on the polemical defensive.

Some party ideologists attempted to counter the either–or framing of Vietnam's options—closed door or full integration into the global economy. Nguyen Huu Cat, an ideologist at the Ho Chi Minh City branch of the party training school, cited Lenin's position on taking advantage of dealing with capitalists when it could be done to advantage. Cat approved expanding economic and technical exchange with capitalist countries to make Vietnam stronger and more globally competitive, and noted that it used to be the case that economic relations followed political relations, but now the reverse was true. In addition, shifting the focus to economic cooperation would strengthen Vietnam militarily and strengthen peace in international relations, which would also contribute to its security. Having made the bow to Lenin's shrewdness in taking advantage of capitalists (Cat discreetly omitted Lenin's alleged comment about the capitalists selling the rope with which they would be hanged[28]) he went on to give a qualified acknowledgment of the paradigm shift about the basic nature of international relations. "The units of commercial production of countries with different political systems can cooperate with each other on the basis of mutual benefit before those countries have official state-to-state relations. Moreover, the requirements of economic development and concepts concerning the strength and national security of a country have undergone a basic transformation which requires putting the means and organization of production on a par with, or even at the forefront of, political, military and economic agencies."

Even though this is an attempt to underline the point that political transformation will not inevitably follow economic relations, Cat ends up endorsing the inevitability of opening up. "This analysis confirms that in order to survive and develop, Vietnam must carry out a policy of opening up and diversification and multilateralization of external relations with all countries, even politically, economically, culturally, and in science and technology, and even with respect to the party and state and popular organizations and nongovernmental organizations."[29]

The priority, though, should be with ASEAN and Asian neighbors. This policy of regional engagement, Cat noted, stemmed from Resolution 13 (1988) of the politburo, which ordered the establishment, "as soon as possible," of a "comprehensive and long-term regional policy toward Asia and Southeast Asia." Cat noted that the shift in ASEAN policy had been ordered years previously, and that "It is not that we have only just now given importance to regional cooperation, first of all with the ASEAN countries."[30]

STRIKING THE BALANCE BETWEEN COOPERATION AND SELF-INTEREST

Following Vietnam's entry into ASEAN, the complexities of striking a balance between assimilation and control over national destiny began to be further specified.[31] But by this time, the integration argument had largely been won, and the idea of a unified and interdependent global economy which compelled Vietnamese participation under rules which would require significant change in domestic policies was no longer seriously contested. However, as the following chapters will show, the aftermath of the Asian financial crisis, the difficulties of expanding economic regionalism in Asia, and the complexities of joining the World Trade Organization all forced Vietnam to examine the tradeoffs of integration in depth.

In 1995 Deputy Foreign Minister Dinh Nho Liem did allude to the tradeoffs which needed further analysis. "Don't simply take the ideological complexion [*y thuc he*] as the foundation for broadening relations," he wrote. In 1991 Vietnam had adopted the policy of becoming friends with all countries. Now it was time to go beyond the [lowest] common denominator (*mau so chung*) of a mutual interest in peace and development. "The things that need to be researched are the right balance between ideology and establishing relations for development[,] clearly recognizing the balance between the economic, political, security and national defense fields," but the "priority is still economic development, production of high-quality goods, and the capacity to compete internationally and at the same time find stable markets."[32]

In the early stages, the debate over globalization and integration revolved around the stark alternatives of learning to live with it, or falling further behind in the economic race and drifting into irrelevancy, a construct which clearly favored the reformers and advocates of integration and extensive international engagement. The idea of a "common denominator" of overlapping but not identical interests between nations was useful to advocates of greater integration, since it presented an image of broad areas of mutual interest, which did not exclude significant differences outside those areas, and thus would allow Vietnam to maintain its distinctive identity even in a condition of interdependence.

Vu Khoan summarized his points about international relations in the post–Cold War era as follows: "Previously, when speaking of independence and sovereignty often people would envision a political closed-door policy along the lines of isolation and economic self-sufficiency. Today, with the bipolar order featuring opposing political–military systems headed by the Soviet Union and America gone, and the world in the process of becoming a new order which is more diverse [*da dang*], the concept of political and economic independence is changing." Now, in a diverse and multipolar world, the countries that "can create for themselves an active and more flexible posture will be in a much better position to preserve their independence and sovereignty." In a globalized world, a country that can leverage its comparative economic advantage will be able to "create a position of maximum influence in international relations, [and] will be that much more able to preserve its standing and sovereignty [*tu the va tu chu*]."[33] This was a significant departure from the view that sovereignty could best be protected by insulating Vietnam from an unpredictable global system.

CONSERVATIVE CONCERNS AND RESERVATIONS ABOUT INTEGRATION

Vietnam's conservatives were hesitant to take this advice to bow to reality and take the risk of opening up in order to learn the rules of the new international game, even though the advocates of engagement argued that Vietnam could take advantage of them and, through deeper international engagement, could come to understand the nature of the new challenges of the post–Cold War era and avoid being victimized by those who understood them better. The conservatives continued to feel threatened by purported schemes of "peaceful evolution." These fears were largely based on the statements of American leaders and others that the collapse of communism in the Soviet Union and Eastern Europe showed that Marxism-Leninism was a historical experiment that had failed, and the last remnants of this outmoded system of government would pass from the scene. In this Western view, the disappearance of communism would happen not by an apocalyptic clash between two rival blocs (the Cold War scenario) but by a process of "peaceful evolution."

Vietnam's conservatives were convinced that the United States and other "hostile forces" were not content to let this historical process play out on its own, but were actively trying to speed it along by a campaign of ideological and political destabilization of Vietnam's communist regime. In his review of events in Vietnam during 1993, Douglas Pike wrote that despite a fairly successful year in domestic and foreign affairs, "The leadership and people of the Socialist Republic of Vietnam (SRV) during 1993 were afflicted by an anxiety syndrome that had about it an ineffable sense of uncertainty tinged with anticipation."[34]

Contemporary foreign press reports cited a variety of perceived threats that underlined the leadership's anxieties, including religious groups, ethnic minorities, and adherents of the former Saigon regime. The *Washington Post* reported that the regime was frustrated with "what diplomats say is continuing 'passive resistance' in the south." Among the problems in the South were the FULRO movement, a coalition of highland ethnic minorities who had been resisting central government control since the late 1950s.[35] FULRO allegedly had external support from Cambodia, but was a localized threat that Vietnamese security officials retrospectively considered to have been "neutralized" after 1992, and it was not the danger that most concerned the party.[36] It was the urban groups, especially those with external connections, that concerned the leadership. An article in the army journal blasted "enemies" in southern Vietnam who "oppose socialism."[37]

This article mentioned such activities as the large black-market trade in Ho Chi Minh City (formerly Saigon), and the influx of western goods mailed by refugees to 180,000 families in Vietnam were intended to "sap our economy." In an extraordinary listing, the journal said the various categories of government "enemies" added up to 14.7 percent of the city's inhabitants.[38]

Clearly, from the view of the conservatives, a model of economic reform that expanded connections between Ho Chi Minh City, the major economic center of the country, and the outside world had many risks, as would a diplomatic strategy of expanding ties with former enemies. It would both empower the former Saigon entrepreneurial and middle class and, in the view of the security branch at least, give them a chance to sabotage the key engine of the Vietnamese economy by work slowdowns, black-marketeering, and other forms of economic sabotage.

It would also benefit the Chinese ethnic minority, which many in the regime still regarded as a Trojan Horse. In 1978, "81 percent of these Hoa, or overseas Chinese, asked to leave Vietnam and . . . most of them still in effect reject Vietnamese citizenship by refusing to accept 'people's identity cards.' In unusually sharp language, the journal said that 'bourgeois Hoa,' encouraged by China and the United States, 'are still the biggest destroyers of the economy of Ho Chi Minh City.'"[39]

These external linkages, and the fears of encouraging them, had a constraining effect on Vietnam's relations with capitalist countries in Europe, America, and Southeast Asia. Clearly some conservatives were still inclined toward the "closure" option that Vu Khoan and others said was no longer possible in the new international system. But they could not openly advocate it, since withdrawal into a bloc of like-minded countries was no longer possible, and detachment from the world system had been overtaken by the party's new line about technological forces driving unstoppable globalization and the necessity of taking advantage of the opportunities it afforded Vietnam's economic development in order to avoid falling further behind. Thus the conservatives were pulled along with the new ideological current, but continued to drag their feet. This is one reason why the reconciliation between Vietnam and the United States, along with ASEAN, can be described as "wary."

In part this insecurity reflected real concerns and in part it was paranoia. It was also partly due to a legacy of the Cold War: many of Vietnam's old-guard leaders were convinced that Vietnam was still the central preoccupation of US leaders, and could not imagine that the country that had dominated world headlines for decades was now at the far periphery of international attention. This was the surviving legacy of the "beauty queen" syndrome discussed earlier—the assumption that Vietnam was still coveted as an object of irresistible desire by those who had once been obsessed with dominating it.

ENLARGING THE CIRCLE OF DECISION MAKING ON NATIONAL SECURITY

In view of this heightened sense of threat in the early stage of the transition to the post–Cold War era, it is curious that Vietnam enlarged the circle of decision making on national defense and security outside the party by establishing for the first time a National Defense and Security committee (Uy Ban Quoc Phong va An Ninh) of the National Assembly, as part of the major constitutional overhaul of institutions in 1992.[40] Some later dissident reports claim that this proliferation of policy centers was part of a leadership power struggle, in which different factions sought to create their own institutional bases. Whatever the validity of this theory, it seems clear that there was an unusually high level of discord among the top leaders in the 1990s, that some-times expressed itself in organizational changes of the party and government (for example, the creation of a standing committee within the politburo). This discord was certainly exacerbated by the new and unprecedented challenges the leadership faced following the collapse of the "socialist world."

In a review of the year 1992 Dorothy Avery, one of the leading US government analysts of Vietnamese affairs, concluded that the internal political balance of power favored the reformers, but the conservatives were able to constrain the pace and scope of reform. The political dynamic resulting from this political friction was an inevitable policy inconsistency, and partial stalemate on key issues. "In fact the growing private sector and the open door foreign policy probably have had a deleterious effect on party control, if not to the degree conservative ideologues and the security establishment feared. Under the circumstances, it is not surprising that Politburo policy, reached by consensus under Secretary-General Do Muoi, has been vacillating and inconsistent at times."[41]

Avery noted that the political activity in 1992 consisted largely of amending the 1980 constitution and restructuring the government. She observed that, "Vietnamese party analysts had come to believe that a prime factor in the demise of East European commu-nism was the concentration of state power in an isolated and rigid party bureaucracy. Restructuring was designed to avoid this fate."[42]

Although the new National Assembly committee did not have a significant voice in security issues, any fragmentation of policy making in the national defense and security arenas ran counter to the attempts in the late 1980s to unify and coordinate security, economic, and diplomatic issues. This attempt to engage institutions outside the party in even the most sensitive issues was perhaps an unintended consequence of the plan to devolve some authority to avoid isolating the party—a lesson drawn from the collapse of the regimes in Eastern Europe.

At a time when it was evident to Vietnam's leaders that there needed to be closer coordination between the diplomatic, economic, and security dimensions of Vietnam's external relations, the modest grant of authority to the National Assembly to participate in decisions once under the exclusive jurisdiction of the party and the relevant ministries is noteworthy. It is probable that the National Defense and Security committee had a limited policy role, but even the establishment of a National Assembly committee dealing with the most sensitive affairs of state security was a signal change from the past. The External Affairs committee of the National Assembly had been in existence for some time (it was established in 1975)[43] but appears to have played a modest role, probably focused on friendship visits and the like.

The establishment of a National Assembly committee on National Defense and Security does not, of course, mean that outsiders would supervise the budget or activities of the military and the security forces. Under the corporate scheme of representation in the National Assembly, all the members of this committee would be delegates from the military and the security branches, on the grounds that they have the requisite "specialized knowledge" to be effective. But even ten years later, it was clear that many less sensitive National Assembly committees had a minimal impact on their area of oversight. For this reason, one proposal was that for these committees, including the National Defense and Security committee, at least a quarter of the members be legislative specialists who could translate their understanding of the subject matter into concrete legislation.[44] Given the fact that most of the key figures in committees such as the National Defense and Security committee were also party members, and leaders in the military and security sectors of the state, it is unlikely that merely adding another hat to their duties reflected a real expansion of political participation in the decision making process.

Moreover, conservatives gained more representation in the party secretariat, with the 1992 addition of ideologist and politburo member Nguyen Duc Binh and Le Kha Phieu, head of the General Political Department.[45] It is an axiom of party organization that those with membership in both the decision-making apex of the party (the politburo) and the body that controls the organizational machinery that translates party decisions into action (the secretariat) are in an especially powerful position. But having to report on military and security affairs to fellow legislators and answer questions was a small but significant step toward increased accountability in the political system.

Wary reconciliation was marked by vacillation, and stops and starts, symptomatic of the overall decision-making process in Vietnam during this period. This pattern had also characterized much of the late Cold War period but now ideological differences on fundamental issues raised by the collapse of communism in the Soviet Union and Eastern Europe exacerbated the underlying ideological differences that stalemated policy in many areas. At the same time, the fragmentation of the power structure at the top either caused, or was reflected in, an elaboration of organizational structures involved in the decision-making process.

Traditional geopolitical considerations and conventional diplomacy had not been overtaken by globalization; rather, new layers of issues had been added to the old problems of diplomacy and security. This required close coordination between economic, political, diplomatic, and security policies. The increasing complexity of external relations required a high level of policy coordination which, even in past years, had been difficult to achieve. On top of this, the proliferation of organizations and institutions with a voice or interest in external relations added to the structural problems affecting efficiency and coordination of decision making in the external sphere.

VIETNAM PREPARES TO JOIN ASEAN

The geopolitical logic of Vietnam's 1991 decision to apply for membership in ASEAN, implemented in 1992, after years of reviling the organization as an enemy and a lackey of China and the United States, is well expressed by the veteran Thai Vietnam-watcher Kavi Chongkittavorn. Although Vietnam was now eager to join ASEAN, membership in this group would not in itself resolve the many external challenges facing Vietnam. Among these were continued reservations about Vietnam on the part of ASEAN countries, a more assertive China, and escalating tension caused by competing claims in the South China Sea. Along with this, Vietnam itself had problems in adjusting to the idea of ASEAN membership, "Before Vietnam's decision to accede to the Treaty of Amity and Cooperation late last year, it had been trying for years to understand ASEAN. In private, top Vietnamese Foreign Ministry officials admitted their country had problems in relating to noncommunist and economically dynamic ASEAN as an entity. They said Hanoi found it easier to handle ASEAN members individually, through bilateral negotiations."[46]

Kavi noted that even as late as February 1990 former foreign minister Nguyen Co Thach was still advocating a new regional organization that would incorporate two blocs—ASEAN and Indochina. This meant that Vietnam would, as leader of the Indochina "bloc," have a status equal to the combined membership of the existing ASEAN. On top of this Thach had advocated that the purpose of this new organization would be to oppose Chinese hegemony—a nonstarter for ASEAN. Eventually Vietnam abandoned this view and agreed to seek membership within the existing framework of ASEAN. In Kavi's view, this was largely for strategic reasons. "Hanoi's new approach is the outcome of a careful calculation. Without being identified with ASEAN, Vietnam could never face the challenges of China's stronger position in Southeast Asia and restricting that influence remains a key foreign policy objective."[47] Having been jilted in its attempt to forge a strategic partnership with China, Vietnam's old fears of its northern neighbor resurfaced.

Economic considerations were also an important factor in Vietnam's decision to join ASEAN. But at least in the beginning, security considerations were more important, as

Kavi's account suggests. Another journalist surveying the region in 1992 wrote: "while analysts admit ASEAN's economies are enough bait for Vietnam to consider joining the organization, they say Hanoi's real motive lies in the renewed security threat from its powerful neighbor, China." The evidence cited was a flare-up in oil-related conflicts in the Spratly Islands. A Vietnam-watcher based in Bangkok, possibly Kavi, said, "Alone against a giant like China, lacking in money and arms, [Vietnam] might feel safer as part of a grouping that shares similar problems."[48]

Although there was not a direct linkage between Vietnam's normalization with ASEAN and its parallel normalization with the United States, Hanoi's leaders had some reservations about membership in ASEAN, and were also ambivalent about the process of normalizing relations with the United States. Nevertheless, diplomatic recognition by the United States and an end to the economic embargo were prerequisites for full engagement in the international economic system. In an era of globalization, to be left outside the core networks of the world economy meant foregoing the best opportunities to "catch up" in economic development. Such isolation also had political and strategic implications.

THE PERILS OF INTEGRATION

On the other hand, the question of whether joining organizations and institutions of the new world order dominated by Vietnam's former adversaries would undermine the SRV's existing institutions and challenge the essential principles of the ruling communist party gave Vietnam's leaders pause. As noted earlier, the issue was whether Vietnam would be assimilated (*hoa nhap*) into the post–Cold War international system, or would integrate (*hoi nhap*) into it. The assimilation model implied the transformation of Vietnam's socialist identity and institutions. The integration model suggested that Vietnam could maintain control over the extent to which it chose to integrate into this system, because the "integration" or, more literally, "joining," would be the result of a choice by Vietnam's leaders. The language of voluntary association also carried the connotation that because the joining was voluntary, the extent of its own transformation after entering into the new international regimes and institutions could be managed by Vietnam.

The perils of reconciliation and global integration, in the eyes of Vietnam's conservatives, are illustrated by their reaction to one form of globalization—the soccer mania that developed in Vietnam during the 1994 World Cup, when much of the urban population watched the games late into the night. Many Vietnamese felt they were actively participating in a global event which linked them to the larger world community of soccer enthusiasts, adopting passionate attachments to one national team or another (of course it was inconceivable that Vietnam itself would ever aspire to reach this level of competition). Vietnam's old-guard conservatives became so alarmed by this phenomenon that they ordered the World Cup semifinal match off the air and replaced it with a eulogy to the recently deceased Kim Il-sung. "Hardline politburo member Nguyen Duc Binh apparently ordered the change from his hospital bed while reformist prime minister Vo Van Kiet was on a trip to Ho Chi Minh City in the south."[49]

MOVING AHEAD TO NORMALIZE RELATIONS
WITH INDUSTRIALIZED COUNTRIES

Establishing formal relations with the United States was important to Vietnam not only because it would end the economic embargo, but also because it would lead to greater access to aid and loans from the World Bank and IMF. For its part, Vietnam was ready to move. By 1992 the Vietnamese government began to buy once-prohibited American soft drinks "by the caseload" for official occasions. This symbolic re-Coca-colonization of Vietnam was apparently popular at the mass level. "'Why don't the Americans come back?' asked Tran Dien, who hawks American soft drinks on a street corner of Ho Chi Minh City, still known by its residents as Saigon and now the bustling if decrepit center of Vietnam's increasingly free market. 'The war is over. The Vietnamese want the Americans to return.'"[50]

This sentiment was not reciprocated from the American side. Despite the resolution of the Cambodian issue, which the United States had singled out as the obstacle to normalized relations, new impediments were raised—most notably the politically sensitive POW-MIA [American prisoners of war and missing in action] issue—and progress toward full diplomatic recognition remained stalled. American policy toward Vietnam was stalemated by internal bureaucratic disagreements and domestic politics.[51] Vietnam felt, with considerable justification, that the George H. W. Bush administration was moving the goalposts by establishing new conditions to replace the now-resolved Cambodian obstacle. But although Vietnam's overtures to the United States and ASEAN did not pay immediate dividends, Hanoi was able to move to broaden its ties on other fronts.

French President François Mitterrand visited Vietnam in February 1993, promising aid and invoking a "special relationship" between the two countries.[52] Vietnam normalized its economic ties with Japan and established formal diplomatic relations with South Korea. In November the Japanese government dropped its fourteen-year embargo against Vietnam and resumed economic relations, which "represented a major step in Vietnam's attempt to reenter the international economic community."[53]

In the case of South Korea, which had fought with the United States in the Vietnam War and had not normalized relations with Vietnam after 1975, the softening of the US position on isolating Vietnam encouraged Seoul to establish diplomatic relations with Hanoi. Because North Korea had alienated Hanoi by supporting anti-Vietnamese factions in Cambodia, Vietnam was receptive to these overtures.[54]

OBSTACLES AND DIFFICULTIES IN ATTAINING ASEAN MEMBERSHIP

This wave of diplomacy with countries on the other side of the old ideological divide was a prelude to the intensification of efforts to mend fences with ASEAN. Vietnam had many reasons for wanting to integrate more closely into the Southeast Asia region, but the ASEAN countries had their own concerns. There was the issue of the growing power of China, which was an important factor in the formation of the ASEAN Regional Forum (ARF), aimed at including China, the US, and other powers in a security dialogue which might defuse regional tensions. Vietnam was clearly a country which had to be "inside the tent" if an effective regional security dialogue were to be established.

Another ASEAN concern was the increased investment in Vietnam, which appeared to be diverted from ASEAN to China, Vietnam, and India, leading to a 40 percent reduction in direct investment in ASEAN countries by the Asian "tigers" in 1993 compared with the previous year.[55] Creating a broader regional economic system might address this diversion of trade and investment.[56] Thus ASEAN had both security and economic incentives to integrate Vietnam more closely into the region.

Although Vietnam had gained observer status in ASEAN in mid-1992, progress toward full membership was slowed by reservations on both sides. This was truly an example of "wary reconciliation." At the end of 1993, Hoang Anh Tuan, one of the foreign ministry's top analysts, wrote that, "Although there is still some hesitation, there is now a growing consensus in Vietnam on the need to become an Asean member. Recent positive results of economic reforms, a thawing in relations with the US, normalised relations with China, as well as improved relations with the Asean states are making membership possible."[57] In his view, the practical results of Vietnam's economic reform as well as progress in normalizing relations with the United States and individual ASEAN states were important factors in removing obstacles to Vietnam's membership in ASEAN. Unlike many other analysts, who viewed continuing tensions between Vietnam and China over territorial issues as providing impetus for Vietnam to join ASEAN, Tuan implied that improved political relations with China are a positive factor, perhaps precisely because the better the political ties, the less likely China would be to view Vietnam's joining ASEAN as an anti-China move.

In a possible reference to the conservatives who were reluctant to join a formerly adversarial organization, Tuan observed that, "Some think that Asean is no longer a relevant instrument to meet new challenges and should be transformed from a sub-regional to a truly regional organisation. Therefore, Vietnam does not necessarily need to be an Asean member but should be part of a new regional organisation." It was not only conservatives who wanted to form a new organization through merger, giving Vietnam equal status with ASEAN in a new entity, but also people like the now-deposed foreign minister, Nguyen Co Thach, who had earlier advocated this expansion and merger approach.[58]

Nevertheless, Vietnam decided to bow to reality and join ASEAN. Editorial comment by the party's newspaper on Vietnam's July 1992 accession to the Bali treaty of amity and cooperation—a general statement of principles of behavior in the region as distinct from organizational membership in ASEAN—reflected Vietnam's fundamental acceptance of the preconditions for integration into the Southeast Asian region on ASEAN's terms. The signing of the Bali treaty "has opened up a new era in international relations in South-East Asia which is in conformity with the general trend in developing countries."[59]

Whatever Vietnam's preferences, it was not in a position to demand entry into ASEAN on the unrealistic basis of an equal merger, or even a transformed ASEAN, as implied by the occasional suggestion from the Foreign Ministry that a new organization would have to be created that would be an amalgamation of the old ASEAN and the old Indochina bloc of countries. Not only would this exacerbate the fears of many ASEAN members that Vietnamese entry would change the nature of the organization and undermine its solidarity and effectiveness, but it was also a remnant of a bygone era when Vietnam dealt with ASEAN on a plane of diplomatic equality.

During Premier Vo Van Kiet's February 1992 tour of Southeast Asia to lay the groundwork for Vietnam gaining observer status to ASEAN, the foreign minister, Nguyen Manh Cam, said, "Let bygones be bygones. . . . It is much better that we all look towards the future."[60] Deputy Foreign Minister Le Mai said, "For 45 years, Southeast Asia has been divided into two groups of countries opposing each other, but now we can be one group, with the same principles of co-existence and cooperation on the basis of equality and mutual benefit."[61] As a supplicant for membership, Vietnam was hardly in a position to make demands.

Recognizing this, Vietnam's first overtures for joining ASEAN were modest in tone, merely requesting to be allowed to participate in a range of ASEAN activities. In response, ASEAN invited Vietnam (and Laos) to participate in an ASEAN foreign-ministers conference as observers.[62]

Vietnam's progress toward entrance into ASEAN required mending fences with key individual members of the organization. Of these, the most important was Thailand, which had played the role of the "front-line state" of ASEAN in dealing with Vietnam during the 1980s, because its own security interests were most directly involved. Thailand would continue to play a central role in Vietnam's application for membership.

Vietnam's leaders remained suspicious of Thailand, not only because of the past conflicts over Cambodia, but also for fear of economic exploitation by Thai economic interests, which Vietnam viewed as rapacious and exploitative. Hanoi first tested the waters of greater involvement with Thailand by dealing with other ASEAN members, such as Malaysia, with which Vietnam had enjoyed better relations, even during the tense period of the 1980s. A Malaysian security analyst observed that Vietnam was becoming more comfortable in dealing with Malaysia and other ASEAN countries—but not yet Thailand.[63]

But Vietnam–Thai relations soon improved, and they led to a resolution of border issues between the two countries. In part, this was due to Thailand's increasing receptiveness to integrating Vietnam into the region. One of the key Thai figures in diplomacy toward Vietnam, Sukhumband Paribatra, then the director of Chulalongkorn University's

Institute of Security and International Studies, acknowledged that the past conflict with Vietnam over Cambodia, and Vietnam's continued adherence to a communist political system, were problems. "These days, however," said Sukhumband, it "is crucial to integrate Hanoi with our cooperative frameworks if lasting peace and prosperity is to be maintained in the region."[64]

Following party leader Do Muoi's visit to Thailand in October 1993, Foreign Minister Nguyen Manh Cam gave a press briefing on the outcome of the trip. In a gesture of reassurance aimed at Thailand and ASEAN as well as China, Cam stated that Vietnam's settlement of conflicting maritime jurisdiction claims would "not affect a third country." He added that improved relations with Singapore and Thailand "conformed 'with the trends of cooperation and development' and went 'beyond the boundaries of political differences.'" Cam acknowledged that Vietnamese membership in ASEAN was not coming soon (within months) but again emphasized that it would happen "at an appropriate time." [65]

The key diplomatic messages in this statement were that Thai–Vietnamese territorial agreements would "not affect a third country"—that is, would have no bearing on China's territorial claims in Southeast Asia—and that Vietnam was willing to focus on economic cooperation, "beyond the boundaries of political differences." This implies that Vietnam would not pursue an amalgamation of blocs, as in the Thach proposal, and would not pursue political objectives within ASEAN, but would join ASEAN for the purposes of regional economic integration and development. In talks with the Thai premier, Do Muoi noted the changed international economic environment as a factor requiring increased regional cooperation.[66]

Despite the economic focus, security issues were very much in play during this phase of Vietnam's normalization with ASEAN. In addition to the bilateral resolution of territorial issues with Thailand, Do Muoi announced Vietnam's intention to join the impending new ASEAN Regional Forum (ARF).[67] The fact that Do Muoi's reinvigoration of Vietnam's ASEAN diplomacy coincided with the establishment of the ARF underlines the salience of security concerns in Vietnam's relations with ASEAN, despite Vietnam's attempt to stress its economic and development aims in the region, and downplay the impact of closer ASEAN ties on any "third party" (China).

When the ARF was established in July 1993, Vietnam was supportive. The army newspaper, which had been generally suspicious of dealings with the noncommunist world, called it "a 'diplomatic victory' for nations in the area seeking a structure for dialogue on Asia-Pacific security. . . . Vietnam, in joining the ARF, had taken another step towards reintegration into the international political arena and had become an important presence which could not be ignored in matters of regional security."[68]

The problems in fitting into ASEAN were not only the legacy of the past, and contrasts in political systems, but also cultural differences. Reflecting both its colonial past and its extensive ties with the West, ASEAN conducted its business in English. Vietnam's francophone heritage was of little use either in ASEAN or in the larger regional and global context, nor was the Cold War legacy of training a younger generation in Russian and East European languages. The foreign secretary of the Philippines commented on the inability of Vietnamese delegates to follow the proceedings during an ASEAN foreign-ministers meeting, and concluded that, "There is a need for them to learn English which is the language of the ASEAN.' ... When ASEAN ministers meet, we all speak English. But with Laos and Vietnam we need interpreters."[69]

Because of its different colonial heritage, which created an elite of French speakers, and its Cold War alignments, which created a younger generation of Russian speakers, Vietnam was the odd man out in a largely English-speaking group of regional elites. At the time of a 1994 ASEAN meeting, ASEAN officials said "it was not Vietnam's political system, nor its economy which was the biggest hurdle to the country's wish for full membership in the regional body. They blamed the lack of fluent English speakers among Vietnam's senior officials."[70]

Vietnamese opinions about the distinctive characteristics and relative utilities of various foreign languages are, of course diverse. But the view of a Vietnamese diplomat is probably not atypical. Steven Erlanger of the *New York Times* described the case of a long-time Vietnamese friend, a diplomat in his forties, who characterized his life as "a definition of cultural dissonance." He was a Northerner with a French education, followed by Maoism and then Soviet Communism. "Now, once again, he admits, shrugging, it's the turn of the smiling, big-handed Americans, whom he fought rather bravely during the Vietnam War. 'For us,' he once said, 'Chinese is the language of the ancient enemy and brother, from whom we sprang. French is the language of love. Russian is the language of arguments. English is the language of money, the language of our future.'"[71] By the end of 1994, the Foreign Ministry declared that it had trained a sufficient number of English speakers to proceed with entry into ASEAN, though it appeared that this was a somewhat optimistic assessment.[72]

ASEAN's tightly knit and clubby group of leaders reflected their colonial heritage. These were not revolutionaries who had struggled to eliminate the vestiges of colonial rule, but the successors to the colonial authorities, and the inheritors of their tastes and perquisites. Prince Norodom Sirivudh, the Cambodian foreign minister at the time, joked that his Vietnamese counterpart, Nguyen Manh Cam, needed to learn golf because it was a favored game of the rest of the ASEAN foreign ministers. "'Golf and diplomacy, which go hand in hand in this part of the world, are relevant because both Vietnam and Cambodia will become members of Asean in future," said Prince Sirivudh."[73] These required cultural adjustments further underlined the point that Vietnam would have to join ASEAN on ASEAN's terms.

VIETNAM'S FINAL PUSH TO JOIN ASEAN

The ending of the US trade sanctions on Vietnam in 1994 gave new impetus to Vietnam's efforts to join ASEAN. One report observed that Vietnam was moving rapidly toward ASEAN membership, but also noted a continuing lack of enthusiasm for Vietnamese membership in some quarters in ASEAN, and among some sectors of Vietnam as well, out of concern that it would lead to a speeding up of reforms and consequent overheating of the economy. For these reasons, some Vietnamese urged delaying full membership until the year 2000.[74] Other reports also noted high-level hesitancy in Hanoi about joining ASEAN in early 1994, fearing that a faster pace would undermine domestic political stability.[75]

For its part, the United States supported Vietnam's membership. The Asian-affairs director of the National Security Council said, "The United States believes that the three Indochinese economies should be re-integrated into the South-east Asian economy and we would be supportive of efforts to bring those three into existing institutions—ASEAN and, down the road, the Asia Pacific Economic Cooperation."[76]

China too was supportive, and emphasized the benefits of Vietnam's membership in ASEAN for regional economic growth and stability.[77] But, as Vietnam's formal admission to ASEAN approached, China issued a warning about Vietnam using ASEAN to back its interests in territorial conflicts with China. "China on Tuesday warned the six members of ASEAN against backing Hanoi in its dispute with Beijing over the Spratly Islands. . . . 'China doesn't want to see the occurrence of such a situation that Vietnam unites with ASEAN countries to deal with China in common. So it is better for ASEAN to be cautious in satisfying Vietnam's demands in this regard,' a Chinese diplomat said."[78]

In contrast to those in the Vietnamese leadership who feared that accelerated membership in ASEAN might adversely affect the Vietnamese economy, Foreign Minister Nguyen Manh Cam underlined the point that the progress of Vietnam's economic reforms made it a good candidate for ASEAN membership. "Domestic results of our economic reforms have laid down a basis to proceed further by expanding contacts and cooperation in specific ways," Cam said.[79] Premier Vo Van Kiet also endorsed this view. He told the secretary-general of ASEAN that, "The positive development of relations between Vietnam and ASEAN countries has become an important factor in the success of the renewal policy being pursued by Vietnam in recent years."[80]

As Vietnam edged closer to ASEAN membership in 1994, it also expanded its plans to solicit massive external development assistance, now that the lifting of the embargo had cleared the way for trade, investment, and loans. Impending ASEAN membership would give Vietnam the credibility and cachet to solicit this assistance. In the summer of 1994, State Planning Minister Do Quoc Sam announced in Singapore that "Vietnam needs about 50 bn dollars in aid and loans over the next six years in order to develop its economy."[81]

ASEAN REACTIONS TO VIETNAMESE MEMBERSHIP

Following the July 1994 ASEAN decision to admit Vietnam as a member, Vietnamese officials began to attend ASEAN meetings.[82] Vietnam's participation in ASEAN led to an immediate response from both ASEAN and Japan to address Vietnam's reconstruction needs, and facilitate its entry into the global economy.[83] ASEAN viewed Vietnamese membership as a way of expanding a regional market and attracting more outside investment.[84] For its part, the Vietnamese Foreign Ministry expressed the hope that ASEAN membership would help clear the way for more extensive Vietnamese membership in the key institutions of the global economy.[85]

Despite the focus on mutually beneficial economic interdependence, some members of ASEAN were still uneasy about Vietnam's impending entry. A leading security analyst in Indonesia worried about Vietnam bringing a confrontational and intransigent diplomatic style into the more conciliatory political culture of ASEAN.[86] Others quietly hoped that Vietnam would offer an additional counterweight to China's growing influence. "The specter of a battle-hardened and resurgent Vietnam hangs over the Association of Southeast Asian Nations (ASEAN) now preparing to embrace their former communist adversary in an economic and political partnership." Although some regional analysts felt that ASEAN intended to use Vietnam and its erstwhile fearsome military reputation as an implied deterrent to Chinese hegemonic ambitions in the South China Sea, Vietnam's foreign minister rejected the idea that Vietnam would play this role. "Our war period is over. We are now speaking of the post–Cold War era where the tendencies of peace and economic cooperation are predominant, not the balance of forces. Cooperation could bring benefit to all," he said.[87] Singapore's Lee Kuan Yew was more blunt. He said Vietnam would inevitably improve its position with respect to the South China Sea, because after joining, "'it will not be simply a bilateral problem, which it has been up to now.' Vietnam will gradually move into a position more like the Philippines, where Asean must take a position on behalf of the Philippines."[88]

The closely interconnected ASEAN security community, long suspicious of Vietnam's military, saw some compensating advantages in Vietnamese membership in the group. "Vietnam's entry into ASEAN last night is set to foster military ties between Hanoi's armed forces and its new regional allies eyeing China's expansion in the Spratlys. . . . 'Closer military ties are likely to be one of the first silent benefits of Vietnam's membership,' one senior official said."[89]

On the other side of the common security interests were persisting, if low-level, tensions between Vietnam and nearby ASEAN members. Some conflicts with neighbors, such as the Thai protests about the treatment of its fishermen who were arrested in Vietnamese waters, reflected the inability of the Vietnamese central authorities to control the policies and actions of provincial authorities.[90] This was another illustration of the way in which "integration" (*hoi nhap*) required real changes in the way Vietnam governed itself. The devolution of power to the provinces, which was a characteristic of Vietnamese politics during the 1990s, created problems in external relations, and had to be reined in from time to time.

Another impediment to Vietnam's full integration into ASEAN was its cumbersome bureaucracy and its tangled proliferation of tax laws, designed to support various sectors of the government. "Several senior ASEAN diplomats have raised fears that Vietnam's complex structure of charges and hefty tariffs are too crucial to the country's developing economy to be tampered with. 'We're not sure of the will of Vietnam to fully participate, especially when middle-ranking cadres realise that cutting tariffs could mean considerable losses in tax revenue short-term,' one said. 'It will be a great challenge for them to meet and us to keep them to it, but I don't expect them to be ready until at least 2010.'"[91]

RISKS AND BENEFITS OF ASEAN MEMBERSHIP FOR VIETNAM

Joining ASEAN carried risks for Vietnam, along with the benefits. Of these, the most important was the possibility that a premature opening of the Vietnamese domestic economy to competition would derail the reform process itself. Robert Templer reported that, "Vietnam's entry into ASEAN is raising concerns among businesses here that lower tariffs and a more open economy will leave them exposed to some formidable rivals among Asia's economic tigers."[92]

As Vietnam prepared to officially join ASEAN in July 1995, Vu Khoan, the deputy foreign minister who had been in charge of the diplomacy with ASEAN, summarized the reasons for joining: "Vietnam's entry into the regional grouping will 'finally end' a decades-long period of antagonistic interregional relations." Khoan added that, "In the present era" Vietnam had come to realize that it "cannot stand outside international organizations to see their members surging ahead."[93] Vietnam officially joined ASEAN on July 28, 1995. Foreign Minister Nguyen Manh Cam said that Vietnam's full membership in ASEAN "constitutes a milestone marking a change in the conjuncture of Southeast Asia fifty years after the end of the Second World War."[94]

Despite the generally upbeat occasion, some ASEAN members apparently had a case of buyer's remorse, and expressed ambivalence about Vietnam's entry to the club. Some worried that ASEAN had allowed its security concerns regarding China to push for a premature addition of communist Vietnam to a group with very different histories, economic systems, and political agendas. "Several expressed doubts about how smoothly Vietnam's backward economy and Communist Party leadership would slot into the group.... Singapore's Foreign Minister, S. Jayakumar, hinted at such concerns warning of 'challenges' ahead if ASEAN was to cope effectively with an expanded membership."[95]

Vietnam's entry into ASEAN was both an attempt to improve the regional economic and security environment (a milieu objective) and a stepping stone for further integration into the world economy. Entry into the World Trade Organization and an ASEAN Free Trade Association (AFTA) would be the logical next moves. Vietnam's fellow ASEAN members had mixed opinions on its readiness to move to the next level of economic integration, and some ASEAN officials complained that Vietnam was dragging its feet in preparing for accession to AFTA in 2006.[96]

Despite these concerns, ASEAN meetings in the aftermath of Vietnam's accession reflected a heady optimism about the prospects for further regional integration. "'Over time, our region's interconnectedness will be as dense as Europe's,' said Singapore Prime Minister Goh Chok Tong."[97] In light of the fact that the 1997 Asian financial crisis, which would shake the entire region, was looming on the horizon, this optimism seems, in retrospect, misplaced.

The director of Vietnam's Southeast Asia Institute presented an overview of the impact of Vietnam's membership in ASEAN in spring 1996. Among other things, Pham Duc Thanh noted that joining ASEAN had made Vietnam more relevant in the overall scheme of global geopolitics, because it added a new dimension to ASEAN's power and influence and, in turn, Vietnam could leverage its influence within ASEAN and on regional and even global politics through a now more "weighty" ASEAN. "At present, when speaking of the role of the big countries in creating a new balance in the region, we see that along with the United States, China, Japan, Russia, and India, people have to acknowledge the growing importance of ASEAN. The linking of the continents of Asia and Europe will strike a new balance between the three centers [Asia, Europe, and North America] and strengthen the global economy."[98]

Thanh argued that Vietnam's membership had enhanced the strategic influence of ASEAN both by increasing the power resources within the group and because of its unique geostrategic position. "Because it holds an important strategic position in the region, Vietnam can be viewed as a relay station [*chiec relai(s)*] between mainland Southeast Asia and island Southeast Asia, and between the Asian members of APEC [Asia-Pacific Economic Cooperation] and the strategic relations that are being cultivated between Asia and Europe. Precisely because of this, Vietnam still has an important role in resolving the political and security issues of the region."[99]

Professor Thanh noted the different views in ASEAN about Vietnam's motives for joining, and argued against the idea that it was merely a self-interested move to increase investment in Vietnam (ASEAN countries provided only 17 percent of total external direct investment in Vietnam, he asserted) and to gain from technology transfer (ASEAN members had a relatively low level of technology, in his view). So, what did Vietnam get out of it, and what did ASEAN get out of it, he asked? The answer was mutual benefit and a more expansive future for Southeast Asia.[100] The same essential argument of equal benefits applied to the security aspect of Vietnam's membership in ASEAN, asserted Professor Thanh.[101]

If the view of the consequences of Vietnam's entrance into ASEAN from the world of Vietnam's government think tanks was positive, the military and security sector of its political system was more skeptical. On the date of Vietnam's accession to ASEAN, Ho Quang Loi, the leading foreign-affairs commentator for the army newspaper *Quan Doi Nhan Dan*, echoed the "merger of two blocs" view that rejected the idea of a one-way assimilation of Vietnam into the organization of its former adversaries. "Vietnam has joined ASEAN; this means the beginning of an integration [*hoi nhap*] for *both sides* [emphasis added]. This is not only important with respect to Vietnam, but for the whole region. A country whose potential has not yet been unleashed [*giai phong*, literally, "liberated"] and which has the promise of rapid economic growth, is joining a region which is registering the fastest rate of growth in the world. This has attracted the special attention of international observers."[102]

Quang Loi supported the view that Vietnam's entry into ASEAN would expand its international influence and make it a more relevant regional and global actor. "At present, ASEAN is the only organization in the world with a regime of dialogue with the big powers of the world as well as the major economic and political centers of the world. At the same time, according to natural logic of calculations of interest [e.g., universal or rational-choice logic and not merely a conclusion drawn from Marxist premises] the big countries will go all out to win ASEAN over. Because of this, Vietnam's entry into ASEAN has become a focus of international life. And precisely because of this, Vietnam's entry into ASEAN has been viewed by international observers as a very sensitive and critical [*nhay cam*] matter in the complex interdependence of international relations in this region."[103]

A year later, Quang Loi had a more qualified view of the significance of Vietnam's accession to ASEAN. "ASEAN, an active regional organization, is viewed as a successful model of gathering dialogue partners [*doi tac*] in 'regional security forums,' but is regarded as still not having enough strength to resolve the big conflicts in the Asia-Pacific continent."[104]

For party ideologists concerned about the impact of association with noncommunist partners in ASEAN, there were a few bright spots. Singapore's one-party state seemed to offer some possible lessons on how to combine economic development and deep engagement with the global economy with the preservation of an authoritarian system. On a visit to a training seminar in Singapore to learn more about how ASEAN did business, Ho Ngoc Minh, a member of the Vietnamese delegation from the top party training school the Ho Chi Minh National Political academy, expressed the view that Singapore's model of strong government economic guidance was a positive model for development.[105]

Other conservatives in Vietnam also found that ASEAN membership had its advantages. Security was no longer something that could be achieved by national efforts alone, especially with respect to transnational crime. The director-general of Vietnam's police told a Malaysian newspaper that Vietnam's access to the Aseanpol criminal database had been useful in "fighting crime within and outside [Vietnam's] borders. . . . With such a database, we will not only keep watch on criminal activities, but also foster closer ties with other police forces in Asean," he said.[106] Thus both the military and security forces, along with party ideologists, saw ASEAN membership as an advantage.

ASEAN MEMBERSHIP AND GLOBAL INTEGRATION

ASEAN membership is actually more revealing about Vietnam's changing worlds than its reconciliation with the United States because that would have happened whether or not the Cold War blocs existed—it was dependent mainly on domestic factors within the

United States, which delayed the attainment of full diplomatic relations until 1995. For one thing, in joining ASEAN, Vietnam had not been swallowed up and "assimilated," but it was far from the merging of equal blocs, which Foreign Minister Thach had once envisaged. Vietnam had to conform to "the ASEAN way," as evidenced in every aspect of its interactions in ASEAN venues and the difficult adjustment of learning how to communicate in an English-speaking environment with the golfing legatees of the elite perquisites of the colonial era.

More seriously, Vietnam now faced a direct comparison with its more economically advanced ASEAN partners. Vietnam would now be measured by the same economic yardstick, which made it more difficult for its leaders to ignore or conceal how far the country had to go to catch up. Writing in the pages of the party theoretical journal, an economist summed up the post-ASEAN challenges for Vietnam. Noting that Vietnam would be forced to cooperate and compete now more than ever, Truong Giang Long added, "our country must cooperate, integrate, and seize opportunities to push our development faster. That it is the direction we have chosen." Whatever the reasons for its economic backwardness (colonialism, war, embargos), the fact remained that it had an underdeveloped economy, an obsolete infrastructure, and little technology.[107]

Aspiring to develop a market economy and integrate into the regional and global economy would require adopting the same basic comparative measures of economic success as everyone else, making it impossible to disguise poor performance. This consideration was clearly a concern for the Vietnamese leadership, to the extent that political legitimacy would be increasingly performance-based, and the main arena of performance would be the economy. Considerations of performance and efficiency might force policies that would reduce party control over important aspects of Vietnamese society. Of these economic yardsticks, the most prominent was average per capita income, which was for Vietnam, "compared with the other countries in the region, still rather far [behind]."[108] In addition to the increased pressure on leaders to perform, since the measure was now efficiency, there was a shift from the equity or redistribution priorities of the old command-economy system—even though international standards of national economic statistics also had measures for equity (percentage of population below the poverty line, gap between the top and bottom quartile in terms of income, etc.) Despite the challenges presented by joining an organization that required playing by rules established by Vietnam's former adversaries, the postmembership assessments of the benefits for Vietnam were largely positive.

The Foreign Ministry official directly responsible for Vietnam–ASEAN relations said that, "After Vietnam joined ASEAN the relations between Vietnam and the ASEAN nations completely changed, and no longer had a confrontational character as before, but increasingly reflected the spirit of 'being in the same meeting, being in the same boat' [*cung hoi, cung thuyen*]. . . . On that basis we were able to resolve many problems that were previously difficult to solve bilaterally, such as delineating the continental shelf with Malaysia, resolving the question of Vietnamese residents in Thailand, and the problem of

refugees with almost all the countries of Southeast Asia." Membership had also strengthened Vietnam's international influence and prestige, he said, and enabled Vietnam to
become a full member of the ARF, which enabled it to deal more effectively with the big
powers. Another plus was that membership in ASEAN had an impact on Vietnamese
domestic opinion in support of integration, in showing that Vietnam could join the
region and engage with the world without losing its independence.[109]

There was, too, a larger context to Vietnam's ASEAN membership. July 1995 was also
a banner month for Vietnam's new diplomacy of diversification and multilateralization.
In addition to establishing formal diplomatic relations with the United States and joining
ASEAN, Vietnam also finalized a trade agreement with the European Union. The conservative voice of Vietnam's army newspaper hailed the signing of an economic and trade
accord with the European Union as an "important step in bilateral relations between
Vietnam and the European Union." Along with the normalization of relations with the
United States and membership in ASEAN, it represented "a further success in the external politics of Vietnam's (Communist) Party and State." The army paper passed over in
silence one part of the ASEAN agreement, "a non-binding clause on Vietnam's human
rights record, contained in the accord."[110]

Vietnam's entry into ASEAN and its simultaneous completion of the long path
toward normalization of relations with the United States seemed to mark an end point
of the process of reconciliation with former adversaries. But it also came at a time when
the international system was in flux, and Vietnamese strategists and theoreticians had a
difficult time in sorting out the larger picture. Their Marxist training in dialectics and
alertness to contradictory historical currents ("contradictions") sensitized them to complexity, but the Marxist framework was severely stretched and did not serve as a clear
guide for determining how these various contending international currents would evolve.

Of the many questions about the future, one of the most distant and abstract was perhaps the most fundamental: if Vietnam's party leaders and ideologists remained convinced that the collapse of socialism in the Soviet Union and Eastern Europe was a mere
bump in the road on the path to communism, what would become of capitalism, which
seemed to be on a roll, with the end of the Cold War and with its apparent success as a
development model, especially in Asia? We will address this question in the following
chapters. It is relevant in this context because it raises the issue of where ASEAN, with its
predominantly capitalist make-up, was headed—and what the long-term implications of
Vietnam's membership in ASEAN were.

Pham Duc Duong, one of Vietnam's leading Southeast Asian experts, catalogued the
various contending forces in his analysis of the implications of Vietnam's entry into
ASEAN and acknowledged the difficulties of analyzing a situation in flux. "Naturally, we
are at a turning point in the history of the world with the organic relations and mutual
impact between two processes of development. This refers to the social revolution from
capitalism toward a socialist direction, and to the scientific and industrial revolution
from industrial civilization to post industrial civilization. Every creed [*tin dieu* = belief

system] is somewhat outmoded [*khong con hoan toan phu hop*], and none of the past methods of getting closer [to an understanding reality] can give us the key to go from the present to the future."[111]

The contending forces identified by Vietnamese analysts were the contradictions between regionalization and globalization, and between integration and nationalism or separatism. The transitions were from a bipolar world to a multipolar world, from a world of arms races to a world of peace. It was also a world of increasing interdependence as well as a world of increasing economic conflict. Duong asserted that the core Cold War arenas like Europe had paradoxically enjoyed stability during the tense standoff between the two superpowers, while the hot conflicts were in peripheral areas like Southeast Asia. Now, he argued, the situation was reversed. All the pent-up conflicts in Europe were reemerging, while Southeast Asia was more quickly stabilizing. Even so, he warned that "in the coming decade Southeast Asia will face tense challenges. Apart from internal questions in each country and in the region at large, the countries of Southeast Asia will have to cope with a world filled with transformations and tense competitions while the ties of interdependence are increasingly close and expanding." "Looked at from the point of view of security," he added—in contrast to his portrayal of Southeast Asia as more stable than Europe—"the danger of destabilization is enveloping Southeast Asia. The question of the 'Eastern Sea' [South China Sea] is bubbling up as a hot point—a very difficult problem to resolve!"

In addition, increases in defense spending in the region, power vacuums, and religious tensions were growing. The fact that Islam had a presence in 150 countries was the specific example Duong used to illustrate the point (in 1995), well before radical Islam had become an international concern. Thanh reflected the dominant view of Vietnamese analysts in asserting that, "From now [1995] to the year 2000 the world, though it is not unipolar (although no one can compete with the United States!) it still is not multipolar though the trajectory toward multipolarity and many centers is still the predominant tendency."[112] From a security perspective, the picture in Southeast Asia from the vantage of the mid-1990s was mixed. Vietnam had improved its security position by joining ASEAN, but there were still clouds hanging over the region.

Although the initial entry of Vietnam into ASEAN seemed to bring about positive results, the apparent stability and prosperity of ASEAN would soon be challenged by the 1997 Asian financial crisis, political instability in Cambodia, and strains over the further expansion of ASEAN. All of this would test Vietnam's commitment to the group, but at the same time give it a voice in shaping a regional response to these crises.

FIGURE 1. Hanoi street 1982. In this prereform year, there was hardly a vehicle in sight. Hanoi was quiet and bucolic, but political tension was high. By 2006 this street was routinely choked with chaotic bumper-to-bumper traffic.

FIGURE 2. Author and deputy director of Vietnam's State Commission for the Social Sciences, Dao Van Tap, 1982.

FIGURE 3. Window display in the State Department Store in central Hanoi, 1982. Enameled pans, prominently displayed, were the height of consumer aspirations at this time.

FIGURE 4. By 2006, the old State Department Store had been demolished and replaced by a glittering new shopping center, whose window displays showed a marked shift in consumer tastes and availability of goods from the socialist austerity of 1982.

FIGURE 5. Vietnamese participants in the Aspen Institute's US–Vietnam Dialogue in 1990. On the left is Vietnam's leading reform economist, Le Dang Doanh, and on the right (front) the mathematician Phan Dinh Dieu, whose early bold calls for reform created a stir in the 1980s and 1990s. In the back (third from left), is the Harvard-trained economist Nguyen Xuan Oanh (known to Americans during the Saigon period as "Jack Owens" for his fluent English). Oanh was very briefly prime minister of South Vietnam in 1964, and was consulted by Party leaders about remedies for the economic crisis in Vietnam in the early 1980s.

FIGURE 6. First joint US–Vietnam conference in the social sciences, on "economic renovation," Hanoi, June 1990. Second from the right is Foreign Minister Nguyen Co Thach, and on the right is Pham Nhu Cuong, a leading figure in the field of ideology at the time. President of the Social Science Research Council, David Featherman is on Thach's right and Bill Turley, who edited a volume of papers from this conference, is next to him.

FIGURE 7. Former senator Dick Clark, organizer of the US–Vietnam Dialogue, meets with Foreign Minister Thach in 1991. Author is on the left, and Bill Nell of Aspen on the right.

FIGURE 8. Senator Clark meets Prime Minister Vo Van Kiet in 1991. Kiet was one of the key figures in Vietnam's reforms.

FIGURE 9. Professor Phan Huy Le, a leading figure in Vietnam's academic and cultural life, and a pioneer of academic exchanges between Vietnamese and foreign scholars. He organized the landmark first conference on Vietnamese studies in 1998.

FIGURE 10. Legendary General Vo Nguyen Giap (fourth from left) lends the prestige of his presence to the 1998 International Conference on Vietnamese Studies.

FIGURE 11. Luu Doan Huynh of the Vietnamese Foreign Ministry's Institute for International Relations. For years he was an *éminence grise*, both for Vietnamese diplomats and visiting foreign scholars, who appreciated his penetrating intellect and candor.

FIGURE 12. Author (right) lectures at the faculty of international relations at the National University of Vietnam in Hanoi, 2007. Prof. Pham Quang Minh, the dean of the faculty is at the left.

6

Uncertain Transition (1996–1999)

ALTHOUGH VIETNAM ESTABLISHED formal diplomatic relations with the United States more or less simultaneously with its entry into ASEAN, the two events had different implications for Vietnam's integration into the post–Cold War world. Entry into ASEAN marked a substantial culmination of the process of diplomatic normalization of relations with the individual members of that organization, as well as a general desire by Vietnam to ensure stability in the region for both security and economic reasons. Joining ASEAN signified Vietnam's entry into an explicit political community and implicit security community in its region. ASEAN membership was politically easier for the Vietnamese leadership than normalization of relations with the United States, but required a greater shift in collective mindset.

The lesson of joining ASEAN was that limited integration in the region was possible without major changes to Vietnam's internal system, albeit with a diminished regional and global stature. Vietnam would no longer be on the front lines of great world events, but simply another Southeast Asian country of limited global impact. It is not surprising that during the late 1990s Vietnam's security dialogues with countries like Australia and Indonesia focused on how to play the role of a middle power, and how to deal with the great powers—this time without a counterbalancing great-power patron.[1] This was another indication that Vietnam was increasingly assessing its security through a realist, rather than an ideological lens. There were clearly strategic and economic advantages to better relations with the United States, but also a perceived greater threat to Vietnam's internal regime and its power holders.

There were few downsides to joining ASEAN and it was relatively unproblematic within the Vietnamese leadership, even though accepting a smaller role in the region within the framework of an organization Vietnam's leaders had once reviled required a greater shift in thinking than the relatively simpler act of accepting diplomatic recognition from the United States. In part, this was offset by the ASEAN stress on non-interference in domestic affairs, which meant that Vietnam's internal political system would not be an issue. And, unlike the United States, ASEAN did not attempt to dictate how Vietnam interacted with the rest of the world by embargos, sanctions, roadmaps, or imposing conditions for membership in organizations controlled or influenced by the United States.

Vietnam's ambivalence about ties with the United States continued after diplomatic relations were established, and was symptomatic of the tortuous progress of reform during the period of uncertain transition from the reactive reform of the late 1980s and early 1990s to its turn-of-the-century decision to embark on a path of comprehensive integration into the global system. It was, however, the very success of limited integration in the late 1980s and early 1990s that reinforced the doubts and backsliding on reform that characterized the period 1996–9.

Vietnam's entry into ASEAN and establishment of diplomatic relations with the United States coincided with what its leaders regarded as the successful completion of the first phase of its reform-era economic development program. In retrospect, said a leading ideologist in 2006, the sense of crisis that had initially impelled the reforms had dissipated by 1995.[2] This caused some Vietnamese leaders to conclude that the previous cautious approach to reform was working, and bolder measures were not needed. Vietnam could develop without fundamentally changing policies and institutions. In some ways it was the perceived success of limited reform that reduced the sense of urgency and contributed to prolonging the period of uncertain transition to the next phase of more extensive reform and integration that characterized the period 1996–2000.

Vietnam's decision to join ASEAN reflected its "new thinking" about international relations, stimulated by the winding down of the Cold War and the lessons drawn from Vietnam's costly occupation of Cambodia. This new thinking was largely prompted by recognition that Vietnam's military actions had not been the most effective means of pursuing its national interests, and that economic development was the key to national strength and well being. This, in turn, required a stable regional and global environment.

From this perspective, other Southeast Asian countries did not represent a security threat to Vietnam, and there were many areas of common interest that Vietnam shared with its neighbors, most of all a shared concern for regional stability and prosperity. Extensive economic integration into the region (ASEAN Free Trade Area, AFTA) was left to the future, but it was understood that there were no fundamental obstacles to this. Vietnam's economic integration into the region was only a matter of time and degree. Vietnam's changed assessment of ASEAN played a significant role in shifting the collective mind set of the leadership from a world view based on a Darwinian zero-sum conception of international relations to a recognition that some situations were, or could be, win-win.

Although Vietnam completed the formal process of diplomatic normalization with the United States in 1995, this normalization had a strategic logic that was independent of the post–Cold War changes in the global landscape. It also had a simple economic logic; ending the embargo and avoiding US opposition to international economic assistance to Vietnam was crucial to its future development. To some extent, improved relations with the United States was a "no brainer" that did not require a substantial shift in mindset among Vietnam's leaders.

Yet some in the Vietnamese leadership were concerned that deeper involvement with the United States would create problems even as it opened up new opportunities. Establishing diplomatic relations with the United States had long held clear strategic and economic advantages for Vietnam, and it had pursued this objective during the post-1975 period of the Cold War. Though many observers feel that Hanoi missed several chances to improve relations with the United States after 1975, it is also true that political conditions in the United States posed severe obstacles to normalization. It is, however, easier to imagine establishment of diplomatic relations between the United States and Vietnam in, say, 1978, than Vietnamese entry into ASEAN at that time because of the influence the United States had in the global and regional systems and any reduction in threat from the United States would be to Vietnam's advantage, especially in view of Hanoi's deteriorating relations with China.

Mutual diplomatic recognition in 1995 was accompanied by dismantling the economic pressures that the United States had imposed on Vietnam, most notably an end to the Cold War-era economic embargo. Still, US–Vietnam relations developed slowly during the 1995–2000 period, in part because Vietnam was hesitant to take the next step toward a bilateral trade agreement and entry into the World Trade Organization, for fear that it would be destabilizing economically and politically. American attempts to establish a security dialogue were largely rebuffed during this period. Key figures in Vietnam's leadership continued to be ambivalent about ties with the United States, and some regarded closer ties as more of a threat than an opportunity.

This view continued to place limits on US–Vietnam cooperation for several years following the establishment of diplomatic relations in 1995. In his overview of events in Vietnam during 1998, Mark Sidel observed that "U.S.-Vietnam relations in 1998 were characterized by both a deepening of ties and frustration. The two countries seem to be simultaneously cooperating and miscommunicating."[3] Some Vietnamese put the blame on the United States. Reversing the image of irresistible attractiveness that Vietnam had once ascribed to itself in explaining the not always wanted attentions of foreigners, a high-ranking Vietnamese diplomat, frustrated by American demands in the difficult negotiations over a bilateral trade agreement, remarked to Sidel, "America is a beautiful lady, but very hard to please."[4] A "senior diplomat" told Sidel that he was convinced that it was America's objective to try to engineer that collapse of Vietnam and the over-throw of its regime.[5] This view was remarkable mainly for the fact that it came from a diplomat rather than from the Vietnamese military or party ideologists.

Closer ties with the United States increased the unease of some of Vietnam's leaders about the impact of "opening up" on what they termed "political stability"—which meant the continued firm monopoly of the party on political and economic power—and heightened their sense of vulnerability. In this chapter we will trace this dialectic of normalization and paranoia, and its contribution to Vietnam's erratic path of reform in the latter part of the 1990s, and its fitful progress toward global integration.

SECOND THOUGHTS ABOUT RISKS OF REFORM

During the last half of the 1990s, reform in Vietnam was slowed by its leaders' second thoughts about the risks of reform, and by difficulties in achieving a clear-cut political transition to a younger generation, and the fact that the potential younger leaders did not have the political weight of their elders. This resulted in a political process that was often indecisive.

There were also differences within the leadership about how much political risk could be tolerated in the opening-up process in order to achieve continued economic growth. In terms of attitudes and temperament, younger did not necessarily mean bolder or more supportive of *doi moi*, opening up, or more receptive to new thinking. Indeed, the transitional generation (such as party leader Le Kha Phieu) were in some ways less committed to change than the older generation they replaced, or more insecure and therefore less willing to accept the risks of change. The combination of a complex and drawn-out leadership succession and the realization that Vietnam would now have to move into a higher-risk phase of reform combined with the cautionary lessons of the Asian financial crisis to make the period 1996–2000 a period of uncertain transition.

We have discussed in previous chapters the deep division within the Vietnamese leadership over the question of whether the primary threat to Vietnam was economic backwardness, and the danger of falling further behind in a brutally competitive world, or the ideological danger to Vietnam's socialist system and party control. Let us recall the account by Deputy Foreign Minister Tran Quang Co about the debate surrounding Vietnam's decision to normalize relations with China. As Vietnam's overall foreign policy was undergoing a sweeping reevaluation in the spring of 1990, some Vietnamese asked, "Why were the other countries in the region worried about China, while Vietnam placed its hopes on China (as a strategic ally)?"; "Was the expansionist hegemonistic face of China the main one, or was it socialism?"; "What was the real nature of 'socialism with Chinese characteristics'?" The related big questions were "What is the main threat to our security and development at present? Is it the threat of falling behind economically or is it peaceful evolution?" and what measures "can be taken to cope with these threats and achieve our objectives ('strategic ally,' 'special relationship')?"[6]

One of the ironies of reform was that its successes made some in the leadership uneasy and insecure. As a report by Nick Cumming-Bruce of *The Guardian* put it, at the end of 1993 (the period that the "peaceful evolution" campaign was beginning to gear up), even as living standards rose and foreign investment increased as Vietnam increasingly opened up, "the success of a pragmatic leadership opening Vietnam to a market economy only underlines the contradictions within a party still dedicated to socialism and a one-party state. A Western observer in Hanoi remarked that, 'It raises the spectre of a dynamic, successful country finding the party increasingly irrelevant, and there are plenty of signs of that.'" Western observers noted the mixed messages in party documents—calls for vigilance against plots to undermine Marxism-Leninism interspersed with new economic reform measures. "'Everything shows they have to abandon Marxism in order to preserve their leading role, but they don't dare to spit it out,' said a reform-minded Hanoi intellectual, himself a party member. 'They create imaginary enemies to make themselves more relevant.'"[7]

To some extent, therefore, the degree of willingness to accept the risks of reform was a function of the desire of many leaders to preserve their power and position. The structural problem the party faced was that its political position was based on a closed monopoly of power, which was threatened by the opening up in the economic sphere that was necessary to promote and maintain prosperity and stability. In simplest terms, the leadership was faced with a choice between a self serving opposition to change that might threaten their position, and the promotion of change inherent in the opening-up process, which would produce development for the good of the country and the welfare of its population.

It must also be said that the author's extensive interviews with scholars, analysts, and diplomats throughout East and Southeast Asia in 1999 and 2000 revealed that most observers felt that Vietnam was becoming more open, cooperative, and at ease with its regional environment. Whatever the hesitations and reservations at the very top of the political system, Vietnam's ASEAN membership provided a new momentum to the process of opening up, which was gradually accelerating despite the high-level ambivalence. This chapter is mainly about the foot dragging of Vietnam's top leadership as they tried to slow the pace of reform and integration, but the late 1990s were also a period where the ground was shifting beneath their feet, and this proved to be the last gasp of fundamental resistance to "changing worlds."

Apart from the political dilemma of reconciling regional and global integration with regime preservation, a key question was whether Vietnam's security should be analyzed through the lens of realism (China as a threat because of its power and proximity), neoliberalism (economics must take top priority because Vietnam's main task was to take advantage of the development opportunities offered by globalization, because economic backwardness was a threat to its international power and influence and a problem for regime stability if a failing economy led to unrest and disaffection), or ideology (China as an indispensable ally in safeguarding the remnants of the socialist world from the plot of "peaceful evolution").

PEACEFUL EVOLUTION: THE DEVELOPMENT OF A CONCEPT

Although the term "peaceful evolution" had earlier been used in other contexts, the concept of peaceful evolution as it evolved into the 1990s was a Chinese formulation adapted by Vietnam's ideologists to describe the new challenge to the beleaguered remnant socialist regimes following the collapse of communism in the Soviet Union and Eastern Europe. In this view, the United States and the capitalist world had not forsaken their ambition of destroying socialism, but had simply updated their strategy and tactics to conform with the new international realities of the post–Cold War world. For those who subscribed to this view, there were clear limits to the level of cooperation with capitalist countries (and the United States in particular) as well as the extent of integration into a capitalist-dominated global system.

A Voice of Vietnam 1994 summary of peaceful evolution described it as "a trick of imperialism aimed at eradicating socialism." A short historical sketch noted that "peaceful evolution" was a strategy that "first came into existence in 1949 when it was first used by the Americans. Shrouded with a complex history, this strategy has gone through many stages and has resorted to various essential tricks such as creating counterrevolutionary public opinion and mass media in the ideological domain, making inroads into the cultural thinking,[8] containing our economic growth and nurturing those economic forces whom they call democratic forces." The commentary observed that, "The 'peaceful evolution' strategy is nothing but a change in the format to conceal the reactionary nature of imperialism." Possibly alluding to Joseph's Nye's recently introduced concept of "soft power" the United States was said to be waging war "with the use of soft tools [*cong cu mem*]."[9]

"Peaceful evolution" is a concept especially relevant to the subject of this study— Vietnam's "changing worlds"—since its central assumption is that the "two worlds" of capitalism and communism will persist in antagonistic struggle until one or the other is eliminated and, therefore, the significance of the end of the Cold War is downplayed by implying that the world remained divided into two antagonistic and irreconcilable groups. This rules out the concept of a stable and lasting unified global system (unless all noncapitalist regimes are eliminated) and is incompatible with the very idea of "globalization"—unless it is understood as strategy of capitalism to dominate the world.

The negative consequences of a reform program that opens Vietnam's economy and society to the outside world were spelled out by Colonel Tran Ba Khoa in the January 1993 edition of the party's leading theoretical journal. He accused the United States of economic and cultural sabotage against Vietnam, citing the embargo, foreign investment which harms local Vietnamese industry, and even cultural exchanges and tourism. "They even used money and goods to bribe our cadres in the form of gifts, thereby degenerating our cadres and party members and persuading them to admire capitalism while criticizing socialism. Other hostile forces have also taken advantage of our open door policy to lead our economy to the path of capitalism and total privatization.

This is another fact that some of us have not realized or have tried to ignore due to the temptation of the green dollars."[10]

A 1993 Chinese study of peaceful evolution, translated into Vietnamese and circulated by the military intelligence branch of Vietnam's army, opened by stating that, "Socialism and capitalism are two social systems [*che do*] that are in fundamental opposition. This opposition and struggle between the two systems has never ceased. From the beginning, international reactionary forces have never abandoned their fundamental stance of enmity and overthrow of socialism."[11] The Vietnamese introduction concurred, "From the birth of socialism, the consistent strategic goal of imperialism has been to destroy socialism," using a number of "the most poisonous schemes, among which is 'peaceful evolution.'"[12]

A few years later the lead translator of the book, the head of Vietnam's Institute for the Study of China, expressed concern that China was employing one of the key tactics of peaceful evolution outlined in great detail in the study, indirect economic pressure, to gain total control over Hong Kong after its 1997 reversion to the mainland. This suggests a significant exception to the idea that the stratagems of peaceful evolution were used only by the capitalists.[13] Even the Chinese studies of peaceful evolution, translated in 1993, noted that the fundamental idea of defeating an enemy without firing a shot (or, as the Vietnamese put it "without gun smoke": *khong khoi sung*) was a staple of ancient Chinese strategy going back at least to the Warring States period, and thus not exclusively a strategy of capitalism.[14]

"PEACEFUL EVOLUTION" AND RELATIONS WITH THE UNITED STATES AND CHINA

Often the threat was vaguely ascribed to "hostile forces" or "imperialism," even though the plans of this amorphous threat were alarmingly specific. The commentary on peaceful evolution mentioned above, from the January 1993 party journal, asserted that "For Vietnam, we realize that imperialism has formulated plans and prepared secret forces to stage a comeback when opportunity permits. The imperialists have also coordinated with reactionary forces in the three Indochinese countries to carry out a multifaceted war of sabotage."[15]

Although it was not always singled out or explicitly mentioned, the main alleged mastermind of peaceful evolution in the 1990s remained the United States. The implication was that closer contacts between the United States and Vietnam could offer America a better opportunity to undermine Vietnam's socialist regime. This connection between closer ties with the United States and heightened fear of the consequences is captured in news reports that the Vietnamese response to the lifting of the US-imposed economic embargo in early 1994 was to escalate the crack down on dissidents and call for heightened vigilance against peaceful evolution.[16]

Although many Vietnamese, including Vietnamese officials, welcomed the dropping of the embargo, some did not. Still, the Foreign Ministry issued a statement noting that on February 3, 1994, "President Bill Clinton declared the lifting of the embargo on Vietnam and proposed the mutual establishment of liaison offices in the two countries. This is a positive and significant decision which contributes to opening a new page in the US–Vietnam relations in the interests of the two peoples."[17] A foreign reporter noted, however, that "The American pill is a nonetheless a bitter one to swallow for some Vietnamese leaders, notably in the military."[18]

It was not the hardened guerrilla fighters from the South, or the combat commanders and veterans of North Vietnamese forces who had struggled against the United States during the Vietnam War that were in the vanguard of reaction against normalizing relations with the United States. The addition of a political general (Le Kha Phieu) to the politburo was done just prior to the formal ending of the embargo. But it was mainly the military intelligence branch that was promoting the threat of peaceful evolution in the early 1990s, primarily through the publication of translations of Chinese books on the subject.

Although many of Vietnam's reformers were privately dismissive of this concept, it had a sufficient hold on the top leadership to provide a continuing check on the pace and scope of reform and integration throughout the 1990s. Not until Vietnam's final acceptance into the World Trade Organization and the responsibilities of being a constructive partner in regional and global integration, especially its role in hosting the APEC conference in 2006, pushed peaceful evolution into the background, did this concept cease to act as a brake on reform and integration into the global system.

As mentioned above, peaceful evolution was not always exclusively attributed to the United States, even though its main expressed concern was with a purported "imperialist" plot to eliminate socialism in Vietnam. Ironically, one of the earliest Vietnamese uses of the term "peaceful evolution" was in the context of alleged Chinese schemes to contest Vietnamese dominance in Cambodia and Laos during the period of the Third Indochina War between Hanoi and Beijing. In 1980, the Vietnamese Foreign Ministry charged that, "In collusion with the United States, and through the agency of Thailand, they are striving to push remnant Pol Pot troops and other Khmer reactionaries back to Kampuchea from Thailand for the purpose of disrupting the Kampuchean revolution and maintaining hostilities along the Kampuchean–Thai border." In contrast to the more direct Chinese intervention in Cambodia, Vietnam charged that China was using subversion to gain a foothold in Laos. "They have increasingly intimidated and threatened Laos, and have stepped up their attempts to bring about a 'peaceful evolution' and foment disturbances in Laos, to drive a wedge between Laos, Vietnam and Kampuchea, and to undermine the solidarity of the three Indochinese countries."[19]

The pre-1989 usage of the term "peaceful evolution" by Vietnam and its allies was as a general description of subversion by political means and psychological warfare.[20] Following the events of 1989, there were two significant developments in the Vietnamese definition and usage of the concept, prior to its relegation to the background in 2006. The first was the Vietnamese response to the collapse of the socialist regimes in Eastern Europe. In 1990, the Vietnamese began to describe this as the result of a Western plot to undermine all socialist regimes. The specific concern at that time was mainly political. Hanoi was worried about Vietnamese dissidents and exiles, who might be used by the United States to destabilize Vietnam's socialist regime.

The second major step in refining the concept of "peaceful evolution" came in 1993–4, and shifted the focus of the concept to economic, cultural, and ideological subversion, and directly addressed the implications of the shrinkage of the once-mighty socialist bloc, and the question of whether or not a single world system (with little room for socialism) was emerging. Vietnam had failed to establish an ideological alliance with China on the basis of socialist solidarity, but it still borrowed heavily from Chinese formulations of the peaceful-evolution concept. The starting point of the Chinese analysis was that the success of the United States in overthrowing socialism in Eastern Europe through the strategy and tactics of peaceful evolution had led to the dissolution of the post–Second World War "Yalta system," that is, the relatively stable coexistence of two antagonistic blocs.[21]

In the view of some Chinese ideologists, the end of the Cold War did not mark the fundamental turning point in international relations that many Western observers assumed, because, in their view, the Cold War continued in a new guise. This also meant, by implication, that the "two worlds" international system would survive the end of the Cold War. Although, in this view, the suppression of the Tian An Men Square demonstrations marked a setback to the alleged American plot to finish off socialism in China, as it had done in Eastern Europe, "We must recognize that the peaceful evolution [aim] of transforming socialism into capitalism remains a harsh reality. 'A World War without gun smoke' as the West has proclaimed is still spreading. . . . From the containment strategy of Truman to today's strategy of 'beyond containment'[22] the forty-year struggle between the two systems has continued unabated."[23] Yet another of the Chinese works on peaceful evolution translated and published by Vietnam's Military Intelligence Directorate in 1993–94 was titled "The world war without gun smoke," another reference to the idea that the fundamental life-or-death conflict between socialism and capitalism persisted, even if the strategy had changed.[24]

One of the few books on peaceful evolution published by the Military Intelligence Directorate during this period that was written by a Vietnamese author and tailored to Vietnamese circumstances argued that America was intent on bringing about the end of socialism in Vietnam in order to finally kick the "Vietnam syndrome." It would do this by promoting economic and political freedom and, if necessary, supplement the soft and unobtrusive tactics of peaceful evolution with violent methods to overthrow the regime.[25] The main focus of the peaceful evolution would be to "push the economy of the Socialist Republic of Vietnam out of the orbit of socialism, privatize and liberalize [*tu do hoa*] the economy in the direction of the capitalist free market."[26] The strategic aim of the "Western world, headed by the United States" would be to "overthrow the socialist state, overthrow the leadership of the Communist Party, negate the ideological construct [*hinh thai y thuc*] of Marxism-Leninism, restore a world system unified under capitalism."[27] Despite the paranoia evident in much of this study of the dangers of peaceful evolution, the conclusion was relatively reassuring. "If we are vigilant, and succeed in our reforms [*doi moi thang loi*], we will continue to have political stability, and will confirm the superiority of socialism, and the peaceful evolution strategy of the Americans and forces opposed to Vietnam will be defeated."[28]

THE EIGHTH PARTY CONGRESS: DEFERRED TRANSITION

Just prior to the Eighth Party Congress in mid-1996, the police carried out a highly publicized raid on Peregrine Capital, a high-profile Hong Kong investment bank, alleging that its foreign manager—a very visible Vietnamese-American—had evaded taxes and violated Vietnamese laws. The raid was a move seen by observers as "one of the strongest signs yet of Hanoi's resolve to wrest back central control over the economy, rein in the private sector, and check foreign cultural influences. Ten years after launching the economic reforms known as *doi moi*, or 'renovation,' party leaders are intent on showing investors who's boss."[29] *Business Week* cautioned that as a result of this and other actions, "Vietnam could fall victim to a classic trap of reaping the easy gains of a newly opening economy without putting the fundamentals in place for the next stage of growth."[30]

In spite of the opaque and often impenetrable barriers to understanding the inner workings of Vietnamese elite politics, there is something approaching a consensus among foreign observers that the Eighth Party Congress was marked by bitter struggle over policies and personnel. As always, it is misleading to analyze this in terms of "reformers" and "conservatives"—especially since the leading "reformist" protagonist, Prime Minister Vo Van Kiet, pushed hard for various reforms precisely in order to strengthen the political control of the Communist Party. Still, it is clear that in the lead-up to the Eighth Party Congress a major struggle took place over the wisdom of speeding market and legal reforms and the need to adopt more fundamental new thinking about Vietnam's present and future.

Robert Templer's valuable reporting from Vietnam in this period presents a vivid picture of the political conflict. He notes the significance of an important letter by Prime Minister Vo Van Kiet, written in August 1995 to other members of the politburo and presenting his vision for the future, nearly a year before the Eighth Party Congress. Templer notes that this letter touched off an intense political struggle, and ultimately diminished the influence of the conservatives. His main point was that the party could no longer vacillate between reform and retrenchment, but had to "cut the Gordian knot of Market-Leninism—the contradiction between the legal needs of a market and the economy and the desire for the party to keep his hands on power." Sounding somewhat like Deng Xiaoping, Kiet said that Vietnam's ideology was outdated and that, "Socialism was what worked." Templer adds that, "Kiet believed the party should give up even pretending to nurture the withered vine of Marxism and instead shelter under the tree of Vietnamese nationalism."[31]

In a 1996 interview with the liberal newspaper *Tuoi Tre*, Kiet replied to a question about the divergence of opinions on political issues and its implication for political stability. He replied, "The old plots of imperialism in previous times have left not a few problems for our national community. The consequences of this must be patiently solved. It is necessary to make concerted efforts to wipe away the prejudices and suspicions about each other. I think that there is not a single Vietnamese, except for those who have resigned themselves to selling out the country, who doesn't want our country to become rich and powerful. And every time we strive to make our country rich and powerful, and our society civilized, we will elicit sympathy and mutual understanding from the community."[32]

Kiet's provocative analysis in his letter to the politburo started from the observation that the dissolution of the two-worlds configuration of the bipolar Cold War era had invalidated many of the fundamental assumptions of Vietnamese policy. Although the new era posed many difficult challenges, he argued, it also offered many opportunities for Vietnam to develop. Kiet came clearly down on the side of those who argued that falling further behind the rest of the world economically was the major threat to Vietnam's security, and that taking risks to engage with the world was essential to ensure its national future.

"In today's world," Kiet told the Politburo, "there is no antagonistic contradiction between socialism and imperialism, but above all there is a quality of diversity and multipolarity which is becoming the most dominant [*noi troi*] element that governs the interactions [*su van dong cua ca moi quan he*] between all states in the world." In addition, globalization was playing an increasingly important role in international relations and rendering the old divisions obsolete. "Many other contradictions which existed during the period when the world was divided into two camps, including even the contradiction between imperialism and socialism, may continue to exist, but they will increasingly be governed by other contradictions and because of this will not longer play their old role."[33]

Using the familiar language of Marxist analysis ("contradictions") Kiet asserted that the world has fundamentally changed, and Vietnam could no longer operate on the basis of the old assumptions. Although Kiet's views did not prevail at the Eighth Party Congress, and many of the reform measures he called for remained stalled for the remainder of the 1990s, this letter seems to be a watershed in the evolution of Vietnam's new thinking about international relations, in that it represents a leader at the very top of the political system explicitly closing the chapter of the "two worlds" mentality and spelling out the logical consequences of abandoning this "us and them" mentality.

To ensure that no one could miss the point, Kiet wrote, "It is necessary to evaluate the true character of the relations among the remaining socialist countries. The truth is that at present four socialist countries remain, although the relations between them remain at a modest level [*quan he voi nhau o muc do nhat dinh*] and they can't act or have the position of a unified economic and political force on the international stage. Speaking of Vietnam's relations with China and the Democratic Republic of Korea, the national-interest character overwhelms (if not obliterates) the socialist character of the relationships among these countries."[34]

Kiet related post–Cold War changes in the international environment directly to Vietnam's decision to integrate into organizations and institutions that once were viewed by Hanoi as bastions of an antagonistic system. "If we don't fully grasp the above points, it would be impossible to explain Vietnam becoming a member of ASEAN, signing a framework agreement with the European Union, and managing to establish international relations that are constantly expanding, and securing an international position that is increasingly better than previously at a time when the socialist world no longer exists." Kiet argued that, paradoxically, the end of the Cold War ideological struggle actually deprived the United States and "other reactionary forces" of a banner to rally anti-Vietnamese global forces, "Because this banner has lost its allure." Kiet directly refuted the "peaceful evolution" argument and contended that the end of the Cold War had made Vietnam's party and regime more secure than ever.[35]

Switching from Marxist polemical terminology, Kiet shifted to the language of traditional values and defined the ultimate purpose of political action as attaining the goal of "prosperous population, strong country, a society that is egalitarian and civilized," which is "the deep aspiration of our people and, at the same time, is also the wish of many developing countries and progressive forces in the world."[36] This formulation neatly combined the traditional modernizing nationalist goal of achieving "wealth and power" with the professed ideals of socialism, "egalitarian society," while identifying Vietnam with the aspirations of a broad category of developing nations and "progressive forces" to downplay the accusation that Vietnam was simply capitulating in joining the rich man's clubs of capitalism. The term "civilized [*van minh*] society" meant that Vietnam should aspire to the highest global levels of culture, education, and technology—a goal without a specific political or ideological content. This concept is discussed at greater length in chapter 9.

Just as important, Kiet attempted to challenge the conservative position that any retreat from an orthodox insistence on state ownership and control of the "commanding heights" of the economy was "a deviation" (*chech huong*). In the context of his remarks on developing nations and "progressive humanity," Kiet went on to assert that, "The various recent theories and models of building socialism may fail, but building a genuine socialist society is still the deep aspiration of the laboring people of the world." However, "We are united in the view that building society in a socialist direction in our country has no precedent, and precisely for this reason we must avoid being formulaic [*cong thuc hoa*] and must take the overall results in attaining the big criterion to cast light on the question of whether or not there is 'deviation' or 'no deviation.'" Kiet specifically cautioned against using the extent of market control by state enterprises and the percentage of private economic activity as measures of "deviations" from the goal of building socialism. State enterprises became a central ideological and policy battleground between conservatives and reformers. As we will see in chapter 7, this thorny issue was a drag on reform and continued to be an unresolved issue throughout the remainder of the 1990s.

One of the striking arguments in Kiet's letter was his insistence that the economy be insulated from political control which, he argued, would lead to manipulation, corruption, and inefficiency. "A strong economy demands that the market reduce to the minimum the manifestations of speculation, abuse of power, monopolies, underground economy, and mafias, and effectively filter out less efficient economic activities and provide a useful confidence to all economic components in society, with the capacity to strongly mobilize them as sources for the process of transforming the economy. In this spirit, it is necessary to be even more steadfast in the socialist direction, and perfect the market even more even more, push the economic activities of the society even more toward marketization."[37] The fundamental point of this argument is that partial reform entrenches a politically manipulated economic system, which leads to corruption and inefficiency. It was Kiet's answer to the conservative argument that Vietnam's limited reforms were successful and that further reform might rock the boat.

Kiet's ultimate purpose in circulating this letter a year before the Eighth Party Congress was to underline the importance of breaking free from the ideological constraints of the past and seize advantage of what he argued was a uniquely favorable moment to accelerate Vietnam's economic development. "Our party has taken up the historical mission for our people of not missing this opportunity. That is precisely the mission of the Eighth Party Congress. One could say that being timid and passing over this opportunity will be a catastrophe for the county and our party will be faced with the danger of being stripped of its leadership—simply because it didn't meet the development needs of the country."

The alternative to "seizing the opportunity" was to fall further, and perhaps fatally, behind. "We stand before the objective demand that our country must become rich, the sooner the better, in order to have the strength to compete and attract all sources [of investment] from outside, in order to maintain our independence and sovereignty while expanding our cooperation and development. . . . As a number of 'tigers' in Asia have done. If we don't do this we will miss the opportunity and lose everything."[38]

The fact that Kiet's letter touched off a political firestorm is testament to the magnitude of the issues raised in it. Templer writes that, "Kiet's letter unleashed one of the most vicious political battles of recent years. There was little support for his views in the Politburo where economic reforms were viewed with suspicion if they weakened the Party's power."[39]

As Templer points out, the fundamental difference between the two groups is how they were affected by the end of the Cold War and its aftermath. In the case of the conservatives, "The collapse of communism shocked [them] deeply. They pinned it on Gorbachev's tolerance of reformers in the highest levels of the Soviet Party and on a sinister Western plot of 'peaceful evolution' that used decadent culture, democracy and human rights to discredit communism."[40] In contrast to his colleagues, Vo Van Kiet drew a different lesson from what he observed in the first half of the 1990s. "Kiet, who had travelled widely in Asia and the West, was shocked by Vietnam's backwardness and poverty compared with its neighbors."[41] Kiet's letter makes quite clear that he strongly opposed political liberalization and its attendant concerns for human rights and democracy, and that his concern was to strengthen party dominance by focusing on the key issues of political power, disengaging from micromanagement of the economy, and overseeing policies that would strengthen its legitimacy.

Although the contending sides clashed over these central issues during and after the Eighth Party Congress, they were not resolved. As in the case of the political succession from the veteran revolutionary generation to those who had matured during the Cold War, the political process in Vietnam was unable to produce a clear-cut result for the remainder of the decade.

AMBIGUOUS OUTCOME OF THE EIGHTH PARTY CONGRESS

At the Eighth Party Congress, the dominant theme was the need for stability. This was also reflected in the personnel decisions of the congress. The expected political transfer of power to a younger generation was postponed, and the aging leadership troika put in place at the previous party congress stayed on in an interim capacity, suggesting an impasse on the next steps in Vietnam's political and economic development. The presence of military and security officials at the highest levels was increased.

A report on the Eighth Congress noted that, "The foreign minister, Nguyen Manh Cam, said party leaders wanted 'a higher degree of intensity' in their drive to modernise. But he added: 'Our task is to maintain social and political order.'" Despite the retirement of some high-level conservative ideologues, the military and security branches increased their representation at the top level of party leadership.[42]

In the end, the desire not to rock the boat in the interests of preserving stability resulted in an ambiguous outcome of the Eighth Party Congress. The anticipated political succession did not take place, and the conservatives succeeded in creating obstacles to forward movement on reforms. Nevertheless, the concerns of Premier Vo Van Kiet and other reformers did leave a mark. The major point of convergence between reformers and conservatives was that by mid-decade Vietnam had definitively emerged from the political and economic crisis of the late 1980s and early 1990s. The congress noted *"Our country has emerged from the serious economic-social crisis* which dragged on for over fifteen years" [emphasis in original].[43]

This was cited by reformers as a reason to push reforms ahead on the grounds that the situation was uniquely (and perhaps only temporarily) favorable. The conservatives cited it as evidence that limited reform had worked well, and pushing the pace of reform would risk destabilization. The reformers' response to this, included in the documents of the Eighth Congress was that "in summing up 5 years of carrying out the resolutions of the Seventh Congress, there was the conclusion: 'the quality and effectiveness of the economy is still low, and the danger of falling further behind is still great.'"[44]

For the first time, the "threats" from the outside that had been alluded to in general and undifferentiated terms were now specified in a party congress document.[45] These will be discussed below. In this context we will note only the tactic of elaborating or "deconstructing" a controversial concept in order to make possible a rank ordering of the various interpretations or definitions of the concept as a prelude to downgrading the less favored interpretation (in this case, attempting to put the threat of "falling behind" as a priority concern, and downgrading the conservative concern with "peaceful evolution").

This same tactic of deconstruction of controversial concepts was employed by reformers with respect to the various components of the economy. In the Eighth Party Congress, the "official" components of Vietnam's economy were defined for the first time and prioritized. "[O]ur party confirmed the components of the economy in our country in the following order: the state economy, the cooperative economy of which the core is the cooperatives [*hop tac xa*], the state capitalist economy, the individual and small merchant economy, the private capitalist economy."[46]

In this case, the itemization and prioritizing did not downgrade an alternative not favored by reformers, but served the purpose of legitimizing the private capitalist component of the economy by inclusion on the list. But in retrospect, the intellectual and political trajectory of reform was clear. As discussed in chapter 7, the Eighth Congress for the first time gave the party's seal of approval to the concept of a "commodity economy," which paved the way for the 2001 Ninth Party Congress endorsing the idea of a "market economy"—a term that was still too controversial to use in 1996.[47]

At the time, the Eighth Congress signaled where the phrase "commodity economy" was headed. "The Eighth Party Congress put forward a very important conclusion: 'Commodity production is not antagonistic to socialism, but is an achievement in development of civilized humanity, which exists objectively, and is necessary for building socialism and even after socialism has been built.'"[48] In terms of polemical strategies, the use of the term "civilized humanity" reflected the view of Kiet and others that there was now a single world standard of achievement, and that in clinging to idea that policies had to have a "socialist character" Vietnam was relegating itself to a backwater by repeating failed experiments.

The underlying issue was about control. Party conservatives clung to the illusion that a dominant state sector could maintain control of the "commanding heights" of the economy, while the reformers did not feel threatened by market forces and wanted to use them to push Vietnam's development. In the end, the conservatives won a pyrrhic victory at the Eighth Party Congress by blocking bolder commitment to reform and identifying "stability" as the main concern of the congress. But some of the conceptual foundations of conservative obstructionism had been eroded.

Perhaps the most important ideological development at the Eighth Party Congress, emphasized in retrospect more than it was at the time, was its new view of globalization. Vu Khoan, who was deputy foreign minister at the time of the congress and later vice-premier, wrote in 2006 that with respect to the evolution of views about integration, "The Eighth Party Congress advanced another step: *globalization, internationalization of the economy and social life is an objective trend*. This was the first time that we had spoken of globalization and assessed that it was an objective trend."[49]

Still, the conservatives attempted to regain the initiative. The military went beyond expressing generalized concerns about "stability" and warned of new plots to overthrow socialism. Once again, military conservatives asserted that far from easing Vietnam's security problems, the dangers to the country would escalate as reforms became deeper and more extensive. Just prior to the Eighth Party Congress, Le Kha Phieu alerted students at the Military Political Academy of "new plots to destroy socialism in Vietnam by the end of the decade." Defense Minister Doan Khue stated that, "We fully understand the inevitable rule that the greater the scale of socialist industrialization, the more difficult our task of maintaining national stability will be."[50]

THE ROLE OF THE MILITARY IN VIETNAMESE POLITICS

At the Eighth Party Congress in mid-1996, five army and police generals were elected to the nineteen-person politburo. This party congress eliminated the party secretariat, the nerve center of the party bureaucracy and a critically important institution responsible for transmitting politburo decisions to the relevant party and state bodies for implementation. Replacing the secretariat was Standing Committee of the Politburo (Thuong Vu Bo Chinh Tri) which, in effect, became the innermost leadership core of the party. In this smaller group, the influence of the military and security sectors was amplified. With the abolition of the secretariat, the power of the party and state administrative bureaucracies was diminished. Although, there was no formal statement describing the exact functions of the Politburo Standing Committee, these may be inferred from the announcement proclaiming its dissolution and the restoration of the party secretariat at the Ninth Party Congress: spokesperson Pham The Duyet said "the Politburo Standing Committee will be dissolved. Under the current circumstances, it is necessary to reestablish the secretariat because the Politburo Standing Committee is no longer an appropriate organizational model, he said. There are now many day-to-day affairs, so the secretariat is badly needed to tackle them, he added."[51]

This suggests that the attempt to focus the top party leadership on policy issues and avoid getting bogged down in details of bureaucratic implementation had been found wanting. It also may refer to the fact that the standing committee may have been viewed as a temporary device to emphasize collective leadership during a sensitive period of political succession, which would not be needed once this process was completed. The other impact of the subsequent decision to abolish the Politburo Standing Committee was to eliminate the distinction between first-tier (standing committee) and second-tier (politburo) membership inherent in the standing committee. (It is revealing that dissident General Tran Do sent his March 29, 1998. letter to the Politburo Standing Committee, rather than the politburo as a whole.)

It is always perilous to attempt any analysis of the inner political dynamics of Vietnam's impenetrably secretive top leadership. Beyond the obvious fact that the standing committee included the leading troika, of the party general secretary (Do Muoi), the premier (Vo Van Kiet), and the head of state (Le Duc Anh), it could be noted that of the remaining two members, Le Kha Phieu was the ranking party person in the military and an alleged protégé of former military chief Le Duc Anh, while Nguyen Tan Dung had been in the military forces in South Vietnam during the war in a variety of capacities, had briefly served as Vice Minister of Public Security (1995–6), later becoming a political and economic troubleshooter and, in 2006, premier.

The military element in the Politburo Standing Committee evidently played a significant role in the mid-term selection of Le Kha Phieu as party leader in December 1997. An April 1997 news analysis by Jeremy Grant of the *Financial Times* attempted to sort out the political maneuvering. President Le Duc Anh had made a political comeback after being restored to health by a team of Chinese doctors. "His return signals the re-emergence of a leadership succession question, shelved at last year's communist party conclave after the main players could not reach consensus on their heirs."[52]

"It has done so not a moment too soon," Grant observed. "Vietnam's reform process has been stalled since that [1996] party meeting. Foreign investors talk of glacial progress on key infrastructure projects that require legal and financial guarantees from the government before they can go ahead. Decision-making in the bureaucracy has all but ground to a halt." In Grant's account, foreign diplomats had noted an intense jockeying for position between reformers and conservatives, which manifested itself in a series of business scandals and commercial disputes in Ho Chi Minh City as the rival sides tried to discredit their opposition.[53]

In addition to the struggle between reformers and conservatives there was a struggle over the sectoral representation of various power groups, especially the military. Grant concluded that "Mr Anh's return to the limelight has far greater significance [than a struggle over policy]: it marks a victory for the Vietnamese military in a long campaign to occupy the political centre stage." The military, whose budget and influence had suffered since the end of the Cambodian conflict as the reformers redirected national priorities to the civilian sector, was now trying to reassert its institutional interests.[54]

Robert Templer observed that, "Now that Vietnam is no longer at war, the military tends to divide into those who see the establishment of a rich military-industrial complex as the key task and those who want to maintain a tight ideological grip on the soldiers. President Le Duc Anh and his protege Le Kha Phieu, now [1998] Secretary General of the Party, are among the ideologues. Neither was popular among those officers who saw the military's role was national defense, not political control." An anonymous 1995 letter called for political reforms and the rule of law. The letter stated that, "There should be no privileges for those who used violence to come to power. . . . We are determined to smash all the selfish, conservative dogmatists who use the guise of the revolution to obstruct the wheel of history."[55] To illustrate the difficulties of understanding the complexities of politics at the top of the political system, some former Southern guerrilla leaders charged that Le Kha Phieu was far from being a protégée of Le Duc Anh. Anh eventually attempted to engineer the removal of Phieu as party secretary general—although it is entirely possible that Le Duc Anh turned against Phieu after he himself was removed from power.[56]

Despite some reformist voices in the military, Vo Van Kiet's insistence on downsizing the state sector and building a legal framework that would limit the exercise of arbitrary power was not well received by other elements in the military and their allies in the politburo. Templer views intra-elite political struggle as essentially concerned with "control of resources and the placement of officials in the lucrative positions of gatekeepers for foreign aid or investment, but they are often framed in the idiom of ideology or in accusations of corruption. These interest groups rarely coalesce around individuals except when threatened."[57]

One of these instances of confrontation between rival groups was, Templer reports, attacks on Kiet by Le Duc Anh and a new member of the politburo, Nguyen Ha Phan. Evidently some of Kiet's supporters in the army were removed, prompting a counter-attack by Kiet's supporters. Nguyen Ha Phan, head of the party's Economics Commission and vice president of the National Assembly was also aligned with the leading ideological conservatives, such as the ailing Dao Duy Tung (soon to be succeeded in this role by his son Dao Duy Quat—an example of dynastic politics at work). Phan was soon dispatched by information that surfaced bringing into question his revolutionary past in the South and he was expelled from the politburo for "serious errors."[58] General Le Duc Anh, who had reportedly demanded Kiet's resignation for circulating the controversial letter, also was subsequently attacked for murky actions in his early revolutionary career (see below).

Carlyle Thayer, perhaps the leading academic authority on the Vietnamese military, observed that the military's unhappiness with reform was due to both budget cuts that were part of the reform program and the fact that the military did not directly benefit from the reforms. Jeremy Grant noted that the resurgent military influence represented by Le Duc Anh and his protégé Le Kha Phieu represented only the political side of they armed forces: "they are less soldiers than 'political commissars,' party ideolog[ues] charged with maintaining communist party ideology in the armed forces."[59]

Some analysts felt that the upsurge of military influence in the party leadership would tilt the tenuous political balance toward the opponents of reform, but others felt that the military was only trying to protect its institutional interests. In this view, the military would tolerate reform as long as it got its cut. "'It's the military ensuring what it considers to be its fair share. They couldn't move to assert total control, even if they wanted to,' said Mr Thayer."[60]

But when Phieu, a military officer, albeit a "political commissar," was designated party leader in late 1997, the conservative views prevalent in the military became more influential. Vietnamese generals in the politburo had not previously been very influential. General Vo Nguyen Giap, the legendary architect of the victory at the battle of Dien Bien Phu, had been unceremoniously tossed out of the politburo in 1982. In the early 1990s, General Doan Khue, the minister of defense, was evidently not an influential figure in the politburo. According to one obituary in 1999, "'He was a man of great ambitions, but he lacked political clout,' said one western diplomat." Apparently he was not much of a politician or strong in interpersonal skills. A diplomat said, "He was a brusque, hard-headed man, who according to his subordinates did not suffer fools lightly." Khue became a politburo member in 1986 and was appointed defense minister in 1991, "at a time when the Vietnamese army underwent a dramatic reduction after decades of war, growing out-moded and ill equipped as a result, observers say. According to one senior advisor, he was a 'a very big general, but all insiders say he did not say anything useful' while a politburo member."[61] With the accession of the political general Le Kha Phieu to the position of party secretary general in December 1997, the military, or at least a sector of it, gained an unprecedented voice at the top of the political system.

BUREAUCRATIC POLITICS OR FACTIONAL MODELS FOR ANALYZING VIETNAMESE POLITICS?

Can we understand the tug of war over the pace and scope of reform in the 1990s in terms of a bureaucratic model of Vietnamese politics, with each sector of the political system attempting to ensure that its institutional interests are protected? Is there a discernable pattern in the interplay of external events, such as normalization with ASEAN and the United States, generational succession in the leadership, and institutional change, such as the short-lived but centrally important substitution of the Politburo Standing Committee for the Central Committee Secretariat, and the ideological debates of this period?

Why was it primarily the military (and specifically the military intelligence branch) that was promoting the dangers of peaceful evolution in the years following the collapse of the Soviet Union? And why did this take the form of reprinting Chinese analyses of peaceful evolution rather than home-grown Vietnamese studies of this threat? At a time when the military forces were being reduced and the military establishment being rele-gated to the background by the focus on economic development, there was a clear insti-tutional interest in keeping alive the fear of external intervention, of maintaining that the Cold War never really ended, and holding out the prospect that "violent means" might be used against Vietnam, even though the party position was that armed conflict in the post–Cold War era was unlikely. And why was it that for the first time in the history of

Communist Party a person whose career had been exclusively within the military was appointed party secretary general?

Perhaps the reason that the military promoted Chinese works on peaceful evolution in the 1993–4 period was that, since the Vietnamese party line did not place the same emphasis on this threat, it would have been politically awkward for the military to step too far out in front on this sensitive issue with its own distinctive viewpoint. The party was constrained by having to consider a multiplicity of factors, its own need for foreign investment, the various constituencies for expanded engagement with the outside world, and diplomatic considerations-none of which directly involved the military. Thus the party's view reflected a composite of perspectives and interests, while the military position was more parochial.

But it is difficult to infer an institutional motive for promoting the concept of peaceful evolution for the Vietnamese military as a whole. For one thing, there was a strong party control system within the military, represented by the General Political Department, that was supposed to prevent the military from developing a separate institutional identity. And the literature of "peaceful evolution" warned against the purported imperialist plot to "depoliticize" or "professionalize" the army precisely on the grounds that it would lead to the army becoming an interest group separate from the party. Yet the 1994 addition of Le Kha Phieu, the head of the army's political department, to the politburo, along with another leading general, raised questions of timing and intent. This was done in early 1994, at the height of the military's campaign to promote the threat of peaceful evolution. There was also the question of whether the net effect was to strengthen the military voice at the highest levels of the party, or the party control of the military.[62]

Still, one possible motive for some of the political elements within the military to espouse the concept of peaceful evolution is that it seemed to link external dangers (the province of the military) to internal dangers (regime security). If the function of the military was no longer primarily to repulse armed attack, what was its purpose in the post–Cold War era? Some speculated that the military would inevitably gravitate toward assuming increasing internal security functions, and that this would bring them into a jurisdictional collision with the security police. Some months prior to his elevation to the top party position in December 1997, Le Kha Phieu engaged in "fraternal talks" with senior interior ministry officials.[63] "'Clarifying the function of each unit and maintaining close cooperation with the People's Army . . . is the prime task of the police force,' the report added." A Western wire-service report commented that, "Phieu made his appearance on behalf of the Politburo, where he has overall responsibility for national security, including internal political control. There have long been tensions between the police and the military, the two most powerful ministries, and in recent years analysts say the military has become more powerful at the expense of the police." One reason given for this development is that the party had concluded that the experiences in Eastern Europe and the Soviet Union in 1989 and after proved that "the army is the best guarantor for its continued rule."[64]

Le Kha Phieu became the head of the party in late 1997, but not without considerable delay and resistance in making the appointment. Internet documents whose provenance and veracity cannot be verified even allege that during his tenure as party secretary general Phieu was the target of a plot by a rogue element of the military intelligence branch. If there is any substance to these allegations, it confirms the difficulties in analyzing the impact of the military as a monolithic interest group. If true, it would also provide a plausible explanation for the instigation of a campaign about peaceful evolution by the military intelligence branch. This would provide any would-be plotters with a political justification to purge any elements within the party who had lost their vigilance and gone too far along the path of reform.

But in Vietnam, nothing is ever simple. Phieu's reputation in Vietnam was as a conservative and an opponent of reform.[65] Moreover, he was clearly on the side of those who stressed the danger of peaceful evolution rather than a target of this group. At the time of Phieu's appointment, Carlyle Thayer observed that, "All his public pronouncements in the 90's have taken this line: Peaceful evolution is the greatest threat facing Vietnam, and the opening up to the outside world brings with it the dangers that outside influences could undermine the party."[66]

Desaix Anderson, who opened the US embassy in Hanoi in 1995 and served until May 1997 as the first American envoy following diplomatic recognition, sought out meetings with conservatives to engage in a dialogue on the subject of peaceful evolution and other concerns. At meetings with Le Kha Phieu, Anderson was told that Phieu's concern was that during the process of economic development "elements in Vietnam would gain wealth and influence and use these in order to try to overturn the socialist system of Vietnam," and that they "might use links with foreign economic interests to attempt to change the political system in Vietnam."[67] For this reason, Phieu was not interested in a development strategy that would create a strong private sector, and "showed great concern for the state of security and society and their possible deterioration in the party did not remain fully in control. He indicated that without state control of the economy, Communist Party political and social control would be endangered."[68]

The main point of this excursion into the uncertain and difficult-to-document territory of interest groups and intra-elite conflict is that, however accurate any specific allegation of intrigue, there is abundant evidence of serious differences within the leadership in Vietnam that is personal, political, and sometimes has policy implications. These divergences in views at the top echelons of the Vietnamese leadership provided space for new thinking and challenges to orthodoxy to develop. They also help explain why obstruction of policy was relatively easy within Vietnam's political system in the 1990s.

When Le Kha Phieu became party secretary general in December 1997, a knowledgeable correspondent noted that, "He backed but urged caution with the open-door policy, warning against the 'blind' following of anything foreign 'as in the current system.' . . . 'Now that the international socialist system has collapsed, an anti-communist ballad of various pitches and rhythms has again been echoing throughout the world,' he warned. . . . 'Capitalism will certainly be replaced as it has already become obsolete and unable to meet the people's welfare needs,' the general declared." [69]

It would be misleading to view Le Kha Phieu as the "army's" voice in bureaucratic politics. As a political officer, he was clearly not a representative of the military professionals. It was reported that he was opposed within the armed forces.[70] Although Le Kha Phieu may have been a political target of some elements in the armed forces for whatever reason, it was a former high-ranking political commissar who was the highest-profile victim of a purge of those who challenged the party by questioning its integrity and direction. General Tran Do, a leading architect of the 1968 Tet Offensive and a hard-line minister of culture in the 1980s, was stripped of his party membership in 1999.

If there was ever a poster boy for the perils of "peaceful evolution" and its threat to the Communist Party, it was Tran Do. Distressed by what he saw as corruption and complacency in the party, Do slid gradually into dissidence and political opposition. In March 1998 the party leadership started a campaign against Tran Do to force him to tone down his criticism. After personal persuasion by Le Kha Phieu failed, the leadership, anticipating support from an expected increase in conservative influence at a forthcoming party plenum, decided, in the words of a Western diplomat, that it was time to "lance the boil and start over with a clean slate." Some interpreted this as a consolidation of power by Phieu, while others thought it reflected his continued inability to dominate the political system. In this view, the Tran Do purge was merely a symptom of political paralysis and policy stalemate. "'Phieu is walking a tightrope,' the diplomat said. 'He's playing people off against each other,' he continued. 'It's apparent in today's policy-making paralysis. Decisions aren't being made. Economic reform has stalled.'"[71]

It was not only the case of General Do, but a reported restiveness among some elements in the armed forces which had, by the late 1990s, become a major concern to the party. Vietnam's first public defense white paper warned of threats and plots to depoliticize the military. "It did not specify who or what the hostile forces were, but diplomats and military analysts said it reflected the party's internal struggles as much as external threats."[72]

These internal struggles, allegedly involving intrigues within the armed forces, were baldly outlined in a 2004 letter by one of Vietnam's leading generals, Nguyen Nam Khanh. In light of his previously expressed hard-line views, General Khanh, like General Do, was an unlikely dissident voice. In 1996, he wrote in the military journal: "Along with the feverish attempts of reactionary, hostile forces to oppose our country, opportunist and rightist elements are trying hard to change our party's political line, organization, and structure to turn it into a social democratic party, which by nature is the product of the bourgeois system. As a result, we must adopt positive measures to smash the hostile forces' dark schemes against our country and must devote efforts to checking the adverse impact of opportunism and rightism to guarantee the conditions for the cause of national renovation to meet the legitimate aspirations of the labouring people and the nation as a whole."[73]

In a 2004 letter to the top party organizations and leaders, widely circulated on the internet, General Khanh, who had been deputy head of the political department of the Ministry of National Defense under Le Kha Phieu, complained of a clique within the Military Intelligence Directorate—the center of the anti-"peaceful evolution" campaign of 1993–4, that was fabricating rumors that top generals and other leaders, including Vo Van Kiet, Phan Van Khai, and Mai Chi Tho, along with General Vo Nguyen Giap and himself, were colluding with the United States, CIA, and Vietnamese exiles. The specific allegations of a plot involving the military intelligence branch and Le Duc Anh, who became head of state, are detailed and extensive, but very hard to evaluate, coming as they do from a political culture that has elevated political disinformation to a form of high art. The fact that well-informed Vietnamese do not specifically deny the authenticity of the Khanh letter and its allegations is suggestive, although I found no one during a trip to Vietnam in 2006–7 who would explicitly confirm its validity to a foreigner either. In the light of the subsequent confirmation of equally sensational charges about political intrigue at the highest levels in the remarkable book *Dem Giua Ban Ngay* [Darkness at Noon] by Vu Thu Hien, it would be premature to dismiss the Khanh letter and its allegations out of hand.[74]

At the very least, this convoluted episode illustrates the complexity of attempting to understand the vagaries of Vietnamese politics through a simple bureaucratic politics model or a factional politics approach. Clearly the army has played a key role in slowing the pace of Vietnam's reforms, but the real motives and exact methods of influence remain hidden from view. General Khanh appears to have been just as hostile to "peaceful evolution" and dubious of the wisdom of "opening up" as the military intelligence branch, but the latter seem to have used this idea as a smokescreen for slandering rivals and undermining their credibility. They no doubt sincerely fear "peaceful evolution" but, if General Khanh's letter is authentic, they are more concerned with maneuvering for power and exacerbating the very divisions they warn against.

The academic researcher is faced with a quandary: in demanding the highest standards of evidence in evaluating these political intrigues, we would be forced to ignore some of the most important motives and dynamics in Vietnamese politics, and thus miss what is really going on. In the case of this book, the political intrigue model complicates the assessment of how crisis and turmoil can provoke collective idea change. Nevertheless, whether or not the opponents of new thinking about the nature of the world and Vietnam's place in it following the end of the Cold War were motivated by different reasons, ranging from sincere conviction or a desire to hold on to power, to even a desire to manipulate hard-line resistance to reform as a political maneuver to gain power, the result in the end was the same. The specter of peaceful evolution gradually lost its power to act as a brake on reform and integration, and the conservatives who promoted it eventually were overtaken by events. Still, this resistance did slow both reform and opening during the uncertain transition to extensive global integration of the second half of the 1990s.

A BALANCING ACT: SLOWDOWN OF REFORM

At the time of his reappointment as party leader in 1996, Do Muoi spelled out the balancing act that slowed reform in the latter part of the 1990s to foreign reporters covering the Eighth Party Congress. One account of this period noted that Do Muoi said, "I think we will have to accelerate our development. . . . Slow development means hunger, don't you think?" He qualified this by stressing the importance of efficiency and stability, but made it clear that there was urgency to revitalizing Vietnam's economic growth. "If reform is too fast, we will make mistakes. If you run too fast and there is something in the road, you may fall down. . . . But at the same time I want to see efficiency and stability. . . . We have to raise living standards. In some areas in Vietnam there are very low living standards. This is my biggest concern."[75]

The replacement of Do Muoi with a new party leader two years later did not resolve the fundamental impasse on reform, resulting from the fact that the leadership had gone too far along the reform path to retreat, but felt increasingly threatened by the specter of letting the process spin out of control. In 1995, Do Muoi remarked "As Lenin taught, we are not afraid of capitalist enterprises, but of not being able to supervise and control them."[76]

Selecting a new party leader was supposed to be done at the 1996 Eighth Party Congress. However, the congress reached an impasse on policy and personnel issues, and the new party leader was not chosen until the end of 1997, with the elevation of Le Kha Phieu to that post. It is not surprising that both the holdover leader reappointed at the Eighth Party Congress, Do Muoi, and Le Kha Phieu, the compromise candidate who emerged from the prolonged process of selecting a new party leader, were sensitive to the need to balance competing interests and constrained from taking bold action either to push reform or to undermine it. A *New York Times* article on Phieu's appointment described this approach in the following terms: "[Phieu's] appointment . . . completes a long-delayed transition in the country's top three posts that involved a balancing act between ideologies, regional interests and power blocs. . . . General Phieu personifies the concern in Vietnam's leadership over the destabilizing effects of the country's sometimes half-hearted steps toward liberalization—a process that is described in Vietnam, as in China, as 'peaceful evolution.'"[77]

As a political general with concerns about "peaceful evolution," Le Kha Phieu would clearly not be an advocate of sweeping reform. At the time of Vietnam's establishment of diplomatic relations with the United States and joining ASEAN, he stated that, "We fully understand Lenin's teaching that seizing the government is difficult, but holding the government in order to organize and build a new society is many times more difficult."[78]

In December 1997, Phieu assumed power at a time of economic slowdown in Vietnam and the unsettled conditions of the Asian financial crisis and at a time of heightened peasant discontent in the countryside, which erupted into violence in the province of Thai Binh in 1997. The *Christian Science Monitor* reported that "Gen. Le Kha Phieu, a shadowy party figure who once called capitalism 'backward' and ensured communist control over the Army, has since said that Vietnam's difficulties are 'very large,' especially as foreign investment and markets shrink in Asia. . . . In a recent report, the World Bank warned: 'Without immediate action, Vietnam's development momentum would be lost.' A boom in foreign investment in the early 1990s faltered last year. Foreign investments dropped 40 percent, its most dramatic decline ever. That threatens the party's hope that rising incomes in Vietnam, one of Southeast Asia's poorest countries, will help keep it firmly in power."[79]

The debate about the pace of reform in the mid- and late 1990s involved what Vietnam's leadership saw as a balancing act, which was required if Vietnam was to open the door wide enough to gain the investment funds necessary to finance its economic development without losing control, and to solicit cooperation in development without creating dependence (as Vietnam had earlier experienced in its relations with the Soviet Union). Vietnamese president Le Duc Anh warned, "Economic cooperation with foreign countries is necessary for development but we should not allow ourselves to become dependant because of short-term considerations as this could have unforeseen consequences for future generations." This attitude certainly complicated Vietnam's announced plan of courting foreign investment, which it hoped would contribute half of the 40 billion dollars need for development until the end of the century.[80]

One of Vietnam's best-known reform economists acknowledged the inevitability of retrenchment in the pace of reform. Do Duc Dinh a director of the Institute of World Economy in Hanoi, said, "In my view, reform will go on normally—neither fast nor slow. He [Phieu] needs to balance the two views in the party."[81] A US official involved in the 1998 trade negotiations with Vietnam said, "They haven't reached any internal consensus, and there are people pushing and pulling in different directions. So we have to wonder, does Vietnam want to wait and be cautious, or does it want to embrace reform?"[82]

Indications that the political and security concerns were becoming an increasing drag on the reform process were already evident in 1996, at the time of the Eighth Party Congress. Several months prior to the convening of the congress a campaign against "social evils" was launched, accompanied by such measures as painting over foreign signs and advertising billboards in some of the Vietnam's cities. "'There was a certain sense for a while this year that perhaps things had stalled out,' said Michael J. Scown, a lawyer with the Washington-based firm Russin & Vecchi who heads the American Chamber of Commerce in Ho Chi Minh City. 'People were wondering whether reforms were going to continue, or whether there would now be a backlash against foreign investment.' . . . 'The real issue under the surface is the issue of national identity,' said Mr. Babson, of the World Bank. 'There is a question where the country is headed.'"[83]

On the eve of the Eighth Party Congress, Ha Dang, former editor of the party newspaper *Nhan Dan* and, in 1996, the head of the ideology department of the Central Committee, summarized the dangers facing the party as "'lagging behind economically; deviation from socialist orientation; red tape and corruption; and peaceful evolution.'

'Peaceful evolution'—what the party fears from such influences as foreign advertising—
is an Asian Communist term referring to a Western conspiracy to impose capitalism by
peaceful means."[84]

The "four dangers" were first enumerated in 1994.[85] As noted above, they were
officially registered in the party documents of the 1996 Eighth Party Congress. These
were: the danger of falling further behind economically, the danger of deviating from the
socialist direction, the scourge of corruption and mandarinism, and the plot and "peaceful
evolution" activities carried out by enemy forces. This was an early attempt to suggest a
formula for balancing the risks and the opportunities inherent in the reform process by
listing the key threats that would have to be evaluated in the risk-assessment process.
Some years later, knowledgeable Vietnamese observers asserted that the rank order of the
newly defined "four dangers" was, in fact, a way of relegating peaceful evolution to the
bottom of the priority list, and that the important point was that Vietnam's economic
backwardness was the most important of the challenges facing Vietnam.[86] In a 2003
article, Ha Dang stated that "none of these dangers should be slighted," which indicates
that even this conservative voice did not give top priority to the threat of peaceful evolution, but also shows that some were opposed to any downgrading of this threat.[87] During
the period of "uncertain transition," conservative voices continued to highlight the
political threats more than the dangers of falling behind economically.

THE ASIAN FINANCIAL CRISIS

The Asian financial crisis of 1997–8 raised many questions for Vietnam's leaders, including the fundamental question of whether the economic danger of falling behind in
development was a more serious threat than peaceful evolution and the related question
of how far Vietnam should go in integrating into the regional and global economy.
Because the military had become increasingly involved in economic ventures to make up
for the budget reductions, these questions directly affected the armed forces. A press
report on the first defense white paper, published in 1998, observed that though it shed
little light on the "sprawling business interests" of the military, it did admit that the regional crisis had adversely affected army businesses.[88]

The involvement of the military in economic activities had now further complicated
its role in the Vietnamese political system by appending a new set of interests and concerns to its traditional defense function. "[Deputy Defense Minister] Hang said that the
greatest threat to Vietnam's national defense would come on the economic front. 'Anything harmful to economic development is also a threat to the national defense,' he said,
adding 'the most dangerous threat is poverty and being left behind.'"[89] Thus any adverse
developments in the regional or global economy would be directly felt throughout the
institutional structure of the Vietnamese state, including the military, which now had an
institutional interest in global and regional economic ties that counterbalanced, and

perhaps outweighed, its stake in promoting the threat of peaceful evolution, at least for those sectors of the military directly benefiting from military enterprises. Still, a vocal ideological core of hard-liners in the military remained opposed to further integration.

A PARTIAL LEADERSHIP TRANSITION

Despite the Cassandras in the military who continued to warn of the perils of integration and engagement in the regional and global system, the general leadership view at the time of the Eighth Party Congress of 1996 was that limited reform had been successful. It had brought clear economic benefits, and the party had managed to keep control of the pace and scope of reform. However, the Asian financial crisis and other challenges compelled the party leaders to break the succession impasse of the Eighth Party Congress at the end of 1997. It had become clear that the stability that was the theme of the Eighth Party Congress could not be obtained without a stronger and more unified leadership, especially in a time of regional turbulence. "Southeast Asia's problems have highlighted the fragility of Vietnam's economy when Hanoi is being pressed by the international community to speed up reforms. The uncertainty has reinforced the position of hardliners such as the general [Phieu] within the party." One army officer said that, "His nomination shows the desire of the party to strengthen its leadership and control and stabilise the political situation."[90]

Observers were surprised at the suddenness of the party decision to elect a new general secretary at a mid-term plenum ostensibly scheduled to discuss economic matters. "'Events have speeded up the decision,' said one western diplomat. 'Normally the party secretary general dies in the job or is replaced by a party congress.'"[91] The complacency produced by the relative success of limited reform in the period between the Seventh and Eighth Party Congresses (1991–6) was jolted by what Carlyle Thayer termed the "four typhoons." The first typhoon was a marked economic slowdown. The second was the outbreak of rural unrest in Thai Binh province in late 1997. Third was an actual typhoon also in late 1997. The fourth typhoon was the Asian financial crisis of 1997–8.[92] "Since the onset of the Asian financial and economic crisis in mid-1997," Thayer wrote in 2000, "the Vietnam Communist Party has convened six meetings of its Central Committee to fashion a policy response. Each of these meetings side-stepped the question of whether or not Vietnam needed to launch a new round of comprehensive economic reforms."[93]

It was in this context of renewed concern and uncertainty about Vietnam's political and economic direction that the delayed generational succession was partially implemented. "The fourth plenum brought to an end to the period of leadership transition that had been under way since the eighth national party congress in 1996, but it did not resolve internal party factionalism between reformers and conservatives." The plenum appointed Le Kha Phieu as party secretary general, replacing Do Muoi, and accepted the resignations of Do Muoi, Le Duc Anh, and Vo Van Kiet from the politburo, to be appointed "advisers" to the Central Committee. "Although these leadership changes have been hailed by the official media as marking a decisive transition to a younger leadership, Do Muoi clearly continues to exercise considerable behind-the-scenes influence."[94]

From the perspective of the year 2000, Thayer concluded that the leadership change had not resolved the impasse over key issues of reform. Le Kha Phieu became leader of the party at the Fourth Plenum in December 1997, but emerged as a compromise candidate, and was forced to play the role of a "consensus builder among the party factions" (as Thayer puts it). This resulted in more caution and indecision about reform.[95]

Thayer observed that the very fact that the Asian financial crisis had not deeply affected the Vietnamese economy was initially cited by the new leadership as evidence of the wisdom of minimizing Vietnam's integration into the regional and global economy. Even so, as we have seen, the unease about the possible spillover of regional instability into Vietnam was a contributing factor to the decision to select a new party leader at the end of the year. Still, the initial response to the Asian crisis was concern but not panic. Evidently, the party leaders had concluded that the installation of Phieu would be sufficient to stabilize the country, and that this political measure would suffice to insulate Vietnam from any problems caused by economic difficulties.

By mid-1998, says Thayer, the Vietnamese leadership realized it had been overoptimistic about escaping the fallout of the Asian economic crisis. Export growth had declined by one-third from the previous year and foreign investment was down to one-quarter of what it had been. "These negative trends reflected Vietnam's dependency on its regional neighbors with whom it conducted sixty percent of its trade and on whom it relied for seventy percent of its foreign investment."[96]

The underlying issue that emerged from this was that partial reform would expose Vietnam to the risks of integration but not provide insulation from them. From the perspective of tracing the evolution of a collective mindset toward acceptance of deep integration, the subject of chapter 7, this setback for the advocates of partial reform was a significant landmark, since it reduced the plausibility of the argument that partial reform would bring adequate benefits to Vietnam, while minimizing the downside of direct exposure to the regional and global economy.

REVIVING THE CHINA CONNECTION: EXPLORING ALTERNATIVES TO FULL REGIONAL INTEGRATION

At the beginning of December 1997, just prior to the installation of Le Kha Phieu as party general secretary, one of China's leading reformers came to Hanoi to tell Phieu that China had found "the right formula" in retaining the core Marxist ideology while jettisoning obsolete ideological strictures. On a visit to Hanoi, Li Ruihan told Le Kha Phieu, that Deng Xiaoping Theory was a "perfect blend of China's national needs with Marxist ideology." But he also suggested that Vietnam would have to find its own distinctive approach to reconciling Marxism with market reforms and global engagement. "He told Mr Phieu that a country would 'blacken or surrogate [*sic*]' Marxism if it failed to adapt it to local conditions."[97] "Mr Li 'also boasted that China was able to modernise Marxism by combining it with "new ideas" and follow a "pragmatic view," in its application.' 'We've taken a bold approach and refuse to stick to an obsolete ideology . . . and achieved new results in our reforms,' he said." The report of Li's visit also observed that "Chinese Communist Party leaders have in recent years toned down their emphasis on Marxist supremacy in talks with leaders from other socialist countries to avoid being described as seeking to be the 'leader' of the socialist bloc following the collapse of the Soviet Union."[98]

Curiously, despite this caution not to copy the Chinese approach to updating socialism to current circumstances, a year later Le Kha Phieu's headed a mission to China, "to study China's valuable experiences." A report on this visit stated that, "'I wish to take this occasion to study China's valuable experiences gained during its building process of socialism with Chinese characteristics,' Phieu told the *Jingji Ribao* Chinese economic newspaper. Analysts say Hanoi is particularly interested in China's reform of the state sector, as Vietnam's 'doi moi' or renovation of the economy is largely patterned on China's model." Part of Phieu's deferential approach was to gloss over elements of conflict in the relationships.[99] Phieu continued to explore the prospects for deepening political and ideological ties with China over the next year.

Alexander Vuving writes, "The deference tradition is alive and well among Vietnam's ruling elites. . . . As expressed by the personal secretary of Vietnamese Communist Party (VCP) chief Le Kha Phieu, the rationale for Vietnam's deference is that 'we live adjacent to a big country; we cannot afford to maintain tension with them because they are next door to us.' The aide used this argument to justify his boss's acceptance of China's terms on a visit to Beijing and Phieu's concessions in the Sino-Vietnamese border pacts of 1999 and 2000."[100] As Vuving also notes, and as Phieu's attempts to shore up ideological ties with China further illustrate, there are a variety of factors involved in this attempt to revitalize the "China card."

In the view of some observers, Vietnamese concerns about the implications of the Asian financial crisis were one reason for this turn toward China. In late 1998, Vietnam's deputy prime minister, Nguyen Tan Dung, told foreign reporters that Vietnam's renewed focus on privatization of state owned industries "had been encouraged by the results seen in China, and noted the Vietnamese leadership paid close attention to China's agricultural policy."[101]

In November 2000, Chinese politburo member Li Tieying visited Hanoi. Phieu told the Vietnamese party newspaper that, "The party, the state and the Vietnamese people still greatly appreciate and cultivate the friendship and traditional cooperation between Vietnam and China." Phieu discussed socialism with Li in a scientific seminar in Hanoi, on "the experiences of Vietnamese and Chinese." Vietnam "greatly appreciates the consolidation and reinforcement of its traditional friendships and global cooperation with China," Phieu said.[102]

This attempt to revive some elements of the ideological solidarity of the "two worlds" era had been criticized by Vo Van Kiet in his August 1995 letter to the politburo, stressing that Vietnam would have to adjust to a "one world" environment. At that time, Kiet had argued that Vietnam would have to develop "in an international environment in which the socialist world system no longer exists. Our country will have to rub elbows [*co sat*] and compete with the entire world, but this will also provide us with the opportunity to expand economic ties with the entire world and give us the opportunity to create and mobilize new forces."[103]

Phieu clearly did not agree with this view and was so intent on engaging China on the ideological and economic fronts that he was willing to downplay the serious security issues that continued to trouble the relationship between the two countries. In 1999, a Western diplomat observed that, "Jiang and Phieu are also likely to downplay contentious issues, although Vietnam 'is still mistrustful of China's strategy' in the South China Sea where the two countries have overlapping claims."[104]

Even the lingering suspicion of China's designs on Vietnamese territory did not prevent the Vietnamese leadership from completing a land-border agreement with China at the end of 1999. Despite disagreements that pushed the negotiations right up to the deadline. Do Muoi and the Chinese had agreed in 1997 to complete such an agreement before the year 2000, the two sides managed to reach a deal settling all disputes along the land border "eight years after normal relations were restored in 1991, ending more than 11 years of diplomatic frost following a bloody border clash in February–March 1979."[105]

This agreement came at a time when China's relations with some members of ASEAN were strained because of China's refusal to sign a "code of conduct," regulating the settlement of territorial disputes in the South China Sea and US–Vietnam relations were in a holding pattern. An Asian ambassador expressed the opinion that "cozying up to China was a good way for Communist Party General Secretary Le Kha Phieu to assure his support among conservatives in the communist elite."[106] The land-border agreement of 1999 was followed by a demarcation of the maritime border between Vietnam and China in 2000.

Although the most visible steps in moving closer to China were made by Phieu after becoming party general secretary in December 1997, the essential groundwork had been laid by his predecessor, Do Muoi. This suggests either the continuing influence of Muoi on major decisions, despite his ambiguous status as an "adviser" to the new leadership, or that Muoi had prevailed in appointing a successor who would continue his policies.[107] In this respect, the political succession remained incomplete until the replacement of Phieu at the Ninth Party Congress.

In the end, Phieu's attempt to "play the China card" came to naught, as had the "Red solution" a decade earlier. China continued to resist his attempts to form a socialist grouping based on ideological solidarity. In the Hanoi meeting with a visiting high-level Chinese delegation in April 1998 the Chinese were careful to state that there was no "socialist axis" developing, and stressed the separate paths of each country. Zeng Qinghong "said that both the CCP and the CPV upheld the combination of the basic theories of Marxism and Leninism with the specific practice. Both parties formulated their targets, policies and guiding principles on the basis of their specific national conditions, he added."[108]

After the replacement of Phieu as party general secretary, there were allegations that he had made too many concessions to China, and had not defended Vietnam's interests. In 2002, Vietnamese dissidents protested the border agreements with China, and a journalist was placed under house arrest after making a two-month tour of the border region which, he hoped, would draw attention to the concessions to China made by the Vietnamese leadership. "Diplomats say the issue remains highly sensitive for Hanoi as the agreements angered nationalist hardliners within the Vietnamese armed forces as well as government critics. 'Dissatisfaction over the concessions made in the agreements was one pretext advanced for the ouster of communist party chief Le Kha Phieu last April,' an Asian diplomat told AFP."[109]

Ironically, one the alleged instigators of Phieu's removal was Do Muoi, who had laid the groundwork for Phieu's China policy.[110] In his 2002 visit to Vietnam, Jiang Zemin tried to repair the strained relationship. He sought a meeting with both Do Muoi and Le Kha Phieu. "Jiang will have the opportunity during his visit to meet both Phieu and his estranged predecessor Do Muoi, who diplomats say used the nationalist card against his heir and longtime protégé during his ouster."[111] As the next chapter will discuss, the "China card" played by Do Muoi and Le Kha Phieu in the late 1990s, which was a major contributor to the impasse (or "uncertain transition" period), was a dead end, and Vietnam subsequently revitalized its policy of global engagement.

WHY NOT A *DOI MOI II*?

Despite the growing recognition that the reluctance to proceed further with integration was a major obstacle to Vietnam's economic development, political caution continued to dominate the party's decision making in the late 1990s. Carlyle Thayer observed that "Vietnam's deteriorating economic circumstances were addressed by the party Central Committee's fifth plenum in July 1998.... But the most remarkable policy response of the fifth plenum was to focus its attention on ideological and cultural issues and to defer a consideration of economic policy."[112]

Thayer poses a key question: Why was it possible to successfully push through comprehensive reforms—*doi moi 1*—in 1986? If it was possible to get consensus on such a major reform effort then, why isn't it possible now? His answer is that "Vietnam adopted 'doi moi 1' in 1986 because of a confluence of internal and external factors. Undoubtedly, the key factors were the major economic crisis that Vietnam faced and the failure of previously adopted policy instruments to address fundamental structural issues."[113]

This analysis supports the findings in the earlier chapters of the present study, including the key point that it was the economic crisis of the early and mid-1980s that ignited the fundamental process of change in Vietnam, even before the crises of 1989 and 1991. Similarly, Thayer argues that it was an absence of a similar sense of crisis and urgency that contributed to a reluctance to re-energize the reform process in the late 1990s. In addition, many conservatives continued to advance the argument that Vietnam's "limited integration into the global economy was a blessing in disguise," which had protected it from the Asian financial crisis. "Today [2000] . . . party conservatives compare calls for 'doi moi 2' with the 'big bang' approach to the reform of socialist economies in Eastern Europe and the Soviet Union. They argue that such policies will only result in internal instability in Vietnam. . . . Such reforms would undermine the basis of their power . . . while the preservation of the status quo offers the possibility of prolonging the party's hegemonic position."[114]

It was in this defensive frame of mind that Vietnam's party leadership entered the twenty-first century. As Nguyen Manh Hung wrote, "In October 1998 the Party in a key Party meeting, decided to back away from economic reform despite dire warnings of an impending economic crisis and concentrate instead on maintaining socioeconomic stability. They maintained this course in 1999."[115] In 1999, "Vietnam's economy continued its decline . . . [but] Vietnam's leadership chose political stability and party supremacy even at the risk of the country 'falling behind.'"[116]

However, as Vietnam approached the twenty-first century, the persuasiveness of the argument that the success of partial reform obviated the need to go farther and faster toward deep integration with the global economy had been severely compromised. In addition, China resolutely refused to identify itself as the core of an alternative to the prevailing global system and continued to remind Vietnam that each country would have to deal with globalization in its own way. As events soon demonstrated, the weakening of the two main rationales used by conservatives to impede the progress of reform (partial reform works, Vietnam could shelter in China's lee from the winds of globalization) cleared the way for a decisive political and conceptual shift among Vietnam's political elite toward accepting the risks of "taking the plunge" into deep integration with the global system.

7

Taking the Plunge (2000–2006)

VIETNAM'S INTEGRATION INTO the Asian region and the global system in the 1990s sometimes seemed to proceed in slow motion, which obscured the extent to which the groundwork was being laid for taking the plunge into deeper interdependence. Despite the powerful constraining influence of conservative forces, which persisted throughout this period and exerted considerable influence in the late 1990s, when the decision was made in 2000 to take the next step in integration by completing the necessary steps to prepare for entry into the World Trade Organization (such as concluding the protracted negotiations with the United States for a bilateral trade agreement), the Vietnamese government moved with uncharacteristic speed and purpose.

As noted in chapter 5, in early 1992, a foreign-aid official observed a new sense of confidence in Vietnam's reform path on the part of premier Vo Van Kiet, who "sounded like a person who had jumped into an unknown ocean of reform without knowing if he would ever reach the shore, and who now, finally, felt certain that he would make it." However, as the previous chapter argues, the sense of bold forward movement faded during the rest of the decade of the 1990s. By the turn of the century, the lost momentum was restored.

In July 2000 a Western diplomat told Agence France Presse, "'Look, China is already well on the way to WTO membership, the leadership here just couldn't resist taking the plunge any longer without any viable alternative strategy.'"[1]

As Vietnam forged ahead with integration, the popular press used the term "striking out into the big ocean" (*vuon ra bien lon*) to refer to the risks and opportunities of playing in the big leagues of the regional and global economy.[2] The implied parallel concept is the prover-bial "home pond" (*ao nha*)[3] in the backyard of a rural house, a modest, safe, familiar, and controlled environment, but one with limited resources and possibilities. The armed forces newspaper used the term "big ocean," in the sense of "not yet ready for prime time," in cautioning that Vietnam's agricultural sector was not ready for "open sea" competition, in an article titled "The peasants cannot possibly swim out by themselves into the 'big ocean.'"[4]

There is a suggestive Chinese parallel to what is translated as "taking the plunge," but it is narrower and more negative than what is intended here: making a firm decision in favor of deep integration in the international system. *Xia hai*, or "jumping into the sea of commerce, initially referred to Chinese party members leaving their official posts to go into private business using their official connections for personal profit."[5] In Vietnam this was more a characteristic of the partial reforms of the 1990s, which encouraged rent-seeking behavior by people with official connections, and something which reformers thought would be reduced by the greater transparency that would come from deep integration. Nonetheless, the signification of breaking with the comfortable confines of the familiar and taking bold and risky action is contained in both phrases—"striking out into the big ocean" (Vietnam) and "jumping into the sea" (China).

There was an increasing sense of inevitability about taking the plunge and some felt that this was not a matter of choice, but a condition of living in the modern world. A writer in the official party journal observed that "At present, it is too late to speak of the issue of whether or not we are ready to jump into the fray [*nhay vao cuoc*] or not. The situation has carried us out into the current with the rolling waves of globalization. We can only strive as hard as possible to swim. It is certain that there will be those who will find their bearings and surge ahead; there will also be those who fall behind, to say nothing of drowning. But that is the basic way of protecting long-term and stable economic security; if not, one will not only fall behind but could be bankrupted by a flood of foreign imports. When that happens, one can no longer speak of economic security."[6]

There appears to have been a "tipping point" at which the stalemate between advocates and opponents of deeper integration was broken, and the momentum toward extensive regional and global engagement became irresistible. Until 2000, conservative opponents of deeper integration had been able to exercise a veto in some key policy areas, or act as a brake on the pace and scope of reform and integration in other areas.

The key question is, what changed around the turn of the millennium to clear the way for a reenergized reform process? A related issue is whether decisions taken during this period were seen by Vietnam's leaders as an irrevocable change of direction, or merely another attempt to balance competing objectives with a hedging strategy. The thesis advanced in this chapter is that it was a departure from the hedging approach of the 1990s. There is yet another issue concerning the actual capacity of Vietnam to follow through on a "deep integration" commitment, but in this context we are first of all concerned with intentions, and only secondarily with capacity to implement the policies required by a deep integration strategy.

As Jeffrey Legro's analysis of collective idea-change proposes, if there was a major break from the hedging of the 1990s, we would expect the explanation to involve some combination of crisis, persuasive alternative paths out of the crisis which could build on established elements of past political discourse, positive and concrete results gained by the new approaches, and discrediting of the old formulas that stood in the way of "new thinking."

That is not precisely what happened here, but it does indicate some directions to search for an explanation of why there was a significant breakthrough in the progress of reform and integration in 2000, with the final accord on the bilateral trade agreement (BTA) with the United States, and a ratification of this approach at the time of the Ninth Party Congress of April 2001. A comprehensive survey of Vietnam's 1975–2002 external policies noted that although the Eighth Party Congress of 1996 had advocated a policy of integration, the Ninth Congress elevated this to a central focus and stressed the need for proactive integration. The Ninth Party Congress added the element of emphasis on deep integration to Vietnam's external policy. "The new point in the external mission statement this time was that the [Ninth Party] Congress strongly affirmed proactive integration into the global and regional economy."[7] The pace of integration accelerated in the interval between the Ninth Congress and the Tenth Party Congress of 2006, which consolidated many of the "opening up" measures and irreversibly committed Vietnam to them. Vietnam's January 2007 entry into the WTO completed this phase of the integration process.

With respect to the "crisis" factor, there had been, in effect, serial crises—or, looked at another way, a single very protracted crisis which started with the economic failures of the post-1975 period and intensified with added layers of problems as the collapse of the socialist bloc unfolded. The main events had been the economic shocks of the 1980s, the end of the Cold War, and the collapse of Vietnam's main Cold War sponsor, the Soviet Union. The repercussions of these events continued to unfold throughout the decade of the 1990s, but the failure of Le Kha Phieu to revitalize an ideological axis with China left Vietnam with only two options—going with the flow of globalization, or attempting to resist the process.

As chapter 6 showed, by the Eighth Party Congress in 1996 the party concluded that the crisis that had started in the 1980s was over. ("Our country has emerged from the serious economic-social crisis which dragged on for over 15 years.") However, the reformers insisted that there was an urgency to the decision about deep integration. Vo Van Kiet's 1995 letter to the politburo warned that "One could say that being timid and passing over this opportunity will be a catastrophe for the county and our party will be faced with the danger of being stripped of its leadership—simply because it didn't meet the development needs of the country."

The Asian financial crisis did not have a major impact on Vietnam, but it did seem to confirm to the conservatives that they had been right in limiting Vietnam's exposure to the turbulent market forces of the regional and global economy. The conservatives also felt that Vietnam's relatively successful rate of economic growth during the 1990s validated the policy of partial reform. In essence, the reformers and conservatives were split over the question of the urgency of deeper integration. Since the conservatives seemingly had a strong argument (partial reform works and deeper reform is risky), and there was no immediate crisis to shake up the polemical stalemate, why was there such an abrupt shift from caution to bold international engagement in 2000–2001?

In part, the answer is that the foundations of the conservative argument had been seriously eroded over the period 1986–2000 and the alternatives they proposed to deep integration had lost their political and polemical power. There was no possibility of reconstituting the two-worlds international system. One prominent alternative to deep integration, the autarky solution, had, as we have seen, already been rejected in the early 1990s, leaving the opponents of opening up no plausible strategic alternative to offer and adapting to globalization as the sole remaining option. The only question was how much and how fast. If the decision was to go with the flow of globalization, it would be necessary to address the question of whether halfway, temporizing measures would involve a lot of risk without corresponding benefits. If so, it would be more advantageous to pursue a deep-integration strategy. After the second collapse of the China card (the first was in 1991), the only issue was how to take the plunge without being swept away by the current.

The only event which could qualify as a "crisis" during the period that Vietnamese leaders made their decision to take the plunge was 9/11, but it was an event that occurred after the fact and had a limited impact on Vietnam. To some extent 9/11 was an international crisis with global repercussions, but the main effect on Vietnam was to alleviate fears of the United States, now that America was preoccupied with terrorism, which not only took pressure off the Vietnamese in the areas of human rights and democracy, but made Vietnam more useful to the United States as a government whose authoritarian ways meant that it would not be used as a base for terrorism. Moreover, the fundamental decision to forge ahead with deep integration had been made prior to 9/11.

The "tipping point" in making the decision to take the plunge was the delayed consequence of the earlier crises, which had put the necessary conditions for extensive engagement in place. These included both the shock of economic failure in the 1980s and the end of the Cold War and the collapse of the Soviet Union. But what happened during the short-lived reign of Le Kha Phieu in the late 1990s to remove the last obstacles to deep integration was a combination of factors which collectively undermined the conservative opposition to opening up. We have discussed the failure of the attempt to carve out a socialist niche in the global system under the wing of China and the nationalist backlash against the territorial concessions that Le Kha Phieu had made to China in a bid for Chinese patronage—which in the end amounted to little and tarnished the nationalist claims of the conservatives associated with Phieu. China insisted that each socialist system had to make its own accommodations with the global market system, and made it clear that China would go its own way and act in its own interests. This seriously undercut the conservative opposition to the deep integration required by engaging in *doi moi 2*.

Another factor that undermined the conservative opposition to a *doi moi 2* was the machinations of some elements of the military and other conservatives, which led to what seems to have been an internal political crisis. One possible consequence of this (though there is no hard evidence) is that the fallout from these intrigues split the conservatives and further weakened their position. On the other side of the coin, the prolonged generational succession was finally completed at the Ninth Party Congress of 1991, and Vietnam's leadership emerged more united and capable of decisive action.

The apparent success of partial reform in the mid-1990s which had seemed to validate the conservative line on going slow and minimizing change was called into question by the end of the decade, as Vietnam's economy had reaped the easy gains of reform, and stalled as the unresolved issues of reform blocked further progress. This, in turn, strengthened the position of the reformers, who had been arguing for bolder action, and brought to the surface again the central issue of whether or not the main danger for Vietnam was falling behind in the race for economic development or risking destabilization by opening up. The conservatives had been somewhat discredited on the national-security front by the failed China card of Le Kha Phieu, criticism of the territorial treaties with China for giving away too much, meddling in political intrigues, and by their own involvement in the widespread networks of corruption, made easier by the partially reformed system, which created artificial monopolies and rewarded political influence which could be translated into cash—the worst of both worlds. Vo Van Kiet had warned in his 1995 letter to the politburo that partial reform would only entrench a politicized economic system and lead to a dead end of corruption and inefficiency. The increasing prominence of corruption as a political issue (Kiet and his own family were not immune from corruption charges) increased the salience of this warning. To the extent that the conservatives were discredited, the reformers gained.

Finally, there had been deep change at the societal level over the past two decades, which had had a major impact on the receptivity to new ideas, created new interest structures in society and new thinking about such fundamental questions as the boundaries between the private and public spheres of life, which altered the political dynamic of the system, and affected public views of legitimacy and national goals and caused a major rethinking of central social issues such as property rights. It is in this area that international relations theory is least helpful, though these deep transformations may, in the end, be the most important explanations for the dramatic changes in policy and political attitudes that took place between 1980 and the end point of this study, 2007.

LAYING THE FOUNDATIONS FOR COMPREHENSIVE
GLOBAL ENGAGEMENT

It took over a decade for Vietnam to enter the WTO. The main arguments for entry had to do with Vietnam's international competitive economic position. After years of American-imposed economic sanctions, Vietnamese leaders were painfully aware of the costs of being excluded from the mainstream of global commerce. Many reformers chafed at the long delay in gaining admission, and pointed out that Vietnam paid for this delay by being forced to accept more stringent conditions than countries that had entered earlier.[8] Reformers also advocated WTO entry because of the impact it would have on Vietnam's domestic economy, strengthening the legal framework of commercial activities, limiting arbitrary state action in the form of subsidies and capricious taxation, and creating a more unified and competitive internal market.[9] For some opponents of deep integration this was precisely the problem; integration would have a profound impact on Vietnam's internal economy by requiring more transparency. This, in turn, would threaten the economic interests of a variety of politically influential groups.

The essential first step toward ultimate membership in the WTO was to negotiate bilateral trade agreements with Vietnam's main trade partners who were members of the WTO. Most important among these was the United States. A bilateral trade agreement (BTA) was put on the agenda following the establishment of diplomatic relations in 1995. The United States insisted that in order for Vietnam to gain full access to the US market, it would have to agree to abide by WTO principles. Vietnam expressed a desire to join the WTO at the time (1995) and established an exploratory committee to prepare the groundwork.[10] Serious discussions with the United States began in 1997 but it soon became evident that completing an agreement would be difficult.[11] Although some of the difficulty in reaching agreement on a BTA was the result of Vietnam's hesitancy in opening up and losing control of critical economic sectors, Vietnam's negotiators argued that the US side had introduced demands in excess of the basic WTO guidelines which were supposed to provide the basis for the agreement.[12] The basic BTA agreement was finally reached in mid-1999,[13] but various problems put off its completion until the following year, and it took yet another year for the ratification process to run its course.

In congressional testimony, US trade representative Charlene Barshefsky commented on what appeared to have been a breakthrough in early 1999, after several years of stalemated negotiations. This was all the more remarkable because the draft BTA went beyond that negotiated by the United States with China, and required more opening up by the Vietnamese. Nevertheless, Barshefsky cautioned in her April 1999 testimony, that this was an agreement in principle, not a completed negotiation.[14] Still, it appeared that a basic agreement had been reached in July 1999.[15]

There are a number of explanations for the delay in completing the BTA, but most accounts assert that Vietnam withdrew its assent to the document after it was made public by the United States.[16] This temporary setback for the BTA indicates that political support for the agreement in Vietnam was still fragile and conservative opposition was strong. Yet, in the end, the economic incentives of proceeding with the BTA outweighed the political opposition as Vietnamese leaders became concerned by a flight of foreign investors, frustrated by the slow pace of economic reform.[17]

Despite the clear economic benefits of an agreement, only a month prior to the signing of the BTA, a well-informed foreign observer predicted that no agreement would be possible until the 2001 Ninth Party Congress, since the fundamental problem was high-level conservative political opposition overriding the economic interests of the state.[18] A senior US trade negotiator observed that "Opposition to the pact comes mostly from Vietnamese businesses that have an interest in keeping the economy closed and those who fear that a liberalized economy could undermine the Communist Party's authority."[19]

A PIVOTAL PARTY MEETING: THE TENTH PLENUM IN MID-2000

At the tenth party plenum, in mid-2000, fear of falling further behind its neighbors and other developing countries became the dominant concern of Vietnam's political leadership. The general expectation that no BTA agreement would be possible prior to the 2001 party congress raises the intriguing question of what took place in the summer of 2000 to break the political deadlock over the BTA. Carlyle Thayer's informed account of this episode offers insight into the complex political maneuvers of 2000, which ultimately led to the decision to take the plunge. "The debate about the pace and scope of economic reforms, and the degree to which Vietnam should open its economy and expose itself to the forces of globalization, became inextricably tied up with consideration of the draft BTA. As the debate wore on, party conservatives became convinced that in order to achieve their objectives of industrializing and modernizing Vietnam by 2020 they needed to reverse the marked decline in foreign investment and step up the rate of economic growth."[20]

The climate of opinion concerning important elements of reform had clearly started to shift in 1998 and 1999, as evidenced by a sudden upsurge in the number of state-owned enterprises that were equitised during this period, after nearly a decade of delay and foot dragging. "During this period [mid-1998 to the end of 1999] an additional 340 state enterprises and elements of state enterprises were equitised. In the year 1999 alone there were 250 state enterprises [equitised,] which was eight times the total number for the preceding seven years. Generally speaking, during this period, the state policy of equitising was better understood by the branches, ministries, and localities."[21] As we shall see, equitising often meant the capture of an enterprise by powerfully connected insiders, but the trend away from the legacy of central-state planning and toward commercialization is significant.

The term which is here translated as state-owned enterprise(s), or SOE is, as Adam Fforde has pointed out, more accurately translated as "state businesses," which had superseded the more narrowly focused term from the central planning era "state enterprises." Fforde was told that during the central planning era "Units were not called state businesses [*Doanh Nghiep Nha Nuoc*] but state enterprises [*Xi Nghiep Quoc Doanh*]. This was because at the time there were simply no private enterprises. Besides, the latter were cooperatives which were part of the socialist economy."[22] Most reporting on Vietnam's state sector continues to use the term "state-owned enterprises," and most English-language sources continue to use the term; in the following discussion, SOEs and "state businesses" will be used interchangeably.

A major development in the promotion and protection of private enterprise also happened at this time. "In 2000, the commercial law came into being and into our life, and fundamentally systematized and made a reality of the freedom to choose the form of commerce, freedom to establish a business, and freedom to manage, freedom to choose the scale, territory, and branch of business, except for a number of professions forbidden by law. The notable point is that these freedoms were systematized and made it possible for ordinary citizens to really benefit from these freedoms."[23] Clearly new energy and a more favorable climate of opinion for reform was building at the end of the 1990s though, as we shall see, political and ideological resistance to some of the most sensitive areas of reform continued to be significant.

Thayer observes that "Vietnam's reform effort gained new momentum after the Central Committee's Tenth Plenum concluded its deliberations in late June and early July 2000. Vietnam issued new implementing regulations for the Law on Foreign Investment (amended in June). According to a communiqué issued after the plenum: '[a]mong the key issues discussed . . . were problems of ownership and economic sectors in the transitional period to socialism; [and] building an independent and autonomous economy in the light of international economic integration.' Of significance was the plenum's debate on the issue of an independent and self-reliant economy and international economic integration."[24]

If there is a precise point in time at which the balance between conservatives and reformers tipped in favor of deeper engagement it was probably mid-2000, as indicated by Thayer's account. "The plenum concluded that there was no other choice but to continue with regional and global integration. The meeting gave its approval for the new trade minister to go to Washington in order to discuss U.S. clarifications. At the same time, long-standing plans to open a stock exchange in Ho Chi Minh City were suddenly given the green light."[25]

The question still remains *why* the conservatives capitulated at this time. There are some intriguing but inconclusive indications that the conservatives overplayed their hand in trying to stall or derail deep integration. The minister of defense, Pham Van Tra, and the army chief of staff were reprimanded for unspecified derelictions of "administrative responsibility" (*khien trach ve trach nhiem quan ly*) by the Party Central Committee on the eve of the 2001 Ninth Party Congress.[26] The best analysis of this critical period is again by Thayer, who notes that Le Kha Phieu faced charges of wiretapping his fellow politburo members, but tried to deflect the responsibility to Tra. A subsequent Party Central Committee meeting voted to replace Phieu.[27]

But even though conservatives like Pham Van Tra survived the leadership transition at the Ninth Party Congress, and continued to write the familiar denunciations of "peaceful evolution" in the party journal,[28] the Ninth Congress made it clear that economic development through deep integration was the key to Vietnam's future. Even Le Kha Phieu, in his last-minute bid to stay in power, felt compelled to acknowledge that the "danger of falling behind" and corruption were the two greatest threats to Vietnam.[29] Following the conclusion of the Ninth Party Congress, this theme was spelled out in greater detail. The report of the congress called for "proactive integration with the international economy."

Globalization was depicted as an unstoppable force, which would require nations of all political and economic colorations to engage with it and try to make it work to their advantage. The analysis of globalization was couched in the familiar (if convoluted) language of Marxism to make it palatable to the skeptical ideologues. "The reason why globalization has such an irresistible force [*suc manh kho cuong*] is that it has an objective reality [*ban chat khach quan*] that is linked to the objective trajectory of mobilization of social production, which is the inevitable result of the development of the forces of production, and the process of economic internationalization." Despite abiding suspicions that globalization advantaged the powerful capitalist countries, standing apart from this powerful tide was not an option.[30]

It is curious that the tenth plenum of the Eighth Central Committee in late June and early July 2000, which Thayer persuasively identifies as the turning point in breaking the impasse on key issues of reform and global integration, is hardly mentioned in subsequent reviews of major political decision points in the party theoretical journal.[31] Press reports just prior to the tenth plenum did not indicate signs of an impending change, noting mainly that the Vietnamese government had become more optimistic about Vietnam's economic situation and that the sharp polemics between reformers and conservatives had noticeably eased off.

An upturn in the Vietnamese economy seems to have revived the interest of foreign investors in Vietnam and strengthened the hand of reformers by suggesting that Vietnam could attract foreign investment without losing control of economic decision making. "Western donors have toned down their criticism of Vietnam's communist authorities after two years of lambasting the slow pace of market reforms, delegates told AFP ahead of the close of an annual review meeting Friday." In part this was due to a rise in global oil prices, which benefited Vietnam, but "the fact remained that Vietnam had managed to achieve growth of six percent in the first half of 2000 despite its failure to heed the dire warnings issued by donors a year ago."[32]

But, as in the mid- and late 1990s, the upturn in the Vietnamese economy also was cited by opponents of deep integration as evidence that partial reform would work, and investors would come even if no major changes were made in Vietnam. "It was not surprising therefore that Vietnamese officials were painting a basically rosy picture of the state of the economy with only a rhetorical nod to donor concerns about the pace of reform."[33]

On balance, the upturn in the Vietnamese economy seems to have favored reform advocates. Diplomatic observers and aid officials noted a more transparent attitude on the part of Vietnamese officials[34] to go along with this more upbeat attitude about Vietnam's economy, but concluded that major decisions still needed to be taken, and that these were unlikely to come before the 2001 Ninth Party Congress. Still, there was some indication that the polarized debate over integration was moving toward resolution. "A year ago in Haiphong, people were virtually shouting at each other—it was left-wing Stalinism against right-wing Stalinism,' [a] diplomat said, referring to the more outspoken champions of free market reform."[35]

It is possible that the revised and more optimistic view about Vietnam's economy was an important factor in clearing the way for a higher level of risk taking, although relatively good economic performance throughout much of the 1990s had been cited by conservatives as a reason not to take the risks of deeper economic engagement with the global economy. The greater transparency and the muting of internal polemics about reform could also have been an indication that decisions had been made which resolved some of the more contentious issues. Moreover, signs of a breakthrough in the BTA negotiations with the United States emerged as the party plenum met. The published communiqué, presented to the press by the archconservative Dao Duy Quat, merely noted that the problem of integration had been a major focus of the plenum and blandly asserted that "The plenum recognized administrative reform as the key task in the process of renovation and economic development in the coming years." Quat highlighted the point that the plenum had upheld the ban on party members engaging in "private capitalist business activities." As for the BTA, he stated vaguely that, "If all obstacles are removed and conditions agreeable to both sides, they will move to signing this treaty."[36]

The BTA breakthrough and other changes that followed this mid-2000 meeting suggest that more happened than was revealed at the time. Possibly the fact that soon-to-be-replaced party secretary general Le Kha Phieu presided over this meeting explains why its importance has been retrospectively downgraded during the tenure of his successor, Nong Duc Manh. But this plenum prepared the major documents that were adopted at the 2001 Ninth Party Congress, so that many of the policy shifts that were attributed to the Ninth Congress had their origins in this mid-2000 meeting or its immediate aftermath. Still, it is an open question why such important decisions were not delayed until the new leadership was in place. Thayer's explanation is that it was a last-ditch effort by Phieu to salvage his position as party leader. "'The stewardship, the leadership, is up for grabs next March. If they miss this opportunity, they are going to go into the party congress with no answer as to how Vietnam is to restore economic growth and reattract foreign investment,' said Dr Carlyle Thayer of the Asia-Pacific Centre for Security Studies in Hawaii. 'It's a question of regime maintenance, of keeping yourself in power.'" A Western diplomat offered the opinion that Phieu not only wanted to stay on as party leader, but aspired to expand his power by becoming head of state as well. "To do that, he has got to convince the party that he has got a firm grip on the economic rudder and is not going to let Vietnam drift yet further behind." He added, using the phrase which echoes the title of this chapter, "Look, China is already well on the way to WTO membership, the leadership here just couldn't resist taking the plunge any longer without any viable alternative strategy."[37] The explanation for this breakthrough probably also involves the combination of factors mentioned earlier (failure of the "China card," perceived shortcomings of partial reform and uncertainties about long-term economic growth despite the recent uptick in the economy, and involvement of conservatives in corruption and political machinations). Another factor may have been that the memories of the Asian financial crisis, which had strengthened the conservatives' warning about the dangers of integration, were fading.

If mid-2000, or even the Ninth Party Congress of 2001, was a major turning point in reform, as Thayer asserts, it was not evident to many other outside observers. One account of the election of Phieu's successor as party leader in 2001 stated that "diplomats noted that the new party chief had never been a champion of economic reform—his career was built precisely on offending neither side of Vietnam's political divide. 'We really shouldn't expect too many changes in Vietnamese policy,' one Western diplomat said. 'Mr Manh is a lifelong apparatchik whose ideological orthodoxy has never been questioned.'" Even the leading reformers sounded cautious. "You may know that in some countries when they had a crisis in the economy, it caused political instability. Vietnam is trying to avoid that," said Prime Minister Phan Van Khai. The patron of the reformers, former prime minister Vo Van Kiet, "echoed his protegé's comments. 'The adjustments we have made must be step-by-step,' he said." A Western journalist concluded that "The caution of the new leadership will be all the greater in the face of persistent rural unrest which was a leading factor in the ouster of Phieu."[38]

These assessments by outside observers remind us of the difficulties of unraveling the complexities of Vietnamese politics. But the underlying problem is the expectation that significant shifts in policy orientation will be immediately visible. This is an argument for taking ideas, including ideological polemics, seriously. Perhaps it is not accidental that an academically trained analyst like Thayer, with long experience observing Vietnamese politics and interpreting political polemics, would see beneath the surface while the diplomats and journalists could not. The theme of this study is that collective mindsets can shift in ways that have significant effects on behavior. We will take up this theme toward the end of this chapter, but we must first return to the issue of behavior, and examine the specific steps taken by Vietnam in pursuit of deeper integration with the global economy.

MOVING TO THE FINAL ROUND OF DEEP INTEGRATION: THE COMPLETION OF THE BILATERAL TRADE AGREEMENT WITH THE UNITED STATES AND NEGOTIATIONS TO JOIN THE WORLD TRADE ORGANIZATION

The story of Vietnam's convoluted path to the final approval of the BTA is murky and hard to untangle. It is clear that conservatives in the politburo initially derailed the 1999 agreement. There was a subsequent attempt to put the blame on minister of trade Truong

Dinh Tuyen, who had negotiated that agreement, for exceeding his instructions. He was removed from his post in January 2000 and Vu Khoan, a senior diplomat, replaced him as Vietnam's chief BTA negotiator. Intriguingly, Vu Khoan had been credited with bringing the land- and maritime-border negotiations with China to a successful conclusion, even though this agreement came under fire for compromising Vietnamese interests—the same charge that some had leveled at Tuyen.[39] A prominent reformer and strong supporter of the BTA later implied that the ousted Tuyen had been made a scapegoat (he was "pictured as a saboteur") and called him "an honest minister."[40]

Tuyen was subsequently reappointed as trade minister in 2002 and played a prominent role in the WTO negotiations. He described the final phase of the 1999 negotiations as "tense" and near breakdown. The agreement itself, he later said, was a framework without the details spelled out, involving issues that proved more difficult than expected. Tuyen later recounted some aspects of this negotiation and portrayed himself as someone who knew how to demand his due in a negotiation. He offered an exchange of gifts in anticipation of a successful conclusion of the BTA negotiations. Tuyen was not altogether pleased when, after giving US deputy trade representative Richard Fisher a carved replica of the Imperial Palace in Hue, Fisher promised to reciprocate with a cowboy hat from his native state of Texas. "When I heard Fisher say he was going to give me a cowboy hat, I was not pleased because when Vietnamese hear the word 'cowboy' they are already put off." In Vietnamese *cao-boi* refers to juvenile delinquents with a swaggering contempt for society, law, and convention, hardly an image that would be pleasing to any Vietnamese, and one which might suggest an out-of-control negotiator who, in *cao-boi* fashion, ignored his instructions, the very charge later leveled against Tuyen. Tuyen didn't get the hat for several years, but he persisted and it was eventually delivered to him long after the negotiation was over and he had been reinstated as trade minister (and he came to view the hat as "beautiful"). This story, he said, showed that he knew how to demand what was owed to him—an indirect way of saying that he defended Vietnam's interest with hard bargaining in the BTA negotiations.[41]

Vu Khoan's explanation of why there was a year-long delay in completing the BTA was that key details remained to be ironed out after the first draft.[42] Tuyen also mentions this, though his critics asserted that the problem was with the framework agreement itself, and not with subsequent disagreements over details. Outside observers concluded that the fundamental problem was not with the economic deal struck in Tuyen's version of the framework agreement, but political opposition to the very concept of an agreement of this type.[43]

The final deal signed in mid-2000 (but not ratified for over a year) had more or less the same elements as the 1999 framework agreement, so it is hard to say that Vu Khoan "got a better deal" than Truong Dinh Tuyen. And it is evident that the fears that had caused the political leadership to back away in 1999 had not been dissipated by the final agreement. "Hanoi and Washington agreed in principle to a pact last July, but Vietnam's

Communist Party Politburo then balked at the deal over apparent concerns it would lose economic and even political control.... Analysts at the time saw the move as a sign Hanoi continued to shun change and was not ready to commit to reforms." Even after the agreement, some Vietnamese feared. "Once the two markets are open, many transnational U.S. firms will flock to Vietnam . . . and state-owned enterprises are afraid the big sharks will eat the smaller ones."[44]

Nor was there any reason for conservatives to believe that the United States had abandoned its alleged strategy of "peaceful evolution." In announcing the completion of the BTA, President Clinton made remarks which must have sounded to Vietnam's conservatives as confirming their worst fears about the connection between opening up and "peaceful evolution."[45] Since the final agreement was not "a better deal" and most of the concerns about the 1999 accord remained, the only logical conclusion is that there was a reconfiguration of Vietnam's political landscape in 2000 that changed the balance of forces between conservatives and reformers, as argued above.

The saga of the BTA was by no means concluded by the signing of the agreement in July 2000. Ratification of the agreement by the United States became entangled in American domestic politics and the transition from the Clinton to the Bush administration. The fact that a human-rights controversy flared up during this sensitive period but did not derail the agreement is testimony to the persuasiveness of the economic logic of the agreement from the American point of view.[46]

Once the BTA concessions had been made, Vietnam could only wait for the US political process to run its course. Congress did not ratify the accord until October 2001. The Vietnamese National Assembly ratified the agreement the following month. Hanoi then accelerated its efforts to join the WTO. Immediately following Vietnam's ratification of the BTA in November 2001 Vietnam invited the head of the WTO for discussions, but was told that the WTO process might be prolonged. WTO director general, Mike Moore, told Prime Minister Khai that "whether Vietnam will become a full member of the WTO in its next meeting, held every two years, depends fully on Vietnam. Vietnam has to negotiate not only with WTO's agencies but also with its 144 member countries bilaterally. Therefore, the process will take time and if even small chances are missed, it will take Vietnam more time to become a full member of the WTO."[47]

AN IDEOLOGICAL TURN IN THE ROAD

The signing of the BTA, along with other key reform measures such as the liberalization of investment laws and the Commercial Law of 2000, which opened significant space for the development of private enterprise, illustrates the breakthrough from the reform impasse that characterized much of the 1990s. Vietnam adopted the concept of market socialism and affirmed the idea of a single global economy, further undermining the "two worlds" view. But significant political and ideological opposition remained. After the

Ninth Party Congress of 2001, however, the opponents of integration were fighting a losing battle, even though resistance to reform persisted. Perhaps the most significant determination from the Ninth Party Congress was that a single global economy existed, and Vietnam would have to integrate into that economy, though it would be able to maintain its political identity as a "socialist market economy."

But the increasing acceptance in Vietnam of the concept of a global market economy not defined by the regime characteristics of its participants seriously challenged the concept of a "socialist market economy" that could function with a considerable degree of autonomy from the larger global economic system, retain its own identity, and play by its own rules, while being deeply engaged with the outside world. It also challenged the view that economic relations with capitalist countries, especially the United States, were dangerous and a potential source of political infiltration and manipulation.

In a remarkable letter to the politburo on the eve of the Tenth Party Congress— reminiscent of a similar letter prior to the Eighth Party Congress (discussed in chapter 6)—when he was still in power, Vo Van Kiet asserted that even in the "two worlds" era Vietnam had been locked into a dependency relationship with the advanced socialist economies, not unlike the economic dependency of the colonial era. "Our economic development continues to be excessively dependent in one direction on the outside world. Before the revolution, the Vietnamese economy was dependent on the policies of the French colonialists. After the revolution, during the Resistance and even after the liberation of the South, our economy was also dependent on the aid of the socialist countries. Now we have moved in the direction of a sovereign economy. . . . However, at present in order to live (in its broadest sense) we still have to be excessively dependent in one direction on the outside world."[48] This formulation accepts the fact of a single global economy, and implies that the Cold War socialist economy was less different from the capitalist economy of the time than the rhetoric of socialist community alleged, since Vietnam was dependent in its relations with both capitalist and socialist countries.

During the Cold War, the view of "socialist" trade, was that it would involve complementarity and a rational division of labor among socialist countries, not competition (regarded by central planners as irrational and wasteful) and market-driven exchanges. Vietnam found this view advantageous, because it situated foreign trade with socialist partners in a political context, and served to conceal the extent to which trade with China and the Soviet Union was essentially a form of subsidized aid. At the same time, the socialist division of labor constrained Vietnam's attempts to move toward an advanced industrialized economy because it was dependent for producer and capital goods on its Soviet and East European trading partners, and supplied them with primary products in return.

Under the global market system there would also be an "international division of cooperation," but one based on economic rationality and comparative advantage as dictated by objective market conditions, rather than the political dictates of the leader of an ideological bloc. "Tied together with economic globalization is international economic integration which, at its core, is economic opening up and participation in the international division of cooperation [*phan cong hop tac quoc te*], which creates conditions for effective coordination between economic potential within the country and the outside, while opening up space and an environment for development by occupying the most suitable niche that can be obtained in international economic relations." In the Vietnamese view, "It is objective economic requirements that have led to widespread participation in the globalized economy by countries of different regimes and political systems."[49]

The director of the reform-minded government think tank, the Central Institute for Economic Management, noted the slow pace of reform in key areas like equitisation of state enterprises and bankruptcy laws, which some reformers regarded as the test case of how much pain the government was willing to tolerate in order to accept market discipline. Dinh Van An noted that "Up to mid-2002 only 828 state enterprises and elements of state enterprises had been equitised, about 3% of the total state enterprises. There are many subjective and objective reasons for this, among them a widespread attitude in many localities that equitisation is a deviation from socialism [*chech huong xa hoi chu nghia*], which gave rise to consternation, timidity, and a failure to strongly push this process forward. . . . With regard to commercial bankruptcy, nine years from the passage of the Bankruptcy Law up to 2003, there had been only 46 enterprises that had declared bankruptcy."[50] In the view of reformers like An, the source of the problem was essentially ideological. "However, the question of new thinking [*doi moi tu duy*] concerning the components of the economy, especially with respect to the meaning and role of private enterprise in our country is not an easy matter. Because this matter conflicts with the traditional concept that still has a heavy influence on the design and determination of the direction for the development and regulation [*dieu hanh*] of society. It is precisely this which makes the *doi moi* measures to encourage the development of private business encounter constant difficulties." An noted that a number of business people "work and worry" at the same time, and fear letting their enterprises grow for fear of being regarded as too big. To avoid this, businesses were split up, profits concealed, and business growth stifled by the fear of becoming too successful and attracting unwanted attention."[51]

The deputy director of the steering committee for *doi moi* and the development of state enterprises gave a more political explanation for the sluggishness of business reform, but also stressed the influence of the "old thinking." While pointing out that the government had intentionally chosen a gradualist path rather than "shock therapy" (*lieu phap soc*), and citing with approval the Chinese approach of "feeling one's way" (*vua lam, vua do*), Ho Xuan Hung offered an organizational and political diagnosis with terminology from the old era to explain why the reforms had not proceed faster. The problem was "lack of a concrete program and plan, lack of close management, to say nothing of being rightist and lacking resolve." Hung added that "The subsidy ideology is still 'weighty' and has not yet been liberated. Ideological dithering and confusion about the direction of development in state business is what has led to hesitation and delay in organizing implementation."[52]

The irony of labeling cadres whose support for marketizing reforms was constrained by residual belief in old-style Marxist ideology "rightists" is worth noting. Perhaps the ease with which the new orthodoxy about market economics could reverse the old "rightist–leftist" labels was the result of appending market economics onto the definition of socialism. "A new breakthrough in thinking and theory regarding market economics came at the Ninth Party Congress (April 2001) which was the first time the concept that our country was implementing a market economy with socialist characteristics was put forth."[53] By appropriating market concepts into the socialist framework, a new orthodoxy was established with full party backing. Thus dissent from this line that took the form of clinging to the old "subsidy" ideology was now by definition "rightist" a label previously used to stigmatize those party members who were excessively cautious in applying or supporting new policies.

To an outside observer, the new thinking embodied in the concept of the "socialist market economy" proclaimed at the Ninth Party Congress could be viewed largely as an exercise in sophistry. The previous party congress had "set forth the very important new concept of the commodity economy and socialism." Now this was regarded as not only being compatible with socialism but "the achievement of the development of human civilization." However, the Eighth Congress had avoided calling this a "market economy." This term appeared officially in party documents for the first time at the Ninth Party Congress. The rationalization that made this term acceptable was that (1) the goal of the market economy was to build socialism, and (2) Vietnam's economy could not at the time be described as a "socialist" market economy because "we are still in the stage of transition" to socialism.[54]

It is tempting to dismiss this formulation as ideological gymnastics and *ex post facto* retrofitting of reality onto the old ideological framework by Vietnam's party theoreticians. But the concept of "market socialism" served two important functions. First, and most important from the perspective of the main focus of this book, it brought to a close the lingering idea that there were two incompatible world systems and removed the major ideological barrier to deep integration and, of course, WTO membership. Second, it redefined the terrain for party ideologists, who would now have to labor to demonstrate that deep integration was actually the salvation of socialism. Following the Ninth Party Congress of 2001, the party leadership initiated a policy review of the theoretical issues that had come up during the two decades of reform, with the intention of resolving remaining controversies and putting to rest any remaining doubts about the path of deep integration in preparation for the Tenth Party Congress and WTO entry. The party's description of the decisions of a March 1, 2003, politburo meeting make it clear that at this time a collective decision had been made to formulate a systematic theoretical and ideological justification for deep integration with the global economy. At this meeting, "the politburo resolved to sum up a number of issues of theory and practice from the past twenty years in order to determine the accomplishments and point out the limitations in the development of our theoretical thinking, to draw some lessons from experience;

discover new theoretical factors and issues and clarify a number of questions about socialism and the path leading to socialism in Vietnam." The party had decided that the time had come to bring the long debate to a close and "come to a conclusion about a number of issues on which there are different opinions, and contribute to supplementing and expanding on the party's policy of *doi moi*, to provide scientific documents in preparation for the Tenth Party Congress."[55]

Nguyen Phu Trong, the politburo member who was in charge of this major review of theoretical and ideological issues related to reform wrote that "Over the two days of 12 and 13 March, 2004, after listening to the steering committee [of the Council on Theoretical Issues] give an overview of their report, the politburo had a discussion and gave the following assessment: 'This is the first time our party has had the conditions to look back over the entire process of *doi moi* over the past, an overview on a large scale, of importance, with rich contents relating to almost all the matters relating to the policy and strategy of revolution in our country. . . . To the present, although there have been not a few difficulties, our country has undergone a fundamental and comprehensive change."[56]

Perhaps the most important consequence of this comprehensive review of the reform process was that it concluded that Vietnam's socialism was fundamentally secure, thus cutting the ground from under the conservatives' continuing warnings that "peaceful evolution" was the foremost danger Vietnam faced, and shifting the focus to development, which favored those who had emphasized that "falling behind" was the main threat to Vietnam. Despite the collapse of socialism in the Soviet Union and Eastern Europe and the global and regional economic crises, Trong said, Vietnam had "not been swept along [*cuon theo*], and has overcome these difficulties to advance step by step." Vietnam had "taken the plunge," but had not been swept away by the current of unpredictable change. It was now ready to take the momentous step toward deep integration of joining the WTO.

FROM IDEOLOGY TO PRACTICE: VIETNAM'S INITIAL EXPERIENCE WITH EXPANDED TRADE RELATIONS FOLLOWING THE BILATERAL TRADE AGREEMENT WITH THE UNITED STATES

Although some party commentary was upbeat about the BTA following its National Assembly ratification,[57] not all elements of the political system were enthusiastic. "The *Cong An Nhan Dan* (People's Police) newspaper, the police's mouthpiece, warned that hostile forces may use the Vietnam–US Bilateral Trade Agreement (BTA) to attack Vietnam." A report on this dissenting view noted that the article was published after the first meeting between the new US Ambassador to Vietnam, Raymond Burghardt, and Deputy Prime Minister Nguyen Tan Dung, which discussed bilateral trade and investment potential. "The BTA may harm Vietnam's economic, commercial and social security.

Hostile forces can also attack the country in the trade arena, making bilateral defense and security problems, that are complicated by historical events, more serious." said the newspaper, which called for "further consideration of national defense and security issues in developing trade with the US, to prevent any possible threat."[58] In other words, the security branch was resisting being sidelined in the policy process, which was now focused on opening up to the outside, rather than the security sector's main task, which was closing down external contacts and influences.

The inevitable commercial conflicts that resulted from expanded trade between the United States and Vietnam created some frictions, but the notable development was an increasing recognition that these conflicts were inherent in a market-based system, and that instead of focusing on how Vietnam was being victimized by external forces—a constant theme in the past—many officials and reformers pointed to the compensating benefits of the BTA. A domestic lobby of American catfish farmers pressured the US government to refuse to allow Vietnamese exports to the United States to be labeled by that familiar name, putting them at a competitive disadvantage. During a review of a year of implementing the US–Vietnam BTA, Vietnam's top reform economist, Le Dang Doanh, commented that, "The more Vietnam exports to the US, the more disputes it will be embroiled in." A reporter from the *Financial Times* noted that, "This idea seems to be gradually hitting home with Vietnamese officials. Many realize now that disputes are commonplace in trade with the US, the world's largest market, as everybody scrambles to hold on to their share of the pie. It is also dawning on the Vietnamese establishment that the BTA is no magic wand with which to wave away all trade problems." Deputy Prime Minister Nguyen Tan Dung stated that, "we cooperate for mutual benefit and will fight for our legitimate rights in accordance with the BTA and international practice. Disputes are normal and show us that integration is not a piece of cake." Nguyen Dinh Luong, a BTA negotiator and adviser to the trade minister, said "any negative outcome in the catfish dispute should be treated as a lesson in equipping local enterprises with the expertise to approach the US market."[59] One of the major differences between the BTA and other negotiated agreements between the United States and Vietnam in the past was that the compliance mechanisms to ensure that the terms of the agreement were adhered to would not involve US government pressure or monitoring. In many respects it would be investors and the market that would pass judgment on how well Vietnam was living up to the BTA commitments. Senior US Commerce Department officials warned Vietnam that failure to live up to the terms of the BTA would "further damage investor confidence and could further stunt Vietnam's already sluggish economy." The United States even offered to assist Vietnam in drawing up legal guidelines that would help realize the economic incentives of the agreement (making Vietnam's market more attractive to investors).[60]

Still, the United States did not want to rely solely on market forces to ensure compliance with the BTA. Unlike the trade agreement between the United States and China, the trade agreement with Vietnam initially mandated annual reviews by Congress which some elements of the Vietnamese leadership feared would be "used as a lever to force greater political and social reforms."[61] But, as Vietnam moved closer to WTO entry, the United States eventually dropped the annual trade review, which largely removed the uncertainties of Congressional politics from US–Vietnam economic relations.

This move from state-to-state compliance mechanisms to market incentives shifted an important element of the security paradigm. In the first place, international competition was now increasingly viewed as a normal aspect of international relations rather than a reflection of political support or opposition. "Trade Minister Vu Khoan also warned of stiff competition ahead for Vietnamese companies. 'Cooperation carries with it an element of competition,' Khoan told the official Vietnam News Agency. 'So it is imperative for us to mobilize all our internal resources and rapidly raise our competitive ability at the national scale, in enterprises and every new product.'"[62]

After five years, the impact of the BTA continued to look positive to Vietnamese trade officials. "After five years of implementing the Commercial Agreement, trade between the two countries has increased 5.54 times (from 1.4 billion USD in 2001 to 7.62 billion USD in 2005)." Deputy Minister of Trade Luong Van Tu added that trade expansion had exceeded the projections of the specialists. Most importantly, it had helped diversify Vietnam's exports beyond agricultural products.[63] The apparent success of the BTA helped sustain momentum for the deeper integration required by entry into the World Trade Organization.

CONSOLIDATION OF THE COMMITMENT TO DEEP INTEGRATION: FROM THE NINTH TO THE TENTH PARTY CONGRESS (2001–2006)

The focus on the linkage between Vietnam's economic future and deep integration with the global economy dominated the period of the Ninth Party Congress (2001–2005) and became the major theme of the following party congress. A party spokesperson stated that this would be the major consideration in selecting the new party leadership in 2006. According to Phan Dien, the Tenth Congress should elect a central committee (Tenth Congress, 2006–2010) "with enough virtue, talent, and character to lead Vietnam to escape the condition of underdevelopment."[64] By 2006 the conservatives now apparently accepted the reformers' view that the main danger was economic backwardness, and the 2001 stress on the dangers of holding back from deep integration were reinforced. In commenting on the draft political report to the 2006 Tenth Party Congress the minister of finance referred to global and domestic challenges outlined by the party secretariat and commented that "The world [situation] does not allow us to fall further behind."[65]

While the conservatives were still able to voice warnings about "peaceful evolution" in 2001, in 2006 Party Secretary General Nong Duc Manh mentioned "peaceful evolution" only once in his address to the Tenth Party Congress, and it clearly was not the central priority. The title of the draft political report of the Tenth Congress makes clear what the focus was: "Raise the leadership capability and energy for struggle of the Party, bring into full play the strength of the entire people, and strongly push forward comprehensive *doi moi* to quickly lead our country out of the condition of underdevelopment."[66]

Former prime minister Vo Van Kiet, in a letter to the politburo prior to the Tenth Party Congress, pointed out that harping on "peaceful evolution" was inconsistent with Vietnam's declared foreign policy principles. Of course, he said, there are hostile forces out there that require vigilance, but it "can't be extreme and lacking good political sense [*nhay ben* = acumen, quick grasp of a changing situation] and done in a simple one-directional us-versus-the-enemy fashion, but must always look at the big picture [*toan cuoc*], and clearly see our power position [*the luc*] at the present time, as well as deeply understanding the interactions between the forces [*the luc*] in the region and the world. The concept of 'peaceful evolution' which we are continually using cannot adequately reflect that kind of vigilance but, on the contrary, has led to the disappearance of a sense of vigilance and has created a reverse impression that is an obstacle for the very task of elevating the spirit of vigilance. I think that we must very judicious [*tinh tao*] in reassessing this matter, especially since we have loudly proclaimed to the world that Vietnam is ready to be friends with all countries of the world and wants to be a reliable partner of everyone."[67]

This was one of the most thorough and direct assaults on the concept of "peaceful evolution." Kiet certainly must have calculated that he would have to confront the issue directly in order to remove it as a constraint on taking the plunge. Again, he built on elements of an existing rhetorical formula but took it in a different direction. Vigilance was indeed necessary, he agreed, but the kind of blind hostility to external influences advocated by the most zealous purveyors of the "peaceful evolution" threat was self-defeating because it led to an indiscriminate blanket labeling of everything from the outside as a threat, and thus actually diminished the spirit of vigilance. Being "judicious" means being discriminating about what the real threats are.[68]

Equally important, Kiet clearly pointed out the contradiction of the partial-reform approach by noting that Vietnam could not treat potential economic partners as threatening enemies while also seeking external participation in its economy and presenting itself as wanting to be "a reliable partner" and "friends with everybody." This disconnect between basic external strategy and hostile rhetoric was self-defeating, he argued. It may have been at this point that the foundation of the 1990s approach to partial reform— reform built on the old assumptions and limited by the aversion to fundamental change— was fatally undermined. The Vietnamese political elite increasingly saw that they could not, in fact, live in a parallel universe. But although this decisive blow to "peaceful evolution" was struck in 2005, the foundations for this had already been laid in mid-2000 as "catching up" became the main obsession of the leadership. The connection between breaking out of the condition of underdevelopment and falling further behind and the Tenth Congress theme of pursuing deep integration was further spelled out by former deputy premier Vu Khoan. "The Tenth Party Congress set forth the goal of 'quickly leading our country out of the condition of underdevelopment' by the year 2010. If we want to do this, we need to employ many measures, among which the two most notable and novel that were raised in the resolution of the Tenth Congress were: *first*, perfect the regime of a market economy with socialist characteristics, and *second*, integrate deeper and more fully into the various global economic regimes [*cac the che kinh te the gioi*]. Integration into the global economy will tie our economy into the regional and global economies on the basis of common rules of the game [*luat choi*]."[69]

The Tenth Party Congress spelled out the connection between deep integration, comprehensive reform, proactive "milieu shaping" diplomacy, and not falling further behind in the global race for economic development. The congress mandated "a faster rate of development with the goal of quickly bringing our country out of its underdeveloped state, to create the foundation for becoming a contemporary type of industrialized society." The foreign-policy corollary was that Vietnam should stress maintaining a "peaceful environment" and creating international conditions that were "more favorable for the program of *doi moi*."[70]

More recent versions of "peaceful evolution" have developed beyond the original implication that it was a strategy by the United States or other "imperialist powers" formulated and executed by the government and specifically targeted on Vietnam and other surviving socialist countries. This was, perhaps, a concession to those party members and others who did not buy the cruder version or thought it was self defeating. "Alongside the absolute majority of opinions in unanimous support," of the concept of peaceful evolution as outlined in successive party congress declarations since the early 1990s, "there have also been the views of those who do not approve of continuing to use the concept of 'peaceful evolution.' The reason is that world peace has led to many changes, the idea is too general and abstract and does not correctly take the measure of the Western countries whose strategies rarely mention 'peaceful evolution' with regard to socialist countries." In addition, the fixation with "peaceful evolution" was criticized for deflecting attention from more direct actual threats, while casting doubt on Vietnam's sincerity in "loudly proclaiming" its willingness to "be friends with the whole world."[71]

The "loudly proclaim" phrase is an apparent reference to the 2005 letter to the politburo by Vo Van Kiet, cited above, who used the same argument and the same language in criticizing "peaceful evolution." In the more nuanced formulation, peaceful evolution is reaffirmed as a serious threat, but not directly linked to specific national policies by the United States or other Western countries. Instead, the analysis cites the publications and transmissions of congressionally funded nongovernmental or quasigovernmental advocacy groups such as the International Republican Institute who criticize Vietnam on human rights or democracy grounds. Even here, there is a silver lining, however. As a result of taking stock of its failure in the Vietnam War, the United States has, in the view of these analysts, opted for a more cost-effective approach. "That involves putting an end to the pursuit of anti-communism by means of war, and instead using its real strength, which is political democracy and economic freedom, as the main weapons to attack authoritarian states [*che do chuyen che*]."[72] In this view the "good news" is that Vietnam is not a specific target of America but simply one of a category of "authoritarian states," and it is the lack of democracy rather than its communist regime per se that is the problem, and it is propaganda and not military invasion that Vietnam must cope with. Presumably it was considered somewhat more reassuring to be in a crowded field of authoritarian states rather than a conspicuous member of the tiny "lonely hearts club" of surviving communist states.

The now retired prime minister Vo Van Kiet, relieved of the constraints of having to appease various constituencies by paying lip service to their concerns, stated unequivocally in an interview that "The biggest danger for Vietnam is falling behind and impoverishment. We have to do what it takes to catch up with the world. Many brothers have set forth many dangers [*nguy co*] but I can affirm that there is one danger. If we can overcome that danger, we will resolve all the other dangers. We have to escape from poverty and reduce the gap between ourselves and other countries so that our people can become wealthy and the country strong."[73]

This concern had also been voiced in Kiet's 2005 letter to the politburo, in which he criticized the draft political report for the Tenth Party Congress for failing to adequately deal with this issue. "It is necessary to clearly and straightforwardly lay out the [policy] directions that have been mistakenly and simplistically categorized as a deviation [*chech huong*], and see if they really are deviant. . . . This matter is really too vague in the report. How could it be that having to catch up with everybody is a deviation, and letting our country fall further and further behind is the right direction? . . . We will suffer losses or will fall behind if, in the impending integration, Vietnam lets other countries expand into [Vietnam], while not actively figuring out how to expand outward."[74] Of course these statements are evidence of a shift in the relative weight of "peaceful evolution" and "falling behind" well after the critical turning point in 2000, but they summarize and illustrate the views that appear to have already become dominant at the turn of the century.

VIETNAM JOINS THE WORLD TRADE ORGANIZATION: PROLONGED NEGOTIATIONS ARE A LEARNING EXPERIENCE ABOUT VIETNAM AND THE WORLD

Many Vietnamese leaders and officials thought that after the completion of the bilateral trade agreement with the United States, entry into the World Trade Organization would be swift and uncomplicated. In fact, the most difficult negotiations were yet to come. During the course of a large number of bilateral and multilateral negotiations along the road to WTO membership, Vietnam learned a great deal about the realities of the global system, and its own place in the world. In addition, it gained valuable experience in how to operate in unfamiliar terrain, and gained a better understanding of how much Vietnam would have to change if it wanted to continue down the path of deep integration in the global economy.

One of Vietnam's top trade negotiators was asked how Vietnam's experience in negotiating the BTA with the United States had affected Vietnam's approach to WTO entry. Deputy Trade Minister Luong Van Tu replied: "Because the signing of the BTA was based on WTO principles, it has contributed to facilitating the country's negotiation process for accession to the world's biggest trade body. As a requirement of the BTA, Vietnam has improved its legal system, thus making it easier for the country's WTO negotiation process."[75] Tu added that, "The negotiation process for the signing of the BTA also helped Vietnam's policy-making agencies more thoroughly understand the nature of globalisation and international integration, as well as WTO rules."[76]

As Luong Van Tu observed, "the signing of the BTA [was] the most comprehensive agreement Vietnam has ever reached with a foreign country." For this reason, it was also a process of education about how the world worked following the Cold War, and Vietnam's role in this new environment. A Vietnamese account of the WTO negotiations noted that the process lasted eleven years and had fourteen rounds of negotiations with twenty-eight bilateral negotiating partners, far exceeding in duration and complexity the two years of negotiations involved in Vietnam's accession to ASEAN.[77]

Luong Van Tu describes the confident mindset of the government following the completion of the BTA with the United States. "We thought that when the bilateral trade agreements (BTA) were finished, then we would have nearly completed the work of joining the WTO, but in fact there were a number of big issues that could not be resolved, such as the textile quotas [*han ngach*] for Vietnam. In addition, we were still subject to the Jackson–Vanik law which was extended each year during the period where we did not have Permanent Normal Trade Relations with the United States."[78]

For much of the decade of the 1990s, Vietnam had been convinced that the door to international acceptance in the major international economic organizations like the WTO was guarded by Washington, and that once the United States decided to open this door, Vietnam could walk straight through. The complex WTO entry negotiation process involved many other countries. Each of the twenty-eight bilateral negotiations undertaken by Vietnam at the request of WTO members presented distinct challenges.

Vietnam thought that some of the negotiations would be unproblematic. In the case of China, there was already an ASEAN trade agreement that included Vietnam and China. Hanoi was confident that there was already a meeting of the minds on the key trade issues involving the two countries, and that the WTO-related bilateral trade agreement would be easy. "When we negotiated with China, there was already a Vietnam-China free trade agreement within ASEAN, so that there was a meeting of the minds [*tu tuong don gian*], and in fact there didn't need to be another negotiation. But with China we still had to go through ten rounds of negotiations, and many of the rounds were tense, with negotiations going through the night."[79]

And despite the completion of the BTA with the United States, there were further contentious issues involving both bilateral questions and US (and European Union) efforts to act on behalf of the institutional interests of the WTO. In a 2006 interview, Deputy Trade Minister Luong Van Tu revealed that "in the course of recent negotiations with the United States, there was a lot of tension. The United States and the European Union were the biggest negotiating partners in the WTO with regard to both goods and services. These negotiating partners negotiated not only for their own interests but also for the interests of the World Trade Organization, so the negotiating demands were wider ranging, deeper, and more varied. This kind of negotiation is very complicated."[80]

One lesson about global integration was that powerful countries could use the rules and institutions of the international economic system to further their own interests at the expense of less powerful nations and newcomers to the game. "Nguyen Dinh Luong, head of the Vietnamese negotiation delegation, said that . . . 'The US has been successful in shifting from the General Agreement on Trade and Tariff (GATT) to WTO to push world trade liberalization to a new level. The US does not sign agreements with partners at a lower level than the WTO.' The result is that new members of the WTO must accept newer conditions than those previously negotiated with the US."[81]

Whereas the BTA negotiations had covered only 300 tariff lines, the bilateral WTO negotiations between Vietnam and the United States involved 9,300. A key issue was negotiating for the granting of permanent normal trade relations, which would eliminate the politicized annual congressional approval of Vietnamese market access to the United States. Vietnam was chagrined to find that the United States wanted to apply the same antisurge protections ("self-defense measures") against Vietnamese imports that it had with China, and its negotiator pointed out that Vietnam was hardly in China's league as an economic power, and did not pose that kind of threat to American commercial interests.[82]

In its WTO negotiations with the United States, Vietnam also discovered how much its internal freedom of action would be constrained by WTO-related obligations. Vietnam's government had passed an edict ordering "assistance" or "support" (*ho tro*) to the textile industry. The translators working for the US and international organizations translated this as "subsidize"—which prompted immediate objections from Vietnam's negotiating partners. Despite the presentation of documents which Deputy Minister Tu asserts satisfied the United States that this "support" did not involve zero-interest loans, and was therefore not a subsidy, Vietnam withdrew the controversial edict.[83]

In addition to learning lessons about give and take in international negotiations and the importance of striving for "win-win" solutions in negotiations—very different from the fiercely adversarial zero-sum international negotiations Vietnam had engaged in during the Cold War, in which even minor concessions were viewed as serious threats to national security—Hanoi also had to reflect on how it was perceived in the world. Vietnam's self-image during the heroic wartime period was of a major international player in global politics that was fighting above its weight class. Its propagandists produced glowing reports of the success of its efforts at "socialist construction" to prove to the world and their own people that Vietnam was developing impressively under the party's leadership. During the WTO negotiations, Vietnam discovered that it would be advantageous to plead poverty and insist on its backwardness; "there is the paradox that although Vietnam has an average per capita income that is under 1,000 US dollars per year, and according to the rules of the WTO lesser developed countries are those which have a per capita income of under 1,000 dollars, Vietnam would not be categorized as a lesser developed country (after considering in addition the standards regarding health, culture, and education). In the economic sphere, our income is low, so we had to negotiate to be accepted as a low income [country]. In the end we were accepted as a low-level developing country. This point was very important, because the WTO granted us a transitional period to implement a number of promises to the WTO regarding the special consumption tax (TTTB, *Tieu Thu Dac Biet*), and the right to engage in commercial activity."[84]

The Cold War era of international posturing was over, and Vietnam now presented itself not as a success story of the neo-Stalinist model of socialist development but as a member of the world community deserving of special consideration for its low level of development. The disconnect between this self-deprecating approach to the world, and commitment to the rules and logic of the market economy, and the continuing insistence of the party ideologists that there was something inherently superior about a "socialist" approach to development, however, was a subject of discussion only among the boldest reformers.

The final and unexpected obstacle to Vietnam's WTO membership was not the United States, or even the European Union, but seemingly innocuous Switzerland, the neutral site of some of Vietnam's most memorable Cold War diplomatic dramas (for example the 1954 Geneva Conference, which divided Vietnam into a communist North and a non-communist South), showing that the new game could be unpredictable. An article titled "The 89th minute" (the final minute of a soccer match) describes the last of many negotiations coming down to the wire with only five hours to go until the expiration of the deadline for the negotiating round. Switzerland was demanding special concessions in the area of maritime transportation in which, despite its landlocked geography, it had a major economic stake. The Vietnamese delegation had feared that other countries would gang up on it in a collusive effort to extract maximum concessions. To their surprise, this did not happen and, in the "eighty-ninth minute," it was only Switzerland that stood in the way of membership. A baffled and frustrated Vietnamese delegation received support from other trade partners, but the delegations were dispersing and going home. It looked like Vietnam's membership bid would be a victim of this impasse. At the last minute, Switzerland relented, the WTO certified that Vietnam had qualified for memberships, and champagne flowed in Geneva.[85]

The leadership's evaluation of the way that WTO membership would affect Vietnam's position in the world was cautious but upbeat. Chief of State Nguyen Minh Triet said that WTO membership by itself was not a guarantee of success in development. It would offer the opportunity to develop, but each nation would have to "have the right stuff" (*ban linh*) to take advantage of the opportunities offered by the WTO, and to avoid the pitfalls of opening up. Triet was confident that Vietnam would make the best of its WTO membership. The wartime legacy of the "beauty queen" imagery of a Vietnam that was irresistibly attractive to foreigners resurfaced in somewhat different form. Triet told a Vietnamese interviewer that, as a result of its WTO membership, "Vietnam is becoming more attractive and beautiful in the eyes of friends every day. Everyone has been won over [*thuyet phuc*] by a safe Vietnam, with its cordial Vietnamese people, warm, friendly, and hospitable."[86] Unlike the victimized damsel of the wartime "beauty queen" image, who was irresistible to predators, the post-WTO Vietnamese image was of a gracious hostess presiding over an island of tranquility in an unsettled world.[87]

The interests of investors and the Vietnamese regime were identical, in this view—stability and predictability. If Vietnam's image as the center of the Cold War vortex of conflict gave it a heroic image at the time, it was now cultivating an image of a safe refuge for investors.[88] Some even questioned the inherent attractiveness of Vietnam, gracious hospitality and stable environment or not. Vo Van Kiet wrote in 2005, "Vietnam's situation is different from the big powers. Vietnam is a relatively small country with an economic strength that is not great, and a market that is not so attractive that others can't live without it."[89]

HAS VIETNAM IRREVOCABLY "TAKEN THE PLUNGE" (AND, IF IT HAS, INTO WHAT?)

There has been some controversy over whether or not Vietnam joined the WTO in good faith, with both the intention and the state capacity to comply with its rules. Certainly the government's public statements have been unambiguous on this point. The minister of agriculture was asked whether, since Vietnam's agriculture would suffer the most from WTO strictures, there would be special protections for this key economic sector. He replied that "Those concerns are well founded. However, if we engage 'in the game' [*tham gia 'cuoc choi'*] of global commerce, we have to accept the regulations for that 'game.' We agreed not to use agricultural subsidies after joining." He expressed confidence that Vietnam's farmers would meet the challenges.[90]

Some argue that Vietnam's leaders took the plunge thinking that they were diving not into a turbulent and unpredictable sea but into a swimming pool with clearly divided lane markers. In this view, Vietnam would swim in the common pool but stay in the lane reserved for "socialist market economies." "Even as it joins the World Trade Organisation on Thursday, completing a three decade-long journey to full integration with the global economic mainstream, Hanoi is formally committed to what it calls a 'socialist-oriented market economy.' What that translates into is preserving a leading role for state-owned enterprises—a goal that could augur frustration for foreign companies clamouring to provide everything from banking services to hypermarkets to telecommunications for Vietnam's youthful, increasingly affluent market of 83m people."[91]

The final chapter of this book will discuss further the question raised by the party's 2004 formal adoption of what Vietnam's party leaders and theoreticians called a "socialist market economy," discussed in the previous section, and what this concept says about Vietnam's future engagement with the world community. In the context of this chapter, the issue will be more narrowly focused on what these leaders expected they would have to give up in order to gain the benefits of WTO membership, and how much integration they had in mind as they took this momentous step. There was certainly no lack of public discussion about the prospective costs of WTO membership. In the summer of 2006, the Vietnamese government organized workshops to convey the magnitude of the changes that would be required of Vietnam. "Vietnam must fulfill many multilateral commitments upon joining the World Trade Organization (WTO) if it is to enjoy the potential benefits brought about from this landmark move," said an announcement of an August 2006 seminar on the WTO adjustments. Nguyen Son, vice office director of the National Committee for International Economic Integration, said "The government must not intervene in the operations of state-owned business in any form, and these businesses must operate under commonly accepted business practices."[92] Reform economist Le Dang Doanh noted that, "Integration is not an end in itself but is a means to develop, and become prosperous. Integration is also a framework to push reforms that are compatible with bilateral and multilateral international commitments."[93]

Some Vietnamese officials downplayed the risks of WTO membership and deep integration, possibly for domestic consumption. One argument advanced by the chief strategist of the State Bank, to allay fears that opening up Vietnam's banking sector would result in domestic banks being submerged by a flood of foreign competition, was that there was no need to worry because the major bank customers would be large state enterprises and no foreign bank in their right mind would "dare" to loan to them, or take the risks of loaning to small and medium enterprises with dubious accounting practices. "The restriction [on foreign banks] which for a long time has been regarded as the most important," he reassured a reporter, "is the restriction that mobilizing money in savings accounts must be in Vietnamese dong." Still, the official did point out that "We also anticipate that after 2010 foreign banks will be able to mobilize capital in Vietnamese dong. By that time there will be practically no restrictions on the activities of foreign banks in Vietnam, and no restrictions in hiring or in the sphere of activities and providing services."[94]

In 2005, several Vietnamese delegations went to the United States to study company law in preparation for new legislation by Vietnam's National Assembly on this subject. Two study missions to the United States for Vietnamese officials, paid for by USAID, were conducted in August 2005, in conjunction with Vietnam's efforts to comply with commitments made under the US–Vietnam BTA and requirements for membership in the WTO.[95] The US government was no longer imposing demands and preconditions on Vietnam, but trying to assist it in complying with commitments Vietnam had willingly assumed.

Some reformers thought the government had not done enough to alert Vietnamese companies to what the post-WTO economic environment would look like, and they were concerned that the fundamental structure of protected enterprises would not be prepared to engage in economic competition where these defenses would not be condoned. "However, Vietnam will also have to open its market for commodities from other WTO members, which poses a great challenge to domestic enterprises. Vietnam will no longer be the market of domestic enterprises themselves," said Dr Le Dang Doanh, a senior economic advisor to the Ministry of Planning and Investment. Doanh pointedly noted that, "Some even think that they have achieved successful results thanks to certain relationships (through bribes for example). Such thoughts and manners will only bring to the brink of bankruptcy when Vietnam further integrates into the world, said the chief economist." He advised businesses "to be aware of a healthy legal environment and an equal playing field with foreign rivals."[96] Doanh's statement suggests the possibility that the government's preparations for post-WTO competition had failed to address some fundamental issues about the nature of Vietnam's SOEs and other matters.

The complex interplay of interests created by the deep and pervasive social and political ties between Vietnamese businesses and enterprises and the power structure posed one of the most difficult issues in the US negotiations with Vietnam, in the interval between the BTA and Vietnam's WTO accession. "In the 1990s Hanoi gave the exclusive right to import and distribute foreign goods to ailing state enterprises, and favoured supporters of the regime. Though today any Vietnamese can import products, many big wholesalers remain politically well-connected. Foreign retailers are seen as threatening the livelihoods of millions of 'mom-and-pop' shops and traditional bazaars, where nearly 90 per cent of retail purchases in Vietnam are still made. 'The feeling all along has been that the Vietnamese know how to sell goods, so why do we need foreigners to come in and do it,' said Tony Foster, an attorney at Freshfields in Hanoi."[97] Despite these clouds on the horizon, US officials seemed very satisfied with Vietnam's record of compliance with its BTA obligations.[98]

For its part, Vietnam expressed its full commitment to deepening global integration, and living up to the commitments it would assume as a member of the WTO. In 2005, Vu Khoan said in an interview with the *Washington Times* that the 1995 decision to apply for WTO entry "indicated Vietnam's determination to integrate itself more deeply into the world economy." Even at that time, Khoan pointed out, Vietnam's economy had achieved such a high degree of global interdependence that this was an inevitable course of action. He further noted that Vietnam had made significant internal changes to prepare for WTO membership. The number of SOEs had been reduced from 12,000 to 4,000 (1,000 of which had been equitised). The private sector in Vietnam had reached 30 percent of GDP by 2005. Vietnam had introduced nearly twenty laws including an enterprise law and investment law, which aimed at creating a "level playing field for all economic sectors." Still, Deputy Prime Minister Vu Khoan cautioned that "Vietnam still has a long and bumpy road ahead to integrate itself fully into the world economy, especially following its accession to the WTO. Vietnam will continue with its efforts to meet international commitments while improving domestic capacity so that it can take part in the game as a responsible new member." He reaffirmed that "Vietnam looks forward to continued support and assistance from the international community so that it can integrate more deeply and effectively in the world economy for shared development of mankind in the process of globalisation."[99] But despite the vows of Vietnamese officials to deepen integration and meet their new obligations, some observers remained skeptical that this would or could be done, and questioned the government's commitments to the necessary reforms.

STATE-OWNED ENTERPRISES: THE BELLWEATHER OF THE IMPACT OF GLOBAL INTEGRATION ON VIETNAM'S ECONOMIC AND POLITICAL SYSTEM

One of the best indicators of what kind of integration Hanoi's political leaders had in mind are the state-owned enterprises or, more accurately, state-owned businesses. This is a complex subject even for specialists, upon whom I will rely. Due to limitations in the author's training and lack of familiarity with the economics of SOEs, the conclusions drawn here must be tentative. Yet this economic question lies so close to heart of the political issues involved with the book's theme of "changing worlds" that it must be tackled.

A journalist for the *Financial Times* of London wrote the following around the time of Vietnam's WTO admission: "In spite of their WTO commitments, Hanoi's communists are still divided over the extent to which state enterprises should be subjected to the pressures of market competition—let alone be relinquished. While giving up control of smaller businesses, the government is simultaneously pumping vast sums of money into some state enterprises, hoping to create national champions similar to the South Korean chaebol."[100] Let us recall that the issue in question here is how much internal transformation would be required of Vietnam as it "took the plunge" and whether or not full integration into the global economy would transform the political economy of Vietnam and, therefore, change the nature of its regime—as the publicists of the "threat of peaceful evolution" alleged.

One study of "the politics of economic restructuring" in Vietnam observed that "SOE reform provides a test case for investigating the relative significance of and the interaction between international and domestic forces in the transition process. Is the Vietnamese state able to control and manage this transition successfully—is it a 'weak' or a 'strong' state in this regard?"[101] There are many other related questions about what SOEs in Vietnam tell us about the nature of the Vietnamese state: is it corporatist, "fragmented authoritarian," or some mix of strong and weak—and how much can we learn about the relations between state and society from examining SOEs? And, as we will discuss in the next section, there is a lively debate about whether or not "policy" has any significant impact on what happens to Vietnam's economy, and the related questions of how much we can learn from study of the rhetoric of state and party leaders—which is the focus of much of this book. Finally, there are questions about the very terminology we use to analyze Vietnamese political discourse ("reformers" and "conservatives") and even whether or not there is any such thing as a "reform" process.

The *Financial Times* article pointed to the view of Vietnam's leaders that even extensive integration in the global economy would not require fundamental political or regime change. In this view, Vietnam was following the same trail to economic transformation as China, "whose economy been transformed into what some call 'capitalism by central committee,' in which the authorities carefully modulate market forces and direct growth."[102]

The problems with a hybrid market system have been extensively discussed. "Many other east Asian countries have also achieved sustained growth and improved living standards for their people through an ad hoc mix of market reforms, statist policies and protectionism, often flouting the so-called 'Washington consensus,' which pushes more aggressive privatisation and liberalisation." wrote Amy Kazmin of the *Financial Times*. However, Kazmin notes that some economists doubted that Vietnam would be able to "transform bloated, inefficient and often deeply corrupt state businesses—which have never operated from a profit motive—into truly competitive companies." The concern was that state-subsidized firms would receive much of the scarce capital that could be used more productively in other ways, compounding the problem of a stressed state banking system already burdened with bad debts from these firms.[103]

Some observers noted the lack of transparency of Vietnamese state enterprises, and contrasted Vietnam's situation with South Korea, which had arrived at an effective mechanism for state assistance to corporations. South Korea had made credit and preferential access to the domestic market for *chaebols* conditional on successful performance, measured by competitiveness in international markets. Some doubted that such market discipline could be applied by the Vietnamese government to its own state enterprises.[104]

The SOEs lie at the heart of the question "how will deep integration in the global economy affect the political and economic system of Vietnam?" Although SOEs employ a small percentage of the Vietnamese labor force, they are a central element of both the economy and the political system. An extremely well-informed veteran of the Vietnamese revolution, often critical of doctrinaire positions, stated that "state enterprises have been the symbol of socialism" and that the leadership "could not give them up."[105] In a 2003 international seminar, deputy prime minister and former trade minister Vu Khoan "defended the much-criticized state-owned sector as necessary to maintain the country's socialist nature." At the first working forum of the Asia Society's 13th Asia Corporate

Conference, Khoan was put on the defensive about Vietnam's weak legal system and lack of transparency. He responded that "We have heard great debate about cloning human beings, but we cannot clone countries either. It is dangerous if all countries are alike."[106]

For many outside observers, SOEs are an anachronistic legacy of the past. Some see them as vestigial remnants of the old central-planning system destined to disappear as Vietnam's economy becomes increasingly marketized and its state industry equitised and run on commercial terms with relatively little interference or intervention from the state. Some critics of Vietnam's reform policies have pointed to the delays and inconsistencies in SOE reform as an indicator of resistance to reform. In this view, the more rapid and definitive the phasing out of SOEs, the more beneficial the result will be to Vietnam's economic development. The leadership's reluctance to transform SOEs (especially with regard to the issues of autonomy of managerial control and subjecting nonprofitable SOEs to penalties which could include bankruptcy and dissolution) is seen as simply delaying the inevitable in Vietnam's full transformation to a market economy. A typical expression of foreign viewpoints on SOEs is the warning to Vietnam issued by a consultative group for Vietnam, at its annual meeting in Hanoi, that Vietnam must wipe out corruption and hasten the dragging pace of SOE reform. "Corruption in Vietnam has a bad impact in investment at all levels." Other concerns were the need for more transparency in public administration and public finance management and the slow pace of restructuring the SOEs.[107]

From the public statements of many Vietnamese officials and observers, it is clear that the problems associated with SOEs are well recognized. "The reform has come along with the encouragement of private sector development and the country's opening to the world, with the State finding that SOEs rely too much on State subsidies and monopolies, but are unable to supply enough essential products to the country. Director of the Investconsul Group Nguyen Tran Bat said that SOEs' monopolies result in society paying unreasonably high costs, and also depresses the economy's competitiveness." Bat observed that, "Most of their products are 20%–40% more costly than imports. While receiving up to 50% of banks' credits, SOEs create only 10% of jobs."[108]

Chairman of the Vietnam Chamber of Commerce and Enterprises, Doan Duy Thanh, said that "people are used to the concept that they do not need to work effectively in the State sector and can live on the State's subsidy and protection. So SOEs are breeding grounds for corruption." The October 2002 party resolution of SOE preserved a state monopoly in many industries. Thanh observed that "Officials in the State sector do not want to lose their economic benefits and, thus, political power, when SOEs are restructured. Unclear policies and laws regarding ownership and private businesses are also hindering people from jumping into SOE privatization and sales." The legacy of the past was also a complicating factor. "People have not recovered their business sense after several campaigns to diminish capitalism in the country late last century. They need to be assured that their investment is legally protected."[109]

The elusiveness of figures on the extent of equitisation of SOEs is underlined by the vague and scattered references to it after Vietnam's WTO entry. A representative article in 2007 mentioned the figure of "3,000 former SOEs" which have been privatized[110] with plans for another 550 by the end of the year.[111] These included major enterprises such as Vietnam Airlines. By 2007, the total number of SOEs was reported to be 1,900.[112] An end-of-year survey of 2006 reported that "The number of state-owned enterprises (SOEs) has been reduced over recent years to only 3.61 percent of the total. But this small number of enterprises still accounted for nearly 55 percent of State provided capital, and provided only 40 percent of the state budget, while employing only about a third of the labor force) as compared to non-state and foreign-invested sectors. It attracts 32.69 per cent of the total of labourers."[113]

The reality behind all these figures is that as Vietnam was joining the WTO, the momentum of equitisation was flagging. As the performance of Vietnam's SOEs deteriorated, "Vietnamese financial institutions are growing reluctant to make loans to government-run companies. This has put a squeeze on companies that, already weak from years of inefficiency, can least endure it. Things are so bad that there have been significant delays in the government's plan to privatize a certain number of these companies." According to a report by a state commission on reform of the state-enterprise sector, "the aggregate capital of the 3,107 former SOEs that became joint stock companies totals only 12% of the combined capitalization of all SOEs. The report also illustrates that the reluctance to convert themselves into private companies is particularly strong among large firms, which should be privatized sooner than smaller entities."[114]

As Adam Fforde's detailed research on SOEs argues, even though there is unquestionably a historic process of shifting from "plan to market," this does not necessarily mean the demise of the SOEs, but he outlines in detail some of the "traps" or transition dilemmas in moving away from the old neo-Stalinist model of central planning.[115] Martin Painter maintains that what appears to some as "slow implementation and apparent incoherence of restructuring policies since 1987," leading to "reform failure," actually shows the reverse. "On the contrary, the state is successfully managing a complex domestic political process in which state business interests defend their commercial privileges against unwelcome restructuring proposals."[116]

Martin Gainsborough argues that, "One of the most prominent themes of the reform years has been the development of businesses with strong roots in the state sector whose growth has involved the hollowing out of public assets. This may have set in train a process that will ultimately lead to the emergence of a new elite but in the story so far the existing elite has been conspicuous among the beneficiaries of the so-called process of reform." His conclusion is that "beneath the veneer of reform with its emphasis on marketisation, it can be seen that the heavy hand of the state is still crucial. Moreover, instead of classic privatisation as envisaged by the multilateral institutions such as the Word Bank, we see a different kind of 'privatisation' by the elite."[117]

Fforde's view of the evolution of SOEs in the past decade and a half suggests that the state is not able to control and benefit from the SOEs as effectively as Painter asserts. And in contrast to Gainsborough's narrower focus on SOEs in terms of control by clusters of self-serving groups in the bureaucratic-managerial elite of the mid-1990s, Fforde examines the changes that occurred in the larger context of the Vietnamese economy, which imply that, as the range of competitive forces expands (due to foreign investment, direct foreign competition, and greater transparency resulting from international agreements and Vietnam's own evolving legal regulations), the ability of state- and party-connected elites to take advantage of partial reform through political connections and pressure may be increasingly circumscribed. Fforde in 2007 took a cautious position on the future evolution of SOEs. He noted that even early on in the reform process SOEs had undergone considerable transformation, and were not quite the neo-Stalinist dinosaurs portrayed by some reformers.[118]

Fforde argues that the SOEs helped cushion the impact of the sudden withdrawal of Soviet aid in 1991 and, by realizing efficiency gains through greater responsiveness to market incentives, they played an important role in regime maintenance through much of the 1990s. Unlike Painter, who views SOEs as strengthening the regime by making greater resources available to it, Fforde notes that Vietnam's economic environment had fundamentally changed by the early 2000s, as a result of the "presence of a dynamic private sector and the foreign invested sector."[119] Gainsborough asserts that "local elite privatisation" and other factors have led to "hollowing out of the state sector."[120]

Fforde's conclusion is that Vietnam's state sector can be viewed in comparative perspective as successful, "Yet viewed in terms of what was possible, it has to be judged a failure. Crucial development problems of the mid-2000s can be blamed centrally upon the limits of SOE change, in particular the failure to break out of the basic model of SOE–state relations, and the associated weaknesses of government and delayed emergence of a private sector."[121]

As the state companies equitise and wean themselves from state subsidies, a distinct corporate entity is created. What this means in political, social, and economic terms is complex and disputed. Economically, the question is who controls the state enterprises that have been equitised? Both Gainsborough and Fforde have studied this issue in great depth. Fforde concludes "It seems clear to me that after 1990 SOEs as a form of property should be looked at in ways that can get behind their formal position as state-owned units to ask simple questions: who controls them, and who benefits from the surpluses created by them? There is abundant evidence to confirm that, whatever answers research may give, they are *not* reasonably viewed as state-controlled." Fforde also concludes that "*it is not SOE managers who effectively control SOEs* [original italics]."[122]

If not the managers, then who controls the SOEs? One possible answer is that they are indirectly controlled through the guidance of the "developmental state," a familiar form of economic organization in East Asia. Another possibility is that the SOE reforms created a quasi-independent business sector, with interests that did not always coincide with those of the state. Fforde writes that a simplified view of the politics of SOEs was that in the 1980s the main state concern was to build up a state business sector and gain its support, while in the 1990s it was largely concerned with finding ways to control what it had created, but with limited success. "If these conjectures are correct, the outcome of this politics was on the one hand to significantly curb trends to emergence of a relatively independent business sector out of SOEs, but on the other hand to fail to re-establish a coherent and relatively united set of control structures."[123]

The deputy chairman of the National Assembly Budget Committee reported that a study of equitisation carried out by this committee found that often equitisation left the old state-enterprise management in control, did not really improve the business, and that the demand for a high percentage of state equity in order to assure control crowded out more productive investment from the outside. "At present the state still retains a controlling interest in 33 percent of the enterprises that have equitised … Many equitised companies still operate under the old form of doing business as a state enterprise from its business plan to the way it divides the profits. In 70–80 percent of enterprises there is still the same leadership group, so that basically the management style has not changed."[124]

The director of the National Assembly oversight group followed up with an even more specific critique of the limited impact of equitisation on state enterprises. "'Following equitisation, there was no change in about 81.5 percent of directors, 78 percent of deputy directors and chief accounting officers. . . . This shows that in reality there are many enterprises which continue to operate as before, in terms of organization, mindset [*tu duy*], technical aspects [*cong nghe*], administration, and commercial philosophy following equitisation, and still look like state enterprises. 'If there is a change, it is only that the old director of the state enterprise have become the new leaders of the equitised company.'"[125]

In contrast to some foreign scholars, Vietnamese studies of the equitisation of SOEs imply that the State has been too effective in maintaining control and that this stultifies needed change in SOEs. The 2006 National Assembly review of the consequences of equitisation concluded that the attempt by the State to maintain a controlling interest in the equitised companies was primarily responsible for a failure to bring about positive change through equitisation, because the state simply used its control to maintain the status quo, and its investment crowded out other investment which might have been more effective in leading to better commercial results. "News concerning the results of the oversight of the National Assembly concerning equitisation [*co phan hoa (CPH)*] has shown that state enterprises [*doanh nghiep nha nuoc (DN)*] holding controlling shares is an obstacle to raising the efficiency of the enterprises."[126]

This National Assembly warning about the shortcomings in enterprise transformation at the time Vietnam was preparing to open up its economy as a consequence of WTO membership, raised some concerns in the Vietnamese press. In an interview with Deputy Prime Minister Nguyen Sinh Hung shortly after the National Assembly's report on the state of equitisation, a reporter asked about the risks Vietnam would encounter if its enterprises were as unable to adapt as had been portrayed. Sinh agreed that there would be problems. "We will integrate, but there will be a path [*lo trinh*], and there will be protection [*bao ho*] for a short time to create conditions for enterprises [*doanh nghiep*]. But if the enterprises don't improve rapidly, and reform and renovate rapidly, they will encounter great difficulties. At present the state-enterprise sector still comprises over 40 percent of GDP."[127] Sinh admitted that under WTO rules, the state was limited in the kind of support it could offer impacted businesses. "Although the 'army' [*doi quan*] of businesses are the main force in joining the WTO, that doesn't mean that they will all be victorious. In this competition, there will be a number of businesses and lines of merchandise that run the risk of defeat. But we have to remember that 'failure is the mother of success' and that the remaining businesses will reorganize and renovate to move forward. When the government signed the provisions for membership in the WTO it placed great faith in the ranks of the businesses."[128]

Sinh's interviewer noted that although when Vietnam joined the WTO it was understood that Vietnam's international competitiveness was the central challenge; "the Economic and Budget Committee of the National Assembly has just reported that there has been nearly no qualitative improvement in our economy." The deputy prime minister could only reply that attracting more foreign investment was the key to improving Vietnam's competitive position, indirectly confirming the seriousness of the National Assembly's findings.[129]

IMPACT OF DEEP INTEGRATION ON VIETNAMESE POLITICS, SOCIETY, AND ECONOMY

As can be seen from the foregoing discussion of SOEs, there are many different views on what they are, to say nothing of how they will be affected by opening Vietnam's economy to the outside world. Let us recall the remark, cited above, of a veteran participant–observer of the Vietnamese political scene, that "state enterprises have been the symbol of socialism" and that the leadership "could not give them up." Adam Fforde poses the question that Vietnamese leaders had to confront during the process of reform: "Upon what would the state rest once it had lost its power, [through] central planning, over the economy in general and the SOEs in particular? How could there be a 'Party without the plan'?"[130]

Much of the analysis of SOEs discussed in the previous section looks at them as captives of special interests, mostly within the party and/or individuals and networks with political connections. This is clearly the reality of many, if not most, of the SOEs, which means that they are somewhat tarnished "symbols of socialism" and something less than reassuring remnants of the socialist regime of the prereform period. At the same time, even the "reformed" SOEs are hardly paragons of market-driven efficiency advocated by some reformers and international economic institutions but have, as many experts have noted, served to preserve the power and interests of party insiders in a changing economic environment. And despite the fact that control of the resources of SOEs by party insiders has in many ways strengthened the party as an apparatus of control, it has not strengthened the state as an agent of development, as some advocates of the "Asian development model" or various ideas of Vietnam as a corporate state have asserted.

From a political point of view, therefore, it could be argued that Vietnam has "taken the plunge" into deeper integration without really transforming the nature of its regime. If this is true, it has several important implications. The first is that, whether or not this result was achieved by accident or design, it is fruitless to focus on ideas and beliefs as explanations for behavioral and institutional change (except to the extent that they might explain attachment to old ideas and resistance to real change). One reason is that, as Gainsborough and others argue, it is interests, not ideas that are the driving force of economic behavior in Vietnam. Another is that the apparent change is illusory—old wine in new bottles—as shown by the ability of the SOEs to adopt the protective camouflage of equitisation and other trappings of market-responsive characteristics, while retaining their old power structure and self-serving behavior underneath.

Yet there are several reasons why the convincing portrait of SOEs as vehicles for the perpetuation of the old power structure does not necessarily mean that ideas and policies don't matter. The first is that, Fforde points out, the larger environment in which they operate, domestic as well as external, has fundamentally changed, and that this inevitably will have a major impact on institutions and interest groups like the SOEs. Two important illustrations of this are the adoption of more elaborate legal commercial codes which make it somewhat easier and safer for private commerce and foreign investment to operate in Vietnam, and the expansion of the foreign business sector, which is now considered a legitimate and integral part of Vietnam's economic system. In this regard, taking the plunge has had real consequences, as both its conservative opponents and its reform advocates argued.

As Nguyen Van Dang, whose views we examine below and whose portfolio covered both the political and policy, and the theoretical aspects of Vietnam's changing economy, wrote in 2005: "Having spent over twenty years in implementing *doi moi*, the viewpoints and ways of the thinking [*quan diem va tu duy*] of the party and state and our people have undergone revolutionary changes in many great and important matters concerning socialism and the road of advance to socialism in our country. There have been extremely important renovations in our theoretical way of thinking [*tu duy ly luan*] and in practice concerning the systems of ownership [*che do so huu*] and the sectors of the economy, along with many renovations of the system for administering the economy, and implementing the democratization of the economy, and renovating the system of distribution and having a clearer grasp [*nhan thuc ro hon*] about the socialist direction." Dang clearly feels that ideas and outlooks have changed and that this has an important impact on policy. An important example he cites in his essay where thinking must change in order to have better policy results is in the role of foreign capital in the Vietnamese economy. "In perception [*nhan thuc*] as well as action, it is necessary to truly regard foreign capital as an important element of the market economy with socialist characteristics in Vietnam."[131] Clearly it required an effort for a generation of party members whose intellectual formation had deeply embedded a view of foreign capital as a vehicle for control and domination of Vietnam to accept it as a welcome and integral part of Vietnam's economy.

However, both Fforde and Gainsborough argue that "policy" is not what drives economic behavior in Vietnam. If it is inexorable economic forces or the interplay of interest groups that primarily explains Vietnamese internal economic dynamics, then ideas and "thinking" (new or old) will not tell us much about the substantial change that has taken place in Vietnam over the past two decades, and a focus on specific decision-making turning points—like "taking the plunge"—would be misleading.

Gainsborough notes studies of reform in China by authors who "have also downplayed the significance of policy," emphasizing instead "the economic logic of change." He cites a study of China which argues that its reforms were more shaped by underlying economic realities and the interplay between politics and economics than by ideology and politics, and which discounts the role of policy choices. This study, by Barry Naughton, "rejects the idea that successful reform was a triumph of the wisdom of the Chinese leadership, who claim to be vindicated in their policies of gradual and partial reform, terming this view 'misinformation' and a distraction from the real dynamics of the reform process in favor of an oversimplified morality tale."[132] With this and other studies of Chinese reforms in mind, Gainsborough concludes that from his research on Ho Chi Minh City policy reform played a relatively unimportant role in the course of events and that he "also downplay[s] the importance of leaders in their role as purveyors in this largely spontaneous process of change."[133]

Fforde takes a more nuanced position on the key question of whether "policy matters." In the context of a discussion of what drove the reforms in Vietnam, Fforde states that, "in my opinion, in the final analysis the answers are to do with a mixture of political and economic logics with how human beings cope with choice under uncertainty: learning through experience. They are not just economic questions but deeply human ones." Fforde remarks that "an economic analysis has to look properly at the interaction between policy and practice, for 'reform' in Vietnam has not been a largely top down process. This is possibly a contradiction in terms, since 'reform' is usually understood as a process consciously initiated i.e. by policy. For that reason it is more helpful to use intransitive terms, such as commercialisation and process, which avoid the implicit assumption that it is policy that plays the determining role." But while warning against stress on top-down change processes and "policy fetishism," Fforde also remarks that to say change came more "from below" does not mean that it came from outside the party and that "it was to a great extent the insider status, as Party members and SOE staff, that allowed SOEs and others to participate in markets and subvert traditional planning. This makes it easier to understand just why a normal private sector took so long to emerge."[134]

As noted in the introduction, this book does not argue that ideas operate in isolation in shaping behavior, but contends that they do provide both motives for action and constraints on behavior. In addition, ideas can be important weapons in struggles over power and spoils of office (some cite this cynical use of ideas as evidence that they are not important in themselves, though I would argue that in these instances ideas also serve as constraints on behavior). Finally, and central to the concerns of the study, when collective idea-change achieves a critical mass it has a clear impact on legitimating the previously impermissible and consolidating the gains of reform to an extent that they are no longer subject to effective political challenge. And, for the most part, the argument for the significance of collective idea change does not depend on whether the idea change preceded and caused behavioral change, or was merely an after-the-fact ratification of a changed reality.

With respect to the specific issue of a struggle over the way Vietnam should engage with a transformed international order, this study does not claim that there are factions (however defined) or clearly defined organized opinion groups. When we use the labels "reformer" and "conservative" it is with full recognition that these are not monolithic or mutually exclusive categories or even identifiable groups or networks.

In the context of this study, there is only one spectrum along which we place reformers and conservatives, and that is one with "fear of falling behind" at one end and "preservation of the socialist regime" at the other. Nationalism plays a powerful role at the "falling behind" pole, and preservation of an ideological belief system (as a source of political power and control based on the ability to define the boundaries of acceptable ideas, as well as an end in itself for many who had grown accustomed to the reassuring certainty of ideological orthodoxy) is the main concern at the other pole. It is the primary argument of this book that the nationalist tendency aimed at keeping Vietnam from falling further behind its neighbors and the rest of the world increasingly prompted Vietnam's leaders to endorse deeper integration and take greater risks in opening up, putting national interest ahead of regime preservation despite the threat to the future of its "socialist" character and even the monopoly control of the Communist Party over important sectors of Vietnamese life.

This does not mean that all reformers are political liberals, or that conservatives do not support some economic reform measures. To forgo the use of these labels because they are problematic in some respects, however, would render it impossible to discuss political trends of the past two decade, and generalizations would simply dissolve into a littered landscape of particularities. The ideas versus interests issue will be examined in greater detail in chapter 9.

In the current context of understanding the decision to "take the plunge," with deeper engagement in the global economic system, the main step is to understand whether it was, in fact, a "decision," or "decisions." It is clearly relevant, but probably not knowable (by an outside academic at least) who took the decision and how it was made, but we can recapitulate some of the factors that might have influenced such a decision from the material presented in this chapter.

At the top levels of the Vietnamese political system there is, at the least, a formal recognition that the reform process has produced change, and that the deeper integration that has been part of the reform process has been accompanied by changes in thinking and perception (if not caused by them). One of many illustrations of this point is an article published in the party's theoretical journal in 2005 by Nguyen Van Dang, the deputy head of the Party Central Committee's Economics Department (Ban Kinh Te Truong Uong). Perhaps not coincidently, Dang is also a member of the party's Central Council on Theory (Hoi Dong Ly Luan Trung Uong), whose chair is the *ipso facto* ideological czar of the party and usually concurrently the head of the Higher Party Training School—the arbiter of ideological orthodoxy.

We will discuss in chapter 9 whether or not the emphasis on ideas is a forlorn attempt by party theoreticians to retrofit ideology to the changes in Vietnam's internal and external realities. Perhaps they take ideas seriously simply because that is their job. For the moment, let us stipulate that while there may sometimes be little congruence between ideology and reality, what the party ideologists define as "acceptable" reality is quite important, because the party still has considerable coercive power to punish or deny, even if its power to shape the underlying social and economic realities in Vietnam has significantly diminished.

In fact, one of the important explanations advanced to understand the breakthrough in Vietnam's official acceptance of a deeper level of global integration is that the influence of those who had previously resisted this faded. The conservatives lost their power to deny this movement, in part because they could no longer maintain the orthodoxy of the "old thinking" and the power of ideological scare tactics ("peaceful evolution" will get you if you don't watch out, or this is a "deviation"!). Here we should recall the point made above that even instrumental use of ideas as weapons of intimidation still has the power to constrain or deter action—but only to the extent that the ideas are still accepted as plausible by important segments of the political elite.

Those who dismiss the role of ideas often point to more direct or persuasive explanations (power struggles, clashing interests, structural economic or social change, forces of history) to explain why the political and economic trajectory of a society moves in one way rather than another. Perhaps it is more useful to look at Vietnam's evolution toward deep integration as a process that had its own logic and momentum, but one which would not have been possible if the constraints of political and ideological orthodoxy had not been removed, especially in a state which, for all its inadequacies still had formidable coercive power—especially the power to deny or negate. "New thinking," in this sense, was a necessary but not a sufficient condition for the reform process to reach the point it had by the year 2006.

It is clear that two decades of reform, along with changes in the world and inside the country, had transformed the ideological landscape in Vietnam. A careful examination of Dang's account of how party thinking on a variety of issues connected to reform had changed is instructive. First, he notes the significant expansion of viewpoints concerning the nature of the Vietnam's economy. "If before *doi moi*, the key was developing the public-ownership economy [*kinh te cong huu*], and in perception [*nhan thuc*] as well as in action there was no acceptance of a multisectoral economy, after that [*doi moi*] there was an affirmation of a multiple forms of ownership economy [*kinh te da so huu*], along with a democratization of the economy. From three forms of ownership: of the entire people [*toan dan*], collective [*tap the*], and private [*tu nhan*], a multisectoral economy was formed; the three forms of ownership did not exist in isolation but were woven together [*dan sen*, intermingled, interdependent] and amalgamated [*hon hop*] in the various production and commercial organizations; a form of amalgamated ownership with a high social level emerged, whose special characteristic was stock ownership."[135]

Dang notes a change in "perception" (*nhan thuc*) of two of the most important features of the reformed economy; the legitimation of private ownership, and the emergence of a multisectoral economy in which various forms of private ownership are intermingled or "amalgamated." This was a key step in legitimating the once-proscribed private sector of the economy. Dang writes that, "The private economy is an important constituent element of the national economy [*nen kinh te quoc dan*]," and that "developing the private economy is a long term strategic matter in developing a market economy with socialist characteristics in our country."[136] Gainsborough rightly stresses the importance of taking a functional rather than a legalistic view of the complex question of ownership and property rights.[137] Still, the formal acknowledgment of the role of private property reflected an important change in party thinking, as the following statement makes clear: "In particular the private economy has evolved from being discriminated against and restricted, has now undergone many fundamental renovations [*doi moi*], which have clearly affirmed each citizen's right to freely do business according the law."[138]

Dang makes it clear that there were still (in 2005) a number of problems that needed to be cleared up because of the demands of integration. Among these were the related issues of the reform of state enterprises and the mobilization of capital and investment funds to enable Vietnamese commercial enterprises to compete in the post-WTO environment. He specifically mentioned the problem of insider equitisation. "Don't allow the continuation of equitisation which is skewed toward closed-door [*khep kin*] purchase by insiders of the enterprise. State enterprises have property rights, and must be self-controlling [*tu chu*] in reality, and accept responsibility in business, in competition, and in accepting risk (don't criminalize business risk). We need to attach responsibility, authority, and rights to the person doing business."[139]

Ha Dang, assistant to party secretary general Nong Duc Manh, published a comprehensive list of the major ideological tenets concerning the opposition between socialism and capitalism that had been progressively revised during the course of *doi moi*.[140] We will discuss these at greater length in chapter 9, but it is a fairly sweeping list of central ideological revisions that had taken place during the course of *doi moi*, suggesting that there had been significant changes in fundamental ideology over the course of *doi moi*. Ha Dang even coined the term "workable socialism," as it was translated by the Vietnam News Agency—although I have been unable to find the Vietnamese term for this concept.[141]

Despite the commitment to deep integration reflected in Vietnam's entry into the WTO, and the fading of the obsession with "peaceful evolution" that had delayed the process, there were still concerns about the risks of immersion in the global and regional economy, as well as the generic risks and uncertainties of the capitalist elements of the Vietnamese economy. In 2007, there were concerns about a potential stock-market bubble and the rush of investors into a market that they assumed only had an up side.[142] Other more traditional concerns about the loss of economic control by the state also resurfaced. It was reported that in Ho Chi Minh City, 30 percent of the economy was under the control of ethnic Chinese by 2007. "Ho Chi Minh City currently has about 500,000 Hoa [ethnic Chinese]—which makes it the region in Vietnam with the most Hoa—living concentrated in districts 5, 6, 10, and 11."[143] Thus reform and associated economic and political developments had brought Vietnam a long way from its harsh repression of the Hoa in the late 1970s (including closing 30,000 small Chinese shops and businesses, banning private commerce, and forcing a massive refugee exodus). In addition, overseas Vietnamese, some who had fled Vietnam as refugees, were enabled by the new openness of the economy to return to Vietnam and establish businesses, thus contributing to the process of national reconciliation, which had foundered in the years after 1975.

By 2008, Vietnamese assessments about the progress in meeting the challenges of adjusting to the deep integration required by WTO membership showed concern, but confidence that the problems could be resolved. Perhaps most significantly, the cultural dimension of the "peaceful evolution" threat involved in opening up to the world received a brief mention in the context of a listing of the early doubts about the process. But the actual issues listed by the party theoretical journal, in a comprehensive summary of progress in problem areas, did not include it among the "seven challenges," in its review of the first year of Vietnam's WTO membership.[144] The three main categories of concern prior to joining were economic (the impact on Vietnam's domestic economy), social (increasing the gap between rich and poor), and political-cultural, including an "increase of political interference from the outside" and the threat of cultural assimilation and the loss of national culture. The assessment of the impact of WTO membership after a year listed seven specific issues in the first two categories, but left out the political-cultural concerns.[145] Perhaps it is simply a question of the area of professional responsibility of the analyst (the principal author just quoted is a university professor of social science). There is still plenty of evidence of the old concerns about "peaceful evolution" in the military and security branches.[146] But the key point is they no longer hold a veto over policy and cannot close the door that has been opened.

To Vietnam's leaders, Vietnam's integration into the global community was presented not as a retreat from previous policies, but as a restoration of Vietnam's rightful place in the international community and an opportunity to actively participate in establishing the ground rules of the evolving international system. Ha Dang, assistant to General Secretary Nong Duc Manh, put it this way: "In joining the WTO and becoming the 150th member of this organization, Vietnam has truly integrated more deeply and comprehensively into the world economy, and not only increasingly becomes part of the market of goods and services of all its members, but also has a position of equality with other members in determining global commercial policy." Vietnam's obtaining permanent normal trade relations with the United States was viewed as a triumph of the regime, as was the removal of Vietnam from the watch list of countries who raised concerns about treatment of religious groups, "Vietnam not only has forced the United States to restore Vietnam's legitimate rights that it should have enjoyed a long time ago, but also to abandon its unilateral inequitable treatment and even completely normalize relations, opening a new page for cooperation in many areas."[147]

Thus Vietnam saw integration as a way of finding a worthy place for itself in the post–Cold War world order, as well as a path to more effective participation in international relations in many noneconomic areas and in the commercial sphere. In the following chapter we will examine the evolution of Vietnam's foreign policy and theoretical views about international relations since the end of the Cold War, and the interplay between diplomacy, security, and development.

8

A Strategy for the Twenty-First Century

AFTER BECOMING A member of ASEAN and establishing diplomatic relations with the United States in 1995, the party convened its Eighth Congress in June 1996 which affirmed that Vietnam would continue a foreign policy that would defend its "independence and sovereignty" while also being "open door" (*coi mo*), multilateral, with diversified external relationships. As Vietnam's leading academic specialist on international relations commented, "It was clear that only if there was peace, stability, and the creation of favorable international conditions, could we concentrate our forces to build the country and successfully achieve the slogan 'rich people, strong country, just society, democracy and culture.'"[1]

There are several notable aspects of this 1996 formulation of Vietnam's diplomatic objectives and outlook on the world, which reflected their new level of integration into the region (ASEAN membership) and removal of the main obstacles to deeper global integration (embargo and nonrecognition by the United States). Along with the earlier 1991 shift to acknowledging a single "international community" and the policy of "becoming friends" with all members of this community, the acknowledgment of a legitimate and inherent diversity in this community that rendered the "us versus enemy" view obsolete made the problem of formulating a coherent strategy for dealing with the external world more difficult. No one should assume that the hard-headed Vietnamese leadership had suddenly been converted to a warm and fuzzy international bonhomie as the essence of their foreign policy, but the idea of "being friends" with "all members of the global community," and the parallel idea of "diversification" (*da dang hoa*) of its external economic relationships did not seem to offer the clear guidelines from which diplomatic and strategic planning could proceed as had the clear-cut Cold War distinction between friends and enemies.

As we have seen, the decision to "take the plunge" into deep integration did not mean that the conservative opposition disappeared. In much the same way that the integration-ists justified their case on nationalist grounds, arguing that if Vietnam was to effectively seek "wealth and power" it would have to accept the risks of becoming fully engaged in globalization, the opponents also used political symbolism with deep resonance in Vietnamese political discourse, in their case anti-imperialism. Indeed several foreign analysts term the conservative opponents of integration the "anti-imperialists." A good example is politburo member and chief party ideologist Nguyen Duc Binh. In 2002, after the decision for deep engagement had been made, Binh continued to assert a neo–Cold War position. "The center of the ideological struggle in the world since the end of the Cold War is the fight against the US government's policy of world hegemony, as reflected by its capital liberalization and human rights theories, according to Nguyen Duc Binh, former member of the Vietnam Communist Party's Politburo, the most powerful body in the country."[2] But by this time Binh was a voice from the sidelines, having lost his politburo status at the Ninth Party Congress.

The Ninth Party Congress of April 2001 added the element of emphasis on deep integration to Vietnam's external policy. "The new point in the external mission state-ment this time was that the Congress strongly affirmed proactive integration into the global and regional economy."[3] In a subsequent politburo decree of November 2001, the beginnings of a diplomatic strategy were sketched out in the form of indicating priorities for Vietnam's external activities. These were: continue to strengthen relations with Vietnam's neighbors and countries that have been traditional friends; give importance to relations with big countries, developing countries, and the political and economic cen-ters of the world; raise the level of solidarity with developing countries and the non-aligned movement; increase activities in international organizations; and develop relations with Communist and workers parties, with progressive forces, while at the same time expanding relations with ruling parties and other parties. Pay attention to people's diplomacy.[4]

Although this checklist was intended to indicate priorities, it did not really do more than identify the various dimensions of Vietnam's diplomacy, without specifying the diplomatic and strategic level of importance of each element, and the relationships between them. In this chapter we will examine each of these elements and attempt to infer the priorities and identify the interconnections. We will first examine the changing Vietnamese evaluation of the nature of the international system and then analyze the connection between Vietnam's commitment to deep integration and its thinking about diplomacy and national security in general terms. Following this we will examine each of the aspects of Vietnam's external policy identified as "priorities" in the checklist above to see if any coherent strategy toward the external world can be discerned.

WHAT KIND OF WORLD ORDER?

Vietnamese analysts and theoreticians characterized the changes in the international system resulting from the end of the Cold War in a variety of ways. In terms of the structure and power distribution of the system, they noted the end of bipolarity, but there were some differences and ambiguities on the key question of whether the new structure was unipolar, multipolar, or some combination of the two, and presented a variety of ideas on what the implications of the different polarities might be.

In this context, let us revisit a point made in the introduction: "the elements in the Vietnamese leadership who became concerned that an attempt to preserve the old system intact would result in losing everything eventually prevailed over those who wanted to cling to the status quo to retain their power and positions." I have argued that the main debate about adapting to the post–Cold War era was essentially between those who wanted to preserve the old political and ideological system intact and those who advocated jettisoning some of the most fundamental ideological assumptions about how the world worked in order to save the system itself. This would inevitably lead to abandoning the contention that the party's legitimacy rested on the claim that it was right in every instance and always had been, in favor of a substantial rethinking of assumptions and a switch to what has come to be known as "performance-based legitimacy."

For both the ideological conservatives and the reformers it was essential to make a correct analysis of the current nature of the international system and the challenges to Vietnam it posed, since the strategy for coping with the challenges of globalization in the twenty-first century would be derived from that assessment. Nguyen Manh Cam, who replaced Nguyen Co Thach as Vietnam's foreign minister and served for the remainder of the decade of the 1990s, commented many years later on the Vietnamese uncertainty about what kind of world would replace the Cold War system.

At the end of the 1980s and the beginning of the 1990s of the Twentieth Century, the international situation unfolded in a very complex way and fundamentally changed. The crisis of the socialist regimes in the Soviet Union and Eastern Europe had a profound impact on every aspect of the world situation. The crisis in the international communist movement was even more serious; the movement for national independence, the movement for improving the people's lives and for democracy of the working class and laboring people of the capitalist countries encountered difficulties. The bipolar world order that had formed after World War II ended. The world moved into a transitional period to a new world order that had not yet been determined, with the development of contradictory currents intermingled with each other.[5]

As we have seen, a few years after the collapse of the Soviet Union, former foreign minister Nguyen Co Thach concluded that there were many elements in the international system counterbalancing American power. Though the United States was formidable, it was not as dominant as it had been in 1950 when "America alone was economically and militarily stronger than all other countries in the world combined." Thach observed that "The fact that China is rising as an economic superpower and the disintegration of the Soviet Union has led to great changes in the relationships among the big countries. America, Western Europe, and Japan have strongly supported the new regime in Russia and supported reforms in Russia, while relations between China and the United States are increasingly tense. . . . The bipolar and tripolar world has become multipolar. And the world is moving from cold war and arms races to an era of economic competition," said Thach in 1995.[6]

A major study of the role of the "big countries" in the post–Cold War world concluded that "International relations has always operated along the axis of big country activities, no matter what kind of a world order there is." The classification of the main actors in the international system that evolved in Vietnam since the Cold War reflects two important conclusions about the world order. The first is that whatever fundamental changes might occur in the international system there will always be a diverse set of main actors, and a wide spectrum of power capabilities. The second is that this diversity makes it inherently unlikely that a purely unipolar system could evolve. This is reflected in the way the key actors in the system are categorized.

Hanoi's analysts settled on a set of definitions in which "great powers" (*cuong cuoc* = strong powers) are a larger and more inclusive category, with a subset of even more powerful "big countries" (*nuoc lon*) which are "a number of key great powers in the contemporary world." These analysts note that others have a somewhat different definition. "People divide great powers into various ranks such as 'superpower' [*sieu cuong*], 'global power [*cuong quoc the gioi*],' and 'regional power' [*cuong quoc khu vuc*]. According to this, superpower is a concept which indicates a country with the strength to determine the totality of important issues in the world, like the United States at present. World powers are countries which play a role beyond their region and have a strong influence on a number of spheres on global scale, such as France, Germany, the United Kingdom, Russia, China, and Japan; and regional powers which have an impact primarily on their geographical region." As we will see, "big powers" are the richest and strongest countries in the international community and possess a wide range of power capabilities.[7]

These Vietnamese international-relations experts implicitly endorse a concept popular in the Clinton administration—that power in the era of globalization depends on being at or near the center of multiple international networks in different spheres of life. Joseph Nye has written that "The United States plays a central role in all dimensions of globalization. Globalization at its core refers to worldwide networks of interdependence. A network is simply a series of connections of points in a system, but networks can take a surprising number of shapes and architectures. . . . Theorists of networks argue that under most conditions, centrality in networks conveys power—that is, the hub controls the spokes."[8] Nye rejects this view, and warns that it misleadingly implies a degree of American dominance that does not, in fact, exist. But it is clear that there is a connection between the idea of comprehensive power, discussed below, and ability to exert influence in many different areas. "America's role," writes Clyde Prestowitz, "according to President Clinton, was to 'be at the center of every vital global network.'"[9]

This is the gist of the conclusion drawn by a Vietnamese task force that was assigned to study the power structure of the new international system that was mandated as part of a larger state research plan covering the period 2001–5. "In the trajectory of globalization, a country or a nation is only viewed as a 'great power' when it has enough ability to dominate [*lam chu*] systems of integration, which means the ability to participate in as many bilateral and multilateral undertakings [*cam ket*] as possible, as well as having the ability to manage these undertakings well in many different dimensions. While the world is becoming increasingly interdependent, the task of mastering these relationships has become a standard by which to measure the power ranking of a state. A great power has to have the power to undertake negotiations and persuade its partners to accept the 'rules of the game' that the great power has laid down. The great powers continue to play an important leading role in the new world order."[10]

In terms of driving forces of the new world system, a party consensus has emerged since the early 1990s that the scientific–technological revolution and the process of globalization driven by the resultant economic forces are the main factors. In terms of the specific power dynamics of the new system, there was considerable discussion of the role of the big countries. Other groups, such as the remnant nonaligned movement were still considered relevant, though this movement had lost its basic function with the disappearance of the two-world system, which defined the alignments that it rejected, and had become an amorphous residual category for lesser developed nations—the losers of the globalization era. Although Vietnam spoke of maintaining ties to its "traditional friends," it certainly aspired to more than tying its fortunes to the remnants of a shattered movement—however much Vietnam's leaders proclaimed that the setback to socialism was only temporary.

Vietnam also needed to find a fitting new global role which, as in the case of Russia during the Gorbachev era (see chapter 1), would "enhance its status" and "preserve its distinctive national identity." For this reason, Vietnam highly valued its ASEAN membership, which gave it a more positive international identity, a greater importance than it would have had remaining aloof from all alignments, or casting its lot with a "lonely hearts club" of remaining socialist countries, which did not share a common vision of socialism, and whose most important member, China, did not want to play the role of maintaining a rump remnant of the once mighty socialist bloc. But what constitutes a "fitting global role" would depend heavily on the perception of how the globalizing world works, and the implications of the opportunities and constraints of the post–Cold War system for Vietnam.

For Vietnam, the idea that the "two worlds" system had been replaced by a "one world" system had taken hold by the turn of the twenty-first century, but it was difficult to also accept the idea of unipolarity, which meant that the one world would be dominated by a single power, the United States. In a broader sense, accepting the idea of US total dominance of the world system would reinforce the idea that globalization inevitably means Americanization, which would place Vietnam's decision to pursue deep integration in a globalizing world in a very negative light.

Some analysts argued that American dominance would be constrained by globalization and international regimes. Nguyen Van Tai, the deputy director of Vietnam's Political Military Academy, wrote a detailed analysis of the positive and negative effects of Vietnam's entry into the WTO on its national military strength. On the plus side, the WTO was an example of an international organization whose legal framework and membership obligations would impose constraints even on hegemonic powers (e.g., the United States). In an unusual linkage of old Marxist concepts with the new realities of a unified global market, Thai noted that the big wars of the twentieth century were caused by conflicts over the "division of the global market," which would now be somewhat constrained by the WTO.[11]

Vietnam's analysts and strategic thinkers had argued throughout most of the 1990s that despite America's overwhelming margin of military superiority over the rest of the world, the world was still fundamentally multipolar, and the key to international stability was the relationship between the great powers in the international system. The implication of this analysis was that deeper integration in the international system was not simply buying into a US-dominated world.

By 2006, this view of the essential multipolarity of the world had been modified in writings of analysts like Tai. "The reality shows that the general tendency is that the process of internationalization of social and economic questions is still a 'unipolar internationalization' that follows the 'leader's whip' of the country with the strongest economic potential." For this reason, the challenges of deep integration should not be underestimated. "And this naturally also brings with it economic conflicts of interest and even the potential possibility of political and social instability. And because we have just officially joined [the WTO] from an excessively low starting point, it is certain that we can't immediately master the basic 'rules of the game' right away, to find a lot of good fortune and advantage. Moreover, in accepting these 'rules of the game' we have to accept the complicated and sensitive new issues that they give rise to like 'soft borders' [*bien gioi mem*], 'information borders' [*bien gioi thong tin*], 'cyber space' [*khong gian dien tu*] . . . Finding where there is a reliable base of support and where there are forces that need to be guarded against is not simple as a result of the transformation of 'designated targets' [*doi tuong*] to 'partners' [*doi tac*]."[12] In some Vietnamese writings on international relations there is a caution that no relationship is pure cooperation or conflict ("partner" or "target"), which can also be interpreted as acknowledging the disappearance of the two-world idea, in which relations on one side were all cooperative "partners" and on the others all adversarial "targets."[13]

At the time the above analysis was written, the author was unaware of the importance of a key foreign policy decision in mid 2003, which amplified the significance of the doi tac-doi tuong terminology. It was not until reading two conference papers in March 2012, that the background to this terminology was clarified. According to Professor Pham Quang Minh, of the University of Hanoi, Resolution Eight of July 2003 marked a major development in Vietnam's adjustment to the post Cold War shifts of alignment in Asia. Up until that time "it was not easy to determine how to play the game, and who shared the same idea." Resolution Eight "provided for the first time the new definitions different from previous ones in Vietnamese foreign policy." One prominent example of this was a new post-Cold War definition of those who are friends and those who are not, which was no longer the traditional dich-ta, but now a distinction between "doi tac" (partners) and "doi tuong" (targets or, as Professor Minh translates it, opponents - still a less adversarial category than "enemy"). These new categories were intended to provide a more subtle and diversified approach to Vietnam's foreign policy and more flexibility to engage with former enemies. In his view this was the most important Vietnamese foreign policy document since Resolution 13 of 1988.[14] Putting this resolution in the context of Vietnam's development requirements, a Party analysis stated "Resolution Eight stressed that in every relationship, whether with partners or adversaries, there was a mix of conflict and cooperation, and in each case it was necessary to simultaneously cooperate and struggle in each form of international relationship."[15]

Alexander Vuvinh also highlights this document's importance. "July 2003 marked the third turning point in the evolution of Vietnam's grand strategy since the 1980s. It was in that month that the Eighth Plenum of the Ninth VCP Central Committee passed a new national security strategy that remove[d] ideology as a criterion for selecting friends and foes. This opened the door for strategic engagement with the United States, which had been identified as a strategic enemy by the preceding national security strategy (adopted in July 1992 but remained unpublicized)."[16] Resolution Eight also had implications for Vietnam's relations with China, since now national interest rather than socialist solidarity was the touchstone for making decisions about Vietnam's national security. Resolution Eight "made us understand more clearly, profoundly, and comprehensively, the mission of defending the socialist Fatherland." While protecting socialism and the Party were prominently mentioned among the national security tasks, so was "protecting the sovereignty, independence and territorial integrity" of Vietnam, and Resolution Eight was cited in connection with "border defense in the new situation."[17]

Another analyst remarks on the complexities of a world that cannot be clearly divided into friends and enemies: "in the regional and international situation at present we must simultaneously build and defend the Fatherland in a very complex international environment, where the line between friends and enemies is not as clear as it was before, and both benefits and costs are involved in every international commercial relationship, as well as short and long term challenges all mixed together." The appropriate response to these security challenges is to make interdependence work for you and embed yourself in as many global networks and bilateral relationships as possible. "The more countries that have an interest in our country manifested through all relationships, the more opportunity we have to become interdependent with them. This is also an opportunity to protect national security in the environment of globalization."[18]

Another formulation qualified the view of a multipolar world that combined unipolarity with multipolarity, but implied that it is a transitional form of world order at the present historical "conjuncture." This term is a legacy of the French (who often speak of what is happening *dans le conjuncture actuel*) that implies an underlying structural process of continual transformation, in which tectonic plates of contradictory deep historical forces grind against each other, and the somewhat related Marxist heritage of seeing the world as a process of antagonistic dialectical trends—hence the implication that a "conjuncture" is only a transitory phase in the march of history.

An analyst from the Ho Chi Minh National Political Academy who specializes in issues of great-power relations and global power structure wrote that; "After the collapse of the Soviet Union, the balance of forces among the big countries began to change in a direction benefitting the United States—the only superpower with a comprehensive national strength, which far surpassed its allies and diplomatic partners [*doi tac*] in every field. For this reason, what replaced the "world order of two superpowers" was a 'conjuncture of one superpower and multiple great powers' [*cuc dien mot sieu, da cuong*]."[19] We will consider this analysis in more detail in the section "Role of the 'Big Countries' and 'Great Powers,'" below.

The current consensus among Vietnamese international relations specialists is contained in the conclusion of the task force on Vietnam and the big powers in the first two decades of the twenty-first century. "One could conclude that there are contradictions between unipolarity and multipolarity, between America and the other big countries in redrawing the political, economic and security map of the world, in contesting for interest and regional influence. With the conjuncture of relations among the big countries like that, the new world order will only be established after another long period." While this is a good thing for Vietnam in that it fosters a balance of power and keeps the United States from consolidating its dominance, a prolonged period in which there is no consolidated "world order" means continual jockeying for power and position, even though this will predominantly take the form of political and economic competition rather than armed confrontation, and will involve "complicated" relations among big powers and between them and smaller powers as they seek to influence the configuration of the new order taking shape.[20]

The security implications of deep integration in a world dominated by the United States and "big countries" (many of which were allies or partners of the United States) remained a source of concern. Foreign investment could be a Trojan Horse for "peaceful evolution," even in the case of countries whose relationship with Vietnam was purely commercial and who therefore were purely "partners" instead of the more complex and threatening alternative form of relationship—"targets." "This could result in defeat, and a defeat that could be more serious than a military defeat." At the same time, countries that could not develop economically would fall further behind.[21]

Despite a decade-long trajectory toward an analysis of the global strategic picture that was increasingly focused on factors supporting peace, stability, and the primacy of economic concerns, some of Vietnam's party analysts are ever vigilant for signs of a re-emergence of familiar global patterns of conflict. Putin's 2007 announcement of a more forward strategic posture, featuring a resumption of regular strategic bomber flights over ocean territory in the Atlantic and Pacific oceans well beyond Russia's borders, was noted in Vietnam with interest. Official Hanoi commentary displayed satisfaction that this assertiveness, aimed at redressing a global power-balance that had tilted too far toward unipolarity, had raised concerns in Washington. And, this commentary pointed out, Russia was not alone in contesting American supremacy, citing the Shanghai Cooperation Organization as a like-minded partner in this new assertiveness. It concluded with the ominous warning that as a result of this new Russian assertiveness "people have even more reason to believe in the prediction of a new cold war."[22]

The debate about the polarity of the world and the distribution of power in it, which seemed to have grudgingly conceded the likelihood of an extended period of American dominance in a quasi-unipolar system, continues to flare up periodically, with each new bit of evidence (such as Russia's increasing strategic aggressiveness) giving rise to the hope that a truly multipolar world is emerging. Toward the end of the first decade of the twenty-first century, the official position was that the unipolarity of the 1990s was ending and that American was losing its grip. The increased assertiveness of not only Russia but other powers, big and small, along with evidence of US economic decline and some of Washington's own guarded official forecasts of a relative decline in strength over the next decade are cited as evidence.

"Thus there is a global power shift, above all in economic strength, which is unfolding. Every time the global economic balance of power changes, inevitably the long-term balance of political power can't help from changing along with it. Global polarity is now undergoing a time of many changes. The United States is no longer the superpower at the summit playing the command role in every international matter as in the previous decade. This has been a process in which the ability of the United States to control outcomes [*chi phoi*] has gradually diminished, and the role of other powers has been rising along with that of middle and smaller power, which is having a greater and greater impact and is becoming the controlling factor."[23]

As in the reaction to Russia's renewed strategic activism in 2007, some party commentators hopefully noted the revival of the leftist movement in Latin America. "After a period of crisis and retreat caused by the collapse of the socialist model in the Soviet Union and the countries of Eastern Europe in the 1980s and the beginning of the 1990s in the twentieth century, a left-leaning tendency has appeared in Latin America that is increasingly turning into a movement in the first years of the twenty-first century."[24]

Raising the possibility of a revival of the socialist movement on the world stage, a Hanoi commentator states that, "Along with the preliminary political, economic, and social accomplishments of the various leftist governments, the point to pay attention to here is that in recent years, the *viewpoint concerning the model and the path advancing to socialism* [emphasis in original] has received the attention of the left-wing leaders in power, and has been raised and discussed by them a lot. . . . [T]his profound transformation in Latin America is now a historical reality which is evidence of the vitality and the development possibilities of socialism, and reinforces the belief in the ideal of communism." Still, the conclusion is that the Latin American left has not yet escaped from American domination, and that the main result has been more distance from the United States and more assertive nationalism and regionalism—in short, a strengthening of multipolarity.[25] Multipolarity is a long way from bipolarity, and it is hard to see how this trend, along with a more assertive Russia, could lead to a "new cold war." It is evident that the nostalgia for the old "two worlds" system is not dead in some circles, but that the prospects of reviving any semblance of the old divisions, even in the form of a loose counterhegemonic coalition, are nil.

VIETNAM'S POSITION IN THE WORLD

One of the central tenets of the constructivist insistence on the importance of ideas in motivating international behavior is that identity issues lie at the heart of the societal consensus, which underlies the formation of national goals. In the case of foreign policy, this involves an understanding of aspirations for a role in the international system that reflects the desired national self-image. Finding an appropriate world role has been a central concern of the Vietnamese political class since the foundation of the Democratic Republic of Vietnam (DRV) in 1945.

Most constructivists stress the importance of finding an international identity that resonates with the cultural values and expectations, after a period of global transformation that requires a redefinition of a nation's place in the world. Recall the case of Gorbachev: "We argue that Gorbachev and his like-minded associates chose the idealistic new thinking over competing foreign policy programs because it offered a new global mission that would enhance Soviet international status while preserving a distinctive national identity."[26] Here we will examine Vietnamese views of their country's post–Cold War role in the world.

In its founding year, the newly independent country of Vietnam had almost no international standing. Phan Doan Nam writes that the early years of the DRV were "an exceptionally difficult and complex period, and there were moments when the fate of the nation was 'a thousand kilos hanging by a thread.' The Democratic Republic of Vietnam had just come into existence and had not yet been recognized by a single country, had no allies, and the economy in the first few years was almost nonexistent. The military forces had not yet been built up and had to simultaneously cope with several hundred thousand foreign troops, including France, Japan, England, [and those of] Chiang Kai Shek, seeking to liquidate the revolution. In that situation, diplomacy was an extremely vital tool and a weapon of the revolutionary government to steer the Vietnamese ship of state past these obstacles."[27]

In some of his writings, Ho Chi Minh preferred to stress the internal factors for the success of Vietnam's independence movement in 1945; "The August Revolution of 1945 was the rising up of an entire people *under the leadership of the Communist Party in the spirit of 'taking our strength to liberate ourselves'*" [italics in original]. Ho added that "This is the first time in the history of the revolutions of colonial and semicolonial peoples that a party that was only fifteen years old had led a successful revolution to seize total power in a country."[28] The events of August 1945, in the party's view, were a distinct contribution to world history, and brought independent Vietnam onto the world stage. The international context of Vietnamese independence in 1945 was crucial, as David Marr has shown,[29] and the revolutionaries had to contend with a bewildering array of challenges from outside forces, which they did by shrewdly combining diplomatic maneuver with internal political mobilization. But while they may have been the among the first revolutionary movements to gain independence (fragile and temporary though it might have been at first), Vietnam did not cast a large shadow on the international arena in 1945.

We have noted earlier Vietnam's pride in being on center stage of world politics during the later phase of the war against the French and then the Vietnam War. "In the last forty years Vietnam and Indochina was the only place in the world that had continuous conflict. . . . and also the only place that in forty years had three international conferences with the participation of all the major countries, members of the UN Security Council. . . . [T]he anti-American Resistance . . . of Vietnam was viewed as a historic confrontation, and Vietnam was regarded as the place where the contradictions of the era were concentrated."[30] As one foreign-policy analyst put it, the years from 1954 to 1975 were "the period of Vietnamese diplomatic activities that attracted the attention of the entire world."[31]

As we have also discussed, the post-1975 period saw the dissipation of international goodwill toward Vietnam because of its internal and external policies, and the ultimate isolation of Vietnam by the 1980s. Nayan Chanda discovered that in the mid-1970s the Chinese called Vietnamese politburo member Le Thanh Nghi "'the beggar' because of his frequent aid-seeking trips to Peking."[32] A Vietnamese foreign-policy expert stated that during this period Vietnam's view of utilizing the main currents of international politics in the 1970s (the "strength of the age") amounted to soliciting aid for Vietnam among its dwindling foreign friends. Eventually aid from China stopped and then assistance from the Soviet Union and Eastern Europe dried up, forcing Vietnam to look beyond its "traditional friends."[33]

This led to the policy of "seeking friends" throughout the international community, regardless of political system or ideological considerations, and a repositioning of

Vietnam from vanguard of the revolution to destitute developing country. By the mid-
and late 1980s, Vietnam's leaders had become painfully aware of the damage that economic mismanagement and belligerent foreign policy had inflicted on Vietnam's
international image. "Why is it," Do Muoi asked at the time, "that Vietnam [has been]
unable to develop to the point that it has become 201 of 203 countries (the most poor and
backward) in the world?" He concluded that "We must be objective . . . and dare to look
straight at the truth of the neighboring countries to draw a useful lesson for our own
people, and not be conceited or conservative. If we are, it will take a long time for
Vietnam ever to raise its head again."[34] This blunt appraisal of how Vietnam was viewed
in the world, as we have seen, prompted Vietnam to reposition itself from revolutionary
vanguard of socialism to needy developing country.

Phan Dinh Dieu in 1988 advocated a modest role for Vietnam while it pulled itself out
of poverty, but once that was accomplished, he saw Vietnam as capable of aspiring to join the
ranks of countries with information economies based on its human capital. "We are part of
the world and have to find our role in the world within a general equilibrium of the system.
What position is the most beneficial to us? That depends on our capabilities. In the short
term this will mean becoming a "hired hand" in the world economy. To get beyond that will
depend on brainpower capable of engaging with the cutting edge issues in a world that is
increasingly becoming an information economy—the third stage of human development."[35]

Vietnamese nationalism demanded more than an identity as a supplicant and fourth-
world basket case, or a helpless bystander in the game of international relations, and its
decision to join ASEAN was significantly influenced by a desire to reestablish a fitting and
influential international image, even if it meant joining ranks with former adversaries as
something of a junior partner. Joining ASEAN had made Vietnam more relevant in the overall scheme of global geopolitics, because "it added a new dimension to ASEAN's power and
influence and, in turn, as a member of ASEAN Vietnam could leverage its influence within
ASEAN and on regional and even global politics through a now more "weighty" ASEAN."[36]

Foreign Minister (1991–2000) Nguyen Manh Cam listed Vietnam's milestones in
integrating into the international community, from ASEAN (1995) to AFTA and ASEM
(1996), APEC (1998), and the WTO (2006). Despite its inexperience on the world conference stage and its limited resources, Vietnam was encouraged by its success in hosting
the meeting of Francophone countries in 1997, which was "the first and biggest international meeting organized in Vietnam." Vietnam was proud of its selection to host an
ASEAN summit only three years after becoming a member, which produced a document
called "The Hanoi plan of action". All these things, along with Vietnam's efforts to "play
its part in resolving global issues," said Cam, "have elevated the role and prestige of Vietnam on the world stage. It is not accidental that Vietnam was shown the confidence of
other countries by being selected to hold important positions in the meetings of the UN
General Assembly. It was voted onto the United Nations Economic and Social Council
(ECOSOC)—the most important agency after the Security Council—and to the executive board of the United Nations Development Program (UNDP), the United Nations

Population Fund (UNFPA), the UN Human Rights Commission, and so on. To develop our profile (*vi the*) even more, Vietnam has begun to campaign to become a nonpermanent member of the Security Council's 2008–2009 term."[37] Vietnam chaired the UN Security Council for the first time in July 2008.

In its new world role, dictated and defined by the strategy of "deep integration" and diversification of relationships, Vietnam's identity is defined now by its constructive contributions to creating a stable world order, conducive to economic growth and development. This is also, to some extent, mandated by the view that higher levels of engagement in a diverse array of global networks are also a measure of power. Such a perspective is somewhat at odds with the position of some party ideologists, who continue to depict the world in familiar Marxist terms as dominated by capitalist powers whose struggle for power and market share dominates international relations. The implications of this view would appear to make close collaboration with many of Vietnam's ASEAN partners somewhat problematic, since they are capitalist, even though not "big countries." The more prevalent view, however, emphasizes the desirability of cooperation with countries in a capitalist-dominated world market, whatever their political system. As in the case of ASEAN, Vietnam sees regional and international memberships as ways of amplifying its voice and influence in the world, through cooperation rather than defiant confrontation or ideologically driven distancing from states with different political systems.

By 2007, Vietnam was quite satisfied with its progress in raising its international profile. "In the last few months of the Year of the Dog [2006], many events connected with our country's international integration successively unfolded, making everyone happy."[38] The first of these was Vietnam's accession to the WTO. Vietnam also successfully hosted that year's APEC meeting, was granted Permanent Normal Trade Relations (PNTR) status by the United States, and was selected to be the Asian country that would be a nonpermanent member of the UN Security Council in 2008–9. A satisfied party assessment of the accomplishments of 2006 contended that these events confirmed Vietnam's rising international status, due to a greater awareness that Vietnam was now not only a gracious host, and a nation with a skillful diplomatic corps, but also "a country with a vibrantly [*nang dong*] developing economy, and a *doi moi* mission that is achieving more and more success, open in cooperation and exchanges with other peoples."[39] Even the gadfly economist Le Dang Doanh, who habitually irritated many in the top leadership by telling them that Vietnam must do better in key economic reforms and in improving competitiveness, said at a politburo briefing in 2005, "We have never seen our position and power as big and strong as present."[40]

COMPREHENSIVE SECURITY

The fact that with more extensive international engagement, Vietnam's national interest involved a combination of elements, and could no longer be simply or solely defined as protecting its sovereignty or regime primarily by military means, suggested the need for a broader concept of security in the post–Cold War era. Nguyen Van Linh outlined an early version of the concept of comprehensive security in 1989, in the context of the failure of Vietnam's military occupation of Cambodia to bring additional security to Vietnam. "You cannot protect the Fatherland without a strong military. But political, economic, and diplomatic [*doi ngoai*] factors also play a key role in the mission of defending the country. We must organize and mobilize each facet: struggle and construction; politics and economics, creating a comprehensive strength [*suc manh tong hop*] to defend the Fatherland, just as we knew how to develop comprehensive strength to defeat the enemy during war."[41] Some international-relations specialists in Vietnamese think tanks write about an extensive array of issues connected with "human security" and abstract threats stemming from natural or structural global conditions, which require a wide range of governmental measures to manage.[42] This section will focus more on those threats that are more conventionally political, economic, and military, and the implications of these threats for "comprehensive security."

The relevance of the concept of "comprehensive strength" was reinforced by Vietnam's conclusion that the collapse of the Soviet Union and the rise to unchallenged supremacy by the United States was due to the fact that one had "comprehensive power" and the other did not. The reliance on one-dimensional military strength of the Soviet Union and neglect of other components of strength had been its undoing. "After the Soviet Union fell apart, the balance of forces among the big countries underwent a clear transformation to the benefit of the United States. It became the sole superpower, with a comprehensive strength in the economic, military, scientific–technological–informational dimensions [in which] America had vastly outdistanced all the countries which were 'strategic allies' or 'strategic opponents,' and they arrogated to themselves the power to violate at will any of the international rules of the game, while other countries, including the big countries, could not do the same."[43]

Another factor that paved the way for the Vietnamese adoption of the concept of comprehensive security was that China had accepted it, indicating that the idea was ideologically suitable for a socialist state, though it also was a universal term that transcended any particular type of regime. A recent study of the role of big countries in the international system observed that "Today, to speak of big countries is to speak of all inclusive [*toan dien*] power of those nations in their comparative relationship with other nations in the international community. They are the richest and most powerful nations among the powerful countries. This strength is 'comprehensive national strength' [*quoc luc tong hop*] (as China calls it), which combines economic, political, military, scientific–technological, cultural, population, territorial, resource, geostrategic position, strengths."[44] The Chinese term is somewhat different ("comprehensive national strength" rather than simply "comprehensive strength") and seems to include more factors than most Vietnamese definitions (including territory, population, and geostrategic position), but the essential meaning is the same. (The Vietnamese analysts say that the actual uses of comprehensive power on the part of big countries are different from medium and small powers.)

Just as the idea of seeking friends everywhere and stressing diversification of foreign relations complicated the task of finding a strategic focus for Vietnam's external policies, the idea of comprehensive security also made it difficult to achieve strategic clarity since, carried to an extreme, the concept turned into a grab-bag of ideas in which everything was related to everything else. Consider the following formulation by party secretary general Nong Duc Manh:

> The content and requirement of the mission of protecting the Fatherland stems from the concept of comprehensive and all-inclusive [*toan dien*] national security. Protecting is not just prevention [*phong ngua*] but in the first instance you have to worry about building up and making yourself strong. Closely combining building up with protection from within each person, each basic organization, anything which benefits the people and the country, and is beneficial to national independence and socialism, must be done with firm resolve. Every political, economic, cultural, social, defense, security, internal, external activity . . . must be firmly grasped and implemented correctly in accordance with the requirement of protecting security in each sphere, each locality that belongs to one's sphere of responsibility, at the same time responding to the general security requirement in accordance with the concept of closely combining the two strategic missions; tying socioeconomic development to national defense and security, and taking socioeconomic stabilization and development to successfully complete the task of industrializing and modernizing the country to provide a firm basis for maintaining political stability, consolidating security and national defense, and providing the conditions for maintaining stability and socioeconomic development.[45]

Despite the convolutions, the basic point of emphasis is clear; comprehensive security aims at preserving stability by emphasizing socioeconomic development.

This can be interpreted to mean that the internal components of security, and political and economic stability produced by successful economic development, are the primary concern, and conventional security and military threats from outside are secondary. Phan Doan Nam writes that "In the past during the war, we created a comprehensive strength by means of coordinating between the three fronts, military, political, and diplomacy. Today, entering a period of peace when the economic mission is at the forefront, diplomacy and economics have to be closely coordinated. Diplomacy has to provide a bridge to bring the commercial enterprises of each country closer together."[46]

Commentaries from a wide range of party, military, and diplomatic analysts of security in the post–Cold War era seem to agree that absolute security and absolute sovereignty are unattainable in the new era, and that the zero-sum concept of single-mindedly asserting "the national interest" as the standard of international behavior, to the exclusion of possible benefits from compromise and cooperative action, is self-defeating. We have seen variations of the view in previous discussions of the shift to accepting the idea of "win-win" outcomes in international affairs. Here let us note the viewpoint of the pseudonymous military-affairs commentators who often provide hard-hitting conservative warnings about subversion ("peaceful evolution") and other threats to Vietnamese security in the military journal *Tap Chi Quoc Phong Toan Dan*. They observe that in today's world, global threats such as terrorism and transnational crime, along with natural disasters, require cooperative efforts, which are "at the same time in the national interests and the key and urgent duty of all countries and peoples in the world. For this reason, the thinking of great powers and hegemonists, and putting one's own national interest above all others, and being "carried on the backs" of other countries, has been assimilated into the concept of ruling the world under the guise of national interest . . . has become an outmoded and dangerous concept, especially when it is dressed up in the form of 'counterterrorism,' and protecting 'human rights' and 'democracy.'"[47]

From the opposite direction of attacking "hegemonists," and reviving the concept of peaceful evolution, these conservative commentators meet the liberal reformers on the point that justification of international action based on absolutizing one's own national interest is "outmoded." As we will see, some Vietnamese analysts question the possibility of achieving "absolute sovereignty" in a globalized world.[48] Although the implication would seem to be that absolute security is also unattainable, the only references to absolute security are critiques of American overreaching in the pursuit of it and claims that Vietnam can achieve "absolute security" in certain limited domestic areas, such as food security,[49] domestic elections,[50] or providing "absolute security" in Hanoi for important international conferences.[51] But the negative implication attached to the alleged US attempt to seek absolute security (it leads to hegemonic behavior) and the fact that even for a superpower it is an unattainable goal suggests that Vietnamese analysts do not take this as a realistic assumption for formulation of strategy.[52] That comprehensive security in the era of globalization involves so many unknowns and unpredictable elements reinforces this. Finally, the whole narrative of the evolution of Vietnamese post–Cold War thinking about security involves an increasing acceptance of the risks of deep engagement in the interest of not falling behind into weakness and irrelevance, and this acceptance of risk logically precludes a search for absolute security, which would require sealing off the country from the outside world.

The concept of comprehensive security is elastic, however, and despite the association of this idea with the Resolution 13 decision to elevate economic development over building a strong military, bureaucratic interest groups feel free to define their constituency as the centerpiece of comprehensive security: as, for example, in the following article by a general who is the political officer of Vietnam's border forces: "In the past period, in the face of complicated developments of the domestic and international situation, our party has renovated its thinking and understanding of protection of the Fatherland in the new situation in timely fashion. . . . National defense and security strength in protecting the Fatherland in the new period is the comprehensive strength of the political, ideological, economic, cultural, social, national security, and diplomatic systems, and the strength of the national unity bloc under the party leadership, and administration of the state of which the army and public security forces are the core."[53]

This point is central to understanding some of the complexities of devising a conventional military security strategy. As we have seen, "comprehensive security" actually downgrades the military component of national security and defines the threats to Vietnam as largely stemming from failure to develop. At the same time, the army and public security forces are the "core" of the regime. The main threat to the military is not a conventional invasion, but anything that weakens its ability to play this core role in defending the regime, "destroying the people's national solidarity, dividing the party, and rendering ineffective the armed and political forces which are the core of the regime."[54]

The lessons of the various "color revolutions" (orange, pink, etc.) in former republics of the Soviet Union, and similar events in former satellite countries in Eastern Europe, have sensitized the Vietnamese leadership to the importance of keeping the military and security forces welded to the fortunes of the party. A retrospective analysis of these political transformations concludes that "The situation of dispersal of power is also a factor which led to the swift decline of the central authority. In addition, the armed forces, security, and intelligence forces were cast outside the sphere of political life, which created an illusion about the use of armed force: it was a case of 'having it, but not really having it' [*co ma khong*]—when the armed forces refused to accept the direct and absolute leadership of the ruling party and state authorities. This also involved a mixing up of a deadly threat [e.g., to the ruling party and government] with the concept of totally equating national defense and security with opposing foreign aggression."[55] In short, the defense of the regime from internal challenge has become as important as defending the country from external threats. In a way, this is Vietnam's extension of the concept of "comprehensive security" to include domestic political threats.

In a series of directives (1989 and 2003), the protocol and regulations for an increasingly close coordination between the armed forces and the public security forces have underlined the fact that the priority security task, as it relates to the application of force, intimidation, coercion, or deterrence, is increasingly seen as internal, involving a wide range of political, cultural, economic, and societal problems that might destabilize the regime. This diversity of threats has contributed to the development of the concept of comprehensive security, and the demand for a much higher level of coordination between the army and the public security forces.[56] In chapter 6 ("Uncertain Transition") we noted the 1997 attempts of Le Kha Phieu to effect a closer linkage between the armed forces and the public security forces prior to assuming the post of party secretary general, and these efforts appear to continue as the line between domestic and external threats is increasingly blurred by globalization.

The relationship between the economic-development goal, which is the clear priority of the regime, and the role of the military–security forces in comprehensive security is not easy to define, not only because of the catch-all nature of the concept, but also because there is little explicit discussion of most of the key national-security problems that might require the threat or use of military or coercive power. And, since Resolution 13 and the decision to downgrade the military–security approach, exemplified by the Cambodian invasion and occupation, in favor of diplomacy, reconciliation, and integration to support economic development, there has been little public discussion of the tradeoffs between the economic and military dimensions of security. These can only be inferred by examining each in turn.

SECURITY AND ECONOMIC DEVELOPMENT IN THE TWENTY-FIRST CENTURY

Since 1986, Vietnam's overall external aims were to ensure that the external environment would be favorable for its priority objective, economic development. Let us recall from chapter 3 the party decree on this subject. "To escape from this difficult situation, in July 1986, the politburo met and issues Resolution 32 which clearly set out guidelines [*chu truong*] and revised diplomatic policies, and moved toward a solution in Cambodia. The resolution clearly stated: the external mission of Vietnam is to have good coordination between the strength of the people and the strength of the age, to take advantage of favorable international conditions to build socialism and defend the Fatherland, proactively [*chu dong*] create a condition of stability for economic construction. It is necessary to proactively move to a new stage of development and peaceful coexistence with China, ASEAN, and the United States, and build Southeast Asia into a region of peace, stability, and cooperation."[57]

In the days of the command economy, economic strategy was largely confined to the domestic plan. "Strategy" was a term applied to diplomacy and military planning. This term might suggest having to formulate contingency response to events beyond control, and in central planning the whole point was that everything was supposed to go "according to plan." Foreign economic strategy, such as it was during this period, consisted largely of soliciting foreign aid. In the age of globalization, however, an external economic strategy is essential. "The process of regionalization and globalization confronts all countries, especially the underdeveloped [*cham phat trien*] and developing countries with new opportunities along with many tough challenges, for which the appropriate response is not to isolate oneself and stand apart from that process. Reality shows that the countries that have an appropriate external economic strategy will be able to both attract strength from the outside (ngoai luc) and develop their internal strength to develop firmly and fast."[58]

There are also important political reasons for defining an explicit external economic strategy. First, the party has staked its future on achieving the status of a developed and industrialized country as proof that its model of "market socialism" works. Second, the competitive demands of the international marketplace and the potential down sides of globalization make it risky to leave Vietnam's fate to chance. Finally, there is a nationalist fear of losing control of the country's destiny, reflected in the following comments by politburo member Nguyen Phu Trong: "There is the idea that, in the conditions of 'globalization' of the economy, opening the door and integrating, raising the question of and independent and sovereign economy, is not very astute and is unrealistic, to say nothing of being conservative and thinking of the old type. Today's world is a unified market, if you need anything you can buy it, if you are short on money you can borrow it, so why advocate building an independent and sovereign economy (?!) [emphasis in original]. Put this way, it sounds reasonable on first hearing, but on careful reflection, it does not have a scientific foundation because it is too superficial and simplistic"[59]

But in keeping with the increasing dominance of the "fear of falling behind" as a greater threat than "peaceful evolution" the stress on economic strategy stands in contrast to the relatively underdeveloped conceptualizing (in the public domain, at any rate) of military security issues. To the extent that security is discussed in the context of economics, it relates largely to two points. First is that diplomacy and strategy are predicated on the assumption that the near future will be relatively peaceful, and there is very little discussion of potential military threats to Vietnam.

One analyst writes that "These days the world has undergone many changes. The danger of aggressive war breaking out has been much reduced as a result of the changes in the balance of power between nations, between the peace-loving forces and the warmongering forces in each country and throughout the world, and as a result of mutual complex interdependence [*phu thuoc lan nhau dan xen phuc tap*] in economics, security, culture, and society, and as a result of the process of globalization and the scientific and technological revolution, along with a human understanding of the value of life and democracy and equality among peoples." But even this fairly optimistic picture is clouded by the concern that there are still remnants of the forces who want to "pursue great power aggression and gunboat diplomacy to seize the land and resources of other countries. For this reason, the danger of aggression is still present for all countries, especially small countries with natural resources or an important geostrategic location on the political, economic, and strategic chessboard of the great powers."[60]

"Because of this," the author concludes, "national security in terms of defending territorial integrity and national resources and its citizens is still a permanent mission of every nation."[61] To the extent that Vietnam needs a strong military, it needs a modernized military, which requires both financial resources and a sophisticated technological base, which can be improved only by economic growth. The other concern is that hostile forces may use the economic open door as a means of exerting pressure on Vietnam.

Not all Vietnamese analysts are as categorical about the urgency or even the relevance of a quest for economic independence in a globalized world. The party theoretical journal which published the cautions of Nguyen Phu Trong cited above also published an article which maintained that, "Naturally, in the trajectory of globalization, one cannot demand absolute sovereignty. Today, we feel that among sovereign nations there can be and needs to be cooperation, integration, linkages, the implementation of regionalization, and corporativization [a literal translation of the term *tap doan hoa*, e.g., development of large state-connected international corporations, like South Korea's *chaebol*] . . . and grasping economic interests to protect national economic security will be done through these mechanisms. This is the direction of development which has had a strategic character since the end of the twentieth century, and will continue to develop and strengthen in the twenty-first century."[62]

We have also discussed the various elements of a new conception of international relations that have direct relevance to the issue of security and development. Among these are; the acceptance of the idea of a single world community and a unified global economy; globalization as an impersonal process affecting all elements of the international system that presents both risks and benefits for nations of the world (instead of being a plot to Americanize the world); the importance of being proactive in shaping a favorable environment to safeguard Vietnam's interests; the idea of interdependence; the replacement of an ideological standard for determining the nature of relations with other countries with a national interest standard and the related shift in emphasis from a paranoid fear of "peaceful evolution" to the threat of falling further behind in the race for economic development; the idea that the national interest cannot be an absolute standard for policy making because of the need to adjust maximum goals to maximize cooperation and support and the acceptance of a "win-win" rather than zero-sum view of international relations; and leveraging membership in regional and global organizations to multiply and extend Vietnam's influence on the world scene.

Of course, the picture of globalization was not entirely rosy. Most Vietnamese analysts agreed that it was a double-edged sword, which presented both opportunities and challenges. Not surprisingly, articles in the military journals tended to be more qualified and negative. "Economic globalization is an objective tendency that draws in participating countries more and more. At the same time this tendency has been dominated [*chi phoi*] by a number of developed countries and capitalist multinational corporations, and contains many contradictions. It has both a positive and a negative side, and involves both cooperation and struggle. The double-faced character of globalization makes it not only an economic and technological process, but also a tense socioeconomic and political–cultural–ideological struggle with opportunities and challenges mixed together in a complicated way."[63] It is significant that this highly qualified view, expressed by members of the Ho Chi Minh Political Academy in the pages of the army's main theoretical journal, is considerably more negative about the threats of globalization than articles from the same higher party school ideologists expressed in the party's own journal, *Tap Chi Cong San*. But even the qualified view represents a significant change from the language of the mid-1990s and earlier.

A good illustration of the implications of these conceptual shifts for the way a new paradigm of the security-development relationship has emerged can be seen in the following excerpt from Vo Van Kiet's important 2005 letter to the politburo. Under the heading "We must strengthen and change direction in economic intelligence," Kiet spelled out the way in which this subject illustrates the changes in the Vietnamese view of international relations.

> Up until now, economic intelligence has always been understood as an action of "us versus the enemy" [*mot hanh dong dich-ta*]. This approach has become outdated, even though it can't be said that it is completely unnecessary at the present juncture. Right now, the important content [of economic intelligence] (with respect to economics), is not an "us versus the enemy" question but an issue of cooperation. Previously the majority of countries used economic intelligence for purposes of stealing information from the opposition while safeguarding their own economic secrets. In the last several decades there have been big changes in many countries. Among them, England, China, and Japan took the lead. Some [social] scientists told me that the words "economic intelligence" [the English term is used in the original] has to be understood as a reconnaissance around the globe to seek opportunities and openings for developing the national economy. Thus, the intelligence mission is not necessarily a form of counter-intelligence, but is really an act of discovery, probing, and determining policy. . . . In this way, the mission of economic intelligence is not necessarily something that should be left to the Ministry of Public Security. It might be placed in the Ministry of Foreign Affairs and coordinated with other agencies, but it could also be put in a research organization [*co quan nghien cuu*].[64]

This represents a major shift from the pervasive security paranoia and the assumption of inherent rivalry and hostility that characterized previous Vietnamese thinking about the nature of international relations. It also brings into question whether or not the role of state security organs is as critical to coping with the contemporary world, as the conservatives maintained.

Vietnam's ideologists have different views on this subject than those on the front lines of government and administration. Nguyen Viet Thao, editor of the journal *Ly Luan Chinh Tri* [Political Theory], holds to the view that information is power and must be strictly controlled, and even cites "contemporary political science"—a field that was only recently allowed to develop in Vietnamese universities because it was seen as a threat to the party's authority to control the interpretation and analysis of all political matters—in support of this view.

> According to the traditional concept, the main basis of power is military strength and economic strength. Today, contemporary political science has added a third foundation which is intellectual and brain power [*tri tue*] which have produced scientific discoveries and industrial secrets. The Western capitalist governments

well understand this point, and have established many strategies of competition with more and more general funds for research and development (R&D [in original]), and constantly carry out intelligence activities to exploit scientific and industrial secrets of the opposition [*doi phuong*], and promulgate strict regulations protecting proprietary advanced technology [*doc quyen cong nghe tien tien*]. This selfish nature of capitalism in incompatible with the lofty socialisitic [*xa hoi hoa*] nature of science and technology, with its role as a direct force of production and with the open door policy characteristic of the globalization trend."[65]

In this concept, only high-minded socialists (or noncapitalists) should be entrusted with the potent economic secrets of contemporary science and technology, which would seem to rule out Kiet's view of a unified global economy and a depoliticized or nonadversarial approach to economic intelligence.

The Tenth Party Congress of 2006 mandated that "building and consolidating a peaceful environment" to create more favorable conditions for *doi moi* and economic development, in order that Vietnam could become an industrialized country by 2020, was the key international task. Vietnam's foreign minister stated that, "At present one could say that our highest national interest is to protect an international environment of peace and stability with the aim of developing the country, protecting our sovereignty and territorial integrity, and protecting the socialist system."[66] This formulation combines milieu goals (protect the international environment of peace and stability) with possession goals (sovereignty and territorial integrity), and implies that regime preservation will depend on "developing the country."

Economic integration is directly linked to the idea of comprehensive power in many analyses. "The goal of economic integration is to create additional sources of power, and create comprehensive strength aimed at moving forward the mission of industrialization and modernization in a socialist direction."[67]

ROLE OF THE "BIG COUNTRIES" AND "GREAT POWERS": VIETNAM'S VIEW OF THE POWER STRUCTURE OF THE TWENTY-FIRST-CENTURY WORLD

Most Vietnamese analysts accept the proposition that globalization has changed the dynamics of international relations, but there is not a complete consensus on how and why, and what are the implications for Vietnam. The analysis of the role of "big countries" in the international system is very important for any discussion of Vietnam's external strategy. If the dynamics of the contemporary world are largely driven by the great powers, Vietnam has the choice of "playing the game" in a balance-of-power sense, by bandwagoning or balancing, or standing apart from the interplay between great powers in the hope that it will be a stable and self-equilibrating mechanism providing the stability Vietnam needs for economic development. In the latter case, Vietnam could either ignore strategic contacts with big powers altogether, or merely ensure that it has good ties with all while not antagonizing any of them. It appears that the "good friends with all" has been the approach adopted. However, some of Vietnam's ideologists express concern for the role played by the "big countries" and stress that their capitalist nature leads to both oppressive collusion against smaller countries and destabilizing opposition to the main countertrend of globalization which, in the view of these analysts, is the economic democratization of world economic system. But despite the public "friends to all" posture, Vietnam has quietly engaged in some diplomacy with big powers that has a quasi "balancing" character.

Phan Doan Nam remarks on the big transformations in thinking about international relations in the last several decades, caused by the scientific–technological revolution and the disintegration of the Soviet Union and the collapse of communism in Europe. These factors have facilitated the development of globalization and interdependence which, in turn, have created a situation in which "Today, there is no country that can dispatch troops to occupy and exploit the resources and labor of other people as happened fifty years ago. This is something that cannot be done and something which is also not necessary. In today's world order, the role of big powers is still very important and sometimes decisive, but the role of small and middle-sized countries continues to increase in deciding the fate of the world."[68]

Not all Vietnamese analysts agree with this proposition. The main alternative perspective is a conventional Marxist analysis which evokes the images of the two-world struggle by placing the capitalist countries that dominate today's world in an ideological framework, with a Marxist view of the political and economic determinants of the global power balance, and insist that the essential nature of most big countries is capitalist and that their motives remain unchanged and fundamentally predatory. Nguyen Viet Thao sounds a notably more strident note about the nature of capitalist countries in today's world than many other analysts and commentators who also appear in the pages of *Political Theory*'s more important sister publication, *Tap Chi Cong San* [Communist Review], the official ideological journal of the Vietnamese Communist Party.

Thao writes that although the collapse of the socialist system of states provided the capitalist countries with a "golden opportunity" to "redraw the political map of the world," there are still some fundamental clashes of interest that prevent them from assuming complete dominance. "At almost the same time, America, Western Europe, and Japan have adjusted their global strategies. The common element in this revision is taking advantage of the historic opportunity to firmly consolidate the leading global monopoly role of capitalism along two main strategic axes; Europe and the Atlantic, and the Asia-Pacific regions, while at the same time creating a strategic encirclement of their leading adversaries, the Russian Federation and China." Switching from ideological confrontation to geopolitical analysis, Thao asserts that the capitalist countries are attempting to control the world by dominating the "heartland" (shades of Mackinder) the key to which is Eastern Europe. The main instrument of this strategy is the expanded NATO.[69]

But another key development is the increasing division of the world economy into closed market systems, the EU, NAFTA, and Japan and the Asian newly industrialized countries. Instead of the conventional Marxist view that these capitalist countries are by nature driven to struggle with others for market share, in Thao's view, groups among the big capitalist powers are colluding to divvy up the world into protected trading blocs. This balkanization of the world market contravenes the main trend of globalization, he argues. "This form of international relations contains within itself the seeds of contraction and partition [*co cum cuc bo*] which runs contrary to open nature of globalization which has an objective character. This kind of international relations has at present, and will continue to have, a destabilizing impact and contains many dangers which could break out." He concludes that "The relations among the developed capitalist great powers [*cuong quoc*] at present is one of cooperation and competition, centripetal and centrifugal, both coordinating with and restricting each other. These multidirectional and paradoxical vectors [*vec-to*] have created dialectical contradictions right in the heart of contemporary capitalism."[70]

Still, the fact remains that many of the big powers are not core members of the capitalist club. Most recent Vietnamese writing on the nature of the contemporary world uses the "one superpower – many great powers" formula in support of the idea that the world is still multipolar, and will become more so in the future. A staple of Vietnamese international-relations writings is the analysis of the reasons why China, Russia, France, Germany, Japan, and India (among others) have an incentive to act in a counterhegemonic fashion, while also stressing their own bilateral strategic tensions with other members of this great-power club.[71] A more discriminating and nuanced view of great-power relations is that "the conjuncture of close cooperation and competitive restriction of each other aimed at the supreme interest of each is a permanent and overarching characteristic of the relations among the great powers in the Asia-Pacific. However, it depends on the location, the specific circumstances, and the specific point in time, in which the cooperative side may be greater than the competitive side, or the reverse. The international community hopes that the great powers in the Asia-Pacific will increase their cooperation by more actively contributing to the trend toward peace and stability, and will push toward cooperation and mutual benefit in regional and world development."[72]

What are the implications of these different views of the role of great powers and big countries in the contemporary world for Vietnam's diplomacy? One survey of the subject concludes that the idea that counterhegemonic balancing will be self-regulating is mistaken because nations always follow their national interest. A prime example is the Russia–China connection, which is, in this view, inherently limited because both countries attach more weight to their ties with the United States than with each other. For this reason, Vietnam should focus on having good relations with all the great powers. This means that Vietnam should not expect a China–Russia axis to counterbalance the United States. The implication is that Vietnam should also maintain good relations with the United States.

Along these lines, Nguyen Hoang Giap, an analyst at the Institute of International Relations, the Foreign Ministry's "think tank," writes: "Over a decade has passed since the end of the Cold War. The big countries like America, Japan, China and—at a certain level—even the Russian Federation, India, and the big countries in the European Union, have all adjusted their policies toward the Asia-Pacific, driven by a strategic concern that has a life-or-death significance." This amounts to increasing their activities in the region to maximize their influence and interest in a variety of areas. "In this environment, Vietnam has step by step showed its proactivity and responsiveness in the way it flexibly pushes each relationship with a big country in the direction of a balance, and strives to achieve the maximum benefit for Vietnam's socioeconomic development, and maintaining political stability, independence and sovereignty, and national security."[73]

Of the "big countries," none loom larger for Vietnam than China and the United States. It is not surprising that this fact has led to occasional strategic linkage between the two in Vietnam's relations with them, but it appears to be less significant than many observers have inferred. Although there have been some hints that Vietnam's expression of displeasure about Chinese behavior to American visitors is evidence of Hanoi's desire to pursue an underground and unacknowledged balancing against China, most informed opinion on this subject rejects this conclusion. (Events since the research for this book was concluded in 2007 suggest that there may be more substance to US–Vietnam strategic cooperation in recent years and the Chinese factor that was deeply submerged in the relationship has risen closer to the surface.)

Vietnam's relations with the United States and China cannot be dealt with extensively here. In both cases, there already exist superb and extensive studies of bilateral relations with Vietnam. Vietnam–China ties have also been touched on in several chapters of this book. In the case of the United States, one could argue that Vietnam mainly wants to ensure that it does not antagonize the United States precisely because of its superpower status, but whatever strategic benefits may be derived from America's global power—as a counterbalance to China, for example—can be had as a free rider, without explicit strategic coordination with the United States, which might incur the displeasure of China, or more than minimal reciprocity, as long as the United States is able and willing to act as a counterbalance to China. As noted below, this last has been thrown into question as a result of America's misadventures in Iraq. This may account for the Vietnamese initiative in 2004 to move beyond its free-rider approach to the United States, as a counterweight to China, to more explicit discussions of this sensitive topic with American officials.

The relatively low profile of strategic issues in US–Vietnam relations following normalization of relations in 1995 is well analyzed by Lewis Stern, in his authoritative account of the evolution of military dialogue between the United States and Vietnam. From his perspective as a participant–observer in the military dialogue between the United States and Vietnam, Stern observes that "Between 1996 and 1997, Vietnam's military leadership concluded that contacts between the U.S. and the Vietnamese military would be a harmless adjunct to the overall normalization process, and a strategically inconsequential commitment. Hanoi would not gain security assurances from this link, and should not suggest that the Socialist Republic was at all invested in the possibility of security cooperation with the U.S. Recognition of basic similarities in regional security views and shared defense concerns, could not be parlayed into a meaningful relationship."[74] Stern writes:

> More to the point, the Vietnamese military leadership firmly believed that the most strategically consequential relationship for Vietnam was its link with China, and that the Sino-Vietnamese relationship should not be jeopardized by any suggestion that Hanoi was receptive to anything beyond symbolic steps toward normal military relations with the U.S. The Defense Ministry, especial the ERD [External Relations Department], went to great lengths to insure that Beijing understood Hanoi's views regarding the relationship with the U.S., and that China was fully informed about all interactions between Vietnam's Defense Ministry and the Department of Defense.... [The Vietnamese] wanted the minimum necessary to keep the U.S. interested in interaction, without allowing the relationship to approach the point of strategic relevance.[75]

In more recent years, especially in the wake of the US occupation of Iraq, Vietnam has begun to explore a higher level of engagement with the United States, and more direct discussion of the China factor in US–Vietnam relations. Raymond Burghardt, the US ambassador to Vietnam, in 2004 reported that for the first time Vietnam's leaders quietly broached the question of greater US involvement in Southeast Asia as a counterbalance to China's growing power.[76] "Upon taking office five years ago, Bush administration East Asia policy focused on two related issues: First, engaging with a rising China in ways which protected US interests in the region; Second, strengthening America's alliances in Asia. By mid-2003 one oft-repeated message the administration heard from opinion leaders in Japan, India, Indonesia, Singapore, and Vietnam, was that while the US had been distracted with Afghanistan and Iraq, China's regional influence had been increasing at America's expense. Vietnam's leadership authoritatively conveyed its concerns about America inattention to Asia during Deputy Prime Minister Vu Khoan's visit to the United States in early December 2003. Khoan alluded to these concerns in his public remarks and was even more forthright in his private meetings with Secretary of State Powell and National Security Advisor Rice."[77]

Vietnam's relationship with China is so fundamental to every aspect of its national life that it is not possible to relegate the topic to a brief discussion of even a sweeping issue like "big powers." For the purposes of this section, a few points will suffice.

The first is that Vietnam–China relations are truly comprehensive, pervading nearly every aspect of Vietnam's existence. The interlocking and comprehensive nature of the China–Vietnam connection is illustrated by a recent visit by a Chinese military delegation to Vietnam in which leading generals on each side "informed each other on the two countries' socioeconomic development, discussed their experiences of building up the armed forces, and reviewed the implementation of protocol between the two defence ministries.... On the same day, Zhang was received by Lieutenant General Nguyen Khac Nghien, a member of the Party Central Committee and chief of the general staff of the Vietnam People's Army."[78] In contrast to the distant and compartmentalized military-to-military relationship with the United States, the Chinese military visit is placed in the larger context of Vietnam's socioeconomic development and party-to-party ties.

The slogan that currently is used to describe the aspirations of Vietnam and China in their relationship was crafted at the beginning of 1999. This was a time when, as we have seen, Le Kha Phieu was attempting to play "the China card" by consolidating political and ideological ties with China. The slogan was "friendly neighbors, comprehensive cooperation, long-term stabilization, looking toward the future" (*lang gieng huu nghi, hop tac toan dien, on dinh lau dai, huong toi tuong lai*). As several Vietnamese analysts later told me, this was hardly an ideological solidarity pact, as indicated by the somewhat lukewarm opening identification of the relationship as one of "friendly neighbors," rather than the militant revolutionary solidarity of the past, reflected in the famous wartime "lips and teeth" image (China and Vietnam are as lips to teeth; when the lips are open the teeth get cold).[79] The other elements of the slogan could also be read as emphasizing a shared interest in development, rather than looking to the past to resurrect old ideological bonds. China, as we have seen, did not want to play the role of managing a "lonely hearts club" of remnant socialist countries, although Vietnam periodically tried to appeal to China's interest in protecting socialism as a means of fending off or deterring predatory or bullying realpolitik behavior. In this sense, the "ideology card" could be seen, from Vietnam's perspective, as a "weapon of the weak."

Perhaps the best analysis of Vietnam's strategy toward China is Alexander Vuving's model of a shifting four-component mix of traditional realism (balancing), socialist internationalism (solidarity), interdependence (enmeshment), and asymmetry (deference). He concludes that there has been a trend toward enmeshment in Vietnam's China strategy. "The integrationists developed their grand strategy out of the realization that falling economically behind other countries in the surrounding region is Vietnam's largest danger. Thus, their preference for economic growth can be seen as a form of internal balancing. And yet, this grand strategy is based on the view that Vietnam's internal economic buildup can only be achieved through integration into the region and the world and through close ties with the West. As their worldview suggests, the integrationists' preferred avenues of dealing with China are balancing and enmeshment. Their aim is to deter China and interlock it into a network of multilateral interests."

"However," writes Vuving, "both the anti-imperialists and the integrationists have encountered serious difficulties in pursuing their preferred pathways. First, China does not share with Vietnam's anti-imperialists the vision of a united front of socialist forces. The strategy of solidarity is therefore not viable. Second, the integrationists constituted—until the Tenth Party Congress in 2006—a minority in the Vietnamese leadership and have never controlled the most powerful office in the country, party general secretary. As a result, Vietnam's pursuit of balancing and enmeshment was halfhearted. Because the integrationists, too, have been socialized in the traditional Vietnamese view of relations with China, some also tend to take the expedient path of deference. Combined with China's preference for Vietnam's deference, these factors explain the steady rise of deference as a salient component of Vietnam's China strategy after the Cold War."[80]

Vuving does not feel that the Vietnamese are locked into a particular approach toward China, but have gone through phases of emphasizing one, or another, or a combination of approaches, depending on circumstances, what seems to be working, and who is in power. The two very different views of the role of China in US–Vietnam relations presented by Burghardt and Stern (above) are examples of this fluctuating pattern, and can be explained by the fact that they are speaking about different time periods. "Vietnam's China policy in the post–Cold War era has not been guided by a single strategy. Nor is there a regular pattern of shifting from one strategy to another," Vuving argues, derived from "a mixture of four different pathways with a changing salience of components. These pathways are the preferred foreign policy approaches of Vietnam's two competing grand strategies." This has led to a Vietnamese China strategy that is a combination of "solidarity, deference, balancing, and enmeshment." Vuving concludes that the fundamental reason for shifts in approach to China is disagreement among elites, especially at the politburo level, and states that "these top decision-makers represent incompatible grand strategies. Thus, the coordination of Vietnam's China policy has yielded less a symphony than a mismatch." A final conclusion, relevant to the topic of this book, is that his study "also demonstrates that it is not power or ideas alone, but the interplay of power and ideas that matters most in shaping the choices of a state."[81]

As far as policy coordination is concerned in the Vietnam–China connection, the combination of murky policy processes and multiple policy stakeholders on both sides would seem to present a formidable barrier to even the most rational state-to-state interactions, adding to the inherent instability in strategic focus found by Vuving. This is well captured in Ang Cheng Guan's account of the seeming confusion over a 1997 Chinese military move against Vietnam in the South China Sea. "Given the opaqueness of the decision-making process in Beijing and in Hanoi regarding the South China Sea . . . [o]ne presumes that there are also different competing groups within Vietnam with interests in the South China Sea, although it is the Vietnamese Foreign Ministry that remains in overall charge. Compared to China, it has often been said that Vietnamese politics is Chinese village politics writ large."[82]

There are other big powers with important ties to Vietnam, such as Europe, India, and Russia, but the relationship in each case is not driven by anything that could be termed a "strategy" or determined by larger strategic considerations. India is, to be sure, a potential counterweight to China, but that does not seem to be the main aspect of Vietnam's relations with it, which go back to India's longstanding support for Vietnam in its prolonged revolutionary struggle.

As in the case of many sensitive issues, Vietnamese analysts present their own views under the guise of citing "international" expert opinion. The consensus seems to be that India is well on its way to becoming a great power, but the economic and sheer size dimensions of its strength are highlighted more than the military or strategic aspects. According to one group of Vietnamese strategic researchers, a country is seen as a great power if it has the following three elements. One is enough strength in terms of hard power, comprising economic, military, and scientific–technological strength. A second factor is a degree of soft power, which comprises its political regime, the character of its people, the level of societal cohesion, its educational situation, the regulatory capacity of the state, and the capability of expanding its influence within the international community. Third is a big population (population over 50 million). Since India qualifies on all these counts, Vietnam's strategic researchers feel that it has the requisite conditions to become a great power. India has shown the desire to play the role of a world power, they argue, including attempting to influence events throughout the Indian Ocean, the Persian Gulf, and the entire Asian region.[83]

Although Vietnam takes note of India's "Look East" policy and its desire for closer relations with ASEAN and more influence in Southeast Asia (and the implicit implications for counterbalancing China in this region), it hides behind ASEAN when the strategic implications of this are discussed. India is attempting to fill the power vacuum left by the retreat of the U.S' and Russia from Asia. "The fact that India became an official member of ARF [ASEAN Regional Forum] in 1995 has to some extent shown the strategic calculations of ASEAN toward this country."[84]

For Vietnam, the benefit of India as a counter to China did not require any strategic coordination. India would do what it did in the region out of its own self-interest and did not require any prodding. "With the strong influence of China in the Southeast Asian region toward the end of the 1980s, the policy makers in India concluded that only India could restrict Chinese influence in this region, and only this would guarantee the role of India in South Asia." In addition, India had concluded that it had important interests in Southeast Asia and that close ties with ASEAN were therefore necessary.[85]

Although Vietnam is, in essence, a free rider on whatever counterbalancing impact India may have in Southeast Asia, and has generally not explicitly raised security issues in its bilateral relations with India, it did sign a joint declaration in 2003 which characterized the relationship as "strategic." "In particular, on the visit of General Secretary Nong Duc Manh to India (May 2003) the two sides put out a joint declaration on the Framework for Comprehensive Cooperation Between Vietnam and India entering the 21st century, with the goal of establishing broad and deep strategic cooperation."[86] What this amounts to, however, seems to be an endorsement of India's desire to play a role in the region, rather than a promise to actively collude with India's activities there. "Vietnam completely supports India's Look East policy—an external policy that India has been following for a long time, aimed at consolidating its international role in an environment that has had many changes since the end of the cold war, especially since the 'rise of China' and the spectacular development of ASEAN. India is guiding its foreign policy along the lines of its international priority of expanding commercial ties with all countries." Instead of being a partner facilitating India's move into the region, Vietnam sees itself as an intermediary. "Vietnam, with its position as a member of ASEAN, ASEM and APEC, is in a strategic position, and will be an important bridge in expanding relations between India and the countries in the region."[87]

A survey of Vietnam's relations with the influential actors in the world contends that "In its relations with the big countries, Vietnam emphasizes developing relations with Japan, Russia, and the EU."[88] Some observers assert that Vietnam's relationship with Russia is primarily commercial.[89] On the other hand, Professor Nguyen Manh Hung observes that "While the concept of "strategic partnership" was never applied to Sino-Vietnamese relations, it was repeated over and over by Vietnamese leaders when they talked about Vietnam relations with Russia and with the former Soviet republics such as Belarus and Ukraine." He further observes that "Russia can also serve somewhat as a counter-balance to Chinese power. During his visit to Vietnam, president Putin said Russia was ready to help Vietnam to modernize its army and provide Vietnam with new and modern technology."[90]

Official Vietnamese enthusiasm for a recently more assertive global strategic posture by Russia illustrates the residual hope among some senior Vietnamese officials, whose sympathies were formed during the era of close ties with the Soviet Union, that some semblance of a strategic relationship between Vietnam and Russia could be restored.[91] Nonetheless, Professor Hung concludes that "There are, however, limits to what Russia could do fulfill a strategic role in Asia to meet the expectation and hope of Vietnam." The amount of trade between the two countries is small, and Russia pulled out of Cam Ranh naval base in 2002, before its lease expired.[92] Whether the 2007 re-energizing of Russia's global strategic presence has any implications for Vietnam remains to be seen, though, given the dangers of arousing China's suspicion that a strategic link between Russia and Vietnam would be implicitly aimed at China as in the past, this would seem an unlikely eventuality.

Vietnam's ties with Europe and the European Union (EU) are both bilateral and multilateral, but without an extensive security component in either case. In the case of the Asia–Europe Meeting (ASEM, essentially a forum for discussion between ASEAN and the EU), there is a political component to the dialogue, and Vietnam claims to be an active participant in discussions about terrorism, new security challenges, and even human rights.[93] Mainly, however, this is a forum designed to maintain or expand the aspect of multipolarity in the world, along with a venue for exchanges on commercial issues. A Vietnamese review of various scenarios for future development concludes that there will be a modest institutionalization of ASEM, but nothing that would suggest the emergence of a significant new axis in international relations.[94]

Even so, the EU—or, rather, mainly the big countries in the EU—can be useful to Vietnam in attaining development and diplomatic goals. "The EU is in an important corner of the world and because of that if Vietnam wants carry out its diversification and multilateralization of international relations with good results, the EU is a traditional partner which can help Vietnam develop these relations."[95]

Japan is an important partner of Vietnam, but is seen primarily in a commercial and regional context, even as Vietnam notes increasing evidence of Japan's aspiration to become a world power. "In the new international setting Japan has begun and continues to pursue a re-adjustment of its development strategy aimed at becoming a complete great power in the future. This is very clearly manifested in the strategy of 'three concentric circles' [*ba vong tron trung tam*] (the US–Japan alliance, Asia–Pacific security, and the United Nations)."[96]

Despite the aspirations of Japan to become a "complete power," presumably by a more overt expansion of its military capabilities, and a global power in the conventional sense, Vietnamese specialists evidently conclude that, for Vietnam at least, the changing Japanese role will take the form of a greater diplomatic activism and stronger attempts to take a leadership role in Asia. "Asia has always had an extremely important position in Japan's development strategy, generally speaking, and in diplomacy in particular. Japan's desired goal in its readjustment of its Asia policy is to increase its role and become a leader of this hemisphere not only in economics but in other areas as well." Still, from Vietnam's perspective the impact will be largely on regional affairs, and mainly still in the economic area. "With these strategic readjustments, in particular in the diplomatic sphere, it is certain that the role of Japan will change. Japan will play a big part in the political conjuncture of the region and the world, both multilaterally and bilaterally." This will not only reinforce multipolarity in the region, but increased Japanese action will have economic benefits for Vietnam. "As Japan's position expands, it will mean that their sharing of responsibility will increase. That will be advantageous in resolving common difficulties, especially financial support and compensation."[97] Again, although Vietnam may reap the benefits of this higher Japanese profile in the region, it will be a consequence of Japan's changing perception of its role and interests and does not require any specific policy changes by Vietnam.

In the final analysis, Vietnam's relationships with the "big powers" are so diverse and differentiated that it is hard to speak of a unified approach to this class of international actors. This does not rule out the possibility that Vietnam is counting on the self-balancing dynamics of big power relations to provide them with what they most want from these countries—stability and peaceful interactions on the world scene. In addition, the conviction that it is economics, not security issues, that dominate international relations in today's world also allows Vietnam to customize its relations with each great power in ways that do not draw it into an explicit security relationship, such as balancing or bandwagoning, but to focus instead on what each can contribute to Vietnam's economic development. But although Vietnam realizes it cannot play with the "big boys" on the international stage, it does feel that it can help shape its regional environment.

THE REGIONAL CONTEXT OF FOREIGN POLICY: VIETNAM
AND ITS NEIGHBORS

Vietnam's regional concerns can be considered on two levels. The first is its immediate neighbor states or "near abroad"; China, Laos, and Cambodia. The second is the Southeast Asian region. The strategic problem posed by Vietnam's immediate neighbors is first of all a very traditional concern with security of borders. The complexity of this task can be understood by considering the following figures: "Our country has a common border that is 1,463 kilometers long and runs along six of Vietnam's provinces and two of China's provinces. The Vietnam–Laotian border is 2,067 kilometers long and runs along 10 Vietnamese provinces and 9 Laotian provinces. The Vietnamese-Cambodian border is 2,067 kilometers long and runs along 9 of Vietnam's provinces and 7 of Cambodia's provinces. The seacoast of our country is 3,260 kilometers, with 550 river estuaries, 68 bays, 53 ports, and 3,000 large and small islands."[98]

In many ways, the "near abroad" of Vietnam's immediate neighbors has been dominated by traditional possession goals, involving sovereignty and borders, while Vietnam's evolving concern with milieu goals—shaping a favorable environment through proactive engagement—was reflected in its decision to reconcile with former adversaries in the region and become a member of ASEAN. Vietnam prized its membership in ASEAN because it proved to be a good way to amplify Vietnam's influence in the world, at least on those issues with which ASEAN could speak with a common voice. It also was a discreet way to counterbalance China in such contentious areas as rival territorial claims in the South China Sea, because Vietnam could stand with other claimants as a group that wanted the matter settled by diplomacy rather than *force majeure*. The "code of conduct" for actions in this area, and the high-minded call for peaceful resolution of disputes were, in this sense, also "weapons of the weak." The fact that ASEAN was at the core of the ARF, for nearly a decade the main forum for discussion of regional strategic issues, also played to Vietnam's advantage.

Instead of emphasizing the loss of cohesion in ASEAN and the dilution of ASEAN's role in Asian security dialogues, Vietnamese analysts have stressed that as the competition of external powers for influence in the region intensifies, the geostrategic importance of Southeast Asia increases, and with it the importance of Vietnam on the regional and world stage. "Entering into the 21st century the importance of this region and ASEAN will not diminish, but will increase because of the constant strengthening of coordinated action and increasing linkages between the members of ASEAN; as a result of the appearance of new opponents, the increasingly fierce contestation [*tranh dua*] among the big countries in the Asian Pacific Region, especially between the United States and China."[99]

In recent years, following its expansion to include all states in Southeast Asia, ASEAN has lost a considerable amount of cohesion and international influence as well. Some critics charge that ASEAN has become a two-tier organization, with the original members on one side, and Vietnam, Laos, Cambodia, and Burma on the other. The rise of China and the emergence of alternative forums for strategic dialogue in Asia (such as ASEAN + 3) and the six-party talks focused on North Korea, sidestepping the ARF, have further diluted ASEAN's impact. Despite the view of some Vietnamese analysts that this is a positive development, because Vietnam's increasing geostrategic relevance will increase as the importance of Southeast Asia to the larger international context grows, all of the negative developments mentioned have complicated Vietnam's hope of using ASEAN as a strategic influence multiplier. It has also narrowed Vietnam's options in dealing with China.

Vietnam's main anxieties about Cambodia involve a concern for China's rising influence in that country, which must evoke memories of the "encirclement" fear that led Vietnam into the Cambodian morass in the first place. Laos, a kind of dependent state of Vietnam for many years, is also increasingly affected by rising Chinese influence.

The strategic involvement that linked Vietnam's "near abroad" with the Southeast Asian region was, in the post-1975 period, Vietnam's invasion and occupation of Cambodia. After the withdrawal and political settlement, Vietnam's relationship with Cambodia appears to be mainly focusing on joint action to control dissident tribal groups that operate on both sides of the border. Vietnam's public security minister spoke of combined actions aimed at "rendering ineffective" the Fulro movement, which has resisted Vietnamese encroachments on the traditional lands and ways of life of the tribal people.[100]

A review of Vietnam's international activity in 2007 stated that "Our top priority remains emphasizing the consolidation and development of relations with the neighboring countries in Southeast Asia, especially with respect to China, Laos and Cambodia, aimed at bringing about new developments in deepening and improving the quality and effectiveness of these relations."[101] The difference between Vietnam's ties with Cambodia and Laos can be seen by the slogan devised to describe the relationship, slightly modified from that used to describe Vietnam–China relations. Vietnam and Cambodia have continued to strengthen their friendship and cooperation in line with the slogan "good neighbors, traditional friendship, comprehensive cooperation, long-term stability." The major difference is that the China–Vietnam slogan does not mention "traditional friendship" and the inclusion of this phrase may be a Cambodian concession in a rhetorical formula which otherwise, as in the case of China–Vietnam, delineates a formal state-to-state connection with the assumption of equality.

Contrast this with Vietnam's insistence on retaining a quasiprotectorate in Laos, described as a "special relationship"—a term once used to describe Cambodia as well, but rejected by the Cambodians as the Vietnamese extricated themselves from their occupation of that country. The official visit of General Secretary Nong Duc Manh to Laos and the reciprocal visits to Vietnam of Lao leaders "have consolidated and strengthened the traditional friendship, and the special relationship of comprehensive cooperation between the two countries." Vietnam and Laos have annual joint meetings of the two politburos, underlining the close party ties between them. "Vietnam is the second biggest investor in Laos, with about 500 million US dollars in registered capital. Vietnam and Laos are actively carrying out a plan to increase the density and durability of border markers. The settling of the border intersections between Vietnam, Laos and China is an accomplishment of special significance."[102]

MILITARY FORCE AND TRADITIONAL SECURITY IN THE ERA OF GLOBALIZATION

Hidden behind a veil of secrecy, the exact nature and functions of the Vietnamese military remain obscure to outsiders. Required by commitments to ASEAN to produce occasional defense white papers in the interests of "transparency" and "confidence building," Vietnam has produced several platitudinous documents that have exasperated rather than enlightened the target audience. Speaking of the first 1998 Vietnamese defense white paper, a Hanoi-based military expert said "The document is of no use at all. It says nothing about mobile forces, nothing about organization, nothing about the navy or airforce." A journalist added that "Long on rhetoric and short on detail, the white paper leaves most crucial questions about Vietnam's military unanswered, and a press briefing by deputy defense minister Trung Hang did little to fill in the blanks. Hang refused to provide an estimate of the size of the army, saying only it had declined from its wartime peak of more than one million to 'some hundreds of thousands'—understood to mean fewer than 500,000. Nor did he shed light on the number of aircraft in its airforce, ships in its fleet, or the army's budget—none of which are in the report. 'Some countries make this information available . . . allow me not to disclose these figures,' he said. Hang said Vietnam's desire was to 'be friends with all nations,' adding that the military's purpose was 'peace not war, friendship not hostility, and that peaceful cooperation with China, the United States and Japan was a top priority.'"[103]

Perhaps, like the Wizard of Oz, there is not much behind the curtain shielding Vietnam's military from public view. It is certainly true that the role of the military in Vietnam's external policy, and even its overall security policies is a far cry from the prominence it had in earlier years. The military's function seems to be largely to provide an important prop of domestic support to maintain the regime in power, and to serve as an economic arm of the government in some sensitive areas like telecommunications and rural development in remote zones, or in sensitive border areas. In the same press conference on the first defense white paper, the military spokesperson said "that the greatest threat to Vietnam's national defense would come on the economic front. 'Anything harmful to economic development is also a threat to the national defense.' adding that '. . . the most dangerous threat is poverty and being left behind.'" As discussed above, the military and public security forces are considered to be "the core of the regime," indicating that the internal function of regime preservation is central to their mission.

In this regard, it is an irony that among the rare instances in which there is public evidence of a potentially destabilizing power struggle in Vietnam, it has involved the military—or, more specifically, an element of the military intelligence branch (see the discussion of the T2–T4 affair in chapter 6). Although the details and implications of this affair remain murky, it is perhaps not unrelated to a subsequent decision to reinstitute the system of party control of the military embodied in the placement of "political officers," with extensive command authority in all major units and branches of the military.

The political officer (or political commissar) system originated in the Soviet Union as a means of bending the former Czarist officers to the will of the party, later as an extension of Stalin's power (suspended temporarily during the Great Patriotic War, when nationalism was the main motivator and military efficiency the precondition of victory). In Vietnam, the political officer system was abandoned in 1982 and replaced by a system of "one person in command."[104]

In July 2005 the politburo issued an order to resurrect the political officer system in the military; the politburo (Ninth Congress) issued Resolution 51/NQ-TW, "Continuing to perfect the system of party leadership and implement the regime of one commander linked with implementing the regime of political commissars and political officers in the People's Army of Vietnam." However, the "one person in command" system was retained.[105] The following year the General Political Directorate of the armed forces issued a decree attempting to clarify the role and sphere of authority of the political commissars or political officers.[106]

The reasons for this revival of the political commissar system are evidently connected with the concerns about the lessons of the collapse of communist regimes in the former Soviet Union and Eastern Europe, discussed above, and possibly the destabilizing actions of elements of the military intelligence branch. A constantly repeated refrain in party and military commentaries on the armed forces is that hostile forces want to "depoliticize" (*phi chinh tri hoa*) and professionalize the armed forces in order to divert them from the task of preserving the Communist Party in power. Vietnamese generals have referred to a plot to "neutralize" (*trung lap hoa*) "depoliticize," and "render ineffective" (*vo hieu hoa*) the armed forces.[107] This is probably one reason why the party has severely restricted many normal country-to-country military liaison and exchange activities.

But even strong conservative support for the idea of maintaining absolute party control over the armed forces did not, apparently, always mean unquestioning acceptance of the authority of specific leaders in the party. We saw earlier that General Nguyen Nam Khanh warned of "feverish attempts of reactionary, hostile forces to oppose our country, opportunist and rightist elements are trying hard to change our party's political line, organization, and structure to turn it into a social democratic party, which by nature is the product of the bourgeois system."[108] Subsequently Khanh, himself a former deputy commander of the General Political Department of the armed forces, was nearly purged from the party for demanding, along with several other former high-ranking military officers, accountability for the alleged misconduct of the former commander-in-chief and later chief of state, Le Duc Anh.[109]

Perhaps it was internal political struggles involving elements of the armed forces rather than concern with increasing the military efficiency of the army that led the reinstitution of the political commissar system, especially in view of the fact that the "one person in charge" doctrine was left in place. It is worth noting that Vo Van Kiet complained about the political commissar system, in his 1995 letter to the politburo, as a holdover from the war years and a symbol and symptom of all the old party control mechanisms that were incompatible with running an effective and accountable government in a period of economic development.[110]

In a 2006 article commenting on the reinstitution of the political officer system, General Khanh said that it was a duty of the political officer "to strictly execute all resolutions and directives from above," whatever the circumstances but, at the same time, to be respectful of minority opinions from lower ranks. He again warned of the dangers of "peaceful evolution."[111] The old problem of drawing a line between the authority of the unit commander and the political officer resurfaced in discussion, as did the question of whether or not the younger generation is producing officers with the "right stuff" to perform the complex tasks of the political officer. "At present, the ranks of political cadres at the basic levels are still under strength, the supply of successors is thin and unstable. Almost all the political cadres from the division and regimental levels and equivalents and below have not undergone the actual experience of the political officer system, and have not yet met the demands and requirements of the new situation."[112]

Because of the expanded concept of comprehensive security, which links the military to a variety of social and economic sectors of society, there is a need to be more explicit about the jurisdictional boundaries within the Vietnamese political system that may involve the military and security forces. In the case of the military forces, the apparent adoption of an in-depth territorial defense strategy that stresses the importance of local militias also requires greater levels of coordination with local authorities. The decision to allow the military to fend for itself in a time of budget tightening had allowed a variety of questionable economic activities to proliferate in the guise of military "self-reliance." These involved a variety of investments based on influence-peddling and corruption (in luxury hotels and the like) and dubious commercial enterprises, which lined the pockets of well-placed military officials, as well as military requisitioning of valuable land for various projects. Eventually, in 2005, the National Assembly attempted to clarify the powers and prerogatives of the military by "regularizing" (*the che hoa*) its legal and constitutional status "In the face of a situation in which many basic issues of principle involving the guarantee of strengthening national defense embodied in various party resolutions and the 1992 constitution have not been regularized by legal documents that have a high level of juridical validity [*hieu luc phap ly cao*]."[113]

The second defense white paper published in 2004 stressed that military force would be the last option for Vietnam. Given the growth of Chinese military power and the fact that most of Vietnam's other security issues do not involve likely conflicts with other neighbors (or with the United States, the only other "big country" which could project power onto Vietnam's territory), this may be a simple statement of fact. "The purpose of the national defence of Vietnam is for peace and self-defence. Vietnam applies all necessary measures to achieve the above-stated goal while respecting the independence, sovereignty, and interests of other nations in conformity with the basic principles of the UN Charter and international laws." Vietnam "consistently advocates neither joining any military alliance nor giving any foreign countries permission to have military bases in Vietnam. Vietnam will never take part in any military activity that uses force or threatens to use force against any other country, but Vietnam is prepared for self-defense against any action encroaching upon its territory, airspace and territorial waters, and national interests." The white paper stated that Vietnam would be "ready to cooperate with other nations in the region and the world in the efforts to solve nontraditional security issues such as transnational organized crimes, illegal drug trafficking, piracy, environmental and ecological degeneration, etc." With respect to sovereignty issues, Vietnam was "always ready to enter into peaceful negotiations to find reasonable and sensible solutions."[114]

General Pham Van Tra, minister of defense from 1997 to 2006, reviewed the new thinking concerning the military and national defense in the journal *Quoc Phong Toan Dan* in 2005. He noted the complexity of the concept of security, which involved many nonmilitary factors such as politics, economics, and culture while, at the same time including more traditional elements, such as the prospect that armed conflict may occur. "We must more clearly understand the constitutive elements and the policies and implementing measures in order to create an national defense strength in the new conditions; the important role of security and external affairs [*doi ngoai*, which implies diplomacy or *ngoai giao*, but is a more inclusive concept], the necessity of close coordination between security and external affairs, and between national defense–security–external affairs with economic construction."[115]

In 2006, the Tenth Party Congress put even more stress on the nonmilitary components of security and national defense. A *Nhan Dan* commentary on the party line enunciated at the congress stated that "National defense is: the maintenance of a country, including the totality of its domestic and external activities by military, political, economic, cultural, and scientific-technological means." The article went on to say, "National defense is not synonymous with military affairs and war. It is carried out in peacetime with the aim of self-protection and defense of the country, but deterrence doesn't have to be passive, and must push back and defeat all enemy plots and be prepared to fight and win if war should break out. The supreme [*toi uu*] military strategy is to preserve the country without having to resort to war, a strategy of appropriately resolving the relationships between economics and national defense and the other activities of society."[116]

Cutbacks in defense spending clearly have affected Vietnam's military options by making it difficult to modernize the force. Discussions on this subject in the military journals are vague and inconclusive. The general in charge of force modernization endorses the goal of retaining the capacity to fight a high-tech war and "win under every form" of warfare. He also notes how Vietnam's force modernization suffered with the collapse of the Soviet Union and the communist regimes in Eastern Europe, but insists that Vietnam is making up for it by a combination of its own efforts and "seeking appropriate ways to restore the traditional relationships," presumably primarily with Russia and the Ukraine.[117]

An even more fundamental question is the issue of what the military needs to be able to accomplish in terms of applying deadly force, which should be the starting point for any discussion of strategy and modernization. Apart from many articles in the military journals concerning the strategy and tactics of other militaries, there is not much explicit or concrete discussion of this key question. A representative example is an article by a senior colonel in the Military Strategy Institute of the Ministry of Defense who discusses an ongoing clash of "three different viewpoints" concerning the level of attrition that the armed forces must be able to inflict to achieve its strategic objectives, from merely wearing down the enemy to complete annihilation.[118] The lack of a consensus on such a basic issue indicates that many fundamental questions of military strategy remain unanswered, possibly because there is no felt urgency to do so.

From the time of Resolution 13 in 1998, military requirements no longer dominated Vietnam's external strategy. Vietnamese forces withdrew from Cambodia, Vietnam defused the threat from China by normalizing relations, and military expenses were cut back in order to focus on the primary task of economic development. The new military posture was to be "just enough" or "sufficiency" (*vua du*), but this formulation did not address the key question; "just enough" for what? The actual role of the military throughout the 1990s was a combination of symbolic supporter of the task of regime maintenance; purveyor of the concept of the threat of "peaceful evolution"; economic entrepreneur engaged in ventures, such as nightclubs and hotels, to provide income for the budget-starved armed forces; lead organization in economic development in remote areas; and the more traditional role of guardian of border areas on land and sea. Whether Vietnam's armed forces were expected to prepare for bigger contingencies, such as a future "big power" attack, was unclear.

In the case of China, Deng Xiaoping told the military at the outset of reforms that their equipment was so outmoded that there was no point in building up the military until the Chinese economy had developed to the point where the burden of greater military expenses could be carried, and a modernized high-tech force could be equipped. (The deficiencies of China's military in terms of training and equipment were starkly exposed in its unsuccessful attempt to "teach Vietnam a lesson" by military invasion in 1979.) Though China has now embarked on the military buildup that Deng promised, it is possible that Vietnam's armed forces are in somewhat the same position as the Chinese military during the earlier years of reform. The steering committee for China–Vietnam relations, formed in 2006, included military and security officials and finance and economic representatives, suggesting that there is a felt need to address security issues in a broader framework in the Vietnam–China relationship.[119]

The public face of this relationship suggests increasingly close contacts between the military establishments in Vietnam and China. An important dimension of the Vietnam–China military-to-military connection is border security and something which seems to approximate "confidence building" in this sensitive area. "The Military Forces of Vietnam and China will cooperate more closely, especially in patrolling the Tonkin Gulf and border areas, agreed Vietnamese Defense Minister Pham Van Tra and his Chinese counterpart Cao Gangchuan at a meeting in Hanoi on April 7 [2006]."[120]

Exchanging experiences about the role of the military sector in economic development appears to be a prominent aspect of this relationship. Phung Quang Thanh, member of the political bureau of the Communist Party of Vietnam, minister of national defence and chief of general staff of the Vietnamese People's Army, on a visit to China in 2006, stressed the importance of high-level mutual military exchanges between Vietnam and China, especially in the area of "cooperation in the national defence industry, so that the two sides could make new contributions to their respective countries and national defence construction."[121]

This linkage of economic and security issues in Vietnam–China relations may be connected to mutual concerns about maximizing oil revenues in the disputed areas of the South China Sea. In a 2005 visit to Vietnam, Chinese vice-president Zeng Qinghong mentioned the prospect of joint exploration of the disputed areas in South China Sea. Zeng linked this to what appeared to be an attempt to define a zone of economic co-operation closely integrating northern Vietnam and southern China. He said China attaches great importance to the construction of the Beibu Gulf economic rim and two economic corridors which respectively links Kunming of China to Lao Cai, Hanoi, Hai-phong of Vietnam, and Nanning of China to Lang Son, Hanoi and Hai-phong of Vietnam."[122]

Economic security has received more attention from the party than military security and strategy in the *doi moi* era, because it is directly related to the top-priority mission of economic development. "The special characteristics of the age are peace, independence, and development, cooperation and struggle. In particular, in globalization economic competition is increasingly fierce. There is no country that does not have to face challenges regarding its economic interests. For this reason, every country takes economic security seriously. And this issue has become the basic foundation and the main target of the strategy of national security." Significantly, in this most important area of government policy, the relevant points of defense against threats to economic security are good economic policy and societal consensus not to be swept into a dependency relationship. "The most dangerous thing in protecting economic security is the paralysis and loss of vigilance of the operating agencies in charge of macro- and microeconomic policy, and of the entire society."[123] We have seen that in the case of military diplomacy between Vietnam and the United States, the need to focus on economic issues has often put military relations on the backburner. In regards to economic security, the traditional instruments of security—the party, the ideologists, and the armed and public security forces—are not relevant.

This does not mean, however, that the Vietnamese military is unconcerned with economic security or the challenges of globalization. We have already mentioned the view of Nguyen Van Tai, deputy director of Vietnam's Political Military Academy, on the possible Trojan Horse character of deep integration. WTO membership is viewed by Tai as a prospective threat to Vietnam's military posture. Although he couches his warning in general and hypothetical terms, the implications for Vietnam are clear. "The countries whose economic potential is not strong enough will be forced to accept a higher degree of risk in competition; accordingly, the possibility of continuing to fall further behind economically is practically a 'death foretold in advance' if they can't find the right prescription to revive themselves. When their turn comes, falling behind economically will certainly lead to dependency in every respect, even regarding their political form of government. For this reason, they can't think of allowing independent investment in the military defense sector. . . . Regarding scientific–technological potential it is the same; if there are no appropriate measures taken, then weakness in the level of science and technology will, under conditions of integration with the WTO, expose even more the inferiority in defense-industry development. . . ." Tai called for new thinking in the military sphere and a more explicit consideration of the tradeoffs between economic interest and military security, but adds that in considering the tradeoffs between "challenges and opportunities" Vietnam should not become so paralyzed by fear of the challenges that it misses the opportunities.[124]

This is a hybrid view that draws on the fear of "falling behind," as a nationalist theme used by reformers to argue for the necessity of deep integration and as the conservative warning that deep integration is simply an open door for subversion and attacks on Vietnam's socialist regime. What is distinctive about Tai's formulation is that it raises the specter of a dependent military–industrial sector, which would compromise Vietnam's ability to defend itself from attack.

The leading foreign expert on the Vietnamese military, Carlyle Thayer, has provided a detailed account of the economic dimension of this sector of the regime. "Since the adoption of *doi moi* Vietnam has taken a number of steps to further sanction the army's role in commercial activities as well as its long-standing involvement in economic development and construction activities." In Thayer's calculation, in 1995 there were an estimated 335 army-run enterprises in Vietnam, employing about one hundred thousand soldiers, or one-sixth of the VPA's standing force. In 1998 "Vietnam launched a second wave of reforms in military-run enterprises aimed at professionalizing the army's commercial activities."[125]

Thayer observes that, "According to Hanh Dung, the Ministry of National Defense 'is structured like a real, if miniature, government.' According to one foreign economist, it is difficult to conceive of any industry in which the military is not involved. The VPA's tentacles reach into every corner of the economy." Businesses run by the military "are involved in the full spectrum of activities from the most basic (laundry and food processing) to the highly advanced (computers and telecommunications). Most army-run enterprises cannot stay solvent by meeting their military contracts alone and must seek outside work. Defense Ministry figures show that 10–20 percent of military enterprise output goes to the army; in other words, up to 80 percent of the army's contracts come from the civilian sector."[126]

From these developments in the military sphere of Vietnam's regime, we can infer that the military as an institution plays a minor role in contributing to either the theoretical or policy dimensions of "comprehensive security." It is ironic that one of the main props of the regime has also been the major threat to regime cohesion and stability, with the alleged intrigues of rogue elements of the military intelligence branch. The lack of evidence of any serious thinking about the role of the armed forces in the larger strategic picture does not suggest that military has either been tasked with formulating such a role or is capable of doing so. There is thus a major void at the center of Vietnam's strategic picture, which in most countries would be filled by the military dimension. Considering the earlier centrality of the Vietnamese armed forces in its strategic thinking, this apparent recusal of the armed forces from serious contribution so Vietnam's thinking about strategic responses to the regional and global environment is somewhat anomalous.

IS STRATEGY AN ILLUSION?

What do we mean by strategy? Many analysts define it narrowly as the relationship of military force to political goals. Richard Betts writes that, "Strategy is the essential ingredient for making war either politically effective or morally tenable. It is the link between military means and political ends, the scheme for how to make one produce the other. Without strategy, there is no rationale for how force will achieve purposes worth the price in blood and treasure." Even in this more narrowly defined realm of strategy there are still complex questions about even the fundamental premise on which it rests. "Politicians and soldiers may debate which strategic choice is best, but only pacifists can doubt that strategy is necessary."[127]

But, says Betts, "Because strategy is necessary, however, does not mean that it is possible. Those who experience or study many wars find strong reasons to doubt that strategists can know enough about causes, effects, and intervening variables to make the operations planned produce the outcomes desired. To skeptics, effective strategy is often an illusion because what happens in the gap between policy objectives and war outcomes is too complex and unpredictable to be manipulated to a specified end. When this is true, war cannot be a legitimate instrument of policy."[128] Of course, the Vietnamese revolutionaries would argue that it was foreign intervention that imposed the necessity for both war and strategy on them, and they take understandable pride in formulating a very sophisticated strategy that minimized their own vulnerabilities and maximized the vulnerabilities of their adversaries.[129]

The issue here, however, is a broader conception of strategy that takes into account the Vietnamese adoption of the concept of comprehensive security and the paramount goal of preserving regional and global stability to facilitate economic development. There is also the fact that Vietnam is not a major power on the world scene, and has only a modest capacity to influence the course of events even in its own region.

One of Vietnam's leading foreign-affairs analysts writes, in an essay that references a number of prominent U.S. international-relations theorists, that in the era of globalization and scientific technological revolution, "the military strength factor is increasingly being viewed in a more comprehensive context. According to this, military strength no longer plays a controlling role as before, while the controlling influence of economics is constantly increasing. Because of this, in the strategies of the big powers (Grand National Strategy) [English term and parenthesis in original], of the world's nations, especially the big countries, there is less of a tendency to rely solely on military strength, but [military strength] is usually combined with other instruments such as economics, political influence . . . [ellipsis in original] to maximize the attainment of their strategic objectives."[130]

It may be useful to consider some parallels and differences between Vietnam and China in the area of external strategy. There are, of course, fundamental differences between Vietnam and China, but they each confront somewhat similar problems in some areas. Each relates diplomacy and overall strategy to economic development, and each preserves a remnant communist regime, which much of the rest of the world considers an anachronism, that places a heavy burden on the political leadership to justify its continuing authoritarian rule and limited accountability at a time of rapid domestic socioeconomic change and the impact of globalization. This might justify at least a brief consideration of some of the writings on China's grand strategy.

Avery Goldstein analyzes Chinese attempts to formulate a comprehensive and integrated approach to the world "by examining the role of diplomacy in China's grand strategy." He argues that "after several years of ad hoc attempts to deal with the new challenges that accompanied the end of the Cold War, a clearer consensus on China's basic foreign policy line began to emerge among Party leaders in 1996. This consensus, tantamount to the country's grand strategy, has provided a relatively coherent framework for the PRC's subsequent international behaviour and the expected contribution of diplomacy to the country's security."[131]

The definition of "grand strategy" employed by Goldstein is the broader view of the term that is used in this chapter. "This consensus constitutes a grand strategy for China in the sense the term is often employed by international relations scholars, the distinctive combination of military, political and economic means by which a state seeks to ensure its national security."[132]

It is instructive that Goldstein does not find the smoking gun of a formal policy document that spells out this grand strategy, but rather speaks of a "consensus" among the leadership. This is also the case in Vietnam and an important reason why it necessary to examine their collective discourse in detail. If there is a "grand strategy" in Vietnam, it would most likely be implicit and reflected in a collective discussion about security by top political, military, security, diplomatic, and economic officials. This would indicate not so much a secret plan as the points of consensus and convergence, the priorities and emphases, the way the various components of "comprehensive security" related to each other, and the shifts in the parameters of "mainstream" views on these issues. Underlying all of this is the reconceptualization of the nature of international relations and Vietnam's place in a globalizing world, discussed above.

Goldstein's account suggests some parallels between China's and Vietnam's strategic aims during the Cold War, and its adjustment to the post–Cold War era. The fundamental differences between the two cases also cast light on the role of grand strategy in Vietnam's changing circumstances. "During much of the Cold War, Beijing's overriding challenge was to ensure a relatively weak China's security in the face of pressing threats from the superpowers. The priority was clearly to address core survival concerns (territorial and political integrity) and the imperatives for Chinese diplomacy were correspondingly straightforward. . . . Today, however, China has greater strength and also believes it faces few immediate threats. In addition to providing for core survival concerns, China's contemporary grand strategy is designed to engineer the country's rise to the status of a true great power that shapes, rather than simply responds to, the international system." In order to defuse concerns about its growing strength, "since 1996 Beijing has forged a diplomatic strategy with two broad purposes: to maintain the international conditions that will make it feasible for China to focus on the domestic development necessary if it is to increase its relative (not just absolute) capabilities; and to reduce the likelihood that the U.S. or others with its backing will exploit their current material advantage to abort China's ascent and frustrate its international aspiration."[133]

Of course, with respect to power, Vietnam's problem is the reverse. The days when Vietnamese were regarded as "the Prussians of the Orient" are long gone. Rather than having to adopt a "neo-Bismarckian" reassurance strategy to defuse potentially destabilizing resistance to its international rise to power, Vietnam must somehow adjust to an ever more powerful China with growing regional and perhaps even global ambitions. It has periodically tried to do so with a special form of reassurance strategy that stresses common ideological ties and shared interest in preserving socialism. With respect to other countries, Vietnam has also adopted a different reassurance strategy (Vietnam wants to be friends with all nations) as part of its reconciliation with former adversaries and reintegration into the Southeast Asian region. Vietnam, like China, has been concerned about possible instability on its periphery.

As Goldstein notes, this is the second of three reasons that have compelled China to formulate a "grand strategy" which stresses reassurance (the first reason is to facilitate a stable environment for development). "[A]lthough the risk of world war remained low, the risk of China's involvement in limited military conflicts over sovereignty disputes along its periphery had grown. Thus, it was important to reduce the growing possibility that others would be united by their anxiety about a purported 'China threat.'"[134]

The third reason is that "although the bipolarity of the Cold War had indeed faded, it had given way to an unexpected era of American unipolarity rather than the dawn of multipolarity. Thus, it was necessary to cope with the resulting potential dangers China saw in surprisingly robust American primacy."[135] We have seen that Vietnam's views on the extent of multipolarity in the post–Cold War international order have also shifted, though the consensus conclusion appears to be that it would be impossible for the United States to consolidate a purely unipolar system. This has important implications for strategy because it allows for the possibility that a form of great-power equilibrium will assure stability, and points away from the need to form a counterhegemonic coalition or even directly participate in the intrigues of great-power balancing. In this regard, Vietnam can be a "free rider" on the self-regulating stabilizing mechanism of the international system which, in turn, reduces the urgency of thinking seriously about large-scale military conflict—in contrast to China.

Perhaps the most important parallel between Vietnam and China is that the search for grand strategy has to take into account new challenges to regime legitimacy and preserving the existing regime and power structure. Given the party's identity of its own interests with those of the nation in both countries, this is the key driving force behind strategic imperatives. Goldstein asserts that "it took until the mid-1990s for Beijing to adapt Deng's strategic logic effectively, in part because the post–Cold War world turned out to be significantly different from the one Deng had anticipated." The collapse of communism elsewhere put more pressure on the Chinese leadership to maintain themselves in power by being successful in economic development.[136]

Ian Johnston's linkage of China's development-centered grand strategy and its status quo orientation to the international system has important implications for Vietnam. As summarized by Katzenstein and Suh, this view holds that "Marketization and a comprehensive security strategy thus go hand in hand in consolidating a fundamentally status quo orientation in policy."[137] While one might argue that China is merely biding its time until its growing power allows it to assert a revisionist role, both with regard to an influence in world affairs more commensurate with its self-image and in redeeming its irredenta (Taiwan and claimed territory in the South China Sea), to complete the task of undoing the dismemberment of China in the nineteenth and twentieth centuries. Vietnam has no such motivation. It has what it wants and is trying to hold on to it.

How would one summarize Vietnam's "grand strategy?" Perhaps the starting point is to note that there is no fully developed or formally articulated "grand strategy," but the elements of one might be inferred from the analysis in this chapter. The starting point would be accepting that a stable status quo in the region and the world serves Vietnam's interests. Much of its earlier strategy was based on the view that the status quo was undesirable and untenable and was aimed at undoing the perceived wrongs inflicted on Vietnam by more powerful actors in the international system. With reunification accomplished and external enemies repulsed or mollified, Vietnam has now turned to the task of making the international system work for its interests, by using what it assumes to be an offsetting system of rivalries among the larger powers in the system, membership in ASEAN as an influence multiplier, and membership in international organizations and regimes to enforce rules which protect its weaker members.

Accepting the status quo does not mean that Vietnam is oblivious to the rapid pace and wide scope of dynamic change going on in the world. But it is seen as change within the system, not change of the system. Continuous and far-reaching change in economics, science, and technology has the potential to be destabilizing, but it is now viewed as a condition of modern life rather than a hostile scheme aimed at Vietnam. Self-strengthening and international cooperation are now considered to be the most effective defenses against the negative consequences of change. A parallel to Vietnam's wartime tradition of "strategic judo"—turning the enemy's strengths into weaknesses—would be taking the negatives of globalization (disruptive change and potential for rapid movement up and down the scale of economic success) and turning them into positives (accelerated innovation and a chance to improve Vietnam's position in the international pecking order).

This seems to be the implication of the many discussions about the perils of "fortune" or "luck" in today's world. For example: "So, what is economic security? It is the capacity of a country to resist the attacks, invasions, and economic impact of external economic forces. Economic security is an environment within the country and internationally which preserves peace and security, creates conditions for the economic system of a nation to develop continuously, with stability and security. In the wave of globalization, all countries participate in a common "game" [*cuoc choi*], and match their strength against the others on the playing field of the international market, with the aim of seizing fortune and grasping opportunities, while casting aside the vicissitudes of fate [*rui ro*], gaining economic advantage, protecting economic security, and increasing the national comprehensive strength, of which the core is economic strength."[138] In today's world, strategy can attempt to cope with uncertainty and reduce risk, but there is no longer the confidence in grasping trends and predicting outcomes that characterized the period when Marxism was the shaping factor of Vietnamese strategic thinking. The old rhetoric of Marxist determinism ("it is no accident that . . .") is rarely heard in twenty-first-century Vietnam. Unlike the "two worlds" era, Vietnam cannot assume that the forces of history inevitably work in the favor of those who are on the "right side" or that those with the right dialectical tools can see the future.

A related point would be that Vietnam has now accepted a proactive approach to international relations aimed at shaping the regional and global environment to provide stability and a favorable environment for development. In a nondetermined environment, each society has to do its best to create favorable conditions to further its interests.

"Nondetermined" does not mean that there are not larger historical forces at work, only that they are not predictable and the outcomes are not inevitable. Adopting this concept and the related acceptance of the idea that the challenges posed by the impersonal forces of globalization do not represent a specific threat from any country or group of countries has altered Vietnam's view of how it will engage with the outside world and has paved the way for accepting the risks of deep integration in order to reap the benefits.

Although Vietnam's declared policy of "making friends" with everyone and moving beyond the paradigm of an "us-against-them" world does not facilitate the kind of discriminating targeting that gave coherence to Vietnamese strategy in the Cold War, one can deduce a hierarchy of objectives and priorities, and the interrelationships among them.

In terms of territorial integrity, Vietnam has always placed top priority on its relationships with its neighbors, attempting to achieve predominant influence in Laos and Cambodia, while neutralizing China's overwhelming size and power. In this regard, Vietnam's decision to abandon direct control of Cambodia and confrontation with China was a fundamental strategic turning point, as was its related decision to place economic development above military defense as a priority, and move from an obsession with defensive possession goals to proactive milieu goals. Better to improve relations with the rest of the region and world, and tap into the benefits of globalization, than to cling to the expensive and unrewarding occupation of Cambodia.

Being more proactive in international engagement does not necessarily require a strategy blueprint, or even effective coordination between the various components of Vietnam's putative strategy. The fact that there does not seem to be a consensus on the role of military force in Vietnam's overall strategy further indicates that there is no integrated plan. Indeed the author was told by an informed foreign military observer in 2000 that he concluded that the Vietnamese military in general doesn't "discuss strategy—i.e., what would you do if . . . —or the modernization of their force."[139]

There is also the question of how a formal comprehensive security plan would be coordinated. One possibility would be that the external-affairs division of the Party Central Committee, whose original function was to coordinate relations with socialist bloc countries at a time when these relations comprised the bulk of Vietnam's diplomacy, would be transformed into a sort of US-style national security council. But this, according to informed observers, has not happened.[140]

Another possibility is that the National Defense and Security Council of the National Assembly, established in 2002, would take on a coordinating and policy role, but this too has apparently not been the case.[141] Based on his extensive research on the defense dimension of Vietnam's external policy, Lewis Stern has shown instances which suggest a rudimentary interagency process to relate military issues to other aspects of external policy. "Between April and August 1997, the Foreign Ministry, the Ministry of the Interior, and the External Relations Department of the Central Committee began to wire the MND's ERD [Ministry of Defense's External Relations Department] into a fledgling process of coordination that involved more regular consultations."[142] Another example of coordination between military and economic policy was the suspension of negotiations concerning the visit of the American secretary of defense while the BTA negotiations with the United States were at a critical stage, presumably to allow for a total focus on the main priority of the moment, which Stern concludes was "an indication that the MND was prepared to live with the results of an interagency process that placed the military relationship in a larger context. and ultimately called for slow and deliberately small steps in military ties."[143] On the other hand, Stern cites examples "of the Defense Ministry's generally cloistered approach to foreign and defense policy issues" and the "habit of refraining from, or avoiding, interagency discussions with the Foreign Ministry," as well as occasions of "freelancing military diplomacy, without coordinating their positions or discussion the consequences of these actions with the Foreign Ministry."[144]

The most likely locus for grand strategy coordination would be, as it always has been, the politburo. Even here, the attempt to establish a minipolitburo (the standing committee of the politburo) in the late 1990s because the collective body was too unwieldy for this kind of detailed policy discussion was abandoned. Moreover, when the foreign minister is not a politburo member, the problems of high-level policy coordination increase. Stern notes some problems in military diplomacy with the United States in 1997 at a time when the new foreign minister, Nguyen Dy Nien, had just assumed the post and was not a member of the politburo, which, he concludes, "blunted the Foreign Ministry's ability to manage policy through a rudimentary interagency approach."[145]

Alternatively the secretariat, which handles the routine policy business of the party, might serve a coordinating function, but the extent to which "comprehensive security" has spilled over into a wide range of nonparty bureaucratic, technical, and even nonstate institutions makes this difficult. This leaves us with the question of whether or not there can be a "grand strategy" without an organizational locus for its formulation and implementation. The probable answer is, no.

Vietnam has adjusted to the end of two-worlds era, but with a domestic political system that is a remnant of that earlier era. The fact that there are still significant areas in which Vietnam's political system inhibits full cooperation with even its closest partners in ASEAN is a case in point. Recall the military spokesperson's plea when explaining Vietnam's first defense white paper; asked to provide details on Vietnam's military forces he replied, "allow me not to disclose these figures." When Vietnam first joined ASEAN, the founding members of that organization triumphantly insisted that it would be on the terms of the original club members. However, the expansion of ASEAN has led to a virtual two-tier organization, and raised questions about the cohesion of the organization and its future—especially in the light of the inexorable growth of Chinese power and development of other forums which dilute ASEAN's influence (ASEAN+3, for example).

Still, Vietnam has made an irreversible choice for deep integration into a one-world system. It is impossible not to wonder how long the tension between maintaining the old domestic institutions and power structure in the face of a profound socioeconomic transformation accelerated by this integration will last. As we have seen, the central axis of debate in Vietnamese politics has been the relative priorities to be given to regime preservation and avoiding falling further behind in a brutally competitive world, and the extent to which these two aims are in conflict. The old nationalist commitment to reform and deep integration, in the interest of seeking "wealth and power," has apparently won out over conservative resistance to any change that would risk the power and position of the current elite. But this story is not yet conclusively resolved.

We move to the final chapter, which will end where we started; with a question about whether or not there are parallel realities in Vietnam—Vietnam's own internal "two worlds." In the introduction, we noted the observation by journalist David Lamb that "if you took away the still-ruling Communist Party and discounted the perilous decade after the war, the Vietnam of today is not much different from the country U.S. policymakers wanted to create in the 1960s." But, of course, "taking away" the ruling Communist Party from the equation in the foreseeable future is highly unlikely. As Lamb implies, the extraordinary thing is that Vietnam has changed as much as it has while maintaining its authoritarian political system, created in a different era and for purposes quite different from the current challenges facing it. The final task of this study is to examine the issue of whether a changing society and an unchanging political system can coexist over the long haul. If, in fact, the party has been the primary engineer of Vietnam's remarkable transformation, and has learned to reinvent its methods and mission, the answer is yes. If, on the other hand, the transformation has taken place not because of the party but in spite of it, the answer might be different. A third possibility is that the party and the society it rules can coexist in parallel universes in which each "does its own thing." It is to this issue we finally turn.

9

Rhetoric and Reality

THIS BOOK HAS been a study of collective idea change. It has attempted to document, analyze, and explain significant shifts in the thinking of the Vietnamese political elite about key issues concerning national security and external policy in Vietnam. But, of course, there are inherent pitfalls in this kind of study. First is the issue of whether the statements on which much of the analysis rests reflect sincerely held convictions or are mere official rhetoric; do they mean what they say? Second is the question of whether or not these statements are expressions of a true change of mind on these important matters of paramount concern to the political elite, or whether they are after-the-fact rationalizations of policy shifts forced on them by the compulsion of changing circumstances: did changing ideas produce changes in behavior or merely reflect them? Did they learn, or merely adapt?

These are complex questions, and probably ones that cannot be definitively answered, although we will try to see what the evidence produced in this study can tell us about them. But perhaps the most difficult issue is the one that will occupy the bulk of this concluding chapter; does the rhetoric have any relationship at all with reality? Are we merely studying a solipsistic community divorced from the larger reality, the larger world, or even its own society? Do the ideology and political rhetoric really matter when it comes down to explaining actual policy and behavior? Does the party do its thing while the rest of society simply goes about its business? Is there a direct relationship between public writing and oral declarations about policy and the policy itself, especially in sensitive areas of foreign affairs and security?

Before addressing this question in detail, and attempting to answer the two preceding questions, let me repeat a point made in the introduction. External affairs and national security issues are different than other political matters in that they are by definition largely the province of the governing authority, the political elites of a society. Unlike, say, economics, which may be determined by spontaneous or structural forces from below, external and security issues are largely decided at the top. In the case of culture, creative artists can ignore or circumvent the attempts of the party and state to control their work in a variety of ways. Although the state can deny a film studio to a director or a theater to a playwright (see the wonderful movie about artistic life and repression in Cold War East Germany, *The Lives of Others*), it cannot deny a canvas to a painter or a piece of paper and a desk drawer to a poet, who can bring their creative imaginings to life even if denied a gallery in which to display or a journal in which to publish. But external relations must go on largely through the institutions of the state, and there has to be a policy to guide these interactions which must also be determined by the state, even in an age of globalization and increasingly transnational ties (in which one of the actors is not a state). Second, it is marginally easier to establish a connection between ideas and policy, and policy and behavior, in the area of security and diplomacy than in most other areas of governance.

One reason it is important to understand collective idea-change in Vietnam is that as the founding generation of revolutionary leaders and their immediate successors leave the scene, politics is less driven by individuals or small-group dynamics, and more by the system itself. In the days of Le Duan and Le Duc Tho in the 1970s and early 1980s, a handful of leaders could dictate ideological orthodoxy, changing it according to convenience and interpreting events to suit their political interests and bolster their power. The post–Cold War Vietnamese system is based on a larger and more consensual sphere of ideas among the political elite. As one observer points out, "Individuals don't move the system in this country' . . . The leaders may change in coming days, he said, but in terms of policy, 'I would expect it to be difficult to spot the difference.'"[1] For this reason, it is important to determine the expanding boundaries of the mental horizons of the political elite, as well as the changing center of gravity.

The repudiation of the old model of central planning and the subsidy system was a shock to the ideational system of the party faithful, and opened the way for further questioning of the idea of a party monopoly of the truth, in turn paving the way for more emphasis on empirical facts, rational persuasion, performance legitimacy, international standards of theoretical reasoning, and less reliance on ideological formulas. The role played by Le Duan and Le Duc Tho in clamping down a coercive lid on any challenge to the old ways of doing things had demonstrably catastrophic results, and paved the way for more reasoned debate. One of the most important legacies of the Le Duan–Le Duc Tho attempts to control opinion by threats and coercion is that the clear negative results have inhibited their successors from doing the same, and this was crucial in opening up intra-elite discussions.

The experience of the 1980s also showed that political power could not bend reality to its will. The negative terms "subjectivism" (*chu quan*) and "acting arbitrarily" or "only according to one's will" (*duy y chi*) became staples of *doi moi* criticism of what had gone before. Policy debate from that time forward increasingly featured rational persuasion, even though this was often constrained by the partial success of the conservatives in placing ideological limits on debate. We have seen the disdain expressed by Prime Minister Vo Van Kiet and others for the ideologists' argument of last resort, the claim that some policy was a "deviation" (*chech huong*) from Marxism, when reason and facts failed to persuade.

The pragmatism characteristic of Deng Xiaoping in China began to be reflected in Vietnamese approaches to policy, especially after the final collapse of the Soviet Union. For all his faults, Do Muoi was a key transitional figure in the evolution of policy debate from fiat imposed by the top to persuasion of key interest and opinion groups. The very immobilism for which he was criticized showed that he was unwilling (or unable) to ram through conservative policies which did not command consensus support. Moreover, the policy stalemate was produced by policy pluralism; there was a mix of reform and conservative approaches, which meant that reform was still alive, if not thriving. The conservatives could slow but not stop the momentum of reform. The fact that persuasion was necessary is, in itself, an indication of the change in the nature of the political elite as the circle whose ideas and opinions affect policy expands. In this sense, the "uncertain transition" of the 1990s was not entirely time wasted, but was a slow-motion gathering of forces for the next stage of reform, deep integration ("taking the plunge").

The year 2000 and the decision to "take the plunge" into deep international integration was another turning point. This seems to be the juncture at which the rearguard actions of the conservatives lost their efficacy and their de facto veto of extensive reform measures no longer worked. Ominous insinuations about "deviationism" and "peaceful evolution" seemed to lose their power to produce a political stalemate by preventing decisive movement toward deep integration. We have argued that, as Legro's model would predict, this was largely a question of discrediting alternatives, as the conservatives were unable to produce a persuasive answer to the question of how else Vietnam might accelerate its economic development, and the specter of contamination and subversion from the outside overwhelming Vietnam as it opened up lost its potency.

INCREASING COMPLEXITY OF INTRA-ELITE DISCOURSE

The pioneers in pushing out the boundaries of political discourse within the elite in Vietnam were the extraordinary few who, while having served the regime with distinction, were distressed at its inadequacies and wanted to save it from itself. Although some of these held positions at the highest levels, most, like Nguyen Van Linh, were too committed to the tradition of discouraging, marginalizing, or punishing dissent to go public.

Indeed, Linh quietly resigned his position in the politburo in 1982 rather than push his case. And, as events of 1989 showed, there were clear limits to how far Linh was inclined to stray from orthodoxy in matters other than economics. He did not, in fact, become "Vietnam's Gorbachev."

For others, with deeper reservations about the party's direction, the harsh repression of Hoang Minh Chinh, former director of the Nguyen Ai Quoc Higher Party School, for allegedly being "revisionist" (pro-Soviet) and involved in conspiracy, was a warning not to rock the boat. If even this orthodox Marxist could be jailed, who could think of posing challenging questions to the party leadership?

We have discussed the new elements of policy debate or contestation that appeared in the late 1970s and early 1980s. Fence-breaking was one. The various research task forces reporting to different leaders were a form of policy development and innovation outside the formal organizational structures of the party and state. The growing challenges to orthodoxy, first by people on the margins of the mainstream like Phan Dinh Dieu, and then increasingly within the mainstream itself, pushed the envelope of concepts and issues that were "on the table." This very expression began to appear in elite discourse, indicating that fundamental issues, which were once taken for granted or too sensitive to discuss, were now on the agenda and open to discussion.

A contributing factor to the erosion of the veto power of the conservatives was the increasing complexity of intra-elite discourse. In addition to the growth in the size and change in composition of the political elite, more channels of formal and informal internal communication and contacts with the outside world clearly had an impact on expanding the range of acceptable policy options and alternatives in collective discussion, of drawing new parameters of "acceptable" discourse, and influencing the political agenda.

IMPACT OF THE INTERNET ON POLITICAL COMMUNICATION

Although documenting the full impact of the internet on Vietnamese elite politics is beyond the scope of this study, it is central to understanding important changes in the flow of ideas in Vietnam. One crucial consequence of the internet explosion is that it provided an alternative channel for the communication of ideas of great political sensitivity, as can be seen by the proliferation of nonauthorized documents used in this study. To cite a few: the memoirs of Deputy Foreign Minister Tran Quang Co, the memoir and letters of Tran Do, and various other letters to the politburo and key party authorities by other important political figures demanding redress for various political grievances tolerated or overlooked by the top party leaders; the policy-focused critiques of Vo Van Kiet (his letters to the politburo in 1995 and 2005) which illustrate a felt need to develop alternative means of communication when party ears are closed at the top, or when channels of communication at the highest level are restricted; Le Dang Doanh's confidential briefing to the politburo widely circulated on the internet; and evidence of internal party discord (the T-2 affair), which once would have been restricted to furtive word–of-mouth transmission among a very closed circle within the elite.

David Marr has carefully traced the interaction between control of intellectual discourse and the development of technology that made this control more difficult, in an informative and insightful book chapter titled "A Passion for Modernity: Intellectuals and the Media." He cites Truong Chinh's seminal July 1948 speech on Marxism and Vietnamese culture as an event that "established boundaries on intellectual activity that the party has continued to demand to the present day [2003]. The ultimate arbiter of truth and beauty were the masses as represented by the party."[2]

"On the eve of reform," some voices began to call for expanding the boundaries of political discussion—but within strict limits. Nguyen Khac Vien, the editor of a series of studies translated into foreign languages and designed to present Vietnam's wartime society and policies in a favorable light to an international audience, called in 1980 for a reduction in political control of the dissemination of information. "When summarizing his argument, Dr. Vien included a diagram that predictably placed the (party) leadership at the center, but then proceeded to draw a direct link between the 'scientific community' and the media. He urged increased grassroots discussion in the media of current policies and performance including opinions contrary to official statements. He especially asked that surveys conducted by social scientists that produced unpleasant results not be restricted to a tiny official audience. Nevertheless, Dr. Vien still felt it necessary to draw a double line on his diagram that separated all intra-elite communication from the profusion of complex, contradictory data arriving from both within Vietnamese society and from the world outside."[3]

Marr's authoritative account of the impact of technology on intra-elite discussion and dissemination of information analyzes the influence of the introduction of the photocopier, the fax machine, and the internet. "During the 1990s, Vietnam experienced a revolution in communications technology which made it possible for intellectuals and others to exchange information as never before."[4] Even media more easily controlled by the government, such as newspapers and television, opened up significantly in the 1990s and after.[5]

Early government attempts to control the internet were soon swamped by technological innovation and the proliferation of access points. By 2007, ten years after the internet had been introduced to Vietnam, nearly 20 percent of Vietnamese had regular access and the target usage rate for 2010 was set by the government at 25–30 percent.[6] In Hanoi, 39 percent of the population used the internet in 2007 (60 percent of these were in the 18–30 age group), and in Ho Chi Minh city the figure was 32 percent.[7]

The limitations of the internet as a communications vehicle for dissident voices in Vietnam are still evident, however. The 2007 arrest of Tran Khai Thanh Thuy, an award-winning journalist and writer, was a clear attempt by the government to combat the use of the internet to circulate ideas that the regime felt challenged its legitimacy and authority. Thuy had posted a number of internet essays calling for greater democracy. As a teacher, novelist, and publisher of a clandestine dissident internet journal, Thuy was a marginal member of the political elite, and had no political protection. Even the eminent Tran Do was purged, although in his case it was for what he said more than the channels through which he communicated. Although some internet communications by members of the elite were pushing the limits of the acceptable, Tran Do was clearly "off the reservation."

Although most of the internet communications by dissident voices in Vietnam relate to demands for more democracy or greater respect for human rights, there have also been some nationalistic postings with national security implications. The most famous case in this regard is that of a computer instructor and cyber dissident Le Chi Quang, who was jailed for four years in 2002 for "posting articles criticising land and sea border agreements forged between Vietnam and China in 1999 and 2000."[8] He had accused the Vietnamese authorities of making territorial concessions to China. Compounding his attacks on the government in a sensitive national-security area, Quang "had also come out in favour of more democracy and incurred the wrath of the authorities for posting articles praising well-known dissidents Nguyen Thanh Giang and Vu Cao. His arrest was part of an ongoing crackdown against intellectuals and dissidents who use the web to circulate news or opinion banned from the tightly-controlled state press."

Of course the government is also aware of the powerful potential of the internet as a means of political communication, and has taken tentative steps to utilize it. At about the same time Quang was being imprisoned for circulating attacks on the government's border agreements with China, the head of the Party Central Commission for Ideology and Culture acknowledged that the internet would be an important vehicle of communication for the party and government. "'The Internet and e-newspapers have had a major impact and proven themselves to be one of the most effective means for disseminating the party's guidelines and the government's policies,' stressed Nguyen Khoa Diem, who is a politburo member and secretary of the Communist Party of Vietnam Central Committee. Diem also described them as a bridge to send news and information from the country to more than two million overseas Vietnamese."[9]

Subsequently, the party began to experiment with the internet as a form of direct leader-to-people political communication. Vietnam's prime minister, Nguyen Tan Dung, "held an unprecedented online chat with citizens Friday, engaging in a frank—but filtered—discussion on topics ranging from corruption to personal advice. During a wide-ranging, three-hour event, Dung defended the state's control of the media, told personal stories of his experiences as a Viet Cong soldier fighting against Americans in the Vietnam War and promised to crack down on rampant corruption.[. . .] Dung, 57, is the highest-ranking government leader to participate in the new online outreach programme by the Communist Party, which outlaws all opposition, in the nation of 84 million people."[10]

The striking aspect of this kind of direct political communication is that it is an implicit admission of the defects within the party and the unreliability of some of its members, which makes the former top-to-bottom hierarchical information- and opinion-delivery systems unsuitable for communications in which the top leadership has to address the deficiencies of those at lower levels and/or pin the blame for problems on them. And, if the middle- and lower-level cadres were the problem in cases of corruption and abuse of power, they clearly would obstruct the political feedback process for which they were the gatekeepers. Moreover, the internet seemed to open the floodgates for voicing of opinions and grievances—some 20,000 questions were submitted to the prime minister in his first internet "chat."[11] In focusing on individual leaders, this form of communication also undermines the carefully crafted image of the party as a monolithic collectivity, which was an essential ingredient of its claim to infallibility. An individual leader might be wrong, but not the "collectivity." On the other hand, the use of the internet and other media may be a device to raise the profile and prestige of the relatively anonymous and uncharismatic current group of leaders.

The internet also spreads political discussion beyond the inner party–state elite policy process and constitutes an added dimension of elite discourse—a triangle consisting of leader communicating directly with ordinary people, with the elite listening in to pick up cues. This is an extension of the traditional practice of the party and state cadres attentively following speeches and proclamations by leaders, with the new twist that it also contains feedback information from below. Party and state cadres can also learn what issues are being brought to the attention of people at the top. And, of course, the internet is a double-edged sword; it is useful for disseminating official messages, but difficult to control, as the lively non-sanctioned and forbidden internet discussion of Vietnamese political topics amply demonstrates.

To some extent this feedback device is an application of new technology to an old concern—identifying problems before they can fester and get out hand. In the early reform period it was "suggestion boxes" placed in public locations.[12] Now it is the internet. Dao Duy Quat, newly appointed founding editor of the party electronic journal and deputy head of the party Commission on Ideology and Culture, described the feedback function of internet communication between party and people as follows: "Through this channel of dialogue, the leadership at each level of the Party and the State can directly hear the voice, the aspirations, and the things that aggravate [*nhung buc xuc*] the people. This will help them understand and supplement the policies and directly lead to the resolution of the things that crop up and create aggravation in society. For this reason, and in the capacity of the organ of opinion of the Central Committee, and with the responsibility and mission of an electronic newspaper, I have proposed to open a channel of dialogue."[13]

The internet is essentially a young persons' medium. "About 86 percent of respondents in the 15–19 age group were comfortable surfing the net, while the 20–24 age group recorded at 74 percent proficiency. Overall, only 45 percent of respondents could surf the web." This is especially significant because of Vietnam's demographics; in 2006, a study found that "69 percent of Viet Nam's population is below the age of 35 with slightly more than half under 25."[14]

However, some of the most dramatic uses of the internet for intra-elite dialogue have come from elderly, retired revolutionary veterans, who are politically protected by their venerable status in the party and by powerful internal party networks. We have already seen illustrations of top-level party debate or discourse through the internet, but the example of one response to a memoir, which the party tried to suppress because it attacked the record of former General Secretary Do Muoi, is especially interesting. It attempted to define some forms of internet political communications, such as memoirs, as a form of protected speech, since they are similar to the authentic and unfiltered voice of mass opinion in traditional orally transmitted communication. In a letter to the politburo and other leading party organs, veteran revolutionary Le Tien defended the memoir of former deputy prime minister Doan Duy Thanh, which contained criticisms of former party leader Do Muoi. He appealed to international standards of conduct: "From ancient times to present in the world no one has forced, and could not possibly force anyone to write a memoir according to the dictates of some power holder, and also cannot arrest a person who has written a memoir under color of whatever authority."[15]

Le Tien also played to the party's longstanding praise for and promotion of "folk" or "popular" literature (*van hoc dan gian*) as an authentic expression of the wisdom of "the people," and argued that writing memoirs did not violate the law because it was not like a formal published document (which implicitly *were* legitimate targets of party censorship) but rather the modern-day version of "orally transmitted literature." He argued that the internet was only a delivery system for what remained a form of authentic popular expression. Le Tien argued that censorship of popular modes of communication was a throwback to the oppression of the feudal state, rather than a hallmark of modernity. "In world history, as well as that of our country, there have never been penalties imposed on various types of popular literature even though those in power in the old days didn't like it."[16]

Le Tien asserted that the character flaws of individual leaders were in the public domain and fair game for open discussion and, moreover, that discussion was an essential source of feedback learning for the party. His promotion of informal channels of discourse was also an implicit defense of the uncensored use of the internet for intra-elite dialogue. "The ideas of those who have retired, of citizens who are not in the machinery of public office, are the reflections of society, and people holding power should carefully listen to them to adjust the way they administer the country, a society that the more modern it becomes the more it needs to encourage all elements of civilian society to participate in administering society and, by carefully listening to their ideas, revise one's own policies." Tien asserted that "The thoughts of people who write memoirs, as well as the thoughts of other people who no longer hold power, in their capacity as citizens, are essential information for the ruling authorities."[17] Although this argument seems aimed at protecting retired members of the political class—retired cadres—it expands the arena of political discussion beyond the circle of currently serving officials and party members and opens the door to opinions expressed by people no longer held in check by organizational discipline.

The combination of the internet and the growing political complexity of the elite produced an expanded virtual political community, which paralleled the official organizational machinery of the party. The internet allowed the circulation of unauthorized memoirs, which constituted part of the political struggle within the elite. Examples are Doan Duy Thanh attacking Do Muoi, and Tran Quynh defending the legacy of Le Duan. Petitions defending a Doan Duy Thanh or Nguyen Nam Khanh or attacking a Le Duc Anh were certainly weapons in the party's internal jockeying among patron–client networks. It also offered the very large and significant group of retired high party cadres continued participation in the party's politics, polemics, and policy debates, forming an enlarged virtual political community along with the active members of the elite. The senior retired cadres also enjoy a form of protected speech because of their revolutionary credentials and because they cannot be threatened with removal from office, and this contributes to opening up the range of views expressed within this virtual community.

THE SPREAD OF OPEN DEBATE

Eventually, even the authorized press featured real clashes of opinion about sensitive issues, illustrated by the reactions to the attempts of some retired conservative ideologues like former politburo member Nguyen Duc Binh to turn back the clock in the lead up to the Tenth Party Congress. Indeed, one of Binh's main concerns was that by soliciting public comment on the draft political report of the Tenth Party Congress, the party itself had opened the door to general discussion of once sacrosanct issues, which in the past were discussed guardedly and behind closed doors.

We will discuss the controversy ignited by Binh in more detail in a subsequent section. But one of his clear concerns was that the growing diversity of views openly expressed within the party was not only detracting from the party's prestige and authority in society at large, but would lead to the collapse of the party itself if not checked. His conclusion about the main reason for the collapse of communism in the Soviet Union was the loss of confidence and belief at the highest levels of the party, which then spread to the rank and file. "The lack of unanimity [*nhat tri*] in the party at present is mainly in the area of awareness [*nhan thuc*, as in political awareness = *nhan thuc chinh tri*]. Since it is a matter of awareness, it must be resolved by awareness, by exchanges of views, discussions, and frank debates in the spirit of comradeship. If you want to do this, you must directly put the issues on which there are divergent opinions on the table, above all the following key issues . . ."[18] We will discuss the specific hot-button issues below.

Fearing that such inner party debate might erode the party's authority if it was visible to the outside, Nguyen Duc Binh proposed to hold these discussions closely within the confines of the party. To overcome the party's reluctance to confront fundamental questions of ideology, Binh proposed that "the Central Committee set up an internal publication, with restricted circulation within the party. It could be called 'Controversies' [*tranh luan* = debates], and would publish articles with differing viewpoints, but would not publish them openly. To guarantee tight control, it could be stipulated, in the statement of principles about the objectives of the publication, that none of the articles would be permitted to attack Marxism-Leninism, Ho Chi Minh thought, or the political line and basic path of the party, although there could be permission granted in special cases to critique this or that concrete viewpoint, or this or that specific policy approach [*chu truong*], but not the basic party line or fundamental principles. The time is ripe for putting out a publication like 'Controversies' because the public or semipublic [*cong khai hay nua cong khai*] differences of views within the party expressed by a spokesperson or distributing documents is very damaging and has created serious discord and division within the Party and society."[19]

Perhaps heeding Nguyen Duc Binh's advice to publish journals of facts and theoretical debates that were more tightly restricted to the party inner circle, at a time when the party has decided to give its main theoretical journal wide internet circulation, several new publications were launched. "Thus as of the beginning of 2007, *Tap chi Cong san* will have four publications; *Tap chi Cong san* (concerning theory and politics as before, appearing once a month); *Tap chi Cong san Chuyen de co so* [basic specialized topics] (once a month); the specialized journal *Ho so su kien* [Digest of events] (twice a month), and *Tap chi Cong san Dien tu* [Electronic communist review] (twice a month)."[20] If this does, in fact, represent an attempt to maintain an enclosed inner "world of the party," even as the party reaches out to the rest of world with the internet version of its theoretical journal, it would appear to contribute to a schizophrenic approach toward reality, with an opening to the outside world (deep integration), but a simultaneous retreat into an interior world decoupled from the larger context in which it operates.

Clearly what upset conservatives like Nguyen Duc Binh has been the failure of the top party leadership to crack down on internal party debate and its spillover into the public realm. As we shall see, he wanted to draw a sharp line between orthodoxy and deviation largely on the basis of reviving the pre-*doi moi* precepts that constituted the "party line" when it really was a literal "line" drawn between orthodoxy and deviation. Almost as aggravating to him was the open discussion in the newspapers, in letters expressing individual opinions on various aspects of the draft political report of the Tenth Party Congress, that had been encouraged by the party leadership. In Binh's views, these things were best handled out of public view and kept within a closed circle. The leakage of leadership controversies in letters circulated on the internet was clearly beyond the pale, by his standards. Ironically, Binh's article was publicly disseminated in the pages of *Nhan Dan* and incited scathing public replies published in more liberal outlets like *Tuoi Tre* (see below).

In terms of keeping debate on sensitive political and social issues within the closed circle of the party, the horse had long ago left the barn. The economic debate that led to *doi moi* raised some of the most fundamental questions about the nature of socialism and the direction in which the party was leading Vietnam. Along with increasingly complex and intractable problems came increasing diversity of views within the party.

Intra-elite discourse was further complicated by the increasing role of specialists in policy questions, especially in the area of economics, where their views on matters like markets often entered terrain previously reserved for party theoreticians and ideologues, but also in many other areas related to Vietnam's development as a modern society. As Vietnam realized that it could not successfully develop in isolation, it opened up and invited the participation of international specialists and organizations to help identify and resolve development problems. The fact that the many in the Vietnamese elite increasingly saw themselves as part of a wider "epistemic community" was an inevitable by-product of opening up (as the purveyors of "peaceful evolution" feared) but was increasingly accepted as a positive aspect of Vietnam's integration into the larger world, and acceptance as a member in good standing of the international community.

FACING THE FACTS

The growing sense of conflict between rhetoric and reality in the 1980s prompted the party leadership to proclaim at the Sixth Party Congress of 1986 that the time had come to face facts. "In the new international and domestic setting, the Sixth Party Congress of 1986, in the spirit of '*looking squarely at the truth, correctly evaluating the truth, clearly stating the truth*,' reassessed the country's situation in strict fashion, and clearly stated the accomplishments and failings, clearly pointed out the shortcomings in strategic guidance, in organizing implementation, in order to set out a comprehensive renovation program for the country."[21]

Much of the following discussion relates to the relationship between the party and the larger society in domestic matters. With the exception of some nationalistic issues such as the question of whether Vietnam's leaders had made excessive concessions to China in border negotiations, most of the concerns of the Vietnamese public have to do with local issues. There are two large exceptions to this generalization, however. One is the pervasive corruption within the system. To the extent that it negatively affects public support for the party and the regime, it makes "performance legitimacy," or "delivering the goods" all the more important.

This puts a premium on the second major issue: success in economic development, which in turn is significantly affected by external policy. The most pressing concern of the vast majority of Vietnamese citizens is having the opportunity to live a comfortable and fulfilling life. To the extent that this depends on how well the party and government seize the opportunities of globalization and minimize its negative consequences to "catch up" with the rest of the world, domestic welfare and external affairs are closely linked, and of direct concern to the "people" and the "masses." In this sense, both Party leaders and ordinary citizens confront the same reality—a world increasingly shaped by external forces that have a powerful domestic impact and cannot be arbitrarily resisted or ignored.

We noted in chapter 5 ("Wary Conciliation") the Chinese use of the phrase "world of the party," which, applied to the Vietnamese context, usefully describes the conviction of the top leaders that they could shape reality outside their "world" to conform to the visions and desires of those who lived inside the charmed circle of party leaders. This was reinforced by the conviction of conservative party members and leaders that definition and interpretation of reality could only be done by the party and within the party, which meant that inconvenient realities could be downplayed, ignored, or contextualized to make them more palatable. The corollary of this is the conviction that ordinary citizens either do not grasp the real situation, or the "big picture," and have to rely on higher authority to fill them in (and thus they will accept the party's view of reality), or they can't be trusted to deal with reality (as Jack Nicholson's character proclaims in the film *A Few Good Men*, "you can't handle the truth!").

It was often the case that the top party leaders were more shielded from reality than was society at large. But the more the top party leaders were directly exposed to these external realities, the more difficult it was to cling to their imagined visions of the world beyond the corridors of power. An illustration of the insular world of the leadership in the period before *doi moi* is Truong Chinh's shock when he made an on-the-spot visit to the South in 1983 and said, "It turns out that everything that we have been told in Hanoi is completely wrong."[22] This started a series of reality checks that led to the reforms.

The international-relations counterpart of this emergence from the closed world of the top party leadership was the series of visits made to southeast Asia by top leaders in the early and mid-1990s, after the collapse of the Soviet Union, which gave some of them their first direct glimpse of the "other" world. The outreach of top leaders that was part of the reconciliation process also helped to defuse some of the more extreme paranoid convictions of the party leaders that had long been reinforced by isolation and secrecy.

The origins of the tendency to let ideology reshape reality was noted by Tran Bach Dang, as cited in chapter 3 ("The Year of Living Dangerously"): "The reality of Vietnam after the revolution is different from what I imagined when I joined the party.... Life has shown us that it is much more complicated. The thing is, we received Marxism in a theoretical sense, not in a full sense, and the information was not very precise. Marxism came to Vietnam through the interpretation of Stalin and Mao Zedong. It was simplified to a great extent. And now we read the classic works of Marx and other founders, and we find that things were not so simple. Though the social conditions under which Marx wrote his works are not the same as now, the principles are the same. Yet those principles were not interpreted precisely correctly."[23] It is certainly not coincidental that this kind of reevaluation of the party's approach to reality came in the late 1980s as the socialist world crumbled.

One of the rare high-level advisers who for several decades has specialized in telling truth to power is the reform economist Le Dang Doanh. His unvarnished advice was not always followed or appreciated, but in 2005 he was invited to give a wide-ranging briefing to the politburo as it prepared for the Tenth Party Congress. Inevitably a transcript of the briefing appeared on the internet. In this briefing Doanh said "We live in a world that is rapidly and fluidly changing. We have to truthfully report to you comrades about who our friends now are. When it comes down to it who can we cooperate with? And will it 'come down to it?' We say we are friends with everyone, well, is Mr. China a friend? Or does he plan to make mincemeat out of us [*lam thit*]? And if he makes mincemeat out of us he will bluntly say so, and won't be subtle [*nhe nhang*]. And in that case, who do we turn to? Mr. India is so good to us, but he is weak. If he's weak how can he help [though] he is very friendly. And as for Mr. United States, he is far away, and has never grabbed anyone's land. Moreover, the United States has a very different civilization from us, our economies are different, our way of thinking is different, so understanding each other is not easy. . . . For example, Taiwan has been very good toward the United States. And it must be said that Taiwan is a democratic regime with a developed technology, and many strong points—so who struck out at Taiwan the quickest? The United States, and no one else. Taiwan's Minister of Economics told me, our best friend is [ourselves] becoming much stronger." He went on to lay out what Vietnam would have to do to become stronger and more competitive in an unforgiving world and stressed the difficulty of this task.[24]

Doanh was criticized by some high party officials for his blunt talk and the fact that (without his knowledge or approval) a transcript taken from a hidden tape recorder was published on the internet. Hearing that Doanh was under attack, former prime minister Vo Van Kiet offered to step in, if needed. "Why didn't they listen to you?" he asked.[25] It seems that "facing the truth squarely" is still more prevalent in some corners of the leadership than in others.

In 2007, before an assembly of top leaders in the propaganda and ideological sectors of the party and leaders of the media, Secretary General Nong Duc Manh said, "I applaud the spirit of looking squarely at the truth that you comrades have shown, not only in correctly evaluating the accomplishments and strong points, but also in clearly pointing out and being strictly self critical about the shortcomings, deficiencies, and limitations in carrying out your tasks."[26] But the question, of course, is who decides what a "correct" evaluation is, and how do the propagandists and the ideologists reconcile the function of molding public opinion and the function of accurate reporting on the extent of the gap between the proscribed rhetoric and the reality?

PUBLIC OPINION AND THE PARTY

An example of the consequences of Vietnam's ideologists taking a fresh look at Marxist theory is the reevaluation of the role of public opinion in the formulation of party policy. For years the Vietnamese party had maintained that because it was the embodiment of the progressive elements in Vietnamese society and had an unerring inside track to the truth through mastery of Marxist-Leninist theory, its own assessment of public opinion was sufficient and authoritative and there was no need for such direct surveys of public attitudes as public opinion polls. Moreover, the fundamental assumption was that public opinion should reflect party policy, and not the other way around. To the extent that there was a gap between what the party wanted and what people actually thought, it was the job of the ideologists to mold opinion into the correct shape.

It was, in fact, policy failure and popular resistance to unworkable and unpopular measures that opened the way to a more systematic inquiry into popular opinion. In a book on the role of public opinion in *doi moi*, the authors ascribe some key policy shifts in agricultural reform to solicitous soundings of mass opinion. The term "the masses" (*quan chung*) is central to any discussion of public opinion, since it refers to ordinary, non-Party citizens, for whom the Party lays down the line. In theory, pioneered by the Chinese Communist Party, the political communication loop is "from the masses, to the masses."[27]

In practice, in Vietnam the communication was increasingly one way—top down. In his 2005 letter to the politburo, Vo Van Kiet pointed to the dangers of "standing above the people." "When we had not yet attained state power, the party had only one single point of support, which was the supporters from the masses [*co so quan chung*]. If the party became distanced from the masses, it would not be protected and enveloped by them and would have been annihilated by the enemy. In the two resistance struggles, if the party had not mobilized the strength of the masses, it could not have played any role. When it became a party in power in peaceful construction, it became estranged from the people and standing above the people is the greatest danger for the party. Becoming distant from the people and standing above the people lead to dictatorship and arbitrary action and losing the confidence of the people. If you lose the confidence of the people, that point of support for the party, you are in danger of losing the party. Precisely for this reason it is necessary to determine clearly and transparently in the party regulations what the responsibility of a party member toward the people is in the sphere of their own operational responsibilities and personal activities."[28]

The passive "masses" have become the dialectical counterpart of the active "party," although this is usually obscured in official discussions of the subject. "Starting from the standpoint of the concept of the masses [*quan diem quan chung*], our party has always regarded public opinion of the masses as important, and has elevated the role of researching the inner thoughts [*tam trang*] and aspirations of the masses, seeing this as an important foundation for determining the policies and policy lines," wrote one party study of the subject. It singled out a number of market reform measures as policies which "stemmed from the practical experiences and from the desires of the people [*nhan dan*]." The study asserted that the party had, as the "mass line" requires taken these inchoate ideas and "proactively" (*chu dong*) translated them into policies that "accorded with the ideas of the party and the feelings of the people."[29]

In fact, in all of the cases cited (the market reforms in agriculture and industry), the policies had been forced on a reluctant party only in desperation and after orthodox measures had clearly failed. It was not so much a matter of the party proactively seeking out public opinion as it was adjusting to changes that had already taken place in society in defiance of party policy.

By the late 1990s, perhaps having learned from this experience, and in an effort to exert more control over spontaneous change by anticipating it and adjusting to it before being forced to do so by *faits accomplis*, the party had incorporated polling data into the policy process, and even validated this by going back to the classic Marxist-Leninist texts. "The task of researching social opinion has become an important element in the system of the party's ideological tasks, helping in grasping, analyzing, integrating, and forecasting the ideological, psychological situations, and aspirations of the masses in society. This helps the party committees in its ideological mission to issue appropriate measures toward each category of target in society."[30]

The theoretical justification for this can be found in several statements by Marx, Engels, and Lenin. "Engels himself wrote 'to have the possibility, at the least, of completing that reform [*cai tao*] there first of all has to be a major step forward in public opinion.'"[31] Of course, Engels was also scathingly critical of public opinion in a constitutional democratic context, and the references to Engels' views on the subject are consistent with past practices of selective quotations from the Marxist classics to support the preferred policy positions of the day.[32]

There are of some crucial areas of life in Vietnam in which the party implicitly acknowledges that it has to go outside the party structure to find out what the political reality is. The best example of this is the question of corruption among party cadres, which the party admits is serious and pervasive. Given this fact, it would be pointless to allow the members of the party machine to have the final say on what people think about their shortcomings, in effect issuing a report card on themselves.

Huu Tho, former editor of the party newspaper, *Nhan Dan*, and head of the party's Central Ideology–Culture Commission (Ban Tu Tuong–Van Hoa Trung Uong), wrote about the problems in controlling corruption. He noted that from 1997 to 1998 the percentage of people polled who thought that the party had been "passive and ineffective" in combating corruption rose from 62% to 72%. "Thus the confidence of the people in the leadership of the party and administrators of the State in anti-corruption is falling; that is the reality and the concern." From this, Huu Tho concludes that "Correctly evaluating the real situation (thuc trang) is a big issue."[33]

It is worth examining the assessments of the top party ideologists about their own views on how close a connection there is between rhetoric and reality in Vietnam. Huu Tho is a major figure in this regard as is the Central Ideology–Culture Commission which he once headed. Mark Sidel wrote in 1997 that "This party group, responsible for overseeing theoretical and cultural issues, is often considered a conservative voice on issues of interest in Vietnamese intellectual and cultural circles. The commission has been led since 1991 by Ha Dang, a relatively conservative official who previously headed the party newspaper *Nhan Dan* and who has had a long career in the party's ideology and cultural apparatus."[34]

The once imposing party newspaper *Nhan Dan*, which used to be faithfully read by the political class to pick up the cues necessary for political survival, is now considered to be dull, unreadable, and largely irrelevant even for the political elite, who prefer to read livelier and more informative papers. Before 1975, *Nhan Dan* often had revealing investigative articles which, within the confines of approved policy, often served as a reality check and feedback mechanism for the party leadership. Investigative journalism in recent times has migrated to other newspapers. As in the past, it rarely critiques the assumptions of policy, but focuses on problems of implementation and issues of incompetence and corruption. External affairs and security issues are still out of bounds for this kind of journalism, however.

It is difficult to assess the extent of the use of polling in Vietnam and its impact on the policy process. In addition to the examples just cited, there are scattered sources that would give us some insight on this subject, such as an opinion survey conducted by Dong Nai province concerning attitudes in the province about party and state activities during the year 2006. In this survey, 3,000 questionnaires were distributed and the response rate was 99.2 percent—which may tell us something about how authentic a public sample this was (nearly 44 percent of respondents were cadres and civil servants, and another 4.5 percent were military, while around 20 percent were peasants). It is also significant that opinion surveys are done by the propaganda section of the Province Party Committee, which is logical (they are entrusted with managing public opinion, among other things) but a conflict of interest, given their responsibility for ensuring that party policies are well understood and enthusiastically received.[35]

With a sample composition like this, we might term the poll a survey of the "attentive public." Still, surprisingly the data indicate that affairs of state are more politically salient than local politics; 93.3 percent paid attention to Vietnam's entry into the WTO and a similar percent followed the APEC conference in Vietnam, while around 57 percent paid attention to the meetings of the Province Party Committee and the People's Committee. The survey concludes that, "The great majority of people are proud and enthusiastic about the great affairs of state (84.9 percent) of which 35.1 percent are very enthusiastic and proud. There are still 22.4 percent who have reservations [*ban khoan*] or find it hard to give a response, and 9 percent feel it is "just all right" [*binh thuong*]." Given the inherent conflict of interest in party- and government-administered opinion polls, some citizens have called for the newspapers to take on this function.[36] Given the tight party control of the press, this seems unlikely, though the few bold and liberal newspapers like *Tuoi Tre* and *Tien Phong* have significantly expanded the range of public information and expression of opinion.

Articles by party leaders now routinely use the slogan of the 1986 Sixth Party Congress, "face the truth squarely."[37] It seems clear that the party leadership is far less insulated from reality than it was during its prereform style of having the top officials screened off from society and the world in secretive and insulated bubble. The decision of the prime minister to submit to responding to direct questions from ordinary people—screened though they were by a platoon of aides and technicians and filtered through an impersonal medium—was a symbolic recognition of the need for a closer link between the top of the party and reality at the ground level.

EROSION OF THE OLD THINKING

Chapter 2 ("On the Eve of Reform") attempted to document the beginning of the erosion of the old thinking. Perhaps the most succinct summation of the process was by the economic historian Dang Phong. "The breakouts in Vietnam were special because they didn't directly 'declare war' on the politics and programs, but usually went abut it with delicacy and indirection. If the policies were like ancient walls of a fortress, the breakout assaults did not use heavy artillery but only cuts with a knife, and were done like the trowel of a mason removing the mortar between bricks on a wall. At some point the knife cuts and the trowel could bring down an entire wall without breaking things or shaking the earth. It was even possible to salvage many of the materials to use for new projects."[38]

An example of building a new conceptual structure from old materials is the 1988 analysis of Phan Dinh Dieu, discussed in chapter 2. Another is the "new thinking" of Bui Tin in 1990, discussed in chapter 4 ("Changing Partners"). Yet another is the analysis of Nguyen Co Thach in 1995 (chapter 5, "Wary Reconciliation") of the implications of the global upheavals, using familiar tropes to arrive at an unfamiliar conclusion. But, of course, in the process of this selective rearrangement of concepts, significant portions of "old thinking" are omitted or rejected or, in some cases, recontextualized in a way that fundamentally changes the meaning of the familiar terms and concepts.

In a 1996 interview, Prime Minister Vo Van Kiet was asked the following rhetorical question: "In the process of seeking out the new, were there any times during which there was a relapse into the old way of thinking [*nhan thuc*]?" His reply was that "When moving from the old to the new, at every level there is a process of intermingling between old and new. For example, at the beginning it could be that surrounding our *doi moi* effort, the struggle between new and old was rather strong. Once your thoughts have fallen into a familiar pattern [*suy nghi thanh thoi quen*], changing them is not easy. Even when *doi moi* had achieved great success, at the same time it had not yet been perfected, the market system manifested not a few problems, which stemmed from its very nature. As a former colony, we had escaped from a society that was run completely on the lines of a market system, and now we are following a socialist economy based on a regime of a directed market system [*co che thi truong co dinh huong*], which we can influence [*co tac dong cua chung ta*] to follow our objectives. The market economy is a product of humanity, but the double-edged nature of it depends on the political system of each country; if you simply let it happen [*buong long*] the damaging side will predominate, if you figure rationally and appropriately the benefit side will predominate." As in many other statements, Kiet warned about the dangers of being hasty and acting according to one's own impulses.[39] The implication is that the solution of the struggle between old and new is a compromise that salvages enough of the old to make the new acceptable and manageable. A deeper implication is that if practical measures can be dressed up enough to be retrofitted into the old ideological framework, without impeding the policy, then this is a way to get consensus on extensive reform.

One of the most interesting contrasts between a lapsed believer who rejected the entire package of the old belief system, and a guardian of the true faith who had made tactical adjustments to salvage it, is a dialogue between Mai Chi Tho and a veteran revolutionary and former comrade–in-arms who had shared a bunker with Tho during some of the fiercest fighting of the Vietnam War. Tho tells the story of his conversations with "Mr. X" during the period (1987–1991) Tho was minister of interior (later minister of public security). Calling him "Mr." (*ong*) indicates that he was no longer in the party—in which case he would have been called "comrade"—and that he had either been purged or had left the party, since it is highly unlikely that someone that close to Mai Chi Tho would not have been a party member at one time. Mr. X did "not accept the viewpoint and line of the party. Although the public security branch had taken measures [*xu ly*], given reminders, and restricted his contacts, this person still did not give in. It appears as though this was not a personal grievance but was a problem [*thac mac*] he had with the party authorities in power."

Tho summoned his disaffected former colleague, now under house arrest in a village on the outskirts of Saigon with a "breeze and a river view," to his Ho Chi Minh City office. Tho offered a "compact": if his old comrade in arms could convince Tho he was right, he would become a convert to his views, but if Tho was able to offer convincing support for his view, then the dissident would have to fall in line. In Tho's account of this exchange, X argued that he deserved his day in court (literally: he was demanding an open legal trial) to defend his views, which were (in Tho's words) that capitalism was right and Vietnam should take the capitalist path. Socialism was wrong, evidenced by the collapse of the Soviet Union and Eastern European communist countries, couldn't be achieved, and forcing the people down that path would lead the country onto a road of misery.[40]

Mai Chi Tho was especially perplexed because this showed that a veteran revolutionary did not accept Vietnam's *doi moi* as an effective or adequate response to the collapse of the Soviet Union. "This time was a period in which there were many strange and pessimistic viewpoints emerging because of the crisis in the socialist camp," said Tho, who countered that the collapse of the Soviet Union was the result of its specific failings, and did not show that the theory of communism was bankrupt. Mr. X was not convinced and pointed to the lack of democracy in Vietnam and the technological achievements of capitalism. Tho responded with an impassioned defense of the role played by communism in liberating oppressed people, in an attempt to elicit old memories of the revolutionary struggle and appeal to the patriotism of Mr. X. Tho also maintained that capitalism had not changed its stripes, and was still fundamentally exploitative.

The argument went on for three days. "Mr X brought out all his bookish theories. The two old friends standing on opposite sides of the ideological battlefront spoke to each other a great deal about theory. After this matter, Nam Xuan [Mai Chi Tho] thought: 'The reason this old friend is still stubbornly resistant, is that we committed errors in practice, absolutizing class character' [*tuyet doi hoa giai cap tinh*]." Tho acknowledged that people were complex, and could not be reduced to one element. There were considerations of individual personality, national characteristics, regional characteristics, occupational characteristics, gender, traditions to be considered as well, "but we only absolutized class character." This was not the fault of Marx or Marxism but of Vietnam's application and understanding of it.[41]

None of this persuaded Mr. X. "There was no 'sudden breakthrough' [*dot bien*] in Mr. X's understanding, but in the end he ran out of arguments and was silent." Tho told Mr. X that it would do no good to go to court. For one thing, Mr. X had broken a lot of laws, and this would all be held against him. Second, although this did not cross over completely into an issue of the "enemy versus us," it was bordering on it [*map me*], and he could easily be exploited. Taking this to court would have foreign journalists poking around and people trying to incite him. "It would create complicated state of opinion in the party and among the people."[42]

Tho proposed to let the matter drop, and that is apparently what happened. Mr. X "was representative of a class of people. The number of people who thought like him was not small. Now, it can be said that there are still people who think like that, but they don't say so out loud."[43] Was this a continuation of the "terrifying silence" that Nguyen Van Linh spoke of in the 1980s? Possibly, but it could have also indicated indifference more than fear or silent resistance. Indifference is, in the end, probably an even greater threat to the maintenance of the old belief system.

A few bold innovators and critics did have the courage to "say so out loud" and would not be relegated to silence. Revealing that the "emperor has no clothes" is shocking but, once accomplished, creates a new base line of acknowledged reality that cannot be rolled back. The prime example is Phan Dinh Dieu, with his electrifying call for the resignation of party leader Le Duan, whose failings as a leader after 1975 were later generally acknowledged within the party, and his bold 1988 article pointing to a different future for Vietnam than the one envisaged by the party at that time. By 1991, elite opinion was beginning to catch up with Dieu, but most were not yet ready to "come out" with their "new thinking." As noted earlier, a group of prominent academics and institute leaders was summoned to a conference in preparation for the 1991 Seventh Party Congress. Dieu repeated what he had been saying for some time, with no evident impact. Finally, the head of the Social Sciences Institute commented that "we all agree with what Dieu said, but only he dared say it."[44]

A graphic description of the crisis of belief along with a detailed account of his own ideological evolution is contained in the book *Dem Giua Ban Ngay* [Darkness at Noon] by Vu Thu Hien, who was once a party insider, and whose father had been for a time the personal secretary to Ho Chi Minh.[45] His decision to speak out cost him many years in jail. Then living in exile in France, Hien spoke of the changes in intellectual atmosphere in a 2006 VOA interview. The interviewer noted that he had said that the situation for writers in Vietnam was now more "open" (*thoang hon*) and asked him to elaborate. "Q. 'You speak of "open," do you mean that writers in Vietnam at present no longer have to "know fear" [*biet so*] as the writer Nguyen Tuan once said?' A. 'I think that the fear has diminished. It has diminished because of the situation, that is, Vietnam now also has to integrate with the world. In the old days, there were more things forbidden. Now the forbidden things have been reduced and the fear has diminished. But there are still some things which must be feared, because if you aren't careful you will encounter problems, even though Vietnam has made great efforts to integrate with the world. For example, in the past, all you had to do was say the slightest thing and you would go to jail, people would be incarcerated for three years, and then there would be another three year term added on, and then another three years, and you would never know when you would get out. Now people are trying hard to change this, so that it is closer to normal human [practice]. Maybe, according to hearsay [*quan thinh*], the fear is still there, it still has a long, drawn-out life. For this reason, the road that the Vietnamese people must take to get to a better place, that is to break out of the envelopment by old, outmoded, and wrong ideas and advance along the same road with human kind, looks like it will be a road fraught with many hardships."[46]

Within the military there was grumbling about the latitude allowed for the public to engage in political debate about party principles and policies in the lead up to the Tenth Party Congress. An article in the journal of the armed forces complained that even constructive ideas and criticism were disseminated too widely, even to the rest of the world, where they were exploited by antiparty elements and "enemy forces." Some of these ideas are "extremely superficial, wrong, and will create confusion and suspicion in the party and among the people." Among those spreading these ideas are "people with a record of participating in the revolution and who have made contributions to the country in positions of not inconsiderable responsibility. And I am very surprised by the attitude, the way of expressing themselves, and the substance of those who are 'contributing ideas' [*gop y*] to the party. Their way of looking at things concerning the country and the leadership of the party is superficial and lacks objectivity, a gloomy monochromatic picture of defeat and error. I ask myself, how is it that they have changed like this."[47]

The answer was that, in addition to having been taken in by "enemy forces," these people were unwittingly doing a "self-engendered evolution" (*tu dien bien*)—in other words, "peacefully evolution-izing themselves" even without direct external instigation.

In addition there were the more blatant cases of opportunists and disgruntled elements engaged in antiparty activity. "Although this is only a small force, if we don't resolutely struggle against their erroneous viewpoints, then with all sorts of tricks and guises, and clever methods, along with linking up with enemy forces on the outside, they will gradually weaken our Party, sow suspicion among the masses and even among a segment of our cadres and Party members. At the beginning this suspicion will erupt only at a few points, but gradually it will spread to become a pervasive suspicion of the entire body of Marxism Leninism and Ho Chi Minh thought, and of the necessity for the revolutionary mission, the goal that we have voluntarily striven to achieve throughout our lives."[48]

THE LAST STAND OF IDEOLOGICAL ORTHODOXY

The "big tent" approach to ideology advocated by people such as Vo Van Kiet, and the willingness of a Mai Chi Tho to let the ideological defection of a former comrade-in-arms pass, struck some diehard conservatives like Nguyen Duc Binh as unprincipled and likely to lead down a path whose end was the casting aside of even the pretense of socialism. In their view, people who questioned the strict party line *should* "know fear." Some conservatives felt that the only way to stop this ideological erosion was to draw a firm line between what is "socialist" and what is not, and to go on the offensive to defend it, accusing the pragmatists of complicity, conscious or inadvertent, with the enemies of Vietnamese communism.

Nguyen Duc Binh had been the politburo's authority on ideological issues, and was for years the head of the Ho Chi Minh Higher Party School, which gave advanced ideological training to higher-level party cadres. Like the party leadership of the Tenth Congress (2006), Nguyen Duc Binh, now retired, also felt that it was time to "face the truth squarely." But in his view the painful truth was that orthodox belief in Marxism and faith in the party's ideological line had dangerously eroded.

"I think that the lack of unity of mind (*nhat tri*) in the party is one of the weaknesses," said Binh in his *Nhan Dan* article. Binh stated that there had been previous admissions of inner party differences, but that the "reasons for it have never been thoroughly analyzed." He suggested that the politburo and the central committee "look squarely at this truth, because the time has come when it can no longer be avoided." Lenin had warned that "Small contradictions and small differences of opinion often create big contradictions and big differences of opinion when people cling to their small errors and try hard not to correct them, or when people commit big mistakes the focus is put on the small mistakes of one person or a few other persons. Disagreement and dissension always spread like this . . . Lenin also said, no one can liquidate us if we ourselves do not commit mistakes. The entire question lies in this word 'if.' If we commit mistakes which lead to dissension then everything will collapse."[49] By implication, Binh indicates that the "mistakes" are not policies that have an adverse impact on society, but lack of vigilance in stamping out heterodoxy or dissidence within the party.

Binh then comments on what he considers to be a lack of conviction and indifference to party doctrine within the party which is leading in a dangerous direction. "A number of cadres, even middle and high level cadres, appear to have a complex, and are embarrassed when they have to speak of socialism and Marxism-Leninism. It looks like they are afraid to get the reputation of being doctrinaire, conservative, not *doi moi*, and perhaps they are for a *doi moi* which abandons socialism and Marxism-Leninism! When they can't avoid speaking of socialism and Marxism-Leninism they will do so, but in reality inside they do not believe in it. Some people, because of limited level of understanding, will say, 'oh well, we don't need to talk about remote abstractions like doctrines [*chu nghia*] or ideals [*ly tuong*], as long as the people are prosperous, the country is strong, the society is just, fair [*cong bang*] and civilized [*van minh*], it's all right. And some people, not because of a low level of understanding, really hold this view, in reality they use this line of thinking [*lap luan*] to avoid the issue and to engage in sophistry [*nguy bien*]. . . . The draft political report of the Tenth Congress states that 'Manifestations of distancing from the goal of socialism have not yet been overcome.' It should add 'to say nothing of going in the direction of increasing.'"[50]

For Nguyen Duc Binh, the time had come to force the issue and make a stand, lest the gradual slide into "liquidating" (*tieu diet*) communism continue. It is noteworthy that he aims directly at those like Vo Van Kiet who were trying to shift the basis of regime legitimation from socialism to nationalism. We have already seen Kiet use exactly the formulation about "prosperous people," "strong nation," and "civilized society" which Binh feels are slogans devised to cover the retreat from socialism.

He wrote in the party ideological journal that "There are some comrades who think that with the collapse of the Soviet Union we no longer need to think about defining the era, because socialism in the world is very remote and that trying to define the era [e.g., how the transition to socialism will evolve and when communism will arrive] is useless and, on the contrary, will created subjective illusions and adventurism in action. . . . there is also the idea that we need a new concept about the [historical] age [we live in] to replace the old, outdated concepts that history has passed by. Today's age, in their estimation, is a postindustrial age, also called the age of post-industrial civilization, or the cyber-age civilization, the civilization of brainpower, etc." There is nothing wrong with these concepts, Binh argues, as long as everyone acknowledges that they are moving toward socialism, rather than a final stage in themselves.[51] He might well have been referring to the debate about Marxist historical periodization stimulated by Phan Dinh Dieu's 1988 article "Some observations about today's era and our path."[52]

It was time to "put everything on the table," (*dat tat ca len ban nghi su*), he said. "Thus we have to pose the question directly; Is our party going to continue to take the socialist path or not? Don't beat around the bush, equivocate [*lap lung*], or be evasive, but answer the question directly. Don't be like some people and reply along the lines of 'yes, but it will be a *doi moi* socialism.' *Doi moi* is a given, but don't play sophistical games, or do a conceptual bait-and-switch [*danh trao khai niem*]." And it is not just a question of paying lip service to socialism as many have done, but manifesting it in action, argues Binh.[53]

Of course, the key question is how is what, concretely, is "socialist" and who defines it? As noted earlier (chapter 2), the pioneer reform thinker Phan Dinh Dieu had already anticipated this question. His answer was "Our goal is socialism. But the concept of socialism is being renovated (doi moi) and we must change our awareness on this subject. And could it be that for us, a poor underdeveloped country, socialism is a goal toward which we are headed, not an immediate objective? The transitional road to it is long, and comprises many stages. We have to determine our goal for the immediate stage," which, he said, is getting out of poverty.[54]

For the conservatives like Binh, this was not enough. A return was needed to clear standards of what was a "deviation" and what was not. Although he acknowledged the complexity of defining "market economy with a socialist orientation," and gave a convoluted explanation of the problem which unwittingly proved his point, he added that it was the combination of introduction of the market element in Vietnam's domestic economy and the challenge of simultaneously adapting to globalization that was especially difficult, and threatened to "dissolve" Vietnam's regime (*hoa tan*) rather than assimilate (*hoa nhap*) into the global system. For Binh, indicators of deep integration such as joining the WTO were mere tactical expedients. "Joining the WTO in and of itself is not an end but a means . . . ," to tap into the "strength of the age" and by acquiring modern technology and taking advantage of the brainpower economy (*kinh te tri tue*), to build the material base for socialism, which is the "central mission of the entire period of transition to socialism."[55]

There were a number of markers that would constitute adherence to "socialist orientation," such as maintaining a major state role in the direction of the economy, but the real battle line was drawn on the question of whether capitalists could be members of the party and whether a party member could engage in private business, especially when it involved employees who might be considered "exploited." This, in turn, cut to the core issue of who and what the party represented. Some in the party wanted to stress its nationalist claim to represent "the people" and felt this was obscured by the outmoded claim to be a party "of the working class" or, at the least, should be added to it. In the end even some veteran party ideologists like Huu Tho, the retired former editor of the party newspaper, wanted to move past the nagging issue of capitalists in the party. Asked by an interviewer about his views on party members doing business in the private sector of the economy, Huu Tho replied, "Previously, the draft political report . . . was right on target: don't restrict the scale [of private enterprise in which party members are permitted to engage]. Following that, a number of people wrote articles in the newspapers criticizing this. So how could we speak of a unanimity and continuity on this? And this morning the comrade party general secretary officially stated that party members could engage in the private economy. I think that this view is supported by the majority of party members and people." On the question of whether the party was still the vanguard of the working class in Vietnam, Huu Tho replied, "I think that this question has been decided for a very long time. The overarching ideology in our revolutionary theory is the ideology of nationalism [*tu tuong dan toc*]. Class must be situation within the nation [*dan toc*], and is a part of the nation, it does not transcend the nation. For this reason, what the draft political report has now said on this is entirely reasonable."[56]

As we have seen, even the former minister of the interior Mai Chi Tho, acknowledged that the party had committed an error in overemphasizing class and class struggle. Binh took a hard line on this issue, and was adamant in rejecting the idea that a party member could be engaged in private business. "Previously there were times when we committed the 'leftist'[57] error and placed to much emphasis on class and class struggle, and had to pay a steep price for it. Today, not a few comrades again commit the error of moving from one extreme to the other, to the point of lightly regarding class struggle and then going on to reject the very existence of classes and class struggle. There is a school of thought [*lap luan*] that contemporary society no longer has classes, but have only different strata and social groups; and that there is no basis for dividing [society] into economic categories because everything is blended together [*hon hop*] and woven together so that the economic basis for determining classes no longer exists." He also rejected the idea circulating in Vietnam that while Marxism-Leninism stressed class, Ho Chi Minh stressed the nation (*dan toc*).[58]

China's rejection of some of the core concepts of traditional Marxism-Leninism, especially the substitution of "harmonious" society for class struggle, which sounded quite a bit like the "blending together" of social and economic differentiation criticized by Binh, certainly complicated the efforts of conservatives to find a bedrock orthodox position where a hard and fast line could be drawn. The fact that the Vietnamese leadership enthusiastically endorsed China's ideological pragmatism and flexibility made a conservative resurgence in Vietnam unlikely. In 2006 Vietnam's National Assembly chairman, Nguyen Phu Trong, reported to the Vietnamese press on a recent China visit. "Q. 'What do [you] think of the China Communist Party's stance on building socialism with Chinese characteristics?'" Trong replied that China "has developed a clear roadmap" and has "decided to put forth the policy of building a harmonious socialist society, and then developing science and building a harmonious society with man in the core. I think these are correct steps. China and Vietnam have many things in common, so we can share our views and learn from each other. The visit provided me a chance to learn how China has turned theory into reality and it has a lot of experience in this area."[59]

Unlike Mai Chi Tho, who was critical of the overemphasis on class, Nguyen Duc Binh singled out collectivism and the planned economy as the major failing of the party in the past. This suggested that the party's shortcomings were organizational and policy errors, and not political or ideological mistakes. "The big deficiency of the model was the absolutization of the central planning system, and absolutization of collectivism, while underemphasizing individual creativity and subjectively and arbitrarily [*duy y chi*] rejecting commodity production and the market system, and allowing a pervasive subsidy system to spread, which suppressed the motive force of direct interest, and by doing this suppressed proactiveness and creativity in economic units and among individual workers."[60] He was willing to jettison extreme central planning and the subsidy system, but not the fundamental political role of class as the defining aspect of the Party and the political system, which, of course, meant that socialism and capitalism would remain irreconcilable systems and that strict limits needed to be placed on how far Vietnam could take the market economy as the basis of its development.

Nguyen Duc Binh's aggressive conservative stand provoked a lively reaction. Nguyen Quang A, who, armed with a Ph.D. in information science obtained in Hungary, made a considerable amount of money in buying and selling computer equipment in the former Soviet Union and Eastern Europe, subsequently became the director of a private bank in Hanoi, and the chairman of the Informatics Council (Hoi Dong Tin Hoc), wrote a scathing reply, published in the liberal paper *Tuoi Tre*. He criticized Binh for using loaded Marxist–Cold War terminology (the "gang of capitalists") that belonged to the distant past, and for calling the collapse of communism in Eastern Europe a "disaster" (ask them if they think it was a disaster, he suggested).

Nguyen Quang A wrote the introduction to the Vietnamese translation of Thomas Friedman's *The World is Flat*, which in 2006–7 was prominently featured as a bestseller in most bookstores in Hanoi and Ho Chi Minh City. He is frequently covered and quoted in the press. A cadre from the Ho Chi Minh Political Academy cited him approvingly as a leading authority on the internet.[61] Nguyen Quang A called former politburo member and therefore heavyweight politician Nguyen Duc Binh "the Professor" to remind readers of his ivory tower background as leader of the Ho Chi Minh Academy where party leaders were instructed in Marxist-Leninist theory. The Professor he implied, was merely recycling abstruse doctrine, divorced from reality, and rendered obsolete by events. Having reduced the once-imposing political figure of Nguyen Duc Binh to a nagging pedant (the "Professor"), Nguyen Quang A asserted that in discussing what had been "put on the table," no one should try to claim a monopoly for their own views. "I don't want to interfere in internal party matters," wrote Nguyen Quang A, "but the decisions of the Communist Party affect the present and future of more than 80 million people."[62]

Rejecting Binh's proposal that all sensitive issues be discussed only behind closed doors within the party, A proposed that "there be open discussion of questions important to the country, among which there may be issues involving the Communist Party, if they want. Whether or not the Communist Party listens is the party's business. I believe that widespread open discussion is good for the country and also good for the Communist Party. What good is organizing debate in a way that cuts off and deters critical ideas? That is an unfair debate." In this spirit a collection of articles by twenty-two different authors, including Nguyen Duc Binh and Nguyen Quang A, who responded to the party's call to contribute ideas on the draft political resolution of the Tenth Party Congress, running to 400 pages, was published in Hanoi.[63]

Nguyen Quang A noted that Nguyen Duc Binh had rested a large part of his conservative case on the proposition that the Vietnamese people had "chosen" the socialist path once and for all, and any deviation from this would be a betrayal of the national will expressed in this choice. The idea of a collective choice at a historical moment in time having eternal validity is absurd, A argued, and "not very Marxist" because history is constant change. (As we have seen, Binh himself used a variant of this argument in asserting that the end of the Cold War and the apparent triumph of capitalism, embodied in globalization, was only apparent because globalization was a prolonged process, not a destination, The destination, which would constitute the "end of history" would be communism.)

Nguyen Duc Binh is quite blunt about what is at stake in his two major articles in *Tap Chi Cong San* elaborating on his views: it is the political survival of the group in power in Vietnam. "There is no ruling class that has not worried about building and protecting its economic base. In the case of socialist countries this is even more the case, because generally speaking socialism cannot be formed spontaneously but has to be consciously built."[64] In other words, once the state disengages from its attempts to control the economy, the whole ruling structure will collapse.

Utilizing the powerful impact of the then current exhibition of life under the "subsidy regime," which was a painful and vivid reminder of where the socialism advocated by Nguyen Duc Binh had led, Nguyen Quang A said, "I won't speak any further of this or that 'orientation.' [You] have not been clear about [what you mean by] orientation, but [say that you are] afraid of this or that person 'deviating'—what is it that you fear? I am afraid that the Professor's version of 'socialist orientation' will take us back to 'Standing in line all day' and probably anyone who has stood in line all day will find it hard to agree with the Professor about the 'State economy with a socialist orientation' and about the path that has been chosen. I think that theory is very important, but it can only develop on the basis of competing ideas or true freedom of thought in an environment where people feel free to speak up, as the venerable Ho said. If there is no freedom for debate then the councils on theory [*hoi dong ly luan*] can turn into 'councils of muddle' [*hoi dong lu lan*] as people often say."[65]

I would like to ask the Professor what is 'the socialist road' without the qualifying phrase 'that was chosen?'" writes Nguyen Quang A.

Probably the Professor will agree with me that the socialist road that had been chosen by all the "socialist" countries prior to 1990 in the previous century has completely failed. . . . If we understand that socialism in Vietnam is doing what it takes to make "the people prosperous, the country strong, society democratic, egalitarian and civilized," and to have peace and stability so that people can realize their full potential and live a quiet life in harmony with each other, and for

Vietnam to avoid perpetually falling behind and to oppose corruption. . . . Party membership will be multiples of what it is now and the Vietnamese people will follow that party with one accord, except if there is another party which pursues these goals more effectively than the Vietnamese Communist Party. . . . So go ahead and clearly state your goals and the means to achieve them and the practical actions to support these goals, and let the people decide. I believe that if you are really clear like this, then you would have to form another Communist Party, which might be called the Vietnamese Communist Party Marxist-Leninist,[66] which would advocate policy approaches like the Professor has outlined in the section titled 'resolutely stick to the socialist road' and compete with the current Vietnamese Communist Party.[67]

This is a classic example of a distinctively Vietnamese style of caustic, taunting humor (*xo*), but also a pointed reminder that Binh is calling for an ideological rollback to a position abandoned by the party, which underlines the irony of a position which calls for party unity and discipline by rejecting the current party line. It is this contradiction which, in the end, dooms the "last stand of the conservatives" to failure.[68]

In another article published in *Tuoi Tre*, Nguyen Quang A again challenges Nguyen Duc Binh by noting yet another fundamental problem with his call for a return to orthodoxy. The largest socialist country in the world, China, has been quite pragmatic in its adjustments of theory to policy, and Vietnamese conservatives cannot, therefore, point to the most important socialist state left in the world to support their case. "I think that in reality terminology does not have to be very significant. The Chinese are very smart; people say they are building socialism with Chinese characteristics, but when asked what Chinese characteristics are, no one can explain it. I think that it is right that people are doing capitalism, but people have to use [the term] socialism with Chinese characteristics in order to mollify those who participated in the 'Long March.' I think that saying one thing and doing another is very smart of the Chinese."[69]

Thus some prominent voices in Vietnam openly proclaim that having a gap between rhetoric and reality is a good thing, because it appeases the conservatives, lets the reformers do their thing, and diminishes the role of ideological polemics in policy debate and political argumentation. In 1998, while Binh was still in office, he presided over a conference on teaching Marxism-Leninism in the universities, which considered the possibility of special bonuses for people teaching these courses—an implicit admission of the academic perception of the undesirability of remaining locked into indoctrination as a career track.[70] Whether there has been a compartmentalization (and marginalization) of ideological specialists, and whether this amounts to an implicit pact to let the Party ideologues do their thing while the rest of society gets on with their lives is not entirely clear, but the frosty reception given Nguyen Duc Binh's appeal to turn back the clock certainly suggests that this is the last stand of party ideological conservatism.

In retirement Nguyen Duc Binh was given a platform to express his views. A volume of his collected articles on ideology and indoctrination from 1977 to 2001 was published on the eve of the Ninth Party Congress. Clearly they failed to have an impact, as the Party Congress took a very different direction than the conservative path advocated in these writings. An 870-page updated version of this was published in 2005, which contained Binh's arguments for continuing to adhere to a "two worlds" model of international relations. Globalization does not mean a unified world economy under capitalism, he asserted, and it is a process not an end state. The end state toward which the process is headed is communism, even though Binh acknowledged that it looked like capitalism had triumphed for the moment, and that the desired communist future was a long way off. "Can we speak of a *unified global economy*? Can we speak of *a global village*?" he asked. "I think that world development has reached the point that it is impossible to have the *structure of a capitalist economy serving* as a unified global economy." As for the two worlds, Binh argued that not only were there still socialist countries on the scene, but "Even in the capitalist world there still exist 'two worlds'—a world of the rich and developed, and a world of the poor and backward."[71]

Even Nguyen Duc Binh was forced to concede that harping on the defects on capitalism to longer went over well in this new "delicate" attitudinal environment, and that the party doesn't need to harangue the people about the evils of capitalism as long as it keeps its internal ranks in line—hence the importance of keeping capitalists out of the party.[72] That effort, however, came to naught. Caught between purifying its ranks and striving to assimilate the most dynamic elements of society, the party has apparently opted for the latter.

Perhaps the main problem the party faces is the corruption of its own members. It is not primarily the cadres in the private sector who are the problem, but the cadres who take advantage of the remaining areas of government control in the economy to use their political power for profit. These party members have a vested interest in maintaining a strong state role in the economy because it provides these opportunities. At the same time, the resultant corruption is a far greater threat to the party's domestic legitimacy than "peaceful evolution."

The Tenth Party Congress pointed out the necessity of having a party watchdog presence in private enterprises—a control function evidently overlooked by conservatives like Nguyen Duc Binh. The Tenth Congress political report says "Party members who are assigned to carry out the private economic activities must set good examples in adhering to the party statute, in abiding by the law, in seriously implementing the State policies and other regulations of the Party Central Committee. Efforts must be made to quickly issue guidelines and instructions for these party members to satisfactorily carry out their tasks while firmly maintaining the qualifications and characteristics of a party member."[73] Whether the party will succeed in keeping its designated agents in the private sector sufficiently "red" over the long run remains to be seen. The question is, "who will transform whom?"

THE NEW ELITE

One reason that the previous section examined the polemics of Nguyen Quang A in some detail is that in age and background he represents the demographic and political experience of the emerging leadership generation. Born in 1946, he served in the army and was then sent to Hungary where he received his Ph.D.[74] He is also an interesting example of a successful entrepreneur, an emerging group in society that will play a large role in Vietnam's economic development and its future in general. As a party member in good standing,[75] the director of a private sector bank[76] director of a private company,[77] and someone who is very visible in the domestic and foreign media, he is well placed to play a central role in the key debate on the issue of whether or not people engaged in private business can be party members. Much of Vietnam's future course will increasingly be shaped by people from this background.

The pre-1945 leaders and those who became active during and just after the August 1945 revolution are mostly gone. As any student of Max Weber would expect, the trend has been away from a star system of politics, in which the first and second generation of revolutionaries played the leading role, to a more "routinized" and bureaucratic constellation of leaders. A number of keen observers of the Vietnamese political scene have commented that the current leadership "belongs to the system" but also note that the system has significantly changed over time and that this leadership generation is distinct from its predecessors. At the time of the 2006 Tenth Party Congress, an unnamed foreign businessman who had been a longtime observer of the Vietnamese political scene said "'Individuals don't move the system in this country.' . . . The leaders may change in coming days, he said, but in terms of policy, 'I would expect it to be difficult to spot the difference.'"[78]

A similar view was expressed in the comment of another anonymous seasoned observer of the Vietnamese scene on the eve of the Tenth Party Congress. "All eyes this week are on Deputy Prime Minister Nguyen Tan Dung. His boss, Prime Minister Phan Van Khai, now 72, is almost certain to step down after nine successful, if bruising years of reform battles throughout the government. Still only 56—a spring chicken in Hanoi's political ranks—Mr Dung was the youngest leader in years to make the Politburo when he joined the ruling body in the mid-1990s. . . . Described as boyish, dynamic and charismatic in private, Mr Dung hails from the Ca Mau Peninsula on Vietnam's southeastern tip. 'We are still waiting for Dung to fully establish his credentials as an out-and-out reformer,' said one Asian diplomat who knows him. 'What we can see is that he is a pragmatist who knows how to work within the system . . . that is important for anyone who wants to get things done here. 'He may be young and dynamic, but he is still a creature of the system.'" Nonetheless, many informed observers feel that a younger leadership will have an impact. "Hanoi-based British academic Martin Gainsborough recently told a group of foreign investors that the importance of generational change could not be underestimated as the country opened up. 'We predict that issues which were once non-negotiable . . . will gradually come onto the agenda,' he said."[79]

Further underscoring the impact of generational change in bringing relatively anonymous leaders to the fore is the following account of what is probably the last hurrah of the revolutionary generation of leaders, with General Vo Nguyen Giap (age ninety-four in 2006) who had been blocked from the top party position by ambitious rivals throughout his career, former party leader Do Muoi (age eighty-nine) the somewhat younger Le Duc Anh (age eighty-six, and controversial for his now clouded past and political machinations against other leaders), the still younger successor to Do Muoi as party leader, Le Kha Phieu (age seventy-five). Greg Torode, reporting on the congress, wrote that

This week's party congress [April 2006] was the last gasp for old revolutionaries as a younger leadership pushes the nation forward. . . . As Vietnam's 10th Communist Party congress closed on Tuesday, four old men sat silently in the front row. Between them, the 'special advisers' represented the entire 75-year history of Vietnamese communism. They date back to the party's earliest days in jungle caves plotting the downfall of French colonial Indochine, to its bloody and victorious war against the US and the former South Vietnam. They helped lead the invasion of Cambodia and the border war against China as cold war tensions turned inward. Finally, they rose during the more recent peace—a 30-year struggle marked by poverty, suspicion and internal battles over the pace of reform. The congress confirmed the need for younger leaders across the party to ensure reforms help Vietnam surge beyond its status as an embryonic Asian tiger economy. The meeting also seemed to highlight that the old men's time had passed, along with their ideological battles. With a combined age of 345, it could be the last time they're seen together at the same event. But they are not going quietly into their dark political night.[80]

In 2006 the Tenth Party Congress not only marked a historic leadership turnover, but also elicited the support of previous leaders for a more open style of politics. "General Giap, his seniority finally unquestioned, has led supporters in a drive to boost reform and force openness within the party, which has struggled to shed its wartime secrecy, party sources said. 'Giap is the last one of his breed left, our last link to Uncle Ho,' said one party official. 'And there is no one who can touch him now, no one to keep him on the sidelines.'" Even the transitional leader Le Kha Phieu, who had tried to slow or reverse the reform momentum at the turn of the millennium now weighed in on behalf of a different kind of politics. Noting the prominence of General Giap and his support of political reform, Carl Thayer wrote that "General Phieu's role has been more surprising. He, too, has been urging internal transparency and an end to corruption in terms that appear to belie his dogmatic image. 'Let's put everything on the table at the congress,' he said, urging an end to the smoke-filled rooms and rubber-stamp political theatre that have decided the leadership in the recent past, including his own rise. 'It's remarkable, he is saying the things that could have got you in trouble while he was in power,' one observer noted. 'That was just five years ago.'"[81]

Not all of the older generation of leaders supported the new direction, but the older conservatives were now increasingly isolated. "General [Le Duc] Anh has proved a darker force. Despite bad health that has dogged him since a massive stroke in 1996, he has still been privately influential, party sources say. He has made life internally difficult for younger reformers, warning the party is under threat. As the hunched, frail figure of General Giap approached his seat, the other leaders rose to greet him and shake his hand. General Anh didn't move. The evidence from the congress, however, suggests General Giap has won his last battle. The session featured robust debate and rigorous internal voting to create a new Central Committee and ruling Politburo—a far cry from the congress 10 years ago when a dead man was 'elected' after dying a day before the official vote." To some observers it seemed that a younger reform leadership had now definitively shifted the course of Vietnamese politics. "Mr [Nong Duc] Manh appears secure and his prime minister is almost certain to be confirmed as Nguyen Tan Dung, who at 56 promises to be the most youthful and dynamic government leader in the history of modern Vietnam. A cautious optimism is palpable on the streets of the cities and among party and government officials. The reforms can't be turned back and are in their healthiest state since the renewal process began 20 years ago. The question, then, is quite how far Vietnam will move and what will it look like in its headlong rush to industrialise by 2020. As reform minded as the new leadership may be, it is clear they are still creatures of the party, if not the revolutionary guard of old. 'Long live the Communist Party of Vietnam,' Mr Manh said as he closed the congress. It was in part pure rhetoric, but also a reminder that the security of one-party rule remains paramount, even as the country moves ahead."[82]

Ho Chi Minh's longtime revolutionary associate, former prime minister Pham Van Dong, gave a gloomy assessment of the state of the party in 1999 and warned that it had lost much of its appeal to the younger generation. "If we do not do anything to improve this situation, in the next five or 10 years our party will become a party of middle-aged and elderly people."[83] It is clear that rejuvenation of the party was a major concern of this revolutionary icon.

Pham Van Dong cautioned that "It is necessary to realize what the truth is, and speak the truth and the whole truth with a spirit of revolutionary will power, and in a serious manner. We must state all issues that must be dealt with and how to deal with them in efficiently and practically. In that spirit, we must emphasize that many people of high authority and power in the party, state, and mass organizations have degraded and degenerated themselves. They are seeking more power, money, and benefits and causing a large part of our people to lose trust in our party. This will lead to resignation, which is the integration of all the grave dangers against us. Some dangers are clear. The others are not so transparent. Some are easy to see, others are hidden."[84]

Cumulatively, the Tenth Party Congress marked a rejuvenation of the leadership. The leadership reshuffle in 1991 brought the average age of the politburo down to sixty-four[85] from seventy-one in the previous term,[86] but in 1996, the average age of the Politburo was again up to seventy-one.[87] In 2006, "the 14 newly-elected political bureau members, including 8 members elected for the first time and 6 members of the Political Bureau from the 9th tenure, are in the age bracket of 56–66, averaging at 59.9. . . . Out of 160 official members of the newly-elected Communist Party of Vietnam's Central Committee (CPVCC) with the average age of 53.5, 79 were elected for the first time. The CPVCC also elected 21 alternate members who are 43.4 years old on average. The 181 CPVCC members include 16 women and 18 ethnic minority people."[88]

The average age of Central Committee members in 2006 (nearly sixty) was even older than the average of the Sixth Central Committee elected in 1986 (fifty-six) but with a significantly different life experience from the 1986 Central Committee of which "Twenty-one members of the new Central Committee were admitted to the party before 1945 (12%); 142 in the 1945–65 period (82%) and 10 in the 1965–69 period (5.9%). Of the party Central Committee, 75 members have got university or higher academic degrees, accounting for 43.3%, and 56 others have graduated from senior high schools (32.3%)."[89] Thus only 10 percent of 1986 Central Committee members had joined the party since 1965, while by 2006 this latter group was certainly the dominant majority. The Vietnamese cabinet appointed in 2002 averaged fifty-six years of age, six years younger than the cabinet they replaced.[90]

Some senior leaders felt that there were areas of party and government work where extensive experience was indispensable and age was a qualification for good judgment rather than a disqualification. Former foreign minister Nguyen Dy Nien was asked if the age qualifications had an impact on diplomacy. "Yes, many Vietnamese diplomats have expressed concern about the new age category used in the selection of party Central Committee members for the 10th tenure. This is because most of our deputy ministers of foreign affairs are more than 60-years-old. Ironically, in the foreign affairs sector only those who have reached the age of 60 or more are considered as becoming mature in their career." Nien expressed the view that perhaps in diplomacy experience was a good thing and therefore the rejuvenation policy should not be applied to the foreign affairs sector.[91]

Another illustration of leadership turnover is in the composition of the Twelfth National Assembly, elected in 2007. Among the 493 people elected to the National Assembly in 2006, 354 were elected for the first time, 164 had a postgraduate level of education and 309 a university level of education. Forty-three were nonparty members, 127 were women, and 87 belonged to ethnic minorities.[92]

As the top leadership experiences generational turnover and brings in a different range of life experience and formative influences, the composition of the younger ranks of the party is also changing. The overall overage age of party members is around forty-five years, but this is considered still too high.[93]

The Communist Party of Vietnam (CPV) admitted 751,700 new members in 2001–05 term, an increase of 42.23 percent compared with previous term, bringing the total Party membership to 3.1 million.

Among the newly admitted Party members, the numbers of women, members of the Ho Chi Minh Communist Youth Union, ethnic minority people, religious followers and intellectuals increased steadily in comparison with the previous CPV Central Committee term, thus contributing to progressive change to the Party's structure.

In 2005 alone, more than 107,000 members of the Ho Chi Minh Communist Youth Union were admitted to the CPV. The average age of new Party members in 2001–05 period was 30.15, a decrease of 0.61 years in comparison with the previous period.

The professional knowledge and working skill of the new CPV members in that period was higher, with nearly 218,000 members holding college or university degrees, an increase of 97.80 percent, and particularly, more than 4,700 new members with post-graduate degrees, nearly triple the previous number.[94]

EPISTEMIC COMMUNITIES: KNOWLEDGE NETWORKS AND THE GROWTH OF COSMOPOLITANISM

What influences will shape the outlook and expectations of this new educated elite? It should not be assumed that the old Marxist framework of analysis is moribund. There are a number of reasons why it will still exert a powerful influence in the thinking of Vietnam's political elite for a long time into the future. However, it is not the survival of Marxism as a theoretical construct that is the primary concern of Vietnam's conservatives, but Marxism as a source of political authority. "After carefully analysing the relations between the theoretical work and the scientific characters of the theses of Marx, Engels and Lenin, Comrade Nguyen Duc Binh criticized the idea of depoliticizing Marxism, saying the demand for the separation of Marxism from politics is totally erroneous."[95] It is the continued official profession of Marxism as a totalistic belief system that divides Vietnam from most of the rest of the world in an era of globalization. Globalization exposes the Vietnamese political class, and larger society, to many influences which are in dynamic tension with the core of the old ideological superstructure.

The world "cosmopolitan" has had a checkered history in Marxist writings, culminating in the paranoia of Stalin at the time of the so-called "doctor's plot," in which Jewish doctors were tarred with the antisemitic smear of "rootless cosmopolitanism." This term, as used by Stalin, indicated not a healthy open-mindedness and receptivity to advanced global practices, but treasonous lack of fixed loyalties to the Soviet Union. All connections with the outside world were deemed subversive. The Jewish doctors were accused of conspiring to murder Stalin. Pravda kicked off the campaign in 1949 by inveighing against "unbridled, evil-minded cosmopolitans, profiteers with no roots and no conscience. . . . Grown on rotten yeast of bourgeois cosmopolitanism, decadence and formalism . . . non-indigenous nationals without a motherland, who poison with stench . . . our proletarian culture."[96]

One doesn't hear this kind of language any more, certainly not in Vietnam, but the idea that there is a world culture out there inimical to socialist values has had a long afterlife in the minds of some of the doctrinaire theoreticians represented by Nguyen Duc Binh. These days the debate about ideological worlds in collision uses more decorous and indirect language, primarily centered around the term "civilized culture" or "civilization" (*van minh*).

We noted the dismissive reference by Nguyen Duc Binh to this term, which he ascribed to those who were trying to lead Vietnam to a noncommunist future. "Some people, because of limited level of understanding, will say, 'oh well, we don't need to talk about remote abstractions like doctrines [*chu nghia*] or ideals [*ly tuong*], as long as the people are prosperous, the country is strong, the society is just, fair [*cong bang*] and civilized culture [*van minh*], it's all right. . . . Today's age, in their estimation, is a post industrial age, also called the age of post industrial civilization, or the cyber age civilization, the civilization of brainpower etc."[97]

This criticized use of *van minh* was, in fact, included in one the key party slogans devised for the 2001 Ninth Party Congress—"National Independence—Socialism, rich people, strong country, justice, democracy, civilized culture"—and routinely repeated by the top leadership since then.[98] For Nguyen Duc Binh and other conservatives, socialism, or at least the imagined ideal of socialism, is the ultimate in "civilized culture." "The Communist Party, according to the conception and ideology of V. I. Lenin and Ho Chi Minh, is the party of intellect, honor, and the conscience of the age, a civilized and virtuous party."[99]

As William Turley has suggested, some of the contemporary overtones of the term "civilized" or "civilized culture" in Vietnamese discourse may hark back to the post-Stalin usage of this term in the former Soviet Union.[100] In the Gorbachev-era debates about reform there were still echoes of the age-old struggle between Western-oriented reformers, advocating "civilized" behavior as emulation of Europe, and the Slavophiles.[101] One would be hard pressed to find similar cultural inferiority complexes at work in Vietnam, historically far more secure in its cultural identity, but given the centrality of the Soviet model in many Vietnamese conceptions of socialism, these doubts about the darker side of the Soviet era must have a residual effect, at least among an older generation of Soviet-educated Vietnamese. Another more explicitly reformist use of the term is the East European equation of "civilized" politics with democracy and human rights.[102]

The idea of a common civilization and common humanity was central to Gorbachev's stunning speech at the United Nations in 1988 which, in effect, declared an end to the two-worlds conception of international politics. "Today we have entered an era when progress will be based on the interests of all mankind. Consciousness of this requires that world policy, too, should be determined by the priority of the values of all mankind."

Gorbachev spoke of "the emergence of a mutually connected and integral world. Further world progress is now possible only through the search for a consensus of all mankind, in movement toward a new world order."[103]

Even closer to the contemporary Vietnamese usage of "civilized" society and conduct is the way Eduard Shevardnadze used the term right after the collapse of the Soviet Union; "If we wish to be a civilized country, we have to have the same laws and customs as the rest of the civilized world."[104] In June 1992 Boris Yeltsin said that "Russia has made its final choice in favor of a civilized way of life, common sense and universal human heritage."[105]

In some contexts, Vietnamese theoreticians speak of a plurality of cultures and civilizations, rather than a single overarching civilization. "The program of global deliberations on the dialogue among the cultures and civilizations for stable peace and development of the United Nations has stressed: All civilizations respect the unity and diversity of humanity. . . . Through dialogue people will tie together all civilizations and accomplishments of civilization to create a common legacy for humanity."[106] Even in the case of this pluralistic view of "civilizations" there is an encompassing "common legacy for humanity."

As was brought out in an interesting 2007 discussion on the Vietnam Studies Group Listserv,[107] there is a natural linkage between "civilized" and "contemporary" or "modern" in that all these terms imply a universal standard of the most advanced standards of thought and behavior—which are worth emulating. Of course, if these are existing standards set by nonsocialist societies, it raises the question of how "socialism," now widely identified in many minds with "out of date," will displace the existing benchmarks of "civilized society," especially in the area of human rights and democracy.

One way of looking at the implications of accepting a universal standard of "best practices" and "best behavior" is that this is a feature of globalization that is beyond the ability of a single nation or even group of nation states to control. What is "civilized" is what most societies accept as desirable standards of conduct. Of course no society can be forced to accept any standards that offend its values and run contrary to its interests, but becoming a participant in the establishment of global standards requires engagement in multiple "epistemic communities."

An authoritative definition of this term is that of Peter Haas in a volume of *International Organization* devoted to the subject: "An 'epistemic community' is a network of knowledge-based experts or groups with an authoritative claim to policy-relevant knowledge within the domain of their expertise. Members hold a common set of causal beliefs and share notions of validity based on internally defined criteria for evaluation, common policy projects, and shared normative commitments."[108]

For the purposes of our discussion, this could be reduced to a simpler formula. An epistemic community is a "network of knowledge-based experts whose expertise within specified issue areas often leads to a common understanding of the nature of the basic problems in their given area, a common set of assumptions and a terminology to deal with these problems, and an entry into the political process which affects those issues." Much of this is taken from Haas's concluding essay (co-authored with Emanuel Adler) in the special issue of *International Organization* on this subject. The stress here is more on the Vietnamese component of such international communities—let us call them "knowledge networks" for simplicity. In fact, since this flurry of attention to epistemic communities in the early 1990s—perhaps in the enthusiasm of the early post–Cold War period—the attention to this concept seems to have diminished. Arms control, which was an early example of experts shaping political debate, was put on the backburner. However, one could make the argument that the idea still has salience in important issue areas such as environment, trade, law of the sea, and global commons, and even in the sensitive domain of security.

But because of the great divide that continues to exist between Vietnam and most other countries, even its close neighbors, resulting from very different political systems, I do not stress the "shared normative values" across national boundaries (though it exists in many issue areas). But the idea of sharing fundamental assumptions and adopting common terminology is an important element of the process of "changing worlds." We have seen how the idea that Vietnam's future was headed in a completely different direction than most of the rest of the world was muted over time by the introduction of new ideas about a "common era" that will last long enough to make Vietnam's ultimate professed destination (communism) so remote as to become a quasi theological, more than a political issue. We have seen the fading of the two-worlds fixation with "peaceful evolution," and its displacement with a common concern for global and regional stability to facilitate economic development. We have seen a shift from zero-sum to win-win thinking, perhaps one of the most crucial effects of Vietnam's engagement in larger knowledge networks.

A striking illustration of the impact of a wider range of information on Vietnamese discourse is the interesting decision of Nguyen Quang A to bypass standard Marxist definitions of "oppression" in his debate with Nguyen Duc Binh about party members and private enterprise. Instead, Nguyen Quang A used various definitions of "oppression" accessed from the English version of Wikipedia (which, of course, also has a Vietnamese version).[109]

The practical implications of expanding the availability of information have been considerable. But more than having access to a greater reservoir of available raw data, it is the familiarization with the larger international universe of ideas and concepts which has the deepest impact. Perhaps the leading edge of Vietnam's engagement with external knowledge communities which led to substantial idea change was with ASEAN and the ASEAN Regional Forum (ARF). The cumulative impact of NGOs should not be underestimated. In a more direct and pragmatic vein, the economists and trade specialists who saw what had to be done to "catch up" with the rest of the world were also affected by their membership in "knowledge networks." The Ford Foundation's annual report of 2005, covering its funding activities for the previous year, lists a remarkable range of projects in Vietnam, including collaborations with institutions like the Ho Chi Minh National Political Academy (which used to focus exclusively on ideological training for higher party cadres), the Institute for International Relations (the think tank and training center of the Foreign Ministry), the Vietnamese Academy of Social Sciences, programs in such sensitive areas as the ethnic minorities of the northern highlands of Vietnam, and a wide variety of programs involving Vietnamese national and regional universities.[110]

Vietnam's universities have increasingly "internationalized" their curriculums, even in areas such as political science and international relations which had long been considered the exclusive domain of the party, and sealed off from contact with any knowledge networks outside the socialist bloc. In 2002 the Ford Foundation, with the approval of the Vietnamese government, commissioned a study of the academic teaching of international relations in Vietnam. One of the mandates of the study was to determine "What are the disciplines/subdisciplines, key concepts, core skills and pedagogical tools that characterize the teaching of IR around the world?"[111] Vietnam's higher-education leadership stresses the importance of "internationalizing" the university curriculums.[112]

The academic study of international relations had a long gestation, starting from the mid-1950s efforts of French-trained professors like Pham Huy Thong to institute a curriculum of world history, which for many years was the only IR-related course of study in socialist Vietnam. Professor Vu Duong Ninh, the pioneer of academic training in international relations, started to develop the world-history curriculum in 1960 with translated books from China and the Soviet Union but, eventually finding these unsuitable, replaced them with Vietnamese materials. In 1981, Professor Ninh taught in Madagascar and was introduced to French books on international relations; on his return, he participated in producing a four-volume series on world history. By 1990, the educational authorities began to see that world history was not in itself a sufficient IR curriculum, and in 1995 an independent international relations faculty was established. The course of studies was further expanded under Professor Pham Quang Minh, Ninh's successor as dean of the faculty of international relations.[113]

In terms of policy-oriented IR analysis, the Institute of International Relations (IIR) has played the major role. It has been the key participant in various Track II security discussions, which have served as an important conduit for the transmission into Vietnam of global ideas and terminology in the fields of IR and security. Vietnam's experience in the ARF and other ASEAN-related forums, has accelerated the incorporation of international concepts and terminology related to security and international issues into Vietnam's conceptual world. The fact that English is the common language of ASEAN has meant that standardization of terminology is essential. Recognizing the importance of direct contact and communication with the outside world, the government has ordered officials to attain English fluency, with mixed results.[114]

Relevant Western books on international relations and security issues have always been translated into Vietnamese, but in the past access to these was largely confined to the policy community "for internal circulation only." An example is the translation of the *Asia-Pacific Security Lexicon* by Paul Evans and David Capie (2002) done for the IIR in that year, but still marked "for internal circulation."[115] Soon, however, this book was on sale in many of the major commercial bookstores in Hanoi. The concept of restricting circulation to a narrow policy elite is deeply entrenched, however. Certainly a Vietnamese translation of a book published in Singapore could not be of major concern to the prying eyes of foreigners, so the only point of restricting circulation would be to maintain an internal monopoly on knowledge. This practice, however, is dying out, and since 2000 there has been an explosion of foreign books commercially available both in Vietnamese translation and in foreign languages in Vietnam. These include texts on international relations and security issues translated from Chinese, carefully labeled "for reference" to underline that they are not necessarily the Vietnamese view.[116]

Moreover, the proliferation of textbooks on international relations since 2000 has created an increasing diversity of approaches to the study of this field. Some books are translations of foreign texts on international relations.[117] Many of the general surveys take the form of historical overviews of contemporary international relations, in the tradition of the "world history" approach and are aimed at providing an "authorized" history of events for a general audience of party and government officials.[118] Some are more specifically targeted for higher-level party training with ideological overtones and a policy focus.[119]

Much of the advanced discussion of international relations theory is done in party schools and the IIR, the Foreign Ministry's think tank and training school. In the IIR's own journal, published and available for subscription since the early 1990s, there has been a recent flurry of articles on various schools of Western thought about international relations.[120] The party's main theoretical journal also publishes articles which introduce its readers to international concepts and terms related to international relations.[121] Even in sensitive areas such as security and defense, Vietnam has adopted concepts and terminology which may not reflect its preferences or actual practices (such as "transparency") but at least there is now a common terminology to discuss the issue.

The fact that most of the advanced theoretical discussions about international relations still take place outside Vietnam universities illustrates the party's determination to continue to exert some control over the extent to which "knowledge networks" influence the development of sensitive areas of political inquiry. Still, the university curriculum in the area of international relations has come a long way since its cautious introduction in the mid-1990s, at least in its aspirations. An example is the preface of another book in the world-history genre of international relations, Professor Ninh's *History of International Relations*, whose first volume was published in 2006. This book is intended for use in the schools along with other more theoretical texts, and aims to provide students with tools to do their own analysis of events.[122]

In view of the great importance that Vietnamese leaders place on attaining a niche in the global "knowledge economy," the role of universities in training students able to function in this demanding role is increasingly vital. As of 2003, Vietnam had over a million university graduates and 100,000 doctorate holders. However, in the view of one educator, "the country's science and technology remains underdeveloped, being unable to produce products competitive with other countries."[123]

This practical concern has led to an increasing willingness of the Vietnamese government to undertake educational partnerships with foreign entities—a major departure for Vietnam's universities, whose insularity was once zealously guarded for fear of allowing them to become centers of heterodoxy in a tightly controlled ideological system. The current foreign partnerships are largely in practical and applied areas. In 2006, Boeing Corporation held a series of workshops with Vietnamese universities, aimed at standardizing and upgrading the engineering curriculum. "'The move to a universally accepted accreditation process will provide a significant benefit to Vietnamese students and universities,' said Patrick Antony, corporate director, Enterprise University Relations for Boeing, and the company's representative to ABET. 'For Vietnamese engineers and companies to compete globally, the world must be able to see that international standards of education are being applied.'"[124]

In areas like business training[125] and economics, foreign partnerships are proliferating as part of the drive to "internationalize the curriculum" in higher education. A report on Prime Minister Phan Van Khai's 2005 visit to Harvard and MIT notes that

> The Vietnamese leader met with Harvard President Lawrence H. Summers. He then briefly visited the John Harvard statue in Harvard Yard and touched the bronze toe of the statue for luck. The Harvard Institute for International Development (HIID) and the Harvard Yenching Institute have enrolled Vietnamese graduates to study at Harvard since 1998. Between 1996 and 2003, the John F. Kennedy School of Government of Harvard has operated the first level of the Fullbright [*sic*] Economics Teaching Programme at the Economics University in Ho Chi Minh City with a yearly funding of 1–1.2m [US dollars] from the Fullbright. On March 23, 2004 . . . Prime Minister Phan Van Khai met with professors from Harvard University and the MIT to discuss how to build a university of international standards in Vietnam.[126]

Although largely aimed at upgrading standards in practical fields, the internationalization of the curriculum will inevitably have an impact in more theoretical areas of the social sciences, such as international relations. As evidenced by the Ford Foundation's annual report of 2005, noted above, sociology and anthropology are rapidly developing as areas for international cooperation.

A related point is the increasingly important role of overseas Vietnamese. "Among nearly 3 million Vietnamese living abroad, about 300,000 people are university graduates and highly skilled workers who have a thorough knowledge of culture, science and technology and economic management. Many of them are leading officials at research institutes, universities and hospitals abroad and international organizations. Every year, about 200 overseas Vietnamese intellectuals have been invited to go back to Vietnam to work with relevant ministries, services, localities, and research institutions. Some of them have been invited to work as advisors to the Prime Minister."[127]

A combination of perceptions has reinforced the influence of knowledge networks in Vietnam. The understanding that increasingly development will require a knowledge-based economy is perhaps the most important. The related understanding that the threats and opportunities of globalization pose the same challenges for every participant in the international system has forced Vietnam to cast a wide net in understanding the reality in which it must operate (recall Vo Van Kiet's redefinition of the function of economic intelligence). The related expansion of travel, commerce, and overseas education has also had an impact. And finally, we should not underestimate the power of the concept of reaching for the "civilized" elements of world society, and the idea that there is a core of accepted advanced norms and practices that should be a guide for all states and societies.

There is no real conceptual counterweight to this one-world concept. Since the gradual dissipation of the illusion of a "Red solution" for some dimensions of international affairs, that would align Vietnam with China, and China's resolute insistence that there is no one "socialist" path to development, but only a "Chinese socialism" or a "Vietnamese socialism," there has been no ideological or political core around which conservatives like Nguyen Duc Binh could coalesce.

SOCIETY, CULTURE, AND POLITICS: GLOBALIZATION AND LOCALIZATION

The Vietnamese elites are the main participants in the knowledge networks that link Vietnamese society to the larger outside world. But these elites are also shaped by cultural forces within their own society. These cultural forces operate at the deepest levels of Vietnamese society and, like the more visible socioeconomic factors that have produced change in Vietnam since 1975, have undergone a profound transformation since that time.

From the impact of cosmopolitan and global forces on the attitudes and actions of the Vietnamese elite in the post–Cold War era, we now turn to the most local and distinctively Vietnamese aspects of societal change. This is a task that requires anthropological skills that are well beyond the range of the present author's training, and thus we will briefly survey some of the rich analyses of recent cultural change in Vietnam by some extraordinary scholars who have produced a corpus of fieldwork and interpretation which has profound implications for our topic.

Vietnam is indeed "changing worlds" in the sense of embarking on a process of deep integration with the larger global system. But the paradoxical consequence of globalization is that it had in many ways led to a revival of local traditions and cultural practices, which have reinforced Vietnam's distinctive identity or, as some would argue, identities—given the powerful resurgence of diverse manifestations of localism. Far from transforming Vietnamese society into a bland replica of some putative globalized model, globalization has opened the way for a resurgence of some of Vietnam's most distinctive traditions, and it has expanded cultural pluralism within Vietnam.

A striking example of this is the impact of the economic reforms—which have featured so prominently in the story of "changing worlds"—on the family, the basic unit of Vietnam's social structure, and on the seemingly esoteric topic of ritual remembrance of the dead, which is a central aspect of family cohesion and has deep cultural significance in Vietnam. Heonik Kwon's remarkable study *After the Massacre* provides a number of keen insights worthy of consideration.[128]

For the decades of the revolutionary conflicts and their aftermath, the Vietnamese state had tried to use a variety of devices such as public monuments to impose its views of what constituted heroic sacrifice, and of which of the deceased were true and worthy members of the authentic Vietnamese community. The goal was to achieve a cultural uniformity and internalization of the party's goals and values which would reinforce the political unity desired by the party. As Kwon and others discovered, however, the state began to lose its capacity to define which members of the community of the deceased were "worthy" and authentic. A vast cultural transformation was set in motion which challenged the capacity of the party and state to shape Vietnamese values in the way they had been able to do during wartime.

During the *doi moi* period, "The villagers incorporated the official monuments to heroic death into their domestic and public spaces, but they also built their own, unofficial cenotaphs and shrines. Unlike the state war monuments, these unofficial sites of hero worship were diverse in form and were used in actuality for remembering a wide spectrum of war deaths. The marginalized, informal remembrance of war dead benefitted from the economic reform and political liberalization initiated in the late 1980s. The economic reform program revitalized family-based agricultural and commercial activities, and it was accompanied by a growing tolerance of traditional religious practices. According to Hy Van Luong, political liberalization permitted the revival of family ancestral worship, through which the revitalized economic unit expressed its moral unity and developed practical kinship networks."[129]

Kwon shows that in Vietnamese culture there is a sense of interactive community between the living and the dead, which led to the large-scale movement of corpses into "a new common location under the proprietorship of a kin group as extended families began to control the land and resources required for this transference of grave sites. Just as the labor force was moving from the impoverished state sector to the revitalized private sector, so the corpses moved from the neglected margins of the centralized command economy to the center of the new private ritual economy."[130]

As Kwon points out "The Cold War split traditional community and family life in Vietnam, and even the identity of individuals. The split historic identity of the Cold War continues to be an unsettling element in family commemorations. How to reconcile the heroic heritage of a revolutionary ancestor with another ancestor's stigmatizing legacy as a counter-revolutionary is a pressing question for numerous families in southern and central Vietnam."[131] The "two worlds" of the Cold War international system were mirrored in the "two worlds" of Vietnam's civil war.

Physical relocation of the politically divided dead was one way of dealing with this. Another way in which the reclaiming of the primacy of kinship over politics helped to reunify these family divisions was by building family temples to commemorate the deceased kin. "The dead were the first to benefit from the economic reform. The first phase brought a large number of displaced remains of the war dead to the family-held graveyards, and this encouraged the development of practical collaboration and moral unity within the families. It prepared the moral and organizational grounds for the revival of unity that was to be crystallized in the community wide activities for the renovation of the ancestral temples. The temples reconstituted the autonomy of the traditional social organizations by providing them with historical depth. . . . The temple, in other words, restored the past to the living and secured the future for the dead."[132]

In a provocative chapter titled "The decomposition of the Cold War," Kwon draws some larger political conclusions from his anthropological research. "The revival of the cult of ancestors was an important part of the changing political relations of the dead. Localized ancestor worship emerged as a power paradigm of history in place of the dominant national hero-worship. Although war heroism and the ancestral cult share many common ideological and esthetic elements, these two social forms also have a few distinctive orientations. Vietnamese war heroism cuts through regional differences, creates homogeneity across differential local unity, and its management is centralized. The Vietnamese ancestral cult, on the contrary, emphasizes regional specificity, reinforces local unity, and its management is highly decentralized."[133]

Kwon notes that during the Cold War, two opposing scholarly views dominated the analytic attempts to frame the larger significance of the events of this period. One was the view that conflicts on the periphery of the spheres of the main antagonists were simply extensions of the primary conflict between the rival superpowers. The other, which Kwon terms "postcolonial," was that the dynamics of conflict in these peripheral areas, mostly former colonies of the West, were shaped by an indigenous nationalist vision and driven by local forces, not by orders from Moscow or Beijing. The critique of the "clients as proxies" view of the Cold War is by now well established, but Kwon adds a critique of the postcolonial view as well, on the grounds that it attributes a monolithic purpose and identity to the indigenous forces that it emphasizes as the true agents of their own history.

"The postcolonial historical perspective, in my view," says Kwon, "has not yet come to terms with the progression of modern political history, in which, ironically, the very 'native point of view' the postcolonial discourse tried to represent has turned into a locally hegemonic force, thus ruling out divergent experience and memories." Many postcolonial interpretations of revolutionary conflict have subscribed to the view of monolithic nationalism (as defined by the revolutionaries) in opposition to foreign intervention, thus obscuring the diversity of these societies. This slighting of cultural diversity can also extend to interpretations of tradition and modernity. In Kwon's view "the revival of ancestor worship in Vietnam . . . is not merely a restoration of traditional social ideals but rather of a countermeasure against dominant political convention."[134]

Still, despite the localizing and diversifying aspects of the return to an ancestor-clan–family cultural base for Vietnamese society, the net effect of this development has been to bind up the wounds of civil war, and achieve a social unity in the face of official preferences for perpetuating the divisions that undergird the party's legitimacy as the victor in a revolutionary conflict. "The revived ancestral worship in Vietnam contributes to undoing the legacy of the war by assimilating the historical political duality of 'this side' and 'that side' to the traditional unity of family (*nha and phai*) and lineage (*ho and toc*). . . . The history of the Cold War is changing in the place of the ancestors. Kinship identity transcends the political bifurcation and—like the nation's drive toward a new socioeconomic form that is also a partial embrace of 'the other side' (or incorporation into the other side, depending on how people look at it)—provides an alternative social unity."[135]

What does this deep cultural transformation have to do with collective idea change at the elite level? A systematic analysis of this question would require another book-length treatment. Perhaps a few personal anecdotes will suggest some answers. During the author's first visit to Hanoi in 1982, seven years after the end of the war, only a very constrained and tense meeting with his wife's only immediate relative in Hanoi (a sister) was permitted. A visiting American could only conclude that normal human relationships with Vietnamese in Vietnam would not be possible in his lifetime, given the overwhelming political and historical baggage involved in such contacts. In subsequent years, family contacts with Americans and Vietnamese-Americans became much easier and more relaxed.[136] Two decades after these tense encounters of the 1980s, many Vietnamese elites were unselfconsciously engaged in purely social relations with foreigners that were unthinkable in the 1980s, and even difficult throughout much of the 1990s. This is a reflection of the fading of the antagonistic "us against the enemy" view that characterized Vietnam during the Cold War, and posed a formidable barrier to meaningful contacts with it.

By 2007, evidence of the resurgence of familism documented by Kwon, Luong, Malarney, and others was even more pronounced. For the first time, the author and his wife were invited to a family occasion with cousins who had been active at high levels in the party's ideological sector. Subsequent discussions with several of these ideologists were open, informative, and suggested a sophisticated effort to adapt party ideology to new circumstances that stood in sharp contrast to their one-time superior, Nguyen Duc Binh. Their general approach might be described as seeking limited political liberalization as a means of preserving party rule. The fact that there was no longer a stigma attached to complex family relations and connections with foreigners, including those with a direct professional interest in sensitive areas of Vietnamese political life, was a telling indicator of the extent to which integration into the global community and the internal reconciliation documented by Kwon have progressed.

Also in early 2007, the author's wife discovered that the residents of a North Vietnamese village had petitioned her cousins to allow the addition of her uncle to the village pantheon, alongside statues of Ho Chi Minh and a memorial to revolutionary martyrs in the village communal house. Although the uncle had suffered painful persecution as a landlord, despite his support of the Viet Minh (an episode vividly described in her family history, *The Sacred Willow*[137]), he was now regarded by the villagers as a benefactor whose now auspicious and protective presence would benefit the village community. In the same year, in her family's native village south of Ha Noi, the state designated the refurbished tombs of her nineteenth-century mandarin ancestors—who had once been reviled by the revolution as "feudalists" and mandarins who were not only oppressing the people but had capitulated to the French—an "official historical and cultural site." It was inaugurated with a festive and well-attended ceremony, with local party officials as prominent guests of honor.

It is not hard to imagine that family stories like these are now commonplace among the Vietnamese elite. Most political commentary by external observers about the impact of the reforms on society, and the implications for political change, has focused on the debate about whether economic reform inevitably leads to the development of civil society which, in turn, creates pressures for democratization. This study does not address this question, or the even more complicated debates about recent developments in state–society relations in Vietnam, beyond what was said in chapter 8 about the controversies concerning state-owned enterprises and discussions in other chapters of debates concerning the extent to which the economic reforms were top-down or bottom-up.

It could be, however, that the resurgence of familism and distinctive local social and religious practices will serve as a kind of buffer against state intrusion into core areas of society, in the same way that "civil society" is alleged to. But while the additional breathing space for family groups and individuals has a profound impact on the way life is lived, it does not necessarily lead to democratization in the way the proponents of the "civil society" scenario predict. Indeed by strengthening patronage networks (including networks of corruption), resurgent familism may lead in a quite different direction. In this sense, the acceptance of the inevitability—and even desirability—of "changing worlds" does not signify an inevitable commitment to democracy as well as market capitalism, or an acceptance of the "end of history" view that all countries will eventually end up as capitalist democracies. There is indeed now one world instead of two, but in the view of most Vietnamese elites, it is a world of diversity—not two models, or one model, but many possible futures.

It seems clear from the observable evidence of how elites function in Vietnam today, that resurgent familism has provided an environment that is congenial to open engagement and deep integration with the rest of the world. In part this is because of the economic benefits that integration and economic reform have conferred not merely on individuals but on family groups—housing, education, private-sector opportunities among them—far beyond the state's capacity to furnish equivalent benefits to an equivalent number.

A VISION FOR THE FUTURE

This is not a book of prognostication. We have traced a significant transformation in the collective mindset of Vietnamese elites about the nature of their society, the world they live in, and the proper relationship between the two. Whether Vietnam will be recognizably the same polity several decades from now is impossible to predict. A summary of the path Vietnam has traveled since the end of the Vietnam War may offer some clues, however.

Was it the post–Cold War transformation of the global power structure that led Vietnam down the path it subsequently took? Or the positive and negative incentives of the global economy? Was the significant shift in collective ideas among the Vietnamese political elite a cause or a consequence of these objective factors? Among these idea changes, three stand out as fundamental and transformational. The first was the rejection of the Marxist central-planning model in the 1980s, and the related undermining of the idea that the party (and its leadership) was always right, far seeing, and wise. The second was the shift from confrontation to accommodation marked by Resolution 13 (1988) and the decision to withdraw from Cambodia, along with the related upgrading of economic development as Vietnam's top priority, and downgrading of military force as the ultimate guarantor of Vietnam's national interests. The third was the 1991 adoption of a policy of "becoming friends" with all countries who would agree to normal relations with Vietnam—which implicitly rejected the zero-sum "us against the enemy" foundation of previous Vietnamese strategic thinking.

These three developments took place in a context of crisis, but the hammer-blow shock did not come until the final collapse of the Soviet Union in 1991. This definitively undermined any possibility of avoiding real change. It marked the beginning of the end for the conservative resistance to reform and opened the way for the subsequent decisions to reconcile with former adversaries, join ASEAN, and to embark on a path of deep integration with the global economy. It was not, therefore, a single "external shock" that led to these changes, but a shock following an extended crisis which had weakened resistance to change that was the *coup de grace* for the old ways. Although Vietnam's current leadership has not abandoned the rhetorical goal of becoming an advanced industrialized socialist country, it is a far cry from the "time just after reunification" which people talked of "as being intoxicating, a time when people could seriously imagine that by following the

Soviet model Vietnam could become an industrialized country by the year 2000, 'after four to five Five Year Plans.'"[138]

Vietnam several decades from now will probably still be ruled by the Communist Party, or some authoritarian version of it, but it will be a significantly transformed party. Dependence on performance legitimacy to sustain its authority will lock it into international integration as will the security model (stability and cooperation) it adopted at the end of the Cold War. Politics will probably not take the form of multiparty competition but sectoral and interest group representation could become much more structured and salient, and perhaps institutionalized into networks of factions within a dominant party, as in Japan's LDP for much of the post-1945 period (a possibility that is of considerable interest to some of Vietnam's ideologists). There will be increasing stress on transparency and accountability, and probably a more prominent political role for the National Assembly.

As specialists on communist political systems have long known, the Achilles heel of the domination by a single party is the problem of finding a way to institutionalize political succession.[139] We have seen that the transfer of power from the generation of political leaders who had gained prominence during the years of revolutionary struggle to a younger generation of more technocratic leaders was prolonged and often led to political stalemate. Whether a less intrusive party and state will reduce the stakes of power holding and alleviate the potential for succession crises, remains to be seen. In some ways, increasing stress on performance legitimacy may also lead to more consensus on who the most capable leaders are. Nonetheless, Vietnam is far from being a state governed by laws or Weberian bureaucratic rationality. Political power, lodged within the party, will probably trump constitutional formalities, legal codes, and administrative rules for some time to come.

As the representation of interest groups becomes more important, the most difficult political task will be finding new ways of regulating interactions between patron–client networks. The expanding size and complexity of the elite will make this more difficult. The tangle of public–private economic relationships may entrench corruption still deeper into the system.

Corruption is at the heart of the intersection between the "refamilization" of Vietnamese society (with implications for reshaping patron–client networks involved in corruption along kinship lines) and the pressures of deep integration and external competition, including the demand of foreign investors for transparency and an even playing field. The external pressures have a complicated impact on Vietnam domestically. On the one hand a more predictable rule of law and greater transparency are important for encouraging foreign investment. On the other hand, the foreign investment raises the financial stakes for individuals and groups with official connections and gives more incentives for corrupt behavior.

There is an important body of scholarship that would dispute this negative symbiosis between integration and corruption. Sandholtz and Gray have done extensive research which leads them to the conclusion that greater degrees of international integration lead to lower levels of corruption, which we define as the misuse of public office for private gain. We theorize that international factors affect a country's level of corruption through two principal channels. One acts through economic incentives, altering for various actors the costs and benefits of engaging in corrupt acts. The second mode is normative. Prevailing norms in international society delegitimate and stigmatize corruption. Countries that are more integrated into international society are more exposed to economic and normative pressures against corruption. We therefore test the following hypothesis: the more a country is tied into international networks of exchange, communication, and organization, the lower its level of corruption is likely to be. The analysis of data from approximately 150 countries strongly confirms our expectation.[140]

Over the long run, this may well be the case in Vietnam, but the experience of the past decade casts some doubt on this hypothesis. Although "prevailing international norms" have had an important impact in other areas of Vietnamese political and economic life (including security concepts and legal reform) in the case of the nexus between refamilization, patron–client relations, and corruption, domestic factors trump external norms and practices. Indeed, the incentives for corruption provided by Vietnam's integration have sometimes combined to exacerbate the problem. Perhaps the most famous recent case of corruption involved two dimensions of integration—misuse of foreign aid funds, and Vietnam's mania for global (especially English) soccer.

The scandal started with a few bets on soccer games $7 million worth of bets and it raised such an uproar here that even the leader of the Communist Party joined in, saying that corruption "threatens the survival of our system." It was a shocking statement, in late April, from the most powerful man in the land and reflected serious concern at the top over one of the most corrosive and intractable problems in this fast-developing country. The head of an organization called PMU18 which managed hundreds of millions of dollars from foreign aid for development and construction placed a bet, reportedly $320,000 on an English soccer match. The subsequent investigation set investigators on a trail of mansions, mistresses, luxury cars and protection money that led to the resignation in early April of the transport minister and the jailing of his deputy. Three men implicated in the scandal had been on a list of nominees to join the Communist Party Central Committee later that month.[141]

Corruption is acknowledged as a pervasive and serious problem by everyone from the top party leaders to the most outspoken dissidents. Since the extent and severity of the problem are not in question, the main points of controversy about corruption center on what the causes of corruption are and what to do about it. The party leadership generally portrays this as a result of moral and political failings of individuals, which can be corrected by cracking down on those who are caught. The larger systemic issues raised by the problem of corruption tend to be downplayed. There is, for example, little direct discussion of the incentives for corruption presented by a mixed economy in which free market payoffs are often dependent on privileged official connections.

Another systemic response to the problem of corruption would be improvement of the legal system which, of course, would have significant implications for Party rule and Vietnamese politics as currently practiced. In some ways, one of the most profound impacts of deep integration will be on the Vietnamese legal system which, in turn, will affect the not only the relations between the state and its citizens, but also interactions with foreigners and the outside world.

Scholarship on the influence of foreign models on the Vietnamese legal system has documented one important dimension of the "epistemic communities" discussed above, namely the opening of Vietnam to a variety of international models of law and legal systems. John Gillespie examines the way in which the post–Cold War changes have affected discourse on law and legal systems in Vietnam, and concludes that "shifts in Marxist economic thinking have made legal borrowing from capitalist countries theoretically respectable, but at the same time, the role of 'state economic management' in the mixed-market economy is unresolved. Legal discourse reflects this uncertainty. It oscillates between the neoliberal legal language that permeates foreign-donor discourse and the ambiguous messages in Party and government writings about 'Party leadership' over the economy. With some notable exceptions . . . legal discourse rarely considers the institutional and epistemological incompatibilities generated by superimposing a rights-based legislative framework over a Soviet-inspired legal system."[142]

This illustrates the point that integration affects not only specific sectors of the political, social, and economic system in Vietnam, but also the relationship among them, as in the case of law, economics, and legislation, mentioned by Gillespie. In his informative analysis of legal change in Vietnam, Gillespie notes that "Legal discourse is learning from new economic ideas, especially concepts sponsored by international trade agreements. Other epistemological barriers are also dissolving. Marxist antipathy toward East Asian culture has been replaced by a 'reality' manufactured to support contemporary development objectives. Utopian yearnings for a model socialist society have been discarded in favour of East Asian developmentalism with 'socialist' characteristics. In the arenas where legal discourse has emerged from the shadow of political discourse, socialist law has become noticeably more legalistic and rule-oriented."[143] His conclusion is that Vietnam is evolving in a direction of "hybrids" between imported laws and legal concepts and "local norms and practices." "In other social arenas, where political and moral discourses remain more powerful than legal discourse and without compelling reasons to legalise or constitutionalise political processes, 'socialist law' is likely to remain faithful to longstanding Marxist-Leninist concepts."[144]

This might serve as a general proposition on how deep integration will affect Vietnam's future development. National interest, in creating a more favorable environment for economic development, will produce more adaptations of the old legal and economic framework, but there will be tensions because of the inherent strain of building new additions onto a sometimes incompatible foundational structure. And, for the foreseeable future, politics and party will trump economics and the law—with the important qualification that the party now sees its future as dependent on successful economic development, which will go a long way toward producing congruence between political and economic objectives.

Beyond these systemic and structural questions is the issue raised by this book: the impact of collective idea change among the political elite of Vietnam. Even if the Communist Party remains the dominant political force in Vietnam for the foreseeable future, it will be a very different party because of the substantial shift in ideas and assumptions about the world among the elite that has taken place over the past several decades, and the continuing reinforcement of this process of idea change by extensive engagement in global "knowledge-based networks."

Two elements of the impact of ideas transmitted through these knowledge-based networks are worthy of particular attention. The first is the hybridity issue mentioned by Gillespie. As in the case of borrowed models of law and legal concepts resting uneasily on the old Marxist foundations, imported ideas in other areas of the political system may lead to incongruity and inconsistency. A combination of the concern about alienating its neighbors (especially China) and a desire to speak the reassuring language of ASEAN and the Track II dialogues have led Vietnam to largely avoid open discussion of the realpolitik dimension of international relations, such as the implications of the rise of China, using bromides such as "stability" and becoming "friends with all countries" to sidestep the question that used to be the starting point of analyzing a strategy for dealing with the world; who are real friends and who are prospective enemies. This contemporary cosmopolitan security discourse is in most respects an improvement over the ideological and confrontational impulses of the "us against the enemy" aspect of the Cold War period, but it also raises the question of how deeply rooted in the mental grooves worn by Vietnam's traditional strategic culture it is. Should crisis or instability challenge the foundations of the hopeful assumptions on which this non-strategy is based, will Vietnam remain wedded to its new thinking about security and international relations?

The main exception to the hope-for-the best approach to security is the diehard conservatives still flogging the threat of "peaceful evolution." But between paranoia and Pollyanna, there appears to have been an atrophy of a once-vibrant (if often doctrinaire) tradition of strategic analysis in Vietnam.

A second element of the impact of ideas from the outside on Vietnam is the differential way in which they affect various sectors of Vietnamese life. The hip-hop crazy younger urban set attending overflow performances in places like the former Soviet Cultural Friendship Palace[145] may not be concerned with neoliberal theories of the impact of integration on development, but they are profoundly influenced by the consequences of these ideas as they play out in Vietnam. These are precisely the people who will be an important component of the next generation of Vietnam's political elite.

An example of how internal changes caused by the social impact of a changing economic system interact with the absorption of global attitudes and values is the changing attitude toward personal wealth and conspicuous consumption in Vietnam. One has only to stroll past the former State Department store in downtown Hanoi to see the advertising emblems of international chic which long ago displaced the humble enameled tin basins—the acme of consumerism when the author made his first visit to that city in 1982. A *Christian Science Monitor* report titled "The Monied Heroes of New Vietnam" observes that "Social attitudes toward public displays of wealth and success are shifting after decades of war and austerity, particularly among the under-24 crowd, which makes up over half of the population. Luxury-brand retailers are vying for consumers who until recently preferred to sock money away or invest quietly in real estate rather than flaunt it. And as Vietnam integrates fully into the world economy—it joined the World Trade Organization in January [2007]—such trends seem likely to grow, as more Vietnamese join the affluent classes and feel more secure about showing off. 'Vietnam is a country that's gone from looking down on entrepreneurs and private businessmen to revering them. This is a culture that worships successful entrepreneurship,' says Than Trong Phuc, country manager for US chipmaker Intel, which is building a $1 billion plant in Vietnam."[146]

The generational contrast in attitudes toward prosperity and egalitarianism, as noted in the introduction, was vividly displayed in the public reaction to the sensational exhibit "Hanoi Life Under the Subsidy Economy" in 2006–7. Recall the comments of curator Nguyen Van Huy: "The younger generation who did not live in the subsidy economy can hardly understand how their parents lived," said Huy. "On weekends, about 2,000 visitors—about five times the usual attendance—pack into the museum. The parking lot overflows with motorcycles and even private cars, which are so new in Vietnam that the museum had to create a special parking place for them. 'Those are the rich people who bring their children to tell them about their life in the past,' Huy said."[147] Even though the parents visiting this exhibit were largely members of the elite, now prospering under the reforms, there was a widespread nostalgia for the solidarity and idealism of the austere era of shared poverty. Hanoi parents reported, with resigned amusement, that the reaction of their children to the privations of their elders was (with a tone of teenage bored exasperation) "you told us already; it was really miserable; you keep repeating it [*biet roi, kho lam, noi mai*]."[148]

It is probably a combination of the resurgent familism stemming from the economic reforms and a widespread global attitude of admiration for those who achieve material success that have reinforced changing views concerning wealth and equality in Vietnam. The consequences of this shift in societal attitudes for the old ideology are profound. At the same time, it leaves open the question of what the future basis of social solidarity will be if prosperity is not equitably shared across classes and regions.

The key question is how changing social attitudes will play out politically. The political sphere in Vietnam is somewhat insulated from outside ideas and models, though it is indirectly affected by the fallout from Vietnam's opening up to the outside world. The party hopes that it can compartmentalize and control these outside influences. But can the development of rule of law in the commercial sphere to reassure foreign investors be walled off from the sphere of political accountability? Given the way in which globalization has paradoxically unleashed diverse currents of localism at the cultural level, it seems that globalization's impact does not come in a standard integrated package. It appears unlikely that outside influences can be as cleanly segregated and controlled as the party hopes.

The essential condition for the trajectory of the past two decades to continue is the maintenance of international and regional stability. This is the basic assumption underlying every aspect of Vietnamese thinking about external strategy and domestic development. Despite the post–Cold War turmoil in other areas, and even in the face of the Asian financial crisis, the stability assumption central to the collective idea-change among the Vietnamese elite has not been seriously challenged. If this continues, so will the process of idea change which reinforces deep integration and engagement with the outside world. But it should be emphasized that it was the dual shock of economic failure closely followed by the collapse of Vietnam's conceptual and political world with the end of the Cold War and disintegration of the Soviet Union that was the indispensable catalyst to the extensive collective idea change that took place in the following years. Should an equivalent combination of global and domestic upheaval take place, another fundamental rethinking of assumptions would no doubt follow. The Asian financial crisis of 1997–8 and the global economic crisis of 2008 certainly challenged the stability assumption, but do not appear to have derailed the leadership's commitment to deep integration, but that does not mean that some future crisis would not lead to a reappraisal of Vietnam's international course.

Barring such cataclysm, Vietnam seems likely to become an increasingly pluralistic society, living in a pluralist world. The two are mutually reinforcing. The prospects for political liberalization seem much more uncertain. But we have seen that political change and idea change are closely, if not always causally, connected. The great obstacles to change in Vietnam during the Cold War were the severely limited conceptual horizons of the political elite, and the lack of persuasive alternatives to the rigid orthodoxies of the day. The discrediting of key elements of the "old thinking" and the immersion into a global world of ideas and "knowledge-based networks" now provide a wide range of alternative approaches to the full spectrum of Vietnam's concerns.

Most recent scholarship on Asian security issues has been syncretic, using a combination of insights from different schools of thought according to their utility and explanatory power in a given context.[149] In calling for "analytic eclecticism," Katzenstein and Sil compiled a book on Asian security in which chapters "share one thing in common in the answers they offer. . . . they all combine insights drawn from a least two of the research traditions [realism, liberalism, constructivism]. The chapters draw on a mixture of insights from the three different research traditions, pointing to the importance of, and relationships between, identity, interest, and power in the adaptation of Asian states' strategic behavior."[150] This book has attempted to follow this "eclectic" tradition, while focusing mainly on ideas, identity issues, values, and perceptions of the political elite.

Jeffry Legro, whose work on collective idea-change has provided many helpful insights for this study of Vietnam's "changing worlds," stresses that his idea is "not to show that ideas 'trump' other traditional factors—specifically power or interest groups—in explaining foreign policy change and continuity, but instead to make sense of how these *ideas interact with other factors in specific ways* to cause outcomes."[151] The power factor of losing its main strategic partner, the Soviet Union, was a decisive precondition for Vietnam's decision to opt for deep integration. So was the failure of its central-planning economic model, and the loss of Soviet economic aid which had, for a time, disguised the failure. If China had taken another path, and had accepted Vietnam's several attempts to create an ideological axis of the remnant communist regimes, the story might have been different. The fact that it took more than a decade from the dual economic-strategic crisis of the 1980s to the final decision to "take the plunge" in 2000, indicates that there was considerable resistance to accepting the risks and uncertainties of deep integration, and that "muddling through" without making substantial changes from the old ways had a logic and an appeal to an important segment of the political elite.

In the final analysis, the factor that probably tipped the balance to a decisive commitment to deep integration was nationalism—the fear of irrevocably falling behind its neighbors and the rest of the world, which had an underlying logic of both power politics and economics. "Falling behind" also would mean accepting the marginalization of Vietnam in the international community, which was unacceptable to most Vietnamese. The necessary facilitating condition was relative peace, with the exception of global terrorism and conflicts in the Gulf and Central Asia (which benefited Vietnam by distracting the United States from making Vietnam an adversarial target because of its political system and related human-rights issues), and stability in the region. Regional stability along with dynamic regional economic growth made joining ASEAN an attractive option, and Vietnamese membership had a strong impact on both its strategic outlook and in its learning curve about the world of its former adversaries. Nonetheless, the sufficient condition for Vietnam to make a clear-cut choice to open up to the world was, in the end, a decisive shift in the center of gravity of the collective mindset of its political elite.

Vietnam has indeed "changed worlds," in the sense that it has adjusted to the end of the bipolarity of the Cold War "two worlds" international structure, largely abandoned its "us against the enemy" zero-sum view of the outside world, and opted for deep integration into a globalized system. This does not, however, mean that it has been swallowed up by the capitalist–democratic world that survived the collapse of its Cold War rival. In this sense, the consequence of Vietnam's "changing worlds" has not been absorption into the world of the Cold War victors, propelled by force of circumstance to proceed down the same path and follow the same model, but a journey from a world of limited intellectual and political horizons and highly circumscribed strategic choices, to the open world of globalization with its challenging mix of perils and opportunities.

NOTES

PREFACE TO THE PAPERBACK EDITION

1. July 2000 is probably the best guess. See David W. P. Elliott, *Changing Worlds: Vietnam's Transition from Cold War to Globalization* (Oxford University Press: 2012), 197.

2. See http://phamvuluaha.wordpress.com/2013/06/20/why-i-write-the-winning-side/.

3. *Changing Worlds*, 40.

4. The two most comparable cases are the writings of the Paris-based Bui Tin, once a Deputy Editor of the Party newspaper and close confidant of General Vo Nguyen Giap, and Vu Thu Hien, whose father was a personal secretary of Ho Chi Minh's.

5. Thomas Fuller, "In Hard Times, Open Dissent and Repression Rise in Vietnam," *New York Times*, April 24, 2013, http://www.nytimes.com/2013/04/24/world/asia/vietnam-clings-to-single-party-rule-as-dissent-rises-sharply.html?_r=0. Huy Duc's real name is Truong Huy San. Born in 1962 in the one-time revolutionary hotbed of Ha Tinh province, he served in Vietnam's military during its occupation of Cambodia, and was subsequently a journalist for the liberal *Tuoi Tre* newspaper until he was terminated for pushing the envelope of criticism too far. In 2012–13 Huy Duc was a Nieman Fellow at Harvard.

6. *BTC II*, 215.

7. See Jeffrey W. Legro, *Rethinking the World: Great Power Strategies and International Order* (Ithaca: Cornell University Press, 2005) and the discussion in *Changing Worlds*, 13.

8. *BTC I*, 256–67.

9. *Changing Worlds*, 39.

10. See note 35 on p. 335 in *Changing Worlds*, which cites the author's own earlier statement to this effect.

11. *Changing Worlds*, 40.

12. *BTC I*, 338.

13. Ibid., 114–31.

14. *Changing Worlds*, 186–87.

15. *BTC II*, 191.

16. Ibid., 405–06.

17. Barbara Crossette, "Hanoi, Citing Famine Fears, Seeks Emergency Aid," *New York Times*, May 15, 1988.

18. *BTC II*, 63.

19. Ibid., 66.

20. Ibid., 212–13.

21. Ibid., 138.

22. *Changing Worlds*, 179.

23. Ibid., 265.

24. *BTC II*, 279.

25. For a discussion of this point, see *Changing Worlds*, 119.

26. Ibid., 193.

27. Ibid., 166.

28. Ibid., 167.

29. *BTC II*, 305.

30. Ibid., 306.

31. Ibid., 387.

32. Ibid., 402–03. Much of this centers around the role of state ownership in Vietnam's economy.

PREFACE

1. See for example the biographical profile of Huynh and his contributions to the conference described in James Blight, Robert Brigham, Thomas Biersteker, and Col. Herbert Schandler, *Argument without End: In Search of Answers to the Vietnamese Tragedy* (New York: Public Affairs, 1999). Huynh passed away in 2010. For a moving and perceptive appreciation of his remarkable life, see Stein Tonnesson's posting on the Vietnam Studies Group Listserv, February 23, 2010.

2. Some papers from this conference are contained in William S. Turley and Mark Selden, eds., *Reinventing Vietnamese Socialism: "Doi Moi" in Comparative Perspective* (Boulder CO: Westview Press, 1993).

CHAPTER 1

1. Gareth Porter, "The Transformation of Vietnam's World-view: From Two Camps to Interdependence," *Contemporary Southeast Asia* 12, no. 1 (June 1990): 5.

2. Ibid., 3.

3. David Lamb, "War is History for Vibrant Vietnam," *Los Angeles Times*, April 30, 2005.

4. Adam Fforde and Stefan de Vylder, *From Plan to Market: The Economic Transition in Vietnam* (Boulder, CO: Westview Press, 1996): 128.

5. For a discussion of Vietnam's traditional fixation with possession goals, see David W. P. Elliott "Vietnam: Tradition Under Challenge," in Russell Trood and Ken Booth, ed., *Strategic Cultures in the Asia-Pacific Region* (New York: St. Martin's, 1999). For the "strategic judo" aspect

of revolutionary Vietnam's diplomacy, see David W. P. Elliott "Hanoi's Strategy in the Vietnam War," in Jayne Werner, ed., *The Vietnam War: Vietnamese and American Perspectives* (New York: Sharpe, 1993).

6. Cited in Aaron L. Friedberg, *In the Shadow of the Garrison State* (Princeton: Princeton University Press, 2000): 3.

7. Fforde and de Vylder, *From Plan to Market*, 63.

8. Ibid., 95.

9. Hoc Vien Quan He Quoc Te, "Thang loi co tinh thoi dai va cuoc dau tranh tren mat tran doi ngoai cua nhan dan ta" [A victory reflecting the spirit of the age and struggle of our people on the diplomatic front] (Hanoi: NXB Su That, 1985): 8–9.

10. Jack S. Levy, "Learning and Foreign Policy: Sweeping a Conceptual Minefield," *International Organization* 48, no. 2. (Spring 1994): 298.

11. Ibid.

12. Although this study does not take a comparative approach, the case of China raises many interesting questions for the study of collective idea change in Vietnam. A vital difference between the two cases is the discrediting of Maoism, which allowed much of the "old thinking" to be swept away as tainted by association with Mao, and the extraordinary figure of Deng Xiaoping, who was an early convinced reformer and used his dominant power position to impose his policies on the political system. In Vietnam, there was not an equivalent figure either in terms of commitment to sweeping reforms or in terms of political dominance that could impose preferred policies despite opposition. With respect to the Soviet Union, the most useful comparative issue (which, however, this study does not attempt to undertake) is the question of the extent to which the need for economic reform in the Soviet Union drove the adjustments in military and foreign policy.

13. Levy, "Learning and Foreign Policy," 300.

14. Ibid., 301.

15. Jeffrey W. Legro, *Rethinking the World: Great Power Strategies and International Order* (Ithaca: Cornell University Press, 2005).

16. Ibid., 11.

17. Ibid.

18. "Foreign policy idea change (and continuity) depends on preexisting ideas. Collective ideas fundamentally shape their own continuity or transformation (1) by setting the terms and conditions of when change is appropriate and (2) constituting the most likely option(s) for the new orthodoxy." Ibid., 13.

19. Ibid.

20. Ibid., 34.

21. Justin Fox, *The Myth of the Rational Market* (New York: HarperCollins, 2009): xi–xv.

22. Deborah Welch Larson and Alexei Shevchenko, "Shortcut to Greatness: The New Thinking and the Revolution in Soviet Foreign Policy," *International Organization* 73 (Winter 2003): 77.

23. Ibid., 78.

24. Porter, "Transformation of Vietnam's World-view," 4.

25. The classic discussion of this theme in early modern Asian nationalism is Benjamin Schwartz, *In Search of Wealth and Power: Yen Fu and the West* (Harper, 1969).

26. Porter, "Transformation of Vietnam's World-view," 5.

27. Ibid., 6.

28. Kay Johnson, "Vietnam Relives the Bad Old Days," Deutsche Press-Agentur, August 15, 2006.

29. Ibid.

30. Ibid.

31. Hoang Tung, "Thoi dai moi, tu tuong moi" [New age, new ideology], text on website of Radio Free Asia (Vietnamese), April 22, 2005; http://www.rfa.org/vietnamese/; see also http://www.wright.edu/~tdung/HoangTung.htm.

32. Serge Berthier interview with Le Dang Doanh, *Asian Affairs*, Spring 2000.

33. Ibid.

34. Ibid.

35. An interesting exception to this generalization is the role played by eminent historians from central Vietnam, Dr. Phan Huy Le in particular, in broadening the horizons of the discipline and fostering extensive scholarly links beyond the socialist countries. Dr. Le's colleague Prof. Tran Quoc Vuong did, however, make some amusing comments about the predominence of the central Vietnam influence in his field. "Speaking of friends who came from Nghe-Tinh . . . I always had a bit of a 'complex' [English in original] . . . about my immaturity (non kem). I was from the Country of the North [*bac ky quac*, a teasing word play on the central Vietnamese pronunciation of "bac ky quoc," itself a self-deprecating reference to the regional insularity and self-importance of the North Vietnamese, as seen by many from other regions]. . . . Nguyen Khac Vien (himself from Nghe-Tinh) . . . told me . . . 'Over half, if not two-thirds of the scientists [the term includes social scientists] at present are from Nghe-Tinh.'" Tran Quoc Vuong, *Khoa Su Va Toi* [The faculty of history and me] (Hanoi: NXB Dai Hoc Quoc Gia Ha Noi, 2001): 132.

CHAPTER 2

1. This is the thesis of Jeffrey Legro, "If there is a default explanation for discontinuous shifts in social ideas," writes Legro, "it is 'external shock'—typically such big events as war, revolution, or economic crisis. . . ." But, he notes, there is a problem with this simple formula: "Similar shocks seem to have different effects: some leading to change and some not." Legro, *Rethinking the World*.

2. Legro is mainly concerned with big powers. The relevant link to the present study of Vietnam is his concern with how national elites "fundamentally reassess their strategies of engagement with the international order."

3. Jack S. Levy, "Learning and Foreign Policy: Sweeping a Conceptual Minefield," *International Organization* 48, no. 2. (Spring 1994), 301.

4. Thus Matthew Evangelista suggests that, "Learning metaphors obscure what is fundamentally a political process," and Allen Lynch argues that the new thinking "is first of all a political rather than an intellectual or conceptual act." Jack S. Levy, "Learning and Foreign Policy," 301. For the importance of economic factors, see Celeste A. Wallander, "Western Policy and the Demise of the Soviet Union," *Journal of Cold War Studies* 5, no. 4 (Fall 2003).

5. Fforde and de Vylder, *From Plan to Market*, 126.

6. Pham Hung speech at the Sixth Party Congress, BBC Summary of World Broadcasts, January 3, 1987.

7. Legro, *Rethinking the World*, 13.

8. Tran Do, "Dai Hoi Nam" [Fifth Party Congress], *Hoi Ky* [Memoir], tap 2, chuong 2 [volume 2, chapter 2]. As is the case with several key documents used in this study, this version of the

memoir was taken from the internet, and its authenticity and provenance cannot be verified. I used the version found on http://ykien.net/bntd_hoiky21.html, and feel sufficiently confident in its authenticity to use it here.

9. The author interviewed Tran Do in August 1982 in his office at the Ministry of Culture at about the time this incident with Le Duc Tho took place. One topic of discussion was a pamphlet authored by Tran Do on the dangers and evils of "decadent culture," a forerunner of "peaceful evolution." At the time I concluded that Tran Do was a hard-line conservative. Subsequently, I was told by a number of Vietnamese that he was, in fact, viewed as something of a patron of the writers and artists, with a real appreciation of artistic creativity, and a "liberal" in terms of matters of artistic freedom—which readers of his tract on "subversive culture" would find hard to image. His subsequent memoir reveals that the reality of that time was far more complex than I could ever have imagined, and once again underlines the futility of outsiders trying to plumb the depths of Vietnamese politics. It is, however, highly unlikely that Do would have become such a visible dissident if he had not felt so outraged and betrayed by Le Duc Tho's conniving attack on him.

10. Le Duc Anh, "Tong bi thu Le Duan nhu toi biet" (ky cuoi) [The Le Duan that I knew: Final installment], *Tien Phong* online, July 10, 2006.

11. Tran Do, "Dai Hoi Nam."

12. Michael Fathers, "An Old Soldier who Clung in Vain to the Spoils of Victory," *The Independent* (London), October 14, 1990.

13. Martin Gainsborough, *Changing Political Economy of Vietnam: The Case of Ho Chi Minh City* (London: Routledge Curzon, 2003), 107.

14. Martin Gainsborough, "Beneath the veneer of reform: the politics of economic liberalisation in Vietnam," *Communist and Post-Communist Studies* 35 (2002), 355.

15. Vo Van Kiet, "Nghi luc va khi phach Pham Hung" [The energy and firmness of purpose of Pham Hung], in Truong Van Sau et al., *An Tuong Vo Van Kiet* [Impressions of Vo Van Kiet] (Ho Chi Minh City: NXB Tre, 2002), 310–11.

16. Vo Van Kiet, "Dong chi Truong Chinh—Tong bi thu cua doi moi" [Comrade Truong Chinh: General secretary of *doi moi*], in Truong Van Sau et al., *An Tuong Vo Van Kiet*, 292.

17. Vo Van Kiet, "Dong Chi Pham Van Dong: Nha cach mang uyen bac va mot nhan cach lon" [Comrade Pham Van Dong: An erudite revolutionary and a great person], in Truong Van Sau et al., *An Tuong Vo Van Kiet*, 297.

18. In June 1985, Mr. Linh was quietly restored to the politburo. Despite opposition from Truong Chinh, the party ideologue, and Le Duc Tho, he was elected party chief at the Sixth Congress in December 1986. Steven Erlanger, "Vietnam, Drained by Dogmatism, Tries a 'Restructuring' of Its Own," *New York Times*, April 24, 1989.

19. "At the beginning he was in charge of socialist transformation in the provinces of the South.... [I]n the end he became a kind of roving inspector [*chung chung*] in the provinces of the South. When the Fifth Party Congress was held [1982] he asked to withdraw from the politburo." Tran Hieu and Manh Viet, "Gap nhung nhan chung cua 'Cuoc xe rao lich su': ky cuoi—'Ong gia can co'" [Meetings with witnesses of the "historic fence breaking," final installment: "The diligent old man"], *Tien Phong* online, June 26, 2006.

20. The most notable of these was the underground memoir of Tran Quynh, a former deputy prime minister, who tried to refurbish the overall historical picture of Le Duan. "Citing the shortcomings, errors, and temporary defeats with the goal of obscuring or blackening the picture of Le Duan, or even denying the role of Le Duan, is an anti-historical and anti-scientific attitude, and

stems from an inglorious attitude of envy. The thing that pains me the most is that after Le Duan's death, the leaders of the country, who had earlier praised Le Duan and who didn't dare to open their mouths to say anything bad about Le Duan have, intentionally or not, let the campaign to blacken his reputation and reject his role spread ever larger. The ink used to blacken his reputation gets darker and darker and the scope of it continues to spread. At the most, a number of people light a candle on the death anniversary of Le Duan, read a speech, do interviews, and write feeble articles for the newspapers." "Nhung ky niem ve Le Duan," *Hoi Ky cua Tran Quynh* ["Reminiscences about Le Duan," Memoir of Tran Quynh], http://www.lmvntd.org/dossier/tquynh.htm.

21. He notes but does not explain the reasons for the fact that "The concentration for reform of the high ranking military officers and civilian civil servants of the puppet authorities was announced to be for two years but in reality dragged out to ten years." And Mai Chi Tho said that the fact that their jailors had to eat the same food "was also something of a consolation to them, even though no one wanted this situation." Nguyen Thi Ngoc Hai, *Mai Chi Tho Tuong Con Dan* [Mai Chi Tho: General and son of the people] (Ho Chi Minh City: NXB Cong An Nhan Dan, 2005), 132.

22. Ibid., 148–9.

23. Ibid., 139–40.

24. A US government profile of the mid 1980s gave the following information: "Mai Chi Tho, the lowest ranking of the new full Political Bureau members, was appointed minister of interior in early 1987. He was a former Ho Chi Minh City deputy secretary and mayor and was believed to have overall responsibility for security in southern Vietnam. Having been a past subordinate of Nguyen Van Linh and Vo Van Kiet, Tho was a strong supporter of economic reform and increased openness in the party. He was born in 1916 and is a brother of Le Duc Tho." http://www.country-data.com/frd/cs/vietnam/vn_appnb.html. The picture of Mai Chi Tho as a reformer in the 2005–6 series of articles on the "eve of reform" is belied by accounts from the 1980s that identify him as firmly aligned with his conservative brother, Le Duc Tho.

25. Tran Hieu and Manh Viet, "Gap nhung nhan chung cua 'Cuoc xe rao lich su'" [Meetings with witnesses of the "historic fence breaking"], *Tien Phong* online, June 19, 2006.

26. Tran Hieu and Manh Viet, "Gap nhung nhan chung."

27. Ibid.

28. Ibid.

29. "Vietnam Gets in the Swing: Once shunned as an indulgence of the bourgeoisie, it is now viewed as a symbol and tool of the Asian country's economic modernization." Amy Kazmin, *Financial Times*, August 8, 2005. "Vietnam Turns to Tennis," Tini Tran, Associated Press, September 28, 2005.

30. Interview in Hanoi, December 2006.

31. Nguyen Minh Nhi, "'Dem Truoc' doi moi; Tuong nhu xa xoi lam" ["On the eve" of *doi moi*: It seems so long ago], *Tuoi Tre* online, December 6, 2005.

32. Xuan Trung and Quang Thien, "'Dem Truoc' doi moi: chuyen doi vo hinh" ["On the eve" of *doi moi*: The invisible transformation], *Tuoi Tre* online, December 10, 2005.

33. Le Duc Tho, 78, who left the politburo when Mr. Linh became party leader and continues to serve as an "adviser," is considered the *éminence grise* of conservative and ideological caution here. He works, in part, through his younger brother, the interior minister, Mai Chi Tho, 66, whose appointment to the politburo is believed to have been part of the elder Mr. Tho's price for retirement. Mai Chi Tho served as Mr. Linh's deputy in Ho Chi Minh City and then got reasonable marks as the city's mayor from people who wanted change. But one Vietnamese official who knows him well

said: "He is Le Duc Tho's brother. He seems an open man, but he is not." Erlanger, "Vietnam, Drained by Dogmatism."

34. Xuan Trung and Quang Thien, "'Dem Truoc' doi moi: chuyen doi vo hinh."

35. For a mid-1970s analysis of the wartime debate over socialist orthodoxy, which maintains that Le Duan wanted to put war production ahead of all other considerations, and Truong Chinh a resolute defender of orthodoxy who feared that cutting corners for the benefit of the war in the South would undermine socialism in the North, see David W. P. Elliott, "North Vietnam Since Ho," *Problems of Communism* 24, no. 4 (July–August 1975): 35–52. This line of analysis would partially support Le Duc Anh's view of Le Duan as a pragmatist and reflects the widespread perception that Truong Chinh was a rigid ideologue—which makes their postwar role reversals all the more remarkable. But see the following discussion by Professor Tran Nham.

36. Vo Van Kiet, "Dong Chi Truong Chinh—Tong bi thu cua doi moi" [Comrade Truong Chinh: General secretary of *doi moi*], in Truong Van Sau et al., *An tuong Vo Van Kiet*, 293.

37. Ibid., 292.

38. Xuan Trung and Quang Thien, "'Dem truoc' doi moi: chuyen doi vo hinh."

39. Kevin Phillips, *American Theocracy* (New York: Viking, 2006): 174–5. In the same vein, see Michael Lind, *Made in Texas: George W. Bush and the Southern Takeover of American Politics* (New York: Basic Books, 2003).

40. Gainsborough, *Changing Political Economy of Vietnam*, 98.

41. Steven Erlanger, "America Opens the Door to a Vietnam It never Knew," *New York Times*, February 6, 1994. He also observes that "Vietnam's aging leadership is bewildered by the decay of a socialist ideology to which they've devoted their lives. The discipline of wartime was long ago cracked by corruption and bureaucracy, and by the siren song of the West."

42. Xuan Trung and Quang Thien, "'Dem truoc' doi moi: chuyen doi vo hinh."

43. Ibid.

44. Legro, *Rethinking the World*, 34.

45. Dang Phong, "Dem Truoc doi moi: 'Bau sua' cua dot pha" [On the eve of reform: "The 'mother's milk' of the breakout"], *Tuoi Tre* online, December 12, 2005.

46. Ibid.

47. Nguyen Thi Ngoc Hai, *Mai Chi Tho Tuong Con Dan*, 138–9.

48. Xuan Trung and Quang Thien, "'Dem truoc' doi moi: Chiec ao cho co che moi" [A cloak for the new system], *Tuoi Tre* online, December 5, 2005. Describes the shutdown of supplies and spare parts for key pieces of machinery in the textile industry which get noticeably worse by the end of 1979 when these could not be imported from the U.S. or Japan because "we didn't play" with them [*ta khong choi*]. In 1979, the party leader of Ho Chi Minh City, Vo Van Kiet, gave political protection to some textile factory managers to "break out" [*dot pha*] and find creative (but illegal) ways to get foreign exchange to import the necessary parts and materials. Ibid. See also Tran Hieu and Manh Viet, "Gap nhung nhan chung cua 'Cuoc xe rao lich su' Ky II" [Meetings with witnesses of the 'historic fence breaking,' part 2], *Tien Phong* online, June 20, 2006.

49. Xuan Trung and Quang Thien, "'Dem truoc' doi moi: chuyen doi vo hinh ['On the eve' of *doi moi*: The invisible transformation], *Tuoi Tre* online, December 10, 2005.

50. Ibid.

51. Tran Hieu and Manh Viet, "Gap nhung nhan chung cua 'Cuoc xe rao lich su': Part IV: 'Dep Loan'" [Meetings with witnesses of the "historic fence breaking," part 4: "Crushing the rebellion"], *Tien Phong* online, June 22, 2006.

52. Ezra Vogel, *Deng Xiaoping and the Transformation of China* (Cambridge, MA: Harvard University Press, 2011): 189.

53. Dang Phong, "Dem truoc doi moi: Uy quyen cua long dan," [On the eve of reform: "The power of the people's support"], *Tuoi Tre* online, December 16, 2005.

54. Ibid.

55. Xuan Trung and Quang Thien, "'Dem truoc' doi moi: Nhung thong diep gui den Ba Dinh" ['On the eve' of *doi moi*: Messages sent to Ba Dinh], *Tuoi Tre* online, December 9, 2005.

56. "Party Congress Shakes Up Politburo," Facts on File World News Digest, April 2, 1982.

57. Tran Hieu and Manh Viet, "Gap nhung nhan chung cua 'Cuoc xe rao lich su': Part IV: 'Dep Loan'" [Meetings with witnesses of the "historic fence breaking," part 4: "Crushing the rebellion"], *Tien Phong* online, June 22, 2006.

58. Ibid.

59. "A conference was recently held in Ho Chi Minh City to study and discuss plans for implementing the Council of Ministers' resolution on protecting socialist property and ensuring social order and safety. Attending the conference were key leaders of various administrative organs, the security forces, the army, the police force and tribunals of provinces from Quang Nam-Danang to Minh Hai; leaders of military regions and army corps; and leaders of the sectors concerned at the central level. Pham Hung, member of the CPV Central Committee Political Bureau and Vice-Chairman of the Council of Ministers, chaired the conference to which he conveyed the Council of Ministers' resolution. Comrade Pham Hung reminded sectors from the central to grassroots levels, localities and units to review their situation extensively; to set forth requirements and measures for quickly reorganizing the management and protection of socialist property; and to launch a revolutionary movement among the people to participate actively in the protection of socialist property and the maintenance of social order and safety and to counter the enemy's scheme of economic sabotage. He also urged them to implement the Council of Ministers' resolution scrupulously so as to contribute to the successful implementation of the 1982 and 1981–85 five-year state plans." "Council of Ministers discusses protection of socialist property," Hanoi home service, 25 August 82.

60. Tran Hieu and Manh Viet, "Gap nhung nhan chung cua 'Cuoc xe rao lich su': Part V: 'Nhung trum cay xanh tren sa mac'" [Meetings with witnesses of the "historic fence breaking,' part 5: "Oases in the desert"], *Tien Phong* online, June 23, 2006.

61. Ibid.

62. Ibid.

63. Linh's "pragmatic revolutionary views were exemplified by Resolution 24/TW (Third Party Congress) after the liberation of the South and unification, to the time he was in the Politburo (Fourth Party Congress) and then withdrew from the Politburo (Fifth Party Congress) and returned to the position of Party Secretary of Ho Chi Minh City, then when he returned to the Politburo toward the end of the term of the Fifth Party Congress, and when he was elected General Secretary of the Party at the Sixth Party Congress—from beginning to end [these views] were absolutely consistent." Tran Hieu and Manh Viet, "Gap nhung nhan chung cua 'Cuoc xe rao lich su': Ky Cuoi—'Ong Gia can co.'"

64. Erlanger, "Vietnam, Drained by Dogmatism."

65. Nguyen Minh Nhi, "'Dem Truoc' doi moi; Tuong nhu xa xoi lam."

66. Vo Van Kiet, "Tong bi thu Le Duan, nha lanh dao kiet xuat cua cach mang Viet Nam, Nguoi hoc tro xuat sac cua Bac Ho" [Le Duan, illustrious leader of the Vietnamese revolution, outstanding pupil of Uncle Ho], in Truong Van Sau et al., *An Tuong Vo Van Kiet*, 286.

67. Ibid., 287.

68. "Dem truoc doi moi; Noi niem cua toi" [On the eve of reform; "My Reflections"], *Tuoi Tre* online, December 13, 2005.

69. Tran Hieu and Manh Viet, "Gap nhung nhan chung cua 'Cuoc xe rao lich su': Ky Cuoi—'Ong Gia can co.'"

70. Ibid.

71. Sophie Quinn-Judge, "Vietnam's Bumpy Road to Reform," *Current History* 105, no. 692 (September 2006): 4.

72. Fforde and de Vylder, *From Plan to Market*, 15.

73. Interview with Vo Van Kiet in Saigon Giai Phong, "Vi ca nuoc, TP HCM phai co buoc dot pha" [For the entire country, Ho Chi Minh City has to have a breakout], *Tuoi Tre* online, September 7, 2006.

74. Referring to Nguyen Van Linh's constant admonition to cadres serving under him, during his exile from the politburo in the early 1980s, that "we have to convince the brothers," an article explained that this meant, "if in the localities we continued to break down and dismantle fences and break out to earn a living, even though it might have some effect, if at the highest levels there is not an agreed policy, it won't work. Because if you have to keep revising and retreating from the initiatives, the situation will be tense and become a mess, the country cannot be stabilized, and development will be impossible." Tran Hieu and Manh Viet, "Gap nhung nhan chung cua 'Cuoc xe rao lich su': Ky cuoi—'Ong gia can co.'"

75. "Dem truoc doi moi; Cong pha 'luy tre'" [On the eve of reform; "Breaking through the 'bamboo hedge'"], *Tuoi Tre* online, December 4, 2005.

76. "Dem truoc doi moi; Chien thang chinh minh" [On the eve of reform; "Gaining victory over ourselves"], *Tuoi Tre* online, December 15, 2005.

77. Ibid.

78. Ibid.

79. Barbara Crossette, "For Hanoi Chiefs, A List of Problems," *New York Times*, December 23, 1986.

80. Ibid.

81. Xuan Trung, "Nguoi cam co doi moi" [The person who held up the flag for *doi moi*], *Tuoi Tre* online, July 1, 2005.

82. Ibid.

83. Xuan Trung, "Nguoi cam co doi moi."

84. Quinn-Judge, "Vietnam's Bumpy Road to Reform."

85. A 1995 report stated that, "Minister Dang Huu chairs the National IT Program Steering Committee (NITSC), and substantial additional leadership and energy is provided by the Deputy Chairman, Phan Dinh Dieu, a French-trained professor of mathematics who led earlier, but essentially stillborn, government IT planning efforts in 1976 and 1984.... Undeterred by the frustrations of the two earlier efforts, the indefatigable Dr. Dieu pushed the draft of a plan by August 1994." "Computing in Viet Nam: Transitions and Choices," *Communications of the ACM* 38, no. 1 (January 1995): 11–16. Reprinted in *Dien Dan*, April, 1995, 20–23, http://som.csudh.edu/cis/lpress/vietsy.htm.

86. Interview in Hanoi, December 2006.

87. "'When the Communist Party declared its acceptance of the free market economy, it meant that this party is not truly a communist party; they have dropped the communist

system,' says Mr Phan Dinh Dieu, a mathematician in Hanoi whose views are tolerated by the party and who is regarded by foreign diplomats as a sort of licensed dissident. 'The result is that the party is transformed from a communist party into a party of power.'" Victor Mallet, "Vietnam Communist Party Sees Writing on the Wall: Observers Believe the Country Will Have to Abandon Marxism," *Financial Times* (London), March 16, 1993. Stein Tonnesson's 1992 interview with Dieu shows how bold his views were, especially in the context of the 1980s and early 1990s: http://hieuminh.org/2012/02/02/interview-with-the-vietnamese-mathematician-phan-dinh-dieu/.

88. Interview in Hanoi, December 2006.

89. "The Vietnam Socialist Party today [15th October] declares that it has terminated its activities after 42 years of existence. In a statement read at the farewell meeting held at the party's office here [Hanoi], the Secretary-General, Nguyen Xien, said that the founding of the socialist party on 22nd July 1946 was aimed at rallying the patriotic and progressive intellectuals trained before the August revolution in 1945. . . . Nowadays, the statement said, there remain very few intellectuals belonging to the pre-revolution generation and those who are members of the socialist party are already very advanced in age. Therefore, at its final congress held on 21st and 22nd July 1988, the party issued a resolution declaring the termination of its activities." "Vietnamese Socialist Party Terminates Activities," BBC Summary of World Broadcasts, October 17, 1988.

90. Phan Dinh Dieu, "Vai nhan thuc ve thoi dai ngay nay va con duong cua ta" [Some observations about today's era and our path], *To Quoc* [Fatherland], Co Quan Trung Uong Dang Xa Hoi Viet Nam [Organ of the Central Committee of the Vietnamese Socialist Party], 9–1988, 1. Emphases in original.

91. Ibid., 4.

92. Nguyen Duc Binh, "Gop y du thao van kien Dai hoi Dang X; Van de tieu chuan dang vien" [Contributing ideas on the draft document of the Tenth Party Congress: the issue of standards for party members], *Tuoi Tre*, February 25, 2006.

93. Phan Dinh Dieu, "Vai nhan thuc ve thoi dai ngay nay va con duong cua ta," 8. Emphasis in original.

94. Nguyen Duc Binh, "Tiep tuc mot cach kien dinh va sang tao con duong xa hoi chu nghia" [Resolutely and creatively continuing along the socialist path], Part 2, *Tap Chi Cong San* [Communist review], 119 (2006).

95. Nguyen Minh Hien, "Giao Duc Trong Doi Thoi Giua Cac Nen Van Hoa Van Minh Vi Hoa Binh Va Phat Trien Ben Vung" [Education in the dialogue among the cultures and civilizations for stable peace and development], *Tap Chi Cong San*, 80 (2005).

96. Clayton Jones, "The Perils of Reform; Vietnam Chief Assails Old-Style Politics," *Christian Science Monitor*, February 2, 1988.

97. Keith B. Richburg, "Vietnam Making Slow Progress on Reforms," *Washington Post*, July 22, 1988.

98. Jones, "The Perils of Reform."

99. Keith B. Richburg, "Hanoi Uneasy about Passing Torch to New Generation," *Washington Post*, July 30, 1988.

100. M. Baker, "And now, Vietnam's Economic War Tears it Apart," Nationwide News Pty Limited Herald, July 12, 1988.

101. Richburg, "Hanoi Uneasy."

CHAPTER 3

1. Steven Erlanger, Esther B. Fein, Edward A. Gargan, Bill Keller, Nicholas D. Kristof, and Philip Taubman, "Voices of the Party Faithful: Searching For A Path in the New Era," *New York Times*, January 22, 1989.

2. "Tong bi thu Nguyen Van Linh va cuoc dau tranh chong cac bieu hien huu khuynh trong cong cuoc doi moi" [Party Secretary General Nguyen Van Linh and the struggle against rightist manifestations in *doi moi*], *Tap Chi Cong San*, 86 (2005).

3. Dang Phong, "Dem truoc doi moi: Uy quyen cua long dan."

4. Keith B. Richburg, "Vietnam Tackles Its Economic Ills; Hanoi's Hopes for New Trade After Cambodia Pullout Fading," *Washington Post*, October 5, 1989.

5. Steven Erlanger, "Hanoi Remains True to Communism, But Party is Making More Changes," *New York Times*, February 11, 1990.

6. Carlyle A. Thayer, "Vietnamese Foreign Policy: Multilateralism and the Threat of Peaceful Evolution," in Carlyle A. Thayer and Ramses Amer, eds., *Vietnamese Foreign Policy in Transition* (New York: St. Martin's Press, 1990): 2–3.

7. Phan Doan Nam, "Ngoai Giao Viet Nam Sau 20 Nam Doi Moi" [Vietnamese diplomacy after twenty years of *doi moi*], *Tap Chi Cong San*, 111 (2006).

8. For a discussion of Vietnam's traditional fixation with possession goals, see David W. P. Elliott, "Vietnam: Tradition Under Challenge," in Trood and Booth eds., *Strategic Cultures*. For the "strategic judo" aspect of revolutionary Vietnam's diplomacy, see David W. P. Elliott, "Hanoi's Strategy in the Vietnam War," in Jayne Werner, ed., *The Vietnam War: Vietnamese and American Perspectives* (New York: Sharpe, 1993).

9. Phan Doan Nam, "Ngoai Giao Viet Nam Sau 20 Nam Doi Moi."

10. Ibid.

11. "Vietnamese Leaders Send October Revolution Greetings," BBC Summary of World Broadcasts, November 8, 1988.

12. "[O]n January 6, 1988, Foreign Minister Eduard Shevardnadze spoke of plans for all Soviet troops to be out of Afghanistan by the end of the year. Two weeks later the Phnom Penh government began to talk of a Vietnamese military pullout. Soviet officials say politely that Vietnam was already beginning to change its mind over Cambodia, largely because of its deepening economic crisis. But they admit encouraging Vietnam to withdraw." Paul Quinn-Judge, "Sino-Soviet Summit: Thawing the Big Chill," *Christian Science Monitor*, May 12, 1989.

13. Karen M Sutter, "China's Vietnam policy: The road to normalization and prospects for the Sino-Vietnamese Relationship," *Journal of Northeast Asian Studies* 12, no. 12 (Summer 1993): 21.

14. Do Muoi, "Giu vung ban chat cach mang, phan dau hoan thanh moi nhiem vu, mai mai to tham truyen thong anh hung cua quan doi nhan dan va dan toc Viet Nam anh hung" [Hold fast to the revolutionary character, strive to complete all tasks, always burnish the heroic traditions of the Vietnamese army and people], *Nhan Dan*, December 22, 1989.

15. "'Very Bewildered' Premier Replies to National Assembly Debate," BBC Summary of World Broadcasts, December 22, 1988.

16. Steven Erlanger, "Vietnam Leaders Reported Deeply Divided," *New York Times*, January 31, 1991.

17. Ibid.

18. "Vietnam moves to counter political unrest," Xinhua General Overseas News Service, Vietnam, December 10, 1988.

19. "Hanoi says it faces serious trials, big difficulties," Xinhua General Overseas News Service, December 13, 1988.

20. Clayton Jones, "Famine Fans Discontent in Vietnam," *Christian Science Monitor*, January 5, 1989.

21. Ibid.

22. Ibid.

23. Ibid.

24. Hoang Chi Bao, "Chu nghia xa hoi trong boi canh chinh tri cua doi moi" [Socialism in the political context of *doi moi*], *Nhan Dan*, August 24, 1989.

25. Richburg, "Vietnam Tackles Its Economic Ills."

26. Kiyoshi Hasagawa, "Vietnam Ending Economic Isolation; But Balancing Ideology against Economic Reform May Prove Tough," *Nihon Keizei Shimbun*, May 26, 1990. Vietnam's per-capita income was estimated by some as $500 in 1990. Philip Shenon, "Vietnam Appeals for Foreign Help," *New York Times*, June 28, 1991.

27. Steven Erlanger, "Vietnam's Vietnam: Scars of Cambodia," *New York Times*, April 9, 1989.

28. Ibid.

29. Ibid.

30. Ibid.

31. Ibid.

32. Nicholas Cummings-Bruce, "Vietnam 'Defeat' as Army Pulls Out: No Glory in Hanoi's Troop Withdrawal," *The Guardian* (London), September 18, 1989.

33. "Nguyen Quang Sang, 56, a noted novelist and screenwriter, lives next door to the former house of the late General Edward Lansdale, the American intelligence agent who did much to form early American policy in Vietnam. He has a son of 16, he said, who is good at engineering. 'To tell the truth, I don't want him to have to participate in warfare as I had to do,' Mr. Sang said. 'I want him to study. And if the war stops, he won't have to go. As a father, I'm very glad.'" Erlanger, "Vietnam's Vietnam."

34. Cumming-Bruce, "Vietnam 'Defeat' as Army Pulls Out."

35. Erlanger, "Vietnam, Drained by Dogmatism."

36. Steven Erlanger, "Hanoi Chief Assails Obstacles to 'Renovation,'" *New York Times*, April 2, 1989.

37. Ibid.

38. Nguyen Dy Nien, "Chinh sach va hoat dong doi ngoai trong thoi ky doi moi" [Foreign policies and activities during the *doi moi* period], *Tap Chi Cong San*, 90 (2005).

39. USSR–Yugoslav Joint Declaration, BBC Summary of World Broadcasts, March 21, 1988.

40. Buoc phat trien cua quan he huu nghi va hop tac Vietnam-Nam Tu [A step in the development of friendly relations and cooperation between Vietnam and Yugoslavia], *Nhan Dan*, September 9, 1989.

41. Steven Erlanger, "Vietnamese Leader, Assailing the West, Ignites Fear at Home," *New York Times*, September 19, 1989.

42. Ibid.

43. "Su Kien Chinh Tri o Ba Lan Van Thai Do Cua Chung Ta" [Our attitude toward political events in Poland]" *Nhan Dan*, August 26, 1989.

44. Interviews with the directors of state industries, "Doi dau voi thu thach, lam gi de vuot qua?" [In coping with the challenges, what can be done to overcome them?], *Nhan Dan*, August 9, 1989.

45. Fforde and de Vylder, *From Plan to Market*, 248–9.

46. Gorbachev's speech to the United Nations December 7, 1988, http://www.cnn.com/SPE-CIALS/cold.war/episodes/23/documents/gorbachev/.

47. "Vietnam's Delayed Support for Soviet Diplomatic Initiative," Xinhua General Overseas News Service, December 21, 1988. Of course, this report from its official news agency also reflected China's impatience with Vietnam's delay in following the Soviet lead in making concessions.

48. Erlanger, "Vietnamese Leader."

49. Nguyen Van Linh's Speech at Seventh Plenum, BBC Summary of World Broadcasts, August 30, 1989.

50. Ibid.

51. Nguyen Van Linh, "Phan dau xung dang la to bao chien dau vi su nghiep cua Dang va nhan dan, vi ly tuong cua chu nghia xa hoi" [Strive to be worthy of the fighting newspaper of the party and the people, for the ideal of socialism], Speech delivered to the cadres, reporters, and editors of *Quan Doi Nhan Dan*, September 25, 1989, *Nhan Dan*, October 19, 1989.

52. Nguyen Van Linh, "Hoc tap de nam vung va van dung dung dan chu nghia Mac-Le-nin" [Study to firmly grasp and correctly utilize Marxism-Leninism], *Nhan Dan*, October 10, 1989.

53. Vu Huu Ngoan, "Doi moi cong tac tu tuong de phat huy truyen thong va bao dam hieu qua lanh dao" [Renovate the ideological mission to develop the tradition and guarantee effectiveness in leadership], *Nhan Dan*, February 12, 1990. Ngoan was a participant in the US–Vietnam Dialogue, organized by former senator Dick Clark of the Aspen Institute in the late 1980s and early 1990s.

54. Erlanger, "Vietnamese Leader."

55. Keith B. Richburg, "Pullout of Troops Said to Aggravate Rift in Hanoi; Moderates Hope Withdrawal from Cambodia Will Bring Quick Benefits From West," *Washington Post*, September 15, 1989.

56. Bui Tin, *Hoa Xuyen Tuyet*, 44–8.

57. Ibid.

58. *Nhan Dan*, October 6, 1989.

59. *Nhan Dan*, October 12, 1989.

60. *Nhan Dan*, October 18, 1989.

61. *Nhan Dan*, October 25, 1989.

62. "Vietnamese Party Leader Makes First Appearance in Six Weeks," UPI, December 6, 1989.

63. Vu Cong Tuan, "Chien luoc kinh te-xa hoi va cach mang khoa hoc ky-thuat o Cong Hoa Dan Chu Duc" [Social-economic strategy and the scientific-cultural revolution in the German Democratic Republic], *Nhan Dan*, October 5, 1989.

64. Pham Van Dong, "Theo con duong cua Cach Mang Thang Muoi, tang cuong tinh doan ket va su hop tac Viet-Xo" [Follow the path of the October Revolution and strengthen the spirit of Vietnamese–Soviet solidarity and cooperation], *Nhan Dan*, November 6, 1989.

65. Do Muoi, "Mo rong va nang cao hon nua hieu qua hoat dong kinh te doi ngoai" [Expand and raise still higher the efficiency of external economic activities], *Nhan Dan*, November 14, 1989.

66. Pham Van Dong, "Theo con duong cua Cach Mang Thang Muoi."

67. Nguyen Van Linh, "Cung co hoa binh, de cao canh giac, phat huy suc manh tong hop de bao ve To Quoc" [Consolidate peace, raise vigilance, develop comprehensive strength to defend the Fatherland], *Nhan Dan*, December 15, 1989.

68. Ibid.

69. Ibid.

70. Ibid.

71. Ibid.

72. "Tong bi thu Nguyen Van Linh va cuoc dau tranh chong cac bieu hien huu khuynh trong cong cuoc doi moi."

73. Ibid.

74. Ibid.

75. Eero Palmujoki, *Vietnam and the World: Marxist-Leninist Doctrine and the Changes in International Relations, 1975–93* (London: Macmillan, 1997): 174–5.

76. Palmujoki argues that "despite the strong emphasis on the concept of a transitional period" at the time of the Sixth Party Congress, "this was not directly reflected in the foreign policy sections of the Party Congress documents. The transitional period entered the foreign policy discussion several months later," Ibid., 200.

77. Luu Van Loi [*Lou Von Loy*] was a civil service official during the French period. During the French war, he wrote speeches and proclamations in the Department for Proselytizing the Enemy. In 1954, he joined the military delegation to the International Control Commission (ICC), where he became a deputy to Ha Van Lau. In 1961, he was named director of the US Department in the MFA and participated in the Geneva Conference on Laos. He participated behind the scenes in many of the secret negotiating initiatives during the 1960s and later served on the Frontier Commission, dealing with China, Laos, and Cambodia, before his retirement. Since retiring, he has written several books on the negotiations with the Americans, both during the secret phase before 1968 and after 1968 in Paris. Source: Brown University News Bureau, June 10, 1997 (prepared in connection with Robert S. McNamara's trip to Vietnam in 1997, assisted by Professor James Blight of Brown, among others).

78. Palmujoki, *Vietnam and the World*, 175–6.

79. As Palmujoki puts it, the "vocabulary relating to international relations reflected the new Soviet approach. The world was not examined on the basis of the simple model of two camps, but as a complicated system with different developing tendencies. The key concept was the interdependence of the world." Ibid., 182.

80. Ibid., 175.

81. Ibid., 180.

82. Palmujoki presents an interesting list of related terms such as *xam nhap lan nhau* ("mutual penetration") and a use of an old term, *su lien kiet* ("alignment"), which had been used to describe solidarity within the socialist camp in the more general sense of interdependence. Ibid., 190–91.

83. Do Muoi, "Giu vung ban chat cach mang."

84. Palmujoki, *Vietnam and the World*, 185.

85. Ibid., 186.

86. "Nguyen Co Thach introduced the concept of regionalism (*chu nghia khu vuc*)" and concluded that "Vietnam's chances of survival may lie in regional cooperation better than in conventional strategy of alignment with ideologically motivated friends." Ibid., 195.

CHAPTER 4

1. Only two years earlier "a delegation from the Nguyen Ai Quoc Institute in Hanoi led by Nguyen Duc Binh, member of the CPV Central Committee and Director of the institute, arrived in the PRK for a visit and to discuss the task of educating cadres in the coming years." "Hanoi Institute Delegation in PRK Discusses Educating Cadres," BBC Summary of World Broadcasts, September 7, 1988.

2. "Cambodian explains party changes to Vietnamese communists," Agence France Presse, October 29, 1991. "Chea Sim thanked the CPV and Vietnamese government for assistance in building the Institute of Sociology, which had already been inaugurated, as a symbol of the bond of friendship, solidarity and cooperation between Cambodia and Vietnam." Chea Sim receives Vietnamese Political Bureau member, BBC Summary of World Broadcasts, November 4, 1991.

3. The author was sitting two rows behind the Vietnamese ambassador and witnessed this example of the "lonely hearts club" in action.

4. Tony Walker, "Castro makes belated pilgrimage to Beijing," *Financial Times* (London), November 27, 1995.

5. Andrew Sherry, "Hanoi sees Cambodian communist party reforms as tactical," Agence France Presse, November 1, 1991.

6. "Do Muoi vows Vietnam will stay communist," Agence France Presse, October 23, 1991

7. Ibid.

8. *Tuoi Tre* interview with Vo Van Kiet, "Cung lam cho dan giau nuoc manh thi se tim duoc diem tuong dong" [Working with each other to make the country rich and powerful will create common ground], in Truong Van Sau et al., eds., *An Tuong Vo Van Kiet*, 134.

9. Ibid.

10. Andrew Sherry, "Beijing summit marks breakthrough for Vietnam," Agence France Presse, November 4, 1991, ". . . according to Vietnamese sources . . . [the] normalization of state-to-state ties and the reestablishment of economic relations will be highlighted during the visit, which will play down the normalization of party-to-party ties, they said."

11. Michael Shari, "Soviet Fall Rattles Asian communists; Strongmen struggle to keep hold on power," *Nikkei Weekly*, October 5, 1991. This article cited North Korea's foreign minister Kim Yong-nam's interview with *Jane's Defense Weekly* in early September. "Western diplomats in Seoul said Kim appeared to be suggesting not a softer line but a harder one. 'It might have been a way of saying, Communism is gone, but what the hell, we didn't need it anyway,' one diplomat said. He cited a speech in late August by strongman Kim Il-son[g] calling for vigilance."

12. *Hoi Ky Tran Quang Co* [Tran Quang Co's memoir]. This remarkable insider's view of Vietnamese diplomacy during the 1980s and early 1990s is widely available online: e.g., http://www.diendan.org/tai-lieu/ho-so/hoi-ky-tran-quang-co/. A Google search will list a number of alternative links. Authoritative Vietnamese sources have confirmed the authenticity of this document.

13. Thanh Tin, "Sac xuan cua dong chay" [Spring colors of the current (of history)], *Nhan Dan*, Xuan Canh Ngo [Year of the Horse], Tet edition, January 27, 1990.

14. Ibid.

15. Bui Tin, *Hoa Xuyen Tuyet* [The thaw] (Irvine, CA: Saigon Press, 1991): 74.

16. Thanh Tin, "Sac xuan cua dong chay."

17. Bui Tin, *Hoa Xuyen Tuyet*, 157–8.

18. "Cuong linh xay dung chu nghia xa hoi trong thoi ky qua do" [Draft program for building socialism in the era of transition], *Nhan Dan*, January 12, 1990.

19. Ibid.

20. Quan Doi Nhan Dan Debate on Military Defence in Draft Chapter, *Quan Doi Nhan Dan*, January 24, 1991, BBC Summary of World Broadcasts, February 26, 1991.

21. Do Muoi, "Giu vung ban chat cach mang."

22. Quan Doi Nhan Dan Debate on Military Defence in Draft Chapter.

23. Ibid.

24. Le Duan, *This Nation and Socialism are One: Selected Writings of Le Duan*, ed. T.V. Dinh Chicago: Vanguard Books, 1976).

25. This quotation is taken from a translation by the author of the first (undated) issue of the "journal" (*dac san*) of the Club of Former Resistants (Cau Lac Bo Nhung Nguoi Khang Chien Cu). The original was obtained by Nayan Chanda, then editor of the *Far Eastern Economic Review*. Because this was circulated clandestinely, there was little identifying information about the circumstances of publication, not even a date. Internal evidence shows that it was probably printed at the end of 1988 or in early 1989.

26. Ibid.

27. Ibid.

28. Truong Giang Long, "Mot so van de trong qua trinh hoi nhap Viet Nam-ASEAN" [Some issues concerning the process of Vietnam's integration into ASEAN], *Tap Chi Cong San*, no. 3 (February 1997): 57–8.

29. *Hoi Ky Tran Quang Co.*

30. Pham Thanh Dung and Dinh Thanh Tu, "Moi quan he giua Dang, Nha Nuoc va cac to chuc chinh tri-xa hoi o Lien Xo truoc day—thuc trang va nhung van de rut ra doi voi Viet Nam" [Relations between party and state and social and economic organizations in the former Soviet Union: The reality and lessons to be learned by Vietnam], *Tap Chi Cong San*, 108 (2006).

31. *Hoi Ky Tran Quang Co.*

32. Ibid.

33. *Tuoi Tre* interview with Vo Van Kiet, "Mot gio voi tan chu tich Hoi Dong Bo Truong Vo Van Kiet" [An hour with the new prime minister Vo Van Kiet], in Truong Van Sau et al., eds., *An Tuong Vo Van Kiet*, 120–21.

34. Bui Tin, *Hoa Xuyen Tuyet*, 151.

35. "Vietnam Politburo Has its Own Reformist," Kyodo News Service, February 9, 1990. This article erroneously identifies Bach as "the Party leader in charge of foreign affairs"—possibly a misreading of his "filter" function described by Bui Tin.

36. "Tran Xuan Bach attends 'frank, open-minded' party debate in Hanoi," BBC Summary of World Broadcasts, January 27, 1990.

37. Ibid. "Analysing recent political upheavals in the socialist countries and our country's actual socio-economic situation, especially its price and market fluctuations in 1989, the participants contributed frank, open-minded opinion about the party's role and its leadership patterns, socialist modality, the connection between socialist democracy and proletarian dictatorship, and renovation of the economic mechanism and the political systems."

38. "Party Plenum Communique Announces Dismissal of Tran Xuan Bach," BBC World Broadcasts, March 31, 1990.

39. Keith Richburg, "Vietnam's Communists Demote Leading Proponent of Political Change," *Washington Post*, March 29, 1990.

40. "In the secretive inner circle of Vietnam's Communist leaders, Bach's greatest offense, according to some analysts, appeared to be allowing his public profile to grow while violating the cherished dictum here that the Politburo must act collectively, without any public sign of disagreement. Some of Bach's speeches have been widely reported in foreign publications, where he was depicted as a new voice for Vietnam's more liberal factions." Ibid.

41. Paul Wedel, "Vietnamese communists celebrate 1975 victory amid doubts," UPI, April 29, 1990.

42. R.G. Ig-nop-ski [R.G. Yanovsky], "Doi moi Dang Cong San Lien Xo, mau thuan va van de dat ra" [Renovation of the Soviet Communist Party, contradictions and issues], *Nhan Dan*, February 9, 1990.

43. Ibid.

44. Nguyen Duc Binh, "Dang trong su nghiep doi moi vi chu nghia xa hoi" [The party in the mission of *doi moi* for socialism], *Nhan Dan*, February 8, 1990.

45. "Combating US Hegemony Tops World Politics Today, Former Politburo Member," *Financial Times*, October 22, 2002.

46. "Chu Tich Hoi Dong Bo Truong Do Muoi tiep dong chi V. K. Gusev" [Premier Do Muoi Receives Comrade V. K. Gusev], *Nhan Dan*, March 3, 1990.

47. Nguyen Van Linh interview with Mainichi Shimbun's Tokuji Hosono, "Chu nghia xa ho nhat dinh vuot qua cuoc thu thach" [Socialism will certainly overcome the challenges], *Nhan Dan*, April 24, 1990.

48. Peter Eng, "Vietnam Cracks Down on Dissidents," Associated Press, June 20, 1990.

49. Bui Tin, *Hoa Xuyen Tuyet*, 108–10.

50. *Hoi Ky Tran Quang Co.*

51. Ibid.

52. Ibid.

53. "Soviet Deputy Foreign Minister Briefs SRV Premier on Malta Summit," BBC Summary of World Broadcasts, December 12, 1989.

54. Michael R. Beschloss and Strobe Talbott, *At the Highest Levels: The Inside Story of the End of the Cold War* (Boston: Little, Brown, 1993): 153.

55. Ibid., 163.

56. *Hoi Ky Tran Quang Co.*

57. Ibid.

58. Ibid.

59. Ibid.

60. Brantly Womack, *China and Vietnam: The Politics of Asymmetry* (Cambridge and New York: Cambridge University Press, 2006).

61. *Hoi Ky Tran Quang Co.*

62. Ibid.

63. Truong Giang Long, "Suc manh sang tao cua Cach Mang Thang Tam" [The power of creativity from the lesson of the August Revolution], *Tap Chi Cong San*, 89 (2005). See also Phan Doan Nam, "Hoat dong doi ngoai cua Viet Nam trong nam qua" [Vietnam's external activities in the past year], *Tap Chi Cong San*, 98 (2006).

64. Truong Giang Long, "Suc manh sang tao cua Cach Mang Thang Tam."

65. Ibid.

66. *Hoi Ky Tran Quang Co.*

67. Ibid.

68. Ibid.

69. Ibid.

70. Ibid.

71. Ibid.

72. Ibid.

73. Do Muoi, "Tiep tuc su nghiep doi moi, doan ket tien len vi thang loi cua chu nghia xa hoi, vi am no hanh phuc cua nhan dan" [Continue the task of *doi moi*, unite to advance for the victory of socialism, for the well being and happiness of the people], *Nhan Dan*, September 2, 1990.

74. Ibid.

75. *Hoi Ky Tran Quang Co.*

76. Terry McCarthy, "Vietnam Turns Down Chinese Offer of Aid," *The Independent* (London), December 12, 1990.

77. Steven Erlanger, "Its Gains Dissipated, Vietnam Tries to Salvage Its Economy," *New York Times*, February 17, 1991.

78. Myron Rush, *How Communist States Change Their Rulers* (Ithaca: Cornell University Press, 1974).

79. Interview in Hanoi, December 2006.

80. Interview in Hanoi, December 2006.

81. Interview in Hanoi, December 2006.

82. Bui Tin, *Hoa Xuyen Tuyet*, 148.

83. Nguyen Phu Trong, "Mot so van de ve con duong di len chu nghia xa hoi o nuoc ta" [Some questions concerning the path toward socialism in our country], *Tap Chi Cong San*, 1 (2001).

84. *Tuoi Tre* interview with Vo Van Kiet, "Mot gio voi tan chu tich Hoi Dong Bo Truong Vo Van Kiet" [An hour with the new prime minister Vo Van Kiet], in Truong Van Sau et al., eds., *An Tuong Vo Van Kiet*, 121.

85. Interview in Hanoi, January 2007.

86. Professor Tran Nham, "Resolutely Follow the Socialist Path—That Is the Principled Stance of the Draft Platform," in the rubric "Contributing Views to the Draft Documents of the Seventh Party Congress," *Nhan Dan*, January 24, 1991, in FBIS-EAS, February 19, 1991.

87. Ibid.

88. Erlanger, "Vietnam Leaders Reported Deeply Divided."

89. Ibid.

90. Nguyen Manh Cam, "Ngoai giao thoi ky doi moi mot giai doan phat trien quan trong cua nen ngoai giao Viet Nam hien dai" [Diplomacy during the *doi moi* period—an important stage of development in contemporary Vietnamese diplomacy], *Tap Chi Cong San*, 92 (2005).

91. Yuli Ismartono, "Looking for New Friends to Help Push Capitalist Program," IPS-Inter Press Service, August 6, 1991.

92. William Branigan, "Vietnam Reaffirms Fealty to Marxism; Hanoi Shocked by Defeat of Allies in Moscow," *Washington Post*, September 6, 1991.

93. Ibid.

94. Nguyen Phu Trong, "Chu nghia da nguyen chinh tri va thu doan chong chu nghia xa hoi" [Political pluralism and the scheme of opposing socialism], *Nhan Dan*, May 30, 1990.

95. Nguyen Trong Thu, "Suc song cua xa hoi chu nghia" [The living strength of socialism], *Tap Chi Cong San*, 12 (1991), 2–6. An early version of this argument published prior to the coup was printed in *Nhan Dan*: Mai Ninh, "Chu nghia xa hoi hap hoi chang?" [Is this the last gasp of socialism?], *Nhan Dan*, June 1, 1990.

96. *Hoi Ky Tran Quang Co.*

97. "China provides first economic aid since 1970s to Vietnam," Agence France Presse, December 2, 1992.

CHAPTER 5

1. Philippe Agret, "Vietnam's Communist Party chief set to visit capitalist centres," Agence France Presse, April 9, 1995.

2. Andrew Symon, "Vietnam in Transition: 'Too Much Change, Too Fast, Will Be Harmful,'" *East Asia News and Features* (Australia) Pty Limited, *Asia Today*, March 1996.

3. Jack Taylor, "Vietnamese Australians Protest Red Carpet Welcome for Hanoi Chief," Agence France Presse, July 28, 1995. See also "Protests Threat for Vietnamese Leaders," *Courier-Mail* (Australia), July 26, 1995, and "Liberal Leadership Split over Do Muoi Snub," *Courier-Mail* (Australia), September 2, 1995.

4. "Writers fell under what Chu Anping, a liberal newspaper editor, aptly called 'the world of the Party.' In this world, the leaders and the administrators gave the writers subjects to deal with; they let them know if they got things wrong, and punished them if they kept getting them wrong. Much has been written about the problems caused by this system. Not nearly enough, though, has been written about the deeper influences that 'the world of the Party' had on Chinese writing." Perry Link, "Chinese Shadows," *New York Review of Books* (November 16, 2006): 33.

5. Borje Ljunggren, "Market Economies under Communist Regimes: Reform in Vietnam, Laos and Cambodia," in Borje Ljunggren, ed., *The Challenge of Reform in Indochina* (Cambridge: Harvard University Press, 1993): 42.

6. "With regard to a host of investment obstacles listed recently by the Federation of Economic Organizations (Keidanren), the Vietnamese leader said, 'These problems are not things that can be resolved in a day.'" "Muoi to Call for Increased Grants, 'Daring' Investment,'" Kyodo News Service, April 3, 1995.

7. Truong Giang Long, "Mot so van de trong qua trinh hoi nhap Viet Nam-ASEAN", 57.

8. Legro, *Rethinking the World*, 11.

9. Ibid., 34.

10. Nguyen Manh Cam, "Phat bieu tong ket hoi thao ky niem 50 nam ngoai giao Vietnam" [Closing sSpeech at a seminar on the occasion of the fiftieth anniversary of the Vietnam diplomatic service], *Tap Chi Nghien Cuu Quoc Te* [Journal of International Studies] So Dac Biet, [special issue], no. 7 (September 1995): 5–9.

11. Ibid., 7.

12. Dinh Nho Liem, "Dan toc Viet Nam, vi hoa binh, doc lap, va phat trien trong cong dong quoc te" [The Vietnamese people, for peace, independence, and development in the international community], *Tap Chi Nghien Cuu Quoc Te* [International Studies], no. 4 (12–1995): 5.

13. Ibid.

14. Phan Doan Nam, "Nhin lai the gioi va Chau A-Thai Binh Duong sau Chien Tranh Lanh" [Looking Back on the World and the Asia-Pacific region After the Cold War], *Tap Chi Nghien Cuu Quoc Te* [International Studies], no. 15 (12–1996): 5.

15. Nguyen Manh Cam, "Phat bieu tong ket hoi thao ky niem 50 nam ngoai giao Vietnam," 8.

16. Ibid.

17. Nguyen Co Thach, "Dac diem tong quat cua tinh hinh the gioi trong 50 nam qua" [Special general characteristics of the global situation over the past fifty years], *Tap Chi Nghien Cuu Quoc Te* [Journal of International Studies], So Dac Biet [special issue], no. 7 (September 1995): 22.

18. Ibid. 12.

19. See chapter 3. The author was present at a 1991 meeting during which Foreign Minister Thach proudly presented former senator Dick Clark with the finished Vietnamese translation of the Samuelson text.

20. Nguyen Co Thach, "Dac diem tong quat cua tinh hinh the gioi trong 50 nam qua," 24.

21. Ibid., 13–19.

22. Ibid., 22.

23. The Wikipedia entry on Khrushchev states, "Soviet premier Nikita Khrushchev famously used an expression generally translated into English as 'We will bury you!' . . . transliterated as *My vas pokhoronim!*) while addressing Western ambassadors at reception in Moscow in November, 1956. The translation has been controversial because it was presented as being belligerent out of context. The phrase may well have been intended to mean the Soviet Union would outlast the West, as a more complete version of the quote reads: 'Whether you like it or not, history is on our side. We will bury you'—a meaning more akin to 'we will attend your funeral' than 'we shall cause your funeral.' The idea of one world triumphing over the other was, however, still central to orthodox communist thinking in this period." The definitive biography of Khrushchev agrees that, "The context, a reference to the Soviet idea of peaceful coexistence, suggested that he was referring to victory in economic and political competition, but many in the West took the remark literally." William Taubman, *Khrushchev: The Man and His Era* (New York: Norton, 2003), 427.

24. Vu Khoan, "An ninh, phat trien va anh huong trong hoat dong doi ngoai," 5.

25. Ibid., 6.

26. Ibid., 4–5.

27. Ibid.

28. "Lenin, who spent most of his life in the West and not in Russia, who knew the West much better than Russia, always wrote and said that the Western capitalists would do anything to strengthen the economy of the USSR. He said: They will bring us everything themselves, without thinking about their future. And, in a difficult moment, at a party meeting in Moscow, he said: 'Comrades, don't panic, when things get very tough for us, we will give the bourgeoisie a rope, and the bourgeoisie will hang itself.' Then Karl Radek, who was a very resourceful wit, said: 'Vladimir Ilyich, but where are we going to get enough rope to hang the whole bourgeoisie?' Lenin effortlessly replied, 'They will sell it to us themselves.'" Alexander Solzhenitsyn, speech to the AFL-CIO, Washington, D.C., June 30, 1975.

29. Nguyen Huu Cat, "Vietnam hoi nhap vao khu vuc vi hoa binh va phat trien" [Vietnam integrates into the region for peace and development], *Nghien Cuu Dong Nam A* [Southeast Asian studies] (February 1996): 28–9.

30. Ibid.

31. An example is the 1997 article in the party theoretical journal cited in chapter 4 (note 28), which characterizes integration as inevitable, but sounds some cautions about ways in which the process of assimilation should be managed. Truong Giang Long, "Mot so van de trong qua trinh hoi nhap Viet Nam-ASEAN," 57–8.

32. Dinh Nho Liem, "Dan toc Viet Nam, vi hoa binh, doc lap, va phat trien trong cong dong quoc te," 6.

33. Vu Khoan, "An ninh, phat trien va anh huong trong hoat dong doi ngoai," 4.

34. Douglas Pike, "Uncertainty Closes In," *Asian Survey* 34, no. 1 [A Survey of Asia in 1993: Part I] (January, 1994), p. 64.

35. William Brannigan, "Resistance in South Frustrates Vietnam," *Washington Post*, January 3, 1993.

36. The minister of public security in 2001 dated the FULRO problem as lasting from 1986 to 1992, although it flared up again in February 2001. Le Minh Huong, "An ninh trong su nghiep xay dung va bao ve to quoc" [Security in the mission of protecting the Fatherland], *Tap Chi Cong San*, 1 (2001).

37. "More troublesome for the government, however, according to diplomats who have visited Vietnam recently, are the activities of Southern Vietnamese who—since the 1975 takeover by the North Vietnamese—continue their passive resistance against Communist rule of South Vietnam and Hanoi's policy of 'socialist transformation' of the region." William Brannigan, "Resistance in South Frustrates Vietnam," *Washington Post*, January 3, 1993. Brannigan also notes a US State Department report of persecution and relocation of Southern Catholics, and harsh measures directed against Cham Moslems. There were also deep frictions between the regime and some Buddhist groups in Hue at this time.

38. The list included "468,000 members of the former South Vietnamese Army; more than 72,000 administrative personnel and police of the old Saigon government; 3,000 leaders and 450,000 members of disbanded political parties; about 400,000 Roman Catholics, who it said make up 13.6 percent of Ho Chi Minh City's population; 60,000 Buddhist monks and 480,000 Vietnamese Chinese." Brannigan, "Resistance in South Frustrates Vietnam."

39. Ibid.

40. Bui Ngoc Thanh, "Ve hoan thien to chuc va do moi noi dung hoat dong cua cac co quan chuyen mon cua Quoc Hoi" [On perfecting the organization and renovating the activities of the specialized organs of the National Assembly], *Tap Chi Cong San*, 19 (2002).

41. Dorothy R. Avery, "Vietnam in 1992: Win Some; Lose Some," *Asian Survey* 33, no. 1 (January 1993): 67.

42. Ibid.

43. Bui Ngoc Thanh, "Ve hoan thien to chuc va do moi noi dung hoat dong cua cac co quan chuyen mon cua Quoc Hoi."

44. One key article on the subject of specialized committees of the National Assembly said that with respect to the National Defense and Security Committee, "every member must be a member of the armed forces or the security police." Bui Ngoc Thanh, "Ve hoan thien to chuc va do moi noi dung hoat dong cua cac co quan chuyen mon cua quoc hoi."

45. Avery, "Vietnam in 1992," 70.

46. Kavi Chongkittavorn, "Vietnam Woos ASEAN as Ally Against China," *Yomiuri Shimbun*, July 12, 1992.

47. Ibid.

48. Yuli Ismartono, "Security, Economic Pressures Goad Hanoi to Join ASEAN," IPS-Inter Press Service, July 15, 1992.

49. "Vietnam Wobbles on the Capitalist Fast-Track: The Party Old Guard Signals its Concern about Unbridled Reform as National Assembly Convenes," *Financial Times*, October 20, 1994.

50. Philip Shenon, "As Foreign Investment Rises, Vietnam Wants the U.S. Back," *New York Times*, December 26, 1992.

51. Thomas Lippman, "Aides at Odds on Response to Vietnam; U.S. Gesture Urged For Help on MIAs," *Washington Post*, December 5, 1992.

52. "Mitterrand Promises More Economic Aid and Closer Relations with Vietnam," BBC Summary of World Broadcasts, February 12, 1993.

53. "Economic Ties with Japan Normalized," Facts on File World News Digest, December 31, 1992.

54. "According to Seoul's statistics, imports from Vietnam rose 38.9% year on year to $47.5 million in the first 10 months of this year, while exports to Vietnam jumped 117.6% to $343 million in the same period, according to Seoul's statistics. South Korean investment in Vietnam has also grown rapidly to total $1.6 billion as of November, the ninth highest of any nation." Makoto Suzuki, "Vietnam, Seoul Establish Formal Diplomatic Ties," *Nikkei Weekly*, December 28, 1992.

55. Yasushi Watanabe, "Investment From Asian NIEs Bypassing ASEAN," *Nikkei Weekly*, December 20, 1993.

56. "The Association of Southeast Asian Nations (ASEAN) is planning to ally with Japan and Taiwan in a regional trade bloc to counter the formation of the North American free trade area (NAFTA), local newspapers reported today. The reports, quoting a high-ranking government official, said the proposed bloc should also include Hong Kong, Vietnam, Myanmar and Kampuchea. The move is expected to be discussed when the ASEAN senior economic official meeting convenes in Manila next Monday." "ASEAN to lure Japan, Taiwan to trade bloc," Xinhua General Overseas News Service, October 15, 1992.

57. Hoang Anh Tuan, "Membership Has its Privileges," *Business Times* (Singapore), October 30, 1993.

58. Recall the comment of a Thai observer cited earlier that, "As late as February 1990, former Foreign Minister Nguyen Co Thach was still calling for the creation of a new regional organization that would incorporate two blocs—ASEAN and Indochina." Chongkittavorn, "Vietnam Woos ASEAN as Ally Against China."

59. "'Nhan Dan' welcomes Vietnam's signing of ASEAN Bali Treaty," BBC Summary of World Broadcasts, August 4, 1992.

60. "Vietnam Premier on Another Fence-Mending Tour," Inter-Press Service, February 28, 1992.

61. "Vietnam seeks observer status in ASEAN," Agence France Presse, January 20, 1992.

62. "Vietnam to join ASEAN in regional cooperation programs," Kyodo News Service, July 22, 1993.

63. "The old perceptions of threat seem to be receding with each ASEAN country enjoying varying degrees of success with the Vietnamese, according to Institute of Strategic and International Studies (ISIS) analyst Bunn Nagara, who recently visited Vietnam. But, he said, 'The Vietnamese are suspicious of the Thais' exploitative business interest, while remaining cautious about staunchly anti-communist Singapore which until 1991 banned its businessmen from investing in Vietnam." "Malaysia: Decades-old Relationship with Vietnam is Paying Off," IPS-Inter Press Service, April 5, 1993.

64. "ASEAN Policy-Makers Seek to Unite Region," IPS-Inter Press Service, March 1, 1993.

65. "Foreign Minister Comments on Do Muoi Visits to Singapore and Thailand," BBC Summary of World Broadcasts, October 21, 1993.

66. "Vietnamese Government Leaders in Bangkok." BBC Summary of World Broadcasts, October 18, 1993.

67. "Do Muoi: Vietnam to join Asean and regional forum," Xinhua General Overseas News Service, October 5, 1993.

68. "Hanoi Welcomes Formation of the ASEAN Regional Forum," Agence France Presse, July 29, 1993.

69. "Asean to help Vietnam, Laos in English training," Xinhua General Overseas News Service, August 2, 1993.

70. "Language a Stumbling Block to Hanoi entry in ASEAN," Agence France Presse, July 23, 1994.

71. Erlanger, "America Opens the Door."

72. "Foreign Ministry officials have privately admitted that preparations for joining ASEAN have been more difficult than expected as few senior civil servants are up to speed on some of the complex trade and legal issues involved. But the government is now confident it will be ready when it is admitted in July at a meeting of ASEAN foreign ministers in Brunei despite the administrative burden of attending the more than 200 meetings a year held by the group." "Vietnam Overcomes Language Barrier to ASEAN: Foreign Minister," Agence France Presse, December 11, 1994.

73. Harish Mehta, "Phnom Penh Leaders Eye Golf, Stability and Trade," *Business Times* (Singapore), August 10, 1994.

74. Leah Makabenta, "ASEAN makes haste slowly to include Vietnam," IPS-Inter Press Service, February 24, 1994.

75. "ASEAN to Boost Cooperation with Vietnam as Step to Membership," Agence France Presse, February 22, 1994.

76. Makabenta, "ASEAN makes haste slowly."

77. "Jiang Zemin expects promotion of Sino-Vietnamese Ties," Xinhua General Overseas News Service, November 22, 1994.

78. "China Warns ASEAN over Supporting Vietnam in Spratly Dispute," Agence France Presse, December 13, 1994.

79. "ASEAN to boost cooperation," Agence France Presse.

80. Sergei Blagov, "Vietnamese Premier Praises Relations with ASEAN Countries," Itar-TASS, February 22, 1994.

81. "Planning Minister says Vietnam needs 50bn Dollars in Aid and Loans," BBC Summary of World Broadcasts, June 8, 1994.

82. "Vietnamese officials will participate for the first time in a meeting of a senior officials of the Association of Southeast Asian Nations (ASEAN) in Brunei's capital of Bandar Seri Pregawan in November, an ASEAN source said here Saturday. . . . In October, prior to the November meeting in Brunei, Vietnamese Vice Foreign Minister Vu Khoan will visit the ASEAN's six member states and the ASEAN Secretariat office in Jakarta, the source said. . . . Meanwhile, Vietnamese Trade Minister Le Van Triet arrived Saturday in the northern Thai city of Chiangmai for a meeting with ASEAN economic ministers who have just concluded their 26th annual meeting here this week. The meeting between ASEAN economic ministers and Minister Le Van Triet, which will begin on Sunday, is the first of its kind. It is intended to familiarize Vietnam with ASEAN's economic cooperation programs." "Vietnam to Join ASEAN Meeting for First Time," Kyodo News Service, September 24, 1994.

83. Keiji Urakami, "Japan, ASEAN to cooperate on Indochina reforms," Kyodo News Service, September 24, 1994.

84. "Asean makes way for Vietnam: Partners give Hanoi extra time to bring in tariff cuts," *Financial Times* (London), April 28, 1995.

85. "Vietnam hopes ASEAN membership leads to APEC, WTO," Kyodo News Service, December 2, 1994.

86. "'Vietnam is used to a very tough way of negotiation. This is not the Asean style,' says Ms Dewi Fortuna of the Centre for Political and Regional Studies at Indonesia's Institute of Sciences." Kieran Cooke, "Asean Gets its First Communist Member: Vietnam's Entry, on the Heels of Normalisation with the US, is a Diplomatic Coup for Hanoi," *Financial Times* (London), July 27, 1995.

87. Leah Makabenta, "Remaking Vietnam's Fearsome Military Image," IPS-Inter Press Service, April 18, 1995.

88. "Vietnam in Asean 'Will Make for Better Bargaining Position,'" Straits Times (Singapore), April 1, 1995.

89. Greg Torode, "ASEAN Plans to Foster Hanoi Military Links," *South China Morning Post*, July 29, 1995.

90. "Industry executives say the problem of fisheries in Vietnam stems from the inconsistency of fishing policies between the central government in Hanoi and the provincial authorities. Hanoi banned the activities of all foreign fishing vessels in February and ordered a review of foreign involvement in its fisheries. But some provincial authorities granted concessions to some Thai companies whose trawlers were then seized and the crews imprisoned by the Vietnamese Navy. Provincial authorities also maintain 'voluntary forces' to patrol waters where Thai and Vietnamese claims overlap. These boats with armed crews have been responsible for some of the violent attacks on Thai vessels." Leah Makabenta, "Vietnam–Thailand: Meeting Eases Tensions on Fisheries," IPS-Inter Press Service, March 11, 1995.

91. Greg Torode, "Vietnam Ready For ASEAN Changes," *South China Morning Post*, July 25, 1995.

92. Robert Templer, "Vietnam, to Feel the Stiff Winds of Competition," Agence France Presse, July 23, 1995.

93. "Vietnam sees ASEAN entry opening 'historical chapter,'" Kyodo News Service, July 7, 1995.

94. Tim Johnson, "Vietnam becomes 7th member of ASEAN," Kyodo News Service, July 28, 1995.

95. Greg Torode, "New Era as Hanoi Signs Up," *South China Morning Post*, July 29, 1995.

96. "The AFTA target date for the other ASEAN economies was 2003, when tariffs would fall to between zero and five percent, but leaders agreed at the summit Friday to speed up the creation of the free trade zone. A target of complaint was the mountain of paperwork required for the various lists of products to be considered under AFTA which Vietnamese bureaucrats delivered up for ASEAN inspection at the last minute. Other officials say that communist Vietnam has made great strides in freeing up its once impenetrable economy, adding that they hope Burma, Cambodia and Laos will follow before the end of the century." Philip McClellan, "Vietnam Takes Cautious Steps towards Free Trade Area," Agence France Presse, December 17, 1995.

97. Ted Bardacke, "Asean outlines ambitious vision of further regional co-operation," *Financial Times* (London), December 16, 1995.

98. Professor Pham Duc Thanh, "Vai tro cua Viet Nam trong ASEAN [The role of Vietnam in ASEAN], *Nghien Cuu Dong Nam A*, March, 1996, p.12.

99. Ibid.

100. Ibid., 14.

101. Ibid., 13.

102. [Ho] Quang Loi, "Viet Nam-ASEAN; Chiec cau trong khung troi sang" [Vietnam-ASEAN, a bridge across the dawn], essay first printed in *Quan Doi Nhan*, July 28, 1995, and reprinted in his book of essays, Quang Loi, *Cuoc But Pha Toan Cau* [The global breakup], (Hanoi: NXB Quan Doi Nhan Dan, 1997): 360.

103. Ibid., 361.

104. [Ho] Quang Loi, "'Cuoc hoa nhac mo ho,' o vong cung Chau A-Thai Binh Duong" [Muddled music in the Asia-Pacific circle], essay first printed in *Quan Doi Nhan*, June 8, 1996, and reprinted in Quang Loi, *Cuoc But Pha Toan Cau*, 289.

105. Siti Rahil. "Teaching Vietnam the ASEAN way," Kyodo News Service, June 10, 1996.

106. "Vietnam Welcomes Inclusion in Network," *New Straits Times* (Malaysia), May 30, 1996.

107. Truong Giang Long, "Mot so van de trong qua trinh hoi nhap Viet Nam-ASEAN" [Some issues concerning the process of Vietnam's integration into ASEAN], *Tap Chi Cong San*, no. 3 (February 1997), 58.

108. Ibid.

109. Nguyen Manh Hung, "Nhin lai mot nam Viet Nam gia nhap ASEAN" [Looking back on a year of Vietnam's membership in ASEAN], *Tap Chi Nghien Cuu Quoc Te* [International Studies], no. 13 (8–1996): 4–5.

110. "Vietnam Celebrates Signing Accord with European Union," Agence France Presse, July 18, 1995.

111. Pham Duc Duong, "Trien vong ve su lien ket va hop tac khu vuc" [Prospects for regional alignment and cooperation], *Nghien Cuu Dong Nam A* [Southeast Asian Studies] (2–1995): 5.

112. Ibid., 5–6.

CHAPTER 6

1. Interviews in Canberra, Australia, June 1999, and Jakarta, Indonesia, July 1999. The author conducted extensive interviews in East and Southeast Asia in the summers of 1999 and 2000 with scholars, diplomats, and security analysts who had a professional interest in Vietnam. This research was made possible by a generous grant from the Smith Richardson Foundation. These interviews were mostly done with an assurance of no direct attribution, and are infrequently specifically cited in this study. Cumulatively they provided indispensible background, especially for the time period covered in this chapter, and presented a remarkably consistent view of Vietnam's evolving attitudes toward the outside world and especially its view of security issues in the Asian and Southeast Asian region.

2. "It was not until nearly ten years into the process of renewal (1995) that the crisis might be considered as over, when the Five-year Plan for 1991–1995, the first half of the 10-year Strategy for Socio-Economic Development (1991–2000), exceeded many of its major targets. From 1996, the country embarked on a new stage of development with the acceleration of industrialisation and modernization. In the following five years (1996–2000), average GDP reached 7.5 per cent while GDP during the year 2000 doubled that of 1990. During the five-year term of the Ninth National

Party Congress (2001–2005), GDP reached an average of 7.5 per cent. Although the quality of future growth remains constrained, world analysts agree that it is a miracle for a nation to reach an average GDP of over seven per cent for 15 consecutive years. Vietnam was thus been compared to a newly emerging dragon." Ha Dang, "Vietnam Official Reviews Development, Urges Efficient Leadership." BBC Worldwide Monitoring, April 13, 2006.

3. Mark Sidel, "Vietnam in 1998: Reform Confronts the Regional Crisis," *Asian Survey* 39, no. 1 (January–February 1999): 96.

4. Ibid., 98.

5. Ibid., 97.

6. *Hoi Ky Tran Quang Co.*

7. Nick Cumming-Bruce, "Seven Years On, Vietnam Is Itching For Prosperity," *The Guardian* (London), December 27, 1993.

8. The author circulated a paper in Hanoi, "Vietnam's Strategic Culture," prepared for a conference in Malaysia, "Strategic Culture in Asia," during the summer of 1994. "Strategic Culture" was a concept in international relations that emphasized the importance of cultural and historical factors in shaping the perceptions of elites about security issues—an alternative to the realist and neoliberal modes of analysis. This quickly resulted in an invitation from a high-ranking Ministry of Public Security official to explain the concept of the paper. The ensuing discussion strongly suggested that "strategic culture" was interpreted by some Vietnamese security officials as "strategy of culture" (which is the literal translation into Vietnamese). The apparent concern was that this paper was a blueprint for using cultural subversion to destabilize Vietnam. This sensitivity to an obscure academic paper suggests the level of anxiety of Vietnamese security officials at the time. The paper was eventually published with the title "Vietnam: Tradition under Challenge," in Trood and Booth, eds., *Strategic Cultures.*

9. "The peaceful evolution strategy has a global character. It does not have any time and space limits. The tempo and the process of this war develop very slowly. Although this war does not give any feeling of fierceness, the results it produces may be very great. The peaceful evolution strategy advocates building and using on-site political forces to set up its base and rally force from within the socialist regime for use as an inside force. In this strategy, the imperialists will play the role of an external strike force. When the situation permits, they will resort to military force." Translated text of a talk by Voice of Vietnam station editor Vu Dinh Vinh, titled "Peaceful evolution strategy: A trick of imperialism aimed at eradicating socialism," BBC Summary of World Broadcasts, Asia, February 25, 1994.

10. Excerpts from Colonel Tran Ba Khoa's article, "Heighten Vigilance against Peaceful Evolution of the Hostile Forces," published in January 1993 issue of *Tap Chi Cong San*, BBC Summary of World Broadcasts, January 16, 1993.

11. Nguyen Huy Quy et al., translators, "Ban ve van de chong dien bien hoa binh" [On opposing peaceful evolution] (Hanoi: Nha Xuat Ban Chinh Tri Quoc Gia, 1993): 9. This was a translation of a 1991 Chinese book published by the People's Security University in the People's Republic of China. The book was designated "for internal circulation only" and published in only 1,000 copies, although other translated Chinese studies of peaceful evolution, translated and published in 1993, were published in the more standard run of 5,000 issues and evidently intended for a somewhat wider audience.

12. Ibid.

13. "Vietnam's concern on investment from Hong Kong, the fourth biggest investor after Taiwan, Japan and Singapore, is much more serious. 'Chinese authorities will interfere in Hong

Kong's economic activities, not using military or administrative measures but economic measures,' said Nguyen Huy Quy, director of the Institute of China Studies in Hanoi." Varunee Torsricharoen Kyodo New Service (Bangkok), January 7, 1997.

14. Dien Bien Hoa Binh Va Chong Dien Bien Hoa Binh [Peaceful Evolution and Opposing Peaceful Evolution], originally published in Chinese by the Social Sciences Publishing House of China, translated and published in Vietnamese by General Directorate II [Intelligence], of the Vietnamese Ministry of National Defense in October 1993, 24–31.

15. Tran Ba Khoa, "Heighten Vigilance against Peaceful Evolution."

16. "Vietnamese authorities, signaling that they do not intend to let the lifting of the US economic embargo threaten political stability, have arrested a leading dissident.... Since the embargo was scrapped in February, the official press has stepped up its warnings against 'peaceful evolution'—a Cold War term for the subversion of communist regimes through economic and social change." Philippe Agret, "Vietnam Sends Signal with Clampdown on Dissent," Agence France Presse, March 20, 1994.

17. "Foreign Ministry Statement on Clinton Decision to Lift Embargo," BBC Summary of World Broadcasts, February 5, 1994.

18. Philippe Agret, "Vietnam has Economic Hopes, Political Fears as US Embargo Ends," Agence France Presse, February 4, 1994.

19. SRV Foreign Ministry Memorandum on Tension in South-East Asia. Source: VNA in English 15:36 GMT, 26 August 1980; Agency "full text" of 26th August, SRV Foreign Ministry Memorandum. BBC Summary of World Broadcasts August 28, 1980; section: Part 3, The Far East; A. International Affairs; 3. Far Eastern Relations; FE/6508/A3/1.

20. In 1985, Vietnam's Cambodian ally denounced, "The enemy scheme of launching a counteroffensive against the revolution in Cambodia [which] takes the form of a subversive war of encroachment whose final goal is to overthrow the regime of the young PRK.... The enemies use not only military means but also a perfidious psychological war and peaceful evolution tricks to sabotage the revolution, corrupt our cadres, and create divisions in our ranks and the Cambodia–Vietnam solidarity." Heng Samrin's Political Report to KPRP Congress, 14 October, 1985, BBC Summary of World Broadcasts, October 18, 1985.

21. "In 1988, America comprehensively implemented the strategy of peaceful coexistence in Eastern Europe, and effectively achieved their desired objective. The powerful changes in Europe dissolved the Yalta regime, which had been the basic face of the world and had existed with stability for many years following World War II." Luong Van Dong et al., "Chien luoc dien bien hoa binh cua My [The American strategy of peaceful evolution], originally published in Chinese by the People's Publishing House of Cat Lam, China, March 1992; translated into Vietnamese and published by Tong Cuc II (General Directorate II), Bo Quoc Phong (Ministry of National Defense), May 1993, 304.

22. This refers to the phrase introduced by President George H. W. Bush in 1989. "Our goal is bold—more ambitious than any of my predecessors might have thought possible. Our review indicates that forty years of perseverance have brought us a precious opportunity. Now it is time to move beyond containment, to a new policy for the 1990s; one that recognizes the full scope of change taking place around the world and in the Soviet Union itself." Speech at Texas A & M University, May 12, 1989.

23. Van Dong et al., "chien luoc dien bien hoa binh cua My," 338.

24. Luu Dinh A, ed., *Cuoc chien tranh the gioi khong co khoi sung* [The world war without gun smoke], (Nha Xuat Ban Chinh Tri Quoc Gia—Tong Cuc II—Bo Quoc Phong, 1994).

25. General Nguyen Anh Lan, ed., *Chien luoc dien bien hoa binh cua de quoc My va cac the luc phan dong quoc te chong chu nghia xa hoi va chong Viet Nam xa hoi chu nghia* [The peaceful evolution strategy of the American imperialists and international reactionary forces opposing socialism and opposing socialist Vietnam] (Tong Cuc II—Bo Quoc Phong, June 1993): 119.

26. Ibid., 148.

27. Ibid., 160.

28. General Nguyen Anh Lan, ed., "Chien luoc dien bien hoa binh cua de quoc My," 162.

29. Frederik Balfour and Joyce Barnathan, "Is Reform Alive in Vietnam?" *Business Week*, July 1, 1996.

30. Ibid.

31. Robert Templer, *Shadows and Wind: A View of Modern Vietnam* (New York: Penguin, 1998): 87.

32. *Tuoi Tre* interview with Vo Van Kiet, "Cung lam cho dan giau nuoc manh thi se tim duoc diem tuong dong" [Working with each other to make the country rich and powerful will create common ground], in Truong Van Sau et al., eds., *An Tuong Vo Van Kiet*, 136.

33. "Thu cua Ong Vo Van Kiet gui Bo Chinh Tri Dang Cong San Vietnam 1995" [Letter sent by Mr. Vo Van Kiet to the politburo, 1995], http://www.lmvntd.org/dossier/0895tvvk.htm. Curiously, this crucial document, sent by Prime Minister Vo Van Kiet to his colleagues in the politburo on August 9, 1995, is extremely difficult to find on the internet, while many other sensitive internal Party documents are widely disseminated by politically engaged persons and groups both inside and outside of Vietnam. I have used the most plausible version of this document that I can find.

34. Ibid.

35. Ibid.

36. Ibid.

37. Ibid.

38. Ibid.

39. Templer, *Shadows and Wind*, 89.

40. Ibid.

41. Ibid.

42. Nick Cumming-Bruce, "Vietnam Reform Comes at Price; Security Chiefs are Taking a High Profile in the Politburo," *The Guardian*, July 2, 1996.

43. To Huy Rua, Hoang Chi Bao, Tran Khac Viet, and Le Ngoc Tong, *Nhin Lai Qua Trinh Doi Moi: Tu Duy Ly Luan Cua Dang 1986–2005* (Sach Tham Khao), Tap. I [Looking back on the process of *doi moi*: Party theoretical thinking, 1986–2005 (reference book), vol. 1] (Hanoi: NXB Ly Luan Chinh Tri, 2005): 64.

44. Ibid., 377.

45. Thai Son, "Day manh cuoc dau tranh chong tham nhung trong giai doan hien nay" [Push the struggle against corruption in the present stage], *Tap Chi Cong San* online, 47 (2003).

46. To Huy Rua, Hoang Chi Bao, Tran Khac Viet, and Le Ngoc Tong, *Nhin lai qua trinh doi moi: Tu duy ly luan cua Dang 1986–2005*, 226.

47. Nguyen Phu Trong, "Doi moi tu duy luan vi su nghiep xay dung chu nghia xa hoi" [Renovate theoretical thinking for the mission of building socialism], *Tap Chi Cong San*, 76 (2005).

48. To Huy Rua, Hoang Chi Bao, Tran Khac Viet, and Le Ngoc Tong, *Nhin lai qua trinh doi moi: tu duy ly luan cua Dang 1986–2005*, 235.

49. Vu Khoan, "Tich cuc va chu dong hoi nhap kinh te quoc te" [Energetically and proactively integrate into the international economy], *Tap Chi Cong San*, 119 (2006).

50. Greg Torode, "Warning of Plots to Crush Socialism," *South China Morning Post*, March 29, 1996.

51. Cao Cuong, "Vietnam Communist Party to Reestablish Secretariat," *Saigon Times Daily*, April 19, 2001. Distributed by Financial Times Information.

52. Jeremy Grant, "Military Tries to Keep Power Base," *Financial Times* (London), April 16, 1997.

53. Ibid.

54. Ibid.

55. Templer, *Shadows and Wind*, 90–91.

56. "At the time of the 11B Plenum of the Eighth Party Congress in February 2001, in the face of the scheme of Le Duc Anh's bad mouthing (noi xau) and blatantly slandering aimed at overthrowing General Secretary Le Kha Phieu, comrade Hai Xo who was working in Hanoi and knew that comrade Nam Thi had sent a letter of denunciation immediately called on Nam Thi to meet with comrades Hai Xo, Nguyen Duc Tam, Muoi Huong and the Central Control Commission to clarify the background of Le Duc Anh . . . " Letter of Pham Van Xo, Dong Van Cong and Nguyen Van Thi to the Politburo, February 2. 2005. http://www.ykien.net/clbdt040.html#dt040e.

57. Templer, *Shadows and Wind*, 91.

58. Ibid., 90–92.

59. Grant, "Military Tries to Keep Power Base."

60. "Gen Phieu is tipped to replace Mr Muoi as general secretary, and is believed to have his blessing. But until this year, he was an obscure figure. . . . As one of five people in the 'inner core' of the 18-member politburo-known as the Standing Committee-he wields significant control over the leadership's agenda. His rapid rise, and conservative stance on issues such as foreign investment and the perceived threat from 'hostile forces' abroad, has led to some nervousness among observers. They fear his rise threatens the careful political consensus between reformists and conservatives underpinning Vietnam's political stability for decades. . . . But others play down such fears." Ibid.

61. Frederik Balfour, "Hardline Vietnamese Conservative Doan Khue Dies," Agence France Presse, January 16, 1999.

62. "The communist party of Vietnam has appointed four new politburo members, including Foreign Minister Nguyen Manh Cam and another army general, while warning Thursday it would block any shift to political pluralism. The central committee meeting ahead of the mid-term national conference which began Thursday nominated Cam, the head of the army's political department Le Kha Phieu, head of the party's control commission Do Quang Thang and one of the party's secretaries Nguyen Ha Phan to the politburo. This expanded the party's ruling body to seventeen members. . . . The adding of a third general to the politburo came as party general secretary Do Muoi was quoted as telling the 647 delegates at the national party conference the communist party must maintain 'political stability' and would not 'accept political pluralism or a multi-party system.' Analysts said the appointment of three-star general Phieu, the third military figure in the politburo, showed that maintaining political power concerned the communist party while it pursues its 'Doi Moi' economic reform drive begun in 1986. 'Security is an important issue,' one Westerner who advises the Vietnamese government said. 'The issue of peaceful evolution is important.'" Michael Collins, "Vietnam Adds General to Politburo, Blocks Political Pluralism," Agence France Presse, January 20, 1994.

63. "Vietnam Ideologue Calls for Closer Police, Military Ties," Deutsche Presse-Agentur, April 28, 1997.

64. Ibid.

65. "Phieu is described by observers as a conservative whose orthodox Marxist ideology will inevitably become a source of tension with the reform-minded cadres. The general favours a more cautious pace of economic reform. Another hindrance is his lack of international exposure. His only experience abroad has been Cambodia, which diplomats said is something one should not want to brag about." "Completing Vietnam's Leadership Trinity," *The Nation* (Thailand), October 2, 1997.

66. Seth Mydans, "A Vietnamese Leader Who is Wary of Markets," *New York Times*, December 31, 1997.

67. Desaix Anderson, *An American in Hanoi: America's Reconciliation with Vietnam* (White Plains, NY: EastBridge, 2002): 179.

68. Ibid., 180.

69. Greg Torode, "Enigma Tipped for Leadership," *South China Morning Post*, July 21, 1997.

70. Pascale Trouillaud, "Vietnam's party chief must bring order to the ranks," Agence France Presse, December 28, 1997.

71. Michael Mathes, "General's Ousting Signals Vietnam Communist Party Jitters," Deutsche Presse-Agentur, January 8, 1999.

72. Greg Torode, "Warning of Bid to Split Military, Party," *South China Morning Post*, July 3, 1998.

73. "Army magazine article warns against opportunism, rightism," Source: *Tap Chi Quoc Phong Toan Dan*, Hanoi, in Vietnamese 14:56 GMT, 31 January 96, 4–7, BBC World Wide Broadcasts, February 2, 1996.

74. This letter can easily be located on the internet. An English-language summary of its contents is on the website of the overseas Vietnamese democracy advocacy group Que Me, http://www.queme.net/eng/e-news_detail.php?numb=143, with a link to the Vietnamese text of the letter. Vietnamese publication titled "Vu An 'sieu nghiem trong' T2–T4" [The "super serious" trial of T2–T4], *Tu Sach Thoi Su VN Va The Gioi* (Arlington, VA: Canh Nam Publishers, 2004): 192–223.

75. Seth Mydans, "Buoyant at 79, Vietnamese Leader Denies Divisions in Party over Reform," *New York Times*, July 1, 1996.

76. Seth Mydans, "Hanoi Seeks Western Cash but Not Consequences," *New York Times*, April 8, 1996.

77. Seth Mydans, "A New Leader for Vietnam Who is Wary of Markets," *New York Times*, December 31, 1997.

78. "General Defines Armed Forces' Role," BBC Summary of World Broadcasts, August 28, 1995.

79. Abby Tan, "Hanoi's Toughest War: Managing the Market," *Christian Science Monitor*, January 29, 1998.

80. "Vietnamese President warns of dangers in economic links," Agence France Presse, May 28, 1996.

81. Abby Tan, "Hanoi's Toughest War: Managing the Market," *Christian Science Monitor*, January 29, 1998.

82. Sidel, "Vietnam in 1998," 97.

83. "Like others who monitor the situation here, Mr. Scown said that both Vietnamese and foreigners were holding their breath now, waiting for the results of the party congress. 'Nobody knows what policies will come out or who the policymakers will be,' he said. 'Everything is on hold. There's also something of the flavor of an American election year with a lot of rhetoric about law and order and protecting traditional Vietnamese values.' For Vietnam today these are new and genuine concerns." Mydans, "Hanoi Seeks Western Cash."

84. Ibid.

85. "The mid-term party conference (January 1994) pushed the summation of the practical realities in carrying out doi moi and put forward measures aimed at stepping up its implementation, while at the same time pointing out the four great dangers facing our country (the danger of falling further behind economically, the danger of deviating from the socialist direction, the scourge of corruption and mandarinism, and the plot and 'peaceful evolution' activities carried out by enemy forces." Nguyen Phu Trong, "Tong ket thuc tien moi nhiem vu trong yeu cua cong tac ly luan hien nay" [Summing up the practical experience, a key task of the theory mission of today], *Tap Chi Cong San*, 14 (2002).

86. Interviews in Hanoi, January 2007.

87. Ha Dang, "Thoi ky moi cua su phat trien" [The new period of development], *Tap Chi Cong San*, 31 (2003).

88. Frederik Balfour, "Vietnam's Defense White Paper Sheds Little Light on Military," *Agence France Presse*, September 24, 1998.

89. Ibid.

90. Pascale Trouillaud, "Vietnam's Party Chief Must Bring Order to the Ranks," *Agence France Presse*, December 28, 1997.

91. Ibid.

92. Carlyle Thayer, "Doi Moi 2? Vietnam after the Asian Financial Crisis," *Harvard Asia Quarterly* 4, no. 1 (Winter 2000).

93. Ibid.

94. Ibid.

95. Ibid.

96. Ibid.

97. Daniel Kwan, "Beijing has 'right blend' of Marxism," *South China Morning Post*, December 8, 1997.

98. Ibid.

99. "Vietnam Communist Party chief to study China's experiment," *Agence France Presse*, February 25, 1999.

100. Alexander L. Vuving, "Strategy and Evolution of Vietnam's China Policy: A Changing Mixture of Pathways," *Asian Survey* 46, no. 6 (November–December 2006): 809.

101. Jonathan Birchall, "Vietnam and China Inch towards more Neighbourly Relations," *Financial Times* (London), February 25, 1999.

102. "Vietnam Stresses Ties of Friendship with China." *Agence France Presse*, November 13, 2000.

103. Kiet, "Thu cua ong Vo Van Kiet gui Bo Chinh Tri Dang Cong San Vietnam 1995."

104. "Vietnam Communist Party chief to study China's experiment," *Agence France Presse*, February 25, 1999.

105. "Vietnam and China sign historic land border treaty," *Agence France Presse*, December 30, 1999.

106. "Another interpretation of the agreement is that China and Vietnam have moved closer, while rapprochement with the United States appears to have stalled. Although Hanoi and Washington agreed in principle on bilateral trade agreement in July, Vietnam shyed away from ratifying it, partly out of deference to China, analysts say. 'This shows that China is gaining on the United States in the race for influence in southeast Asia,' said one Asian ambassador." "Vietnam and China sign historic land border treaty," Agence France Presse, December 30, 1999.

107. "Le Kha Phieu and Do Muoi stressed the CPV's policy to adhere to the socialist road and its strategy to implement overall reforms . . . Zeng [Qinghong] especially praised the smooth power transition completed at the fourth plenary session of the CPV's Eighth Congress last December and the National Assembly last September." "Vietnamese Leaders Call For Closer Ties With China," Xinhua General Overseas News Service, BBC Worldwide Monitoring, April 4, 1998.

108. Ibid.

109. Steve Kirby, "Jiang heads to Vietnam amid new sensitivity over ties," Agence France Presse, February 26, 2002.

110. "During his April 1998 trip to Vietnam, Zeng Qinghong said that the three visits to China by Do Muoi made a significant contribution to promoting the friendly cooperation between the two parties and two countries." "Vietnamese Leaders Call for Closer Ties with China," Xinhua General Overseas News Service, BBC Worldwide Monitoring, April 4, 1998.

111. Kirby, "Jiang heads to Vietnam."

112. Thayer, "Doi Moi 2?"

113. Ibid.

114. Ibid.

115. Nguyen Manh Hung, "Vietnam in 1999: The Party's Choice," *Asian Survey* 40, no. 1 (January–February, 2000): 100.

116. Ibid., 98–99.

CHAPTER 7

1. Steve Kirby, "Growing Gap with Neighbors Forces Vietnam to Sign US Trade Deal," Agence France Presse, July 13, 2000.

2. A representative usage of this term is the following statement in an article which was part of a series published in the newspaper *Tuoi Tre* under the general heading "striking out into the big ocean": "As we know, and people have already spent a lot of time discussing 'going out into the big ocean' of the WTO, and the matter of comprehensive integration. At the same time, with the specific commitments concerning opening the door to cultural and informational services, we can see that the impact will not be excessively strong or sudden." "Cac cam ket WTO co hieu luc: Hieu dung ve 'mo cua' van hoa" [The commitments of the WTO are effective: Correctly understanding the cultural "open door"], *Tuoi Tre* online, January 14, 2007.

3. Every Vietnamese knows and treasures the saying "we return to bathe in our own pond; whether it is clear or muddy, the home pond is always better" (*Ta ve ta tam ao ta, du trong du duc, ao nha van hon*).

4. "Nong Dan khong the tu boi ra 'bien lon'" [The peasants cannot possibly swim out by themselves into the big ocean], *Quan Doi Nhan Dan*, March 8, 2007. This phrase came to be used to deplore the short-sighted behavior of peasants victimizing themselves by abandoning potentially

more reliable long-term sources of income to change over to rice cultivation because of the short-term incentives of the global market. "Khong the de nong dan 'tu boi'" [We cannot let the peasants "swim on their own"], *Tuoi Tre* online, July 4, 2008. Here the usage suggests the costs of abandoning rational land-use planning (a vestige of the centrally controlled economy) for spontaneous, and short-sighted, profit-driven individual behavior which, it is alleged by some officials, leads the individual not only to act contrary to the collective good, but against long-range personal interest.

5. "The growing number of Chinese government officials 'jumping into the sea of commerce' and forming their own companies could lead to a resurgence in official profiteering, a mainland newspaper has warned. Official profiteering, or guandao as it is colloquially known, was rampant in the late 1980s as officials used their power and influence to sell off state controlled goods on the private market at huge profits." Geoffrey Crothall, "Profiteering fear as officials turn to business," *South China Morning Post*, April 10, 1993.

6. Van Quang, "An ninh kinh te trong toan cau hoa kinh te" [Economic security in economic globalization], *Tap Chi Cong San* online, 41 (2003).

7. Vu Duong Ninh [editor-in-chief], *Ngoai giao Viet Nam hien dai 1975–2002* [Contemporary Vietnamese diplomacy, 1975–2002] (Hanoi: Hoc Viet Quan He Quoc Te, 2002): 110.

8. For example, see interview with Pham Chi Lan "Cham gia nhap WTO thua thiet lau dai" [Late entry into the WTO will inflict lasting damage], *Tien Phong* online, September 28, 2006.

9. Vo Van Phuc, "Tac dong cua viec gia nhap To Chuc Thuong Mai The Gioi den cac dia phuong" [The impact of joining the WTO on local areas], *Tap Chi Cong San* online, 119 (2006).

10. "MFN now likely, but US wants slice of consumer market," *East Asia News and Features* (Australia) Pty Limited *Asia Today*, November, 1995.

11. "'The two sides are miles apart,' said a Hanoi-based lawyer who has seen a copy of the 80-page draft agreement which US negotiators delivered to their Vietnamese counterparts. Others agree, saying that it could take up to two years for the former wartime foes to hammer out an agreement acceptable to both sides." The United States was concerned about the favored position of Vietnamese State Owned Enterprises and Vietnam's human rights record. "Vietnam and US Move Ahead on Bilateral Trade Agreement," Agence France Presse, September 24, 1997.

12. "According to one of Vietnam's negotiators and Deputy Head of the Ministry of Trade's Division for Europe-America Affairs, Nguyen Van Binh, the US side wanted to include an entire investment chapter to the agreement, while WTO does not require a separate agreement on the issue. Moreover, the Vietnamese side argued that the US requirements relating to investment environment improvement for US companies operating in Vietnam are even higher than regulated by WTO." "Vietnam: A Bridge Too Far," *Vietnam Economic News*, September 28, 1998.

13. Frederik Balfour, "US, Vietnam agree in principle on landmark trade accord," Agence France Presse, July 25, 1999.

14. "After the opening of diplomatic relations, we began negotiations on a Bilateral Commercial Agreement in 1996. The talks proceeded very slowly for three years. However, our work this year has proceeded rapidly, culminating last month with an agreement in principle that, when completed, will fundamentally change Vietnam's trade regime and contribute to a broader liberalization of its domestic economy." Testimony of Ambassador Charlene Barshefsky, U.S. Trade Representative, before the Senate Foreign Relations Committee Subcommittees on International Economic Policy and Asia-Pacific Affairs, Subject—American Trade Negotiations With Vietnam, Federal News Service, August 4, 1999.

15. "The United States and Vietnam on Sunday reached an agreement in principle on a bilateral trade agreement marking the final step towards full economic normalisation 24 years after the end of the Vietnam War," Balfour, "US, Vietnam Agree in Principle."

16. "The two sides reached an agreement in principle in July 1999," said one report, " but Vietnam walked away from the deal after it was circulated widely among its leading government officials." Edward Alden, "US and Vietnam near trade deal," *Financial Times* (London), July 11, 2000.

17. Ibid.

18. "No Vietnam–U.S. trade pact this year," Deutsche Press-Agentur, June 14, 2000.

19. "U.S. Aide Is Pessimistic on Hanoi Trade Accord; Politburo Is Hesitating on Pact, Official Says," *International Herald Tribune*, September 11, 1999.

20. Carlyle Thayer, "Vietnam in 2000: Toward the Ninth Party Congress," *Asian Survey* 41, no. 1 (January–February 2001): 181–8.

21. Do Mai Thanh, "Nhin lai qua trinh co phan hoa doanh nghiep nha nuoc nuoc ta" [Look back on the process of equitising state businesses in our country], *Tap Chi Cong San* online, 102 (2006).

22. Adam Fforde, *Vietnamese State Industry and the Political Economy of Commercial Renaissance: Dragon's Tooth or Curate's Egg?* (Oxford: Chandos Publishing, 2007): 60.

23. Dinh Van An, "Phat trien cac loai hinh doanh nghiep trong nen kinh te nhieu thanh phan" [Development of the various commercial enterprise types in the multisectoral economy], *Tap Chi Cong San* online, 57 (2004).

24. Thayer, "Vietnam in 2000."

25. Ibid.

26. "Thong bao hoi nghi lan thu 11 (lan 2) Ban Chap Hanh Truong Uong Dang khoa VIII" [Announcement of the eleventh plenum (second session) of the Eighth Party Congress], *Tap Chi Cong San*, no. 7 (April 2001): 4. See also "Party Plenum Reprimands Defence Minister, Army Chief," BBC Monitoring Asia-Pacific, March 25, 2001.

27. Ibid., 82.

28. Pham Van Tra, "Tang cuong quoc phong-an ninh, bao ve vung chac To Quoc Viet Nam xa hoi chu nghia trong tinh hinh moi" [Strengthen national defense and security, firmly protect the socialist republic of vietnam Fatherland in the new situation], *Tap Chi Cong San*, no. 8 (April 2001).

29. Party Secretary General Le Kha Phieu, "Hoan thanh tot nhat moi cong viec chuan bi cho dai hoi lan thu IX cua Dang" [Finish up the very best the preparations for the Ninth Party Congress], *Tap Chi Cong San*, no. 3 (February 2001): 4.

30. Nguyen Thuy Anh, "Chu dong hoi nhap kinh te quoc te" [Proactively integrate with the international economy], *Tap Chi Cong San*, no. 12 (June 2001).

31. A computer search through 2007 of the downloaded text of the contents of *Tap Chi Cong San*, which has been online since 2001 finds no mentions of the Tenth Plenum of the Eight Central Committee, although many other plenums are cited for political decisions that are considered especially important by the party.

32. Steve Kirby, "Western Donors Tone Down Criticism of Slow Pace of Vietnam Reforms," Agence France Press, June 23, 2000.

33. Ibid.

34. "Whereas two years ago Vietnam did not publish a budget at all and in 1999 it made only a "very modest presentation," this year it presented donors with a detailed public spending review

covering a full 75 percent of total expenditure. 'The overall story is that public money is spent well and that there is an increased openness in explaining that information,' Steer said." Kirby, "Western Donors Tone Down Criticism."

35. Ibid.

36. Cao Cuong, "Party Plenum Pledges Further Integration," *Saigon Times Daily*, July 5, 2000.

37. Kirby, "Growing Gap with Neighbors."

38. Ibid.

39. "In January the politburo removed trade minister Truong Dinh Tuyen from his post in what many believe was punishment for exceeding his mandate in supervisions of the trade talks." Khoan, sixty-two years old, was characterized as "a savvy English speaker renowned for his superb negotiating skills, local sources said, confirming that the minister played a key role in brokering the recently signed land border agreement between Vietnam and its northern neighbour China." "U.S. Will not Re-negotiate Terms to Vietnam Trade Deal," Deutsche Press-Agentur, February 22, 2000.

40. Interview in Hanoi, January 2007.

41. "Chiec mu cao-boi va nhung mon no biet doi" [The cowboy hat and the things owed that I knew how to demand payment for], *Tuoi Tre* online, February 8, 2005.

42. "Vietnam–U.S. Trade Agreement Should Benefit Both Countries, Says Vietnamese Official," Xinhua General Overseas News Service, June 30, 2000.

43. Anthony Salzman, chairman of the Hanoi Branch of the American Chamber of Commerce in Vietnam said "I would infer there is a profound debate going on about whether opening markets is the way to achieve national prosperity," In his view "Opposition to the pact comes mostly from Vietnamese businesses that have an interest in keeping the economy closed and those who fear that a liberalized economy could undermine the Communist Party's authority." Thomas Crampton, "U.S. Aide Is Pessimistic On Hanoi Trade Accord; Politburo Is Hesitating on Pact, Official Says," *International Herald Tribune*, September 11, 1999.

44. "Vietnam Buoyed, Anxious over Historic U.S. Trade Pact," Deutsche Press-Agentur, July 14, 2000.

45. "We hope expanded trade will go hand in hand with strength and respect for human rights and labor standards. For we live in an age where wealth is generated by the free exchange of ideas and stability depends on democratic choices. By signing this agreement, Vietnam takes an important step in the right direction." "Remarks by the President on the Announcement of Vietnam Bilateral Trade Agreement," US Newswire, July 13, 2000.

46. A Catholic priest had publicly urged the United States not to approve the BTA until the Vietnamese government improved its human-rights record. Despite a personal warning from a State Department official that the subsequent arrest of this priest might adversely affect the BTA ratification, the BTA was approved by Congress in October 2001. Immediately after this Hanoi imposed a stiff fifteen-year sentence on Nguyen Van Ly. "Arrest of Vietnam Priest Won't Help Trade Pact, U.S. Official Says," Deutsche Press-Agentur, May 18, 2001. "Vietnam Sentences Catholic Priest to 15 Years in Prison," Associated Press, October 19, 2001.

47. "Vietnamese Premier Hopes Visit by WTO Head to Help 'Quick' Accession." BBC Worldwide Monitoring, December 3, 2001.

48. Vo Van Kiet, "Dong gop y kien vao bao cao tong ket ly luan va thuc tien 20 nam doi moi" [Some ideas on the concluding summary report on theory and practice of twenty years of *doi moi*], April 2005, http://www.ykien.net/tl_viettrung90.html.

49. Nguyen Thuy Anh, "Chu dong hoi nhap kinh te quoc te" [Proactively integrate with the international economy], *Tap Chi Cong San*, no. 12 (June 2001).

50. Dinh Van An, "Phat trien cac loai hinh doanh nghiep trong nen kinh te nhieu thanh phan."

51. Ibid.

52. Ho Xuan Hung, "Thach thuc va trien vong doi voi doanh nghiep nha nuoc" [The challenges and prospects of state enterprises], *Tap Chi Cong San* online, 110 (2006).

53. Le Xuan Tung, "Nhung dot pha tu duy ly luan ve kinh te thi truong o nuoc ta" [New breakthroughs in thinking and theory regarding market economics in our country], *Tap Chi Cong San* online, 65 (2004).

54. Nguyen Phu Trong, "Doi moi tu duy luan vi su nghiep xay dung chu nghia xa hoi" [Renovate theoretical thinking for the mission of building socialism], *Tap Chi Cong San* online, 76 (2005).

55. Ibid.

56. Ibid.

57. "Hanoi Radio Hails 'Positive Progress' in US–Vietnam Relations in 2002," BBC Worldwide monitoring, December 19, 2002.

58. "Police Force in Vietnam Warns Over Security Threats from BTA," *Vietnam News Briefs*, March 20, 2002.

59. "Vietnamese Officials Feel Less Tense About Trade Disputes with the US," *Financial Times Information*, January 7, 2003.

60. "U.S. Official Says Vietnam Trade Pact Is Key to Investor Confidence," Deutsche Press-Agentur, August 23, 2000. Vietnam subsequently acknowledged substantial US support on helping Vietnam prepare to meet its WTO commitments. "USAID Support to Vietnam's WTO Commitments Fulfillment Acknowledged," Thai Press Reports, January 24, 2007.

61. "U.S. Official says Vietnam Trade Pact Is Key to Investor Confidence."

62. "U.S., Vietnam Sign Bilateral Trade Agreement—Trade Pact Opens U.S. Market, Brings More Competition," *Saigon Times Daily*, July 17, 2000.

63. Luong Van Tu, "Nhung chang duong di den quy che thuong mai binh thuong vinh vien Vietnam Hoa Ky" [Stages along the road to permanent normal trade relations between Vietnam and the United States], *Tap Chi Cong San* online, no. 122 (2007).

64. "Ban Chap Hanh, Bo Chinh Tri se thay doi rat nhieu" [There will be a great deal of change in the central committee and politburo], *Tien Phong* online, April 14, 2006.

65. Comments of Minister of Finance Nguyen Sinh Hung in "Dai Hoi X: Dai bieu gop y cho bao cao chinh tri" [The Tenth Party Congress: Delegates offer ideas on the the political report], *Tien Phong* online, April 19, 2006.

66. *Tien Phong* online, February 3, 2006.

67. Vo Van Kiet, "Dong gop y kien vao bao cao tong ket ly luan va thuc tien 20 nam doi moi."

68. Influential voices in the party echoed Vo Van Kiet, signaling that the time had come to de-emphasize "peaceful evolution" and focus more on "falling behind." One account of the evolution of thinking about international relations over the course of the doi moi period said that "This is a process in which there has been a shift from raising high the banner of ideological consciousness (that is, class) to the banner of national interest (since the time of Doi Moi) as the main standard to assess the situation and formulate external policies." Chu Van Chuc, "Qua trinh doi moi tu duy doi ngoai van hinh thanh duong loi doi ngoai moi" [The process of renovating

thinking about external affairs and the formation of a new policy line on external affairs], *Nghien Cuu Quoc Te*, no. 58 (September 2004).

69. Vu Khoan, "Tich cuc va chu dong hoi nhap kinh te quoc te."

70. Nguyen Dy Nien, "Nam bat thoi co, vuot qua thach thuc thuc hien thang loi duong loi doi ngoai Dai Hoi X Cua Dang" [Grasp the opportunity, overcome the challenge of victoriously implementing the external policy of the Tenth Party Congress]. *Tap Chi Cong San* online, 108 (2006).

71. Major General Bui Phan Ky, "Con khong chien luoc 'dien bien hoa binh' chong Viet Nam?" [Is there still a strategy of "peaceful evolution" to oppose Vietnam?], *Quoc Phong Toan Dan*, 4–2006, 36.

72. Ibid.

73. Interview with former prime minister Vo Van Kiet by an overseas Vietnamese-American journalist, *Dien Dan Forum*, March 13, 2007.

74. Vo Van Kiet, "Dong gop y kien vao bao cao tong ket ly luan va thuc tien 20 nam doi moi."

75. "Trade Agreement With US is Good Beginning to Vietnam's WTO Bid," *Financial Times Information*, June 16, 2005.

76. Ibid.

77. "Cang thang dam phan WTO: Nhung chi tiet moi tiet lo" [Tense WTO Negotiations: The details that have just now been revealed], *Tuoi Tre* online, November 7, 2006.

78. Ibid.

79. Ibid. In an interview with the original BTA negotiator, Truong Dinh Tuyen, who had been recalled to duty to assist in the WTO-related negotiations with the United States. Tuyen was asked—rhetorically—whether the May 2006 negotiations with the United States were the "most tense." "Tren chin tang gioi, hoi chuyen dam phan WTO" [Nine stories up, discussing the WTO negotiations], *Tien Phong* online, February 12, 2007.

80. "The final negotiation with the United States was the most tense. It stretched out for four days and three nights to resolve the remaining obstacles." "Cang thang dam phan WTO: Nhung chi tiet moi tiet lo."

81. "Vietnam Finds WTO Negotiations with US Harder than BTA," *Financial Times Information*, Vietnam News Briefs, April 12, 2005.

82. Luong Van Tu, "Nhung chang duong di den quy che tuong mai binh thuong vinh vien Vietnam Hoa Ky" [Stages along the road to permanent normal trade relations between Vietnam and the United States]" *Tap Chi Cong San* online, 122 (2007).

83. "Cang thang dam phan WTO: Nhung chi tiet moi tiet lo."

84. Ibid.

85. "Phut 89" [The 89th minute], *Tien Phong* online, February 18, 2007.

86. "Toi cung phai tu nang minh len de hoi nhap" [I too will constantly have to improve myself to integrate], interview with Nguyen Minh Triet in *Tien Phong* online, February 16, 2007.

87. The dissident intellectual Ha Si Phu, however, continued to use the "damsel in distress" image, comparing Vietnam to a girl caught in between two rival athletes (e.g., big and strong suitors), China and the United States, competing for her favors. Ha Si Phu, "Viet Nam nhu mot co gai ma dang chung chien giua hai chang luc si" [Vietnam is like a girl between two athletes trying to win her favor], Radio Free Asia, April 11, 2005.

88. Vietnam's attractiveness to European investors, in the party's view, is that "First, EU businesses place great importance and highly appreciate the political stability and guaranteed

security in Vietnam in the past years." Dinh Manh Tuan, "Viet Nam gia nhap WTO co hoi va thach thuc doi voi cac doanh nghiep vua va nho cua EU" [Vietnam's WTO entry and the challenges with regard to small and medium enterprises of the EU], *Tap Chi Cong San* online, 125 (2007).

89. Vo Van Kiet, "Dong gop y kien vao bao cao tong ket ly luan va thuc tien 20 nam doi moi."

90. "Nong nghiep va nong dan se vuot qua thach thuc" [Agriculture and peasants will overcome the challenges], interview with Minister of Agriculture Cao Duc Phat, *Tien Phong* online, February 19, 2007.

91. Amy Kazmin, "In Beijing's Footsteps," *Financial Times* (London), January 8, 2007.

92. "WTO a firm helping hand," *Saigon Times Magazine*, August 31, 2006.

93. "Mot Quoc Hoi cua hoi nhap, doi moi, va phat trien" [A National Assembly of integration, *doi moi*, and development], *Tuoi Tre* online, March 24,2007.

94. Interview with Le Xuan Nghia, Vu truong Vu Chien Luoc, Ngan Hang Nha Nuoc [Director of the strategic section of the State Bank], "Mo cua ngan hang: Khong so canh tranh ve van con bao ho?" [Opening the doors of the banking sector: Is there no need to be afraid of competition because there will still be protection?], *Tien Phong* online, April 12, 2005.

95. "Study Missions to the US Conducted For Vietnamese Officials," *Financial Times Information*, August 10, 2005.

96. "Vietnam Businesses Advised to Renew Themselves for Effective Integration," Thai Press Reports, August 8, 2006.

97. "US Trade Expert Extols US–Vietnam Trade Relations," *Asian Pulse*, January 20, 2005.

98. Ibid.

99. "Vietnam's Bid for WTO Membership Reflects Its Strong Global Integration," *Financial Times Information* Global News Wire, Asia Africa Intelligence Wire, May 3, 2005.

100. Kazmin, "In Beijing's Footsteps."

101. Martin Painter, "The Politics of Economic Restructuring in Vietnam: The Case of State-owned Enterprise 'Reform,'" *Contemporary Southeast Asia* 25, no. 1 (April 2003): 21.

102. Kazmin, "In Beijing's Footsteps."

103. Ibid.

104. Ibid.

105. Interview in Hanoi, January 2007.

106. "Vietnam rejects 'clone' development, defends state businesses," Deutsche Press-Agentur, March 6, 2003.

107. "International Donors Warn Vietnam to Wipe Out Corruption, Hasten SOE Reform," *Financial Times Information*, December 3, 2003.

108. "Government Determined to Push Up SOE Reform," *Financial Times Information*, February 5, 2002.

109. Ibid.

110. Oliver Jones, "A Giddy Ride in Booming Vietnam," *South China Morning Post*, March 4, 2007.

111. "Vietnam earmarks another 550 state-owned firms for privatization in 2007," BBC Monitoring Asia Pacific, February 1, 2007.

112. "71 State-Owned Firms to Offer Shares to Public," *Toronto Star*, January 3, 2007.

113. "Vietnam Reduces State-Owned Enterprises to 3.61 per cent of Total Firms," BBC Monitoring Asia Pacific, December 8, 2006.

114. Takeshi Hasegawa, "Vietnam Far Behind Privatization Goal," *Nikkei Weekly*, August 28, 2006.

115. Fforde, *Vietnamese State Industry*.

116. Painter, "Politics of Economic Restructuring in Vietnam," 20.

117. Gainsborough, *Changing Political Economy of Vietnam*, 106. He notes that "Furthermore, instead of politicians fighting over policies on ideological grounds, we see rent-seeking and the use of policy instruments and so-called corruption cases as part of power struggles to defend such commercial interests."

118. Fforde, *Vietnamese State Industry*, 222.

119. Ibid.

120. Gainsborough, *Changing Political Economy of Vietnam*, 39.

121. Fforde, *Vietnamese State Industry*, 225.

122. Ibid., p.217.

123. Ibid., p.220.

124. Interview with Dang van Thanh, Deputy Director of the National Assembly Budget Committee, "Co phan hoa chua thoat canh nua chung" [Equitisation has still not escaped from being only a halfway measure], *Tuoi Tre* online, September 19, 2006.

125. "Khong the chu dao bang cach giu nhieu von" [One can't possibly maintain the initiative by holding a lot of capital], *Tuoi Tre* online, September 22, 2006.

126. Ibid.

127. Interview with First Deputy Prime Minister Nguyen Sinh Hung, "Chinh phu dat niem tin rat lon vao doi ngu doanh nghiep" [The government puts great faith in the ranks of enterprises], *Tien Phong* online,October 19, 2006.

128. Ibid.

129. Ibid.

130. Fforde, *Vietnamese State Industry*, 200.

131. Nguyen Van Dang, "May van de ve che do so huu va thanh phan kinh te o nuoc ta" [A number of questions concerning the ownership system and the economic sectors in our country], *Tap Chi Cong San* online, 97 (2005).

132. Gainsborough, *Changing Political Economy of Vietnam*, 104–5.

133. Ibid., 105.

134. Fforde, *Vietnamese State Industry*, xx.

135. Nguyen Van Dang, "May van de ve che do so huu va thanh phan kinh te o nuoc ta."

136. Ibid.

137. "Drawing on the work of Jean Oi and Andrew Walder, property rights are understood here in terms of Harold Demsetz's notion of property as a 'bundle of rights'. These are subdivided into three kinds of rights—control, income, and transfer—while there is also recognition that there are a variety of ways such rights might be enforced, ranging from formal law to social custom." Gainsborough, *Changing Political Economy of Vietnam*, 24.

138. Nguyen Van Dang, "May van de ve che do so huu va thanh phan kinh te o nuoc ta."

139. Ibid.

140. Ha Dang, "Kinh te thi truong qua cac buoc doi moi tu duy" [The market economy over the course of the stages of ideological renovation], *Tap Chi Cong San* online, 127 (2007).

141. "Despite Vietnam's ongoing social, economic, and political problems, its achievements over the past twenty years have prevented collapse akin to that of the Soviet Union and

ensured the development of 'workable socialism' according to Assistant to the Party General Secretary Ha Dang. Reviewing the doi moi, or renewal process, the senior official said the country's ongoing problems included corruption and a lack of economic competitiveness. He said the political system and the party's leadership needed to be 're-invigorated.'" "Vietnam official reviews development, urges efficient leadership," BBC Worldwide Monitoring, April 13, 2006. The VNA English-language report of this speech also uses the term "workable socialism." "Renewal process results in great achievements," *Vietnam Thong Tan Xa* [English], April 13, 2006.

142. "Straits Times lo ngai ve chung khoan Viet Nam" [The *Straits Times* worries about the Vietnam stock market], *Tien Phong* online, April 24, 2007.

143. "TPHCM: 30% doanh nghiep do nguoi Hoa lam chu [Ho Chi Minh City: 30% of enterprises are headed by Hoa], *Tien Phong* online, February 22, 2007. See also Steve Kirby, "Saigon's Chinatown Bounces back from Dark Years after 1975," Agence France Presse, April 28, 2000.

144. Pham Dinh Nghiem and Hai Quang, "Bay thach thuc doi voi Viet Nam sau mot nam gia nhap WTO" [Seven challenges for Vietnam one year after joining the WTO], *Tap Chi Cong San* online, 151 (2008).

145. Ibid.

146. Nguyen Duc Thang, "Am muu, thu doan 'lat do chinh tri trong hoa binh' cua My va phuong Tay o cac nuoc Trung A va Dong Au thoi gian qua" [Recent plots and schemes of the Americans and Western countries to achieve "peaceful political overthrow" in countries of Central Asia and Eastern Europe], *Tap Chi Cong San* online, 150 (2008.

147. Ha Dang, "Hoi nhap quoc te va vai tro lanh dao cua Dang ta" [International integration and the leading role of our party], *Tap Chi Cong San* online, 123 (2007).

CHAPTER 8

1. Vu Duong Ninh, ed., *Ngoai Giao Viet Nam Hien Dai 1975–2002* [Contemporary Vietnamese diplomacy, 1975–2002] (Hanoi: Hoc Viet Quan He Quoc Te, 2002): 109.

2. "Combating US Hegemony Tops World Politics Today; Former Politburo Member," *Financial Times Information*, October 22, 2002.

3. Vu Duong Ninh, *Ngoai Giao Viet Nam Hien Dai*, 110.

4. Ibid.

5. Nguyen Manh Cam, "Ngoai giao thoi ky doi moi mot giai doan phat trien quan trong cua nen ngoai giao Viet Nam hien dai."

6. Nguyen Co Thach, "Dac diem tong quat cua tinh hinh the gioi trong 50 nam qua" [Special general characteristics of the global situation over the past fifty years], *Tap Chi Nghien Cuu Quoc Te* [Journal of International Studies], So Dac Biet [special issue], no. 7 (September 1995): 22.

7. Nguyen Xuan Son and Nguyen Van Du, *Chien luoc doi ngoai cua cac nuoc lon va quan he voi Viet Nam* [External strategy of the big countries and their relations with Vietnam] (Hanoi: NXB Chinh Tri Quoc Gia, 2006): 14–15.

8. Joseph Nye, *The Paradox of American Power* (New York: Oxford University Press, 2002): 91.

9. Clyde Prestowitz, *Rogue Nation* (New York: Basic Books, 2003): 34.

10. Nguyen Xuan Son and Nguyen Van Du, *Chien luoc doi ngoai cua cac nuoc lon va quan he voi Viet Nam*, 16–17.

11. Nguyen Van Tai, "Thoi co va thach thuc doi voi suc manh quan su quoc gia khi Viet Nam gia nhap WTO" [Opportunities and challenges with regard to military strength when Vietnam joins the WTO], *Tap Chi Cong San*, 121 (2006).

12. Ibid.

13. "Proactively, creatively, flexibly, and nimbly deal with each external issue based on the situation of each target, and each relationship, and each concrete matter; don't be inflexible, over-eager or hasty. Organically link the two faces of international cooperation and conflict and deeply grasp the dialectical relationship between a 'partner' and a 'target.'" Ngo Chi Nguyen, "Cong tac doi ngoai thoi ky doi moi thanh tuu van bai hoc kinh nghiem" [The external mission in the *doi moi* period: Accomplishments and lessons], *Tap Chi Cong San*, 93 (2005).

14. Pham Quang Minh, "Vietnam and Korea in East Asian Pacific Regionalism," paper delivered at the Fourth Annual Koret Conference, The Walter H. Shorenstein Asia-Pacific Research Center, Stanford University, March 2, 2012.

15. Nguyen Manh Hung, "Thuc hien nhat quan duong loi doi ngoai doc lap tu chu hoa binh hop tac va phat trien" [Uniformly carry out the independent and autonomous policy of peaceful cooperation and development], Tap Chi Cong San, 114-2006.

16. Alexander Vuvinh, "Vietnam Between China and the United States: Historical Experiences, Perceptions and Strategies," paper delivered at the Fourth Annual Koret Conference, The Walter H. Shorenstein Asia-Pacific Research Center, Stanford University, March 2, 2012.

17. Vo Trong Viet, "Bao ve vung chac chu quyen bien gioi, vung bien cua to quoc trong tinh hinh moi" [Solidly protect the Fatherland's borders and maritime zones in the new situation], Tap Chi Cong San, 109-2006.

18. Doan Van Thang, "An ninh quoc gia trong boi canh toan cau hoa" [National security in the environment of globalization], *Nghien Cuu Quoc Te*, no. 58, 9–2004, 100.

19. Ha My Huong, "Quan he giua cac nuoc lon khu vuc Chau A Thai Binh Duong" [Relations among the big countries in the Asia-Pacific region], *Tap Chi Cong San*, 107 (2006).

20. Nguyen Xuan Son and Nguyen Van Du, *Chien luoc doi ngoai cua cac nuoc lon va quan he voi Viet Nam*, 261–4.

21. Nguyen Van Tai, "Thoi co va thach thuc doi voi suc manh quan su quoc gia khi Viet Nam gia nhap WTO."

22. Truong Luu, "May bay cu, chien luoc moi" [Old airplanes, new strategy], *Tap Chi Cong San*, 135 (2007).

23. Tran Ba Khoa, "The gioi don cuc hay da cuc?" [A unipolar or a multipolar world?], *Tap Chi Cong San*, 155 (2008).

24. Nguyen Khac Su, "Khuynh huong xa hoi chu nghia buoc dau cua canh ta My La-Tinh" [The socialist orientation in the first phase of the Latin American left], *Tap Chi Cong San*, 141 (2007).

25. Nguyen Khac Su, "Khuynh huong xa hoi chu nghia buoc dau cua canh ta My La-Tinh," *Tap Chi Cong San*, 141 (2007). For another upbeat account of the prospect for a revival of the global communist movement see Nguyen Hoang Giap and Nguyen Thi Que, "Phong trao cong san quoc te trong giai doan hien nay" [The international Communist movement in the present stage], *Tap Chi Cong San*, 141 (2007).

26. Deborah Welch Larson and Alexei Shevchenko, "Shortcut to Greatness: The New Thinking and the Revolution in Soviet Foreign Policy," *International Organization* 73 (Winter 2003): 78.

27. Phan Doan Nam, "Ngoai giao Viet Nam 60 nam dau tranh va truong thanh" [Sixty years of Vietnamese diplomatic struggle and maturation], *Tap Chi Cong San*, 89 (2005).

28. Nguyen Trong Phuc, "Cach mang thang tam nam 1945 va tu tuong Ho Chi Minh ve xay dung nha nuoc phap quyen xa hoi chu nghia cua dan, do dan, vi Dan" [The August 1945 revolution and Ho Chi Minh thought concerning building a socialist constitutional state of the people, by the people, and for the people], *Tap Chi Cong San*, 21 (2002).

29. David Marr, *Vietnam 1945: The Quest for Power* (Berkeley: University of California Press, 1997).

30. Hoc Vien Quan He Quoc Te, *Thang loi co tinh thoi dai va cuoc dau tranh tren mat tran doi ngoai cua nhan dan ta* [A victory which reflects the current age and our people's struggle on the diplomatic front] (Hanoi: NXB Su That, 1985): 8–9.

31. Phan Doan Nam, "Ngoai giao Viet Nam 60 nam dau tranh va truong thanh."

32. Nayan Chanda, "Brother Enemy: The War After the War," (Orlando: Harcourt Brace Jovanovich, 1986), 27.

33. Nguyen Tan Dung, "Ve duong loi va chien luoc phat trien kinh-te xa hoi cua Dang tai Dai Hoi IX" [On the party policy line and strategy of socioeconomic development at the Ninth Party Congress], *Tap Chi Cong San*, 4 (2001).

34. David W. P. Elliott, "Dilemmas of Reform in Vietnam," in Turley and Selden, eds., *Reinventing Vietnamese Socialism*, 80–81.

35. Phan Dinh Dieu, "Vai nhan thuc ve thoi dai ngay nay va con duong cua ta," 8.

36. Professor Pham Duc Thanh, "Vai tro cua Viet Nam trong ASEAN" [The role of Vietnam in ASEAN], *Nghien Cuu Dong Nam A* (March 1996): 12.

37. Nguyen Manh Cam, "Ngoai giao thoi ky doi moi mot giai doan phat trien quan trong cua nen ngoai giao Viet Nam hien dai."

38. Ha Dang, "Hoi nhap quoc te va vai tro lanh dao cua Dang ta" [International integration and the leading role of our party], *Tap Chi Cong San*, 123 (2007).

39. Ibid.

40. "Bai thuyet trinh cua Tien si Le Dang Doanh truoc Bo Chinh Tri" [Briefing of Dr. Le Dang Doanh to the politburo], Radio Free Asia, November 3, 2005: http://www.rfa.org/vietnamese/in_depth/2005/03/15/Le_Dang_Doanh_Interview_part1_VHung/.

41. Nguyen Van Linh, "Cung co hoa binh, de cao canh giac, phat huy suc manh tong hop De Bao Ve To Quoc" [Consolidate peace, raise vigilance, develop comprehensive strength to defend the Fatherland], *Nhan Dan*, December 15, 1989.

42. Ta Minh Tuan, "An ninh con nguoi va nhung moi de doa toan cau" [Human security and global threats], *Tap Chi Cong San*, 153 (2008).

43. Ha My Huong, "Cuc dien quan he quoc te giua cac nuoc lon nhung nam dau the ky XXI" [The conjuncture of international relations among the big countries in the first years of the twenty-first century], *Tap Chi Cong San*, 36 (2003).

44. Nguyen Xuan Son and Nguyen Van Du, *Chien luoc doi ngoai cua cac nuoc lon va quan he voi Viet Nam*, 15–16.

45. Nong Duc Manh, "Giu vung moi truong hoa binh on dinh de phat trien kinh te xa hoi la loi ich cao nhat cua dat nuoc" [Firmly maintaining a peaceful and stable environment for socio-economic development is the highest interest of the country], *Tap Chi Cong San*, 40 (2003).

46. Phan Doan Nam, "Ngoai giao Viet Nam sau 20 nam doi moi."

47. Dong Duc and Pham Lien, "Quan niem dia-chien luoc thoi ky 'hau chien tranh lanh'" [The concept of geostrategy in the post–Cold War era], *Tap Chi Quoc Phong Toan Dan*, 12 (2005), 48.

48. "[I]n the trajectory of globalization, one cannot demand absolute sovereignty," Van Quang, "An ninh kinh te trong toan cau hoa kinh te." See discussion below.

49. Hoang Binh Quan, "Dinh huong chien luoc phat trien kinh te xa hoi cua tinh Tuyen Quang" [Setting the strategic direction for socioeconomic development in Tuyen Quang province], *Tap Chi Cong San*, 125 (2007).

50. Vu Thi Loan, "Nang cao trach nhiem cua he thong chinh tri va cong dan to chuc thang loi cuoc bau cu dai bieu Hoi Dong Nhan Dan cac cap" [Raise the responsibility of the political system and the citizens in organizing elections for People's Councils at all levels], *Tap Chi Cong San*, 57 (2004).

51. Phan Doan Nam, "Hoat dong doi ngoai cua Viet Nam nam 2006" [External affairs activities of Vietnam in 2006], *Tap Chi Cong San*, 122 (2007).

52. "America has exploited its absolute superiority to seek absolute security for itself and holds that 'the events of 11-9-2001' are a national security challenge to America, to its way of life and values, but one which can be exploited to use counter terrorism to consolidate the position and dominance of America." Phan Doan Nam, "Ve su dieu chinh chien luoc an ninh quoc gia cua My" [On the revision of American national security strategy], *Tap Chi Cong San*, 55 (2004).

53. Vo Trong Viet, "Bao ve vung chac chu quyen bien gioi vung bien cua To Quoc trong tinh hinh moi" [Firmly protect the sovereignty of the Fatherland's ocean border in the new situation], *Tap Chi Cong San*, 109 (2006).

54. Major General, Professor, Dr. Nguyen Phung Hong, general editor of *Tap Chi Cong An Nhan Dan* [People's security magazine] of the Ministry of National Security, "Nang cao hieu qua phoi hop hoat dong cua cong an va quan doi tren cac dia ban chien luoc" [Elevate the effectiveness of coordination between the public security forces and the armed forces in the strategic areas], *Tap Chi Quoc Phong Toan Dan*, 6 (2006), 29.

55. Vo Thu Phuong, "'Cach mang mau sac' nhin lai va suy ngam" [The "color revolutions": Reflections and reconsiderations], *Tap Chi Cong San*, 109 (2006).

56. Nguyen Phung Hong, "Nang cao hieu qua phoi hop hoat dong cua cong an va quan doi tren cac dia ban chien luoc."

57. Phan Doan Nam, "Ngoai giao Viet Nam sau 20 nam doi moi."

58. Nguyen Tan Dung, "Ve duong loi va chien luoc phat trien kinh-te xa hoi cua Dang tai Dai Hoi IX."

59. Nguyen Phu Trong, "Xay dung nen kinh te doc lap tu chu va chu dong hoi nhap kinh te quoc te" [Build an independent and sovereign economy and proactively integrate into the international economy], *Tap Chi Cong San*, 2 (2001).

60. Doan Van Thang, "An ninh quoc gia trong boi canh toan cau hoa" [National security in the environment of globalization], *Nghien Cuu Quoc Te*, no. 58 (September 2004): 100.

61. Ibid.

62. Van Quang, "An ninh kinh te trong toan cau hoa kinh te."

63. Nguyen Hoang Giap and Nguyen Thi Que, "Nhan thuc the gioi va su phat trien tu duy doi ngoai cua Dang ta trong thoi ky moi" [Our party's understanding of the world and the development of thinking about the external world in the new period], *Tap Chi Quan Doi Toan Dan*, 12-2005.

64. Vo Van Kiet, "Dong gop y kien vao bao cao tong ket ly luan va thuc tien 20 nam doi moi."

65. Nguyen Viet Thao, "Quan he giua cac nuoc tu ban phat trien trong boi canh toan cau hoa" [Relations among the developed capitalist countries in the environment of globalization], *Tap Chi Cong San*, 106 (2006).

66. Nguyen Dy Nien, "Nam bat thoi co, vuot qua thach thuc thuc hien thang loi duong loi doi ngoai Dai Hoi X cua Dang" [Grasp the opportunity, overcome the challenge of victoriously implementing the external policy of the Tenth Party Congress]. *Tap Chi Cong San*, 108 (2006).

67. Pham Van Hung, "Toan cau hoa van xu huong van dong cua dong chay von quoc te" [Globalization and the direction of the flow of mobilizing international investment], *Tap Chi Cong San*, 15 (2002).

68. Phan Doan Nam, "Nhung xu huong chu yeu cua quan he quoc te hien nay va 15–20 nam toi" [The main trends in international relations at present and over the next fifteen–twenty years], *Nghien Cuu Quoc Te* 57 (June 2004): 21–2.

69. Nguyen Viet Thao, "Quan he giua cac nuoc tu ban phat trien trong boi canh toan cau hoa".

70. Ibid.

71. See, for example, Ha My Huong, "Cuc dien quan he quoc te giua cac nuoc lon nhung nam dau the ky XXI."

72. Ha My Huong, "Quan he giua cac nuoc lon khu vuc Chau A Thai Binh Duong."

73. Nguyen Hoang Giap, "Phat trien quan he voi cac nuoc lon trong chinh sach doi ngoai doi moi cua Dang va Nha Nuoc ta." [Development of relations with the big countries in the party and state's external relations in *doi moi*], *Tap Chi Nghien Cuu Quoc Te* 61 (6–2005).

74. Lewis M. Stern, *Defense Relations Between the United States and Vietnam* (North Carolina: McFarland, 2005): 224.

75. Ibid., 224–5.

76. The following paragraphs are based on the author's "The United States and Southeast Asia: Fading Hegemony and Stalemated Regionalism," a paper presented at the conference "American and Asia: Changing Strategic Relations," organized by the Keck Institute of Claremont McKenna College, April 10, 2008.

77. Raymond Burghardt, "US–Vietnam: Discreet Friendship Under China's Shadow," Yale Global Online, 2005: http://yaleglobal.yale.edu/display.article?id=6546.

78. "Vietnamese, Chinese Armies Discuss Development Issues," *Financial Times Information*, November 30, 2006.

79. See Brantly Womack, *China and Vietnam: The Politics of Asymmetry* (New York: Cambridge University Press, 2006), especially chapter 6.

80. Vuving, "Strategy and Evolution of Vietnam's China Policy," 821.

81. Ibid., 823–4.

82. Ang Cheng Guan, "Vietnam–China Relations Since the End of the Cold War," *Asian Survey* 38, no. 12 (December 1998): 1133–4.

83. Trinh Cuong, "An Do voi muc tieu tro thanh cuong quoc" [India and the goal of becoming a great power], *Tap Chi Cong San*, 75 (2005).

84. Vo Xuan Vinh, "ASEAN trong chinh sach huong dong cua An Do" [ASEAN in the "Look East" policy of India], *Tap Chi Cong San*, 125 (2007).

85. Ibid.

86. Nguyen Thu Phuong, "35 nam quan he Viet Nam–An Do" [Thirty-five years of Vietnam–India relations], *Tap Chi Cong San*, 122 (2007).

87. Ibid.

88. Nguyen Hoang Giap, "Phat trien quan he voi cac nuoc lon trong chinh sach doi ngoai doi moi cua Dang va Nha Nuoc ta."

89. Nguyen Quang Thuan, "Quan he kinh te thuong mai Viet Nam–Lien Bang Nga trong boi canh quoc te moi" [Economic and commercial relations between Vietnam and the Russian Federation in the new international setting], *Tap Chi Cong San*, 116 (2006); and Dinh Cong Tuan, "Quan he kinh te Vietnam–Lien Bang Nga trong boi canh quoc te hien nay" [Economic relations between Vietnam and the Russian Federation in the current international setting], *Tap Chi Cong San*, 105 (2006).

90. Nguyen Manh Hung, "Vietnam and the Major Powers: Economic Renovation, Political Stability, and Foreign Policy," paper presented at the EuroViet V Conference, Saint Petersburg State University, Russia, May 28–30, 2002.

91. See the article by Truong Luu, "May bay cu, chien luoc moi."

92. Nguyen Manh Hung, "Vietnam and the Major Powers."

93. Trinh Cuong, "ASEM va su tham gia cua Viet Nam trong ASEM" [ASEM and the participation of Vietnam in ASEM], *Tap Chi Cong San*, 66 (2004).

94. Nguyen Thu My, "ASEM: Cac kich ban phat trien trong nhung nam sap toi" [ASEM: Scenarios for its development in the coming years], *Tap Chi Cong San*, 116 (2006).

95. Nguyen Hoang Giap, "Phat trien quan he voi cac nuoc lon trong chinh sach doi ngoai doi moi cua Dang va Nha Nuoc ta."

96. Nguyen Duy Dung, "Dieu chinh chien luoc doi ngoai cua Nhat Ban trong boi canh quoc te moi" [Re-adjustment of Japan's external strategy in the new international setting], *Tap Chi Cong San*, 119 (2006).

97. Ibid.

98. Vo Trong Viet, "Bao ve vung chac chu quyen bien gioi vung bien cua To Quoc trong tinh hinh moi" [Firmly protect the sovereignty of the Fatherland's ocean border in the new situation], *Tap Chi Cong San*, 109 (2006).

99. Tran Khanh "Vi the dia chinh tri Dong Nam A thap nien dau the ky XXI" [The geopolitical position of Southeast Asia in the first decade of the twenty-first century], *Tap Chi Cong San*, 19 (2002).

100. Le Minh Huong, "An ninh trong su nghiep xay dung va bao ve To Quoc" [Security in the mission of building and protecting the Fatherland], *Tap Chi Cong San*, 1 (2001); and Nguyen Tuan Khanh, "Gia Lai: Tiem nang va phat trien" [Gia Lai: Potential and development], *Tap Chi Cong San*, 51 (2004).

101. Phan Doan Nam, "Hoat dong doi ngoai cua Viet Nam nam 2006" [External affairs activities of Vietnam in 2006], *Tap Chi Cong San*, 122 (2007).

102. Ibid.

103. Balfour, "Vietnam's Defense White Paper."

104. Lieutenant General Pham Hong Cu, "Suy ngam ve su ra doi va phat trien cua che do chinh uy, chinh tri vien" [Reflections on the origins and development of the political commissar and political officer system], *Tap Chi Quoc Phong Toan Dan* 6 (2006), 16–19.

105. Ibid.

106. Phuong Minh Hoa, "Tam tam tri cua nguoi chinh uy chinh tri vien trong giai doan cach mang moi" [The heart and mind of the political commissar and political officer in the new revolutionary phase], *Tap Chi Cong San*, 111 (2006).

107. Senior Lieutenant General Phung Quang Thanh, politburo member, commander of the general staff, and deputy minister of defense, "Nhiem vu co ban ve cung co quoc phong, xay dung

quan doi nhan dan trong tinh hinh moi" [The basic mission of consolidating national defense and building the people's army in the new situation], *Tap Chi Quoc Phong Toan Dan*, 6–2006, 3.

108. "Army Magazine Article Warns against Opportunism, Rightism," Source: *Tap Chi Quoc Phong Toan Dan*, Hanoi, in Vietnamese 1456 gmt 31 January 96, 4–7, BBC Worldwide broadcasts, February 2, 1996.

109. "I also heard that Senior Colonel Minh Quang, the party secretary of the party chapter in which Senior Lieutenant General Nguyen Nam Khanh participates in party activities said: 'The party chapter, which is comprised of senior colonels, major generals, lieutenant generals, and senior lieutenant generals, among which is Senior Lieutenant General Le Ngoc Hien, the former chief of staff of the People's Army of Vietnam, proposed to place Senior Lieutenant General Nguyen Nam Khanh in the category of most outstanding party member, with the a strict spirit of struggle and criticism, and stern resolve to build a strong and clean Party. The party chapter also [considered] the idea of purging Senior Lieutenant General Nguyen Nam Khanh and unanimously rejected it.'" Letter of Tran Dai Son to the preparatory committee for the Tenth Party Congress, October 3, 2005, http://www.ykien.net/trandaison05.html. See also Radio Free Asia interview with Nguyen Thanh Giang, July 3, 2005.

110. "We need to quickly get over the remaining influence of the manner of running the country [as if it was] in wartime, with the special characteristics like the political commissar system, with power to make decisions on the spot, localism, a mechanism of deploying cadres according to political requirements, the party machine as a parallel hierarchy [*bo may cua dang song trung*], but in reality standing above or displacing the state machinery, a regime with unclear lines of authority and weaknesses in professional competence as a result of using the principle of 'the collective leads and the individual is responsible' [for carrying out decisions made collectively], etc." Letter of Vo Van Kiet to the politburo, August 9, 1995, http://www.lmvntd.org/dossier/0895tvvk.htm.

111. Senior Lieutenant General Nguyen Nam Khanh, "Pham chat, dao duc, loi song va phong cach lam viec cua nguoi chinh uy, chinh tri vien quan doi nhan dan Viet Nam" [The character, virtue, way of life, and work style of the political commissar and political officer in the People's Army of Vietnam], *Tap Chi Quoc Phong Toan Dan*, 3–2006, 13–14.

112. Senior Colonel Le Khuong Me [deputy director of the Organization Department of the People's Army of Vietnam], "Chuc nang, nhiem vu va cac moi quan he cua co quan chinh tri trong quan doi nhan dan Viet Nam" [The role and mission and the relationships between the political organizations in the People's Armed Forces of Vietnam], *Tap Chi Quan Doi Nhan Dan*, 4–2006, 13.

113. General Nguyen Van Rinh, "Quan diem, noi dung co ban cua luat quoc phong va viec trien khai thuc hien luat" [The concept and contents of the basic national defense law and the implementation of law], *Tap Chi Quoc Phong Toan Dan*, 8–2005, 6.

114. "Vietnam Publishes National Defence White Paper," *Asia Pulse* (Australia), December 13, 2004.

115. General Pham Van Tra, Politburo member and Minister of Defense, "Nhin lai 20 nam doi moi tu duy ve nhiem vu quan su, quoc phong, bao ve To quoc trong thoi ky moi" [Looking back at twenty years of new thinking on the military and national defense mission of protecting the Fatherland in the new period], *Tap Chi Quoc Phong Toan Dan*, 8–2005, 1.

116. "Xay dung nen quoc phong toan dan vung manh" [Build a strong and stable national defense of all the people], *Nhan Dan*, September 9, 2006.

117. Lieutenant General Nguyen Hoa Thinh [director of the Center For Military Science and Technology and Military Industry], "Nhin nhan su doi moi va phat trien trong khoa hoc-cong nghe quan su" [Recognizing renovation and development in military science and industry], *Tap Chi Quoc Phong Toan Dan*, 11–2005, 16–17.

118. Senior Colonel Nguyen Dong Thuy, "Ban ve hoat dong tac chien chien luoc trong chien tranh bao ve To Quoc" [Discussing the strategic combat activities in war to protect the Father-land], *Tap Chi Quoc Phong Toan Dan*, 6–2006.

119. The announcement of the Steering Committee for Vietnam–China Cooperation stated that "The Vietnamese Committee is headed by Deputy Prime Minister and Foreign Minister Pham Gia Khiem and its members are leaders from the Central Foreign Relations Committee, the Foreign Ministry, the Ministry of National Defence, the Ministry of Public Security, the Ministry of Planning and Investment, the Ministry of Trade and the Ministry of Finance." The composition of the Chinese membership was analogous. "Steering Committee for Vietnam–China Cooperation Established," *Financial Times Information*, Global News Wire, November 15, 2006.

120. "Vietnamese, Chinese Armies to Work More Closely," *Financial Times Information*, April 10, 2006.

121. "Vietnam Hopes to Step Up Military Ties With China," *Financial Times Information*, August 10, 2006.

122. "China, Vietnam likely to complete border demarcation work before 2008, Chinese vice president says," Xinhua General Overseas News Service, October 19, 2005.

123. Van Quang, "An ninh kinh te trong toan cau hoa kinh te."

124. Nguyen Van Tai, "Thoi co va thach thuc doi voi suc manh quan su quoc gia khi Viet Nam gia nhap WTO" [Opportunities and challenges with regard to military strength when Vietnam joins the WTO], *Tap Chi Cong San*, 121 (2006).

125. Gérard Hervouet and Carlyle A. Thayer, "The Army as a Political and Economic Actor in Vietnam," in Christopher Goscha and Benoît de Tréglodé, eds., *Naissance d'un Etat-Parti: Le Viet Nam depuis 1945. The Birth of a Party-State: Vietnam since 1945* (Paris: Les Indes Savantes, 2004): 355–81.

126. Ibid.

127. Richard K. Betts, "Is Strategy an Illusion?," *International Security* 25, no. 2 (Autumn, 2000): 5–50.

128. Ibid.

129. See David W. P. Elliott, "Vietnam: Tradition under Challenge," in Trood and Booth, eds., *Strategic Cultures*, and David W. P. Elliott, "Hanoi's Strategy in the Vietnam War," in Werner, ed., *Vietnam War*.

130. Hoang Anh Tuan, "Khai niem va viec su dung suc manh quoc gia va suc manh quan su trong quan he quoc te hien dai" [Conceptualizing and using national strength and military strength in contemporary international relations], *Nghien Cuu Quoc Te*, no. 62 (9–2005).

131. Avery Goldstein, "The Diplomatic Face of China's Grand Strategy: A Rising Power's Emerging Choice," *China Quarterly* 168 (December 2001): 835–6.

132. For this broad understanding of grand strategy, as distinct from military strategy, Goldstein cites the following ("The Diplomatic Face of China's Grand Strategy, " 835); Paul Kennedy, "Grand Strategy in War and Peace: Toward a Broader Definition," in Paul Kennedy, ed., *Grand Strategies in War and Peace* (New Haven: Yale University Press, 1991); Barry Posen, *The Sources of Military Doctrine: France, Britain, and Germany Between the World Wars* (Ithaca: Cornell University Press,

1984); Richard Rosecrance and Arthur A. Stein, eds., *The Domestic Bases of Grand Strategy* (Ithaca: Cornell University Press, 1993); Thomas J. Christensen, *Useful Adversaries: Grand Strategy, Domestic Mobilization, and Sino-American Conflict, 1947–1958* (Princeton: Princeton University Press, 1996).

133. Goldstein, "The Diplomatic Face of China's Grand Strategy," 835.

134. Ibid.

135. Ibid.

136. Ibid., 837.

137. J. J. Suh, Peter J. Katzenstein, and Allen Carlson, eds., *Rethinking Security in East Asia: Identity, Power, and Efficiency* (Stanford: Stanford University Press, 2004): 27. Johnstone's essay in this volume (pp. 34–96) is titled "Beijing's Security Behavior in the Asia-Pacific: Is China a Status Quo Power."

138. Van Quang, "An ninh kinh te trong toan cau hoa kinh te."

139. Interview in Hanoi, July 2000.

140. Interviews in Hanoi, December 2006 and January 2007.

141. Interviews in Hanoi, December 2006 and January 2007.

142. Stern, *Defense Relations*, 235.

143. Ibid., 234.

144. Ibid., 205, 222.

145. Ibid., 206.

CHAPTER 9

1. "Vietnam Top Leaders Ask to Resign." Agence France Presse, June 24, 2006.

2. David G. Marr, "A Passion for Modernity: Intellectuals and the Media," in Hy V. Luong, ed., *Postwar Vietnam: Dynamics of a Transforming Society* (Lanham: Rowman & Littlefield, 2003): 267.

3. Ibid., 277.

4. Ibid., 289.

5. In addition to Marr, see Russell Heng, "Media in Vietnam and the Structure of its Management," in David Marr, ed., *The Mass Media in Vietnam* (Canberra: Department of Political and Social Change, Australian National University, 1988).

6. "Viet Nam's Internet Usage Rate Skyrockets," *Financial Times Information*, May 18, 2007.

7. "39 percent of Hanoians use Internet," Vietnam News Agency, February 1, 2007.

8. Philippe Perdriau, "Vietnamese 'Cyber-Dissident' Jailed for Four Years," Agence France Presse, November 8, 2002.

9. "Party Official Calls for 'Proper Controls' on Internet Use," *Financial Times Information*, September 20, 2002.

10. "Vietnam's Communist Prime Minister Reaches out Online," Deutsche Presse-Agentur, February 9, 2007. Though it was touted as an internet chat, the event itself was not in real time. Dung sat in front of a computer, but did not type. Instead, a team of assistants read off questions to him. As he answered the questions verbally, transcribers typed furiously to post the results on the official government and Communist Party websites within an hour. Though the questions were screened, those that were allowed were frank. One person asked about incompetence of government.

11. "20,000 Questions for Vietnam Prime Minister's First Online 'Chat,'" Deutsche Press-Agentur, February 7, 2007.

12. "Vietnam's new leader, Nguyen Van Linh, was hailed last April [1985] for a novel idea among his communist comrades: placing a suggestion box in Ho Chi Minh City (formerly Saigon)." Clayton Jones, "Vietnam installs 'innovative' new party chief," *Christian Science Monitor*, December 19, 1986.

13. Interview with Dao Duy Quat, "Chu Tich Nuoc se doi thoai truc tuyen voi dan" [The president of the country will directly engage in dialogue with the people], *Tien Phong* online, February 23, 2006.

14. "Teenagers Rule the Internet in Viet Nam," *Financial Times Information*, November 6, 2006.

15. Le Tien, December 7, 2005 letter to the politburo, party secretariat, and party Central Control Commission, "Dang khong duoc trung tri tac gia 'Lam nguoi la kho'" [The party cannot punish the author of "To be a person is hard"]., To "be a person" means to be person of integrity and moral force: http://www.ykien.net/doanduythanh16.html.

16. Ibid. "When it is transmitted to the written page then that form of orally transmitted literature circulates on paper, and today with the new technology the printing is very beautiful and it is even circulated on the internet. These newly developed technologies are only a tool to help transmit the content of what used to be orally transmitted literature in a way that makes contact more convenient."

17. Ibid.

18. Nguyen Duc Binh, "Xay dung dang ta that vung manh" [Building our party to become truly strong], *Nhan Dan*, February 23, 2006.

19. Ibid.

20. "Dong Chi Truong Tan Sang lam viec voi ban bien tap *Tap Chi Cong San*" [Comrade Truong Tan Sang has a working session with the *Communist Review* editorial board], *Tap Chi Cong San*, 131 (2007).

21. *Ban Tu Tuong-Van Hoa Trung Uong* [Central Ideology-Culture Commission], *Doi ngoai Vietnam thoi ky doi moi* [External relations in the period of *doi moi*] (Ho Chi Minh City: NXB Chinh Tri Quoc Gia, 2005): 41–2.

22. Tran Hieu and Manh Viet, "Gap nhung nhan chung cua 'Cuoc xe rao lich su': Part V: 'Nhung trum cay xanh tren sa mac.'"

23. Erlanger et al., "Voices of the Party Faithful."

24. "Bai thuyet trinh cua Tien si Le Dang Doanh truoc Bo Chinh Tri [Briefing of Dr. Le Dang Doanh to the Politburo], Radio Free Asia, November 3, 2005; http://www.rfa.org/vietnamese/in_depth/2005/03/15/Le_Dang_Doanh_Interview_part1_VHung.

25. Interview in Hanoi, January 2007.

26. "At the opening of the countrywide conference on information and culture, Secretary General Nong Duc Manh says 'I applaud the spirit of looking squarely at the truth'" [*Toi hoan nghenh tinh than nhin thang vao su that*], *Tien Phong* online, February 27, 2007.

27. Although it would require further research to prove this, a selective survey of the use of the term "mass line" in Vietnamese Communist writings shows that it is generally used to indicate the need for cadres to set a good example for the people and do good things for them, rather than to take the ideas of "the masses" as a starting point for a Chinese style policy feedback loop. See also the discussion in David W. P. Elliott, "Revolutionary Re-integration: A Comparison of the

Foundation of Post-Liberation Political Systems in North Vietnam and China," Ph.D. dissertation, Cornell University, 1976, 420–44.

28. Vo Van Kiet, "Dong gop y kien vao bao cao tong ket ly luan va thuc tien 20 nam doi moi."

29. Luong Khac Hieu, ed., *Du Luan Xa Hoi Trong Su Nghiep Doi Moi (Sach Tham Khao)* [Social opinion in the mission of *doi moi* (reference book)] (NXB Chinh Tri Quoc Gia, 1999): 65.

30. Ibid., 71.

31. Ibid.,.51. "From the standpoint of the doctrine of dialectical materialism, Marxism-Leninism has pointed to the enormous role of the various aspects of state of mind [*tinh*: that is a very general and complex term, which indicates "mind," "intellect," "mental state," "morale"—among other dictionary definitions; in Marxist usage it is essentially the dialectical counterpart to the material aspect of life], among which is social opinion [public opinion] which emanates from the decisive historical role of each strata of the people."

32. "The whole English Constitution and the whole of constitutional public opinion is nothing but a big lie which is constantly supported and concealed by a number of small lies whenever at one point or another its true nature appears a little too openly in the light of day. And even if a person comes to the realisation that the whole of this construction is but untruth and fiction, even then he still adheres to it, indeed more tenaciously than ever, so that the empty words, the few meaninglessly assembled letters, should not fall apart, for these words are after all the pivot on which the world turns, and with them the world and mankind would of necessity plunge into the darkness of chaos! One cannot but turn away in deep disgust from this tissue of blatant and concealed lies, of hypocrisy and self-deception." Engels also said that "The struggle is already on. The Constitution is shaken to its foundations. What form the immediate future will take emerges from what has just been said. The new, alien elements in the Constitution are democratic in nature; it will become evident that public opinion too is developing in a democratic direction; the immediate future of England will be democracy. . . . But democracy by itself is not capable of curing social ills. Democratic equality is a chimera, the fight of the poor against the rich cannot be fought out on a basis of democracy or indeed of politics as a whole. This stage too is thus only a transition, the last purely political remedy which has still to be tried and from which a new element is bound to develop at once, a principle transcending everything of a political nature. This principle is the principle of socialism. Vorwärts!" no. 84, October 19, 1844; see http://www.marxists.org/archive/marx/works/1844/condition-england/ch02.htm.

33. Huu Tho, "Mot so van de ve van hoa trong giao doan cach mang moi" [A number of issues concerning culture in the new revolutionary stage], published in *Tap Chi Thong Tin Cong Tac Tu Tuong*, 5–1998 and reprinted in Huu Tho, "Theo Buoc Chan Doi Moi (Binh luan bao chi)" [In the footsteps of *doi moi* (newspaper editorials)] (Hanoi: NXB Chinh Tri Quoc Gia, 2002): 508–9.

34. Mark Sidel, "Generational and Institutional Transition in the Vietnamese Communist Party: The 1996 Congress and Beyond," *Asian Survey* 5 (May 1997): 448: "In the pattern of generational change, Ha Dang is retiring and thus was not elected to the new CC. After the 1996 Congress, Nguyen Huu Tho, editor-in-chief of *Nhan Dan* since 1992 and a member of the 1991 and 1996 CCs [Central Committees], was named to head the commission. Before heading *Nhan Dan*, Tho had served as its deputy editor (until deputy editor Bui Tin's defection) and earlier as vice-chair of the Commission for Ideology and Culture."

35. Dong Nai Province, "Bao cao ket qua dieu tra du luan xa hoi nam 2006" [Report on the investigation of opinion in society, 2006], http://www.dongnai.gov.vn/thong_tin_KTXH/mdocument12052007/mlfolder.2007-04-12.6775931936/mlfolder.2007-04-13.0264374171/mlnews.2007-04-16.9640151559.

36. Vu Tien Phuoc, "*Tuoi Tre* nen dung ra dieu tra du luan xa hoi" [*Tuoi Tre* should take it upon itself to investigate public opinion], *Tuoi Tre* online, September 3, 2006.

37. "'The Tenth Party Congress has the task of looking squarely at the truth in order to review and objectively and comprehensively evaluate the weaknesses and shortcomings, and at the same time draw lessons from the implementation of the resolutions of the Ninth Party Congress,' said State Chairman Tran Duc Luong in opening the Tenth Party Congress." Article titled "Nhin thang vao su that" [Looking squarely at the truth], *Tuoi Tre* online, April 19, 2006. See also Nong Duc Manh (secretary general of the Communist Party of Vietnam), "Nhin thang vao su that, danh gia dung, su that de dua ra duoc nhung quyet sach dung dan" [Facing the truth squarely, correctly evaluating the truth in order to put forth the right policies], *Tap Chi Cong San*, 8 (2002).

38. Dang Phong, "Dem Truoc doi moi: Uy quyen cua long dan."

39. *Tuoi Tre*, interview with Vo Van Kiet, "Cung lam cho dan giau nuoc manh thi se tim duoc diem tuong dong" [Working with each other to make the country rich and powerful will create common ground], in Truong Van Sau et al., *An Tuong Vo Van Kiet*, 135.

40. Nguyen Thi Ngoc Hai, *Mai Chi Tho Tuong Con Dan* [Mai Chi Tho: General and son of the people] (Ho Chi Minh City: NXB Cong An Nhan Dan, 2005): 188–9.

41. Ibid., 192–3.

42. Ibid., 193–4.

43. Ibid., 194.

44. Interview in Hanoi, January 2007.

45. Vu Thu Hien, *Dem Giua Ban Ngay: Hoi Ky Chinh Tri Cua Mot Nguoi Khong Lam Chinh Tri* [Darkness at noon: The political biography of a person who doesn't engage in politics] (California: Van Nghe, 1997).

46. "Tro chuyen cung nha van Vu Thu Hien" [Conversing with the writer Vu Thu Hien], BBC broadcast in Vietnamese, February 23, 2006, http://www.voanews.com/vietnamese/archive/2006-02/2006-02-23-voa13.cfm.

47. Manh Dung, "Phai chang do la y kien dong gop chan thanh voi Dang" [Could it be that these are sincere contributions of ideas to the party]? *Tap Chi Quoc Phong Toan Dan*, 4–2006, 18.

48. Ibid., 19.

49. Nguyen Duc Binh, "Xay dung dang to that vung manh" [Building our party truly strong], *Nhan Dan*, February 23, 2006.

50. Ibid.

51. Nguyen Duc Binh, "Tiep tuc mot cach kien dinh va sang tao con duong xa hoi chu nghia" [Resolutely and creatively continuing along the socialist path], part 2, *Tap Chi Cong San*, 119 (2006).

52. See discussion of this essay titled "Some observations about today's era and our path," in chapter 2. Dieu portrayed humanity as going through three stages; from agricultural production, to production of machines, and then to the stage of "informaticizing" (*giai doan tin hoc hoa*) the world.

53. Nguyen Duc Binh, "Xay dung dang to that vung manh."

54. Phan Dinh Dieu, "Vai nhan thuc ve thoi dai ngay nay va con duong cua ta," 8.

55. Nguyen Duc Binh, "Tiep tuc mot cach kien dinh va sang tao con duong xa hoi chu nghia," part 2.

56. Interview with Huu Tho, Lao Dong, April 4, 2006, http://www.ykien.net/daihoiX.html.

57. "Leftist" (*"ta" khuynh*) is always placed in quotes to indicate that it is not entirely a true allegation. Most party conservatives feel that "leftism" is merely a spirit of overexuberance by

dedicated party members whose hearts are basically in the right place. It is like saying "so called" leftism. Rightism (*huu khuynh*), the opposite political error, is never put in quotes, to indicate that there is a large element of truth in applying this label.

58. Nguyen Duc Binh, "Xay dung dang ta that vung manh."

59. "New development in China–Vietnam relations," *Financial Times Information*, April 17, 2007.

60. Nguyen Duc Binh, "Tiep tuc mot cach kien dinh va sang tao con duong xa hoi chu nghia" [Resolutely and creatively continue along the socialst path], part 1, *Tap Chi Cong San*, 118 (2006).

61. Interview in Hanoi, January 2007.

62. Nguyen Quang A, "Doi loi cung GS. Nguyen Duc Binh va gop y voi Dang Cong San Viet Nam" [A few words with Professor Nguyen Duc Binh and some suggestions for the Communist Party of Vietnam], http://www.viet-studies.org/kinhte/NQA_talawas.pdf. Parts of this article were published in *Tuoi Tre*, February 28, 2006. *Ptyalize* published the entire article on the internet.

63. *Tranh Luan de Dong Thuan* [Reaching consensus through debate] (Hanoi: NXB Tri Thuc and Tap Chi Tin Hoc & Doi Song, 2006). This also includes an article by Nguyen Quang A.

64. Nguyen Duc Binh, "Tiep tuc mot cach kien dinh va sang tao con duong xa hoi chu nghia," part 2.

65. Nguyen Quang A, "Doi loi cung GS. Nguyen Duc Binh va gop y voi Dang Cong San Viet Nam."

66. This is a dig at the dogmatic approach of Nguyen Duc Binh. During the Cultural Revolution, some splinter Maoist groups throughout the world called themselves the Communist Party of X (Marxist-Leninist) to signify their break from the orthodox pro-Soviet Communist Parties of their countries.

67. Nguyen Quang A, "Doi loi cung GS. Nguyen Duc Binh va gop y voi Dang Cong San Viet Nam."

68. Ibid.

69. Tien Si, "Nguyen Quang A noi ve bai viet cua ong Nguyen Duc Binh," phan 1 [Dr. Nguyen Quang A speaks about the article written by Mr. Nguyen Duc Binh, part 1], Radio Free Asia interview, March 13, 2006.

70. "The delegates asked the party, state, and universities to provide preferential treatment to lecturers of Marxism-Leninism to encourage them to work more effectively and to set a good example for Vietnamese students." "Teaching of Marxism-Leninism at Colleges Reviewed," BBC Worldwide Monitoring, July 1, 1998.

71. Nguyen Duc Binh, "Ve toan cau hoa—May van de phuong phap luan va phuong phap tiep can" [On globalization: Some questions of methodology and methodological approaches], in Nguyen Duc Binh, *Mot So Van De Ve Cong Tac Ly Luan Tu Tuong va Van Hoa* [Some questions of the theoretical, ideological, and cultural missions] (Hanoi: NXB Chinh Tri Quoc Gia, 2005): 781–4.

72. "In order to avoid some delicate aspects that might arise in this psychological environment, our country does not necessarily have to proclaim it and widely propagandize about state capitalism. But in the theoretical and political understanding, and ideology and party line, especially within the party and among the leading political and administrative cadres" there must be a firm understanding of "the leading role of the worker's class." Nguyen Duc Binh, "Tiep tuc mot cach kien dinh va sang tao con duong xa hoi chu nghia," part 2.

73. "Full Text of Ninth Party Central Committee's Political Report" adopted at the 10th National Congress of the Communist Party of Vietnam, held in Hanoi, 18–25 April 2006; as carried by Vietnamese newspaper *Nhan Dan* website on 7 June. BBC Worldwide Monitoring, June 30, 2006.

74. "Su thay doi lon trong tu duy cua Dang" [The big change in the party's thinking], *Tuoi Tre* online, February 28, 2006.

75. Dai Hoi Chi Bo CNTT [Congress of the Information Technology party chapter], "Khoa Hoc Cong Nghe Thong Tin" [Information Technology website], September 16, 2006, http://cntt.hnue.edu.vn/users/new/index.php?option=com_content&task=view&id=46&Itemid=44.

76. Chairman of VP Bank, "Vietnam's Banks Fail to Link ATM Networks For Growth," *Asia Pulse*, May 24, 2006.

77. Director of the 3c Company, "Hopes of Nissan Plan Expire," *Vietnam Investment Review*, October 22, 2001.

78. "Vietnam Top Leaders Ask to Resign."

79. Greg Torode, "Creative, Young, Loyal: Hanoi Eyes Future Leaders," *South China Morning Post*, April 21, 2006.

80. Greg Torode, "Changing Guard," *South China Morning Post*, April 28, 2006.

81. Ibid.

82. Ibid.

83. "Former Party Official Pham Van Dong Discusses Party," BBC Worldwide Monitoring, May 18, 1999. "The party's relationship with the young generation: young people these days are not too keen about joining the party. The party's relationship with the intellectuals: intellectuals also do not pay much attention to the party membership. These three groups of people do not want to join the party because they have seen so many party organizations and members failing to behave like communists and who do not deserve to be in a Ho Chi Minh's party. We should consider seriously the fact that the average age of our party members at present is 64 [! this was, in fact the average age of the politburo at that time; the average age of party members actually held steady at around forty-four years old between 1995 and 2005]."

84. "Former Party Official Pham Van Dong Discusses Party," BBC Worldwide.

85. Paul Wedel, "New Vietnamese Communist Leader Takes Power," UPI, June 1991.

86. Philip Shenon, "Vietnam Party Vows to Maintain Absolute Power," *New York Times*, June 25, 1991.

87. "Jostling begins in Vietnam's leadership ranks," *Financial Times* (London), April 29, 1996.

88. "New Communist Leaders Ensure Gradual Reform, Foreign Media Says," *Financial Times Information*, April 26, 2006.

89. "Composition of New Central Committee Analysed," BBC Summary of World Broadcasts, January 3, 1997.

90. "Vietnam Announces Sweeping Cabinet Reshuffle," Kyodo News Service, August 8, 2002.

91. "Foreign minister concerned over new age category for party selection," BBC Worldwide Monitoring, May 6, 2006. "I have seen many young diplomats in the world today; yet, a large number of noted diplomats are old and still work effectively. I think that it would benefit our foreign affairs sector the most if old, experienced Vietnamese diplomats were elected to the new party Central Committee. Currently, Vietnam has many deputy foreign ministers who have been working with this sector for more than 35 years and have gained vast experience in this field."

92. "493 dai bieu Quoc hoi khoa XII" [493 representatives elected to the Twelfth National Assembly], *Tien Phong* online, May 30, 2007.

93. "Mr. [Tran Dinh] Hoan, who is also a member of the Politburo, suggested the Party should have more young members to carry out its missions in the future, adding that the average age among its membership decreased rather slowly, from 44.9 in 1995 to 44.35 in 2004." "Communist Party Urged to Recruit More Youths," *Financial Times Information*, March 17, 2005.

94. "Vietnam: More than 751,000 New CPV Members Admitted in Five Years," *Financial Times Information*, April 17, 2006.

95. Nguyen Duc Binh, "Nguyen Duc Binh Reports on Party's Need for Improved Theoretical Work," BBC Summary of World Broadcasts, June 20, 1992.

96. http://en.wikipedia.org/wiki/Rootless_cosmopolitan, accessed February 22, 2012.

97. Nguyen Duc Binh, "Tiep tuc mot cach kien dinh va sang tao con duong xa hoi chu nghia," part 2.

98. Nguyen Tan Dung, "Xay dung nen kinh te doc lap, tu chu theo dinh huong xa hoi chu nghia" [Build an independent and sovereign economy with a socialist orientation], *Tap Chi Cong San*, 26 (2002).

99. Nguyen Duc Binh, "Phan dau vi mot dang tri tue, danh du, van luong tam cua thoi dai, mot dang dao duc,van minh" [Struggle for the party of intellect, honor, and the conscience of the age, a civilized and virtuous party], *Tap Chi Cong San* online, 86 (2005).

100. I am indebted to William Turley's Vietnam Studies Group Listserv communication of June 13, 2007, for raising the issue of the Soviet connection of "civilized" and further discussion about "modernity," especially the comments on this thread by Ho Hue Tam Tai, Joseph Hannah, George Dutton, Bill Hayton, Ed Miller, and Adam Fforde.

101. This was vividly captured in a 1988 article by Seweryn Bialer. "But the strongest feeling one now encounters in the Soviet Union is shame; shame at the country's backwardness, at the brutality of Soviet life, at the lack of beauty, at the militaristic order at a time of worldwide revolution of democratic participation, at the drunkenness and social pathology that is everywhere. This feeling is encountered not only among the elite and the intelligentsia, but also among ordinary people. Sometimes in discussions with Westerners the shame is camouflaged by artificial arrogance or bitter humor, but it is nonetheless an angry, deep, and uncompromising shame, and a quest for respectability by the standards of civilized countries. It is a shame that is most fully expressed in typically Russian heart-to-heart talks with friends that last long into the night. Such a deep, almost desperate shame is a powerful weapon in Gorbachev's arsenal. It provides a major psychological basis for his efforts." Seweryn Bialer, "Gorbachev's Program of Change: Sources, Significance, Prospects," *Political Science Quarterly* 103, no. 33 (1988): 457.

102. "1) The government can be dismissed, and the dismissal takes place in a civilized way. To us Eastern Europeans, it is quite clear what is meant by dismissing ruling figures or groups in an uncivilized way; they are murdered, become victims of a coup d'état, are executed or imprisoned after their dismissal, are removed by an uprising, and so on. 2) Democracies use an electoral procedure for civilized dismissal. The procedure is controlled by laws complemented by conventions." Janos Kornai, "What the Change of System from Socialism to Capitalism Does and Does Not Mean," *Journal of Economic Perspectives* 14, no. 1 (Winter, 2000): 36.

103. Gorbachev's speech to the United Nations, December 7, 1988.

104. Eduard Shevardnadze, "No One Can Isolate Us, Save Ourselves. Self-Isolation is the Ultimate Danger" *Slavic Review* 51, no. 1 (Spring, 1992): 119.

105. *Time Magazine*, July 6, 1992. Thanks to William Turley for this citation.

106. Nguyen Minh Hien, "Giao duc trong doi thoi giua cac nen van hoa van minh vi hoa binh va phat trien ben vung" [Education in the dialogue among the cultures and civilizations for stable peace and development], *Tap Chi Cong San*, 80 (2005).

107. See William Turley's Vietnam Studies Group Listserv communication of June 13, 2007.

108. Peter M. Haas, "Introduction: Epistemic Communities and International Policy Coordination," *International Organization* 46, no.1 (Winter 1992): 27.

109. Nguyen Quang A, "Doi loi cung GS. Nguyen Duc Binh va gop y voi Dang Cong San Viet Nam."

110. See http://www.fordfoundation.org/pdfs/library/ar2004.pdf.

111. Ramses Amer, Sherry Gray, Nguyen Vu Tung, Advisory Report to the Ford Foundation: Renovating Undergraduate Teaching of International Relations / Studies in Vietnam Hanoi, Vietnam: 2004.

112. Interviews in Hanoi, December 2006 and January 2007.

113. Interview in Hanoi, December 2006.

114. "These days, it's not unusual to see a Vietnamese government official speaking with foreigners in English. This was rare five years ago. Under the pressure of international integration, learning English is becoming a real requirement for many officials at every level." Tran Le Thuy, "When Leaders Learn English," *Saigon Times Magazine* (*Financial Times Information*), July 11, 2002.

115. Thuat Ngu, *An Ninh Chau A-Thai Binh Duong* [Asia-Pacific security lexicon] (Hanoi: Hoc Vien Quoc Te, 2003).

116. Vuong Dat Chau, ed., *An Ninh Quoc Te Trong Thoi Dai Toan Cau Hoa* (sach tham khao) [International security in the age of globalization (reference book)] (Hanoi: NXB Chinh Tri Quoc Gia, 2004).

117. Paul R. Viotti, Mark V. Kauppi, *Ly Luan Quan He Quoc Te* [International relations theory], (Hanoi: Hoc Vien Quan He Quoc Te, 2001). Translated and published by the Institute of International Relations.

118. Hoang Van Hien and Nguyen Viet Thao, *Quan He Quoc Te Tu 1945 den 1995* [International Relations from 1945 to 1995] (Hanoi: NXB Chinh Tri Quoc Gia, 1995).

119. *Giao Trinh Quan He Quoc Te: He Cu Nhan Chinh Tri* [International relations curriculum: BA in politics track] (Hanoi: NXB Ly Luan Chinh Tri, 2005): 7. The political and practical policy focus of this text is made clear in the preface. "International relations and the external policy orientation (called International Relations for short), is a basic course of study for the training program for leading Party and popular association cadres in the Ho Chi Minh National Political Academy. This course of studies will equip the student [with a knowledge of] many questions regarding politics and international relations among nations in order to elevate their understanding concerning the motivation of the world revolution and Vietnam [and] on that basis to understand and absorb the new external policy line of our Party and State."

120. Some examples are; Nguyen Thanh Huong, "Chu nghia tu do moi va quan he (kinh te) quoc te hien nay" [Neoliberalism and contemporary (economic) international relations], *Nghien Cuu Quoc Te*, no. 24 (June 1998); Vu The Hiep, "Cac truyen thong ly luan quan he quoc te" [The various theoretical traditions in international relations], *Nghien Cuu Quoc Te*, no. 57 (June 2004); Vu The Hiep, "Quan diem chu nghia hien thuc ve quan he quoc te" [Conceptions of realism in international relations], *Nghien Cuu Quoc Te*, no. 59 (December 2004); Doan Van Thang, "Chu

nghia tu do tu mot cach nhin" [A perspective on liberalism], *Nghien Cuu Quoc To*, no. 64 (March 2006); Nguyen Vu Tung, "Tim hieu ve chu nghia tan bao thu" [Understanding neo-conservatism], *Nghien Cuu Quoc Te*, no. 57 (June 2004): Dinh Thi Hien Luong, "Chu nghia khu vuc: cac truong phai tiep can ly thuyet" [Regionalism: The theoretical approaches of the various schools of thought], *Nghien Cuu Quoc Te*, no. 60 (March 2005).

121. Tran Van Trinh, "An Ninh phi truyen thong: Mot khai niem moi va huong hop tac moi" [Non-traditional security: A new concept and a new direction for cooperation], *Tap Chi Cong San*, 109 (2006).

122. Vu Duong Ninh (chu bien), *Lich Su Quan He Quoc Te* [History of international relations], vol. 1 (Hanoi: NXB Gia Duc, 2006). See also the international-relations text written by two scholars from the National University of Hanoi: Nguyen Quoc Hung and Hoang Khac Nam, *Quan He Quoc Te: Nhung Khia Canh Ly Thuyet va Van De* (Sach Tham Khao) [International relations: Theoretical elements and issues (reference book)] (Hanoi: NXB Chinh Tri Quoc Gia, 2006). "This course of study is aimed at providing students with the basic understanding of the process of evolution of relations among nations, and the big transformations in international relations. From there, students will have taken the first step toward have the foundation to analyze events that have taken place, and training in the ability to forecast the situation in the face of the changes that are taking place in the political life of the world. This course will be coordinated with other courses in the training program (theory and international relations, international economics, international law, and Vietnam's foreign relations) which will guarantee [attainment of] an intellectual grasp of history and, at the same time, evoke reflections on the past and present, which will have both a theoretical and a practical significance for the international integration of our country."

123. "Vietnamese Scientists Call for Training of Capable Leaders in Science," *Financial Times Information*, March 26, 2003.

124. "Boeing, Vietnam Universities Work Together on Accreditation Standards," *Financial Times Information*, December 21, 2006.

125. "It came as a surprise when Phung Thi Van Anh applied for a training course in business management at the Hanoi School of Business. To many, there was no need for this influential woman, who heads the management board of the renowned Bank for Investment and Development of Vietnam (BID), to receive further training. But this isn't just any course. This is the International Executive Development Program for top managers organized by the Hanoi School of Business (HSB) in cooperation with the Amos Tuck School, a part of the US Dartmouth College. The program is tailored for managers and entrepreneurs in different economic sectors who want to perform work more effectively, develop firms and advance management careers." Ngoc Hai, "Upgrading the business brain," *Vietnam Investment Review*, August 6, 2001.

126. "Vietnam Premier Meets Academic Leaders in Boston," BBC Worldwide Monitoring, June 26, 2005.

127. "Overseas Vietnamese Intellectuals Encouraged to Take Part in National Construction," *Financial Times Information*, August 16, 2005.

128. Heonik Kwon, *After the Massacre: Commemoration and Consolation in Ha My and My Lai* (Berkeley: University of California Press, 2006).

129. Ibid., 68.

130. Ibid., 69.

131. Ibid., 75.

132. Ibid., 81.

133. Ibid., 155.

134. Ibid., 161.

135. Ibid., 163.

136. See the family history by Mai Van Elliott, *The Sacred Willow: Four Generations in the Life of a Vietnamese Family* (New York: Oxford University Press, 2000).

137. Ibid.

138. Fforde and de Vylder, *From Plan to Market*, 128.

139. Myron Rush, *Political Succession in the USSR* (New York: Columbia University Press, 1965).

140. Wayne Sandholtz and Mark M. Gray, "International Integration and National Corruptions," *International Organization* 57 (Fall 2003): 761.

141. Seth Mydans, "Vietnamese leaders uneasy as integrity erodes," *International Herald Tribune*, May 5, 2006.

142. John Gillespie, "Changing concepts of socialist law in Vietnam," in John Gillespie and Pip Nicholson, eds., *Asian Socialism and Legal Change: The Dynamics of Vietnamese and Chinese Reform* (Canberra: Asia Pacific Press at the Australian National University): 59.

143. Ibid., 67.

144. Ibid., 68.

145. "When Vietnamese teenager Nguyen Manh Nam first started breakdancing, he didn't dare tell his parents about his passion for the hip-hop culture born on the city streets of far-away America. 'I persuaded my father by showing him breakdance films I downloaded from the Internet,' said the dreadlocked 17-year-old. 'Little by little, he grew to like it. Now he even practices it a bit when I'm not at home.' This week, Nam's parents and thousands more will get the chance to see him and members of the 'Big Toe Crew,' the communist country's first and best known hip-hop dance group, make their big-stage debut on a national tour. Together with Niels 'Storm' Robitzky from Berlin and French partner Sebastien Ramirez, they will interpret Vietnam's infamously chaotic street traffic in the high-energy dance and video performance 'Xe Co' (Vehicles). . . . For the Vietnamese group, the opening show in the capital's Soviet-built Friendship Palace is a coming-out performance of sorts for a cultural movement that still turns heads and raises eyebrows here. 'Hip-hop was introduced to Vietnam by students who had studied abroad,' said Nguyet Viet Thanh, 33, the leader of the group that has grown since 1992 from five to 30 dancers with about 30 more unofficial members. 'Hip-hop is my biggest hobby. People first thought it was just for fun, just a fashion. My family thought I would follow it for maybe two or three years . . . but now things have changed.' State censors Monday gave the go-ahead for shows in Hanoi, Danang and Ho Chi Minh City on a tour supported by the French and German cultural institutes that has no political message but may still challenge some audiences." "Hanoi hip-hoppers bring street cred to Soviet-built culture palace," http://www.breitbart.com/article.php?id=070110033524.2yixlwoi&show_article=1, January 9, 2007.

146. Simon Montlake, "The Monied Heroes of a New Vietnam," *Christian Science Monitor*, March 13, 2007.

147. Kay Johnson, "Vietnam Relives the Bad Old Days," Deutsche Press-Agentur, August 15, 2006.

148. Interviews in Hanoi, December 2006 and January 2007.

149. See Alagappa's discussion of "pathways to order" where he concludes that "no approach is sufficient by itself to sustain order. Features of the different approaches usually coexist and over-lap." Muthiah Alagappa, *Asian Security Order: Instrumental and Normative Features* (Stanford: Stanford University Press, 2003): 63.

150. Peter J. Katzenstein and Rudra Sil, "Rethinking Asian Security: A Case for Analytic Eclecticism," in Suh, Katzenstein, and Carlson, eds., *Rethinking Security in East Asia*, 29–30.

151. Legro, *Rethinking the World*, 13.

INDEX

Printed in Great Britain
by Amazon

81393555R00255